Dictionary of Business Biography

Dictionary of Business Biography

A Biographical Dictionary of Business Leaders
Active in Britain in the Period 1860–1980

edited by

David J Jeremy

Research Fellow, Business History Unit
London School of Economics and Political Science

deputy editor

Christine Shaw

Research Officer, Business History Unit
London School of Economics and Political Science

Volume 2
D-G

London
Butterworths
1984

England	Butterworth & Co (Publishers) Ltd, 88 Kingsway, LONDON WC2B 6AB
Australia	Butterworth Pty Ltd, SYDNEY, MELBOURNE, BRISBANE, ADELAIDE, and PERTH
Canada	Butterworth & Co (Canada) Ltd, TORONTO
	Butterworth & Co (Western Canada) Ltd, VANCOUVER
New Zealand	Butterworths of New Zealand Ltd, WELLINGTON
Singapore	Butterworth & Co (Asia) Pte Ltd, SINGAPORE
South Africa	Butterworth Publishers (Pty) Ltd, DURBAN
USA	Butterworth Legal Publishers (Mason Division), ST PAUL, Minnesota
	Butterworth Legal Publishers, SEATTLE, Washington; BOSTON, Massachusetts; and AUSTIN, Texas
	D & S Publishers, CLEARWATER, Florida

© London School of Economics and Political Science 1984

ISBN for the complete set of volumes: 0 406 27340 5
for this volume: 0 406 27342 1

Typeset by Whitefriars Composertype Ltd, Chichester
Printed by The Whitefriars Press Ltd, Tonbridge

Introduction and Acknowledgements

Volume II of the *Dictionary of Business Biography* adds 189 biographies of entrepreneurs active in Britain (excluding Scotland which is covered by a parallel project at the University of Glasgow) since 1860 to the 271 biographies in volume I. The purpose of the *Dictionary* and the principles upon which individuals have been selected have been indicated in the Introduction to Volume I. Suffice it to say here that our aim is to cover the whole gamut of business from mining and manufacturing to public utilities, construction, distribution and financial and miscellaneous services. Academics, civil servants, trade unionists and agriculturalists have been excluded where their involvement in the business world was incidental to their central career. Those still active in business have also been excluded.

The acknowledgements in Volume I cover succeeding volumes but inevitably the preparation of additional volumes produces further obligations. First and foremost the editor is most grateful to the contributors who have so willingly supported the project. Their names and affiliations are given below. The editor's work of assessing entries covering such a wide range of business activity has been greatly helped by the generous co-operation of referees, mostly economic historians in academic departments. Besides those listed in Volume I the following must now be mentioned:

David Bebbington, Clyde Binfield, Roger Dyson, David Fanning, Ralph Gabriel, Andrew Marrison, T M Megaw and Nick Tiratsoo.

In addition to private individuals, a number of learned institutions have aided the *DBB's* editorial functions. The staff of several county record offices and local history libraries (particularly at Leeds and Newcastle upon Tyne), as well as the staff of the Institutions of Civil and Mechanical Engineers, the Royal Artillery Library and of a number of registries of universities and colleges, have kindly supplied us with information about various subjects' places of birth and dates and details of education and qualifications.

The editor is grateful too to members of the *DBB*'s Advisory Board, particularly Professors Hannah and Barker and Dr Reader, whose advice has helped to shape both the project and individual entries.

Within the editorial team high levels of commitment and co-operation on everyone's part have allowed us to meet the tight deadlines and budgets faced by the *DBB* project. The enormous burden of word processing has been borne by Miss Kiely, Miss Kidner and Mrs Peake (who joined the project in December 1983 when Miss Kidner left). Their stamina and good humour have been indispensable. At a critical moment we also had some inputting assistance from Ms Eve Mason, secretary of the Business History Unit. While Mrs Peake has maintained the *DBB* office's secretarial functions, Miss Kiely has taken over the work of collecting birth and marriage certificates and Dr Geoffrey Tweedale has done most of the bibliographic research for this volume. Mark Dixon and Carol

Watson, graduate students in the Business History Unit, have also helped by collecting probate valuations and miscellaneous items of information.

The editor has read and commented on every entry, normally imposing the usual *DBB* format; Dr Shaw has been responsible for the final editing of most of the F entries. Proofing has been shared between the editor, deputy editor and Dr Tweedale.

The illustrations, assembled by Miss Kiely, are designed to act as 'triggers' to the imagination: showing portraits of some of the entrepreneurs and a selection of their workplaces, products or primary documents. We are grateful to all those who have helped by providing illustrations and again, for any unwitting invasions of copyright (which we have tried to rectify), we apologise.

Once more I would like to underscore my gratitude to everyone who has supported the *DBB* project in any way, emphasising that none, besides the editor, is responsible for the editorial faults that remain.

David J Jeremy

Contents

List of Contributors to Volume 2

(affiliations at the time of writing)

Margaret Ackrill	Academic Visitor Business History Unit, London School of Economics and Political Science.
Alison Adburgham	Wadebridge, Cornwall.
J K Almond	Senior Lecturer in Metallurgy, Department of Mechanical Engineering and Metallurgy, Teesside Polytechnic.
Colin Baber	Lecturer, Department of Economics, University College Cardiff.
Philip S Bagwell	Professor Emeritus in History, Polytechnic of Central London.
T C Barker	Emeritus Professor of Economic History, London School of Economics and Political Science.
D S M Barrie	formerly Chairman, British Railways (Eastern) Board and General Manager, British Railways, Eastern Region.
O A Beckerlegge	York.
Victor Belcher	Assistant Editor, *Survey of London,* Greater London Council.
Mona S Black	Swanland, North Ferriby, Humberside.
Michael R Bonavia	formerly Academic Visitor, Economic History Department, London School of Economics and Political Science.
Jonathan S Boswell	Senior Lecturer, The City University Business School, London.
Gordon Boyce	formerly Research Student, London School of Economics and Political Science.
Emily Boyle	Lecturer, School of Marketing and Business Policy, Ulster Polytechnic.
Trevor Boyns	Lecturer, Department of Economics, University College, Cardiff.
Keith Brooker	Lecturer, Department of Business Studies, East Yorkshire College of Further Education.
Kathleen Burk	Lecturer, Department of Humanities, Imperial College of Science and Technology, London.
Michael F Bywater	Librarian, Institute of Chartered Accountants in England and Wales.

W A Campbell	Lecturer, Department of Inorganic Chemistry, University of Newcastle upon Tyne.
M J Cannons	Redditch, Worcestershire.
John Cantrell	Department of History, Manchester Grammar School.
Geoffrey Channon	Principal Lecturer, Department of Humanities, Bristol Polytechnic.
Andrew Christie	Dale Centre, Loughborough, Scotland.
J F Clarke	Principal Lecturer, Department of Geography and Environmental Studies, Newcastle upon Tyne Polytechnic.
D C Coleman	Emeritus Professor of Economic History, Pembroke College, Cambridge.
D A Collier	Department of Economic History, Mid-Warwickshire College of Further Education.
Edward Connell	Lecturer, Extra Mural Department, University of Leeds.
T A B Corley	Senior Lecturer, Department of Economics, University of Reading.
Tom Corran	Fielding Newson-Smith Ltd.
Phillip L Cottrell	Senior Lecturer, Department of Economic and Social History, University of Leicester.
Robin Craig	Senior Lecturer in Economic History, Department of History, University College, London.
R P T Davenport-Hines	Research Officer, Business History Unit, London School of Economics and Political Science.
Alun C Davies	Senior Lecturer, Department of Economic History, The Queen's University, Belfast.
P N Davies	Senior Lecturer and Head of the Department of Economic History, University of Liverpool.
J R Edwards	Senior Lecturer in Accountancy, Department of Accountancy and Financial Control, University College, Cardiff.
Ruth Dudley Edwards	London.
R W Ferrier	Company Historian, BP, Britannic House, London.
Sidney Flavel	Salisbury, Wiltshire.
Roderick C Floud	Professor of History, Birkbeck College, London.

G R M Garratt	Esher, Surrey.
Brian Gee	Senior Lecturer, Science Education Unit, College of St Mark and St John, Plymouth.
Antony C Gilpin	London.
John Goodchild	Principal Local Studies Officer and Archivist, Wakefield M D Libraries.
Jill L Gosling	formerly Research Assistant, Business History Unit, London School of Economics and Political Science.
T R Gourvish	Senior Lecturer, School of Economic and Social Studies, University of East Anglia.
J Greenacomb	Assistant Editor, *Survey of London,* Greater London Council.
Carl E R Grundy-Warr	Department of Geography, University of Durham.
C Gulvin	Principal Lecturer, Department of Economics and Economic History, Portsmouth Polytechnic.
Leslie Hannah	Professor of Business History and Director, Business History Unit, London School of Economics and Political Science.
Charles E Harvey	Senior Lecturer in Economics and Business History, Department of Humanities, Bristol Polytechnic.
Roy Hay	Lecturer, School of Social Sciences, Deakin University, Victoria, Australia.
John Hibbs	Director of Transport Studies, Business and Management Studies, City of Birmingham Polytechnic.
Robin Higham	Professor, Department of History, Kansas State University, USA.
John O Hitchcock	Sevenoaks, Kent.
J A Holloway	Director of Press and PR Services, Smiths Industries PLC.
Graeme M Holmes	Senior Lecturer, Department of Economics and Banking, University of Wales Institute of Science and Technology.
A C Howe	Lecturer, Department of International History, London School of Economics and Political Science.
David Iredale	District Archivist, Moray District Record Office, Forres, Moray.
R J Irving	Personnel Director, Imperial Inns & Taverns Ltd.

D T Jenkins	Lecturer, Department of Economic and Related Studies, University of York.
David J Jeremy	Research Fellow, Business History Unit, London School of Economics.
David S Johnson	Lecturer, Department of Economic and Social History, The Queen's University, Belfast.
Aubrey Jones	Industrial Fellow Commoner, Churchill College, Cambridge.
Edgar Jones	Group Historian, GKN PLC.
Geoffrey G Jones	Lecturer, Economic History Department, London School of Economics and Political Science.
John King	London.
R M Kirk	formerly Research Student, Department of Economics, University of Salford.
Jack Kitchen	Professor of Accountancy, University of Hull.
David Kynaston	formerly Research Student, Department of Economic History, London School of Economics and Political Science.
Jean Lindsay	Department of History, Ysgol John Bright, Llandudno, Gwynedd.
Duncan McDowall	Senior Research Associate, The Conference Board of Canada.
Sir Peter Masefield	formerly Chairman of British European Airways and the London Transport Executive.
William M Mathew	Lecturer, School of Economic and Social Studies, University of East Anglia, Norwich.
D John Morton	Historical Information Officer, Royal Doulton Tableware Ltd.
Michael S Moss	Archivist, University of Glasgow.
Robert Murphy	formerly Research Student, Economic History Department, London School of Economics and Political Science.
Norman Mutton	Principal Lecturer, Department of Government and Economics, City of Birmingham Polytechnic.
Chris Niblett	Glossop, Derbyshire.
Paul Nunn	Principal Lecturer in Economic History, Department of History, City of Sheffield Polytechnic.

Maurice E Ogborn	formerly General Manager, The Equitable Life Assurance Society.
R H Parker	Professor of Accountancy, Department of Economics, University of Exeter.
Henry W Parris	University of Reading.
Denys C S Pegg	Company Archivist, Pearl Assurance PLC.
D C Phillips	Archivist, Institute of Agricultural History and Museum of English Rural Life, University of Reading.
M H Port	Professor of History, Queen Mary College, University of London.
Veronica Rady	Head of Records Management and Archives, Shell International Petroleum Co Ltd.
John B Rae	Senior Professor Emeritus, Department of Humanities and Social Science, Harvey Mudd College, California, USA.
J Gordon Read	Keeper of Archives, Merseyside County Museums, Liverpool.
W J Reader	Texaco Visiting Fellow, Business History Unit, London School of Economics and Political Science.
M C Reed	Honorary Lecturer, Department of History, University of Glasgow.
Peter N Reed	Assistant Director, Merseyside County Museums, Liverpool.
Hew F Reid	Director of Studies, Department of Furniture Technology, Buckinghamshire College of Higher Education.
Jack Reynolds	Honorary Visiting Lecturer, University of Bradford.
David J Richardson	Headmaster, Laxton School, Oundle.
Michael Robbins	London.
Richard Roberts	Lecturer, Department of History, University of Sussex.
Mary B Rose	Lecturer, Department of Economics, University of Lancaster.
D J Rowe	Lecturer, Department of Economics, University of Newcastle upon Tyne.
William D Rubinstein	Senior Lecturer, Department of Social Sciences, Deakin University, Victoria, Australia.
Roger Ryan	Department of General and Adult Education, Southport College of Art and Technology.

Christine Shaw	Research Officer, Business History Unit, London School of Economics and Political Science.
E M Sigsworth	Reader in Humanities, School of Humanities, Humberside College of Higher Education.
Jack Simmons	Professor, formerly Department of History, University of Leicester.
Judy Slinn	London.
P E Smart	formerly with The Institute of Bankers, London.
Barbara M D Smith	Lecturer, Centre for Urban and Regional Studies, University of Birmingham.
Richard Storey	Archivist, Modern Records Centre, University of Warwick Library.
Michael Stratton	Lecturer, Institute of Industrial Archaeology, University of Birmingham.
Jennifer Tann	Reader, Management Centre, University of Aston.
Dennis Teesdale	Publicity Manager, Babcock Woodall-Duckham Ltd.
Richard Trainor	Lecturer, Department of Economic History, University of Glasgow.
Geoffrey Tweedale	Researcher, Business History Unit, London School of Economics and Political Science.
Lady Gillian Wagner	London.
David H E Wainwright	Economic and Social Research Council, London.
Ronald B Weir	Lecturer, Department of Economics, University of York.
Joyce F Wheatley	London.
John F Wilson	Lecturer, Department of History, University of Manchester.
J S G Wilson	Emeritus Professor of Economics and Commerce, University of Hull.
R G Wilson	Senior Lecturer in Economic History, University of East Anglia, Norwich.
Robert J Wyatt	Wokingham, Berkshire.
Basil S Yamey	Professor of Economics, London School of Economics and Political Science.
Stephanie Zarach	London.
Jonathan H Zeitlin	Research Fellow, King's College, Cambridge.

Notes to Readers

1 Biographies are in the alphabetical sequence of subjects' family names. In the case of *hyphenated* surnames the first name in the compound family name determines the sequence.

2 In entry headings the title 'Lord' has been confined to barons, holders of the lowest degree in the British peerage; holders of degrees above baron have been given their exact peerage title, 'Viscount', 'Duke' etc. Peers are all listed in the alphabetical sequence of *family* names, not titles.

3 Place names are normally used according to the contemporary usage pertaining to the particular entry.

4 County boundaries are usually those prevailing before the reorganisation of local government in 1975.

5 For a note on British currency usage, see abbreviations (below), under £.

6 Foreign words have not been italicised.

7 The place of publication in bibliographical references is London, unless otherwise stated.

8 In the case of books running to several editions, bibliographical information is provided for the first or major edition.

9 Cross references to entries in the *Dictionary of National Biography*, *Who's Who of British Members of Parliament* and *Who Was Who* are regularly provided in the lists of sources but in many cases contributors have relied on ampler or more recently discovered sources.

10 On probate: the biography of any *DBB* subject dying in England or Wales includes the gross valuation of his/her estate where this has been recorded in the probate calendars at Somerset House, London, under a civil system commenced in January 1858. These figures should however be used with great caution, bearing in mind the following caveats:

(a) Before 1898 probate was required in respect of personalty only ie only 'moveables' like personal effects, stocks and shares and bank credits but also leaseholds.

(b) From 1898 onwards (following the Land Transfer Act of 1897) the probate valuation included realty, or immovable property like land and houses.

(c) Valuations of both personalty and realty always included unsettled property ie property in the absolute possession of the testator and not preserved in any way for future generations by some legal act of settlement.

(d) Settled land (ie that tied up by acts of settlement) was included in the probate calendar figures from 1 January 1926 under the Settled Land Act of 1925.

(e) Inter vivos gifts were not included in probate.

(f) Gross probate valuations of estates are those made before the deduction of funeral expenses and debts due on the estate.

(g) Prior to 1881 the value of an estate was given in round figures eg not exceeding £450,000 or £500,000 etc.

(h) The figures given in these entries are taken from the calendars at Somerset House and therefore miss any Scottish, Irish or foreign probates, unless these are specifically identified.

For further historical notes on this complex subject see Josiah Wedgwood, *The Economics of Inheritance* (Harmondsworth, Middlesex: Penguin Books Ltd, 1939 ed); Colin D Harbury and D M W N Hitchens, *Inheritance and Wealth Inequality in Britain* (George Allen & Unwin, 1979); William D Rubinstein, *Men of Property. The Very Wealthy in Britain Since the Industrial Revolution* (Croom Helm, 1981).

11   Subjects' writings. These do not include unpublished works. Where these are known they are cited as an unpublished source.

12   Company reports have been regarded as an unpublished source.

13   Patents have been classed as writings.

Abbreviations

AA	Automobile Association *or* anti-aircraft
AC	Alternating current
& Co	and Company
ADC	aide-de-camp
AEG	Allgemeine Elektrizitäts Gesellschaft
AEI	Associated Electrical Industries
AFC	Air Force Cross
AG	Aktiengesellschaft (joint-stock company)
AGM	Annual General Meeting
AIOC	Anglo-Iranian Oil Co
am	ante meridien (before noon)
APCM	Associated Portland Cement Manufacturers
APOC	Anglo Persian Oil Co
ARP	air-raid precautions
ASE	Amalgamated Society of Engineers
Aslef	Associated Society of Locomotive Engineers and Firemen
ATA	Air Transport Auxiliary
ATV	Associated Television
b	born
BA	Bachelor of Arts *or* British Airways
BAT	British American Tobacco Co *or* British Automobile Traction Co Ltd
Bateman	John Bateman, *Great Landowners of Great Britain* (Harrison, 1879).
BBC	British Broadcasting Association
BBFT	British Bank for Foreign Trade

BC & CC	British Cocoa & Chocolate Co
BCe	Birth certificate from General Register Office, St Catherines House, London WC1B 6JP
BCe (Scots)	Scottish birth certificate from The Registrar General, New Register House, Edinburgh EH1 3YT
BDA	Bradford Dyers' Association
BDC	British Dyestuffs Corporation
BEA	British European Airways *or* British Electricity Authority
BEF	British Expeditionary Force
BET	British Electric Traction Co
bhp	brake horsepower
BICC	British Insulated Callender's Cables
BIDC	Bankers' Industrial Development Corporation
BISF	British Iron and Steel Federation
BL	British Library, Great Russell Street, London WC1B 3DG
BLPES	British Library of Political and Economic Science, London School of Economics, Portugal Street, London WC2A 2HD
BMC	British Motor Corporation
BMH	British Motor Holdings
BMMO	Birmingham & Midland Motor Omnibus Co Ltd
BMPM	Bowater's Mersey Paper Mills Ltd
BOAC	British Overseas Airways Corporation
Boase	Frederic Boase, *Modern English Biography, Containing Memoirs of Persons Who Have Died since 1850* (6 vols, Truro: Netherton & Worth, 1892-1921).
BP	British Petroleum
BPC	British Printing Corporation
BPCM	British Portland Cement Manufacturers

Bros	Brothers (used in company titles)
BS	Bachelor of Surgery (Britain) *or* Bachelor of Science (USA) *or* Bristol-Siddeley
BSA	Birmingham Small Arms
BSc	Bachelor of Science (Britain)
BSC	British Steel Corporation
BST	British Stockbrokers' Trust Ltd
Bt	Baronet
BT	Board of Trade
BTC	British Transport Commission *or* British Trade Corporation
Burke's Landed Gentry	(Burke's Peerage Ltd. Various editions since 1836; edition identified by date).
Burke's Peerage and Baronetage	(Burke's Peerage [Genealogical Books] Ltd. Various editions since 1826; edition identified by date).
BVC	British Vacuum Cleaner
ca	circa
CB	Companion of the Bath
CBE	Commander of the Order of the British Empire
CBI	Confederation of British Industry
CEGB	Central Electricity Generating Board
ch	chapter
CIE	Companion of the Order of the Indian Empire
Cif	cost, insurance, freight
C-in-C	Commander-in-Chief
CIWL	Compagnie Internationale des Wagons-Lits
CME	Chief Mechanical Engineer
CMG	Companion of the Order of St Michael and St George

CND	Campaign for Nuclear Disarmament
Co	Company
Col	Colonel
comp	compiled, compiler
Complete Peerage	George Edward Cokayne, *The Complete Peerage of England, Scotland, Ireland, Great Britain and the United Kingdom, Extant Extinct or Dormant* (13 vols, St Catherine Press, 1910-59).
C Reg	Companies Registration Office file(s); microfiche versions of the files have been obtained from Companies Registration Office, 55 City Road, London EC1Y 1BB.
C Reg(w)	Notes made from company files subsequently despatched to the PRO and there subjected to a random destruction rate of 80–90 per cent.
CRO	County Record Office
Crockfords	*Crockfords Clerical Directory* (various editions, 1858 to present).
cwt	hundredweight (112 pounds, avoirdupois)
d	died
d (following a monetary figure)	pence [See note under £ at the end of this list]
DAB	*Dictionary of American Biography* edited by Allen Johnson and Dumas Malone (22 vols, New York: Charles Scribner's Sons, 1928-1944). The abbreviation also covers supplements to the *DAB*.
DBB	*Dictionary of Business Biography*
DCe	Death certificate from General Register Office, St Catherines House, London WC2B 6JP
DCL	Doctor of Civil Law *or* Distillers Co Ltd
DCM	Distinguished Conduct Medal
DCO	Dominion, Colonial and Overseas (Barclays Bank DCO)
DD	*Directory of Directors* (annual, East Grinstead: Thomas Skinner Directories, 1880-1983).
DH	de Havilland
DL	Deputy-Lieutenant

DLB	*Dictionary of Labour Biography* edited by Joyce M Bellamy and John Saville (6 vols, Macmillan, 1972-82, in progress).
DLitt	Doctor of Letters
DNB	*Dictionary of National Biography* edited by Leslie Stephen and Sidney Lee (63 vols, Oxford University Press, 1885-1933). The abbreviation also covers supplements to the *DNB*.
DSc	Doctor of Science
DSC	Distinguished Service Cross
DSIR	Department of Scientific and Industrial Research
DWB	*Dictionary of Welsh Biography down to 1940* edited by Sir John Edward Lloyd and R T Jenkins (London: The Honourable Society of Cymmrodorion, 1959).
EAC	Employers' Advisory Council
ECSC	European Coal and Steel Community
Edwards seminar paper.	Almost 450 papers, chiefly by businessmen and women presented in Professor Ronald S Edwards' Seminar at the LSE, 1946-1973, on 'Problems in Industrial Administration' (in BLPES Manuscripts). A number of these papers were published in *Business Enterprise* (Macmillan, 1959), *Studies in Business Organisation* (Macmillan, 1961) and *Business Growth* (Macmillan, 1966) edited by R S Edwards and H Townsend.
EE	English Electric
EEC	European Economic Community
EEF	Engineering Employers' Federation
EFTA	European Free Trade Association
Elliott research notes.	The biographical research notes on British MPs (mostly of the twentieth century) compiled by the late Anthony Elliott and kindly loaned to the *DBB* project by his widow Mrs Thea Elliott.
EMGAS	East Midlands Gas Board
EMI	Electric & Musical Industries
Erickson workcards.	Biographical workcards prepared by Professor Charlotte Erickson on steel and hosiery leaders, for her book *British Industrialists. Steel and Hosiery, 1850-1950* (Cambridge: Cambridge University Press for the National Institute of Economic and Social Research, 1959) and kindly loaned by her to the *DBB* project.

ETU	Electrical Trades Union
F	Fahrenheit (temperature)
FBI	Federation of British Industries
FCS	Fellow of the Chemical Society (now FRCS)
FCSDA	Fine Cotton Spinners' & Doublers' Association
fl	floreat (flourished)
FO	Foreign Office
fob	free on board
Foster, *Alumni Oxonienses.*	Joseph Foster, *Alumni Oxonienses, The Members of the University of Oxford 1715-1886* (4 vols, Oxford: James Parker & Co, 1891).
FRS	Fellow of the Royal Society
GB	Great Britain (England, Wales and Scotland)
GBE	Knight *or* Dame Grand Cross of the Order of the British Empire
GCVO	Knight *or* Dame Grand Cross of the Royal Victorian Order
GDP	Gross Domestic Product
GEC	General Electric Co
GER	Great Eastern Railway
GHQ	General Headquarters
GKN	Guest, Keen & Nettlefolds
GLC	Greater London Council
GmbH	Gesellschaft mit beschränkter Haftung (private limited liability company)
GNP	Gross National Product
GRA	Greyhound Racing Association Ltd
GWR	Great Western Railway
HC	House of Commons
HLRO	House of Lords Record Office

HM	His/Her Majesty/Majesty's
HMS	His/Her Majesty's Ship
HMV	His Master's Voice
Hon	Honourable
HP	Handley Page
hp	horsepower
HT	High Tension
HTS	Hilton Transport Services
IAL	Imperial Airways Ltd
IBA	Independent Broadcasting Authority
ibid	ibidem (the same source as the one previously quoted)
ICAEW	Institute of Chartered Accountants in England and Wales
ICE	Institution of Civil Engineers
ICI	Imperial Chemical Industries
IEE	Institution of Electrical Engineers
IG	Interessengemeinschaft (combine)
IME	Institution of Mechanical Engineers
Inc	Incorporated
JISI	*Journal of the Iron and Steel Institute*
JP	Justice of the Peace
Jr	Junior
KBE	Knight Commander of the Order of the British Empire
KCB	Knight Commander of the Order of the Bath
KCIE	Knight Commander of the Order of the Indian Empire
KCMG	Knight Commander of the Order of St Michael and St George
KCVO	Knight Commander of the Royal Victorian Order

KG	Knight of the Order of the Garter
KLM	Koninklijke Luchtvaart Maatschappij NV (Royal Dutch Air Lines)
kV	kilovolt
kW	kilowatt
£	£: see end of list
lb	pound(s), weight
LBC	Left Book Club *or* London Bicycle Co
LCC	London County Council
LCD	London, Chatham & Dover Railway
Lieut Col	Lieutenant Colonel
LLB	Bachelor of Laws
LLD	Doctor of Laws
LMS	London, Midland & Scottish Railway *or* London Missionary Society
LNER	London & North Eastern Railway
LNWR	London & North Western Railway
LSE	London School of Economics and Political Science
Ltd	Limited
MA	Master of Arts
MAP	Ministry of Aircraft Production
MBE	Member of the Order of the British Empire
MC	Military Cross
MCe	Marriage certificate from General Register Office, St Catherine's House, London WC2B 6JP
MCe (Scots)	Scottish marriage certificate from The Registrar General, New Register House, Edinburgh EH1 3YT
MCe (Irish)	Irish marriage certificate from The Registrar General, Oxford House, 49/55 Chichester Street, Belfast BT1 4HL (Northern Ireland), or The Registrar General, Custom House, Dublin 1 (Southern Ireland)

MCWF Co	Metropolitan Carriage, Wagon & Finance Co
MD	Doctor of Medicine
mk or MK	Mark
MM	Military Medal
MMS	Methodist Missionary Society
MP	Member of Parliament
MSc	Master of Science
MSS	Manuscripts
MVO	Member of the Royal Victorian Order
MW	megawatt(s)
NAAFI	Navy, Army, and Air Force Institutes
NATO	North Atlantic Treaty Organisation
NCB	National Coal Board
NCO	non-commissioned officer
nd	no date
NEDC	National Economic Development Council
NER	North-Eastern Railway
NHS	National Health Service
NLR	North London Railway
np	no place
NPA	Newspaper Proprietors' Association
NRA	National Register of Archives, Quality House, Quality Court, London WC2A 1HP
NSPCC	National Society for the Prevention of Cruelty to Children
NV	naamloze vennootschap (limited company)
OBE	Officer of the Order of the British Empire

OB St John	British Order of the Hospital of St John of Jerusalem
ODI	Overseas Development Institute
OPEC	Organisation of Petroleum Exporting Countries
OTC	Officers' Training Corps
P&O	Peninsular & Oriental Steamship Co
PA	Press Association
passim	here and there
PATA	Proprietary Articles Trade Association
PC	Privy Councillor
PD	*Parliamentary Debates* (Hansard)
PEP	Political and Economic Planning, now the Policy Studies Institute, London
PFR	Prototype Fast Reactor
pH	measure of hydrogen in concentration (indicating level of acidity)
PhD	Doctor of Philosophy
PLA	Port of London Authority
PLC (*or* plc)	public limited company
pm	post meridien (afternoon)
PP	*Parliamentary Papers*
pp	privately printed or published
PrC	Probate Calendar in Principal Registry of the Family Division, Somerset House, Strand, London WC2R 1LP
PRO	Public Record Office, Chancery Lane, London WC2A 1LR, or Ruskin Avenue, Kew, Richmond, Surrey TW9 4DU
psi	pounds per square inch
Pty	Proprietary (private limited company in Australia and South Africa)
PVC	polyvinyl chloride

qqv	cross reference to several other entries
qv	quod vide (which see; cross reference to another entry)
RA	Royal Artillery *or* Royal Academician
RAC	Royal Automobile Club
R&D	research and development
RAeS	Royal Aeronautical Society
RAF	Royal Air Force
RAFVR	Royal Air Force Volunteer Reserve
RAOC	Royal Army Ordnance Corps
RASC	Royal Army Service Corps
RC	Royal Commission
RCA	Radio Corporation of America
RE	Royal Engineers
REA	Royal Exchange Assurance
REME	Royal Electrical and Mechanical Engineers
rep	reprinted
RFC	Royal Flying Corps
RIBA	Royal Institute of British Architects
Rly	Railway
RM	Royal Marines
RN	Royal Navy
RNAS	Royal Naval Air Service
RNR	Royal Naval Reserve
RNVR	Royal Naval Volunteer Reserve
RO	Record Office
RPM	resale price maintenance

RSA	Royal Society of Arts
Rt Hon	Right Honourable
RTZ	Rio Tinto-Zinc Corporation
RUSI	Royal United Services Institute
s (following a monetary figure)	shillings [see note under £ at the end of this list]
SA	Société Anonyme (limited liability company)
SC	Select Committee
Scots DBB	*Scottish Dictionary of Business Biography,* Department of Economic History, Glasgow University
SE&CR	South Eastern & Chatham Railway
SHAEF	Supreme Headquarters, Allied Expeditionary Forces
Singer, *History of Technology.*	Charles Singer, E J Holmyard, A R Hall and Trevor Williams (eds), *A History of Technology* (7 vols, Oxford: Clarendon Press, 1954-78).
SMT	Securities Management Trust
SOAS	School of Oriental and African Studies, London University
SR	Southern Railway
Sr	Senior
SSRC Elites data.	Biographical workcards from SSRC project on 'The Economic Worth of Elites in British Society since 1880' conducted by Professor H J Perkin of Lancaster University, and kindly loaned by him to the *DBB* project.
STOL	Short take-off and landing
sv	sub verbo (under the heading cited)
TA	Territorial Army
TD	Territorial Decoration
TDG	Transport Development Group
Times *Prospectuses.*	*Prospectuses of Public Companies Including the Number of Bonds Drawn and Cancelled. Reprinted from the Advertisement Columns of the Times* (biannual, Times Publishing Co Ltd, 1891-1964).

TNPG	The Nuclear Power Group
TUC	Trades Union Congress
TV	television
UAC	United Africa Company
UCL	University College, London
UDC	Urban District Council
UERL	Underground Electric Railway Co of London
UK	United Kingdom (England, Wales, Scotland and Northern Ireland)
USA	United States of America
USAF	United States Air Force
V	volt(s)
VCH	*Victoria History of the Counties of England*
Venn, *Alumni Cantabrigienses*	John Venn and J A Venn, *Alumni Cantabrigienses. A Biographical List of All Known Students, Graduates and Holders of Office at the University of Cambridge, from the Earliest Times to 1900* Part II *1752 to 1900* (6 vols, Cambridge: Cambridge University Press, 1946-54)
V/STOL	vertical or short take-off and landing
VTOL	vertical take-off and landing
Will	Will of subject (unless otherwise stated) in Principal Registry of the Family Division, Somerset House, London WC2R 1LP
WPM	Wallpaper Manufacturers
WW	*Who's Who* (annual, Adam & Charles Black, 1849-1983).
WWMP	Michael Stenton and Stephen Lees, *Who's Who of British Members of Parliament. A Biographical Dictionary of the House of Commons* (4 vols, Hassocks, Sussex: Harvester Press, 1976-81).
WWW	*Who Was Who, 1897-1980* (8 vols, Adam & Charles Black, 1920-81).
WWW Theatre	*Who Was Who in the Theatre, 1912-1976* (Detroit: Gale Research Co, 1978)
YMCA	Young Men's Christian Association

£   Pound (monetary). In all entries, for dates before 15 February 1971 (when Britain switched to a decimal currency) the pound quoted is the old one, ie divided into 20 shillings each of 12 pence. Monetary sums under this old system are expressed as follows: £2 12s 6d. The decimal system abandoned shillings and divided the pound into 100 pence. The conversion rate for shillings is therefore one (old) shilling of 12 pence to five decimal pence.

ERRATA

p 356   title should read Sir Charles William Ewing Fielding.

p 583   title should read Frederick Godber, Lord Godber of Mayfield, Sussex.

*Sir David Dale (taken from J C
Carr and W Taplin* History of the
British Steel Industry *Oxford:
Basil Blackwell, 1962).*

DALE, Sir David

(1829-1906)

Iron and steel manufacturer and railway manager

David Dale was born in Moorshedabad, Bengal, on 11 December 1829; his
father, also called David Dale, was serving in the East India Company, as
a judge of the city court. David, the second son, was named after his
illustrious great-uncle, the founder of the New Lanark Mills and father-in-
law of Robert Owen. Though Dale's career as a prominent manufacturer
with an enlightened interest in good industrial relations fits into this
honourable family tradition, the major influence on David Dale as a child
was, in fact, his mother. His father died at sea on 23 June 1830 while he
was coming home with his family on furlough. David's mother, Ann
Elizabeth, daughter of Rev George Douglas of Aberdeen, settled at
Darlington, where she was admitted into the Quaker community in 1845.
David was brought up as a Quaker, and his industriousness and integrity,
together with his calm and dignified bearing, constantly reminded those
who had dealings with him of his membership of this denomination.
However, in his later years he came to dislike some of the developments
that had taken place within the Quaker community, and he resigned from
it in about 1888.

Educated privately in Edinburgh, Durham and Stockton, David Dale
began his business career in 1846 in the offices of the Wear Valley
Railway, moving from there to the offices of the Stockton & Darlington
Railway. Showing a flair for finance, at the age of twenty-three he was
appointed secretary of the Middlesbrough and Guisborough section of the
line. Six years later, he became the partner of William Bouch, the lessee of
the Shildon Locomotive Works, near Darlington, who had the contract to
work the Darlington and Stockton section of the line with its heavy
mineral traffic. Bouch took care of the practical arrangements, Dale of the
finances; together they built up a successful locomotive-building and
- repair works, before Dale ceased to be a partner in the early 1870s.

It is not clear whether Dale left his railway employment during his
partnership with Bouch, but his continued involvement with the affairs of
the Darlington branch led to his appointment, about the time he ceased to
be Bouch's partner, as managing director of the Stockton & Darlington
Railway. In 1881 he became a director of the North-Eastern Railway, and
was chairman of the NER Way and Works Committee at the time of his
death.

Despite his long association with the railways, Dale's reputation as a
businessman rests above all on his association with the Consett Iron Co.
His introduction to the Consett Works occurred in 1858, when Dale was
appointed as inspector of the works for the creditors of the insolvent
Derwent Iron Co. Within a few years the new administration was in
trouble too and in April 1864 a new company, the Consett Iron Co, bought

the assets of the Derwent & Consett Iron Co, which included 18 blast-furnaces and 500 acres of freehold land, for the bargain price of £255,000. Dale was appointed one of the joint managing directors, though he seems to have left the day-to-day running of the works to his colleague Jonathan Priestman. In 1869, Priestman resigned and his position was filled by a new general manager William Jenkins (qv), whom Dale had persuaded to come to Consett from the Dowlais Iron Co. Dale continued as managing director until 1873 and served as chairman from 1884 to his death. He and Jenkins turned the Consett Iron Co into the most profitable iron and steel firm in the country. The average profits of the company, as a percentage of the capital employed (share capital, reserves, loans, and undistributed profits), during the first fifty years of the company's life were 19.1 per cent, the average dividend over the same period 23 per cent. The peak profit of £672,000 after tax and interest came in 1900 when the issued capital was £1.5 million. Contemporaries attributed this success largely to the quality of Consett's management, a view endorsed by a recent study of the firm's profitability. Though not responsible for any major technical innovation, Jenkins kept a close and canny eye on technical developments in the industry, and the plant at Consett was always updated. Jenkins was mainly responsible for the decision to specialise in the manufacture of plates after the collapse of the rail trade in 1876, and for the decision to begin production of steel in 1883. By 1887, Consett was the largest steel-plate producing works in England and was a major supplier of the local shipbuilders, as well as exporting throughout the world. A wide range of other iron and steel products was produced as well, including much coal from the company mines, which yielded about 1.5 million tons a year by the turn of the century.

Dale contributed to the success of the company in several ways. He was largely responsible for the consistently sound financial policy of the company, especially the placing of large sums to reserve, and the cautious (by the standard of his contemporaries) policy of dividend payment which did so much to ensure its continuous prosperity. It was he who assured the company of regular supplies of ironstone. In 1872, at a time when domestic haematite prices were rising fast, Dale set up the Consett Spanish Ore Co to enable the Consett Iron Co to take a share in the produce of a Spanish iron-ore concern, the Orconera Iron Ore Co (Dale eventually became chairman of both these companies). Dale's influence and attitudes did much to keep relations with the employees of the firm consistently good. In this period, when other iron and steel firms in the area suffered from troubled industrial relations, there was little internal disturbance at Consett. The few strikes, particularly those of the Consett miners, were called in sympathy with regional or national actions. Dale took great interest in the social and educational facilities provided for the workers (who numbered about 6,000 in 1893) and their families; these facilities included an infirmary, schools for well over 1,000 children, and reading-rooms.

Dale's reputation as an industrial conciliator spread beyond Consett. Soon after a costly six-months strike in the North of England iron-trade in 1866, Dale first proposed the formation of an arbitration board. He pursued the proposal in 1868 while secretary of the local Iron Manufacturers' Association. By February 1869, when the men of several works suggested the establishment of a Board of Arbitration on the model as again and again he has shown himself perfectly able to take care of himself without consideration for any liability he may have incurred by way of guarantees' {MB, Madders' diary, 12 Dec 1907}. As late as 1914 he was reportedly 'in a strait' {HLRO, Bonar Law Papers, 35/5/48, Arthur Steel-Maitland to Law, 18 Dec 1914}.

In the 1890s Dalziel became involved in the Cie Internationale des Wagons-Lits which had been founded in 1876 by a Belgian engineer named Georges Nagelmackers (1845-1905). Initially Dalziel was concerned to attract English travellers to CIWL's Continental services, but his influence in the company increased by the marriage of his only child Helen, who died 21 December 1910, to René Nagelmackers (d 1929), the founder's son. In 1902 Dalziel joined the Conseil d'Administration of CIWL and together with a financier called Lucien Villars helped to re-organise railway operations and to fund investment in rolling-stock. He obtained a large shareholding in CIWL, 'carrying with him other large British financial interests which gradually have become the most powerful influence in the company' {PRO, FO 371/11859, Memo in Ralph Glyn to Sir Austen Chamberlain, 14 May 1926}. In 1919 he was elected president of the Conseil d'Administration and president of the Comité d'Administration in 1924. His board comprised one Austrian, two Belgians and Spaniards, three Italians and British, and seven French: it proved a hard task to adjust the conflicting interests and to harmonise such diverse factors. Dalziel himself was said to represent £3.5 million in bonds and £2.5 million in CIWL shares at market value in 1926.

In 1906-7 Dalziel bought the British Pullman Palace Car Co, which had been formed in 1882, from its American owners. At that time only three British railways had Pullman services: the London, Brighton & South Coast; the London & South-West with two cars; and the Highland, with two sleepers. Of these, only the Brighton run was financially successful. Dalziel proved ruthless in his quest for profits, investing solely in viable routes and scrapping loss-making services, beginning with the Highland in 1907. The first Pullman carriages manufactured in Britain were seven cars supplied by Metropolitan Carriage & Wagon Co's Lancaster works, which were in service as the *Southern Belle* on the Brighton route from November 1908 until December 1924. The first electrically hauled Pullmans were two cars introduced in 1910 on the Metropolitan Railway's line from Aylesbury and Chesham to Aldgate: these were supplied by the Birmingham Railway Carriage works, which met most of Dalziel's rolling-stock needs at that time. At a joint meeting in Birmingham of 1910 between the Institution of Mechanical Engineers and the American Society of Mechanical Engineers, 'Dalziel expressed the opinion that main line electric working in this country was not only commercial but comparatively imminent' {*Times Engineering Supplement* 3 Aug 1910}. Initially Dalziel's Drawing Room Cars Co was the financial medium for his purchases of equipment, but in 1915 he re-organised the group and registered the Pullman Car Co with £250,000 ordinary capital. This was increased to £500,000 in 1920, with £625,000 preference shares issued in 1923 at the time when CIWL was increasing its stake in Pullman.

Dalziel was also a director until 1910 of the De Mello Brazilian Rubber Co Ltd, formed in 1906 with issued capital of £465,000 to develop 700,000 acres on the River Acre in Brazil. He was a director for many years of the

Liberian Rubber Corporation, which was registered in 1905 with £270,000 issued capital to obtain a complete rubber monopoly in Liberia.

He headed several Anglo-French retailers and wholesalers. In 1899 he became the first chairman of Aux Classes Laborieuses Ltd, a British registered company (initially with £250,000 ordinary and £375,000 cumulative preference shares) which operated as drapers and general furnishers in Paris. He was an original director from 1901 and chairman from 1902 of Bloch & Behr Ltd, wholesale Paris clothiers registered in London with £65,000 ordinary and £64,000 preference shares issued. In 1913 Bloch & Behr was reconstructed to become Les Galeries Universelles Ltd, wholesale clothiers, grocers and bakers, of which Dalziel was again chairman. Another company operating in France of which he was a director from 1907 until his death was the Elysée Palace Hotel Co, which had been formed by CIWL but had met financial difficulties. Before the war he also successively became a director and then chairman of Charles Drecoll Ltd, dressmakers and furriers of Paris and Vienna. Dalziel received the Légion d'Honneur in 1907.

Dalziel masterminded another example of Anglo-French commercial collaboration: the taxicab business. In 1906 he formed the General Motor Cab Co Ltd, capitalised at £500,000, of which he was initially vice-chairman, and then chairman 1907-12. This, together with the United Motor Cab Co of which he was the first chairman in 1907-8, introduced motor taxicabs to London, following their success in Paris. Both companies used French-built cabs, French-patented taximeters and French directors, although Godfrey Isaacs (qv) was also involved. By July 1907 Dalziel could declare 'that a new English industry, with immense prospects, has been established' {*Times* 2 July 1907}. The next year he conceived the Provincial Motor Cab Co which enjoyed less success and was wound up after the outbreak of war. George Dalziel at this time became a director of the New York Motor Cab Co, Davison Dalziel became pre-war chairman of the Brussels Motor Cab Co (in which the Nagelmackers family were concerned), and it was stated in 1910 that he was 'interested in motor cab undertakings in Berlin and New York' {*Times* 17 Jan, 7 Dec 1910}. Dalziel was involved in the French motor-car industry by 1900, and was chairman from 1907 of the British company, Charron Ltd, which owned the Paris motor-cab manufacturers Automobiles SA Charron, Girardot et Voigt, and had initially £304,000 issued capital.

Dalziel was narrowly defeated when he contested Brixton as the Unionist candidate in 1906, but after siting General Motor Cab's great garage in the constituency the next year, he was victorious in the general election of January 1910, and represented Brixton (with a hiatus in 1923-24) for almost seventeen years. His nephew Nigel Claudian Dalziel Colman (1886-1966) succeeded him as MP for Brixton 1927-45 and received a baronetcy for political services in 1952. Dalziel gave little attention to the House of Commons. His first speeches in 1916 were very brief and concerned new laws affecting stockbrokers. He did not once speak or submit a written question throughout the Parliament of 1918-22, and was one of the Unionist MPs, mostly businessmen like Douglas Vickers and Vernon Willey (qv), who did not attend the Carlton Club meeting which voted to withdraw from the Lloyd George coalition in 1922.

William Knox D'Arcy with his wife Elena (seated, centre) and his children outside their house in Wandal, Rockhampton, Queensland, Australia (courtesy of British Petroleum Company plc).

except the five northern provinces (those adjoining the border with Russia) in return for 16 per cent of the profits.

H T Burks, a geologist, was chosen to investigate briefly and an engineer, George B Reynolds, to drill. The difficulties were formidable: the terrain inhospitable, the locality was lacking in resources and the political situation unstable. Nevertheless after first drilling unsuccessfully in the west of the country, Reynolds persevered in the south west before finally striking oil at Masjid-i-Suleiman in May 1908. D'Arcy who originally wanted only to float a company, found himself working the concession, with costs vastly exceeding his expectations — almost £250,000 before the discovery well. He tried to interest other concerns in raising further capital. Eventually the Burmah Oil Co, with some encouragement from certain members of the Admiralty, joined D'Arcy in a Concessions Oil Syndicate in 1905 and furnished further funds on strict terms, including operational control which was managed locally by Reynolds. Further injections of cash were made in 1907 and 1908, but Burmah showed signs of reluctance to commit itself to further finance until the two wells then being drilled produced oil — which they did. Consequently on 14 April 1909 the Anglo-Persian Oil Co (APOC) was formed, with the Burmah Oil Co holding most of the shares. D'Arcy surrendered his rights in return for 170,000 Burmah shares, a seat on the board of APOC and the reimbursement of the expenses he had already incurred, £203,067 19s 6d. D'Arcy remained an interested and attending director until his death. By grasping the opportunity to acquire his oil concession in Persia, he had as much claim as anybody to be regarded as the founder of the oil industry of the Middle East.

William Knox D'Arcy died on 1 May 1917 leaving £990,988 gross.

R W FERRIER

Sources:

Unpublished

BCe.

MCe.

PrC.

Published

BP Shield International Mar 1972.

Ronald W Ferrier, *The History of the British Petroleum Company: The Developing Years 1901-1932* (Cambridge: Cambridge University Press, 1982).

WWW.

DARTMOUTH, 6th Earl of Dartmouth
see LEGGE, William Heneage

DARWIN, Sir Horace

(1851-1928)

Scientific instrument manufacturer

Horace Darwin was born at Downe in Kent on 13 May 1851, the fifth and youngest son of the celebrated naturalist Charles Darwin and his wife Emma née Wedgwood. As a boy he was somewhat delicate in health but,

Sir Horace Darwin (courtesy of the Science Museum, London).

with the help of private tuition, he qualified to enter Trinity College, Cambridge, in 1871. After graduating in the mathematical tripos of 1874 he took up an ordinary apprenticeship in the iron foundry of Messrs Easton & Anderson of Erith, Kent. During this time he became an associate member of the Institution of Civil Engineers (1877) and of the Institution of Mechanical Engineers (1878). At the end of his training he returned to Cambridge and remained there for the rest of his life.

The 1870s at Cambridge University saw the gradual recognition of the claims of natural science as a subject for study and research. Laboratories were developed in chemistry, engineering, physics and physiology although the early workers experienced considerable difficulty in obtaining specialised equipment for their researches. As a result A G Dew-Smith, a wealthy amateur experimenter, took up the challenge to supply much needed items to Michael Foster, a professor in the physiological laboratory, by providing initial finance for a small workshop in Panton Street. There the business was in the hands of a capable mechanic, Robert Fulcher. Both Dew-Smith and Foster were known to the Darwin family and it is not surprising, therefore, that Horace Darwin should have joined this venture when he returned to Cambridge. Following the termination of Fulcher's interests in 1880, Darwin entered into partnership with Dew-Smith and the Cambridge Scientific Instrument Co was officially founded on 1 January 1881.

The reputation of the company was earned through excellent craftsmanship and Darwin's flair for design. Geometric design, based on principles established by James Clerk Maxwell, was a particular feature of Darwin's approach to mechanical problems and this is well-exemplified in the company's first successful product, a microtome popularly called the Cambridge 'Rocker'. By 1884 trade had grown sufficiently to warrant a move to larger premises in Tibbs Row. Important orders came from a

Sir Horace Darwin — The Cambridge Rocking Microtome. A successful product based on early application of the principles of geometric design (courtesy of the Science Museum, London).

variety of sources: Lord Rayleigh requested a synchronous motor; Sir Francis Galton needed anthropometrical instruments; the Kew Observatory commissioned cloud cameras; and the Board of Trade sought a temperature-regulator. Characteristically Darwin would immerse himself in the problems of the investigators and then quickly design an item to suit their needs. Rarely was he interested in the actual construction of an instrument once the prototype or model had been approved. Individually-made items had, of course, to be separately priced and it was an initial failing of Darwin to underprice the finished artefact, showing little conception of how to charge for materials and labour. This was quickly rectified in 1885 when, with a majority holding of the company's shares, he took over the chairmanship and responsibility of running the business. Dew-Smith retired in 1891.

In 1895, when the business was transferred to purpose-built premises in Chesterton Road, a limited liability company was formed with a nominal capital of £10,000 of which £5,235 was issued. At that time electrical measuring methods began to appear and Darwin was quick to obtain sole manufacturing rights for devices such as H L Callendar's potentiometric recorder for temperature measurement. Indeed, temperature measurement became a speciality under Robert S Whipple (qv) who joined the firm as Darwin's personal assistant in 1898. Whipple, an inventive man himself, helped to pioneer the introduction of instrumental methods of control in certain industrial processes and, in later years, relieved Darwin of business worries by taking a strong lead in the company's affairs. Darwin, by contrast, saw a future in the development of electromechanical devices and items such as the Einthoven electrocardiograph and the Duddell oscillograph. In the same year that Whipple joined the company, Darwin's foreman of long standing, W T Pye (qv), left to help his son set up a general instrument making business which eventually specialised in radionics and became renowned as Pye Radio Ltd. Another pioneer in the electrical instrument field who gained his initial experience under Darwin's guidance was Henry Tinsley.

In recognition of his numerous contributions Darwin, in 1903, became the third brother in the family to be elected FRS. About this time his interests turned to aviation and the problems of mechanical stress and navigation in flight. He was appointed to the government Advisory Committee for Aeronautics and during the First World War took office as chairman of the Air Inventions Committee. Meanwhile, as part of the war effort, the company informally joined forces with the London firm of R W Paul. It was rationalised that the latter should deal with medical equipment while the Cambridge base should concentrate on secret war work. The two companies officially amalgamated in 1921. For his wartime services Darwin was created KBE in 1918.

Darwin married Emma Farrer, daughter of Thomas Henry Farrer Esq, later First Lord Farrer, in 1880 and they had three children. Aside from business concerns Darwin took a keen interest in local government and was elected Mayor of Cambridge for 1896-97. Also he took a special interest in mentally handicapped children. He died on 22 September 1928 leaving £111,699 gross. Although his only son, Erasmus, had been killed in the First World War, family interests in the company were maintained. Despite takeovers and subsequent dismembering of the company in more recent times an offshoot still trades as the Cambridge Instrument Co and on its board (1982) is a grandson of Horace Darwin.

BRIAN GEE

Writings:

'On a Self-recording Barometer' *Proceedings of the Cambridge Philosophical Society* 5 (1883-86).

(with C V Burton) 'Side-slip in Motor Cars' *Engineering* 78 (1904).

'Scientific Instruments, Their Design and Use in Aeronautics' *Aeronautical Journal* 17 (1913).

(with C C Mason) 'Instruments, the Design of Scientific' *Dictionary of Applied Physics* 3 (1923).

Collections of Cambridge Scientific Instrument Co instruments are kept by the Whipple Museum (Cambridge) and Science Museum (London).

Sources:

Unpublished

Cambridge University Library Archives Department, Papers of the Cambridge Scientific Instrument Co.

BCe.

MCe.

PrC.

Published

Cambridge Instrument Co, '50 Years of Scientific Instrument Manufacture' *Engineering* 159 (1945).

----, '75 Years of Successful Endeavour, 1881-1956' (the company, 1956).

Cambridge Review 26 Oct 1928.

DNB.

Richard T Glazebrook, 'Sir Horace Darwin FRS, KBE' *Nature* 122 (1928).

James R Moore, 'On the Education of Darwin's Sons' *Notes and Records of the Royal Society of London* 32 (1977).

Proceedings of the Royal Society of London 122A (1929).

Times 24 Sept 1928.

Venn, *Alumni Cantabrigienses.*

Robert S Whipple, *Journal of Scientific Instruments* 6 (1929).

----, 'Reminiscences of an Instrument Maker' *Journal of Scientific Instruments* 19 (1942).

WWW.

Sir Samuel Davidson (courtesy of Mr David Johnson).

DAVIDSON, Sir Samuel Clement

(1846-1921)

Inventor and manufacturer of ventilation equipment

Samuel Clement Davidson was born in Ballymachan, County Down, on 18 November 1846, the youngest child in the family of five boys and three girls of James Davidson and his wife Mary née Taylor. His father, a Non-subscribing Presbyterian, was a successful farmer who had branched out into flourmilling in the city of Belfast. Samuel was educated at the Royal Belfast Academical Institution which he left at the age of fifteen. After two years of private tuition he went into the offices of William Hastings, a Belfast surveyor and civil engineer. There he learned the rudiments of engineering and gained a lifelong love of mechanical experimentation.

As a younger son, in a small family firm, he could not hope to succeed to his father's inheritance. (His eldest brother, John carried on the family milling business, becoming a JP and a member of the Belfast Harbour Board, while the second brother, James, took up hunting in India and Ulster, earning thereby the sobriquet 'Nimrod'.)

In 1864, through the influence of a cousin in India, James Davidson, Samuel found employment on an Indian tea plantation. Later, with some financial help from his father, Samuel became co-owner of the estate, and after James Davidson's death in 1869 bought out his cousin's interest and obtained sole control. Enjoying independence and financial security at the early age of twenty-five, Samuel Davidson spent the rest of his life gratifying his taste and talent for mechanical invention. From 1869 until 1881 he spent most of his time in India where he engaged variously in the mapping out of tea plantations, and investigating the means by which the processing and packaging of the commodity might be improved. He also became a consultant in tea production to the Government of India. Davidson returned briefly in 1873 to marry Clara Coleman, a grand-daughter of John Ritchie, the founder of shipbuilding in Belfast; they had three daughters (one of whom died as a child in India) and two sons who both predeceased their parents. In 1881 he came back to Belfast to establish his own engineering business initially employing only seven men. This firm was later to operate under the trademark 'Sirocco', named after the hot wind that blows from North Africa to Italy, a reference to the features of the drying machines Davidson later developed.

Tea consumption was rising rapidly in the later nineteenth and early twentieth centuries, a result of increasing incomes and temperance. From 1864 (the year Davidson went to India) until 1921, the year of his death, UK consumption rose over four and a half times. As the public's taste became more discerning, the demand for quality tea grew even faster. Davidson, almost single-handedly, enabled this demand to be fulfilled. The main problem in producing high-quality tea in large quantities lay at the drying stage. The old method whereby the leaf was dried over charcoal fires was crude, slow, and all too frequently produced inferior tea. The bulk of Davidson's inventive activity between 1864 and 1898 was devoted to perfecting the methods by which tea was dried. The problem lay in creating a hot blast of air that would dry the tea rapidly. At first Davidson's inventions were based on the principle of rising hot air, but he was dissatisfied with them as 'even when the height of the chimney' was 'greatly increased there was still insufficient draught to draw the air through anything but a few lightly loaded trays' {MaGuire (nd) 19}. More and more he turned his attention to experimentation on the development of fans. By the lengthy process of trial and error he gradually improved his machines and in 1898 finally achieved success with the invention of the Sirocco Forward Bladed Centrifugal Fan. The same year the business became a limited company, Davidson & Co Ltd, trading under the name of Sirocco; it was capitalised at £170,000 comprising 10,000 £10 ordinary shares and £70,000 in 5 per cent debentures. By the early twentieth century the firm employed over a thousand men in Belfast alone and the Sirocco factory extended over four acres.

Although Davidson's work on the development of fans for tea drying proved to be his most enduring contribution, he also revolutionised virtually all other aspects of the process of tea manufacture, from the receiving of the green leaf at the factory to the packaging of the final product. But the fan he had initially invented for drying tea was to prove adaptable for other purposes, ventilation of mines and ships, for example. (Ironically, given Davidson's pronounced patriotism, nearly every ship in the German fleet sunk at Scapa Flow was equipped with 'Sirocco' fans.) Subsequently, after Samuel's death, the company produced variations of the basic design for use in air raid shelters, power stations, meat and vegetable dehydration plants and aircraft. Under his successors, A Agar and F G MaGuire (his son-in-law), the company set up subsidiaries in South Africa and Australia; in March 1960 it became a public company and in 1972 was taken over by the South African combine, Abercom Investments Ltd.

When Davidson died he had over 120 patents to his name. Most of them were for tea processing machinery and fans, but he also invented a predecessor of the bazooka, the 'Hand Howitzer'. Although the British military authorities showed little interest, the American Government saw the potential of the weapon and decided to manufacture it on a large scale. However, the First World War came to an end and the project was shelved. Davidson made inventions in many other areas: belt rivets, steam engines, the production of special beverages from tea, coffee and cocoa, the manufacture of peat briquettes, and machinery for processing raw rubber.

In his early years Davidson had been a keen sportsman: for six years 100 yards champion of East Bengal, and the North East Rifle Association champion in 1873. In his later years he enjoyed photography and motor vehicles but, most of all, mechanical experimentation which provided both livelihood and hobby. He belonged to the Institution of Mechanical Engineers, the Society of Arts, and the Institute of Directors. His only recorded office, however, was in 1915 when he was elected president of Belfast Chamber of Commerce. Although asked many times to sit on the local council he refused, preferring to devote his time to his experiments.

Politically he was described as 'loyal to the core' {*Belfast Telegraph* 19 Aug 1921} and was 'a staunch friend and generous supporter of the Ulster Volunteer Force' {*Belfast Newsletter* 19 Aug 1921}. However his devotion to Unionism did not prevent his strenuous opposition to the expulsion of Roman Catholic workers from the factory during the riots of both 1912 and 1920.

Samuel Davidson's success stemmed less from entrepreneurial ability than from sheer inventive talent. On 22 June 1921 he was made a KBE and on 18 August of the same year he died; in his will he left £185,817 gross (£65,025 gross in London).

DAVID S JOHNSON

Sources:

Unpublished

PrC.

Private correspondence with Mr Edward MaGuire, grandson of S C Davidson, and Mrs Wendy Pratt, great-granddaughter of S C Davidson.

Published

Belfast Newsletter 19 Aug 1921.

Belfast Newsletter 200th Anniversary Supplement 1 Sept 1937.

Belfast Telegraph 19 Aug 1921.

Alexander Ibbetson, *Tea from Grower to Consumer* (Pitman, 1910).

Edward D MaGuire, *The Sirocco Story* (Belfast: Davidson & Co, nd).

Brian R Mitchell and Phyllis Deane, *Abstract of British Historical Statistics* (Cambridge: Cambridge University Press, 1962).

WWW.

DAVIES, David

(1818-1890)

Railway contractor, coalmine and dock entrepreneur

David Davies was born in the village of Llandinam, Montgomeryshire on 18 December 1818. He was the eldest of a large family born to David Davies and his wife Elizabeth, who had moved there from Cardiganshire. The family belonged to the Calvinistic Methodists, whose strong religious and temperance principles were to govern David Davies all his life, to the extent that when in his railway-building days he was moving locomotives to working sites by road, they were not allowed to continue the journey on the Sunday.

After education at the village school, David Davies began work at the age of fourteen under his father, who combined small farming with the craft of a master sawyer of timber. The boy not only developed a notable skill with woodworking tools, but soon evinced a remarkable degree of judgement in the quick and accurate estimating of quantities and dimensions in building work generally. Beginning in a small way locally, Davies, before he was thirty, had successfully entered the field of public works contracting for local authorities and others within his immediate area. The spread of railways across South and mid-Wales enabled him to widen his field of action.

Between 1855 and 1870 Davies built nearly 150 miles of railway, including most of the Cambrian Railways system with its mountainous section east of Machynlleth, which is still in use today. In nearly all these projects (the exception being his partnership with Thomas Savin, which Davies himself severed), he displayed great ability in the choice of his associates, assistants and workmen, among them (Sir) James Szlumper, and the great Brunel's gifted son, Henry Marc Brunel.

The two greatest industrial achievements of Davies' life came after middle age. Having successfully exploited the quarrying of limestone while building railways in Pembrokeshire, he was struck by the immense potential of the Rhondda Valley coalfield with its huge reserves of the world's finest steam coal. In 1864, therefore, he formed with his associates a consortium to acquire the lease of mineral rights in the upper part of the valley. After much frustration and anxiety, Davies's workmen struck the rich steam coal seam more than 600 feet down, during a last despairing week in which, such was their personal loyalty, they had offered to work for nothing. From this initial success stemmed two of the most powerful combines of the age: David Davies & Co and its successor the Ocean Coal Co, whence came his nickname, 'Dai Davies yr Ocean'. In 1890 his first four collieries were employing nearly 3,400 men and producing over one million tons of coal a year.

By the standards of the time, they seem to have been good employers. The housing built for Davies's workers in parts of the Rhondda Valley was in some quarters highly regarded. And in the 1870s, on at least two occasions, the miners employed by David Davies & Co elected, in a free choice, to accept their employer's wage scale rather than that of the coal owners' association, which the firm left for some years (rejoining in 1889 when a conciliation board replaced a 'sliding scale' committee).

Davies's last and most successful venture came in his closing years. Cardiff docks, saddled with obsolete facilities, could not cope with the rapidly expanding traffic in steam coal from the Rhondda and Aberdare valleys. Shipment coal traffic was not only being delayed at Cardiff itself, because of ships having to wait for berths, but also by congestion on the Taff Vale Railway, with its monopoly of rail traffic between the Rhondda and Aberdare Valleys and Cardiff. When the Cardiff townsmen resisted a new expansion of their docks, David Davies and his associated freighters sought a new deep-water port on Barry Sound, directly linked by rail to the Rhondda Valley above Pontypridd (and later to the Rhymney and Monmouthshire Valleys). Although the first bill for the Barry Dock & Railways Co failed to pass in 1883, it succeeded the following year. The docks and initial elements of the railway system were brought into use in 1889, and were instantly successful, so that the Barry Co, which was one of the last major undertakings of the railway age, became also one of the most prosperous. Barry eventually became the largest coal-shipping port in South Wales.

Davies had been deputy chairman to the Earl of Plymouth in the formation of the company and the construction of the docks and railways. But he did not long survive to enjoy his large personal triumph within that of the Barry venture.

Davies' horizons broadened beyond Wales and his own firm. He attended the opening of the Suez Canal (1869), advised the Czar of Russia on railways (1870), and later still became a director of British-invested railways in Spain and Brazil. At home he contributed generously to the establishment of the University College of Wales, Aberystwyth, of which he was treasurer, 1875-87. In the House of Commons, as Liberal MP for Cardiganshire, 1874-86, he was an honest but not outstanding Parliamentarian. His rather homespun speeches were mainly confined to issues close to his heart, such as temperance, land tenure, and employers' liability. But as with the Cambrian Railways board (from which he resigned after presenting, at the company's general meeting in 1879, an impulsive, caustic and perhaps tactically ill-timed criticism of current management), he was unafraid to speak out against the party lines on issues about which he felt strongly.

Throughout his increasingly busy working days, Davies never forsook the obligations of religious and family life. His marriage in 1851 to Margaret Jones (1814-94) afforded him the staunchest of supporters, to his life's end. They had one son, Edward (1852-98). Worn out perhaps by the exertions, strains and anxieties of his last project, David Davies died on 20 July 1890, leaving £404,424 gross.

Edward's son, David Davies, followed in his grandfather's footsteps in politics, education and commerce. He served as Liberal MP for Montgomeryshire, 1906-29, and as president of the University College of Wales, Aberystwyth. He was deputy chairman of both the Barry and the Cambrian companies, and the last chairman of the Cambrian Railway Co.

After their amalgamation with the Great Western Railway in 1922, David Davies Jr joined the GWR board. His numerous public services and benefactions were recognised by elevation to the peerage as Baron Davies of Llandinam in 1932.

D S M BARRIE

Sources:

Unpublished

Proceedings of various Parliamentary Committees on Bills of railway companies with which David Davies was associated.

PRO:

RAIL 23 Barry Railways Co (originally Barry Dock & Railway Co).
RAIL 65 Brecon & Merthyr Tydfil Junction Railway Co.
RAIL 92 Cambrian Railways Co.
RAIL 491 Midland Railway Co, Hemel Hempstead Branch.
RAIL 559 Pembroke & Tenby Railway Co.
RAIL 253/764 Van Railway Co.
RAIL 1057/2984 Vale of Clwyd Railway Co.
RAIL 1007/332 David Davies as builder of Vale of Clwyd Railway.
RAIL 1057/1006 Barry Railways; Letters of David Davies, deputy chairman 1887-90 and of his son Edward Davies, managing director of the company, 1890-97.
RAIL 1057/1010 Barry Railway Co: Memorial Statue to David Davies.

Published

Derek S M Barrie, *The Barry Railway* (Blandford Oakwood Press, 1978).

Ivor Bulmer-Thomas, *Top Sawyer. A Biography of David Davies of Llandinam* (Longmans, 1938).

Martin Daunton, *Coal Metropolis: Cardiff, 1870-1914* (Leicester: Leicester University Press).

Charles P Gasquoine, *The Story of the Cambrian* (Wrexham: Woodall, Minshall, Thomas & Co, 1922).

Goronwy Jones, *David Davies (1818-1890), Llandinam* (Gwrecsam: Hughes a'i Fab, 1913).

Evan D Lewis, *The Rhondda Valleys. A Study in Industrial Development, 1800 to the Present Day* (Phoenix House, 1959).

PD.

Davies and Hailey Rimell, *History of the Barry Railway* (Cardiff: Western Mail, 1923).

WWMP.

DAVIS, Sir Edmund Gabriel

(1862-1939)

Company promoter and mining financier

Edmund Gabriel Davis was born at Tuorak, near Melbourne, Australia, on 3 August 1862, son of Samuel Davis, a Jew of French extraction, by Josephine Bensusan. He was educated at Highburn House, St Leonards-on-Sea, and at Collège Chapstal, Paris, where he studied art. At the age of seventeen he went to Cape Colony to recuperate his glands and entered his uncle's general store, Bensusan of Capetown, which specialised in ostrich feathers. He recovered his health during a year spent alone with natives, and dressed only in shorts, collected guano (bird droppings) on an island which he leased off the Cape Coast. He laid the foundation of his fortune by borrowing £1,000 and with it buying up a large number of hopeless debts in German South West Africa. He pursued the debtors, and recovered a large amount. With the proceeds he made in 1888 his first company flotation, the Bechuanaland Exploration Co of which he was chairman. In January 1889 he married, at St Petersburgh Place Synagogue, Bayswater, his cousin Mary Zillah (1866-1941), daughter of Arthur Halford, formerly Hyam (1841-1903), of 8 Pembridge Square, Notting Hill Gate, by Orovida Halford (1841-1915). His father-in-law (and uncle) left £110,283. Another member of the Halford family was Sir Edward Manville (qv). The Davises were a devoted but childless couple; she had a talent for making exquisite patterned fans and needlework shawls, which were exhibited in London on several occasions. Her brother, Alfred Halford (1868-1943) was a prominent London stockbroker.

After his marriage Davis settled in London, becoming partner with a German called Wertheimer in Jacob Picard & Co, foreign agents, of 27 Old Jewry. As a member of the Picard firm Davis received many propositions for developing overseas resources, and emerged in the 1890s as a financier specialising in mining and mineral deposits of a speculative character. He floated numerous companies to exploit the natural wealth of Africa, Australasia and China, and joined the board of many of them as a London financial contact rather than as a mining executive. He also financed the Singapore electric tramway.

Simultaneously, while other financiers exploited the gold and diamonds in southern Africa, he concentrated on its neglected resources of coal and base metals. His interests in lead, copper, tin, zinc, asbestos, vanadium, manganese and tungsten made him one of the greatest individual forces on the world's commodities markets. He had a gift for organising cartels or cornering key-supplies: thus he was chairman of the Wankie Colliery, Rhodesia's sole coal-mine, upon which the Congo Union Minière depended for supplies. He also registered in London in 1911 the Chrome Co Ltd which by 1915 controlled all the world's chrome output except for one Krupp mine in New Caledonia and one independent but semi-derelict mine at Turkiros in Norway. 'Mr Davis the Chrome King' was both chairman and managing director of this company {PRO FO 382/335, minute of 11 Aug 1915 by AR}, which he converted into a private concern in 1923. During the First World War he advised the Admiralty, Ministry of Munitions and Contraband Section of the Foreign Office on mineral policy, and cut the supply to Germany of chrome ore needed as a hardening agent for high-grade steels in big guns and motor vehicles.

One deal that brought Davis notoriety concerned the Chinese Engineering & Mining Co. Herbert Hoover (the future President of the USA) and his English partner C A Moreing (qv) took advantage of the Boxer crisis of 1900-1 to force a Chinese mandarin Chang yen-mao to transfer the valuable Kaiping collieries to an Anglo-Chinese limited company. This was formed in London as the CEM by Davis, who became its first chairman. The Chinese shareholders were not issued with CEM shares worth £375,000 to which they were entitled, but were instead sent Bearer Warrants which carried no voice in the company's affairs unless personally presented for registration in London two days before any general meeting of the company. Aided by fraudulent telegrams from the Belgian Banque d'Outremer, Davis played flagitious tricks with CEM's accounts, capital structure and share ownership until control passed to seven Belgian directors headed by Colonel Thys, who had previously acted as King Leopold's chief jackal in the Congo. The subsequent controversy, including an English lawsuit of 1905, caused an outcry in Britain, and did much harm to British commercial interests in China in the pre-war period.

Davis was active in developing German South West Africa in 1888-1914, for which he received German decorations in 1899 and 1905. He accompanied Cecil Rhodes to Berlin in 1899 and extracted the Kaiser's permission for the Cape to Cairo telegraph to pass through German territory. In 1900, with the help of Albert Ballin, he obtained from Dusseldorf quick-firing field guns for use in the Boer War, despite the German Government's neutrality. An occasion in 1914 when he acted for the Germans caused some scandal. In 1911 Davis became chairman of the Consolidated Nyassa Co, a British holding company which controlled the Companhia do Nyassa, whose assets it sought to protect after the Portuguese revolution of 1910. The Companhia had been chartered by the Portuguese Government in 1891 to develop 10,000 square miles of Mozambique, and its main revenue was a hut tax that yielded £31,430 in 1912. In the early summer of 1914 Davis arranged for 229,590 of Consolidated Nyassa's 368,444 shares to be sold to a group of German banks acting at the German Government's behest. Germany thus acquired management of Portuguese Nyasaland for £114,795 and major complications ensued. 'Davis is no friend of England', complained one director of the Companhia {PRO FO 371/2086, Sir Robert Edgecumbe, memo of 16 Sept 1914 to Home Secretary}; 'I know Mr Edmund Davis well', a diplomat minuted, 'He is cosmopolitan and in spite of his patriotic sentiments probably considers nothing but his pocket' {ibid, Sir Walter Langley, Nov 1914}.

In the early 1920s Davis was a director of over fifty companies, but renounced many of his directorships in 1925 on joining the board of the British South Africa Co. His memory for detail was prodigious, and he kept in his head meticulously accurate information on all his interests. 'He is a sharp business man', wrote Dr Jameson of De Beers and BSA, 'requiring watching' {PRO FO 371/2440, Sir Leander Starr Jameson to Robert Williams 13 Nov 1914}.

Davis owned a house in Notting Hill, Palazzo Desdemona in Venice, Chilham Castle near Canterbury, and bought Villa La Fiorentina at Cap Ferrat from Sir Arthur Du Cros (qv). These homes were filled with his stupendous art collection. His Rodin statuary was unrivalled, and he had an almost illimitable passion for buying old masters and moderns. He sometimes boasted that he could have made as much money from art as he did from finance and mining. He presented a collection of modern British paintings to the Luxembourg Gallery in Paris in 1912-15, for which he was created an Officier of the Légion d'Honneur. In 1935-36 he gave another collection to the South African Art Gallery. Five of his pictures were stolen from Chilham in 1938: two Gainsborough portraits were later recovered, but paintings by Rembrandt, Reynolds and Van Dyck were not.

A London magistrate from 1918, knighted in June 1927, he was active in Kentish charities and was High Sheriff of the county in 1930. Although once president of a Liberal association, he announced his support of the Conservatives in 1930. He endowed the King's School Canterbury with scholastic exhibitions in 1929, and also bequeathed the school £5,000 for musical and medical scholarships. Both Middlesex and St Thomas's Hospitals received £25,000 under his will. His residual legatee was London University, where he established Davis scholarships in medicine, law and engineering to benefit students born in Rhodesia. He played little part in the Jewish community.

Davis, who was a great gourmet, died suddenly at Chilham on 20 February 1939, leaving £394,518. His widow left £14,925 in 1941. Described in 1906 as 'the notorious Edmund Davis — a Jew who would cheat his blind grandmother at cards', and then compared to such fraudulent promoters as Jabez Balfour (qv), Horatio Bottomley (qv), E T Hooley (qv) and Whitaker Wright (qv) {Lo Hui-Min (1976) 376}, he was panegyrised posthumously by one politician of Cabinet rank as 'a veritable Napoleon of finance ... Napoleonic not only in his unflagging zest in his new schemes of financial conquest but in his outward appearance ... He took the most eager delight in giving pleasure to others, and no trouble was too much if he was to provide an agreeable surprise to a friend' {L C M S Amery (1939)}.

R P T DAVENPORT-HINES

Writings:

letter suggesting that multinational companies should hold their annual meetings in London *Times* 19 Dec 1911.

Sources:

Unpublished

British Library, Additional MSS 48929, folios 209-11, letter of Eastern Investment Co to Sir Edgar Vincent, 3 Feb 1897, in papers of Lord D'Abernon.

House of Lords RO, Bonar Law papers 65/2/34, letter of Sir William Plender to Sir Horace Hamilton 19 Sept 1917.

Hopton Hall, Wirksworth, Derbyshire, papers of Philip L Gell.

PRO, Kew, Colonial Office and Foreign Office papers.

Rhodes House, Oxford, papers of George Cawston in British South Africa Company collection.

State Library of New South Wales, Sydney, Mitchell Library, papers of G E Morrison.

MCe.

PrC.

Information from Professor Ian Phimister.

Published

Julian Amery, *Approach Past* (Hutchinson, 1973).

Leo C M S Amery, tribute in the *Times* 22 Feb 1939.

----, *My Political Life* (3 vols, Hutchinson, 1953-55) 1 and 3.

Ellsworth Carlson, *The Kaiping Mines, 1877-1912* (Cambridge, Massachusetts: Harvard University Press, 1957, 2nd ed 1971).

Joseph M Chuubi, 'Archives of the Broken Hill Division' *Business Archives* 48 (1982).

Description des Ouvrages de Peinture, Dessins et Aquarelles de l'Ecole Britannique Moderne Offerts à la France par M Edmund Davis (Paris: Luxembourg Gallery, 1915).

Paul H Emden, *Jews of Britain* (Sampson, Low & Co, 1943).

Financial Times 21 Feb 1939.

Lewis H Gann, *A History of Southern Rhodesia* (Chatto & Windus, 1965).

Herbert C Hoover, *Memoirs: The Years of Adventure 1874-1920* (Hollis & Carter, 1952).

Lo Hui-Min (ed), *The Correspondence of G E Morrison 1895-1912* (Cambridge: Cambridge University Press, 1976).

Edward Jessup, *Ernest Oppenheimer* (Rex Collings, 1979).

Jewish Chronicle 24 Feb 1939.

Simon E Katzenellenbogen, 'British Businessmen and German Africa 1885-1919' in Barrie M Ratcliffe (ed), *Great Britain and Her World 1750-1914* (Manchester: Manchester University Press, 1975).

David J Murray, *The Governmental System in Southern Rhodesia* (Oxford: Clarendon Press, 1970).

R Murray-Hughes, 'Sir Edmund Davis' *Northern Rhodesian Journal* 6 (1965).

Times 21, 22, 23, 24 Feb (3rd and 4th editions only) 1939.

Alfred J Wills, *An Introduction to the History of Central Africa* (Oxford University Press, 1967).

WWW.

W A Daw (courtesy of C A Daw & Son Ltd).

DAW, William Adams

(1856-1908)

Builder

William Adams Daw was born in Torquay on 13 July 1856, the son of Charles Adams Daw, a builder, and his wife Martha Catherine née Matthews.

While he was still an infant his parents migrated to London, where his father, in company with a brother, William Bennett Daw, joined a third brother, Nicholas Fabyan Daw, who had already established himself in the capital as a partner in a short-lived mercantile firm. The three brothers then engaged in speculative building in a small way, initially in the vicinity of Earl's Court, and later in Kensington and Paddington and St Marylebone. From 1865 to 1871 their firm was known as Daw Brothers. The partnership was then dissolved. Nicholas Fabyan Daw retired from active participation, although he assisted in subsequent building ventures, chiefly as an investor, and took a close interest in the running of the business until his death in 1900. William Bennett Daw operated as a builder for a short while, seemingly independently, in the Notting Hill area but by 1875 he had returned to Devon, where he remained for the rest of his life.

The building business was left in the hands of Charles Adams Daw, who was soon joined by his son. William Adams Daw quickly took over the principal managerial role in the firm, and it was under his direction that the business grew and prospered. For over thirty years the firm of C A Daw & Son was one of the most reliable of the medium-sized speculative-building concerns operating in West London. It built over 150 large houses, chiefly in Kensington, but also in Bayswater and Mayfair, as well as several blocks of flats including Campden House Chambers and Hornton Court in Kensington and Eaton Mansions in Cliveden Place, Belgravia.

While at the height of his powers, with his business in a flourishing condition, W A Daw contracted pneumonia and died suddenly on 30 March 1908 at the age of fifty-one. He left a widow, Isabel, a step-son by a former marriage of his wife, whom he had taken into the business, and four children under the age of twenty-one. At his death he had a big house in Ealing and a sporting lodge in Hampshire and employed a coachman, a gamekeeper, several gardeners and a large house staff. His effects were valued at £189,774 gross. By his will the bulk of his estate was left in trust for his children. (His father, C A Daw, was then still alive, but he was in his eighties and had taken no part in the business for many years; he died on 3 September 1913).

Some two months before his death W A Daw had entered into an agreement to build a mansion block at Nos 37 and 38 St James's Place, Westminster, on the Crown Estate. The need to carry out this contract and honour other business commitments, while protecting the interests of his descendants, led to the formation in 1909 of a small private company, C A Daw & Son Ltd, in which shareholding was for many years restricted to members of the family. The company still exists, at the premises in Palace Gate, Kensington, which were built and first occupied by C A Daw & Son in 1884, and is now concerned with property management, repairs and maintenance. The present chairman is a grandson of William Adams Daw.

VICTOR BELCHER

Sources:

Unpublished

C A Daw & Son Ltd, London, records.

Greater London RO, Middlesex Deeds Register; district surveyors' returns.

CReg: C A Daw & Son (103,661).

BCe.

PrC; Will.

Interview with Major A F Daw.

Published

Post Office Directories.

G Dawnay, portrait in pencil (taken from T E Lawrence's Seven Pillars of Wisdom*).*

DAWNAY, Guy Payan

(1878-1952)

Merchant banker

Guy Payan Dawnay was born at St James's Palace, London, on 23 March 1878, elder son of Hon Lewis Payan Dawnay (1846-1910), of Beningbrough Hall, Yorkshire, by Lady Victoria Alexandrina Elizabeth Grey (1853-1922), daughter of General Charles Grey, and aunt by marriage of A M Grenfell (qv). His father was second son of the Seventh Viscount Downe, and having served as a colonel in the Coldstream Guards was Conservative MP for Thirsk and Malton 1880-92; he left £188,870. Dawnay was educated at Eton (1891-95), and Magdalen College, Oxford. He served in the Yorkshire Militia (the Green Howards) 1895-99, but on the outbreak of the Boer War joined the Coldstream Guards, his father's regiment, with which he served until 1911. He fought in South Africa, and received several decorations, including the DSO (1902). Dawnay was adjutant of the Guards Depot 1904-6 (MVO 1907), and after attending the Staff College at Camberley (1908), spent three years on the staff of the Committee of Imperial Defence. He was recalled to the Army in 1914, and proved a brilliant intelligence officer and tactician. As Deputy Chief of General Staff to Lord Allenby, he was strategist of the Palestine campaign of 1917-18:

> Dawnay's cold, shy mind gazed upon our efforts with bleak eye, always thinking, thinking. Beneath this mathematical surface he hid passionate many-sided convictions, a reasoned scholarship in higher warfare, and the brilliant bitterness of a judgment disappointed with us, and with life ... As each [strategic] work of his was ruined he withdrew further into the hardness of frosted pride, for he was the stuff of fanatics {Lawrence (1935) 383}.

He was created CB and CMG (1918), promoted to honorary major general (1919), and awarded high decorations from France, Italy, Russia and USA. He remained on the Army Reserve until 1933.

After the Armistice he contemplated forming a fourth political party free of the vested interests of existing parliamentary groups, together with two maverick right-wing MPs, Aubrey Herbert and George Lloyd, and a former military colleague who became a Bethnal Green social worker, Sir Wyndham Deedes. Dawnay was founding editor of the *Army Quarterly* in 1920-29, and corresponded with many of the most prescient soldiers of his day.

In 1921 Dawnay became chairman of Gordon Hotels, a company which operated, amongst other hotels, the Mayfair, Grosvenor and Victoria in London; the Cliftonville, Margate; the Grand, Broadstairs; the Burlington, Eastbourne (sold 1927); the Royal at Dieppe; the Bristol at Beaulieu, Alpes Maritimes; and different Metropole hotels at Cannes,

£90,000. From 1900 Dawson was chairman of Chilworth Gunpowder, a British company set up under the Anglo-German general pooling agreement of the explosives trade. He was also concerned with the Whitehead Torpedo Works at Fiume in which Vickers bought a holding at the Admiralty's request in 1906, and was chairman of the Whitehead factory at Weymouth. He was a director of Wolseley Motors until its control was lost by Vickers in 1926.

Knighted in 1909, Dawson was listed until the very last moment to receive a barony in the New Year's Honours of 1917. His name may have been deleted because of the widespread, but sometimes misplaced, hostility towards the big armament firms, of whom he was regarded as 'chief spokesman' {Bodleian, Addison diary 1 Feb 1916}. He was at the heart of Vickers' munitions production in the First World War, and received a baronetcy in 1920.

In 1915-16 Dawson was involved with a Canadian speculator, Grant Morden, in launching the manufacture in Britain of cellulose acetate by the British Cellulose & Chemical Manufacturing Co. Dawson initially held £1,000 in debentures and 2,104 shares each of 6d nominal value, and was beneficial owner of another 12,250 6d shares. The Explosives Syndicate of Vickers, Chilworth and Nobel later put in capital, and after unscrupulous 'bulling', the 6d shares of 1916 were worth £14 10s in 1918. This was the basis of the so-called 'dope scandal' first publicised by a critical report of the Select Committee on National Expenditure in 1918 and examined in 1919 by the Cellulose Enquiry committee chaired by Lord Sumner. Dawson's reputation suffered in this affair, with its overtones of war-profiteering, and was further injured by a lawsuit between Admiral Sir Percy Scott and Vickers in 1920 which was caused by Dawson's careless dealings with Scott over the matter of royalty payments on his patented naval gun-sights. At one stage Mr Justice Coleridge interrupted Dawson's evidence to comment 'that will not do: I was not born yesterday' {Times 3 July 1920}, and after judgement was given in the admiral's favour, Dawson offered to resign from the Vickers board.

Dawson remained a decisive and powerful force in Vickers during the group's financial and managerial crisis in 1920-26 following the purchase of the rolling-stock and electrical interests of Dudley Docker (qv). Thus in 1920 he was, in addition to Vickers, a director of William Beardmore & Co, British Cellulose & Chemical Manufacturing, British Lighting & Ignition, British Refrigerating Co, James Booth (1915) Co, Canada Steamship Lines, Canadian-Vickers, Caton Engineering (a torpedo company entering liquidation), Centrifugal Separators, Chilworth Gunpowder, T Cooke & Sons (optical instrument makers), Elma Gear Box Co, Electric & Ordnance Accessories, Ferro-Concrete Ship Construction Co, Isle of Watney Estates, Lancashire & Cheshire Insurance Corporation, Manufacturers Estates & Assets Co, the Menco-Elma Syndicate, Metropolitan Carriage Wagon & Finance Co, the Moler Fireproof Brick & Partition Co, Placencias arsenal in Spain, Scrapers Ltd, S E Saunders Ltd, Vickers-Petters, Siebe-Gorman, Variable Speed Gear, Vickers-Terni in Italy, Whitehead Torpedo, and Wolseley Motors. All of these companies were subsidiaries of, or had business relations with, Vickers.

The appointment of the ordnance specialist Sir George Buckham (1863-

1928) to the Vickers board after the war, followed after 1925 by the rise on the naval side of Dawson's protégé Sir Charles Craven (1884-1944), and finally the appointment of Sir Noel Birch (qv) to take charge of land armaments in 1928, diminished Dawson's role in Vickers. He was the main backer on the Vickers board of their renewed interest in airship development, and was responsible for their support in 1924-30 of Sir Dennistoun Burney (qv) and his Airship Guarantee & Construction companies. The resultant R 100 airship, though it proved a technical success during flights in 1929-30, was a commercial failure. Its building cost of £460,000 was on top of a base charge of £110,000, and as the British Government only paid £350,000, Vickers lost £220,000. 'When you see an airship, think of Vickers', they had proclaimed in 1924 {*Vickers News* July 1924}, but by 1930 Craven wrote 'the sooner this blot on our management is forgotten the better... the Admiralty think we were mad ever to touch it' {Vickers microfilm R334, Craven to Sir Mark Webster Jenkinson 23 Mar 1930}. Dawson was an expansive, ebullient man, whose enthusiasm was contagious to his subordinates, but the rumbustious attitudes which he had developed in Vickers' armaments heyday before 1914 were unsuited to the difficult conditions of disarmament and world-wide arms surpluses that prevailed after 1918.

Dawson received the Royal Society of Arts' Silver medal, and was awarded the first Gustave Canet gold medal from the Junior Institution of Engineers in 1909. He was president of the Junior Institution of Engineers in 1912-13, Prime Warden of the Fishmongers' Company in 1920-21, a leader of the Knights of the Round Table Club, and in February 1931 became Knight Principal of the Imperial Society of Knights Bachelor. He was a member of the Institutions of Civil Engineers and Mechanical Engineers, and held decorations from Spain and Japan. In 1916 he formed a pressure-group, the London Imperialists, intended to secure the election of business-minded MPs for London constituencies; this was later re-organised as the British Commonwealth Union, on whose executive committee he sat in 1918-25.

He married at Bayswater in 1892 Louise (1870-1935), daughter of John Miller Grant. His brother-in-law Percy Grant (1867-1936), after many years residence at Buenos Aires, joined Vickers in 1917 as London representative, of their Sheffield Works, and was afterwards special director in charge of commercial sales (1921), joint general manager of the London Office (1922-26), and finally had charge of their train lighting department. Dawson's only surviving son, Sir Hugh Trevor Dawson (1893-1976), worked for Vickers in 1919-30 and was appointed to control their plywood interests in 1922. Dawson's two daughters married brothers called Micklem, whose youngest brother Commander Sir Robert Micklem (1891-1952) joined Vickers from the Navy in 1919, becoming managing director of engineering and shipyards in succession to Craven in 1944 and chairman of Vickers-Armstrongs, 1946-52.

Dawson held 2,200 ordinary shares in Vickers in April 1898, 8,407 shares in April 1900, 10,642 in March 1905 and 17,491 in May 1912. By May 1920 he held 28,021 ordinary shares in his own name and 49,242 shares together with other directors or relations (excluding 209,000 shares as an executor of Albert Vickers). Having sold 21,600 shares in June 1930, he seems to have owned at his death some 16,144 shares in his own name and 40,586 in association with others. He dropped dead on 19 May 1931 at his house at Elstree, leaving £257,589 gross.

R P T DAVENPORT-HINES

Writings:

The Engineering of Ordnance Gustave Canet lecture of 30 June 1909 (Percival Marshall, 1909).

letter on boy scout movement and labour relations *Pearson's Magazine* Oct 1911, reprinted in Sir Robert Baden-Powell, *Workers or Shirkers?* (C Arthur Pearson, 1911).

Education after the War, with Special Reference to Engineering (Bolton: Glensdale, 1916).

letter on Lord Haig's servicemen's appeal *Times* 11 Aug 1920.

Preface to H B Pratt, *Commercial Airships* (Thomas Nelson, 1920).

paper on operation and construction of commercial airships *Engineering* 22 Oct 1920.

letter on retention of airships *Times* 11 July 1921.

article on commercial airships *Brassey's Naval Annual 1921-22* (William Clowes, 1921).

statement on imperial airship service *Times* 31 Oct 1923.

views on imperial trade *Times* 15 Sept 1925.

Sources:

Unpublished

Bodleian Library, Oxford, papers of Lord Addison.

British Library, papers of Oakely Arnold-Forster and Sir Henry Campbell-Bannerman.

Churchill College, Cambridge, papers of Reginald McKenna.

House of Lords RO, papers of Sir Patrick Hannon.

PRO, papers of Admiralty, Air Ministry, Cabinet Office, Foreign Office, Ministry of Munitions and War Office.

Scottish RO, papers of Sir Arthur Steel-Maitland.

Tyne and Wear RO, papers of Lord Rendel.

Vickers House, Millbank, London SW1, Vickers microfilm.

BCe.

MCe.

PrC.

R P T Davenport-Hines, 'The British Armaments Industry during Disarmament 1918-36' (Cambridge PhD, 1979).

Published

Donald C Coleman, 'War Demand and Industrial Supply: the Dope Scandal 1915-19' in Jay M Winter (ed), *War and Economic Development* (Cambridge: Cambridge University Press, 1975).

R P T Davenport-Hines, 'Vickers' Balkan Conscience' *Business History* 25 (1983).

----, *Dudley Docker* (Cambridge: Cambridge University Press, 1984).

John D Scott, *Vickers* (Weidenfeld & Nicolson, 1962).

Times 2, 6 July, 8 Dec 1909, 12 Dec 1912, 22 Dec 1921, 10 May 1922, 2 June 1923.

Ronald Clive Trebilcock, *The Vickers Brothers* (Europa, 1977).

WWW.

DEELEY
see **MALLABY-DEELEY, Harry C**

DE FERRANTI, Sir Gerard Vincent Sebastian

(1893-1980)

Electrical and electronic equipment manufacturer

Gerard Vincent Sebastian de Ferranti, born at Tedworth Square, Chelsea, London, on 16 February 1893, would normally have had little chance of succeeding his father as chairman of the family electrical business, because he was the second son in the family of seven born to Sebastian Ziani de Ferranti (qv) and his wife Gertrude Ruth née Ince. Vincent and his elder brother Basil (b 1891), were both educated at Repton and their childhood was more than comfortable. Their father, however, encouraged them to take an interest in engineering, and Basil went to Sheffield University for a two year course in mechanical engineering, while Vincent had to make do with a workshop apprenticeship with Yarrows of Scotstoun, the shipbuilders. All this changed during the First World War, when Basil was killed in 1917 while on active service with the 24th Heavy Artillery Group at Messines. Vincent also joined up, with the 67th Field Company RE, and saw active service at Gallipoli and in the Middle East, coming home with the rank of captain and the MC.

He also returned as heir-apparent to the company, and he made a conscious decision to commit himself to building up a successful business. As proof of this, he purchased with his own money 1,800 ordinary shares. His grandfather, Francis Ince, warned him that the investment was by no means lucrative, but Vincent replied that now he had an incentive to increase its value. This typified his approach, for throughout his career the underlying theme was the attempt to run the business successfully and to safeguard his investment. In this sense, he differed from his father, who pursued engineering perfection rather than a high return on capital employed; but Vincent's formative years occurred in the period when his father lost control of his firm, and Vincent was anxious that this should never happen to him.

One thing Vincent did share with his father was his faith in the future of electricity, and between 1919 and 1921 he assisted in building up the transformer department. In 1921 he took over its management and with an able team of engineers established the Ferranti name in the market for the largest, most advanced transformers: in 1921 they won an order for the first 110 kV transformer ever received in Great Britain, for New Zealand; in 1925 Vincent and his engineers demonstrated the first ever 1,000 kV arc on their advanced testing apparatus, which also sold well; and during the construction of the Grid network, between 1929 and 1932, Ferranti won almost one-third of the transformer contracts for the largest three-phase transformers. Vincent and his father had been first to demonstrate the latter's practicability, showing a considerable saving on the conventional method of using three single-phase transformers. As a result of their pioneering work on high tension distribution, the Ferranti reputation in transformers was maintained for over forty years.

Vincent was appointed a director of the company in 1924, and was sent on a world tour, visiting Canada, the United States, New Zealand, Australia and South Africa. He met the company's agents and established contact with all the most important customers in these vital export markets. By the time of his father's death in 1930, he had consequently been educated in the running of a high technology company in an industry with extensive contacts around the world. As a further indication of his willingness to risk his own money in the company he was to run, he also borrowed £77,500 from the Westminster Bank to buy enough ordinary shares from his father's estate to give himself the controlling interest, owning a quarter of the shares held by the Ferranti family and a family trust (which together represented 80 per cent of the ordinary voting shares). Now he could run the company as he thought best: as he always said 'there's no substitute for 51 per cent'.

One of his first major steps in the 1930s was to strengthen the radio department, by investing in valve-manufacturing facilities. Vincent always

DE FERRANTI Sir Gerard Vincent Sebastian

Sir V S de Ferranti (centre) with senior Ferranti transformer staff, in front of the 75,000 KVA, 132,000 V Transformer built 1930–32.

took a special interest in radio, using it as a popular front for the general electronics business. To his disappointment, the radio department made consistent losses throughout its history, largely because it was unable to increase its poor share of the market, dominated by Mullard under S S Eriks (qv). Nevertheless, the Ferranti electronics effort increased in sophistication, with the development of special valves, cathode-ray tubes, and X-ray tubes, and by the late 1930s their expertise was being used to equip Britain's defences with the new radar devices developed by Robert Watson-Watt and his team. In connection with the rearmaments drive of the late 1930s, Ferranti also began to manufacture fuses for both the War Office and the Admiralty, and the Moston radio works were considerably expanded, with government money, to produce fuses quickly and cheaply.

Initially Vincent had been keen to rejoin the Royal Engineers, and he served in France as Commander of the 242nd Field Company from October 1939. Unfortunately, however, he was involved in the débâcle at Dunkirk and soon found himself back in Britain, where the Director-General of Munitions Production directed him back to Hollinwood. Here he spent the rest of the war years. During the war over 90 per cent of the company's resources were committed to the military effort and by 1945 Vincent found himself running six factories, compared to only two in 1939, as a result of government contracts.

After the war, he was keen to re-establish the company's staple trades in their export markets, and the sales teams embarked on extensive overseas efforts. One area where he felt Ferranti could do well was in the American market, and as a contribution to the drive for dollars in the difficult fifteen years after 1945 Ferranti exported almost £3 million worth of transformers to the United States. The transformer department was also considerably expanded, and the largest transformer factory in Europe was built in the early 1950s, at Chadderton in Lancashire, to satisfy the growth in demand. Vincent also gave the newer departments a chance, for there was a potentially vast market for the expertise acquired during the war, particularly in radar, electronics and aircraft instruments. This decision to broaden the base of the company's activities proved very successful. The Edinburgh plant, originally a wartime factory, became one of the most important British producers of airborne radar equipment in the 1950s. Vincent's agreement allowing the company's instrument department to manufacture a Manchester University-designed computer established Ferranti as market leaders in the computer business.

Entirely new projects were begun, often under government development contracts, the most notable being the 'Red Duster' project started in 1949 in association with the Bristol Aeroplane Co. This eventually produced the Bloodhound guided missile, the most successful of its type built in this period, because it came up to specification and was delivered on time. In connection with this project, Ferranti engineers also began to investigate the possibilities of semi-conductors, and by the late 1950s Ferranti was producing a wide range of silicon diodes and rectifiers, being the first on the market with the former. This was the start of the microelectronics revolution, in which Ferrantis participated. The Bloodhound project made excessive profits for the company but by the time this emerged Vincent had retired.

Although Vincent de Ferranti became a renowned figure in the international electrical industry, he found time to talk to his employees. This genuine interest helped to establish a humane tone to the management of the company. At the same time Vincent was the boss: he took the title of managing director in 1934. Although the number of factories increased, and were geographically widely dispersed, from Bracknell in the South, to Manchester and Edinburgh in the North, and in principle each manager was given a degree of freedom in the running of his department, in effect Vincent's presence could always be felt. Through careful vetting of financial statements, and by introducing a system of presenting estimated results for each department to the monthly board meetings, he could keep his finger on the vital pulse, the flow of capital. Between 1930 and 1963, when he retired as chairman, the net worth of the company increased from £600,000 to £12 million, and the capital employed rose from £800,000 to £22 million. At the same time, the labour force grew from 4,800 to almost 20,000. Clearly, expansion of this kind had to be organised very carefully, the more so if Vincent were to retain control. Government finance for certain factories, most notably at Wythenshawe and in Edinburgh, obviously played an important role, but Vincent was always careful to ensure that expansion would not strain the company's resources. One might argue that this prevented an even greater growth, but it is difficult to envisage, and would be totally hypothetical, how much greater the company could have grown with such a restricted market as Britain for advanced electronics, at a time when the American market was expanding much faster. Vincent's achievement was to build a company based on advanced engineering which by 1963 was among the first three British companies in electronics and aircraft instrumentation (ranked by sales), the base upon which it has continued to expand.

Despite the demands of his expanding business, Vincent took an active role in the general affairs of the British and international electrical industry. In 1946, he became the first son ever to follow his father as president of the Institution of Electrical Engineers (IEE), having been a member of the IEE Council since 1933. He was also on the Council of the British Electrical and Allied Manufacturers' Association from 1930, and became its chairman in 1938, thereafter taking an active role as a vice-president from 1946, president in 1957 and a member of the president's Advisory Committee between 1961 and 1963. On the international scene, he was elected chairman of the International Executive Committee of the World Power Conference in 1950. He also held office in such bodies as the International Commission on Large Dams, the International Electrotechnical Commission and the Conference Internationale des Grands Réseaux Electriques à Haute Tension.

Vincent de Ferranti was made an honorary fellow of the Manchester College of Science and Technology; an LLD of Manchester University; and a DEng of Melbourne University. He was knighted in 1948, largely for his contribution to the war effort. Vincent de Ferranti in 1919 married Dorothy Hettie Campbell Wilson, daughter of Reginald Page Wilson, an engineer; they had two sons and three daughters. Sir Vincent died on 20 May 1980 leaving £377,612 gross. The family firm, a public company since 1905 but not quoted on the London Stock Exchange until 1978, remained in the hands of the family. Vincent's elder son Sebastian (b 1927) succeeded him as chairman.

JOHN F WILSON

Sources:

Unpublished

Ferranti Engineering Ltd, Chadderton, Oldham, Lancashire, archives.

BCe.

MCe.

PrC.

John F Wilson, 'The Ferrantis and the Growth of the Electrical Industry, 1882-1952' (Manchester PhD, 1980).

Published

T J Lunt, *Sir Vincent de Ferranti* address at Memorial Service (pp, 1980).

WWW.

DE FERRANTI, Sebastian Ziani

(1864-1930)

Electrical equipment manufacturer and inventor

S Z de Ferranti (courtesy of the IEE).

Ferranti's father, Cesar Ziani de Ferranti (1831-1901), established a successful photographic business in Ostend where he met and fell in love with a beautiful concert pianist, Juliana Szczepanowski (previously married to Stanislas Szczepanowski, a Polish guitarist). After meeting her father, William Scott, a well-known portrait painter in the North of England, Cesar decided to move to Liverpool to form a partnership with Scott and build up a lucrative photographic business. Cesar and Juliana were married in 1860, and set up home in Havelock Buildings, Liverpool, where their only son, Sebastian Ziani, born on 9 April 1864, spent the first eight years of his life.

In 1876, after two years at a Hampstead preparatory school, the young Ferranti was sent to St Augustine's Boarding School, Ramsgate, where the Benedictine monks recognised in him a friendly disposition and lack of conventional academic application. They encouraged him to work in his own field, and his parents helped in most of his demands, even when his attentions turned towards steam engines, a puzzling hobby for the child of such artistically-orientated parents. His interest in things-mechanical was encouraged by an older step-brother, who had joined the Merchant Navy and qualified as an engineer. By the late 1870s, Sebastian was eagerly reading as many technical books as he could lay his hands on, whether sent by his family or supplied by his helpful teachers. Such was his fascination that in 1879 he announced that he was going to University College, London, to study under the eminent engineer Sir Alexander Kennedy, and that he hoped to become a 'Manufacturing Engineer'.

Unfortunately, due to a serious cerebral thrombosis, Ferranti's father was unable to support his son at university, and after only two terms he was forced to leave and find himself work, in the summer of 1881. Life at University College had been enjoyable, for the laboratories were a paradise in which to develop his blossoming inventive ability, but the theoretical work proved harder for him to grasp because of his lack of academic application. By this time, his imagination had been captivated by the electrical experiments and literature that were occupying the minds of both scientists and businessmen. After receiving assistance from a local amateur electrician, and reading avidly on the subject, Ferranti was developing his own ideas. A spell in the laboratories of Siemens at Woolwich contributed immensely to his grasp of the techniques involved. By the early months of 1882 he had interested two men, Alfred Thompson, a photographer, and Francis Ince, a solicitor, in his ideas, at a time of intense activity on the electrical scene. Although Ferranti was then only eighteen, in September 1882, he became the principal member of the new firm Ferranti, Thompson & Ince Ltd.

Ferranti — Rope-driven 10 KV, 1 MW alternators and Hick Hargreaves engines at Deptford Power Station as depicted in 'Electrical Industries' 19 July 1889 (courtesy of Ferranti Ltd).

Ferranti had been largely self-taught, but he now had to seek support from others. His precocious enthusiasm, however, proved insufficient to guarantee a steady source of business and his first company failed by 1885, despite the backing of a prominent electrical pioneer, Robert Hammond (qv). Ferranti was undaunted by this lack of success. He persuaded one of his original partners, Francis Ince (later to become his father-in-law), to join him in a new venture, manufacturing a wide range of Ferranti electrical equipment, most notably the world's first mercury-motor meter and a revolutionary form of transmitting AC using parallel-connected domestic transformers. The meter provided a staple source of business while a London electricity supply company, Sir Coutts Lindsay & Co of Kensington, installed the Ferranti transmission system in their Grosvenor Gallery station.

The Kensington-based company, and equally its re-sited station at Deptford, established Ferranti as one of the foremost exponents of the AC method of electricity transmission and as a manufacturer of the largest type of alternators, transformers and cables. The contract also proved very lucrative, for besides Ferranti's salary as chief engineer of £3,000 per annum, which was high by contemporary standards, the firm supplied most of the equipment.

Unfortunately, the Deptford station was a commercial failure, due to the problems faced by Ferranti and his team in a larger scheme of distribution than any previously supplied by a single station, while the potential market was restricted by government intervention, in the form of the Marindin Inquiry of 1889. Ferranti left Lindsay's company in summer 1891. Nevertheless, he had established the principles of centralised electricity supply. For his courage in putting his words into practice so early, Ferranti was recognised by his contemporaries as one of the most important electrical pioneers.

The demands made on Ferranti's manufacturing business by the Deptford contract strained the Ferranti-Ince partnership and the problem was scarcely relieved by the formation of a limited liability company in 1890, S Z de Ferranti Ltd. The company's nominal capital of £100,000 was composed of 8,000 £10 ordinary shares and 2,000 £10 preference shares, but Ferranti himself took 6,000 of the ordinary shares and financiers were reluctant to invest in a company where they would have no control.

The lack of working capital proved to have serious consequences over the next fifteen years. Although the company moved from London to larger premises in Hollinwood, near Oldham, in 1896, the heavier departments were never able to deliver promptly, while creditors incessantly knocked on the door. Ferranti's insistence upon continually improving the large steam-alternators was also another factor affecting the company's liquidity and ability to meet delivery dates. Various short-term palliative measures were taken, but the most important relationship that evolved was between the company and Parr's Bank, for bank overdrafts became the only means of maintaining liquidity. Security for these loans was Ferranti's shares in British Insulated Wire Co, given to him in 1892 in exchange for the use of his patents covering high tension cables. Eventually, a new company was formed in 1901, Ferranti Ltd, with a nominal capital of £300,000, but again Ferranti took the controlling interest and it took two separate issues to sell 120,000 £1 preference shares. Largely because it lost markets to competitors, especially the firm of Sir William Siemens (qv), the company failed in 1903. This was a great shock to Ferranti, who severed direct connections with the manufacturing business to concentrate on experiments he had begun in 1901 on, amongst other things, turbines and electric drive for textile machinery.

Over the period 1905-14 Ferranti remained a director and major shareholder in Ferranti Ltd, which was reorganised in 1905, but was excluded from the company works by the banks involved in the reorganisation. At the same time he undertook research for other companies like Vickers and J & P Coats. It was also a period in which he capitalised upon his reputation within the industry generally, acting as consultant to several of the large power supply schemes then appearing. His income was also complemented by the sale of some of his patents, most notably No 21,032 of 1904 concerning a steam stop-valve which he was able to sell to J Hopkinson & Co, of Leeds: between 1906 and 1921 Ferranti received a total of £31,874 in royalties on this patent. During this period, Ferranti strengthened his reputation within the industry, and in 1910 and 1911 he was elected president of the IEE, the first time one man had served two consecutive terms. He was also appointed president of the British Electrical & Allied Manufacturers' Association (BEAMA), whose object was to establish reasonable prices from monopoly purchasers in the face of competition from the Americans and Germans, who had protected home markets. At the same time, Ferranti Ltd had been reorganised by three chartered accountants, one of whom died in 1914 leaving a management vacancy into which Ferranti jumped. Never again did he diverge from his earlier ambition to become a manufacturing engineer.

During the First World War Ferranti used his connections with Vickers to secure several defence contracts for the company, amounting in value to over £1.75 million. He was also mainly responsible for effecting the change-over to munitions production, mostly of 5 inch high explosive shells for the War Office. The profit from these contracts was used to finance a programme of improving the company's electrical products, particularly the transformer, and establishing modern research facilities in all departments.

In 1923, Ferranti developed one of the most successful audio-frequency transformers for wireless, enabling the firm to enter one of the fastest growth industries of the inter-war period, the radio industry. In fact, between 1918 and 1930, in his role as technical director, Ferranti instilled the ethos of research into the very fabric of the company, hiring academic scientists to assist internal work and making the firm's products as reliable and as innovative as any in the country, indeed in the world. An indication of this is that during the construction of the Grid network between 1928 and 1931, Ferrantis were given transformer orders by the newly constituted Central Electricity Board worth over £750,000, accounting for almost one-third of that market. Ferranti and his son Vincent (qv), who was manager of the transformer department, persuaded the Commissioners to use three-phase transformers, rather than a bank of three single-phase ones, resulting in a considerable saving to the project.

Ferranti spent a lifetime in the pursuit of his dream of centralising electricity supply, and by the time of his death this dream was coming to completion. His activities on behalf of such organisations as the Electrical Development Association, of which he was president in 1927, and the Electrical Association for Women, also ensured that the domestic use of electricity was widely publicised. His own personal wealth was intrinsically connected to that of the firm (except in the period 1905-14), and by 1930 its fortunes improved markedly, compared to the early years: between 1913 and 1930 profits grew from £10,062 to £68,749 while the labour force increased from 1,752 to 4,773. Ferranti came to recognise that if the accountants on the board were given some influence in running the business, and he remained in charge of the technical department, the company would be in a better position to capitalise upon the expansion of the electrical and electronics industries, and the performance figures illustrate the success of this policy.

Ferranti never used his influence to enter politics, even at the local level, preferring instead to comment on contemporary problems in his speeches to associations, and spending the bulk of his time improving the products of his firm or working to strengthen the electrical industry. For this reason he was never given wider acclaim, although his contemporaries within the technical world recognised his contributions to electrical engineering: in

1912 the University of Manchester conferred on him an honorary doctorate; in 1924 he was awarded the Faraday medal by the IEE, the highest distinction of that Institution and only the third ever received; and in 1927 he was given the ultimate accolade from the scientific fraternity when he was elected FRS.

Sebastian de Ferranti in 1888 married Gertrude Ruth Ince, five years his junior and the daughter of Francis Ince, his partner; they had three sons and four daughters. He died on 13 January 1930.

JOHN F WILSON

Writings:

Sebastian de Ferranti took out 176 patents.

'How to Win a Lock-Out' (Manchester & District Engineering Trades Employers' Association, 1897).

'Coal Conservation, Home-Grown Food and the Better Utilisation of Labour' (Presidential Address to the IEE, 1910).

'Prime Movers' (James Watt Lecture, 1913).

'Electricity in the Service of Man' (Faraday Lecture, 1928).

Sources:

Unpublished

Ferranti Engineering Ltd, Chadderton, Oldham, Lancashire, archives.

Science Museum, London, artefacts.

MCe.

John F Wilson, 'The Ferrantis and the Growth of the Electrical Industry, 1882-1952' (Manchester PhD, 1980).

Published

F Bailey, *The Life and Work of S Z de Ferranti* (1931).

Ian C Byatt, *The British Electrical Industry, 1875-1914. The Economic Return to a New Technology* (Oxford: Clarendon Press, 1979).

DNB.

Gertrude Z de Ferranti and Richard Ince, *The Life and Letters of Sebastian Ziani de Ferranti* (Williams & Norgate, 1934).

Kenneth G Ponting, 'The Textile Inventions of Sebastian Ziani de Ferranti' *Textile History* 4 (1973).

Wilfred L Randell, *S Z de Ferranti and his Influence upon Electrical Development* (Longmans, Green & Co, 1946).

Arthur Ridding, *S Z de Ferranti* (Science Museum, 1964).

WWW.

DE HAVILLAND, Sir Geoffrey

(1882-1965)

Aeroplane manufacturer

Geoffrey de Havilland was born at Magdala House, Terriers Wycombe, Buckinghamshire, on 27 July 1882, second son of Rev Charles de Havilland (1854-1920), clergyman, and his first wife Alice Jeanette (1854-1911), daughter of Jason Saunders, an Oxford landowner and business man. His childhood was tense and unhappy. His father was irascible, opiniated, frustrated and engulfed by a succession of financial crises; among his eccentricities was the hoarding of ripe pears and ducks' eggs in his study which stank of rotten and decaying matter. His mother was a lachrymose woman, harassed by her improvident and inconsiderate husband, and eventually went into a depressive decline.

de Havilland was educated at Nuneaton Grammar School, Oakfield preparatory school at Rugby, and St Edward's School, Oxford, where in 1898-99 he 'suffered under a hard and unapproachable warden who gave the whole place an unsatisfactory tone' {de Havilland (1961) 24}. At this stage he was destined for the church, but from childhood he and his brother Ivon (1879-1905) were fascinated by mechanical engineering, perhaps in reaction to their father who disliked anything mechanical or electrical. As early as 1896 the two boys, subsidised by their tolerant maternal grandfather, installed an electric plant in the family home, and around 1900 the pair bought their first motorcar, a Panhard. The joy and excitement of tinkering with this confirmed their ambition to become mechanical engineers despite paternal opposition.

In 1900-3 de Havilland trained at the Crystal Palace Engineering School, and was then apprenticed at Rugby to Willans & Robinson Ltd, manufacturers of steam, gas and turbine engines. In 1905 he became a draughtsman at 30s a week with Wolseley Motors in Birmingham, but he resented 'doing uncongenial or dull jobs under harsh orders and a harsh regime' headed by Herbert Austin (qv) and J D Siddeley (qv), and resigned after a year {de Havilland (1961) 43}. He then worked for two years with the Motor Omnibus Co, but around 1908, with his imagination inspired by the flights of Wilbur Wright, he persuaded his grandfather to advance him £500 or £1,000 to design and build an aircraft. His first employee in the business was Frank Trounson Hearle (qv) who in 1914 married de Havilland's fiery socialist sister Ione (1885-1953); de Havilland himself married at Fulham in 1909 Louise Thomas (1881-1949), the daughter of a Welsh engineer and formerly governess to his sisters and companion-help to his mother. His wife made the fabric coverings of the first de Havilland aircraft on a hand-turned Singer sewing machine which she continued to use until her death.

Neither de Havilland nor Hearle had seen an aircraft fly when they began work, but after several reverses, in December 1910, they sold a

Geoffrey de Havilland (courtesy of British Aerospace plc).

machine for £400 to the Royal Aircraft Factory at Farnborough, to which de Havilland was recruited to supervise development and to design machines. The Superintendent of the factory, Mervyn O'Gorman (1871-1958), gave him generous support, despite unscrupulous criticism by Pemberton Billing. In August 1912, flying one of his own machines, de Havilland reached 10,500 feet and gained a new British altitude record. In January 1914 de Havilland was appointed an inspector of aircraft in the Aeronautical Inspection Directorate, but he felt 'miserable and wasted' {de Havilland (1961) 93} at leaving design work, and in May 1914 became chief designer for the Aircraft Manufacturing Co (Airco) of George Holt-Thomas (qv). His initial salary was £600 per annum with commission of £50 per aircraft for the first 50 sold in any year, and £25 per aircraft after the fiftieth.

When war erupted he was commissioned in the Royal Flying Corps, but soon returned to design work and test flying for Airco. Of the 20 distinct de Havilland types produced in the First World War, his most successful machines were the DH2 single-seat fighter, the DH4 general purpose biplane, the DH9 two-seater bomber and the DH10 high-speed twin-engined bomber. The pressure of work was such that he had a serious nervous breakdown in 1918. He received the Air Force Cross in 1919.

Holt-Thomas was an unscrupulous publicist who fancied himself 'a Napoleon in business, conceiving and carrying out large financial schemes' {*Economist* 7 Jan 1922} in association with men like 'that little bounder' Sir Sefton Brancker {PRO FO 371/11964, Sir Malcolm Robertson to Sir Robert Vansittart, 11 Mar 1927}. When these schemes

Geoffrey de Havilland seated centre, with founder directors of the de Havilland Co Ltd (courtesy of British Aerospace plc).

began to disintegrate, Thomas tricked Percy Martin (qv) into committing Birmingham Small Arms to buy Airco early in 1920. Airco then transpired to have liabilities of £1.3 million and was put into liquidation.

Following the closure of Airco early in 1920, de Havilland raised £20,000 and registered de Havilland Aircraft Co Ltd in September 1920. Another £10,000 was advanced in 1921 by a dilettante named Alan Butler, who joined the board and after considerably increasing his investment, served as chairman 1924-50, replacing an unsatisfactory nominee of Holt-Thomas. Indeed, de Havilland eschewed becoming chairman or managing-director of his business, as he begrudged all time spent outside the technical side: he later opined that money was 'a very necessary evil that brought with it irksome responsibility and a high nuisance' {de Havilland (1961) 108}. The company's first great commercial success was the Moth two-seater, the first prototype of which was designed by de Havilland and completed in 1925. In the next seven years some 7,278 Moths of different marks were built in Britain, and by 1928 the company was investigating proposals to build factories for Moths in places as diverse as Afghanistan and Finland. The company were active abroad as early as 1924, when several machines were sold in Czechoslovakia and an air service concession was obtained in Romania; but with the advent of the Moth, their sales push extended to the Dominions, Africa, South America and the Orient. The quality of their salesmen varied: one diplomat reported that the 'business inefficiency' of de Havillands, and their Bucharest agent Wing-Commander Crosbie, was unparalleled and 'singularly disheartening' {PRO FO 371/13701, Overseas Trade despatch 203 of Richard J E Humphreys, 2 May 1929}.

The phenomenal success of the Moth, which cost £650 in 1925, was due to its simple but practical design, sturdy construction and cheap upkeep;

Sir Rowland Hill's introduction of the penny post in 1840, with the aid of the latter's brother Edwin, by designing a machine for folding the envelopes which from then on covered letters; at the Great Exhibition of 1851, of which he was a juror and influential committee member, he had a working model on display.

From the early 1850s onwards, under his direction, the firm diversified out of such goods, which clearly had a finite demand, into government contracts for printed articles needed in vast quantities. In 1853 it started printing revenue stamps for the Inland Revenue, and from 1879 to 1911 supplied the whole of Britain's postage stamp issue. Inland postal orders came later, in 1881. In 1855 the firm won the contract for all postal requirements in India, which took up two whole floors of the Bunhill Row factory; orders from the colonies and many foreign countries followed. De la Rue's first currency notes were made in 1859, for Mauritius.

These substantial contracts for security printing, often won against stiff opposition, necessitated very close attention being paid to every scientific and technical aspect. Now reliable but not too costly printing techniques had to be devised, and care given to the precise specification of the paper and inks used, the colours, gums and varnishes. The laboratory which Warren had set up in the 1840s was one of the earliest in a British firm, and in 1854 he engaged as his scientific assistant Hugo Müller (1833-1915), who became a distinguished chemist in his own right, a partner in the firm and from 1898 to 1902 a director after it became a public company (1898). Outside the printing business they jointly designed the first factory distillation of well oil in the world, of Burmese crude oil, to extract paraffin wax for Price's Patent Candle Co Ltd, and in 1857 published their analysis of the oil. Between 1853 and 1855, Warren registered no less than five patents over these refining methods, which proved very profitable to him. Yet he was just as much at home with more mundane tasks; the firm printed considerable quantities of coloured biscuit labels for Huntley & Palmers, and once, in the Palmer brothers' presence, he improvised, with three pieces of coloured paper, a tricolor as a design for the Napoleon biscuit, to be launched for the Paris exhibition of 1867.

In 1859 Thomas de la Rue retired at the age of sixty-five. That year the firm had sales of £110,000 and profits of £12,600 (11.5 per cent on turnover): profit in 1839 had been only £3,000. For the next decade Warren and his younger brother William Frederick (1825-70) ran the firm together in great harmony, their peace of mind broken only by outbursts from their quarrelsome father, reinvigorated as he was by a new young wife. By a thorough overhaul of the firm's whole organisation, the brothers carried it to a high degree of efficiency, and in 1869 Warren felt ready to retire, in order to devote himself to scientific study. Within months William Frederick died of cancer and he had to return to his desk. When he finally retired in 1880, three of his sons, Warren William, Thomas (later Sir Thomas) Andros and Ernest (later Sir Ernest) de la Rue, were in charge of the firm. Sales that year were £334,000 and profit £62,000, or 19.5 per cent on turnover.

Short and tubby, Warren seems to have lacked the flaws and failings that to a less respectful generation bring even the most eminent of Victorians to life. Even his religious views, or lack of them, apparently remained hidden. He was remembered as being a combination of a man of affairs and a scientific amateur of the highest type; the scarcity of such men in Britain after about 1870 was later blamed on 'the worthlessness of our public school system' {*Proc Royal Soc of London* 95 (1919) xvi}. Certainly, his public-school educated sons and grandsons reduced a once highly prosperous company to a low ebb by the time that the last was edged out in 1923.

Despite failing eyesight, Warren de la Rue was active to the last, dying on 19 April 1889; he left over £305,956 gross.

T A B CORLEY

Writings:

(with Charles Button) *A Series of Tables of the Elementary and Compound Bodies Systematically Arranged* (1843).

(with A W Hofmann) *Annual Report of the Progress of Chemistry, and the Allied Sciences* (1849).

(with Hugo Müller) 'Chemical Examination of Burmese Naphtha, or Rangoon Tar' *Proceedings of Royal Society* 8 (1856) repr in *Philosophical Magazine* 13 (1857).

(with Balfour Stewart and Benjamin Loewy) *Researches on Solar Physics* (pp, 1865-68).

On the Solar Eclipse of August 18th, 1868 ... Extracted from the Monthly Notices of the Royal Astronomical Society (Strangeways & Walden, 1869).

Patents:

1853 (1,748)

1854 (1,051, 2,719)

1855 (843) (with G F Wilson)

1855 (2,002).

Sources:

Unpublished

Reading University Library, De la Rue Co Ltd archives.

MCe.

Published

T A B Corley, *Quaker Enterprise in Biscuits: Huntley & Palmers of Reading, 1822-1972* (Hutchinson, 1972).

—, *History of the Burmah Oil Company I, 1886-1924* (Heinemann, 1983).

DNB.
Charles C Gillespie (ed), *Dictionary of Scientific Biography* (16 vols, New York: Charles Scribner's Sons, 1970–80) 4.

Lorna Houseman, *The House That Thomas Built: The Story of De la Rue* (Chatto & Windus, 1968).

Nature 90 (9 May 1889).

Times 22 Apr 1889.

Trevor I Williams (ed), *A Biographical Dictionary of Scientists* (Adam & Charles Black, 1969).

DELOITTE, William Welch

(1818-1898)

Accountant

William Welch Deloitte (courtesy of Deloitte, Haskins & Sells).

William Welch Deloitte was born in London in 1818, the son of a secretary to a well-known firm of provision merchants, and his wife who was the daughter of a West Indies planter named 'Welch'. Reputedly his paternal grandfather was a Count de Loitte who had fled from the revolutionary reign of terror in France during 1793, finding refuge in Hull. Nothing is known of Deloitte's early years but having spent twelve years on the staff of E Edwards, an Official Assignee in Bankruptcy, he established his own practice in 1845 at the age of twenty-seven. This experience proved valuable because at this time the bulk of an accountant's duties fell in the field of insolvencies; his first office, 11 Basinghall Street, was close to his former employers and, significantly, the bankruptcy courts. Living over these premises, Deloitte had gathered some 87 clients (mostly individuals or partnerships) by the end of his first twelve months in practice and within two years had expanded so far as to employ ten clerks. Under his control the firm continued to grow so that by 1897 there were 70 staff and by 1900, shortly after his death, its fee income had risen from £7,597 in 1874 to £41,193.

An event crucial in the success of Deloitte's firm was his appointment in 1849 to assist the shareholder auditors of the Great Western Railway; not least because he could mention the commission as a measure of his integrity and ability when writing to bankrupts named in the *London Gazette* offering to prepare their statements of account prior to an appearance in court. The GWR's shares had been falling in value and the proprietors increasingly concerned for the company's well-being, recorded in February 1850 that 'the auditors have been assisted for the first time throughout a laborious examination of all books, accounts and documents of the company by a public accountant [Deloitte] whom they appointed without previous communication with any individual connected with the company' {PRO, RAIL 250/65, p166}. Although initially taken aback by this proposed action, once the directors had satisfied themselves in August

1849 that the auditors' 'sole object was to strengthen their hands and inspire general confidence in the management' {*ibid* 250/127, p2}, the directors first agreed to the continuance of such an arrangement and then offered the voluntary retirement of four members from their twelve-strong board. The replacements having been duly elected from the shareholders in September 1849, the directors then recommended that such a system of auditing be made legally compulsory and in January 1850 it was formally recorded that Deloitte had assisted in the examination of the accounts {*ibid* 250/127 p238}. Deloitte proceeded in this fashion until 1887 when he was personally appointed as one of the two shareholder auditors; a position he retained until his retirement in 1897. The conflict of interest created thereby was pointed out by one of the shareholders, but the audit committee in 1889, denying that this had been done because the engagement of his firm as accountants was on the eve of termination and might not be renewed, asserted that to fulfill the roles of both auditor and accountant increased his responsibility to the shareholders. When Deloitte retired the audit passed to his firm which continued to hold the appointment even after nationalisation when the railway company became, in effect, British Railways, Western Region.

In this connection it was said that Deloitte devised the double-account system, though Quilter, Ball & Co, another firm much involved in railway auditing, were also mentioned among the originators. The double-account method had the great advantage of segregating revenue expenditure from capital expenditure; depreciation was not charged but expenditure on both maintenance and renewals was written off to revenue. The technique, which was laid down as the statutory form of railway accounts in the Regulation of Railways Act of 1868, offered a considerable advance on most current practice.

Deloitte (who audited the Langham from 1883, and the Savoy Hotel from 1890) was also the originator of a system of hotel accounting which was subsequently widely adopted. Unlike many City practices, he built up a strong industrial base among his clientele, auditing not only railway companies (Lancashire & Yorkshire, West London Extension, and the South Wales Railways as well as the GWR and a large number in South America), but also docks, collieries and ironworks, including the Vulcan Foundry Co, Powell Duffryn (from 1864 and still clients) and the Ocean Coal Co of David Davies (qv). However, the practice was not exclusively industrial: from 1889 Deloittes audited the Prudential, were joint auditors of the London Stock Bank, 1882-1918, and had many newspaper commissions including, from 1886, *The Observer*.

As an indication of his probity and standing Deloitte was called to investigate various frauds, one committed against the Great Northern Railway in 1857 and another that occurred within the Great Eastern Steamship Co in 1870. His inquiries were not only designed to discover the culprit and to devise methods of preventing its recurrence but also to reassure the anxious shareholders that matters had been effectively resolved. In the case of the GNR inquiry, Deloitte originally estimated that the cost of the work would be £7,000, requiring the employment of 30-50 clerks — the basis of his charges being three guineas per day for a principal and one and a half guineas for a clerk. The inroads that financing the employment of this many staff made on his capital impelled him to seek a partner and a 50 per cent share in the firm was sold to Thomas Greenwood, an accountant who seems to have acted as share registrar to the GWR, for £800. The directors of the GNR, unhappy with the potential cost of the investigation, dismissed the firm before its inquiries were complete. Deloitte took the unusual step of protesting in a long letter to the *Railway Times* and a lengthy wrangle over the fees payable began. Wrottesley suggests that £3,397 was eventually paid. When Greenwood left the firm in 1867 his share of the partnership capital was then worth £6,000. The other partners admitted by Deloitte (Henry Dever, 1867-97; Alfred Richard Hollebone, 1867-73; and John George Griffiths, 1869-1902) were all promoted from within the firm having begun their careers as articled clerks.

Deloitte was closely associated with Sir Daniel Gooch (qv), Sir John Pender (qv), Sir George Elliot and Cyrus Field and the other pioneers of submarine telegraphy so that his firm secured the audit of almost all the large cable companies, including Telegraph Construction & Maintenance Co. This dominance probably arose because he knew Sir Richard Glass who, as a cable maker, was involved with many of the early companies. One source {Kettle (1958) 9} noted that they had been friends at school but the *DNB* entry for Glass records that he had originally worked as a clerk for an accountancy firm and could have met Deloitte in that context.

An important aspect of Deloitte's career concerned his close involvement in the formation and early days of the English Institute of Chartered Accountants, of which he became its fourth president in 1888-89, having served as the vice-president from 1884. He had been an original council member of its predecessor, the Institute of Accountants in London, and on its foundation in 1880 became a council member of the English Institute. Deloitte was also a founder of the Chartered Accountant's Benevolent Association and later its president. He had, in addition, been a member of the Manchester Society of Accountants joining because he had an office in the city, which practised under the style of Deloitte & Halliday. Yet the partnership with James Halliday ceased in 1877 and no other branches were opened in the UK until one was established at Cardiff in 1912 (though Deloitte had staff permanently stationed in Wales long before then); overseas the New York branch opened in 1910, one set up in Buenos Aires in the 1890s having a very short life. W W Deloitte should, however, be credited with the foundation of a major accountancy firm, that through internal growth and merger was to become, under the style Deloitte, Haskins & Sells, one of the 'Big Eight' international practices.

When he retired in 1897 aged seventy-nine, Deloitte was the oldest practising accountant in London. He was a long serving freemason with over fifty years' membership. After he moved in about 1858 to a substantial house in Southall, Middlesex, he became something of a local celebrity, building Holy Trinity Church and, in 1897, six almshouses for the poor. Parties of London friends attended his well-spread Sunday dinners at Southall. He was said to have been a man of great determination, sound judgement and exceptional business ability. John Gane, an accountant who left his employ in 1870 to set up on his own, described him as 'an alert, decisive little man with just a touch of austerity in his manner; this, however, covered a kind heart' {Kettle (1958) 6 }.

DELOITTE William Welch

William Deloitte married twice. He had at least one child, a daughter. Deloitte died on 23 August 1898, leaving £74,707 gross.

EDGAR JONES

Sources:

Unpublished

PRO RAIL 250/65 GWR General Meetings of Proprietors 1845-1857, 14 Feb 1850, p 166; and RAIL 250/127 GWR Minutes of General Committee 1849-1850, 9 Aug 1849, p 2.

PrC.

Published

The Accountant 27 Aug 1898.

The History of the Institute of Chartered Accountants in England and Wales 1880-1965 (1966).

[Sir Russell Kettle], *Deloitte & Co 1845-1956* (Oxford: pp for Deloitte Plender Griffiths & Co at the University Press, 1958).

Robert H Parker (ed), *British Accountants, A Biographical Sourcebook* (New York: Arno Press, 1980).

VCH Middlesex 4.

John Wrottesley, *The Great Northern Railway* (3 vols, Newton Abbot: David & Charles, 1979-81) 1.

DENNIS, John Cawsey   and   **DENNIS, Sir Herbert Raymond**
(1871-1939)   (1878-1939)
Commercial vehicle manufacturers

John Henry Cawsey Dennis was born at Huntshaw, Devon, on 20 February 1871, the son of William Henry Dennis, a farmer, and Susanna née Cawsey. John showed an early interest in machinery and after his education at Taunton College, and against his parents' wishes, he became apprenticed to an ironmonger at Bideford where he learned to repair a wide range of metal ware, from cooking pots to farm machinery and bicycles.

Prior to completing his apprenticeship John Dennis successfully applied for the position of ironmonger's assistant with Messrs Filmer & Mason at Guildford, Surrey, and, unknown to his family, he moved there in 1894. In his spare time he built himself a bicycle, and being short of money, he displayed it for sale in a local tailor's window. It quickly sold and John turned his attention to building bicycles for sale as a side-line.

Anxious to extend his knowledge of the supply and manufacture of parts he joined Brown Bros, a London firm of parts factors, where he learned much about machined engineering components. On returning to Guildford in early 1895 he opened on his own account a shop at 94, High Street, the Universal Athletic Stores, to sell mainly cycles of his own manufacture, with parts supplied by Brown Bros. After considerable success with his 'Speed King' and 'Speed Queen' models, he persuaded his brother Herbert Raymond, then aged seventeen years, to leave Devon to partner him in his growing enterprise.

Herbert Raymond Dennis was born on 25 June 1878 at Huntshaw, near Torrington, Devon, and was educated at Wellington School, Somerset. His sound and imaginative commercial sense aptly complemented his brother's considerable engineering flair. The subsequent success of Dennis Bros owed much to these combined gifts which formed the basis of their roles as joint managing directors once the business was incorporated in 1901.

In the late 1890s John and Raymond began to experiment with motorised tricycles. Their first car-tricycle of this design was exhibited in 1899. The first (modified) production models appeared in 1901 as 4.5 hp 3-speed vehicles with front-mounted De Dion engines. Later models employed Astor, and, predominantly, White & Poppe engines of 4.5 to 8 hp. The reliability of these early models won the company the Dewar Trophy in 1907 which persuaded the Post Office to order a large fleet of Dennis delivery vans.

From around 1900 the Dennis brothers realised the potential of 'industrial' motors. Their first commercial vehicle, a 15 cwt van sold to Harrods, was built in 1904 and by 1907 Dennis made four different types of lorries and vans up to 4 tons loading, ranging in power from 18 hp to 40 hp, and in price from £575 to £830. By 1914 Dennis was one of the country's leading lorry makers and provided over 7,000 3.5 ton 'subsidy' vehicles to the War Office during the First World War.

Dennis Brothers' reputation as manufacturers of fire-engines began in 1908 when one such vehicle was sold to the City of Bradford. The London fire brigade was converted to Dennis fire-engines in 1910 after a jet of water was sent over the dome of St Paul's cathedral by two Gwynne turbine pumps. By 1937 over 250 fire-engines, and numerous trailer pumps had been supplied to the London Fire Service alone. About one hundred turbine pumps were also sold to the War Office between 1914 and 1918. Success meant changes in organisation, finance and location. The original partnership was changed to a private company in 1901 capitalised at £30,000 involving outside funds provided by customers and associates, one of whom, Nicholas Andrew, was chairman of the company from 1914 until 1945. In 1913 Dennis Brothers went public with an authorised capital of £300,000 which was increased to £600,000 in 1919. In 1912 the company moved its premises from a backyard workshop to the Barracks in North

J C and H R Dennis — Dennis fire engine 1914.

Street and later to Woodbridge Hill, Guildford, which became the scene of subsequent expansion.

The inter-war years saw the continued growth of Dennis Bros. Although the production of load-carrying vehicles, of up to 12 tons capacity, continued, the firm found itself in stiff competition from larger manufacturers using batch-production methods. Thus Dennis Bros increasingly concentrated on fire-fighting equipment, on municipal vehicles such as gulley-emptiers and dustcarts, and on buses, the latter based mainly on the very successful 'Lancet' chassis introduced in 1931. Large motorised lawnmowers were also made.

John and Raymond Dennis's contribution to the British heavy vehicle industry was considerable. John possessed sufficient mechanical insight to avoid steamers, and also to eschew chain drive from the outset. His most significant engineering contribution was the invention of the worm drive to the rear axle patented in 1904, which incorporated a multi-start thread enclosed with worm wheel and differential gear in a vertically divided casing. This powerful, efficient yet quiet final drive was adopted by many other manufacturers of heavy vehicles and was retained by Dennis into the 1950s.

Raymond's forte lay in publicity and marketing. From the 1890s elaborate steps were taken to stimulate interest in the firm's products: lessons in bicycling and cycle maintenance were given, competitions were organised. Raymond publicised Dennis cycles by racing, winning eleven prizes in 1900 alone. A ten-feet high cycle mounted on a dray was exhibited in the Queen Victoria Jubilee procession at Guildford. Having been fined for driving a motorised tricycle up Guildford's 1 in 11 High Street too fast, the firm used the incident as a publicity weapon, 'on the sworn testimony of the law'. The St Paul's cathedral fire pump display was another example of bold marketing. And as early as 1908 Raymond undertook an overseas sales drive which he repeated in 1919 with a 60,000 mile world tour to research markets and set up agencies to handle Dennis exports.

Clearly John and Raymond Dennis were entrepreneurs in the 'buccaneering' mould who successfully exploited the new technology based on the internal combustion engine. Both were hard-headed but fair-minded businessmen. They operated a non-contributory benevolent fund for their workforce who called no strikes while John and Raymond ran the business. When White & Poppe, the Coventry-based petrol-engine manufacturers, taken over by Dennis in 1919, was transferred to Guildford in 1933, several hundred good quality, low rent houses were constructed by the Dennis management for the migrating workers, the settlement becoming known as Dennisville.

Raymond Dennis was knighted in 1920 for his war supplies services. In 1922 he married Sybil, daughter of Sir Leonard Llewelyn KBE DL of Newport, Monmouthshire, who was a Government Minister in charge of non-ferrous metals in the First World War. She bore Sir Raymond four sons and a daughter. Conservative in politics, Sir Raymond once declined an invitation to stand as an MP. Not active in religious matters, he enjoyed yachting, golf, hunting, fishing and motoring.

John Dennis had similar interests, and also served as a JP. In 1904 he married a local woman, Dora Baker, who bore him one son in 1905. On Dora's death in 1934 John married her sister Julia Elizabeth.

Both brothers died within three months of each other in 1939; Sir Raymond on 20 May, John on 27 August. Sir Raymond left £281,739 gross and John Dennis left £213,578 gross.

C GULVIN

Sources:

Unpublished

BCe.

MCe.

PrC.

Interviews with John C R Dennis, Lady Sybil Dennis.

Published

Commercial Motor 2 Feb 1945.

'Dennis 1894-1979' *Bus Fayre* Feb 1979.

George N Georgano (ed), *The Complete Encyclopedia of Motor Cars, 1885 to the Present* (3rd ed, Ebury Press, 1982).

----, *Complete Encyclopaedia of Commercial Vehicles* (Iola, Wisconsin: Kraus Publications, 1979).

Guildford City Outlook May, Oct, 1939.

Pat Kennet, *Dennis* (Cambridge: Patrick Stephens, 1979).

Motor Traction 7 Sept 1907.

Richard Twelvetrees and Pepys Squire, *Why Dennis and How* (Guildford: pp, 1945).

Who's Who in Surrey 1936.

WWW.

DENNISON, Aaron Lufkin

(1812-1895)

Watch manufacturer

Aaron L Dennison was born at Freeport, Maine, USA on 6 March 1812, one of nine children of a shoemaker. His family moved to Brunswick in 1824, and in 1830 he was apprenticed to a watchmaker, James Carey. Three years later he joined the Boston watchmakers and jewellers, Jones, Low & Ball and in 1839 he started his own business, repairing and selling tools and materials. In partnership with E Howard, D P Davis, and S L Curtis in 1849 he established a factory to produce watches using interchangeable machine-made parts. Located firstly at Roxbury, Massachusetts, and after 1855 at Waltham (where it took its name, the Waltham Watch Co), with Dennison as managing director (at a salary of $1,200 per annum) the firm became renowned as the pioneer of American watchmaking enterprises, and Dennison became famous as the father of the American watchmaking industry. After financial difficulties and disagreements with his partners, Dennison left the company in 1862, and from 1863 to 1870 he lived in Zurich, organising the Swiss end of an early multinational enterprise in which some components (escapements and trains) were made in Switzerland, whilst others (plates and barrels) were made in the USA, and assembled in Boston, and later in Melrose, Massachusetts.

While much is known about Dennison's celebrated but financially unsuccessful career in America, much less is known about his ultimately successful English enterprise. At first, after the failure of the Melrose Watch Co in 1870, Dennison settled at Handsworth, near Birmingham. The Melrose machines were bought by the English Watch Co, which later became the Anglo-American Watch Co of Birmingham, with Dennison as manager at a salary of £350 per annum. Then, in 1874, aged sixty-two, he started his own firm, Dennison, Wigley & Co (later the Dennison Watch Case Co of Villa Road, Birmingham). He abandoned attempts to make a whole watch, and concentrated instead on the manufacture of watch cases. He designed machinery for making them and patented a screwed bezel. His cases were of superior quality and attractively priced. He supplied a number of British and American firms and cornered an important market, through his old Waltham contacts, by supplying the Waltham company with nearly all the silver cases required for their English trade. By 1886 his factory employed 100 workers and had an annual output of 60,000-80,000 watch cases. Dennison himself stayed in active control of the firm until about a month before his death, on 9 January 1895. He was survived by his wife, two sons, and two daughters, and he left £6,238 gross. In the First World War the firm made military watch cases and service compasses. The family controlled the firm until the 1920s.

ALUN C DAVIES

Sources:

Unpublished

PrC.

Published

Paul Chamberlain, *It's about Time* (New York, 1941; repr 1964).

The Dial (June 1920 - Feb 1927. Twenty five issues; at first issued monthly, and then bi- and tri- monthly, by Dennison Watch Case Co Ltd, Birmingham).

Horological Journal 29 (Oct 1886), 37 (Feb 1895).

Charles W Moore, *Timing a Century: History of the Waltham Watch Company* (Cambridge, Massachusetts: Harvard University Press, 1945).

J C Roche, 'The History, Development and Organisation of the Birmingham Jewellery and Allied Trades'. (M Com, Birmingham; published as a supplement to *The Dial* 1927).

Arthur Tramayne, *One Hundred Years after. Being a Little History of a Great Achievement* (Birmingham: Dennison Watch Case Co, 1912).

DENT, Sir Francis Henry

(1866-1955)

Railway manager

Francis Dent was born at Holyhead, Anglesey, North Wales on 31 December 1866, the son of Captain Charles Bayley Calmady Dent RN, the London & North Western Railway Co's marine superintendent at Holyhead, and his wife Corrina née Coureaumelli. Francis began his railway career at seventeen years of age in the general manager's office of the LNWR at Euston. Two years later he transferred to the office of the superintendent of the line, then under the imaginative leadership of G P Neele, who quickly recognised his abilities by making him his principal outdoor assistant in 1889. At the end of 1893 Dent was moved to Chester as assistant district manager of the Chester and Holyhead district. His promotion to district manager in 1899 caused no surprise and he took in his stride the additional duties of goods manager in 1901. His success in organising the freight business in North Wales ensured his selection as goods traffic superintendent of the Metropolitan district a few months later when the company needed an able man to deal specifically with goods traffic congestion at Broad Street. The board assumed that a large and expensive extension of the station would be needed, but Dent contrived a well thought out bonus scheme for the goods staff which accelerated the turn round of goods and rendered unnecessary the projected expansion of the station area.

In 1907 he left the service of the LNWR to become chief goods manager of the South Eastern & Chatham Railway managing committee. His subsidiary title as assistant general manager foreshadowed his succession to the position of general manager which he assumed in 1911 at a salary of £3,000 per annum, a figure which was increased to £4,000 a year later. In his new post his main problem was how to overcome the congestion of goods and passenger traffic in the south-eastern approaches to the capital. In a report to the managing committee on 21 January 1912 he recommended the electrification of the network using alternating current and overhead collection as the main answer, although in the same year he began the reorganisation of Charing Cross and Holborn Viaduct stations. Lack of funds prevented electrification of traction before the First World War but the general manager's scheme for replacing steam power by electric power in the Ashford Works was endorsed.

Dent took a more realistic and understanding view of the claims of labour than did many of his contemporaries. Although he told the members of the Royal Commission on the Railway Conciliation Scheme of 1907 that he disliked the proposal that full-time trade union officers should represent the railway staff at national level, because, he asserted, their influence would be to undermine discipline, Dent did not object to trade union representatives speaking for the railway employees at sectional council level. In this he was in advance of the views held by the majority of general managers of his day.

His long and varied experience as a goods manager persuaded him by 1912 that the nationalisation of the railways would bring substantial advantages. In a notable article in the Jubilee Edition of *Railway News* in 1914 he claimed that 'an enormous reduction in shunting expenses' would result from the creation of a national pool of freight cars and 'the extinction of the private owners waggon'. Changes of the magnitude he envisaged were announced in 1955, the year of his death, under the Railway Modernisation Plan.

Dent's skills as a freight transport organiser were in much demand in the First World War. In April 1915 he was directed by the Railway Executive Committee to supervise the recruitment of railway staff for service in the various theatres of war. In the autumn of 1916 he investigated railway organisation in Egypt and Salonika. His achievements were recognised by the British Government through the grant of a knighthood in January 1916; by the French Government which awarded him the cross of the Légion d'Honneur; and by other leading British railwaymen who elected him chairman of the Railway Clearing House General Managers' Conference in 1918.

Although Dent resigned as general manager of the SE & CR in 1921 and thereby ended his full-time professional career, he continued to play an active part in the formulation of railway policy. He served on the board of the Southern Railway in its early years. He visited Austria as president of the Commission which re-apportioned the rolling stock of the former Austrian State Railways. He served as chairman of the Railway Clearing House for nearly twenty years (from 9 March 1929 until 8 January 1948); he was governor of the London School of Economics; and one of His Majesty's Lieutenants for the City of London.

He married in 1902, Helen Janet, daughter of Richard Mottem of Denham, Buckinghamshire. She died in 1920. There were two sons of the marriage. He married, secondly, Winifred Grace Culling, daughter of W A C Freemantle. He died on 4 June 1955, at his home in Havant, Hampshire, leaving £4,359. His brother Charles, also served the LNWR, being appointed superintendent of the Liverpool district in 1900.

PHILIP S BAGWELL

Writings:

PP, RC Railway Conciliation Scheme of 1907 (1912-13) Cd 6014.

Presidential Address, London School of Economics and Political Science, Railway Students' Association, delivered 22 Oct 1912.

'The State Acquisition of the Railways' *The Jubilee of the Railway News* (1914).

Sources:

Unpublished

PRO RAIL 633/32, South Eastern & Chatham Railway Managing Committee, Minutes of Meeting.

BCe.

PrC.

Published

George P Neele, *Railway Reminiscences* (Wakefield: E P Publishing Ltd, 1974).

Oswald S Nock, *The South Eastern and Chatham Railway* (Ian Allan, 1961).

Railway Gazette 8 Apr 1921, 10 June 1955.

Times 6 June 1955.

WWW.

DENT, Joseph Malaby

(1849-1926)

Publisher

Joseph Malaby Dent (courtesy of J M Dent & Sons Ltd).

Joseph Malaby Dent was born in Darlington on 30 August 1849, the fourth son of George Dent and Isabella, daughter of Hugh Railton of Staindrop, County Durham. George Dent was a house painter; when that business failed he turned music-teacher. Joseph's formal education was limited to a few years at elementary school, but an accident in infancy which lamed him for life fostered a passion for reading which he never lost.

On leaving school at thirteen, Joseph Dent was apprenticed to a printer, and then to a bookbinder. In 1867 he left for London to finish his training there, joining an elder brother who worked for Waterlows the printers. Dent celebrated the completion of his apprenticeship in 1870 by marrying Hannah Wiggins, who helped to run the boarding-house where he and his brother lived; soon after he set up his own bookbinding business in a workshop rented at 3s a week.

Dent's business slowly grew, although he was always short of capital and often hard put to meet the weekly wage bill. Only repeated loans from a grocer, George Carter, helped him to survive these difficult years. In November 1887 Hannah died, and within two months Dent's factory in Great Eastern Street, which he rented at £250 a year, burned down. The sympathetic Carter refused to accept Dent's insurance money as payment of his capital debt and offered to advance more money to help him start again. Three months after a new factory was completed in July 1888, Dent issued the first two volumes of the Temple Library, the *Essays* of Charles Lamb, and thereby fulfilled his boyhood ambition to become a publisher.

The Temple Series began with limited editions on hand-made paper, but then the issue of a cheap but well-made pocket edition of Shakespeare led to the real beginning of his career as 'The Prince of Reprinters'. For some years the annual sales of the forty volumes of this edition, published from 1894 to 1896, reached over 250,000. At that time this was the largest-ever sale of Shakespeare's plays, a record of which Dent was very proud. Dent's desire to make the best English, and then world, literature freely available in inexpensive editions whose printing and binding should be worthy of the texts was the inspiration behind his reprint series, including the Everyman Library. He liked to feel 'that in earning our living we were doing really useful work' {Dent (1928) 139}.

From its inception in 1906 the Everyman series took up most of the resources of the business. It was intended as 'a democratic library' of 1,000 volumes 'at the democratic price of one shilling' {Dent (1928) 126}, to be published in batches of fifty at a time, with a minimum print run of 10,000 for each volume needed to cover costs. A factory at Letchworth, which cost £20,000 for premises and plant, had to be built to cope with the binding of the series. When a new publishing-office was built in London to replace one which had been taken over from Macmillans in 1897 stock-room for two million volumes had to be provided to maintain the Everyman list.

Dent miscalculated the finances of the Everyman series, although its very success caused much of the difficulty because the early reprinting of the first volumes absorbed resources intended for the next batch. Nor could he meet the costs of the new buildings from his own capital: when a limited liability company, J M Dent & Sons, was set up in 1909 its nominal capital was only £9,500. He was forced to borrow from a bank and to obtain extended credit from his paper-makers. Throughout his business life Dent rarely escaped from such liabilities; although he was usually treated well by his creditors, he came to consider 'usury' as the 'prime cause of social oppression' because he thought it encouraged people to get power over others by their capital {Dent (1928) 204}. His financial trials also made him far from generous in the royalties he paid to his authors or the wages he paid to his staff: more than one person saw him burst into tears when asked to pay out money.

But Dent never allowed financial or practical difficulties to stand in the way of his ambitious publishing schemes. His son Hugh, who was his father's 'right hand in administrative work' {Dent (1928) 73}, supplied that attention to administrative detail of which Joseph Dent confessed himself to be incapable. Hugh was the managing director of the company while Joseph was chairman for life. Paxton and Austin (Joseph's sons by his second wife, Alexandra Main, whom he married in 1890) also joined the firm; when they were killed on active service in the First World War Hugh's brother John came to take their place. The war also delayed completion of the publication of the Everyman series, for wartime restrictions slowed down the rate of publication of additional volumes, but before his death Dent did have the satisfaction of knowing that all the debts incurred by the series had been paid, and that capital reserves of over £100,000 had been accumulated.

As well as his major reprint series, Dent published many educational works. Much against his will he was forced to bow to the general practice of selling educational books at non-net prices: he was an early supporter of Frederick Macmillan's (qv) net book scheme. He also commissioned new works, including the Mediaeval Towns series which was inspired by his first visit to Italy in 1890. Dent became an enthusiastic traveller, and as well as making repeated visits to Europe he travelled to America several times to cultivate the American market, which was a very important outlet for his books.

Dent was a 'master-builder of books' {Mumby (1949) 296}, unusual among the publishers of his day in that he was far more ready to accept advice on literary matters than on questions of book production such as the selection of paper or binding-styles. His London publishing-office long retained the character of a workshop and office combined, and when his binding factory was moved to Letchworth he regretted the loss of daily contact with his workers. Whether his binding employees missed him is a moot point: his appalling temper and 'despotic rule' {Swinnerton (1937) 89} in the London publishing office gave his staff the impression of living on the edge of a volcano and made it hard for him to keep good men.

In 1920 Dent gave up general oversight of the business, although his interest in new books and in the details of their production persisted to the end of his life. Business had left him little time for outside activities, except for his enthusiastic participation from his earliest days in London in the activities of Toynbee Hall, where the atmosphere of undogmatic piety and educational endeavour greatly appealed to the Congregationalist in him. In his semi-retirement he devoted much time to various associations including the League of Nations and the Nursery School movement. He died on 9 May 1926, leaving £14,276 gross.

CHRISTINE SHAW

Writings:

(Hugh R Dent, ed), *The Memoirs of J M Dent, 1849-1926* (J M Dent & Sons, 1928).

Sources:

Unpublished

C Reg: J M Dent & Sons (Holdings) Ltd (105,139).

BCe.

MCe.

PrC.

Published

DNB.

Frank A Mumby, *Publishing and Bookselling: A History from the Earliest Times to the Present Day* (Jonathan Cape, 1949).

Ernest Rhys, *Everyman Remembers* (J M Dent & Co, 1931).

Frank Swinnerton, *Swinnerton: An autobiography* (Hutchinson & Co, 1937).

—, *Background with Chorus: A Footnote to Changes in English Literary Fashion between 1901 and 1917* (Hutchinson, 1956).

Times 26 May 1926.

WWW.

DE PAULA, Frederic Rudolf Mackley

(1882-1954)

Accountant

F R M de Paula from The Accountant *26 June 1926.*

Frederic Rudolf Mackley de Paula was born in Hendon, Middlesex, on 23 July 1882, the son of Friedrich Moritz Alphonse Felix de Paula (d 1902), a solicitor and partner in the City practice of Carey, Warburton & de Paula, and his wife Ellen Harriet née Mackley. Frederic had one brother (Waldemar, who was to become a respected City stockbroker) and three sisters.

Frederic de Paula was articled in 1901 to Charles F Cape & Co, chartered accountants of 12 Coleman Street, EC. Apparently Cape had a taste for hunting in the winter, and Frederic used to say this circumstance made it necessary for him to learn quickly, because Cape was inclined to look to his clerks to carry major responsibilites during his absences. Frederic learned to some purpose, and was placed fifth and seventh in order of merit in the 1903 and 1905 examinations of the Institute of Chartered Accountants in England and Wales (ICAEW). It is interesting that first place on each of these occasions was taken by Gilbert Garnsey (qv).

Frederic went into practice on his own account as a chartered accountant in 1909. He was joined in practice in 1910 by Edgar John Turner, and in 1913 by John Strickland Lake. The firm of de Paula, Turner, Lake & Co still continues under the same name in the City, though Frederic resigned his partnership in 1929.

He early showed an interest in teaching, providing auditing lectures from 1908 for the Chartered Accountants' Students' Society of London (CASSL). At that time, Lawrence Dicksee, lately resigned from his part-time chair in accounting at Birmingham University, was giving bookkeeping and accounts lectures for the CASSL finalists. Dicksee was then in his seventh year as part-time lecturer in accounting at the LSE; Frederic de Paula took over Dicksee's CASSL lectures in 1910 in addition to his own auditing course.

Two of de Paula's lectures on auditing delivered to CA Students' Societies around the country in 1911 and 1912 were later reproduced in *The Accountant*, as was a more specialised auditing lecture. This work, with his CASSL teaching, determined him to write his own book on auditing which would tackle the subject in a more fundamental way than the few previous works (including pre-eminently Dicksee's) then available. *Principles of Auditing* first appeared in 1914, went to a second edition in 1917, and a third in 1920. He undertook his own last major revision of the text for the eleventh edition in 1951.

de Paula was one of the young accounting practitioners who left their firms during the First World War. He was first employed at the Ministry of Munitions, where he worked under Sir Eric Geddes (qv) and George Beharrell. When the latter went to France, de Paula took over his work, following him to GHQ in France shortly thereafter as an Assistant Director-General of Transportation with the rank of lieutenant colonel. He was gazetted OBE (military division) and twice mentioned in despatches. His war-time experience of large-scale organisation and administration made its mark on him.

He was demobilised in 1919 and returned to his practice. In 1919 also, the LSE was extending its commerce programme and Dicksee (who had held a personal chair at LSE for some years) was appointed in 1919 to LSE's first established chair in accounting. de Paula joined Dicksee in 1920 as lecturer in accounting and business methods. A readership in accounting and business organisation was established in 1924 and de Paula was appointed to it. When Dicksee retired in 1926, de Paula succeeded him as professor of accounting, still on a part-time basis. He resigned the chair in 1929, along with his senior partnership in de Paula, Turner, Lake & Co, to join Dunlops and rejoin his wartime superiors, Sir Eric Geddes and Sir George Beharrell who were its chairman and managing director respectively.

In the early and mid-1920s Frederic de Paula was already committed to two accounting goals which he pursued virtually through the remainder of his working life. His first concern was to facilitate business investment and managerial control by the provision of improved and more relevant information, principally through fuller disclosure and greater comprehensibility in corporate financial reporting. His second was the improvement of standards of financial management and control within large organisations. In the long term he aimed to underpin advances in these areas by improvements in the education and professional training of accountants.

The main obstacle to improvements in corporate financial reporting in the early 1920s was the widespread employment of the 'secret reserve'. Use of this device had become common in bank balance sheets by the 1880s, with the intent of protecting investors following the disastrous bank failures of the 1860s and 1870s. The idea was that, in good years, directors would put part of their company's profits to reserve without disclosing the transaction to shareholders (lest they press for higher dividends). Later, if profits fell, the amounts previously put to reserve could be transferred back (again without disclosure) to bolster profits from current trading. The company's reported profitability could be thereby stabilised, and dividend payments satisfactorily maintained. By the turn of the century the bona fide use of the practice had the backing of the highest authorities.

After the First World War, however, some accountants like Lawrence Dicksee and Gilbert Garnsey (qv), and others with wider interests like Sir Josiah Stamp (qv), had become anxious at the increasing extent of reliance on secret reserves. There was the obvious danger that they could lend themselves to manipulation. This apart, there was the risk that published accounts might begin to mean little or nothing. But until the early 1930s the reformers' views were not representative of general professional and business opinion.

Frederic de Paula supported the progressives on disclosure, arguing through the 1920s that the virtues of secrecy were exaggerated, and the policy a mistaken one, leading to distrust. In 1931, the Kylsant case, involving Lord Kylsant (qv), chairman of the Royal Mail Steam Packet Co, startled the City and the business world. It turned on issues of financial disclosure to shareholders. De Paula dealt with it, and with its implications, in the sixth edition (1933) of *Principles of Auditing*.

In his practice de Paula had encouraged clients to improve standards of disclosure, receiving public approval for this work in the financial press, for example, for the presentation of the 1929 accounts of Temoh Tin Dredging Ltd. His move to Dunlops in January 1930 (as chief accountant and later as controller of finance) gave him greater opportunities. He persuaded the Dunlop board to present their 1929 accounts in the general form worked out for Temoh Tin. When Dunlops' 1931 accounts appeared, they again attracted favourable comment at least in part because they included comparative figures for the previous year.

In the design and preparation of Dunlops' 1933 accounts, however, he made (from the point of view of the accountancy profession and the business world in general) a momentous contribution by the inclusion of consolidated statements, with a clearly compiled statement of profit for the year, showing how the amount available for dividend had been built up. The Dunlop company was emerging from the depression and its board was able to report increased profits and to recommend an increased dividend. Within the profession the Dunlop accounts of 1933 were regarded as a model for accounting reform to which the Council of the ICAEW pointed its members.

Frederic de Paula's ideas on an enlarged corporate role for accountants were publicised first in a lecture delivered at the LSE in 1926, when he became professor of accounting, on 'The place of accountancy in commerce'. He expressed his aim of raising the status of accounts departments within major companies so that they would rank equally with the principal executive departments. He saw the chief accountant as the chief financial officer of the whole company, who would be responsible to the general manager for the finances of the business and its financial control. When at the end of 1929 de Paula moved to Dunlops, his work on financial management and control, and the development of budgetary control, represented his greatest contribution from the point of view of the Dunlop board. He described it in a number of public lectures through the

1930s, including one to the British Association for the Advancement of Science in 1933.

Early in the Second World War de Paula was lent by Dunlops to the War Office, where he held the appointment of Deputy Director-General of Progress and Statistics, and where he worked on the supply of munitions until recalled to Dunlops early in 1940. Soon after, he became seriously ill and retired from Dunlops at the end of 1941 when he joined Harding, Tilton & Hartley Ltd (later to be known as the British Van Heusen Co) as vice-chairman and joint managing director. He became chairman of that company and served also, especially in the later years of his career, on the boards of other important companies, including the English, Scottish & Australian Bank Ltd; F P & F L Impey Ltd; Powers-Samas Accounting Machines Ltd; Electric & Musical Industries Ltd (and various of its associated and subsidiary companies); Brush Electrical Engineering Co Ltd; and others. He served on the Executive Committee of the British Institute of Management, and was for a number of years a member of the Grand Council of the Federation of British Industries, and its vice-president, 1951-53. He served on the FBI's Taxation Committee from 1932 to 1950, having been its chairman from 1941. He also chaired the FBI sub-committee on Government Contract Cost Investigations which reported in the early 1940s.

At the beginning of the 1940s also, within the ICAEW there was a move to open the Council to younger members and especially to members directly employed in industry and commerce. There had been pressure for such changes both from within and from outside the accountancy profession, and the Council of the ICAEW set up a Taxation and Financial Relations Committee in 1942 to promote discussion on business and financial problems with provincial members, and especially to promote liaison between members in practice and in industry. Regional sub-committees were established in the various ICAEW district societies.

The ICAEW's T and FR Committee still functions under the title 'Technical Advisory Committee'. Its first meeting was held in July 1942 under the chairmanship of Harold M Barton (qv). Barton resigned the chairmanship in March 1943 and de Paula succeeded him. His election to the Council of the ICAEW, as its first non-practising member, followed in December 1943. de Paula had earlier persuaded Stanley W Rowland, a partner in Dicksee's firm since 1924 and for many years lecturer in accounting at LSE, to act as secretary to the Committee.

The T and FR Committee secured permission to consider 'general questions of accounting principles and procedure'. The Council's first *Recommendations on Accounting Principles* appeared in December 1942. They dealt with the treatment of tax reserve certificates, and war damage contributions, premiums and claims. Three further recommendations published in March 1943, also dealt with wartime matters such as war taxes, but included recommendations on the treatment in accounts of proposed profit appropriations, something for which de Paula had long argued.

Under his chairmanship of the T and FR Committee, the Council published in October 1943 and February 1944 the important Recommendations VI and VII on reserves and provisions, and on the disclosure of the financial position and results of subsidiary companies in

move was thwarted by the board of BOAC and Basil (later Sir Basil) Smallpeice (qv) remained in charge of the main company. D'Erlanger's four years as chairman of BOAC were not a great success. The airline was in a low state due to the Comet I disasters, d'Erlanger's health was failing, and although he was able to order Boeing 707's, he also agreed to buy Vickers VC-10s at Ministerial insistence. The main management problem was that d'Erlanger worked out of his flat in town and met the Minister without his managing director, which made for poor relationships and bad decisions. At the same time parliament was beginning to probe nationalised industries and public comprehension of the importance of cost-accounting was just beginning to emerge. BOAC's profitability was still over the horizon when d'Erlanger left, a time in which such issues as the 'national interest' versus commercial policy and BOAC's financing had yet to be resolved.

In many ways, Sir Gerard (he was knighted in 1958 and then put on the BOAC payroll), suffered during both his spells as chairman of nationalised British airlines because he took over at times of critical transition, operating with a collection of second-hand equipment or of new, untried British types, and with totally unsatisfactory concepts of long-term strategy and financing. In both cases his tenure was followed by that of more dynamic and outgoing chairman, Lord Douglas of Kirtleside (qv) at BEA and Sir Matthew Slattery at BOAC, who were willing to defend their interests and had the resources to do so. 'Pops' was too much a humane Jewish gentleman-financier, though a skilled pilot of wide experience, to do political battle.

In 1937 he married Gladys Florence, daughter of H J Sammut, by whom he had one son and two daughters. For his ATA work he was created a CBE in 1943. He died at home in London on 15 December 1962 at the age of fifty-six; he left £317,043 gross.

ROBIN HIGHAM

Sources:

Unpublished

PrC.

Personal knowledge.

Published

Lettice Curtis, *The Forgotten Pilots* (Henley-on-Thames: G T Foulis, 1971).

DNB.

Robin Higham, *Britain's Imperial Air Routes 1918 to 1938* (Shoe String Press, 1960).

Garry May, *The Challenge of BEA: The Story of a Great Airline's First 25 Years* (Wolfe, 1971).

Times 17 Dec 1962.

WWW.

Leo d'Erlanger (courtesy of Mr John King).

D'ERLANGER, Leo Frederic Alfred

(1898-1978)

Merchant banker, aviation and Channel Tunnel promoter

Leo Frederic Alfred d'Erlanger, born in London on 2 July 1898, was one of the first members of the remarkable family of European bankers to be born in England. His half-German, half-American father, Baron François Rodolphe d'Erlanger, was not involved in the family business; his mother, Elisabetta Barbiellini-Amidie was the daughter of Pope Leo XIII's chamberlain and Pope Leo was his godfather. After schooling in France, Leo went to Eton and Sandhurst, living during his formative years with his uncle, Baron Frederic who, with his brother Emile, ran the family bank in London.

From Eton and during the First World War, Leo went to Sandhurst, subsequently serving under Gort in France, where he suffered shell-shock. When he returned to England, Leo joined the family bank, Erlangers Ltd, which his great grandfather had formed in Frankfurt in 1840 (it later moved to Paris while the London branch of 1870 became the major enterprise). In 1927 Leo became a partner in the bank, director in 1939 and finally chairman in 1944. The bank specialised in corporate finance, acceptance credit business and foreign exchange and while Leo became an experienced banker, he remained an entrepreneur. He ran the bank as a benevolent autocrat. In the 1920s the bank's main business was in international loans to foreign municipalities and states, but the scope for expansion was severely curtailed when in 1934 the Bank of England requested London banks not to call in loans to German corporations. It was probably largely due to Leo's efforts that Erlangers was one of the first merchant banks to pay attention to financing British industries, consequently acquiring a first rate list of corporate commercial clients.

Apparently Leo never learned to fly, but he developed a passionate interest in the aviation industry. His first involvement was as substantial shareholder, but through nominees, in Imperial Airways Ltd, formed in 1924. His interest was a joint one with one of his best friends from Eton days, Esmond Cecil Harmsworth (later Second Viscount Rothermere) who joined the airline's board in 1934. Leo thought he might have an interesting hand to play in international negotiations, particularly with the French, but such an opening eluded him, though he was involved in negotiations for a pool of receipts on the Marseilles route.

When at the beginning of 1935 a small and recently publicly floated airline, Hillman's Airways, came on the market following the death of its founder, Edward Hillman (qv), Leo purchased it. Putting his younger cousin, Gerard (qv) onto its board, Leo some months later merged Hillman Airways Ltd with the airline interests of Whitehall Securities Ltd to form British Airways Ltd. The latter airline subsequently became the Government's second chosen instrument in developing civil aviation, with the aid of government subsidies and mail contracts. The airline was encouraged to concentrate on European services which the larger Imperial Airways had with good reason neglected because of its Empire services. Leo avoided direct personal involvement in pioneering businesses in case their demise might compromise him; instead he used nominees to represent his interests, although many years later he doubted whether this had been the wisest policy. In 1935 he was involved in proposals for a British air service to South America together with Harmsworth and Whitehall Securities, but international politics frustrated the plans which were never implemented before the outbreak of war.

Leo's influence on the manufacturing side of the airline industry was much greater. As a merchant banker, he helped to raise capital for the de Havilland Aircraft Co following a request from its chairman, Alan Butler, who was another Eton friend. Other clients included Short Brothers while, at the request of Whitehall Securities, Leo appointed a man to sort out the problems of the flying boat manufacturers Saunders Roe. Most important was the encouragement he gave to the production of the successful Rolls Royce Merlin engine which was subsequently used in the Spitfire, Lancaster bomber and Mosquito aircraft. In a series of meetings in Slough between Leo, Roy Fedden (qv) the chief engineer of the Bristol Aeroplane Co, Col Devereux managing director of High Duty Alloys Ltd and Ernest Hives (qv) director of Rolls Royce, the production plans for the Merlin engine were formulated. During the Second World War, Leo recognised with Devereux that salvation lay in the re-processing of scrap aluminium and other metals in short supply and set up International Alloys for the purpose. He also played a crucial part in rescuing the chemical firm Alginate Industries Ltd and was a significant figure in its development over a long period.

Upon the fall of France in 1940, Leo asked F W Winterbotham of MI5 to get the principal French aeronautical engineers and their plans for heavy under-carriage hydraulics, which were ahead of Britain's, to England. After this was accomplished, the French worked with Dowty's (qv) staff near Gloucester, subsequently providing the undercarriage for the successful Lancaster bomber. Leo also brought his influence to bear on the efforts of Winterbotham to obtain authorisation for experimental work by Barnes Wallis which culminated in the bouncing bomb (or dam buster).

One of Leo's less successful projects was the Channel Tunnel scheme. On the death of his uncle Baron Emile (1866-1939), chairman of the Channel Tunnel Co since 1911, he first became interested. When he believed that he had a duty to shareholders to keep the company alive until the tunnel was built, Leo gave the scheme his support. He persuaded the new chairman of the company Sir Herbert Walker (qv), who had been general manager of the Southern Railway until 1937, to re-appraise the project; Walker subsequently became a powerful advocate of the Tunnel. Little progress was made until 1956, when Leo as chairman succeeded in interesting the Suez Canal Co. The latter wanted to develop a successor business to the Canal, on which their lease would run out in 1968, although in the event it was nationalised by the Egyptian Government that summer. After Leo announced at the Channel Tunnel Co's 76th AGM in May 1957 that the Suez Co would have a major interest in the plan, speculation followed and inflated the value of the company's shares.

In July 1957 the Channel Tunnel Study Group was formed to include French and American interests. The Group's scheme was later adopted by the British and French Governments and Leo was removed from the centre of negotiations, but not from the forum of debate and pressurising. Over ensuing years his time was increasingly occupied in lobbying, lecturing and explaining the need for a Tunnel to a variety of audiences ranging from politicians to some who should have needed no convincing such as the Lecture and Debating Society of British Rail's Southern Region, in 1965.

Eventually the Conservative Government decided in favour of the Tunnel, a decision for which Leo was to a degree responsible. In October 1972, an agreement was signed between the British and French Governments and the Tunnel and financing companies. A further agreement was signed in 1973, but by this time Leo had ceased to be the principal financier associated with the Tunnel. In 1974 he resigned from the Channel Tunnel Co, earlier renamed Channel Tunnel Investments Ltd. Leo's dream was not realised in his lifetime. Following a change in Government in 1974, a review of the project resulted in British withdrawal. Leo was reported as having said that he would have a reserved seat in the first train to travel through the Tunnel, but if he were then dead, his coffin was to be dug up and placed in the train!

His banking activities ended no more happily. After the merger of Erlangers Ltd with Philip Hill Higginson in 1959, he was not appointed chairman of the new company and resigned as vice-chairman of Philip Hill Higginson Erlanger's Ltd and from the board of Philip Hill Investment Trust in 1961.

Leo married in 1930 Edwina Prue, an American whom he had earlier pursued across the world; they had two children. In some ways Leo was a paradox: a disciplined creature of habit who ignored convention; a champion of national causes who abhorred publicity; a devout Catholic given to the quaintest superstitious practices; and a man born to wealth who lived off toast. He was also a man of immense courtesy and charm and consequently was very persuasive. In 1974 he left England to become a tax exile at the exquisite Arab palace his father had rebuilt in Tunisia.

Leo died in Geneva on 25 October 1978.

JOHN KING

Sources:

Unpublished

PRO Air Ministry files, Kew.

Author's correspondence with Leo d'Erlanger 1975-78.

Author's interview with Leo d'Erlanger, May 1978.

Private information supplied by M R Bonavia, Rodolphe d'Erlanger (Leo's son), W R Merton and F W Winterbotham.

Published

Daily Telegraph 26 Oct 1978.

Sunday Express 25 June 1972.

Times 26 Oct 1978.

WWW.

DE ROTHSCHILD
see ROTHSCHILD

DE STERN
see STERN, Sir Edward

DEUCHAR, James

(1849-1927)

Distiller

Born in Scotland in 1849, James Deuchar moved to Tyneside as a very young man, together with his three older brothers (Alexander, George and Robert). Originally James took the license of the *Argyle* public house in High Street, Gateshead and then, together with his brother George, he went into partnership in 1868 with John and James Meikle as 'wine, spirit, ale and porter merchants' at the *Half Moon* inn, 14 Bigg Market, Newcastle upon Tyne. In 1870 the firm widened its activities, when Meikle and Deuchar purchased the Arthurs Hill Brewery in Bell Street, Westgate Road, Newcastle. The partners were now in a position to supply their own licensed houses with beer and from small beginnings rapidly took over a number of public houses on Tyneside. In 1880 James Deuchar left the partnership and set up on his own, taking the *Ridley Arms* in Percy Street, Newcastle, where he commenced his own brewery operations. He quickly built up a large licensed trade and in 1888 purchased the Monkwearmouth brewery and maltings of J J & W H Allison at Sunderland, subsequently closing the smaller Ridley Arms Brewery. In 1895 the company adopted limited liability as James Deuchar Ltd, and went public in 1898, although only just over £100,000 of debentures were sold to the public, all of the ordinary shares being retained by the Deuchar family. At this time the assets of the company were given as £616,000, and included 45 freehold hotels and public houses (including large hotels in Sunderland, Tynemouth and Newcastle) and 31 leasehold public houses. Profits in the three years to 1898 averaged over £30,000 per annum. James Deuchar became chairman and managing director of the new company, of which his brother Robert and Thomas Gillespie of Gillespie Bros & Co were also directors.

Robert Deuchar had meanwhile followed his younger brother's example, by purchasing the Sandyford Stone Brewery in Newcastle and was to do so again in 1897, when he formed Robert Deuchar & Co Ltd, a company which also developed a considerable presence in the brewing and licensed trades on Tyneside and Wearside. While James and Robert had made the step from being innkeepers to being brewers and wine and spirit merchants, the remaining brothers did not develop beyond innkeeping, although Alexander started a bottling business in City Road, Newcastle, where he bottled beers for the firms of both James and Robert.

Increasing demand for pale ales of the Scottish and Burton types led both firms to re-direct their brewing activities. Although Robert was by then dead, his firm acquired the Duddingston Brewery of Simpson & McPherson in Edinburgh in 1910, while James Deuchar purchased William Ross & Co, which had the Lochside brewery and maltings at Montrose. James Deuchar Ltd developed 'Lochstrong' pale ale, which, together with the firm's strong brown ale, was brought to Tyneside by steamer from Scotland.

Increasing profitability enabled the brothers to develop a more expansive lifestyle. Robert moved from Newcastle to Shortridge Hall near Warkworth in 1891 and when he died on 8 June 1904 he left an estate valued at £270,907 gross. Even Alexander, whose business had expanded less rapidly and seen less diversification, left £141,299 when he died on 6 August 1913.

James Deuchar outlived his brothers and remained chairman of James Deuchar Ltd until his death in 1927. At that time his company owned about 150 public houses and hotels in Northumberland and Durham, including three of the four largest hotels in Newcastle, the *Grand*, *County* and *Turk's Head*.

James Deuchar invested heavily in agricultural land in north Northumberland and in Roxburghshire, partly, no doubt, with the aim of controlling barley supplies for his maltings. When he died Deuchar owned 7,000 acres in Northumberland, at Middleton and Ilderton, and 6,000 acres on the estate at Stichill near Kelso, where he lived in Stichill House. He married a Miss Henderson of Birmingham and had three sons (one of whom, James Wilson Deuchar, succeeded him as chairman of the company) and four daughters. When James Deuchar died on 12 December 1927, he left an estate valued at £1,331,716.

D J ROWE

Sources:

Unpublished

P Chilton and M Poppleston, 'History of Brewers in North East England' (typescript, Newcastle Central Library).

J J W Deuchar (courtesy of the Norwich Union Insurance Group).

DEUCHAR, John James Walker

(1851-1911)

Actuary and insurance company executive

John James Walker Deuchar was born at Edinburgh on 24 September 1851, the youngest of five sons of John Deuchar (1786-1863), lecturer in chemistry at Edinburgh University, and his wife Jane Walker, daughter of James Walker an Edinburgh publisher. The family, who were Presbyterians, owned Morningside Park, Edinburgh, with its modest mansion, and had achieved renown for their artistic and scientific talents. J J W Deuchar's grandfather, David Deuchar (1742-1808), was a prominent etcher who acted as seal engraver to the Prince of Wales and was patron of the young artist Henry Raeburn (later Sir Henry Raeburn).

After being educated at the Edinburgh Institute of Glasgow University until the age of seventeen, J J W Deuchar followed an elder brother, David (1843-1905) into the Standard Life Insurance Co as an actuarial trainee in 1868. Eight years later he became a fellow of the Faculty of Actuaries — the professional body for Scotland — and moved to the City of Glasgow Life Office as the company's assistant actuary. Whilst there, he studied law through early morning lectures at Glasgow University; served as a public valuer of friendly societies for Scotland; became an examiner for the Institute of Accountants and Actuaries of Glasgow; and played a leading part in founding the Insurance and Actuarial Society of Glasgow in 1881.

Wider professional recognition came in 1883 with his election as a fellow of the London based Institute of Actuaries. Like his brother David, then, who at thirty-one became manager of the Caledonian Fire & Life Insurance Co in 1874, J J W Deuchar was ready to accept heavy responsibility at a comparatively early age. Indeed, in 1887 the Norwich Union Life Insurance Society chose him as the first person to hold jointly the posts of actuary and secretary to its organisation whilst he was still only thirty-five. The Society had opened in 1808 and initially grew rapidly. However, during the mid-nineteenth century poor investment results led to falling bonuses — the means by which policy holders share in a life office's profits — and made the Norwich Union far less competitive than many of the progressive new insurance firms opening in the Victorian period. Its problems were compounded by directors who had become highly conservative. For instance, in the 1870s they gave little support to Deuchar's predecessor as secretary when he tried to increase the Society's commitment to endowment assurances, even though these policies were attracting the bulk of all new business in the late Victorian life insurance market. Instead, they concentrated on their well established business in whole life insurance policies. Under the actuary who preceded Deuchar this class of business had been run very soundly but with a mounting inability to attract new policyholders. Whereas new sums insured annually had risen to an early peak of £815,000 in 1818, the average slumped to between £200,000 and £250,000 from the 1840s to the 1880s. Consequently, the Society was gradually failing even to match the business lost from policy surrenders and claims among its ageing body of policyholders.

J J W Deuchar therefore faced an immense task in 1887. Failure to introduce reforms could have easily led to an irreversible decline and eventual closure or absorption by a more progressive rival. Fortunately, he found an ally in George Forrester who was president of the Society, 1888-98. As a newcomer to the board twenty years earlier, Forrester had tried in vain to persuade his fellow directors to handle most business in sub-committees rather than taking even the most routine decisions at their main board. Yet, with Forrester's backing, Deuchar stressed the urgency of the need for change and persuaded the directors to adopt a committee system based on those used by the leading Scottish life offices. This allowed routine matters to be filtered out prior to the main board which, as Deuchar intended, now found more time to discuss strategy. He then put forward meticulously planned proposals for expansion. Sensitive to the directors' conservatism he did not press for overseas growth initially. Business from Western Europe became of some importance in the mid-1890s and a South African branch was opened in 1893 which emerged as the Society's largest source of overseas premiums in the Edwardian period.

Even so, Deuchar's emphasis remained with the British market where he achieved rapid growth well in advance of any significant overseas contribution. By 1890, annual new business already stood at £1 million, rose to £2.2 million only ten years later and reached £5 million on the eve of his retirement in 1910. Whereas the Society's results were overshadowed by at least 20 British life offices when he arrived, it ranked second only to the Prudential throughout the 1900s.

The key to Deuchar's success lay in his ability to tackle the complex range of problems arising from life insurance management and his secretarial role, while also finding time to remain an innovative actuary who fully grasped the technical difficulties facing the Society. Moreover, he realised that impressive new business figures did not in themselves guarantee long term success. Accordingly his investment advice — with board agreement — aimed to maximise yields on the expanding life fund without jeopardising its capital value. Head office administration also became more efficient. Bad life risks were, for instance, easier to avoid following his creation of a selection committee of medically qualified directors. Routine administration costs were also held to a minimum. Above all he disliked costly press advertising and canvassing, preferring instead the recognition arising from offering improved bonuses and a more flexible range of policies, among which endowment assurances now dominated.

Growth also required an increased clerical staff. Whereas only ten clerks were employed at head office when Deuchar arrived, their number rose to about 120 over the next twenty years. In some respects he was a strict manager. He extended the clerks' daily attendance by an hour; defined their responsibilities more clearly; and allocated their previously undivided work to six specialised departments, each under a senior clerk. Meanwhile, though, he ended the Society's practice of working on Saturday afternoons and introduced a fortnight's annual paid holiday for every clerk. He also encouraged his staff to gain professional qualifications — an area largely ignored before his arrival — and as business expanded the more able clerks found opportunities for promotion at head office or in one of the branches.

Indeed, the tireless energy which Deuchar displayed as a young man never faltered. At first his methods met with scepticism in the insurance press which gently implied that the Norwich Union was mistaken in departing from its traditionally conservative style of management. By the 1900s, though, as the Society's bonuses improved and expenses were held down, this outlook changed with, for example, the *Post Magazine* referring in 1905 to the Society's 'brilliant expansion of the last decade' {*Post Magazine* 66 (1905) 609}.

Of course, to some degree he fell into the right place at the right time. He appears to have been a modest man and was the first to point out that he had taken over an actuarially sound life office. Moreover, he was fortunate to have had the support of George Forrester during the crucial period when there was a need to convince the doubters that his new approach would work. Yet, he made the best of these opportunities.

Other interests played a minor part in his life. After pressure from his friends, for instance, he became a Conservative councillor at Norwich in 1907, but his chief efforts in this field lay, characteristically, in local education. His other interests included golf, whilst he was an honorary freemason and he maintained a link with his origins through the Norwich Scots Society of St Andrew.

Once established at Norwich his sense of fulfillment lay principally in his responsibilities with the Life Society. Perhaps, also, the pressures of these duties were responsible for the serious breakdown in his health in 1910 which forced him to resign. As a gesture of their respect for Deuchar the directors immediately elected him onto the board. Despite a rest in Egypt, where it was hoped that he would recover from the effects of pneumonia, he died on 6 June 1911 before having made any further contribution in this new role. Moreover, although said to be a 'Financier of great reputation in the insurance world' {*Norfolk News* 10 June 1911}, Deuchar's income from the Society never seems to have risen much above £3,000 a year, while his total estate at death was a modest £14,287. Deuchar's policy of creating new posts for well-qualified senior officials as business expanded allowed the board to choose his successor, Davidson Walker, from within the Norwich Union rather than recruiting elsewhere.

Deuchar, who married and had two sons and two daughters, was predeceased by his wife.

ROGER RYAN

Writings:

Income-Tax Tables for the Year from 5th of April 1865 to 5th April 1866 (Edinburgh: Bell & Bradfute, 1866).

Table of Income Tax to be Deducted at Whit Sunday 1873 (Edinburgh: Bell & Bradfute, 1873).

'On Negative Policy Values' *Journal of the Institute of Actuaries* 19 (1881).

'Some Account of the French General and National Insurance Companies' *ibid*.

A Sketch and the History of the Science of Life Contingencies (C & E Layton, 1882) also in *Transactions of the Insurance and Actuarial Society of Glasgow* 1882.

'On the Non-actuarial Departments of Life Assurance Business' *ibid* 1885. Also published separately in 1885.

Sources:

Unpublished

The Faculty of Actuaries, Edinburgh, information supplied by W Wallace Mair.

The Institute of Actuaries, London, information supplied by Mrs A H Sutcliffe.

The Mitchell Library, Glasgow, information supplied by J A Fisher.

Norwich Union Insurance Group, records used with special permission.

PrC.

PrC (Scots).

Roger J Ryan, 'A History of the Norwich Union Fire and Life Insurance Societies from 1797 to 1914' (East Anglia PhD, 1984).

Published

H W Andras (ed), *Historical Review of Life Assurance in Great Britain and Ireland* 5th ed (1912).

Robert N W Blake, *Esto Perpetua, Norwich Union Life Insurance Society* (Norwich Union Life Insurance Society, 1958).

Bourne's Insurance Directory 1914.

Eastern Daily Press 10 June 1911.

C A Ingram, *Four Score and Four: The Story of the Insurance and Actuarial Society of Glasgow* (Glasgow: 1967).

'The Late Mr David Deuchar' *Journal of the Chartered Insurance Institute* 7 (1904).

William Mair, *Historic Morningside* (Edinburgh: Macniven & Wallace, 1947).

Norfolk News 10 June 1911.

Norwich Mercury 10 June 1911.

Post Magazine 52 (1891), 54 (1903), 65 (1904), 66 (1905), 67 (1906), 70 (1909).

Charles J Smith, *Historic South Edinburgh* (Edinburgh: Charles Skilton, 1979).

DEUTSCH, Oscar

(1893-1941)

Cinema chain owner

Oscar Deutsch, photograph by Vandyk (courtesy of Mr David Deutsch).

Oscar Deutsch was born in Balsall Heath, Birmingham on 12 August 1893, the son of Leopold Deutsch, a general dealer, and his wife Leah née Cohen. His mother was a Polish Jewish immigrant; his father, likewise Jewish, came from Betzho Transchener Komitat in Hungary. They met and settled down in Birmingham where Leopold developed a thriving scrap metal business, until in 1904 he lost his life in a domestic accident (possibly falling off the roof of his home), leaving £2,925 gross. Oscar, the only son, was eleven at the time and the business passed into the hands of Adolf Brenner, Leopold's cousin and partner. Oscar completed his education at the local King Edward VI Grammar School, and at the age of seventeen joined the family firm (Deutsch & Brenner) becoming a director at the age of twenty-one. He remained with the firm during the war.

There was little chance of Oscar Deutsch gaining control of the firm which his father had founded, for his uncle had two sons, both older than Oscar. So in 1920 he grasped an opportunity to utilise his talents more fully. Two former school friends, Michael Balcon (qv) and Victor Saville (Salberg), set up a film distribution company (Victory Motion Pictures Ltd) as Midland agents for C M Woolf's (qv) thriving W & F film company. Deutsch agreed to become chairman. Saville and Balcon soon left for London, where, with Deutsch's financial support, they began film production. Deutsch stayed in Birmingham (he was still involved with Deutsch & Brenner) and expanded his interests into the exhibition side of the industry. He acquired a company called the Midlands Amusement Co which gave him control of two cinemas. More cinemas were acquired in the next few years and in 1928 he collaborated with other prominent Birmingham businessmen to build a cinema at Brierley Hill, Staffordshire.

These were dangerous days for small exhibitors, a plethora of sound apparatus was being put on the market as alternatives to the highly expensive American Western Electric and RCA systems. Deutsch found none of them satisfactory and persuaded the British Thomson-Houston Co to let his own technical expert, Sidney Swingler, research an adequate sound system in their laboratories. The consequent BT-H apparatus proved to be by far the most successful of the alternative systems. It was marketed by a company called Sound Equipment Ltd with Deutsch as chairman. Within eight months of operation 300 sets had been installed. In 1930 Deutsch, again in collaboration with Birmingham businessmen, built his first Odeon in the Birmingham suburb of Perry Barr. He was now vice chairman of the Midland branch of the Cinematograph Exhibitors Association, and in 1931 became chairman. Having survived the coming of sound, the worst years of the depression, and a hefty increase in Entertainment Tax, the film industry could look forward to somewhat brighter prospects. In 1933 Deutsch opened five new cinemas, bringing his circuit strength up to 26. In 1934 he built 17 more and by 1936 he had 142 cinemas, making his the fourth largest circuit in the country.

Deutsch's achievement is indicative of both the strength and limitation of the new industrial growth that occurred in Britain in the 1930s. Rather than attempting to break into the traditional strongholds of popular entertainment, like the West End, the inner London suburbs, or central areas of big provincial towns, Deutsch built his Odeons almost exclusively in new centres of prosperity and population growth, most of which (South Harrow, Worthing, Lewes, Colindale, Sidcup, Ipswich, Brentwood, Uxbridge, Luton, for example) were in the South East of England.

In contrast to the massive cathedral-like cinemas built in working class areas in the late 1920s and early 1930s (most notably the 'Astorias' and the 'Granadas') Deutsch was concerned to provide relatively small, intimate cinema theatres which would entice the inhabitants of the new suburbs and dormitory towns from their new homes. He conceived the idea of 'brand-selling' his cinemas, utilising the economies of standardised design to achieve high standards of comfort and service. Odeons were built explicitly as Odeons, clearly marked by the massive use of cream faience tiles and bold red lettering. By building his own cinemas rather than acquiring other people's Deutsch was able to achieve a uniformity which could be consciously exploited as an image. He consistently retaliated to critics who accused him of 'over-building' by claiming that his cinemas attracted an audience hitherto untouched by the cinema. At the same time he employed architects who designed Odeons such as those at Kingstanding (Cecil Clavering), South Harrow (A P Starkey), Crewe (Budge Reid) and Camberwell (Keith Roberts) as some of the boldest and most exciting buildings of the 1930s.

Suburbanites were wooed by the unimpeachable respectability of the

Odeon cinema, its tastefulness, its modernity, but also by the conscious attempt by Deutsch and his associates to plan their cinemas as intensely local institutions. In terms of design, size and booking policy the Odeon chain was the most thoroughly integrated of the large cinema circuits, yet the individual cinemas were set up as autonomous companies, for strong commercial reasons. Local businessmen and tradesmen were encouraged to invest, contracts were normally awarded to local builders, which helped to win local council building licences, and elaborate opening ceremonies were organised, with Deutsch and the local mayor always present. Once open, every attempt was made to encourage regular patronage; for example at Shirley, near Birmingham, an 'Odeon Car Club' was organised by the manager, who led his patrons on regular Sunday treasure hunts, picnics and visits to stately homes.

However attractive the cinema and however friendly the manager, success could only be guaranteed if a regular supply of first-class films could be provided. Paradoxically, for the intensely patriotic Deutsch, the problem stemmed mainly from the need to show the compulsory quota of British films which had been imposed on exhibitors and distributors by the 1927 Film Quota Act. With most of the production facilities owned by the two rival circuits, Gaumont British and Associated British Picture Corporation, Deutsch along with most independent exhibitors often had to rely on the dreadful 'Quota Quickies' produced on minimal budgets for the American distributors. However, United Artists, the smallest of the American 'Majors', decided to enter more wholeheartedly into production in England and saw the advantage of an alliance with the new circuits. By the middle of 1935, United Artists had a sizeable interest in the County and Odeon circuits which were now ensured a supply of quality films. In May 1937 Odeon and County merged, putting Deutsch in control of a circuit of 250 cinemas, the third largest in the country.

In July 1937 the loose congeries of Odeon interests were consolidated into a £6 million company. Deutsch's policy of concentrating his cinema interests in the areas of population growth paid off well but the lack of Odeon cinemas in key London and provincial centres now proved something of a handicap in securing equitable renting terms from the big American distributors. Henceforth, Deutsch concentrated on acquiring cinemas on central sites which would make Odeon a truly national circuit. This process reached its culmination in November 1939 when he took over the Paramount-Astoria circuit, 18 of the largest and most opulent cinema theatres in the country.

For almost the whole of his career in the film industry Oscar Deutsch was a sick man, but even during the later stages of his illness he managed to organise a routine by which his ability to work was virtually unaffected. In 1935 the Odeon head offices were transferred to London, and Deutsch took up residence at the nearby Dorchester Hotel. Brief rests in the mid-morning and early evening generally allowed him to continue operating, from the lounge of the Dorchester, until two in the morning. On Friday afternoon he returned to his family in Birmingham, spending much of his weekend on the affairs of Singer's Hill Synagogue of which he was warden and president.

Deutsch was a stern disciplinarian and unabashedly paternalistic. Managers were required to dress immaculately and liable to find themselves in deep water if discovered wearing a lounge suit rather than tails for the evening performance. On the other hand, he made himself eminently approachable and tried hard to stick to his habit of knowing the first names of all his employees, despite their rapid multiplication. He offered trade union recognition and good wages and working conditions in return for the high level of service he demanded.

Although he had no political ambitions he was quick to realise the full significance of Hitler's rise to power and became a vociferous advocate of rearmament. Through the agency of Sir Michael Bruce he was instrumental in securing the safety of large numbers of German Jews, and once war did break out he made his cinemas available to organisations like the Red Cross, the ARP, and Services Welfare.

He was also determined to back British films despite the fact that the articles of association of Odeon Theatres explicitly precluded the company from financing film production. Deutsch managed to get round this by promising to book the film if it was made, a guarantee which considerably reduced the problem of raising loan capital. (In fact this contravened Film Act provisions against 'blind booking' but the Board of Trade was enlightened enough to turn a blind eye to what in the circumstances was a laudable transgression). His last public engagement was the première of the highly successful *49th Parallel* which had been financed in this way. In the late 1930s he also participated in forming the Scophony Co, which was involved in the early development of television.

The constitution of the Odeon Theatres board bears witness to the fact that he had not achieved his spectacular success unaided. As well as his erstwhile collaborators, Stanley Bates and W G Elcock, were three United Artists directors, Sir E M Mountain (qv), the managing director of the British & Dominions and Eagle Star Insurance Co; the merchant banker, Philip Hill (qv); and the man who succeeded him as chairman, J Arthur Rank (qv). There was no doubt though that the courage, foresight and sound business judgement of Oscar Deutsch provided the essential catalyst to that success.

Oscar Deutsch married Lily Tanchan in 1918; they had three sons. The eldest, Ronald, was established at Deutsch & Brenner; David, the son who had been destined to go in to the Odeon was only fifteen when his father died; though he worked for the Rank Organisation in the 1950s he found more success as a freelance producer and, like the youngest brother, Gerald, as a writer. Oscar Deutsch died of cancer of the colon on 5 December 1941, leaving £285,601 gross.

ROBERT MURPHY

Writings:

Oscar Deutsch regularly contributed an article to the New Year Edition of the *Kinematograph Weekly,* and a paper to the Cinematograph Exhibitors Annual Conference throughout the 1930s.

Sources:

Unpublished

C Reg: Sound Equipment Ltd (now Eassams Ltd) (344,836); Odeon Cinema Holdings (now Rank Group Holdings) (280,573); Odeon Theatres (now The Rank Organisation) (324,504).

BCe.

PrC.

David Deutsch, unpublished essay on Oscar Deutsch and interview, 8 October 1980.

Published

Sir Michael W S Bruce, *Tramp Royal* (Elek, 1954).

—, *The History of Odeon* (Birmingham: Odeon Theatres, 1937).

Allen Eyles, 'Oscar and the Odeons' *Focus on Film* 22 (Autumn 1975), 23 (Winter 1975) letters from John Fernee and Brian Bulgin.

PEP, *The British Film Industry* (PEP,1952).

Times 6 Dec 1941.

Alan Wood, *Mr Rank. A Study of J Arthur Rank and British Films* (Hodder & Stoughton, 1952).

DEVONPORT, 1st Viscount Devonport
see KEARLEY, Hudson Ewbanke

DEVONSHIRE, 7th Duke of Devonshire
see CAVENDISH, William

DEWAR, Thomas Robert

Lord Dewar of Homestall, Sussex

(1864-1930)

Whisky blender and distiller

Thomas ('Tommy') Robert Dewar was born in Perth on 6 January 1864, fifth of the seven children of John Dewar, a wine and spirit merchant, and his wife Jane née Gow.

The last quarter of the nineteenth century saw the development of a number of highly successful firms in the Scotch whisky industry amongst which one of the most successful was John Dewar & Sons Ltd of Perth, founded in 1846 by John Dewar, the son of a crofter. At the time of his death in 1880 the business was very much a local one though it returned sufficient profits to sustain Dewar's sizeable family. Two of his seven children, John Arthur (1856-1929), his second surviving son, and Thomas Robert, joined the firm in 1879 and 1881 respectively. Together they were to create a firm whose product became a household name. Profit figures offer some indication of their achievement. When the founder died annual profits were a mere £1,321. By 1900 they were £59,000 and by 1925 when the firm merged with the Distillers Co Ltd they were £1,198,154.

The nature of the firm's expansion is difficult to understand without an appreciation of the quite different characters of the two brothers. The elder, John, was a cautious dour individual almost wholly absorbed in financial and administrative matters. Tommy, by contrast, was a flamboyant extrovert whose main skill lay in selling. John spent his whole career based in Perth whilst Tommy pioneered new markets in England and overseas.

Like his elder brother, Tommy was educated at Perth Academy and apprenticed to a spirit dealer. Following his father's death he returned to Perth in 1881 and worked for his brother until admitted to a partnership in 1885. Earlier attempts to expand sales in England had been unsatisfactory and at the age of twenty-one Tommy moved to London to canvass customers. Initially only a modest improvement in sales resulted but in 1890 John secured substantial credit facilities for the purchase of grain whisky from the Distillers Co Ltd. The resources set free by the Distillers' credit were used to accelerate the accumulation of whisky stocks rather than, as the more colourful accounts of Tommy's sojourn in London would have it, on advertising. This reflected the more acquisitive priorities of the elder brother and the importance of mature stocks for the reputation of a proprietary brand. By 1891 when Tommy Dewar left London the firm's sales had expanded more than two and a half fold. This performance was to be surpassed by his next venture in exporting.

By the early 1890s intense competition at home had produced a growing interest among Scotch whisky firms in exports and the appointment of overseas agents was becoming a commonplace. What distinguished

Tommy's approach to exporting was its sheer scale. Between 1891 and 1893, determined to establish Dewars on a world-wide basis, he toured some 26 countries, appointing 32 agents. World sales trips became a hallmark of the firm's approach to exporting. Tommy embarked on another world trip in 1898 and by 1914 the firm's representatives had undertaken five such campaigns.

If the creation of a thriving export business was Tommy Dewar's greatest achievement it was also critically important for the firm's standing in the trade. For although Dewars continued to enjoy expanding home sales despite the declining demand for spirits in Britain after 1900, exports were considerably — almost three times — more profitable than home sales. With the largest volume of export sales amongst the big three blending firms (Buchanans, Dewars and Walkers), Dewars were well placed in the amalgamation discussions which began in 1909. Although an amalgamation proved unattainable in the pre-war years, Buchanan and Dewars merged in a holding company, Scotch Whisky Brands Ltd in 1915. This was subsequently renamed Buchanan-Dewar Ltd in 1919 and merged along with John Walker & Sons Ltd and the Distillers Co Ltd in 1925. Tommy Dewar was appointed managing director of Scotch Whisky Brands but played a lesser part than his brother in the discussions leading up to the final merger. Both brothers were appointed to the board of the DCL in 1925.

Outside the trade Tommy Dewar enjoyed the friendship of many of the leading personalities of the time including Harry Lauder, Thomas Lipton (qv) and the Prince of Wales. Business and the wealth it generated gave him entrée to Edwardian society and he developed extensive sporting interests, especially in horse racing where he registered as an owner in 1897 and was elected to the Jockey Club in 1927. He was one of the earliest of Scotch whisky men to realise the importance of sports sponsorship as a form of marketing symbolised in numerous Dewar cups and trophies.

Wealth also gave him the freedom to indulge in public service, first on London County Council, 1892-95, then as Sheriff of London, 1897-98, and in 1900-6 as Unionist MP for St George's-in-the-East division of London. Public honours included a knighthood in 1901, a baronetcy in 1917 and a peerage in 1919. Lord Dewar never returned to his roots in Perth though the city benefited from his generosity. He purchased an estate in Sussex where he pursued his passion for breeding thoroughbreds, not just race horses but poultry, pigeons, goats, ponies and greyhounds. He also found time to write a number of books, all crammed full with his idiosyncratic views and spiced with his own epigrammatic humour popularly known as 'Dewarisms'.

Lord Dewar died on 11 April 1930, news of his death being announced, perhaps appropriately, in the racing columns of the *Times*. His estate was valued at £5,015,542. He was unmarried and a substantial part of his estate went to his nephew John Arthur Dewar, a director of the DCL.

RONALD B WEIR

Writings:

A Ramble Round the Globe (Chatto & Windus, 1894).

Experiences of Prohibition in the United States, Canada and New Zealand and also of the Gothenburg System (Spottiswoode & Co, 1895).

Toasts and Maxims (Greening & Co, 1906).

(with Joseph Simpson) *Great Scots* (George Pulman & Sons, 1914).

Sources:

Unpublished

John Dewar & Sons Ltd, Perth, Board Minute Books.

PrC.

Ronald B Weir, 'The Development of the Distilling Industry in Scotland in the Nineteenth and Early Twentieth Centuries' (Edinburgh PhD, 1974).

Published

John L Anderson, 'History of the House of Dewar' *DCL Gazette* Apr 1929 — Jan 1930.

Times 12 Apr 1930.

Ross Wilson, *Scotch* (Constable, 1970).

WWW.

DEWRANCE, Sir John

(1858-1937)

Chairman of engineering and coal-mining companies

John Dewrance was born in Peckham, London, on 13 March 1858, the third child and only son of John Dewrance and his wife Elizabeth née Curtis. His father had helped to build George Stephenson's *Rocket*, and later became locomotive superintendent of the Liverpool & Manchester Railway. He went into partnership with Joseph Woods, founder of a small engineering business in Southwark, London; in 1842, after Woods's death, Dewrance became sole proprietor and the firm was renamed Dewrance & Co. Dewrance Sr died in 1861.

John Dewrance the younger was educated at Charterhouse and King's College, London, where he studied science, specialising in chemistry. Later, he was an engineering pupil of his stepfather, Colonel John Davis, who had assumed the direction of Dewrance & Co during Dewrance's minority. In 1879 Dewrance joined his stepfather in control of the company, and Colonel Davis soon retired from the business.

The following year Dewrance formed a research laboratory and took over the staff of Professor Barff, conducting and supervising experiments on lubrication, on the protection of iron from rust, on corrosion, and on the production of aluminium by electrolysis. He himself took out over 100 patents, the first when he was only nineteen. The laboratory eventually developed into the Albion Chemical Co, with a factory, covering two acres, manufacturing cyanide, but Dewrance was forced to close it before the First World War because of undercutting by German manufacturers of cyanide in the British market.

Little is known of Dewrance's direction of his own engineering company, which manufactured valves, pressure gauges and other parts for steam engines. The company was a private one, and Dewrance was sole proprietor until his death. But evidently Dewrance had achieved some reputation as an administrator as well as an engineer, for on 5 April 1899 he was elected a director and chairman of Babcock & Wilcox Ltd.

Babcock & Wilcox had been formed in 1891 to acquire for £190,000 the business of water-tube steam boiler manufacturers, other than in the USA and Cuba, of the Babcock & Wilcox company of New York; it was completely independent of the American company. Since its formation it had been consistently profitable, and had acquired a reputation as a well-managed and well-administered concern.

During Dewrance's chairmanship, the company maintained its reputation as a financially sound and well-run business. The issued capital of the company increased from £320,000 in 1899 to £4.6 million in 1929. All this increase was due to the capitalisation of reserves, and the issue of bonus shares and rights. The company had an excellent profit record. In 1904, for instance, net profits were £289,749, enough to allow payment of a 50 per cent dividend (the actual dividend paid was 20 per cent). Babcocks continued to perform well through the trade depression of the early 1920s: it was not until 1926 that their profits were hit, partly by the coal strike and the General Strike, and declined from £844,752 in 1925 to £745,948 in 1926 (gross manufacturing profit). The early 1930s were a difficult period for Babcocks; in 1931 there were insufficient orders to keep the factories fully employed, one factory, at Lincoln, was closed to reduce costs.

It was not just the general trade depression that was taking its toll. The death in 1927 of Sir James Kemnal (qv), manager of the British branch of the American Babcocks' from 1883, and a managing director of the British company since its formation in 1891 (sole managing director from 1898), brought other difficulties in its wake. Dewrance, complaining that Kemnal had not kept him informed about the affairs of the company, did not want to appoint another managing director, and experimented by appointing a general manager and an assistant general manager. This new arrangement did not work well, and Dewrance was forced to appoint another managing director in 1932.

It is impossible to say what Dewrance's own role was in the direction of the affairs of Babcock & Wilcox during his long chairmanship, which lasted until July 1937 (he retained a seat on the board even then). His many other interests and activities must have precluded his taking an active part in the day-to-day running of this business, and his complaint that Kemnal had kept him in the dark about the company's affairs suggests that he may not have had a very decisive voice in the planning of company strategy either.

Dewrance's other business interest was in the Kent coalfields (he lived in Kent until 1926). He was chairman of the board which took over Kent Coal Concessions and the associated companies (which had a total issued capital of £1,035,045 and £295,000 of debentures in 1912) after their founder, Arthur Burr (qv), was forced to withdraw in 1914 from the direction of their affairs by dissatisfied shareholders. Dewrance was one of the largest shareholders in Kent Coal Concessions, but there were about 3,000 of them, and none held more than a few thousand pounds worth of shares. The war saved the Concessions group, because debenture holders were persuaded to accept the postponement of the payments of interest due to them, and landowners to accept the postponement of the rents due for their minerals, until six months after the end of hostilities. Neither Dewrance nor any of his colleagues drew any fees for their work in attempting to sort out the results of Burr's financial mismanagement; Dewrance gave the group a loan of £23,150 on a mortgage. After the war, the company's continued financial difficulties and growing debts forced the directors to sell off large areas of land to companies who would work them, despite the difficulty of persuading landowners to modify the terms of leases to make them sufficiently attractive to prospective purchasers. In 1922 Dorman Long, under Sir Arthur Dorman (qv), bought 17,466 acres of leasehold, and 2,374 acres of freehold land, for a total of £75,798. Although this left the Concessions group with 5,479 freehold acres, and 12,097 leasehold, it ceased to play an important role in the development of the coalfield.

During the First World War Dewrance served on a number of committees of the Ministries of Munitions and of Labour, and on a Treasury committee. For many years he took an active part in the affairs of several professional societies, being a member of the Institution of Civil Engineers, president of the Institution of Mechanical Engineers in 1923, president of the Institute of Metals, 1926-28, and president of the Engineering and Allied Employers' National Federation, 1920-26. In 1923 he served as Master of the Worshipful Company of Armourers and Braziers, and was an honorary member of the Institute of Royal Engineers, an associate member of the Royal Engineers' Board, a member of the Iron and Steel Institute and of the Institute of Naval Architects. His continued interest in research, and his forceful advocacy of the financial and scientific advantages of co-operative research, took him onto many research committees, including the General Board of the National Physical Laboratory and the Engineering Research Board. He was a fellow of King's College, London, and a member of the Commercial Degrees Committee of the University of London. During 1920-30 he was a governor of the London School of Economics. He was created a KBE in 1920, served as High Sheriff of Kent in 1925, and raised to a GBE in 1928.

In 1926 Sir John moved from Kent to Wretham Hall, Thetford, in

Norfolk. The management of this estate, and his passionate interest in all country sports (he was a good horseman, shot and fisherman) absorbed much of his time in later years. He also took an interest in local associations, such as the local branch of the British Legion, and the Thetford Chamber of Trade, YMCA and Ex-Servicemen's Club. Kindly, unassuming and courteous, Dewrance seemed the very model of an 'English gentleman'.

He married Isabella, daughter of the engineer Francis Trevithick, and granddaughter of the inventor Richard Trevithick, in 1882. She died in 1922; they had one son and one daughter. Sir John died on 7 October 1937, leaving an estate proved at £589,171.

CHRISTINE SHAW

Writings:

President's address *Proceedings of the Institution of Mechanical Engineers* Oct 1923.

PP, Evidence to Coal Industry Commission (1919) Cmd 360.

Sources:

Unpublished

MCe.

PrC.

Information from R W M Clouston, Babcock & Wilcox PLC.

Sir Kenneth Hague, 'The Development and Organisation of Babcock & Wilcox Ltd' (Edwards seminar, paper 230, 18 Nov 1958).

W Johnson, 'The Development of the Kent Coalfield' (Kent PhD, 1972).

Published

Circulator Jan 1938.

DNB.

Economist 26 Apr 1924, 17 Apr 1926, 16 Apr 1927, 21 Apr 1928, 23 Apr 1932.

Proceedings of the Institution of Mechanical Engineers 1937.

A E Ritchie, *The Kent Coalfield, its Evolution and Development* (Iron and Coal Trades Review, 1920).

Statist 21 Apr 1906, 26 Apr 1909, 30 Apr 1910, 22 Apr 1911, 27 Apr 1912, 19 Apr 1913, 2 May 1914, 6 May 1916, 12 May 1917, 18 May 1918, 14 May 1921, 28 May 1923.

Times 8 Oct 1937.

Who's Who in Engineering 1923.

WWW.

Alick Sydney Dick (courtesy of Mr Alick Sydney Dick).

DICK, Alick Sydney

(1916-)

Motor car manufacturer

Alick Sydney Dick was born at Massingham, Norfolk, on 20 June 1916, the younger of the two sons of Walter Dick, a medical practitioner, and his wife Mabel Ernestine née Buckell. Early in Alick's life his father moved to Chichester and developed a respected family medical practice. Alick was educated at Chichester High School and Dean Close School, Cheltenham.

By the age of sixteen Alick had developed an interest in engineering generally and in motor vehicles in particular. After attending the College of Aeronautical and Automobile Engineering in Chelsea, he moved to Coventry in 1933, where his uncle, Major Sydney Dick, introduced him to John Black (later Sir John Black), managing director of Standard Motors. In 1933 the Standard Motor Co was producing cars for the volume market known as 'Flying Standards'. By 1937 John Black had rescued the firm from indebtedness, turning the company into one of the UK's 'Big Five' motor manufacturers with an annual dividend of over 20 per cent. Through Black, Alick obtained a student apprenticeship in Standard's press toolroom at a wage of 18s 6d a week. Though family connections — Major Dick and John Black were brothers-in-law, married to the daughters of William Hillman (qv) — had facilitated Alick's entry into the motor industry, subsequent promotion was achieved through a mixture of luck, tremendous drive and enthusiasm. His ability was recognised quickly and he displayed an aptitude for shouldering responsibility. In 1936 he was appointed a buyer of aero engines for shadow factories and by the outbreak of the Second World War he was production and material controller in a shadow aero engine factory. Four years later he was undertaking similar duties for Standard's Mosquito aircraft production programme.

After the war Dick developed a close and enjoyable working relationship with John Black, as his personal assistant, and was elevated to the position of assistant managing director on his thirty-first birthday, in 1947. Though his personal shareholding in the company was small, Alick, who had been instrumental in Black's resignation following several disagreements between Black and the Standard board, succeeded Black on 7 January 1954. Aged thirty-seven, Dick was the youngest chief executive in the industry in charge of the fourth of the 'Big Five' UK motor manufacturers, with 11,000 employees and an 11 per cent share of the UK motor manufacturing industry in 1954. By 1953 the company's capital was £6 million (increased to £9 million in November 1954) and its after tax profit £644,330. The cars it produced included the Vanguard and Triumph sports car ranges. Dick owed everything to John Black but his style of leadership contrasted sharply with that of his predecessor, for he was willing to delegate authority and to hold regular board meetings.

Dick's handling of labour relations occasionally made him unpopular with trade unions, but generally he was regarded as being a tough, fair-minded, decisive employer. It was his decision, for example, to declare men redundant during the re-tooling of Standard's Banner Lane plant in 1956, thereby provoking a fourteen-day strike. Equally it was he who brought the company back into line with other major manufacturers by rejoining the Engineering Employers Federation in 1957, thus terminating the Standards' union agreement of 1948. In turn this enabled him to revise Standards' bonus payments system in order to check the above-average wage rises the company had previously experienced. Moreover the gang system was re-organised into smaller units to improve labour mobility. During Black's reign the shop stewards had been given considerable responsibility for the running of the factory. So Dick attempted to regain greater control of the shop floor by improving management-labour communications, although he still continued to work through powerful shop stewards.

Throughout Dick's reign Standard-Triumph (formed in 1945 when Standard bought the Triumph Motor Co) faced the basic problem of low profitability and insufficient capital resources to compete successfully in the volume car market. The motor giants, BMC and Ford, were taking over available body-suppliers (such as Fisher and Ludlow) and facing Standard with a risk of being left without adequate body supplies. Dick was aware of Standard's vulnerability as a small mass-producer with little control of the market, and was prepared to approve a merger if it left Standard-Triumph as the dominant (or at least equal) partner. Subsequent merger negotiations with Rover (twice) and the Rootes Group (in 1956) failed mainly because they would not allow Standard a large enough share in the proposed amalgamation. Meanwhile Standard's partners in tractor production, Massey Ferguson, had secretly bought a substantial shareholding in the company and accused it of subsidising its car business from tractor production. Ever since the Canadian firm, Massey-Harris, had taken over Fergusons in 1953 relations between the two companies had deteriorated, so eventually the partnership was dissolved with the Banner Lane Tractor Plant being sold to Massey-Harris for £17,650,000 in 1959.

To replace the loss of the profitable tractor business Dick announced an ambitious car expansion programme involving an attractive new model, the Herald. It was his initiative to go outside Standard's weak in-house design team to the Italian stylist Michelotti for the design in order to produce a competitive substitute to rivals, such as the Morris Minor. Furthermore £12.5 million was made available for new investments in a large modern assembly hall at Canley; the purchase of component suppliers like Mulliners (bodies) and Alford & Adler (front suspensions); the purchase of Hall's Engineering in Liverpool (Speke), as a basis for their own body division, a development which they realised would take until 1965 to complete. Dick would have preferred the plant to have been in Coventry, but government regional policy dictated the new location. The success of this imaginative expansionist programme depended on growing output and demand. Unfortunately Standard's attempts to become more competitive by improving product range and increasing production capacity were frustrated in 1960-61 by a world recession, which halved output levels, a credit squeeze (Dick was very critical of changes in production schedules induced by government 'stop-go' policies) and a consequent financial crisis forcing Dick into retrenchment measures. £1.2 million of capital expenditure was cancelled and sports car production reduced. Thus the company's recent acquisitions proved unprofitable by significantly adding to costs at a time when sales remained stagnant.

Dick (now chairman) knew the company had to merge or die. He successfully negotiated acceptable sales terms with Leyland, makers of trucks and lorries, concluded on 31 November 1960. Standard-Triumph International was no longer economically viable as an independent marginal producer in a highly competitive market. In the 1960-61 recession it was rapidly losing ground and its share of UK car production had fallen from 13.2 per cent in 1947 to 8 per cent in 1960. In this situation Leyland, looking for a partner to help it diversify its product range, must have seemed like a fairy godmother to Dick, who admits that Leyland paid 'a ridiculous price' (£18 million) for Standard. 'They could have beaten us down quite a bit, and we would *still* have been prepared to sell out' {Langworth and Robson (1975) 234}. A clash of personalities between Henry Spurrier (qv), Leyland boss, and Dick, who 'felt like a Cavalier suddenly cast among Roundheads' {Turner (1973) 51}, led to Dick's resignation as head of the car side of the business in August 1961. He felt that Leyland 'did not really understand the motor industry' (oral, Alick Dick, Sept 1978). Equally, Leyland were critical of Dick's management style, accusing him of extravagance. In the thirteen months to 'the end of 1961 Standard-Triumph made a loss of £7 million. All Dick's forward plans for expansion were reversed after his departure, capital expenditure on the car business was cut and the overdraft reduced.

Despite the pressures of running a struggling car firm Dick, nevertheless, achieved considerable distinction in the motor industry. In 1957 he was president of the Society of Motor Manufacturers and Traders, and in 1961 was awarded the Benjamin Franklin medal of the Royal Society of Arts. He has always taken an active interest in the local economy and was chairman of the Coventry Chamber of Commerce in 1957-58.

Outside the motor industry he served as a governor of the College of Aeronautics at Cranfield, 1960-63. His recreational interests include sailing and spending time on the family farm at Hill Wootton, near Kenilworth, Warwickshire, with his wife Betty Melinda Eileen née Hill (daughter of Benjamin Alan Hill, an engineer) whom he married in 1940. They have three sons; the eldest Michael, also entered the motor industry.

After leaving Standard Triumph Alick Dick held other directorships including those of Nickolds Automatics Ltd and Royston Industries, of which he was managing director, 1963-67. In 1967 he became UK purchasing consultant for Volkswagenwerk AG, Wolfsburg Audi NSU Auto Union AG, Ingolstadt, based in Coventry, but ceased to be directly involved in top management.

CARL E R GRUNDY-WARR

Sources:

Unpublished

University of Warwick, Modern Records Centre, papers of Standard Motor Co and TGWU files on Standard.

BCe.

MCe.

Interviews with Alick Dick, Sept 1983.

Information from Dr Stephen Tolliday.

Published

Coventry Evening Telegraph 1 Oct 1956, 28 Aug 1959.

R Langworth and G Robson, *Triumph Cars: The Complete 75-Year History* (1975).

Sunday Observer 21 June 1959.

Graham Turner, *The Leyland Papers* (Pan Books, 1973).

WW 1982.

DICKINSON, Sir Arthur Lowes

(1859-1935)

Accountant

Arthur Lowes Dickinson was born in London on 8 August 1859, to Cato Lowes Dickinson, a portrait painter, and his wife Margaret Ellen née Williams. He was educated at Charterhouse and King's College, Cambridge, where he obtained a first in mathematics in 1882. In the following year he began articles with the accountants, Edwards, Jackson & Browning. He was awarded first prize in the professional intermediate examination of the Institute of Chartered Accountants in England and Wales in 1883, and joint first place in the final in 1886. That year he also became a fellow of the Institute of Actuaries, reflecting his continued interest in mathematics. Dickinson joined the firm of Lovelock, Whiffin & Dickinson as its junior partner in 1888 and in 1901 he was approached by Edwin Waterhouse (qv) to take charge of Price, Waterhouse & Co's American practice.

In 1901 Price, Waterhouse's American activities employed a professional staff of 24, split between offices in New York and Chicago; in 1911, when

Dickinson retired as senior partner, there were 11 offices in the United States, Canada and Mexico, employing 145 professional staff. One of the largest clients acquired during Dickinson's stay was United States Steel, a huge corporation formed from the vertical integration of companies involved in activities ranging from mining to the marketing and distribution of finished steel products. The link between the two organisations was mutually beneficial. Dickinson and William J Filbert of US Steel together did much innovatory work solving financial reporting problems associated with a large-scale business enterprise. The accounts of US Steel for 1902, which contain the best-known early example of a consolidated statement, attracted widespread acclaim as a breakthrough towards full and meaningful financial disclosure. Pioneering lectures outlining much of the theory and practice of consolidated statement preparation were subsequently delivered by Dickinson to the International Congress on Accounting at St Louis in 1904 and to the School of Commerce, Accounts and Finance, New York University in 1905. With the help of two other professional accountants, William M Lybrand and Robert H Montgomery, Dickinson did much to bring about the widespread adoption of economic entity-based financial reporting procedures in the United States.

Dickinson, with the other British accountants working in the United States, exerted a strong influence on professional development in the USA. The first professional American accounting association was established in 1886, but progress had been slow. As president of the Federation of Societies of Public Accountants in 1904 and later as secretary of the American Association of Public Accountants in 1905, Dickinson helped instigate the merger of the two bodies so that the accounting profession could speak with a single authoritative voice on the various issues debated during this period of rapid economic growth. He was heavily involved in arranging the 1904 International Congress on Accounting, and the paper which he read, entitled 'Profits of a Corporation', was a major contribution to the academic success of that meeting.

Dickinson returned to Great Britain in 1913 and remained a partner in the London office of Price, Waterhouse until his retirement in 1923. He was a member of the ICAEW's council, 1914-28, and maintained an active involvement in professional developments. During this period Dickinson criticised British accountants for confining their attention to purely legal responsibilities, thereby ignoring their ethical obligations. A widely published paper presented to the Royal Statistical Society in 1924 drew attention to the lack of business statistics published either for general consumption or for the shareholders of public companies. The importance of full financial disclosure was again the subject of a 1926 paper in which he also stressed the social responsibilities of business.

> The present idea that a business belongs only to those who own the capital therein must give place to a new spirit that it belongs to all who contribute to its success, whether as capitalists or as brain or manual workers, and is a trust for the benefit of the consumer and the nation. This is a high ideal ... and while one of the keys to it is a better understanding, with goodwill and co-operation between Capital and Labour, another is held by the accountant, whose province is to devise and propagate methods by which all

the essential facts in industry may gradually become the property of the community { *The Accountant*, 23 Oct 1926}.

These were far-sighted views and it was not until 1948 that the notion of extreme confidentiality in financial matters gave way significantly to the concept of maximum practical disclosure.

Dickinson was also critical of the professional accounting examinations which he believed erred in the direction of too narrow a technical approach, and his textbook of 1913 which covered a broad range of accounting topics, provided accounting students and practitioners with a deeper understanding of the nature, scope and limitations of accountancy than did most contemporary texts. A feature of Dickinson's work was his ability to combine theoretical solutions with practical expediency. Dickinson, a company director as well as a professional accountant, was determined to help devise satisfactory solutions to a wide range of financial reporting problems and, in choosing between alternative procedures, he gave particular attention to the virtues of conservatism, consistency and objectivity. Many of the procedures which he favoured gained widespread acceptance and there can be no doubt that, through his writing, Dickinson made a significant contribution to the development of the 'generally accepted accounting procedures' on which company accounts are still based.

During the First World War Dickinson was active in the public service as financial advisor first to the Controlled Establishments Division of the Ministry of Munitions and later to the Controller of Coal Mines. Other public work undertaken by Dickinson included membership of the Miners' Welfare Committee, the Commerce Degree Committee of the University of London and the Board of Governors of the London School of Economics. He was knighted in 1919 for government service during the war.

Dickinson married in 1888, Mary Kathleen Jennings, daughter of William Jennings, manager of a finance company and actuary. Sir Arthur Lowes Dickinson died on 28 February 1935, leaving £27,168 gross.

J R EDWARDS

Writings:

'Life Assurance Accounts' *The Accountant* 6, 13 Aug 1887.

'Interest and Sinking Funds' *ibid* 10 Oct 1891.

'The Duties and Responsibilities of the Public Accountant' *ibid* 26 July 1902.

(ed) *Official Record — 1904 Congress of Accountants* (New York: Federation of Societies of Public Accountants, 1904).

'National Organisation' *ibid*.

'The Profits of a Corporation' *The Accountant* 22 Oct 1904 (also published separately in New York).

'*Some Special Points in Corporation Accounting; A Lecture Given 3 Mar 1905, Before the School of Commerce, Accounts and Finance, New York University* (np, 1905). Also in *The Accountant* 7 Oct 1905.

'Some Special Points in Accountancy Practice' *ibid* 22 Apr 1905.

'The Profession of the Public Accountant' *ibid* 27 May 1905.

'The Duties and Responsibilities of the Public Accountant with Regard to New Issues of Stocks and Bonds' *Journal of Accountancy* Nov 1905.

'Notes on Some Special Problems Relating to the Accounts Holding Companies' *The Accountant* 19 May 1906.

'Accounting Practice and Procedure' *ibid* 12 Dec 1908.

'The Economic Aspect of Cost Accounts and Its Application to the Accounting of Industrial Companies' *Journal of Accountancy* Mar 1911.

'Fallacy of Including Interest and Rent as part of Manufacturing Cost' *ibid* Dec 1911.

Accounting Practice and Procedure (New York: Ronald Press, 1913. Repr Houston Texas: Scholars Book Co, 1975).

(with William M Lybrand and F H Macpherson) *Accounting for Modern Corporations, Prepared for the Instruction and Training of Students of the American School* (Chicago: American School, 1922).

'Publicity in Industrial Accounts. With a Comparison of English and American Methods' *The Accountant* 4 Oct 1924.

'The American Association of Public Accountants' *ibid* 28 Nov 1925.

'The Construction, Use and Abuse of Cost Accounts' *ibid* 23 Oct 1926.

Report ... on the System of Accounting, Audit and Statistics of the Railways Owned and Managed by the Government of India, 1926-1927 (3 parts, np, 1927).

'The General Principles of an Efficient System of Transport Accounting' *Journal of the Institute of Transport* Mar 1932.

Sources:

Unpublished

BCe.

MCe.

PRC.

G E Richards, 'History of the First Fifty Years, 1850-1900' (typescript history of Price Waterhouse & Co, 1950).

Published

The Accountant 21 July 1923, 9 Mar 1935.

Chester W DeMond, *Price Waterhouse in America: A History of a Public Accounting Firm* (New York: 1951, reprinted New York: Arno Press, 1980).

George O May, *Memoirs and Accounting Thought* (New York: Ronald Press, 1962).

Mary E Murphy, 'An Accountant in the Eighties' *The Accountant* 26 July, 2, 9, Aug 1947.

—, 'English Audit Practice 1913-1929' *ibid* 16, 23, 30 Aug 1947.

—, 'British and American Contrasts in Accountancy' *ibid* 6, 13, 20 Sept 1947.

—, 'Arthur Lowes Dickinson: Pioneer in American Professional Accountancy' *Bulletin of the Business History Society* Apr 1947.

— (ed), *Selected Readings in Accounting and Auditing Principles and Problems* (New York: Prentice Hall, 1952).

Gary John Previtts, Foreword to Dickinson, *Accounting Practice and Procedure* (1975).

WWW.

A H Dixon (taken from Tracey and Pike Manchester and Salford (1899)).

DIXON, Sir Alfred Herbert

(1857-1920)

Cotton manufacturer

Alfred Herbert Dixon was born in London on 22 February 1857, the son of Henry Hall Dixon, and his wife Caroline, third daughter of Thomas Lynes Esq of Hackleton House, Northamptonshire. Henry Hall Dixon was the best-known of Victorian racing journalists, although trained as a barrister and the son of Peter Dixon, a wealthy cotton spinner of Carlisle. Dixon was only thirteen when his father died but it is likely that he had by then imbibed a spirit of sporting bonhomie and a firm sense of religion. Educated at Kensington Grammar School and Brighton, Dixon began a career in textiles as an apprentice with the Reddish Spinning Co Ltd, of which his uncle was a director. The Reddish firm was headed by William Houldsworth (qv), a connection which was to be crucial in later years. At Houldsworth's suggestion, Dixon, in 1876, joined the Manchester firm of A & G Murray, one of the earliest of cotton firms, then showing signs of entrepreneurial decline. It thereby provided an ideal opening for Dixon's evident managerial talent. In 1881 he became managing director of Murrays, remaining so until 1897. Here Dixon gained his mastery of the cotton trade, as mills and machinery were completely remodelled, and Murrays re-emerged in the forefront of fine-spinning firms.

Complaints of competition and under-cutting in the fine-spinning trade preceded the formation in 1898 of the Fine Cotton Spinners' and Doublers' Association Ltd under the chairmanship of (by then) Sir William Houldsworth. Its practical creation, however, was largely Dixon's work, although the conception and financial promotion owed much to Scott Lings, the managing director of the Reddish Spinning Co. The FCSDA initially amalgamated 31 firms in the fine-spinning and doubling sector, and was to be the largest and most successful of the early mergers in the Lancashire textile industry. Dixon guided its expansion as managing director and chairman of the executive until 1917, when he became chairman. Although in structure the firm has appeared to historians as a loose holding company, it was tightly controlled from the centre under the keen eye of Dixon who combined the vision necessary to tackle large problems with the determination to oversee day-to-day administration. He thus became the vital co-ordinator of the machinery of the Association, whose early features included centralisation of finance, and of the purchasing of raw cotton and stores, and some degree of rationalisation of production, although marketing remained the responsibility of component firms. Individual firms continued to be managed by vendor families but Dixon was careful to insist on management agreements, with bonuses to encourage efficiency. Production, investment and labour relations were subject to a strong central lead, which decisively curtailed family managerial autonomy and was, therefore, an important reason for the success of the firm, where other early combines such as the Calico Printers' Association faltered.

In the longer term, the FCSDA was shaped by Dixon as a more completely vertical firm, and one with a more complete dominance, but never a monopoly, of fine-spinning. The firm acquired a colliery, a substantial share in Carver's, exporters of Egyptian cotton, in 1900, and invested in cotton plantations in the American South in 1911. By 1909, 50 businesses were included in the Association — which controlled over 4 million spindles and employed over 30,000 workers, making it the largest employer in British manufacturing industry. Dixon's interests in scientific research and the welfare of labour were also reflected in company policies: a research department, one of the earliest in the textile industry, was created in 1915, while superannuation schemes were set up in 1902 and 1919.

The success of the Fine Spinners under Dixon's guidance is well attested by capital growth and profitability. Between 1899 and 1920 share capital rose from £5.44 million to £9.14 million, net assets from £5.54 million to £11.65 million, while over the twenty-two year period dividends averaged nearly 9 per cent, considerably higher than for any textile combine other than Coats. The last balance sheet Dixon was to sign revealed record profits (£1.14 million net), the product of the post-war boom. Most importantly, however, Dixon, alarmed at the future prospects of the industry, refused to over-capitalise during the cotton boom. The more impatient shareholders bit on the muzzle but Dixon thereby laid the basis for the Fine Spinners' relative prosperity during the 1920s by ensuring that capital valuation represented earning assets in the medium term. He thus deserved Bowker's encomium, 'perhaps the wisest as the most courageous' of cotton men {Bowker (1928) 40}.

Beyond the Fine Spinners, Dixon played a highly influential role in the entrepreneurial politics of Lancashire. He had aided Sir Charles Macara's (qv) efforts to organise Manchester employers, and it was, therefore, against his advice that the Fine Spinners joined the Bolton Masters' Association in 1898. With his encouragement, however, the latter joined Macara's Federation of Master Cotton Spinners in 1905. Dixon was active in the Federation, particularly in its labour and conciliation work, and

The head office of the Fine Cotton Spinners' & Doublers' Association Ltd, St James Square, Manchester (taken from The Fine Cotton Spinners' and Doublers' Association *(1909).*

became its president shortly before his death. Dixon was also an ardent supporter of the International Cotton Federation, led by Macara, frequently contributing to its congresses before 1914. On its revival in 1919 he became its president, sharing Macara's vision of it as a businessman's 'League of Nations', a model for international co-operation. Dixon's importance in international business diplomacy was further recognised in his leadership of the British delegation to the World Cotton Congress at New Orleans in 1919, and he was to have presided at the Manchester Congress of 1921. Just as the Fine Spinners had acquired extensive overseas interests so Dixon had become an internationally-minded business leader. In particular, he attached much importance to the extension of supplies of raw cotton, and after the war became a strong advocate of the Empire Cotton Growing Movement. Dixon's belief that business interests should be collectively organised also found expression in his participation in the formation of the Federation of British Industries in 1916. He sat on several of its early committees, and did much to extend its base in Lancashire, acting as first chairman of the Manchester branch.

Dixon's most prominent role, however, was as chairman of the wartime Cotton Control Board. His choice was a testimony to his standing among masters and men, respected for his knowledge of the trade, his broad-mindedness, and his sympathy with the workers. He combined, in the words of Hubert Henderson, 'a high measure of devotion to duty, resourceful vigour, shrewdness, tenacity of purpose, even obstinacy' with 'the graces of a singularly gentle and winning personality' {Henderson (1922) 10}. As a result, the Board fell very much under his personal sway and policy direction. Set up in June 1917, it successfully kept the cotton industry working with a minimum supply of raw cotton, and without either the alienation of the business community or the demoralisation of the workforce. Output was restricted by limiting the percentage of machinery to be employed, while unemployment benefits were paid to those out of work with funds raised by levies on employers. The Board did not end all friction between employers and men, particularly as wages were seen to fall in real terms, while profits were often spectacular. Even so, when disputes did arise it was further testament to Dixon's authority that he was called on to mediate. In many ways, the Board was among the most successful exercises in the wartime regulation of industry, and this was, in no small part, due to Dixon under whom the Board was more an extension of the collective regulation of the cotton trade than an instrument of the state. Dixon retained the goodwill of masters and men, while winning that of Government. He was rewarded with a baronetcy in 1918, and went on to become a valued contributor to the post-war Board of Trade Advisory Council.

Dixon's leadership in the cotton trade was additionally recognised by a directorship of the Manchester Royal Exchange (1910-20) and his presidency of the Textile Institute (1920). His activities were always hampered by poor health. Politically, he was neither active nor committed. Always a ready subscriber to charities, he was only to emerge publicly as a patriotic citizen through chairing the committee which organised the raising of the Manchester 'Pals' Battalions in 1915. He also served for a considerable period as Vicar's warden of Chelford Parish Church. As a young man, he had played cricket for Heaton Norris, and had been among Manchester's best-known amateur actors.

In 1880 he married Caroline, daughter of Henry Sandford, manufacturer, of Cringle Hall, Manchester. Sir Herbert died at Warford, Cheshire, on 10 December 1920, of the bronchial asthma from which he had long suffered. A son had died in childhood but he was survived by his wife and daughter. His wealth at death, £233,157 gross, was largely the product of managerial rewards, carefully garnered.

A C HOWE

Writings:

'Egyptian Cotton Prospects' *Report of the Seventh International Cotton Congress, Brussels* (1910).

Preface to Arno Schmidt, *Cotton Growing in Egypt* (1912).

(with E Tootal Broadhurst) 'A Record of the Manchester City Battalions' in F Kempster and H C E Westropp (eds), *Manchester City Battalions of the 90th and 91st Infantry Brigades* (1915).

'The Peace Treaty and American Opinion' *Manchester Guardian* Anglo-American Number, 27 Jan 1920.

'The World's Textile Conference at New Orleans' *ibid.*

President's Address, *Journal of the Textile Institute* 11 (1920).

Introduction to J S M Ward, *Cotton and Wool* (1921).

Sources:

Unpublished

Courtaulds Ltd, Northern Spinning Division, Manchester, papers of the Fine Cotton Spinners' & Doublers' Association Ltd, Directors' and Executive Committee Minutes, 1898-1921.

PRO, BT 7; 197/1; RECO 1/768.

University of Warwick, Modern Records Centre, CBI Predecessor Archive, FBI Minutes and correspondence.

Published

Alderley and Wilmslow Advertiser 17 Dec 1920.

Benjamin Bowker, *Lancashire under the Hammer* (L & V Woolf, 1928).

Cotton Factory Times 17 Dec 1920.

Fine Cotton Spinners' & Doublers' Association, *The Fine Cotton Spinners and Doublers' Association* (Manchester: the firm, 1909).

Hubert D Henderson, *The Cotton Control Board* (Oxford, 1922).

The Jubilee Distaff, 1898-1948 (1948).

Hon Francis Lawley, *The Life and Times of 'The Druid' (Henry Hall Dixon)* (Vinton & Co, 1895).

Henry W Macrosty, 'Business Aspects of British Trusts' *Economic Journal* 1902.

—, *The Trust Movement in British Industry. A Study of Business Organisation* (Longmans, Green & Co, 1907).

Manchester City News 11 Dec 1920.

Manchester Guardian 11, 13 Dec 1920.

Manchester of Today (Historical Publishing Co, 1888).

Textile Mercury 16 Dec 1920.

Textile Recorder 15 Dec 1920.

Times II, 15 Dec 1920.

William B Tracy and W T Pike, *Manchester and Salford at the Close of the 19th Century: Contemporary Biographies* (Brighton: W T Pike & Co, 1899).

WWW.

Raylton Dixon (courtesy of Cleveland County Council).

DIXON, Sir Raylton

(1838-1901)

Shipbuilder

Raylton Dixon was born in Newcastle upon Tyne on 8 July 1838, the second son of Jeremiah Dixon of Ambleside, who occupied 'a responsible position in a banking firm', and Mary née Frank. After a childhood education in private schools he went at 'an early age' to learn shipbuilding as an apprentice at Coutts & Parkinson of Willington Quay on Tyneside. Knowledge gained there of iron shipbuilding was enhanced during his three years (1856-59) at the famous yard of Charles Mitchell at Walker so that when he moved to the rapidly growing industrial region of Teesside he became manager of the Middlesbrough shipyard of Richardson Duck in his early twenties. Within three years the ambitious young man joined with Thomas Backhouse to take over the yard together with two small adjacent yards. Raylton Dixon's brother Wayman was also involved in working the shipyard and when Backhouse retired in 1873 the Dixons carried on alone. The shipyard was then turning out vessels up to about 1,300 tons with an annual output less than 5,000 tons.

By 1882 Dixon had increased the shipyard's output to more than 27,000 tons, only three North East coast yards exceeded that tonnage in that year. The quality of the yard's work was such that they built their first naval vessel in 1875 and Dixon was one of the few pioneering the use of mild steel for ship construction, building his first vessel in this material in 1878. Sensitive to the response of his workers to the new material he reported favourably on their reactions. His approach to shipbuilding was flexible and so he argued the merits of 'composite ships' (iron frame-wood hull) in the 1880s and built such a vessel for the Royal Navy in 1883.

The continued expansion of the shipyard resulted in the formation of a limited liability company in 1897 and by 1901 the yard had an annual output capacity of 40,000 tons, with a work-force of about 2,500. In all nearly 500 ships were turned out under his supervision for the principal shipping lines including the P&O Line.

Sketches of Sir Raylton Dixon & Co's Cleveland Dockyard, from Northern Review *1889.*

Dixon joined the Institution of Naval Architects in 1868 and was twice elected to Council; although he never presented a paper, his thirteen or so contributions to the discussions indicate his wide grasp of technical knowledge and his company's pioneering activities such as the early use of

113

electrical tools. He was also a member of the North East Coast Institution of Engineers and Shipbuilders and contributed to the discussions at the Iron and Steel Institute.

Apart from his shipbuilding interests he was amongst the group of businessmen who supported his friend the graduate chemist S A Sadler (1842-1911) in the formation of a limited liability company for chemical manufacturing in 1883; this company employed about 500 and Dixon was still a director at the time of his death. He was also on the board of the engineering company Robert Stephenson & Co and Elder Dempster Shipping Co of Liverpool.

Deeply involved in the politics of Middlesbrough, he played a leading part in establishing the Conservative Club there but he failed to win the seat in the 1885 general election. Dixon was a member of the town council in 1868-74 and 1878-84 and was elected mayor in 1888. In 1863 he was among the 40 businessmen who met to form the local chamber of commerce. One civic and commercial matter to which he gave particular attention was finding a satisfactory means of transporting people and goods across the River Tees; although his proposal for a transporter bridge was rejected, his shipyard built the ferry steamer that was ordered. He served on the Board of Guardians and was a JP for the town from 1872 and on the commission of the peace for North Yorkshire from 1885. In 1890 he was knighted for public services and given the freedom of the borough.

Dixon had a wider range of interests than most of his fellow North East coast shipbuilders; he was a major for eighteen years in the 1st North Yorkshire Artillery Volunteers; he enjoyed shooting as well as caricature drawing and photography and became the first president of the Tees Amateur Boating Club. He served on two local hospital governing bodies and he made modest donations to these.

In 1863 Dixon married Elizabeth Walker of Glasgow, by whom he had two sons and six daughters. Sir Raylton Dixon died on 28 July 1901 leaving £134,080 gross.

J F CLARKE

Sources:

Unpublished

BCe.

PrC.

Published

Engineer 2 Aug 1901.

William Lillie, *The History of Middlesbrough* (Middlesbrough, 1968).

Newcastle Daily Journal 27 July 1901.

Northern Review 1890.

Transactions of the Institution of Naval Architects 43 (1901).

Transactions of the North East Coast Institution of Engineers and Shipbuilders 17 (1900-1).

WWW.

DOBSON, Sir Benjamin Alfred

(1847-1898)

Textile machinery manufacturer

Benjamin Alfred Dobson was born at Douglas, Isle of Man, on 27 October 1847, the first child (of three) of Arthur Dobson and his wife Henrietta Elizabeth née Harrison. After leaving the family firm of textile machinery makers in Bolton, his father had worked as an engineer in Belfast. Dobson grew up in a relatively affluent home and was educated at Carlisle Grammar School and the Collegiate Institute in Belfast, where he studied engineering. His first job was with the Belfast & Northern Counties Railway as a mechanical engineer. In 1869, after working there for two years, he was promoted to manage a locomotive department. Later in the same year he moved to Bolton, where on the invitation of his uncle, Benjamin Dobson, he started work at Dobson & Barlow's.

His first year in Bolton was occupied by spending a number of weeks in the different machine departments, working with the outfitters in mills, and visiting a number of the firm's overseas customers in France, one of their largest foreign markets. When his uncle retired in December 1871, owing to ill health, Benjamin Alfred became a partner in Dobson & Barlow alongside T H Rushton (son of a Bolton banker). At first his responsibilities included the foundries, the smithy and all machine tools in the works, but he soon assumed a more general managerial role. During the twenty-seven years that he shared in its management, the firm more than doubled in size, largely due to the increasing importance of the foreign market, and in 1898 maintained a workforce of nearly 5,000. Dobson & Barlow specialised in producing machinery to spin fine counts of cotton yarn.

Dobson was an active manager who sought to improve the production process, advance the design and technology of the firm's machinery (he took out 85 patents and in 28 of them he was the sole patentee), and promote the firm's products by travelling extensively. His commitment to technical progress may be discerned by his active sponsorship of technical education within Bolton, his involvement in the Institution of Mechnical Engineers, and his lectures and books on textile processes. The technical books were reprinted several times and translated into both French and German.

He was active in the Bolton Chamber of Commerce, and the Bolton Iron Trades Employers' Association (serving as president of both organisations). Considering these involvements and his deeply-held Conservative political beliefs, it is not surprising that he strongly opposed any attempt by his workforce to challenge managerial authority. In 1887 during a strike lasting six months, Dobson & Barlow drafted in men from outside in an attempt to defeat the dispute. Similarly in the lock-out of 1897 Dobson was prominent in resisting the demands of the Amalgamated Society of Engineers.

Throughout his entire adult life Dobson was involved in public affairs as an active member of the Conservative Party. He became a member of Bolton Town Council in 1874 and, twenty years later, he was elected mayor — subsequently being consecutively re-elected three times. Through his business and political interests Dobson was a key personality in the small group of employers who dominated all aspects of life in Bolton in the late nineteenth century.

In the Queen's Diamond Jubilee Honours List (1897) he received a knighthood; he was also made a Chevalier of the Légion d'Honneur by the French Government, in 1878, for his services to the French textile industry, and received the Voluntary Decoration for twenty years service in the Bolton Infantry Volunteers, in which he held the rank of lieutenant-colonel.

In 1876 he married Coralie Palin of Southport (who died in 1904), the daughter of a civil engineer, by whom he had six sons and three daughters. Dobson died on 4 March 1898, leaving an estate valued at £240,134 which included a large country residence, Doffcockers, that he had bought in 1886.

ROBERT KIRK

Writings:

The Principles of Carding Cotton. The Manufacture of Card Wire and the Grinding of Cards (Bolton: G S Heaton, 1892).

Some Difficulties of Cotton Spinning (Bolton: G S Heaton, 1893).

'Lighting of Workshops' *Proceedings of the Institution of Mechanical Engineers* 1893.

Humidity in Cotton Spinning (Bolton: G S Heaton, 1894).

'Electric Welding' *Proceedings of the Institution of Mechanical Engineers* (1894.)

A Visit to Cotton Land (Bolton, n.d.).

Sources:

Unpublished

Mr B G P Dobson, Haverthwaite, the Diaries of Sir B A Dobson, 1869-1874.

Lancashire R O, Platt-Saco-Lowell Archive.

G Evans, 'Social Leadership and Social Control: Bolton 1870-1898' (Lancaster MA, 1974).

Published

Bolton Chronicle May-Nov 1887.

Bolton Journal and Guardian 26 July 1890, 19 Mar 1892, 4 Mar 1898.

Bolton Municipal Officer Feb 1906.

'A Boltonian', *Evolution of a Textile Machine Works* (Bolton: 1925).

Benjamin Palin Dobson, *The Story of the Evolution of the Spinning Machine* (Bolton, Manchester: Marsden & Co, 1910).

Dobson & Barlow Ltd, *134 Years of Progress 1790-1924* (Bolton: 1924).

—, *Samuel Crompton, The Inventor of the Spinning Mule* (Bolton: 1927).

The Engineer 11 March 1898.

Engineering 11 March 1898.

Harold Hamer, *Bolton 1838-1938, a Centenary Record of Municipal Progress* (Bolton Corporation, 1938).

Industries of Lancashire: Part First: The Premier County of the Kingdom (1889).

Patrick Joyce, *Work, Society and Politics: The Culture of the Factory in Later Victorian England* (Brighton: Harvester Press, 1980).

Manchester Guardian 5 Mar 1898.

Proceedings of the Institution of Mechanical Engineers 1898.

Textile Manufacturer 15 Mar 1898.

Textile Mercury 12 Mar 1898.

Textile Recorder 15 Mar 1898.

Times 5 Mar 1898.

Transactions of the Manchester Association of Engineers 1898.

WWW.

DOBSON, Sir Roy Hardy

(1891-1968)

Aircraft manufacturer

Roy Hardy Dobson was born in Horsforth, Yorkshire, on 27 September 1891, the son of Horace Dobson, a warper in a woollen mill, and his wife, Mary Ann Dobson née Hardy. He served his apprenticeship with T & R Lees, a small engineering firm in Hollinwood, near Manchester. He lived there with an aunt, and became engaged to a Mancunian girl while working in London for a year as an installation engineer for James Pollock, Sons & Co, agents for oil engines. That short southern interlude was decisive for he saw Freddie Rainham flying at Brooklands. In 1914 Dobson returned to Manchester, approached A V Roe (qv) the aircraft designer and constructor for a job, and was accepted with the promise that he would be released from the drawing-office after six months. Roe kept his word, and Dobson became an engineer, developing a shrewd business sense to complement his engineering skills. He learnt to fly, and held Aviator's (ie. pilot's) Certificate No 8,086 together with Engineer's 'A' Licence No 1,051, of both of which he was justifiably proud.

He joined Avro, as the firm was generally known, just as its 504 trainer was going into a long and successful production run and as aviation itself was developing rapidly under the stimulus of the First World War. Exempted from military service because he was in a reserved occupation, he moved during the war from one department to another gaining experience. In 1919 he was appointed works manager, rising to general manager in 1934. A V Roe, which had come under the control of Crossley Motors, was sold to J D Siddeley (qv) in 1930, becoming part of the Armstrong Siddeley Development Co, and in 1935 became a subsidiary of the Hawker Siddeley Aircraft Co Ltd when Armstrong Siddeley merged with Hawkers. Dobson was elected to the board of A V Roe in 1936, and was appointed managing director in 1941 when John Siddeley retired from that post. During this period the firm grew. In the early 1930s it produced 795 Tutor trainers for the RAF and customers abroad. Then came the twin-engined Anson Coastal reconnaissance bomber/transport/trainer of which some 7,195 Mark I's were built by the parent company by 1945. Just as Dobson got into his stride as general manager came the order for the Manchester twin-engined heavy bomber of the 1936 programme, of which only 200 were built. By 1939, A V Roe employed about 5,000 men; Dobson expected the number of employees to double within a year when a new factory, costing £1 million, would be completed.

The Manchester was not a very successful aeroplane, largely because of unsatisfactory engines. In 1941 Dobson backed the conviction of his chief designer, Roy Chadwick, urged on by Rolls-Royce, that the plane would be much improved by fitting four Rolls-Royce Merlin engines, which had been designed for fighters rather than bombers. Dobson overcame the reluctance of the authorities to divert any Merlin engines from the production of fighters. The new plane, the Lancaster, was the most successful bomber produced by either side during the war; 7,374 were built in England and Canada.

Dobson initiated and managed the manufacture of the Lancaster in quantity in Canada, creating airframe and aero engine facilities there. After the war Dobson arranged for Avro to buy these factories, which he set up as subsidiaries, A V Roe Canada Ltd and Orenda Engines Ltd, with himself as chairman. These Canadian companies designed, as well as manufactured, aircraft. A V Roe Canada cooperated with the Canadian Government in the development of an advanced fighter, the Arrow, in the 1950s. Technically successful, the project was too ambitious for Canada's limited military resources and requirements, and was eventually cancelled. Possibly because he had come to realise the limited scope for such projects in Canada, Dobson had already diversified the interests of A V Roe Canada, with particular emphasis on railway engineering.

At the end of the war, Britain had 27 airframe companies, and eight aero engine companies. Four of the airframe units, including Avro, were nominally part of Hawker Siddeley, but each of these four had a very free hand to run its own affairs, and competition between them was fierce. New aircraft were becoming ever more complex, and the development and unit costs of any significant new civil or military aircraft demanded resources which no single firm could command. Successive Governments made it clear to the industry that fewer and larger firms were needed, but failed to insist strongly enough to overcome the resistance of the leaders of the industry, many, like Dobson, being fiercely individualistic. The bitterest rivalry among those firms putting in proposals for one military aircraft (the OR339) was between Avro and Hawker, another firm in the Hawker Siddeley Group; neither proposal was accepted. However, Avro did successfully design and build the radical delta-winged V-bomber, the Vulcan, which met a 1947 Air Staff specification, but did not enter service until 1957.

In 1958 Dobson became managing director and vice-chairman of Hawker Siddeley, of which he had been appointed a director in 1945. Like other leading figures in the industry, he could no longer delay confronting the need for rationalisation, or the need for a more clearly-defined working relationship with the Government. It was Dobson who initiated the acquisition by Hawker of the de Havilland, Blackburn and Folland companies in 1960, thus ensuring that Hawker Siddeley would emerge as one of the two main British airframe companies. The other was the British Aircraft Corporation, formed in 1959-60 by the merger of Bristol, English Electric Aviation and Vickers Armstrong. The Government had promised in 1960 that future projects would be concentrated as far as possible on BAC and Hawker Siddeley, but the two groups felt that it failed to observe the spirit of its undertaking. A joint protest meeting was held in July 1961, at which Dobson was present. It was agreed to tell the Government that the companies would no longer authorise the expenditure of their own resources, beyond the stage of feasibility studies, on defence projects for which the Ministry of Aviation had not issued a firm contract. Dobson argued that no design work for government projects should be placed with companies outside the two main groups, and said that government delays in reaching and confirming decisions were now such that final production on defence projects could not be undertaken in the right time scale, and the Ministry was using this as an excuse to buy abroad. After this meeting, Hawker Siddeley and BAC made several separate representations to the Government, but still did not succeed in getting a clear statement of the Government's long-term aerospace requirements.

Dobson became chairman of Hawker Siddeley in 1963; by then Hawker Siddeley was a group with 112 companies, and a total labour force of 127,000. Following the Labour victory in the general election of October 1964, it was announced in February 1965 that two Hawker Siddeley projects for the RAF, the P1164 supersonic Harrier, and the HS681 transport, had been cancelled. The Labour Government supported the idea of a merger between Hawker Siddeley and BAC, a project about which the companies themselves were none too keen. In such an uncertain climate, Dobson, both as managing director and as chairman, initiated projects to diversify and extend Hawker Siddeley's interests into other fields of engineering, particularly diesel engines and electrical equipment. He retired from the chair in 1967.

All his life Dobson was never one to stand on ceremony either up or down the scale. He was quite prepared to strip off his jacket and show workmen how a job should be done, that it could be done within the time allotted, and that they were being fairly paid for doing it. Though basically a genial person, he was capable of exploding when he felt it was necessary for the good of the cause, whether against workers, management or Government bureaucrats. He had the capacity to inspire great devotion in those who worked closely with him, provided they could stand the pace he set.

Dobson was awarded the CBE in 1942, and knighted in 1945; he served as a JP for Ashton-under-Lyne from 1946. He was a Conservative, and a practising member of the Church of England. He was elected an honorary fellow of the Royal Aeronautical Society in 1956, and was a member of the Council of the Society of British Aircraft Constructors, serving two terms as president 1948-49, and 1962-63. His chief recreations were sporting — shooting, fishing, and sailing — but he also enjoyed photography.

In 1916 he married Annie, daughter of George Smith, a spinner. They had two sons and a daughter. One son was killed in an air accident and his wife predeceased him in 1954. Dobson died on 7 July 1968, leaving an estate proved at £121,794 gross.

ROBIN HIGHAM

Writings:

'Development and Organisation of Hawker Siddeley Group Ltd' in Ronald Edwards and Harry Townsend (eds), *Business Growth* (Macmillan, 1966).

Sources:

Unpublished

BCe.

MCe.

PrC.

Published

The Aeroplane Directory, 1961.

Centenary Journal, Royal Aeronautical Society, 1866-1966 (Royal Aeronautical Society, 1966).

DNB.

Charles Gardner, *British Aircraft Corporation, a History* (Batsford, 1981).

A J Jackson, *Avro Aircraft since 1908* (Putnam, 1965).

Harald Penrose, *British Aviation: The Ominous Skies 1935-1939* (HMSO, 1980).

Times 9 July 1968.

WWW.

DOCKER, Sir Bernard Dudley Frank

(1896-1978)

Industrialist

Bernard Docker as a child (courtesy of Dr R P T Davenport-Hines).

Bernard Dudley Frank Docker, the only child of Frank Dudley Docker (qv) and his wife Lucy Constance née Herbert, was born on 9 August, 1896, at Rotton Park Lodge, Edgbaston, Birmingham. This house was adjacent to the factory of the family business of Docker Bros, paint and varnish manufacturers, which, in 1907, was absorbed into the Metropolitan Carriage Co.

Comfortable financial circumstances surrounded Bernard's youth in Birmingham and Kenilworth. He was educated at Harrow 1911-13, leaving after an attack of pneumonia. He was afterwards taught by private tutors of indifferent quality and crammed for the Oxford University entrance examination by A L Smith, later the Master of Balliol College. In the autumn of 1915, just before Bernard was due to go to Oxford, his father appointed him to a job in munitions production at Metropolitan Carriage, his father's major concern. This was probably to protect him from the military conscription that was expected, and came, shortly afterwards.

In 1918, when Bernard was only twenty-one or twenty-two years old, his father, then chairman of the Metropolitan Carriage, Wagon & Finance Co

(MCWF Co) secured his election to the company's board of directors. The headquarters of the firm were at Saltley in Birmingham. Thus, Bernard, facilitated by family connections and money, moved early and easily into the boardroom; but he did so without business skills or experience. At no time, it is thought, did he take day-to-day executive responsibility for the running of a business, other than his own investment affairs.

He served as deputy chairman of the MCWF Co, 1924-27, though since 1920 this had been a Vickers' subsidiary, and he continued in some other directorships linked to the MCWF Co until the end of his working life. Little is known of these activities. Bernard's progress in the Vickers' empire cannot have been helped by his father's resignation from Vickers in 1920 and his characteristic belligerence. However, in 1926, on the recommendation of Dudley Docker and the committee investigating Vickers' recent mismanagement, Bernard Docker was appointed to the industrial management board of Vickers, his father serving also as an honorary member. This management board, described publicly as made up of men of 'proven ability' {*Times* 8 Apr 1926}, served the main board for a few years.

Bernard's first major chairmanship was that of Birmingham Railway Carriage & Wagon Co in the late 1920s. Appointed director in 1929, he became deputy chairman and, then, chairman during 1930. He was then described by a welcoming director as 'absolutely cradled in the rolling stock industry' {*Times* 23 Feb 1929}. The exigencies of the time required a chairman resident in either London or Birmingham and able to be in daily touch with the managing director. Docker is said to have devoted an enormous amount of time to the company; he was said to have influence, experience and ability and to have made almost a lifetime's study of the rolling stock industry, having recently retired from another position in the industry (at MCWF Co obviously).

Davenport-Hines suggests that Bernard, baulked at MCWF Co, may have turned to this other rolling stock company to make his mark on that industry. The managing director of this company was H J S Moyses, later a co-director at BSA prior to the 1956 affair. This company, unlike BSA, paid regular dividends in the 1930s. Bernard remained chairman until 1960. Then, control switched hands and, over the next few years, manufacturing ceased and the vast factory on the Smethwick-West Bromwich-Birmingham boundary was converted into the Middlemore Industrial Estate; the company later became the First National Finance Corporation. Perhaps coincidentally, the new chairman, F D O'Brien Newman, lived like Bernard at an apartment at Claridge House.

Bernard's principal claim to fame was his chairmanship of the BSA Group from 1940 to 1956. Dudley Docker had become a director of this company in 1906 and had been deputy chairman, 1909-1912. It is ironic that it was he who, in 1910, master-minded BSA's purchase of Daimler Motors for it was the affairs of that side of the BSA business that led to his son's dismissal from the BSA board in 1956. Dudley Docker was also a party in the reconstruction of BSA in 1931-2 and a director of BSA in the early 1940s. It has been suggested by Davenport-Hines that Dudley Docker, through his influence with the Midland Bank (BSA's bankers), forced Bernard onto the BSA board as chairman and managing director in 1944 just prior to his own death; the description of the event may be accurate (though I have found no supporting evidence) but Bernard first became a director of BSA in 1939 before his father's term started and was chairman in 1940. From 1940 he also acted as managing director, unpaid apparently until 1952. This happened when the existing managing director, Geoffrey Burton, went off (while retaining his job at BSA) to be Director General of Mechanical Equipment at the Ministry of Supply, 1940-45. Burton's knighthood in 1942 possibly made Bernard think he should have more than the KBE his public services earned him in 1939.

Bernard, and, more particularly, James Leek, the general manager, saw BSA through its mammoth wartime task as munitions manufacturer. Leek was a director at BSA in 1936 and senior enough to take the gun factory out of seventeen years of mothballs in 1937 after a visit to the Leipzig Trade Fair and a sight of Hitlerism. Leek was day-to-day general manager at BSA during the war years and was in charge of the 28,000 workers in 67 factories scattered round the country by the end of the war. During these years Bernard lived at Great Missenden and Mayfair.

After the war he and Leek, as his indispensable lieutenant (especially on the motorcycle side), saw BSA re-establish itself in world markets. On the motorcycle side, Ariel and then Triumph were acquired from Sangster (qv) in 1944 and 1951 and new markets in Europe and the USA developed, albeit before competitors had recovered from the war in Europe. Production of cycles, steelwork, machine tools, cars and taxis, guns and components as well as motorcycles, and services to these, continued as munitions were abandoned. In 1956, Bernard pointed to the fivefold increase in BSA's profits during his regime but, though profits were never as high again, some of the credit for that growth must go to wartime contracts in Bernard's early years. Group trading profits (excluding sums brought forward from the previous year and before depreciation, taxation and dividends) were £0.8 million in 1940, £1.3 million in 1948 and £2.8 million in 1956 on net usable assets of £5.8 million in 1940, £15.0 million in 1948 and £24.0 million in 1956 (fixed and current assets less current liabilities) — a moderate rate of return of 14.3 per cent, 8.7 per cent and 11.7 per cent in the supposedly boom time for the group. Sangster, by 1961, had pushed the rate of return up to 17.0 per cent by selling the cycle and Daimler subsidiaries rather than by improving profits.

A personal note needs to be injected here. Briefly, for divorce followed within little more than a year, Bernard had been married to an actress, Jeanne Stuart, from April 1933 to June 1934. Thereafter for long periods, he lived with his father at The Gables, Kenilworth, or at a series of flats in London, usually in Mayfair. Then, in 1949, Bernard married Lady Collins née Norah Turner. For a reputedly shy man, this must have entailed considerable adjustment. Lady Docker (1905-1983) was irrepressible but had had moments of tragedy in her life. Her father committed suicide when she was sixteen years old, leaving the family of four children almost penniless. Her mother bought the *Three Tuns* public house in Sutton Coldfield but the future Lady Docker apparently refused to work behind the bar. She later became a dancing teacher and then a dance hostess at the Café de Paris in London where, after several years, she met her first husband. She married twice and was widowed twice in the next few years. Both these husbands were millionaires so that her financial circumstances drastically changed. Her first husband, by whom she had a son, was

Clement Callingham of the wine merchants, Henekeys, a firm of which Bernard was later to become a director. Callingham died in his forties. The widow, on his advice apparently, married Sir William Collins of Cerebos Salt and Fortnum & Mason fame, but he too died. In 1949, at the age of forty-three, she married Bernard, then aged fifty-three. These details are mentioned because Lady Docker was a 'character' who quickly moved into her third husband's business life. Her name and his are synonymous with wealth, extravagance, mink coats, diamonds and the luxury yacht *Shemara* (though this, with its crew of 32 was bought by Bernard in 1938 long before he met Lady Docker) and with public incidents arising out of her ladyship's energy and their combined carelessness of tongue and reputation. It is important to emphasise that both she and Bernard had personal fortunes to maintain their unquestionably great spending; the finances of BSA and other companies were not concerned except marginally. Lady Docker could see in her own life the rewards to beauty over hard work and she came to advocate a matching policy for BSA to attract attention to its products. She advocated that Daimler should move away from the narrow royalty trade into a more mass market, even proposing the production of a smaller family car. The famous gold-plated Daimler and five other special cars and her dress bills and parties implemented this policy, ostensibly for the benefit of the firm. But the BSA Group board feared that the new Daimler image would lose them their royal patronage without getting rid of the persistent losses on the car side.

It seems that Lady Docker interfered and, indeed, set about gaining control of Daimler with determination. She won over Bernard; she became a director of Daimler's subsidiary, Hoopers, the car-body builders; and R E Smith, her brother-in-law, moved into a management post at Daimler and at Carbodies, where he became a director. Bernard started to act at Daimler without informing the Group board. Opposition to both Bernard and his wife grew.

The boardroom row that ensued at BSA between January and August, 1956, is important for several reasons. It ended with Bernard's dismissal by the board and his failure to reverse this at shareholders' meetings in 1956 and 1957. It coincided with the end of the good times at BSA as motorcycle leadership began to slip away and alternative products failed persistently to take off. The first acts of Sangster, the new chairman, were to sell the pedal cycle side to Raleigh in 1957 and to appoint a new group managing director to succeed the retiring James Leek. Daimler and the car companies (but not Carbodies) were sold to Jaguar in 1960. The new appointment of Eric Turner (qv) as chief executive was followed by failures of communication and division between BSA, Small Heath, and its Triumph sister concern at Coventry with damaging effects that were never retrieved. And the boardroom row represented what is believed to be the first occasion when an institutional shareholder, Prudential Assurance Co, BSA's largest shareholder, was induced to intervene in the affairs of a company publicly and decisively. According to Lady Docker, they held 218,000 shares compared to the Dockers' 120,000. The anti-Docker group of directors, led by Sangster and Leek and worried both about losses at Daimler generated by over-production and about Docker's intransigence in its management, had called in the Prudential to support them. Docker, caught between the board and his wife, failed to meet the challenge and went down fighting bitterly, even taking time on ITV to state his case. He ceased to be a director of BSA on 31 May 1956. Incidentally, his cousin, Noel Docker (1894-1975), voted against him at the board meeting; those who voted for him, like Moyses, left the board at the same time. An era of BSA was over.

Aside from BSA and Metropolitan Carriage, Bernard shared his father's link with the Belgian Société Financière des Transports et d'Énterprises Industrielles (Sofina) and with Electric & Railway Finance (Elrafin). Bernard was a director of the first of these by 1925 and, by then, he was also briefly a director of the family firm, Docker Bros, within the Vickers group until its sale to Pinchin Johnson in 1927, and of five others, including Patent Shaft & Axle Tree. He resigned from the board of Associated Electrical Industries in 1929. Twenty five years later, in 1950, he was director of sixteen companies and chairman of eight of these. The list included, apart from BSA and its subsidiaries, Birmingham Railway Carriage and others concerned with land and estates (Metropolitan Surplus & Country Estates), finance (Midland Bank and Guardian Assurance), railways, tramways and electric power, including some French and South American ones (in this, too, following his father). One of these, Anglo-Argentine Tramways, especially exercised Bernard's attentions when in 1947-48 the Foreign Office tried to stop Peron from nationalising the company. Bernard also became a director of James Booth & Co in 1915; John Wilkes, Sons and Mapplebeck, two old Birmingham metal firms, in 1930; and much later, in 1957, of Henekeys until it was sold through him to Charles Forte.

After leaving BSA in 1956, Bernard was associated with a number of ventures including a small domestic airline, the sale of an anti-pollution liquid and the provision of offices for company use, in addition to other commitments, until 1968 and retirement to Jersey.

Bernard Docker's civic involvements were confined to his early and middle years. He was appointed a JP in Warwickshire in 1924, the year in which his uncle, Ludford Docker, was High Sheriff of the county. Again, this appointment came through family influence.

Bernard was chairman of Westminster Hospital in London from 1936 and, after donating £25,000 to it in March 1939, was created KBE in June 1939. Apparently, this knighthood dissatisfied him and, in 1941-42, he made a discreet, though vigorous and unsuccessful, effort to obtain a baronetcy. After the nationalisation of the health service, which he vocally opposed in 1943-48, he served as chairman of the Friends of Westminster Hospital, 1948-53. His longest service in this field, however, was given to the Children's Hospital (King Edward VII Memorial) in Birmingham. He joined the management committee here as early as 1919 at the age of twenty-three and acted as president from 1936 to nationalisation in 1948. He was a member of the King Edward's Hospital Fund for London and chairman of the Council of the British Hospitals Association for many years. Bernard's interest in hospital funding may also derive from his father's pre-war interest in medical charity and factory health provision: MCWF Co had a representative on the Children's Hospital in 1918. Bernard was also a member of the Navy League in 1940 and a fellow of the Royal Geographical Society. Rather differently, he had only a brief spell in the political limelight when he launched a campaign to secure public expenditure cuts in 1953.

There were a number of unhappy incidents in Sir Bernard and Lady Docker's rather public lives which did nothing to enhance their reputations. In 1953, Bernard was fined £50 with costs for committing a breach of the Exchange Control Act, 1947; this was apparently in connection with the *Shemara*. This seems to have led in January 1953 to his angry resignation from the board of the Midland Bank just in time to forestall a resolution to remove him. He also left Guardian Assurance at this time. The Midland was one of the directorships in which he followed his father. There was also the dispute in 1958 with Prince Rainier that led to the Dockers' exclusion from Monaco and France. Probably then, as at other times, over indulgence in alcohol made the Dockers intransigent. Then, there was the bill for Lady Docker's clothes which neither the Inland Revenue nor BSA wished to treat as a necessary business expense of the chairman in 1956.

Sadly, recollection of these incidents and of the gold-plated Daimler took up much of Bernard's obituary in the *Times* {24 May 1978} at the end of what was described as a 'notable but controversial business career'. His very passing on 22 May added a new incident. His last illness left him blind and bedridden in a Bournemouth nursing home. A distressed Lady Docker, however, was only able to visit him intermittently from her tax haven abroad.

On a wider view, however, Bernard was considered a 'shrewd and hardworking director, with considerable flair and powers of quiet leadership, fundamentally a man of integrity, but flawed by obstinacy and impervious to criticism; a combination of qualities not so uncommon in business life at the top' {*ibid*}.

Surprisingly, Bernard was said to have been a quiet, shy, self-effacing man, who worked best away from the public eye. With matching guile, he continued his father's quiet financial activities but also found pleasure in collecting paintings, in friendly company yachting at sea, and on the golf course. His last years were spent in retirement with Lady Docker at St Helier, Jersey. Previously he had lived at Great Missenden and at Stockbridge in Hampshire; the latter estate was sold in 1966 for £400,000. Lady Docker died on 12 December 1983.

BARBARA M D SMITH

Writings:

letter on Westminster Hospital *Times* 17, 21 Apr 1939.

letter on London hospitals *ibid* 9 Dec 1939.

letter on physiotherapy *ibid* 15 June 1940.

letter on health services *ibid* 10 June 1943.

letter on voluntary hospitals *ibid* 4 Apr 1944.

letter on national health service *ibid* 17 June 1944.

letter on social insurance *ibid* 7 Oct 1944.

letter on voluntary work for hospitals *ibid* 8 Sept 1945.

letter on health service plan *ibid* 12 Apr 1946.

letter on voluntary work for hospitals *ibid* 28 May 1948.

letter on death of C M Power of Westminster hospital *ibid* 8 Mar 1954.

letter on his withdrawn gift (1952-53) to British Hospital in Paris *ibid* 22 Dec 1954.

letter on East road accidents *ibid* 23 Apr 1960.

The Docker Digest (an occasional newsletter circulated by Sir Bernard Docker ca 1956-58) concerned with his public expenditure and BSA campaigns — there are copies in Lord Wootton's papers in the Bodleian Library, Oxford.

Sources:

Unpublished

BCe.

MCe.

Published

Birmingham Post 29 Dec 1978, 12 Dec 1983.

Richard P T Davenport-Hines, *Dudley Docker* (Cambridge: Cambridge University Press, 1984).

Directory of Directors.

Norah Docker, *Norah. The Autobiography of Lady Docker* (Allen, 1969).

Reports of the Children's Hospital King Edward VII Memorial Birmingham 1919-48 (in Birmingham Reference Library).

Barry Ryerson, *The Giants of Small Heath. The History of BSA* (Foulis, 1980).

Barbara M D Smith, *The History of the British Motorcycle Industry 1945-75* (Centre for Urban and Regional Studies, occasional paper No 3, 1980).

Stock Exchange Year-Book.

Times 8 Apr 1926, 23 Feb, 21 Nov 1929, 25 Feb 1931, 22, 24 Apr 1958, 24 May 1978.

WWW.

DOCKER, Frank Dudley

(1862-1944)

Industrialist and financier

F Dudley Docker (courtesy of Midland Bank archives).

Dudley Docker (familiarly known as DD) was born at 130 South Street, Smethwick, on 26 August 1862, the fifth and youngest son of Ralph Docker (1809-87), a solicitor practising in Smethwick, who was for many years coroner for East Worcestershire and Clerk of Smethwick's Board of Health. His mother, Sarah Maria Docker (1830-1900), was daughter of a prosperous horse-dealer named Richard Sankey, and married Ralph Docker despite being his deceased wife's sister. Dudley was educated privately and briefly in 1873-74 at King Edward VI Grammar School, Birmingham, before joining his father's law firm, in which his second brother, Edwin (1854-1926), eventually became senior partner. Legal work proved uncongenial, and, in 1881, together with another brother, William (1858-1923), he started the firm of Docker Brothers, dealers in stoving black varnish, with premises underneath two arches of the Great Western Railway in Allcock Street, Birmingham. The fourth brother, Ludford (1860-1940), joined them in 1886, and, thereafter, expansion was steady. Around 1887, Docker Brothers began to make their own varnish, and a factory in Rotton Park Street, Ladywood, was bought for just under £2,000. Ludford and DD jointly inherited their father's entire estate, worth £4,121, in 1887 and this was probably ploughed into the business. A London office and depot were opened near Bishopsgate in 1894, and increasing amounts of paint and varnish were supplied to rolling-stock makers, railways and shipping lines.

All the Docker brothers were good cricketers, and their reputation as sportsmen was a help to the business. Dudley Docker was one of Warwickshire's strongest batsmen in the 1880s, making the highest score at the inaugural match at the Edgbaston ground in 1886 and playing against Australia in 1887. Both he and Ludford Docker served for several years on the Warwickshire Cricket Club's committee, but resigned after a policy disagreement in 1892.

Docker married, on 17 August 1895, in Edgbaston, Lucy Constance (who died at Monte Carlo, 6 February 1947, leaving £187,000), daughter of John Benbow Hebbert (1809-87), a solicitor, sometime Clerk to the Birmingham Justices and Major in the Birmingham Volunteer Rifle Corps, and his wife Lucy Julia, daughter of John Aston of Edgbaston. Their only child, Bernard (qv), was born in August 1896.

In May 1899, Docker Brothers was registered as a limited liability company with authorised and issued capital of £150,000 in £5 shares, divided equally between ordinary and 5 per cent cumulative preference shares. Its first chairman, J P Lacy, was also chairman of the Birmingham rolling-stock makers, Brown Marshalls, and of the Patent Shaft & Axle Tree Co, and was a former director of Kynochs, the ammunition makers.

Dudley and Ludford Docker became joint managing directors, and by June 1906 its £5 shares were quoted at £20 each.

It was through Docker Brothers' connections that DD was able, in 1902, to mastermind the merger of five of the rolling-stock companies. This deal was not only the basis of his personal fortune, but was also the source of his great personal prestige in the Midlands, and the foundation of his political and industrial influence in the region. Although Docker was not a director of any of the companies concerned, he conceived the amalgamation scheme, and carried it through with his tenacious bargaining, financial adeptness, psychological acuity and grasp of detail. The constituents of the merger comprised the Lancaster Railway Carriage & Wagon Co, the Oldbury Railway Carriage & Wagon Co, the Ashbury Railway Carriage & Iron Co (Manchester), Brown Marshall and the Metropolitan Railway Carriage & Wagon Co, the latter two both of Saltley in Birmingham. The new combine, of which Docker became chairman in April 1902, was called the Metropolitan Amalgamated Railway Carriage & Wagon Co, and originally had issued capital of £864,802, of which £90,000 comprised preference shares and the residue was ordinary capital. The combine inherited debentures totalling £107,250 but Docker gave priority to liquidating these, and only £30,000 were outstanding in November 1902.

Docker had previously been recruited in 1899 by J P Lacy to the board of the Patent Shaft Co, bridge-builders and constructional engineers at Wednesbury, whose expertise in axles and tyres complemented the wagon companies' manufacturing of wheels. It was, therefore, logical for Patent Shaft to join the new combine, and this deal was finalised in November 1902. This was not their last acquisition, for Metropolitan Carriage bought Docker Brothers for £264,375 in 1907, and in 1915 made merger overtures to Guest, Keen, Nettlefolds.

Rolling-stock makers were Britain's first true assembly industry; under Docker's leadership from the combine's Saltley headquarters, considerable economies and rationalisation were effected. The Oldbury and Saltley works were re-built after 1902, and over £300,000 was invested in modernising the Wednesbury facilities. Brown Marshalls' works were closed in 1908, and the Lancaster factory was unused from 1909 until requisitioned as the Caton torpedo works in 1915. A new factory was acquired in mid-decade at Manage in Belgium to feed the English works with materials and components at prices which were unobtainable in Britain. Intimate relations were maintained with the United Electric Car Co, and the combine had many dealings with British, American and German electro-technology, as well as colonial, Chinese and South American railways. The British Empire Bridge-Building Co was a joint Canadian subsidiary with the Cleveland Bridge Co of Darlington (1910).

Many of Docker's co-directors at Metropolitan Carriage were mediocre and he so dominated decisions that the combine's success was completely identified with him. There were managerial strains until at least 1906, and although Docker prided himself on spotting new talent, he was continually disappointed by his managers. The change of the company's name in 1912 to the Metropolitan Carriage, Wagon & Finance Co (MCWF) emphasised the importance which Docker attached to the group's financial activities. Apart from financing many of his customers,

Docker had accumulated reserve funds of £450,000 by 1910 and all additions to land, buildings and plant were written off to revenue in 1902-19.

His prestige as head of the largest rolling-stock makers in Britain and as one of the two biggest employers in the Midlands put Docker in demand elsewhere. Although he declined a directorship of the United Counties Bank in 1908, he joined the board of the Midland Bank in October 1912 and, throughout the chairmanships of Sir Edward Holden (qv) and Reginald McKenna (qv), remained one of its most powerful forces until his death. He became a director of Birmingham Small Arms in 1906, and, having contemplated accepting the chairmanship in 1908, served as deputy-chairman 1909-12. In 1910 he master-minded BSA's purchase for over £600,000 of Daimler Motors: although this deal created temporary cash difficulties in the group, in other respects he helped to stabilise BSA during its troublesome attempts to diversify further into civilian products after 1906. He was also a director of W A Laycock Ltd, railway plant and stores and electric light fitters (1900-3); O C Hawkes Ltd, Birmingham glass manufacturers (1904-5); John Wilkes, Sons & Mapplebeck, Birmingham metal-rollers and copper-smelters (1904-5); and W T Avery Ltd, weighing machine manufacturers at Smethwick (1908-10).

He became a JP for Warwickshire in 1909, and was made a CB in the Coronation Honours of 1911 for creating Metropolitan Carriage's heavy artillery battery after the Territorial Army Act of 1907. Among other local honours he was a life governor of Birmingham University, and endowed its Docker scholarships for the children of Metropolitan Carriage's employees. In 1919 he became one of the founding external members of the new Engineering Faculty Board at Cambridge University, and afterwards raised large sums for an engineering building.

His political activism increased after 1905. He detested 'professional politicians', despised the establishment in Whitehall and Westminster and was an outspoken advocate of a 'Businessmen's Government' to arrest British industrial decline. He declined an invitation to stand as the Conservative candidate at Wednesbury in 1908, but was an active president of the Conservative Association there until 1919. In 1909-14, he offered financial backing to parliamentary candidates of all three parties in at least five Midlands constituencies (Wednesbury, Coventry, Nuneaton, and East and Central Birmingham), and his brother Ludford was adopted at Stratford-on-Avon. These candidates' policies resembled those of the pressure group which he launched in 1910, the Business League. Drawing membership from all classes, the League opened branches throughout the Midlands, and at Bristol in 1912: it lobbied for 'a Business Government with business men', a non-partisan Minister of Commerce, complete reform of the Diplomatic and Consular services, Imperial Preference, tied loans and the use of counter-tariffs against international competitors. Docker's avowed intent was for the League to break the stranglehold of traditional party alignment with a new corporatist spirit, and he achieved some local success in this before the outbreak of war.

He was a progressive in industrial relations, who spoke and wrote widely about the importance of 'personal atmosphere' and the 'psychological' element in man management. Following strikes organised by the Workers Union he was instrumental in founding the Midland Employers Federation in 1913, and was president of its successor body, the National

Employers Federation, until its absorption by the Engineering Employers Federation in 1918. In addition he was associated with the National Alliance of Employers and Employed.

Press power also interested him. Before 1909, he influenced the editorial policies of the *Birmingham Gazette* by offering to invest £10,000 in it, and his interest continued until at least 1912. He probably had a similar arrangement with the *Midland Advertiser*, and, as late as 1942-43, tried to buy the *Birmingham Post* group. In 1912, Unionist Central Office asked him to buy the *Daily Express*, and in May 1914, they persuaded him to buy the *Globe*, London's oldest evening newspaper, for £5,000. Through his company, Business Newspapers, Docker exercised direct control of editorial policy until the *Globe*'s sale in October 1919. Its xenophobia and right-wing dissidence led to its temporary suppression under the Defence of the Realm Act in 1915, and Docker's appointment in 1917 of an editorial consultant, Leo Maxse of the *National Review*, increased its virulence. He also invested in Egyptian newpapers around 1926-28.

In April 1915 Docker became chairman of the Birmingham Munitions Output Organisation, and later in the war, MCWF became the largest manufacturer of British tanks. Docker saw the war as a 'mighty solvent' which offered Britain's last chance to reconstruct society on corporatist lines which might prevent Germany and American rivals from spoiling British industrial hegemony. He became a leader of the manufacturers' movement, characterised by P B Johnson as the 'trade warriors' or 'productioneers'. Early in 1916 he gave evidence to the Huth Jackson Committee on post-war trade relations, and later that year was also an animating force on the Board of Trade's Committee on Financial Facilities for Trade (1916), which led to the formation by Royal Charter of the British Trade Corporation with Lord Faringdon (qv) as governor. Docker was amongst the first subscribers to the Corporation's capital, and joined its board in 1917. He also served on the Faringdon committee on the re-organisation of Commercial Intelligence (1916-17), which led to the formation of the Department of Overseas Trade. The workings of the DOT were severely criticised in Docker's dissentient minority report as a member of the Cave committee examining government machinery for dealing with Trade and Commerce (1919). He was also a member of the McCardie committee, appointed by the Minister of Munitions in 1918, to investigate the Midlands 'Embargo Strikes'; and, in 1919, joined the Advisory Council on the Liquidation of the Ministry of Munitions. Among productioneers, Docker was foremost in organising the Federation of British Industries, of which he served as first president from July 1916 to October 1917. Inspired by the example of the Superior Council of Industry and Commerce which had been formed by the Belgian Government in 1890, Docker wanted the FBI to be a 'Business Parliament' supplanting some of the responsibilities of the Westminster Parliament for industrial legislation. He was also associated with the British Manufacturers Association formed in 1915 and reconstituted in 1917 as the National Union of Manufacturers. He emerged in 1918 as a force in another productioneers' group, the British Commonwealth Union. Subsequently he became a vice-president of both the Tank Association and the British Electrical and Allied Manufacturers' Association.

Docker led the war-time merger movement by negotiating in 1918 the joint purchase, for £1.2 million, by MCWF and Vickers, of the British Westinghouse Electrical Co, subsequently known as Metropolitan-Vickers. Later, in March 1919, he persuaded Vickers to buy MCWF for the over-valued price of £12.1 million, and joined the Vickers board. His professed hope was that this vast combine would repeat in Britain the success which AEG and Siemens had achieved in Germany, but various circumstances defeated this strategy.

The foregoing indicates only part of Docker's efforts at industrial reconstruction in 1916-19, and the subsequent betrayal of his hopes soured him. The FBI became 'a Frankenstein monster which he could not allay' {HLRO, BL 83/6/6 Sir Joseph Lawrence to Bonar Law, 2 Aug 1918}, whose members rejected his Protectionism, his progressive stance on labour relations and his wish that the Federation would become a Business Parliament supplanting at least some of the responsibilities of the House of Commons. By 1920, Docker had withdrawn from FBI activity in disgust. His hopes that the British Commonwealth Union would provide the nucleus of a manufacturers' party in the Commons were also frustrated after 1918, although he consented to serve as the Union's president in 1922-25. Other disagreements led to his resignation as a director of both the British Trade Corporation and Vickers during 1920, and the collapse of post-war reconstruction plans convinced him that Britain would never re-organise itself properly to regain industrial supremacy.

Through nominees, he remained crucial to Vickers' development in the 1920s. He represented them in the unsuccessful discussions of 1924 on the merger of the Austin, Morris and Wolseley motor companies, and was the most important member of the Advisory Committee which engineered Vickers' drastic reconstruction in 1926. He was the intermediary in the controversial sale of Metropolitan Vickers to General Electric of America in 1928, and also had charge for a time of the merger talks between MCWF and Cammell Laird. After 1929, Vickers discouraged his involvement in the company.

Docker was also an active railway director. He served on the boards of the Stratford-upon-Avon & Midland Junction Railway in 1909-12 and of the Metropolitan Railway from January 1915 until February 1934, when it was absorbed by the London Transport Passenger Board. In 1921 he became a director of the London, Brighton & South Coast Railway, and, following the re-grouping of 1922, was a director of the Southern Railway, 1923-38. He was an outstanding influence on all three boards, taking particular interest in finance, electrification, rolling-stock orders and political liaison.

After the Armistice, he became increasingly involved in the Société Financière des Transports et d'Entreprises Industrielles (Sofina), the Belgian public utilities and electrical engineering trust led by Dannie Heineman. He was Sofina's senior British participant, although it was not until 1927 that he was able to attract Sofina's orders to Britain. The most ambitious project in which Docker interested Sofina was the hydro-electric development of the Aswan Dam, which he estimated in 1929 would require capital of £30 million. Sofina led him into high-level international dealings with other electro-technological interests, and, indeed, in 1929, he was rumoured to be working to gain control of Sofina. Another Belgian-registered trust in which he was concerned was the International Sleeping Car Syndicate of Davison Dalziel (qv) and he played a part in the acquisition by Dalziel's Pullman Car Co of Thomas Cook & Sons in 1927.

In 1921 Docker formed the Electric & Railway Finance Corporation (Elrafin), part of whose issued capital of £500,000 was held by Sofina, and this private finance house was the vehicle for many of his dealings until the Second World War. He was also connected with the British Stockbrokers Trust of Lord ffrench (qv) and dominated the powerful Birmingham Advisory Committee of the Midland Bank from July 1923 until his death.

Docker was a confidante and advisor of Sir Arthur Steel-Maitland, the Minister of Labour during 1924-29, and helped Sir Victor Wellesley to frame the proposals which resulted in 1934 in the formation of the Economic Relations Section of the Foreign Office. The offer of a barony by the Baldwin Government was withdrawn in May 1929 after objections from orthodox circles in the City of London.

During the crisis in the affairs of BSA in 1932-34, Docker's intervention was decisive in saving the group. He was responsible for Arthur Pollen (qv) succeeding Sir Edward Manville (qv) as chairman and the re-organisation of management and executive directors in December 1933 was his conception. He formally re-joined the BSA board in 1943, and, in June 1944, within a month of his death, secured by sheer force of personality the succession of his only son, as both chairman and managing director of BSA. He had contracted a heart ailment around 1938, and, in conjunction with tonsillitis, this led to his death, after a brief illness, on 8 July 1944 at Coleshill House, Amersham. The bulk of his estate, valued at £887,692, devolved in trust for his son.

Docker was a strange and complex character. He could be jovial, frank, diplomatic, discreet, and had a great power to sway men's minds and to win support from all classes. The mentor of many younger industrialists and politicians, his business mind was always bold, flexible and opportunistic. His memory for people and details was unusually retentive, and his financial sense was honed to the finest point. But, at the same time, he was a backstairs 'fixer' who eschewed limelight, a man who was readily embittered and pursued some quarrels with unnecessary acrimony, a man who could be brutal, ruthless, over-calculating, over-impatient and who was taciturn to the brink of inarticulacy. As a political force, he was awkward and naive, and as a visionary, he was sometimes disruptive. However these paradoxes are resolved (the depressive anxiety, caused by overwork, of which he complained in 1912-20, was doubtless important), Docker remains one of the prime forces of the British merger movement, and an unusually active and explicit exponent of British corporatism. Owing to his preference for working through nominees, it is unlikely that the full range of his interests will ever be known.

R P T DAVENPORT-HINES

DOCKER Frank Dudley

Writings:

letter on A J Balfour's Birmingham speech in *Midland Advertiser* 25 Sept 1909.

letter on Canadian business immorality *Times* 9 July 1911.

'The Labour Unrest: the Businessmen's View' *Daily Mail* 8 June 1912.

'Protection: A Power to Bargain', letter in *Midland Advertiser* 29 June 1912.

Open Letter to Sir Algernon Firth dated 24 July 1912, published in *Midland Advertiser* 17 Aug 1912, and other newspapers.

letter advocating higher salaries for Birmingham municipal officials *Birmingham Gazette* 2 Feb 1914.

'Foreign Loans and British Industries' *Economist* 7 Feb 1914.

'The Port of Finance' *Financial News* 26 Oct 1914 (reprinted *Globe* on same date).

letter advocating Ministry of Munitions *Times* 22 May 1915.

PP, Report of Committee on Financial Facilities for Trade (1916) Cd 8346.

'Causes of Industrial Unrest' article in *Sunday Times* 2 Sept 1917, reprinted in *Journal* of British Electrical & Allied Manufacturers Association, Oct 1917.

Essay in Stanley J Chapman (ed), *Labour and Capital after the War* (John Murray, 1918).

'The Industrial Problem', article in *National Review* 72, (Nov 1918). Reprinted as a pamphlet in 1919 by the British Commonwealth Union.

'The Large View in Business', *Ways and Means* 27 Sept 1919.

PP, Report of Committee to Examine the Question of Government Machinery for Dealing with Trade and Commerce (1919) Cmd 319.

letter on picketing in *Times* 19 Jan 1927.

Sources:

Unpublished

BLPES, papers of Tariff Commission.

Bodleian Library, Oxford, papers of Lord Addison and Lord Woolton.

Cambridge University Library, papers of Earl Baldwin of Bewdley.

Churchill College, Cambridge, papers of Earl of Swinton.

Greater London RO, Metropolitan Railway papers.

House of Lords RO, papers of Lord Beaverbrook, Bonar Law, Lloyd George, Sir Patrick Hannon, Lord Wargrave, and Lord Willoughby de Broke.

Midland Bank Archives, Poultry, London.

PRO, papers of Board of Trade; Foreign Office; London, Brighton and South Coast Railway; Ministry of Munitions; Southern Railway; Stratford-upon-Avon & Midland Junction Railway.

Scottish RO, Edinburgh, papers of Sir Arthur Steel-Maitland.

Sheffield University Library, papers of W A S Hewins.

Trinity College, Cambridge, papers of Edwin Montagu.

University of Warwick Modern Records Centre, papers of Birmingham Small Arms and Federation of British Industries.

Vickers House, Millbank, London, Vickers microfilm collection.

West Sussex County RO, Chichester, papers of Leo Maxse.

BCe.

MCe.

DCe.

PrC: Dudley Docker's will dated 24 November 1943; Lucy Constance Docker's will dated 24 July 1946.

Published

Birmingham Daily Post 11 Nov 1887, 10 July 1944.

Birmingham Gazette 11 Nov 1887, 10 June 1907, 10 July 1944.

Stephen Blank, *Industry and Government in Britain* (Farnborough: Saxon House, 1973).

Richard P T Davenport-Hines, *Dudley Docker, the Life and Times of a Trade Warrior* (Cambridge: Cambridge University Press, 1984).

Economist 3 June 1911, 22 May 1915, 3 June 1916, 9 June 1917, 1 June 1918.

Globe 1914-19.

Paul B Johnson, *Land Fit for Heroes* (Chicago, 1968).

Robert Jones and Oliver Marriott, *Anatomy of a Merger: History of GEC, AEI and English Electric* (Joanathan Cape, 1970).

Midland Advertiser 1908-19.

Sir Charles Tennyson, *Stars and Markets* (Chatto & Windus, 1957).

John A Turner, 'The British Commonwealth Union and the General Election of 1918' *English Historical Review* 93 (1978).

— (ed), *Businessmen and Politics 1900-1945* (Heinemann, 1983).

Vickers News 1919-28.

WWW.

DORMAN, Sir Arthur John

(1848-1931)

Steel manufacturer

Arthur Dorman was born at Ashford, Kent, on 8 August 1848, the son of Charles Dorman, a currier and later a coal and timber merchant. He was educated at Christ's Hospital. After a brief period in Paris, he was apprenticed at the age of eighteen to C J Johnson of Richardson, Johnson & Co at Stockton-on-Tees. There he acquired close experience of commercial operations, manual labour and iron-making techniques in a small iron plant. On marrying at twenty-five, his occupation was returned as metal broker. In 1876 Dorman formed a partnership with Albert de Lande Long to manufacture iron bars and angles for shipbuilding. They acquired an existing plant, the West Marsh ironworks, which had 20 puddling furnaces, a shingling hammer, a puddled iron rolling mill and a 14-inch finishing mill. Soon the firm was operating several works and challenging Belgian and German dominance in the iron girder trade. Moving from iron to steel as its basic material, in the early 1880s it installed open-hearth steel furnaces, first using iron made from imported hematite ores, switching later to the basic process of Gilchrist and Thomas (qqv) which drew on local ores. Capacity doubled between 1889 and 1896. By 1901 Dorman Long's labour force of 3,000 was producing about 180,000 tons of finished materials a year.

During the early 1900s the balance swung towards vertical integration and growth through merger. The rate of expansion in iron and steel production slowed to about 55 per cent between 1906 and 1913. But forward diversification intensified into constructional engineering and bridge building, rolling mills, wire works, rails, and sheet works. Backward linkages embraced iron ore mining and collieries. Much of this was secured by mergers. In particular, control of Bell Brothers, an illustrious and highly diversified local firm, larger than Dorman Long and headed by the distinguished, now aged Sir Isaac Lowthian Bell (qv), was obtained by 1902. A take-over of another substantial local firm, the North Eastern Steel Co, soon followed. Overseas activities included subsidiaries in Australia and South Africa, and constructional work in a variety of countries which brought increasing prestige. By 1914 Dorman Long had overtaken or absorbed its predecessors to become the dominant, although not unchallenged, iron and steel firm on Teesside. More, with some 20,000 employees and annual finished materials outputs of around 400,000 tons, it was now one of Britain's largest steel producers.

In all of this Arthur Dorman was the main spearhead, generally as both chairman and managing director. The limited evidence suggests a towering personal dominance of decision-making, much resilience through successive economic cycles, and great courage in times of adversity, for example in the early 1890s. There were serious strains as when Dorman retired temporarily in 1901-2 on stated grounds of fatigue: 'I have been constantly at it now for thirty years' {BSC, NERRC chairman's speech, AGM, 11 Sept 1901}. There were, too, occasional misjudgements. For example, in 1904 and 1909 Dorman freely admitted that he had been 'too sanguine' and 'mistaken' in forecasting good times immediately ahead {ibid, chairman's speech, AGM, 7 Dec 1904, 7 Dec 1909}. Heavy investment in new plant and equipment required considerable nerve particularly during recession periods and particularly insofar as profits needed to be ploughed back rather than distributed, leading to low dividends and shareholder criticisms. By 1911-14, however, there were substantial increases in both profits and dividends.

Behind Dorman's consistent expansion lay an obvious zest for risk-taking, an enjoyment of substantial, though not enormous wealth, an interest in technical improvement: also, very important, ideals of nationalism and empire, and a quasi-patriarchical concern to sustain Middlesbrough jobs and local pride. On the other hand, the expansionism involved some faults. In particular, the large-scale mergers proved a mixed blessing organisationally. They left a heritage of elderly, non-executive and politically-motivated appointments on the Dorman Long board; also there was much separatism, and both Bell Brothers and the North Eastern Steel Co remained largely unabsorbed, sowing the seeds of subsequent weakness.

The First World War brought a renewed phase of rapid growth. Dorman Long produced about one-half of the high explosives shells used by the army. It started to construct a large new £4.5 million, government-assisted steelworks at Redcar, chiefly for ship-plate. Several substantial companies were acquired mainly for their raw materials, notably Sir B Samuelson & Co Ltd (bought for £1.4 million in 1917) and the Carlton Iron Co (bought for £950,000 in 1919). The firm's partially overlapping and outdated multi-plant operations remained largely concentrated in Middlesbrough. Dorman, made a KBE in 1918 and a baronet in 1923, pressed forward enthusiastically with continued economic optimism and large-scale spending until late 1920.

During the 1920s the combination of recession with the firm's massive size, complexity, organisational looseness and recent acquisitions ideally required a drastic switch to efficiency pursuits. But here Dorman largely failed, permitting the development of a syndrome of 'elderly dominance, proud traditionalism, absentee grandee directors, primarily dynastic promotions at the top and general managerial inbreeding' {Boswell (1983) 214}. Now an old man, Dorman persisted as chairman, flanked by the even more aged Sir (Thomas) Hugh Bell (qv). Although he handed over the managing directorship to his son Arthur in 1923, Dorman's dominance in decision-making continued. He took few steps to renovate a board over-weighted with elderly relics of previous mergers and younger dynasts with inferior abilities. His son Charles (1875-1929) was not a notable success as finance director and vice-chairman and died before his father. His more competent younger son, Arthur (1881-1957), educated at Rugby and Cambridge, lacked the potential to be a dynamic successor. Although financial stringency largely ruled out production rationalisation, other efficiency improvements, now increasingly urgent, were neglected. Management and financial controls were weak. Still an expansionist,

Dorman stuck to the short-cycle, upward trend view of economic affairs he had successfully practised over several decades, showing courage but also inflexibility. Some of this expansionism helped the firm, notably further developments in constructional work, particularly overseas. A new bridge building department secured the celebrated £4.25 million Sydney Harbour Bridge contract, although this eventually produced a loss. However, continued growthmanship involved not only failure to rationalise but also some largely mistimed ventures, for example in Kent, and considerable financial misjudgement, highlighted by a massive £3.5 million debenture issue in 1923 which chronically increased the firm's debt ratio and contributed to an extreme degree of over-capitalisation.

By the late 1920s Dorman Long was one of the industry's weakest firms both managerially and financially despite much continued technical expertise and new activities overseas. A merger in 1929 with its large and even more ailing neighbour, Bolckow Vaughan, brought mixed short-term results. The bankers, now very powerful, pressed for still more ambitious North East Coast mergers but left the top management unchanged. Although deaf and, at times, tired, irascible and depressed, Dorman held on until his death in early 1931. Even then a managerial revival was to be delayed until the late 1930s. The firm's weaknesses were by now deeply ingrained and its further tribulations were to include the breakdown of the project for a merger with the South Durham-Cargo Fleet group in 1933.

Dorman was a paternalistically-minded employer and an effective morale builder who devoted much attention, for example, to planning Dormanstown, a plain and cheaply-constructed housing estate for employees, built in 1917-18 to ensure a labour supply for the newly-developed Redcar site. He moved assuredly from a partly self-made background to a gentlemanly state, living in a solid, neo-Gothic mansion at Nunthorpe, near Middlesbrough; relishing shooting and farming; and enjoying a large private library. He built and endowed the nearby Anglican church; supported local hospitals and technical education, and endowed a museum in Middlesbrough in 1904 to commemorate his eldest son's death in the Boer War. Many of the firm's local philanthropies persisted through the depressed 1920s. After serving for some years as a county councillor and standing as a Conservative Parliamentary candidate in 1892, Dorman restricted his political activities to occasional public eloquence on behalf of tariff reform. His presidency of the National Federation of Iron and Steel Manufacturers in 1923-24 produced no major initiatives.

Dorman was a tall, imposing figure, big in more than physical ways, an impressive speaker and leader, who enjoyed his work through most of his long career, rewarded himself well and found it hard to delegate. Like many brilliant founder-entrepreneurs, he was better at conquering new fields than controlling the firm efficiently when it grew really large. His last period of gerontocracy, dynastic weakness and inefficiency, superimposed on economic stress, should not be allowed to obscure his very substantial achievements nor his great qualities of intrepidity, resourcefulness and flair.

Dorman married Clara Lockwood, daughter of George Lockwood, a Stockton merchant and shipbuilder, in 1873; they had four sons and three daughters.

Sir Arthur Dorman died on 12 February 1931 leaving £132,173 gross.

JONATHAN S BOSWELL

Writings:

'Development of the Basic Open Hearth Process in Cleveland' *Proceedings of the Cleveland Institute of Engineers* Nov 1925.

Sources:

Unpublished

Bank of England, Central Archives Section, London: Securities Management Trust papers; Bankers' Industrial Development Co papers.

British Steel Corporation; Midland Regional Records Centre, Irthlingborough, Northants: National Federation of Iron and Steel Manufacturers' records.

British Steel Corporation, North East Regional Records Centre, Middlesbrough, Cleveland: Dorman Long records particularly directors' minutes; annual general meeting, proceedings and chairman's speeches; financial files; Colliery Committee; correspondence relating to investments; papers on South Durham merger; Britannia Works; Sidney Harbour Bridge contract; Bridge Department; papers on Dormanstown Estate; papers on amalgamation with Bell Brothers; papers relating to Bell Brothers, North Eastern Steel Co, Sir B Samuelson & Co, Carlton Iron Co, Bolckow Vaughan.

PRO, BT/55/38; BT/56/14, 21 and 37; CP/189/30.

BCe.

MCe.

PrC.

Interviews in 1981 with R S H Capes, J Jack, E T Judge, Agnes Tubman (née Lyons), retired officials of Dorman Long.

P H Andrews, 'Report on Teesside Blast Furnaces' (unpublished report, 1928), lent to author by J K Almond.

Erickson workcards.

D C D Pocock, 'A Comparative Study of Three Steel Towns: Corby, Scunthorpe and Middlesbrough' (Dundee PhD, 1969).

P Stubley, 'The Churches and the Iron and Steel Industry in Middlesbrough, 1890-1914' (Durham MA, 1979).

S Tolliday, 'Industry, Finance and the State: an Analysis of the British Steel Industry in the Inter-war Years' (Cambridge PhD, 1979).

Published

Jonathan S Boswell, *Business Policies in the Making, Three Steel Companies Compared* (George Allen & Unwin, 1983).

Duncan L Burn, *The Economic History of Steelmaking, 1867-1939* (Cambridge: Cambridge University Press, 1940).

James C Carr and Walter Taplin, *History of the British Steel Industry* (Oxford: Basil Blackwell, 1962).

C A Hempstead (ed), *Cleveland Iron and Steel: Background and Nineteenth Century History* (British Steel Corporation, 1979).

North-Eastern Daily Gazette 12 Feb 1931.

Teesside Chamber of Commerce Journal Feb 1931.

Times 13 Feb 1931.

Charles Wilson, 'Dorman Long' *Steel Review* 6 (1957).

WWW.

DOUGLAS, George

(1858/59-1947)

Woollen and worsted dyer

George Douglas (courtesy of Bradford Dyers).

George Douglas was the son of David Maitland Douglas, a manager and later a partner in the Bradford stuff merchanting firm of A & S Henry, and his wife Margaret née McConnell. George was educated at Bradford Grammar School before joining his father's firm, where he gained technical and commercial experience. In 1877 he attended the Yorkshire College and in the following year joined the famous firm of Edward Ripley & Son, dyers of Bowling near Bradford. He became responsible for the development and reorganisation of Ripleys to enable the firm to cope with a wider variety of trade and with technological innovations. He progressed to become general manager and junior partner.

The problems of unremunerative prices, severe competition and quality of output faced by the dyeing industry in the 1890s persuaded Douglas to press for the reorganisation of piece dyeing in Bradford and district. It was through his enterprise and organising ability that the Bradford Dyers' Association was founded. Ripley's was the oldest and largest of the firms to enter the combination. The BDA was, perhaps, the most successful of the industrial combinations in the textile industries in the 1890s. Formed in 1898, it brought together, initially, 22 firms in the Bradford piece dyeing trade, about 90 per cent of the business. Floated with a capital of £3 million, the intention of the Association was to sustain remunerative prices for dyeing (average profits of the member firms were 7.86 per cent of their total purchase price of £2,870,640) and to meet foreign competition by effecting economies and improvements in production through the pooling of technical expertise and through the centralisation of administration, purchasing, distribution and accountancy.

The Association subsequently expanded, incorporating many other dyeing businesses in Yorkshire and further afield. By 1906 the BDA employed about 7,500 people, mostly men. Douglas became a joint managing director of the BDA (with Sir Milton Sharp and Sir W H Ackroyd) and was appointed the sole managing director in 1909, a position which he held until his retirement in 1945. He was also chairman from 1924. By capital measures the BDA ranked as the seventeenth largest industrial company in 1905 but in the textile depression of the inter-war years, only fifty-eighth in 1930. Douglas successfully accomplished improvements in piece dyeing, reorganising plant and developing specialisms within the Association, and maintained profitable business for it until the problems of the 1930s. He was recognised for his business acumen, his planning ability and his labour leadership. A very hard worker himself, he was often described as being friendly, courteous and generous to others. He supported actively the Society of Dyers and Colourists of which he was a founder member. He was elected a vice-president from 1894 to 1912 and then president from 1912 to 1914, and made an honorary life member in 1934. Although an advocate of free trade, he argued for subsidies to help the industry in the 1930s and was a leading light in the pressure for industrial reorganisation in textiles at this period.

George Douglas's leisure activities focussed mainly on fishing and shooting. He lived, from 1908 onwards, at Farfield Hall near Addingham in West Yorkshire, amid an estate of 500 acres on the banks of the River Wharfe and was renowned for his love of fishing and shooting both there and in Scotland. Douglas was married and had a son and a daughter. His wife died in France in 1923. Douglas died on 26 November 1947, leaving £391,248 gross.

D T JENKINS

Sources:

Unpublished

PrC.

SSRC Elites data.

'The Bradford Dyers' Association Ltd' (A short typescript history in the possession of the Association, dated 1950).

Published

A F Ewing, *Planning and Policies in the Textile Finishing Industry* (Bradford University Press, 1972).

David T Jenkins and Kenneth G Ponting, *The British Wool Textile Industry, 1770-1914* (Heinemann, 1981).

Journal of the Society of Dyers and Colourists Apr 1948.

Henry W Macrosty, *The Trust Movement in British Industry. A Study of Business Organisation* (Longmans, Green & Co, 1907).

Peter L Payne, 'The Emergence of the Large-Scale Company in Great Britain, 1870-1914' *Economic History Review* 2nd ser 20 (1967).

Telegraph and Argus (Bradford) 26 Nov 1947.

To Mark a Notable Occasion in the History of the Bradford Dyers' Association Ltd 1946 (A booklet issued to commemorate the Centenary Meeting of the Conference of Works Councils of the Association).

DOUGLAS, William Sholto

1st Lord Douglas of Kirtleside

(1893-1969)

Airline executive

Lord Douglas of Kirtleside (courtesy of Sir Peter Masefield).

William Sholto Douglas was born in Oxford on 23 December 1893, the second (and eldest surviving) son of Robert Langton Douglas and of his first wife Margaret Jane née Cannon. At the time of Sholto Douglas' birth, his father was an ordained curate, assistant chaplain of Merton College, Oxford, and secretary of the Church of England Temperance Society. He was a direct descendant of Sir William Douglas, the First Earl of Queensberry (1595-1640). When Sholto Douglas was still an infant, his father took his family to Italy where Langton Douglas was, for a time, British chaplain in Siena and Perugia and beginning to be absorbed in Renaissance art. The family returned to England in 1898 and in 1900 Langton Douglas accepted an appointment as Professor of Medieval History and Dean of the Faculty of Art at Adelaide University in Australia. He left his wife and family with her parents at Tooting in South London. The separation ended in divorce in 1900, with Langton Douglas departing from Holy Orders and leaving his first wife and three small boys very hard up in London.

In these circumstances the Douglas boys started their education at St Mary's Church School at Balham where Sholto also sang in the choir at St John's, Tooting Bec. At the age of eleven he went on to Emmanuel School, Wandsworth, and then, in 1905, his father having returned to Italy and having begun to prosper in the art trade, he and his two brothers, Bob and Archie, were sent to Tonbridge Preparatory School as day boys. Their mother moved to Tonbridge to gain the reduced fees accorded to local residents. In 1907 Sholto passed the entrance examination into Tonbridge School, where he worked hard, did well, played rugby for the first XV, rowed and became a leading member of the Tonbridge School OTC. In 1912 he won a classical scholarship to Lincoln College, Oxford, and went up in October of that year. In what was to be his only year at the University, Sholto Douglas immersed himself in non-academic opportunities; he rowed for Lincoln College, played in the Oxford University rugby trials, sang in the Bach Choir and began to attend meetings of the Fabian Society. Even more significantly, he joined the Artillery Section of the Oxford OTC and paid much attention to learning to ride.

The First World War broke out during his first long vacation and, with a number of his colleagues from Lincoln College, Sholto Douglas immediately volunteered for service in the Royal Artillery. He was commissioned in August 1914 and saw several months' service with the Royal Horse Artillery in France. Then on 26 December 1914, Douglas transferred from the RHA to the Royal Flying Corps for artillery observation duties with No 2 Squadron, RFC, at Merville. After training as a pilot, he flew in the thick of the air fighting in 1915-18. From September 1917 until the end of the war he commanded No 84 Squadron, RFC and RAF, proving himself a fine leader and a competent fighter pilot. He finished the war as a lieutenant colonel, with an MC, a DFC, a French Croix de Guerre and three times mentioned in dispatches. In April 1919 Douglas joined Handley Page Transport Ltd at £500 a year as chief pilot with Commercial Pilot's Licence No 4. On 1 May 1919, he flew the first post-war commercial air service between Cricklewood, London, and Didsbury, Manchester, followed on 2 September 1919, by flying the first Handley Page service on the London-Paris air route between Cricklewood and Le Bourget. In October 1919, however, in a mood of post-war depression, he resigned from Handley Page, contemplated joining his father as an art dealer and then was on the point of going to Calcutta for Andrew Yule & Co, jute merchants, when a chance meeting with his old chief, Sir Hugh Trenchard, persuaded him to return to the Royal Air Force. During the twenty years between the wars, Sholto Douglas advanced steadily in his now chosen professional Service career and, when the Second World War began on 3 September 1939, Air Vice Marshal Sir W Sholto Douglas was Assistant Chief of the Air Staff at the Air Ministry in Whitehall. By the end of the war he was made Air Officer Commanding-in-Chief, British Air Forces of Occupation in Germany — a post he himself disliked intensely in 'an atmosphere of misery and starvation' {Douglas (1966) 306} To his disappointment, in June 1946 Sir Arthur Tedder was made Chief of the Air Staff but, in some compensation, Douglas was created KGCB and a Marshal of the Royal Air Force. He wished to retire but Prime Minister Attlee prevailed upon him, as a duty, to take over from Field Marshal Montgomery as Commander-in-Chief and Military Governor of the British Zone of Germany. In later years, Douglas looked on his eighteen months in this command as the most unhappy of his career — facing with abhorrence his duty of signing death warrants, including those which followed the Nuremburg Trials.

Douglas returned to England in November 1947, having completed seven years as a Commander-in-Chief and, in the New Years Honours List of 1948 he was raised to the peerage as Lord Douglas of Kirtleside. He now looked forward to retirement to the countryside while endorsing his early links with the Fabian Society at Oxford, by joining the Labour Party and taking his seat on the Labour benches of the House of Lords.

Lord Pakenham (later the Earl of Longford), who had been Chancellor of the Duchy of Lancaster, responsible for the British Control Commission in Germany, now became Minister of Civil Aviation. He persuaded Sholto Douglas to accept an appointment to the board of the British Overseas Airways Corporation and, on 14 March 1949, to take over from Gerard d'Erlanger (qv) as chairman of British European Airways. Douglas thus came back full circle to British civil aviation and air transport, with the first stages of which he had been involved thirty years before. Douglas accepted his new position with quiet enthusiasm and during the next fifteen years, until he retired on 31 March 1964, headed with distinction an airline which became not only profitable but the leader in Europe and to North Africa and the Near East. When Lord Douglas came to BEA at Keyline House on the edge of Northolt Airport, the airline was carrying some 750,000 passengers a year (who flew 207 million passenger/miles) and a revenue of £7 million but was suffering serious losses, which reached £2.8 million in 1949-50. Douglas, consistent with his social philosophy, questioned the need for a public undertaking to make a commercial rate of return. He did however believe that it should make sufficient profit to pay interest on its capital and to cover fluctuations in demand, calculating that optimally revenue should exceed all expenditure by about 5 per cent. That position was reached in 1954-55 when, for the first time, a small profit was recorded. When Douglas retired in 1964 BEA was carrying 5.6 million passengers a year, with a revenue of £60 million and a net profit (after interest on capital) of rather more than £3 million a year. BEA, under Lord Douglas, met and encouraged demand for both business and leisure travel into Europe by a differential fares policy and by re-equipping the airline with new aircraft of increased earning capacity. Tourist fares at reduced rates were introduced by BEA on their International Services in April 1953 and by April 1954 traffic increases of more than 18 per cent were recorded, rising from 1.4 million to almost 1.7 million passengers. By the late 1950s BEA was also substantially increasing its carryings of cargo, having in 1959-60 achieved a 28 per cent increase in all forms of cargo and mail compared with a 17 per cent increase in passenger traffic.

Under Douglas BEA met rising demand for passenger and cargo traffic initially by relying on the Vickers Viking and Douglas DC-3 aircraft. By the late 1950s 64 Vickers Viscount of various marks were in service with BEA. By the time Lord Douglas retired, BEA was being equipped with jet aircraft. The shift to jets had been held up by a series of tragic accidents to the De Havilland Comet I, in 1953-54. Comet II's were restored to service in 1957 and Comet 4Bs with BEA in 1960. Concurrently with the Comet 4, BEA introduced the Vickers Vanguard turboprop airliner. Generally the trend was towards larger aircraft which achieved lower costs per seat mile, both stimulated and supported by the increase in traffic.

Under Lord Douglas BEA also made moves towards closer airline co-operation in Europe. But so long as Britain was outside the EEC and its

Air Union, BEA was obliged to make commercial agreements with countries outside the Common Market. With the soaring fixed and variable costs of larger and more jet airliners, smaller European countries outside the EEC found it advantageous to charter aircraft from BEA, as did the Portuguese airline TAP (chartering Viscounts), or to hire BEA's technical services, as did the Greek airline Olympic. These arrangements made a profit for BEA, rising from £63,000 in 1954-55 to £3.0 million in 1963-64.

Douglas brought quiet authority, absolute integrity and a lifetime of command and of knowledge of aviation to the airline. He gave unswerving support to his chief executive, from 1949 to 1955, Peter Masefield (qv), who concentrated on the running of the airline, while Douglas handled the board and the politicians with a direct firmness which brooked no interference while he looked after BEA's international affairs. In 1956-57 Douglas was elected president of the International Air Transport Association (IATA). He inspired confidence and respect throughout the international air transport industry while proving himself to have a sound business sense.

Douglas thus achieved success in three quite different careers — as a fighter pilot and squadron commander during the First World War, as an air officer commanding-in-chief throughout the Second World War and as the chairman of a state-owned airline from 1949 to 1964. To each of these different responsibilities he brought qualities of leadership and determination. Outwardly dour and sometimes brusque to the point of rudeness, he was at heart sensitive and shy, one of the kindest of men with a keen eye for attractive women. He always gave an air of forthright assurance, though inwardly was sometimes hesitant. A stocky figure, of about medium height, he was looked on as a typical John Bull type who, nevertheless, engendered pride and affection in his staff. To the distinction of being Commander-in-Chief longer than any other allied officer of either of the two world wars, he added that of being chairman of a nationalised industry for longer than anyone else before or since.

Douglas first married Mary Howard in October 1919. This marriage was dissolved in 1933 when he married Joan Lesley Denny, daughter of Colonel Henry Denny. Douglas' second marriage was dissolved in 1955 and he then married Hazel Walker, widow of Captain W E R Walker, by whom, to his delight, he had a daughter, Catherine. Lord Douglas of Kirtleside died on 10 February 1969, leaving £34,138 gross.

SIR PETER MASEFIELD

Writings:

Years of Combat (Collins, 1963).

Years of Command (Collins, 1966).

'Development and Organisation of British European Airways - 1949 to 1960' in Ronald S Edwards and H Townsend (eds), *Business Growth* (Macmillan, 1966).

Sources:

Unpublished

BCe.

MCe.

PrC.

Personal knowledge.

Published

DNB.

WWW.

DOUGLAS-PENNANT, George Sholto Gordon

2nd Lord Penrhyn

(1836-1907)

Estate and quarry developer

George Sholto Gordon Douglas-Pennant, Lord Penrhyn (courtesy of Jean Lindsay).

George Sholto Gordon Douglas-Pennant, who succeeded as Second Baron Penrhyn in 1886, was born at Linton Springs, Yorkshire, on 30 September 1836, the son of Hon Edward Gordon Douglas-Pennant (1800-86) who was raised to the peerage in 1866 as First Baron Penrhyn of Llandegai. His mother Juliana Isabella, his father's first wife, was the eldest daughter and co-heiress of George Hay Dawkins-Pennant of Penrhyn Castle, who was the cousin of Richard Pennant, created Baron Penrhyn, County Louth, in the peerage of Ireland, and developer of Penrhyn Quarry at Bethesda near Bangor. Richard Pennant died in 1808 leaving no issue; the title became extinct and his estates, in North Wales and Jamaica, passed to George Hay Dawkins who assumed the additional name of Pennant. George's father assumed the name Pennant by royal licence in 1841, after the death of his father-in-law, George Hay Dawkins-Pennant, in December 1840. From 1885 to 1907 George Sholto Gordon Douglas-Pennant was the owner of Penrhyn Quarry and played a central role in one of the fiercest disputes in British industrial history.

George's mother died on 23 April 1842, when he was only six. This early loss may have had some effect on his character, which was authoritarian and stubborn, yet seemed to crave affection and respect. He was educated at Eton, 1850-52, and then at Christ Church, Oxford. He joined the Royal

Caernarvon Rifles as lieutenant in 1856, was appointed captain in 1858 but then resigned his commission in December 1860. George's father was Honorary Colonel of the Royal Caernarvon Rifles and later of the renamed 4th Battalion Royal Welch Fusiliers. This military background confirmed George Douglas-Pennant's belief in the workers' discipline and unquestioning obedience.

The North Wales slate industry was dominated by the two largest quarries in the world in the 1870s: Penrhyn at Bethesda and Dinorwic at Llanberis, which was owned by the Assheton Smiths. Both were organised on quasi-feudal lines, with provision of cottages, hospitals, pensions and benefit clubs, and this continued until the First World War. Other slate mines and quarries in Caernarvonshire and Merionethshire were less aristocratically organised and labour relations were more harmonious. The industry expanded rapidly in the mid-Victorian era: profits were high and a large export market developed. Narrow gauge railways helped to solve the transport problem and fleets of schooners carried the slate from the ports of Portmadoc, Caernarvon and Port Penrhyn at Bangor. The workers did not share in the prosperity: their wages rarely exceeded £1 a week even though some of their work was highly skilled, and most of it involved some element of danger. Depression in the building trade, however, from 1878 to 1890, hit the slate industry and prices fell. It was during these years that labour relations among the slate workers, especially among those in Penrhyn quarry, reached their nadir.

In 1874 the North Wales Quarrymen's Union had been formed and despite strong managerial opposition more than 2,000 of the 3,000 Penrhyn workers became members. In 1885 the First Baron Penrhyn handed over the quarry to his son George, and it was from this year until 1903 that he waged a desperate struggle to maintain the old paternalistic and autocratic traditions against the inroads of trade unionism.

One of the first actions of George after he succeeded his father as Second Baron Penrhyn in 1886 was to terminate the Pennant Lloyd agreement of 1874 which had granted several concessions to the men. From October 1885 to March 1886 the men at Dinorwic Quarry were locked out after they had held a mass meeting to discuss their grievances. In 1886, however, Lord Penrhyn tried to present himself as a kindly father-figure to his workmen, offering to pay half the cost of their excursion tickets to London. The men expressed their gratitude and Emilius Alexander Young, the new chief manager of the quarry, who master-minded some of Lord Penrhyn's actions, said that this generosity increased the good feeling existing among the men.

Lord Penrhyn's determination not to increase wages in the 1890s ended any prospect of continuing good labour relations. The men's efforts to present their grievances to Lord Penrhyn by means of an elected committee were seen as rebellious, and E A Young suggested that the leading 'malcontents' should be dismissed. The men became increasingly discontented with harsh discipline and low wages, especially as Lord Penrhyn's profits (estimated at about £100,000 per annum in 1898-99) were rising as a result of the building boom in the 1890s. There were labour difficulties in other quarries, but nowhere did the disputes reach such depths of mutual hatred and distrust between labour and management as at Penrhyn. From the end of September 1896 to August

Penrhyn Quarry, Bethesda, about 1890 (courtesy of Jean Lindsay).

1897 the men were locked out after their grievances had been set aside and over 70 men had been suspended, largely because they joined a deputation which tried to put the men's requests to Lord Penrhyn. The lock-out ended with virtually no concessions to the men. The union was not recognised and there was some victimisation of the ring-leaders who were not taken back on various pretexts.

Lord Penrhyn and E A Young became members of the National Free

Labour Association in London in 1897. After 1898 trade became worse because the imports of foreign slates increased. The number of unionists at Penrhyn was reduced by victimisation, and in 1900 the collection of union subscriptions was prohibited in the quarry, because it was claimed some workers were being bullied into paying. Both management and labour were prepared for a confrontation. Lord Penrhyn saw himself as the champion of the principles of laissez-faire. The men fought desperately to improve their position by means of collective bargaining.

In 1900 the Penrhyn workmen lost control and violence broke out against the contractors who let bargains or allocations of slate to the quarrymen. This resulted in Lord Penrhyn instituting proceedings against 26 men, most of whom had not joined in the violence. The quarrymen marched to Bangor on the day of the trial, when 20 out of 26 were found not guilty, and for this they were suspended from work for fourteen days. On 19 November work resumed but eight galleries, worked by the leaders of the men's committee, were not let. The men refused to start work the next day and on being told to start work or leave, they left. The quarry was then closed.

The lock-out lasted until June 1901 when Lord Penrhyn re-opened his quarry with virtually no concessions. About 400 non-unionists were taken on after careful vetting. Lord Penrhyn addressed the men in the quarry, 'congratulating them on their pluck, and their determination to act as free agents with regard to their own labour' {*Slate Trade Gazette* 7 (1901) No 41, p. 149}. A gold sovereign was given to each of these workmen. The re-opening of the quarry seriously divided the quarrymen and their families. Personal malice and quarrels abounded. Those who returned (usually members of the Church of England) were seen as traitors, and violence was directed towards them and their families. Bethesda became the centre of bitterness and in 1901 a detachment of the Queen's Bays was sent to Bethesda to maintain the peace. At the beginning of 1902 a company of Staffordshire Infantry and half a squadron of the 7th Hussars were sent to Bethesda at the request of Colonel Ruck, the Chief Constable.

Lord Penrhyn received support from other employers for his uncompromising stand; but there was also widespread sympathy for the men. The *Daily News*, partly owned by George Cadbury (qv), and the *Daily Chronicle* gave sympathetic accounts of their struggle. Some of the men sought work in neighbouring quarries or moved to South Wales and the coal-mines. Others could find no work and were left destitute. William Jones, MP for Caernarvonshire, referred in November 1902 to 1,200 men at Bethesda, plus widows and families whose breadwinner had gone to find work, who had to rely on charity and very small union allowances. Meanwhile the strike was helping the tile industry and the proportion of foreign slates to the home trade rose to new heights. Those workmen who were employed acknowledged their subservient position and grateful thanks were sent in a resolution, after a mass meeting, to Lord Penrhyn for his 'constant kindness... at all times, but especially in times of sickness and distress' {*ibid* 7 (1901) No 43, p. 18}.

All attempts to bring the dispute to arbitration were resisted by Lord Penrhyn. In March 1903 he sued William John Parry, the men's champion, for libellous statements which had appeared in the *Clarion*. Damages and costs to the amount of £2,508 were awarded to Lord

Penrhyn. The Penrhyn Choir toured the country to gain money for the men and contributions came in from all over the country.

On 14 November 1903, however, the men capitulated and the strike ended. The quarrymen were invited to apply by letter individually to be taken back. There were many who were rejected, and no boy was taken on if any member of his family had taken part in the strike. Those who returned completely capitulated to Lord Penrhyn. Bethesda did not recover quickly from the strike: the value of property fell; many of the quarrymen and their families emigrated; and many of old Penrhyn workmen lived out the rest of their lives unemployed, depressed and impoverished. Neighbourly spirit was destroyed by the split between the 'traitors' and the others and left a lasting legacy of bitterness. The union became insignificant until after the First World War.

Trade was depressed in the early years of the twentieth century, and in November 1905 Lord Penrhyn reduced wages by 2s in the £. This reduction aroused little protest. Lord Penrhyn had triumphed insofar as the men's spirit was broken, but for both parties the struggle had been suicidal.

Apart from the quarry, Lord Penrhyn was a typical landowner, enjoying hunting, shooting and fishing. His interests included horse-racing and he was elected to the Jockey Club in 1887. He was master of the Grafton hounds from 1882 to 1891. He was a DL and JP for Caernarvonshire. He numbered royalty and politicians among his friends: the Prince and Princess of Wales were entertained at Penrhyn Castle in 1894, and Sir Michael Hicks-Beach, the Chancellor of the Exchequer, was a visitor to the quarry and castle in 1896. He was also an active councillor on Caernarvonshire County Council where he was said to be concerned about the problems of the unemployed and to be 'extremely just — stern... aspiring to do justice' {*Gwylior* 19 Mar 1907}. He was a founder of the North Wales Property Defence Association and he owned about 72,000 acres, including land in Northamptonshire. The Pennants were always regarded as good landlords, and in February 1908 when unveiling a stained glass window at St Cross Church, Talybont, near Bangor, in memory of the 'late Lord Penrhyn', Humphrey Ellis, one of his tenants, said 'His philanthropy was proverbial, and his generosity to the poor unbounded'. {*Slate Trade Gazette* 13 (1908) No 121, p. 259}

In 1866 Douglas-Pennant was elected Conservative MP for Caernarvonshire, but in the election of 1868 he was opposed by a Liberal, Thomas Love Jones-Parry, who won the seat by the narrow margin of 148 votes. Workers known to be Liberals were thereafter victimised in his father's quarry; and in the election of 1874, despite the Secret Ballot Act, George regained his seat. In 1880, however, he was decisively defeated by the Liberal candidate Watkin Williams QC. This defeat embittered George who felt personally betrayed by the electors of Caernarvonshire.

He married first, in 1860, Pamela Blanche Rushout (d 1869) the daughter of Sir Charles Rushout, Bt; they had one son and six daughters. He married secondly, in 1875, Gertrude Jessy, the daughter of Rev Henry Glynne, rector of Hawarden; they had two sons and six daughters.

To many of the quarrymen's descendants his name survives as a symbol of injustice, cruelty and the 'iron hand of wealth'. Lord Penrhyn died on 10 March 1907, not in his vast, chill Penrhyn Castle, but at his London residence, Mortimer House, Halkin Street, SW, and was buried near his country estate of Wicken, Stoney Stratford. He left £634,642 gross.

JEAN LINDSAY

Sources:

Unpublished

Gwynedd Archives, Caernarvon, Penrhyn MSS.

University College of North Wales Bangor, Penrhyn MSS.

MCe.

PrC.

Information from Patrick Strong of Eton College, and from Norman Holme of the Regimental Museum, the Royal Welch Fusiliers.

Published

DNB.

Genedl Cymraeg 5 Sept 1905, 18 Aug 1908.

Gwylior 19 Mar 1907.

R Merfyn Jones, *The North Wales Quarrymen 1874-1922* (Cardiff: University of Wales Press, 1981).

Jean Lindsay, *A History of the North Wales Slate Industry* (Newton Abbot: David & Charles, 1974).

PP, RC Labour (1891-94) C 6708-I.

Slate Trade Gazette 3 (1896-97) Nos 13-20; 7 (1901) No 43; 13 (1908) No 121.

Times 12 Mar 1907.

J Roose Williams, 'Quarryman's Champion' *Transactions of the Caernarvonshire Historical Society* 24 (1963).

WWMP.

DOULTON, Sir Henry

(1820-1897)

Pottery manufacturer

Sir Henry Doulton (1820-1897) from a drawing by Frederick Sandys (courtesy of Doulton & Co Ltd).

Henry Doulton was born in Vauxhall Walk, South London, on 25 July 1820. He was the second of eight children born to John Doulton, a potter, and his wife, Jane née Duneau. Five years before Henry's birth, John Doulton had invested his life savings of £100 in a small riverside pottery in Lambeth. It was one of many in this area of South London producing a range of utilitarian salt-glazed stoneware.

Because of his bookishness, it was thought that of all the Doulton children, Henry would become a scholar. John Doulton was prepared to spend generously on Henry's education and future. But the boy surprised everyone by announcing that he would like nothing better than to become a practical potter and at the age of fifteen he entered the family business.

Henry proved his genuine enthusiasm for the firm by rising at 6.00 am to ring the bell which summoned the hands to work. Then he took his place among them. It was originally planned that he would be apprenticed to his father for several years but Henry proved so zealous and so quick that at the end of eighteen months, there was nothing more for him to learn.

With his rapidly-acquired knowledge of all aspects of the pottery trade, from the preparation of the clay to selling the ware, Henry Doulton was soon to play a leading part in running the firm. Under his guidance it developed and expanded, taking over a number of less efficient rivals in the process. By the late 1830s the company added architectural terracotta and garden ornaments to its range; but Henry Doulton was already looking ahead, and decided that the firm should become involved in the sanitary revolution which in the 1840s developed in London and the big new industrial cities.

The firm became the Lambeth Pottery and began the large-scale production of stoneware drainpipes and conduits, many of which, sunk underground in London and other cities, are still in use today. Although unromantic compared with some of the later ware for which Royal Doulton is famous, sanitaryware sales regularly accounted for the bulk of the firm's turnover and profits and permitted subsequent expansion into tableware, Doulton figures and character jugs.

At about the time of the sanitaryware boom, many designers were coming out of art schools keen for experience of industry. John Sparks, the principal of the Lambeth School of Art, persuaded Henry Doulton to employ a few of his students on an experimental basis. In the late 1860s, a few of these students produced efforts based on traditional historical styles, and this early studio ware was received enthusiastically in 1867 at the Paris Exhibition and in 1871 at the International Exhibition in London. But it was the Philadelphia Exhibition of 1876 which finally

Royal Doulton Showrooms (left) and terracotta factory on the Albert Embankment as they appeared early in the twentieth century (courtesy of Doulton & Co Ltd).

clinched the relationship between art and industry — and led to a close bond between the company and the American continent.

Potteries all over the country now began setting up their own art departments. With the Lambeth Studios flourishing, and with factories set up in Rowley Regis, St Helens and Smethwick, Henry Doulton now turned his attentions to North Staffordshire, the traditional home of the ceramic industry.

In 1877 he acquired an interest in a medium grade earthenware factory in Nile Street, Burslem. During the nineteenth century the factory had been through various changes in ownership and now had 160 employees and eight bottle ovens. Child labour was still in use and the conditions at the factory were less than attractive. Initially, the Doulton incursion into Burslem was not successful, and there were rumours that the big potter had taken on more than he bargained for. But the threat of failure spurred Henry on, and he threw himself wholeheartedly into the Burslem endeavour. In 1882, the firm became Doulton & Co, Burslem. Henry Doulton made some managerial changes and eventually a team of talented artists began working at Nile Street, marking the start of the great Doulton tradition. By the end of the nineteenth century, the Nile Street pottery had a world-wide reputation. In 1895 the firm employed over 4,000 people in the sanitary and faience works combined. When in 1899 the company became limited its authorised capital was £1,100,000 (£516,666 issued).

Doulton married in 1849 Sarah (d 1888) daughter of John L Kennaby. They had one son and two daughters. On Queen Victoria's Silver Jubilee in June 1887 Henry Doulton was knighted. Following a serious operation ten years later he died at his home in Kensington on 17 November 1897. Sir Henry Doulton left £310,544 gross

D JOHN MORTON

Sources:

Unpublished

PrC.

Published

Daily Telegraph 20 Nov 1897.

DNB.

Desmond Eyles, *The Doulton Burslem Wares* (Barrie & Jenkins for Royal Doulton Tableware Ltd, 1980).

Edmund W Gosse, *Sir Henry Doulton: The Man of Business as a Man of Imagination;* edited by Desmond Eyles (Hutchinson, 1970).

WWW.

DOVE, Frederick John

(1830-1923)

Builder and contractor

Frederick John Dove was born in Islington, North London, on 23 June 1830, the fifth in a family of ten born to William Spencer Dove (1793-1869) and Ann Isabella née Dixon, both his father and maternal grandfather being builders. William Spencer Dove was then establishing himself as a builder in Islington, but had started his working life as a carpenter at Sunbury-on-Thames.

F J Dove (courtesy of Dove Bros Ltd).

In 1852 the partnership of Dove Brothers was formed. The three partners were all sons of William Spencer Dove: William Warren Dove (1822-80), Benjamin Dixon Dove (1824-92) and Frederick John Dove (1830-1923). Under the deed of co-partnership their father retained overall superintendence of the business with rights of access to all accounts, agreements, etc. It is, however, doubtful if he played a major part in the business during the years immediately preceding his death. In the 1860s a fourth brother joined the partnership, Henry Charles Dove (1840-95).

In 1854 Frederick married Marian Ann Prime, daughter of a Barnsbury builder. Four sons were born between 1855 and 1868.

By the 1850s Dove Brothers were already building a number of new churches and restoring older ones. This was to become a most important part of the firm's expansion in the next thirty years. In the 1860s some of the churches were small and losses occurred on a number of contracts, but gradually profits rose. During this period the firm was based in Studd Street, Islington, where business hours were from 6.0 am to 5.0 pm daily. Architects with whom Dove Brothers were then associated included A D Gough, Benjamin Ferrey, G G Scott, G E Street, A W Blomfield and A Webb. More than 50 new churches were built by 1869 and 130 by the end of the century.

In 1871 Dove Brothers obtained the contract for the foundations of the new Law Courts in the Strand. At £32,894 it was their largest contract to date but they made no profit from it, losing £1,323. The Law Courts contract was followed by several in and around the Inns of Court, including what was probably Dove Brothers' first office building contract (1873). Their office building activities continued in the years that followed and consisted of unspectacular extensions and alterations until 1886 when they obtained the contract to build the Bank of England's New Law Courts branch for £34,925. In 1874, Dove Brothers undertook their first hospital work, at the Charing Cross Hospital. In the years to 1905 ten other hospital contracts followed. The eleven contracts together had an aggregate value of £44,119. In 1907 Dove Brothers obtained the contract to build a new out-patients' department at St Bartholomew's Hospital. The contract was for more than £120,000 and stands in marked contrast to the modest hospital contracts which had preceded it. The contract for University College School at Hampstead, built in the years 1905-7 for £140,000 stands in a similar stark contrast to the school contracts which had preceded it.

In 1881 Dove Brothers opened an office in the City of London, at Tokenhouse Buildings, King's Arms' Yard, whilst retaining their existing office and premises in Islington. Frederick John Dove was in charge of the City Office when it opened and from it he controlled the bulk of the partnership's secular building activities. Church work, now often restoration or enlargement, was still important to Dove Brothers but a much smaller percentage of their total work. From the mid-1880s Frederick John Dove emerged in virtual control of the partnership. His eldest son Frederick Lionel Dove (1855-1932) became a partner with a 10 per cent share of the profits in 1893. Dove Brothers became a limited liability company in 1905 with Frederick John Dove as the governing director and chairman and Frederick Lionel Dove as managing director.

Under the effective control of Frederick John Dove, Dove Brothers

The building of Westminster Central Hall (courtesy of Dove Bros Ltd).

continued to diversify their building operations. In the 1880s powder mills (ie gunpowder factories) and cold stores were constructed. In the later 1890s a number of breweries and bakeries were built. And in 1902-3 three contracts for the erection of artisans' dwellings with a total value of £79,159 were undertaken. One avenue of diversification which was attempted and abandoned was ship-fitting: in 1890 the SS *Sea King* was fitted out by Dove Brothers but it was their one and only contract in this field. Church building continued to be a major part of their business and in 1902 they obtained their largest church construction contract prior to Frederick John Dove's retirement: £43,000 for the Church of the Ascension at Victoria Docks.

Dove Brothers maintained a reputation for high quality in areas of traditional craftsmanship, such as wood carving, whilst beginning to apply new building techniques involving the use of iron, steel and cement. A number of their churches and secular buildings, were iron- or steel-framed, including Australia House in the Strand, the monumental stone exterior of which disguises the rectilinear steel structure within (completed in 1918, three years after Frederick John Dove retired). They were also among the first London builders to use reinforced concrete, in the Motor Bus Garage at Hackney (1906), Central Hall, Westminster

(1906-11), the Colonial Bank, Jamaica (1909) and the German Sailors' Home in East London (1910).

Prior to 1914 it was very unusual for British builders to operate overseas. Holland & Hannen, with a branch in South Africa, were virtually the only firm with continuous overseas operations. Dove Brothers obtained their work in Jamaica, on the basis of expertise in the use of reinforced concrete. Their other pre-war overseas contract was the teak roof for Grahamstown Cathedral, which was pre-fabricated in Islington. The nature of this contract emphasises Dove Brothers continuing reputation for high quality craftsmanship.

The last building completed in Frederick John Dove's active period was the firm's most important contract in the Edwardian era, Wesleyan Methodist Central Buildings (now known as Central Hall, Westminster). A prestigious building, it had an inner dome which was then the largest reinforced concrete dome in Britain. Outside the firm, Frederick John Dove had many interests connected with the building industry. One of the founders of the London Master Builders' Association, he was its president in the years 1882-85. He was also president of the Institute of Builders, 1893-94. Like other members of the Dove family he was associated with a City livery company, being a past master of the Tylers' and Bricklayers'. For over twenty-five years he served as a churchwarden at St Mary's, Hornsey Rise, and for almost fifty years he was treasurer of the Islington Dispensary.

He lived long enough to see his grandson, William Watkins Dove (1897-1967) join the firm in 1920. On 18 December 1923 he died at Mount House, Monken Hadley, the home of his son, Frederick Lionel Dove. His estate was valued at £43,697 gross.

Frederick Lionel (1855-1932) had worked with his father for many years and he became in 1923 the new governing director. In his turn he was able to extend the business until, in the early 1930s, it employed 600 people. On his own death in 1932, his sons William Watkins and Arthur Norman (b 1902), both already directors, took over. William was appointed governing director and held this position until his death in 1967. Arthur became the last of the Doves to be in the firm, being managing director from 1967 until his retirement in 1970.

JOYCE WHEATLEY

Sources:

Unpublished

MCe.

PrC.

Published

David Braithwaite, *Building in the Blood: The Story of Dove Brothers of Islington, 1781-1981* (Godfrey Cave Associates Ltd and Dove Bros Ltd, 1981).

Times 21 Dec 1923

A F Down (courtesy of T A B Corley).

DOWN, Sir Alastair Frederick

(1914-)

Oil company chairman

Alastair Down was born at Kirkcaldy, Fife, on 23 July 1914 the elder son of Frederick Down, an officer of the 12th Bengal Cavalry, and his wife Margaret née Hutchison. Educated at Edinburgh Academy and Marlborough College, in 1938 he qualified as a chartered accountant in Edinburgh. He later described himself as the prototype of the school-leaver who is keen to go into industry: bright but perhaps a little on the indolent side. Seeking a career that would provide an opportunity for travel, he obtained a post with the Anglo-Iranian Oil Co and was stationed in Palestine until 1940.

Already a territorial officer in the Royal Scots regiment, he joined the colours in 1940. A spectacular period of service in the Western Desert and Egypt followed, during which he was awarded the MC and MBE and twice mentioned in despatches. That period came to an abrupt end when he was wounded and lost the sight of his right eye. Thereafter he had to be content with staff headquarters posts, first with the Eighth Army in Italy, and later with the First Canadian Army: he was made an OBE in 1944 and ended the war as a colonel. For his work with the Canadian Army in the Netherlands, he was appointed a knight commander of the Order of Orange Nassau. The Staff College he underwent in 1942 helped to instil into him qualities that were to be of sterling value in his subsequent career: the ability to extract the essentials from written or verbal reports, to issue clear and incisive directions, and to be ruthless when absolutely necessary.

After demobilisation in 1945, he spent the next thirty years progressively moving up the hierarchy of Anglo-Iranian, later renamed British Petroleum. In 1947 he married Marjorie Hilda 'Bunny' Mellon, the daughter of Bertram Mellon, a mining engineer; they had two sons and two daughters. When in 1954 the company began operations in Canada, he was appointed chief representative there, becoming in 1957 president of the BP Group in Canada. From 1962 to 1975 he served in London as a managing director of British Petroleum. In that post, when in 1963 his company and Shell made a take-over bid for the Burmah Oil Co, he had the task of personally presenting the offer to the latter's chairman. After the failure of that bid, he kept a watching brief on the activities of Burmah Oil, which in 1909 had been the parent of British Petroleum and was still the largest single shareholder after the British Government, holding 23 per cent of British Petroleum ordinary shares.

The need to maintain such a watching brief arose from the fact that in the 1960s and early 1970s Burmah Oil, with the prospect — which became reality in 1963 — of having its original Burmese assets bought out by the new independent Republic of Burma, diversified into a range of oil and non-oil activities. The top management of British Petroleum was concerned at the possible conflict of interest, particularly as two Burmah Oil directors were board members. Among Burmah Oil's acquisitions were Castrol, Halfords and the US Signal Oil & Gas Co, and it also entered into substantial obligations in connection with a large tanker acquisition programme and with the interests it now had in the North Sea.

The scale of financial over-commitment, later described as injudicious, nearly proved fatal to Burmah Oil after the OPEC price rises of 1973-74 and the subsequent plunge in British stock exchange values. In December 1974, faced with the threat of having to default on some of its debts, Burmah Oil was compelled to seek a loan from the Bank of England. With government approval, the Bank provided guarantees, for a maximum of one year, but only on stringent conditions; notably, that the company's holding of British Petroleum shares should be sold outright to the Bank at the current (depressed) stock market price, and that a new chairman and board of directors should be appointed.

In January 1975 Down, a deputy chairman of British Petroleum since 1969, was chosen as the chairman of Burmah Oil. At the age of sixty he was taking on what was probably the second most arduous job in British industry at that time: second only to the chairmanship of British Leyland. 'Those who didn't say I was mad said that they admired my courage', was Down's characteristically low-key comment. He saw his role primarily as leader of a team. At a time of low morale for the company, he sought to restore to it a sense of direction. While he himself was in almost daily contact with the Department of Energy and the Bank of England, between them monitoring every major decision, his hand-picked top management team travelled the world to negotiate agreements vital to the company's survival. As the new managing director he brought in Stanley J Wilson, formerly of Mobil Oil.

For Down and his colleagues, the first priority was to decide which assets would have to be sold off, especially those likely to yield high cash proceeds and those with very heavy capital outlay commitments. They did succeed in retaining subsidiaries, such as Castrol and Halfords, that were fortifying the over-committed company with good cash flows. However, several areas were of special concern: above all the tankers and liquid natural gas carriers where substantial future expenditure could be anticipated. The process of reducing the tanker fleet from over 40 to ten by 1982 proved very costly, but by 1979 tanker operations were once more back into profit. The largest single group of assets (at nearly £300 million) were the American interests, mainly the recently purchased Signal. With the backing of the British Government, the company was able to delay the sale until a fair offer was received. That sale, and a successful negotiation over natural gas carriers, completed the company's main rescue plan, and its long-term recovery now seemed to be assured.

While working closely with the Bank of England, Burmah Oil in 1976 instituted legal proceedings against the Bank for the recovery of its former British Petroleum shares, which it claimed had been taken over at an unfair price. The consequent delay was caused by government refusal, on grounds of crown privilege, to disclose certain key documents; the company unsuccessfully contested this refusal up to the House of Lords. The case itself was held in the High Court during 1981, but was lost by

Burmah Oil, which decided not to take it to appeal. Meanwhile the company had returned to overall profitability in 1978, the year in which Down was knighted.

In February 1980, Down retired from full-time duties with the company, remaining part-time chairman while Wilson became chief executive. Down then joined the Scottish-American Investment Co Ltd and the Royal Bank of Canada as a part-time director: in 1977 he had become a non-executive (and the only non-US) director of TRW Inc of Cleveland, Ohio. He also served as honorary treasurer of the Field Studies Council from 1977 to 1981.

When he finally retired from the chairmanship in June 1983, Burmah Oil's turnover had risen from £916 million in 1975 to £1,537 million in 1982; whereas in 1975 a £24 million loss had been made, in 1982 pre-tax profits were £81 million. In 1980 he was the Hambro Businessman of the Year, and in 1981 he was awarded the Cadman Memorial Medal, presented every four years by the Institute of Petroleum for outstanding services to the oil industry. In his earlier years he had pursued the outdoor recreations of shooting, golf and fishing, but of these he enjoyed all too little during his gruelling eight and a half years with Burmah Oil.

T A B CORLEY

Sources:

Unpublished

Burmah Oil Co Annual Reports, 1974-82.

Sir Alastair Down, Address given to London Branch of Institute of Petroleum, 26 Nov 1979.

MCe.

Interview with Sir Alastair Down, 20 Dec 1983.

Published

Accountant 30 Jan 1975.

Accounting 28 Feb 1975.

BP Shield International Feb 1975.

Executive World Aug 1981.

Financial Times 24 Jan 1975, 10 Dec 1979.

Financial Weekly 29 Feb 1980.

International Management Aug 1978.

Petroleum Review 35, No 418, Nov 1981.

WW 1983.

Sir George Dowty (courtesy of Dowty Group Services Ltd).

DOWTY, Sir George Herbert

(1901-1975)

Aircraft components manufacturer

George Herbert Dowty was born at Pershore, Worcestershire, on 27 April 1901, the seventh and twin son of William Dowty, a druggist and chemist of Pershore, and his wife Laura née Masters. He was educated at the Royal Grammar School, Worcester. After technical training at the Victoria Institute, Worcester, he joined Heenan & Froude, precision engineers engaged in hydraulics, and then worked as a draughtsman with British Aerial Transport, Dunlop, and A V Roe, where he did the undercarriage for the Cierva Autogyro at the age of nineteen and the new Avro types at the rate of several a year. He learned a lot from H P Folland, then chief designer of the Gloster Co, to which he moved in the mid-1920s. There he concentrated on streamlined rubber pads for compression springs and for reducing drag; he also began to accumulate patents, and publish. From 1928 to 1931 he desperately sought financing for his ideas.

His first big break came in 1931, when at the age of thirty, he gambled on an order from Kawasaki in Japan for six pairs of his internally sprung and braked wheels, which Gloster had miscalculated in costing. He rented a loft, hired two part-time craftsmen, and made up the sets in the evenings. (And thus became the first British specialist aircraft accessory firm). Once the Japanese order was completed, he had to keep alive with a variety of odd orders for metal labels, film developing dishes, and the like, while still perfecting undercarriages. The original internally-sprung wheel was soon overtaken by the low-pressure tyre and the small wheel hub, but this led to a revival of interest in the shock-absorber strut, of which Dowty had considerable experience. At the same time wheel brakes came into use which eliminated the tailskid and called instead for shock-absorbing tailwheel struts and self-centering mechanisms. This in its turn coincided with other aspects of the technical revolution in aircraft manufacture including all-metal construction and higher wing-loadings. The result was that whereas Dowty got an order to do fixed undercarriages for the Gloster Gauntlet (1934) and the follow-on Gladiator (1937), his big coup came with the order from Sydney Camm (qv) for the retractable undercarriage for the Hawker Hurricane (1936).

About this time Dowty realised that the conventional hydraulics industry could not help the aeronautical world and he therefore moved into the field because of the power-drive needs of both undercarriages and flaps. The big problem to be solved was that of sealing high-pressure fluids at 3,000 psi, or about three times the current working pressures. Here again Dowty's knowledge of rubber and lubricants came into play and his firm began to shoot ahead. It led also to work on 'O' rings and better pistons and machining, as well as careful attention to better

George Dowty standing on an Avro Lancaster undercarriage function test rig at his company's Arle Court factory near Cheltenham, Glos. Some 22,000 Lancaster undercarriage units were produced (courtesy of Dowty Group Services Ltd).

production techniques. Ultimately these advances led to the 50,000 psi system installed in the mid-1950s in the Lockheed F-104.

By 1935 his firm was in cramped space and when the Cheltenham Council refused to allow him to expand, he got loans from his sister, Mrs Fell, and from A W Martyn of Glosters; Martyn became chairman of the company (until his death in 1947) and in September 1935 the whole firm moved to Arle Court outside Cheltenham. This became Dowty's residence and headquarters combined where most of his design work was carried out. In 1936 he converted his business into a public company, Aircraft Components Ltd, which had an authorised capital of £200,000. The private company was bought for £35,000 cash and 400,000 fully paid 5s shares of which Dowty received 222,000. At this time his salary was £1,200 per annum. In 1940 the firm's name was changed to Dowty Equipment Ltd. Dowty secured his market share by rapid innovation, registering many patents including a number for developments in liquid springs. Rearmament and the rapid expansion of the RAF created new demand for his products and made Dowty a business success, as reflected in the firm's high dividends which rose from 5 per cent in 1936-37 to 25 per cent in 1938-39 and 10 per cent in 1939-40. Expansion also forced on him mass production. Dowty was now the acknowledged expert on undercarriages and served on Royal Aeronautical Society technical committees.

Dowty's work on the hydraulic oleo leg aroused interest in the South Wales coal industry and he soon successfuly demonstrated that the same principles could be applied to pit-props, which could then be used over and over again. Once his idea was accepted, he led his team of designers and engineers to conceive of a whole roof-support system, introduced after the war (1947). In all this he was 'a benevolent employer ... a generous, friendly, but intensely demanding chief' {*Times* 9 Dec 1975}. Later he moved into railway buffers and other applications of his knowledge of shock-absorbing devices.

During the Second World War Dowty's aeronautical hydraulic work included the development of feedback systems for gun-turret controls and for the operation of variable and constant-speed propellers; this eventually led him to develop powered flying controls for jets. Another aspect of jet development was fuel metering systems, in which his company also specialised as one of the chief ancilliary firms in the British aircraft-aerospace industry. Jet-engine work started in 1943 in co-operation with de Havilland on the DH-1. The heights, speeds and temperatures of supersonic jets posed new challenges which the Dowty Group, as it was becoming, kept meeting under its leader's inspiration with equipment such as the Vapour Core pump, a constant-speed device for fuel delivery in variable quantities. But the company, hamstrung by the 100 per cent wartime profits tax, was short of cash. Dowty himself suffered nervous breakdowns.

In the 1950s further advances were made in coal-mining where again aeronautical knowledge was applied to produce not only walking supports, whose manufacture began in 1957, but also automatic, electronically-controlled mining equipment which allowed for a variable face to be worked remotely, starting in 1964. At the same time, Dowty, was involved in the development of hydraulic controls for tractors and other machinery. This in its turn led to an interest in the general problems of loading and unloading and of electro-hydraulic servo-mechanisms. His work on vibration and fatigue failures in aeronautics led him to apply the new knowledge to railways, whose main problem he came to realise was that their goods trains moved at much lower speeds than their passenger traffic. Partly through his work British Railways by 1966 were producing goods wagons capable of 150 mph speeds based upon aeronautical engineering principles.

In 1954 Dowty Group Ltd was formed to bring together all the firm's diverse interests. Dowty himself remained on the board until his death.

Dowty logo (courtesy of Dowty Group Services Ltd).

The company opened subsidiaries in Canada and the USA. Later the American factory on Long Island was closed and Canadian activity was concentrated in Ontario. Each of the subsidiary companies, such as Dowty Nucleonics, Dowty Seals, Rotol Ltd, was a separate entity with its own board of directors. Dowty also relied heavily on subcontracting. Though Dowty once said, 'Although scientific methods can be useful, I believe that business is still much more an art' {Edwards and Townsend (1961) 34}, he implemented an apprenticeship programme and recruited graduates.

Outside his own firm, Dowty was chairman of the Industrial Development Board for Malta, 1960-63, succeeding Lord Hives (qv); and then chairman of Boulton Paul in 1968.

Dowty's own achievements were recognised in 1937 with the award of the Edward Busk Memorial Prize and in 1955 of the Royal Aeronautical Society gold medal for the Advancement of Aeronautics. He became a member of the council of the Royal Aeronautical Society in 1946 and president in 1952-53. He was vice-president and then president of the Society of British Aerospace Companies, 1960-61, and treasurer of the SBAC, 1961-68. He was also honoured in his own locality with the freedom of Cheltenham (1955) and Tewkesbury (1964). A DL of Gloucestershire, he was knighted in 1956.

Like many engineers, Dowty seems to have been apolitical; he also seems to have had no known religious preference. He was a close friend of Sir Roy Fedden (qv) with whom he had a long association because of their working proximity — and they occasionally went fishing together, though it is not clear that Sir George fished. His recreations were bloodstock breeding, cricket, curling (he captained England in 1962), tennis, snooker, golf, and work. He married in 1948 at the age of forty-seven Mrs Annie B Lockie of Canada; they had one son and one daughter. Sir George Dowty died on the Isle of Man, 7 December 1975, at the age of seventy-four.

ROBIN HIGHAM

Writings:

'Development and Organisation of the Dowty Group Limited', in Ronald S Edwards and Harry Townsend (eds), *Studies in Business Organisation* (Macmillan, 1961).

'Aviation the Pacemaker' *Centenary Journal, Royal Aeronautical Society, 1866-1966* (Royal Aeronautical Society 1966).

Sources:

Unpublished

BCe.

Published

Bill Gunston, *By Jupiter! The Life of Sir Roy Fedden* (The Royal Aeronautical Society, 1978).

Sir Robert Hunt, 'The Life and Work of Sir George Dowty' *Aerospace* Nov-Dec 1981.

Derek N James, *Gloster Aircraft since 1917* (Putnam, 1971).

Lionel T C Rolt, *The Dowty Story* (Newman Neame, 1962).

Times 9 Dec 1975.

Times *Prospectuses* 91 (1936).

WWW.

DOXFORD, Sir William Theodore

(1841-1916)

Shipbuilder

Sir W T Doxford (courtesy of J F Clarke).

William Theodore Doxford was born at Bishopwearmouth, County Durham near Sunderland on 1 February 1841, the first of four sons in a family of ten of the merchant shipwright William Doxford and his wife Hannah (1814-95), daughter of a glassworker, Robert Pile. Within a few months of his birth his father was declared bankrupt on the failure of the small wood shipbuilding yard which he worked in partnership with a fellow shipwright called Crown. Doxford Sr returned to work at his trade as a craftsman but was able to re-establish the partnership in 1845 and this time it survived until 1851, when once more it seems William Doxford returned to working as a shipwright and some time as a timber merchant. In 1858 Doxford Sr opened a shipyard at Pallion on the south bank of the River Wear, where he was joined by the young William Theodore, whose previous education was described as at Bramham College. The shipyard made very modest progress until in 1864 Doxfords joined the other three Sunderland yards that were building in iron. Within five years the site at Pallion was extended. Output in 1864 was 3,109 tons and eight years later reached 9,574 tons.

In order to build its own marine engines in 1878 the Doxfords erected engine and boiler shops and a younger brother, Robert Pyle (1851-1932), who had learned his engineering under William Allan at the Scotia works, took charge of this part of the business. When William Doxford Sr died in 1882, aged seventy years, all four sons were involved in the management of the business. Soon afterwards the output of the shipyard was challenging for the leading position on the River Wear.

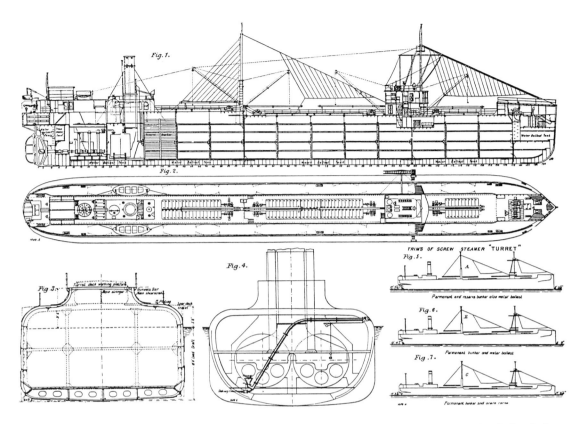

Plan of the screw steamer 'Turret' constructed by Messrs William Doxford & Sons Ltd, Sunderland taken from Engineer *26 May 1893 (courtesy of J F Clarke).*

Doxfords' management were always prepared to encourage initiatives and in 1875 they built their first naval vessels. Twelve years later the company installed oil burning boilers, something of a novelty, in a torpedo boat, but failed to sell the idea to the Admiralty. William Theodore was the key figure in the family management, although the technical ideas came from a variety of sources — technical staff as well as management. The introduction of the 'turret ship' in 1891 proved both popular and profitable. That year a limited liability company was formed, with a capital of £200,000, all owned by the Doxfords.

The yard launched more than 106,000 tons of shipping in 1906, while in the years 1905 and 1907 the company built a greater tonnage than any other shipyard in Britain. Untypically of the industry, the firm devoted resources to research and one of the outcomes was the Doxford diesel engine, one of the very few successful British designs of this type of engine for marine work. Under the engineer K O Keller, design and experimental work started in 1906 and by 1914 there was a successful trial engine. By 1914 profit was £161,000 and the company's capital £450,000.

Doxford was deeply concerned with labour relations; his own family background made him very well aware of the hardships arising from

Drawing of SS 'Turret Age' taken from Shipping World *1 September 1893 (courtesy of J F Clarke).*

fluctuations in the shipbuilding trade. He was a firm but fair employer and played a major role in the successful operation of the Conciliation Board established at Sunderland during the depths of the depression in November 1885. A profound understanding of the essential principle of conciliation was shown by Doxford, in his evidence to the Royal Commission on Labour in 1892, when having pointed out that there were no means 'of enforcing decisions' he continued 'personally I think that position is better than if we had . . . power to compel compliance' {*PP*, RC Labour (1892) C 6894, 429}. He was 'very strongly in favour of strong unions, both on the part of the men and the employers' and said 'the stronger the unions are the less likely there will be strikes' {*ibid*, p 431}. Always active in the employers organisations, Doxford frequently represented Wearside on the National Federation of Shipbuilding Employers and was chairman of the Wear Shipbuilders' Association from 1908 to 1912.

A Unionist in politics, in 1895 he became the first Conservative MP to be elected in Sunderland for forty years; knighted in 1900, he retired from parliament in 1906. He was actively involved in local affairs, serving on the Sunderland Town Council and as a River Wear Commissioner as well as being a magistrate in both the town of Sunderland and County of Durham; he was also a DL of the county.

Doxford was a foundation member and second president of the North-East Coast Institution of Engineers and Shipbuilders; he joined the Institution of Naval Architects in 1878, was elected a Council member in 1896 and vice-president in 1908. The latter's obituary notice described

Doxford as being 'associated with all the principal developments in shipbuilding and marine engineering from the days of wooden ships' {*Transactions of the Institution of Naval Architects* 49 (1917) 233}. Doxford contributed greatly to the work of both institutions and was a very frequent contributor to discussions.

In 1863 he married Margaret, daughter of Richard Wilkinson, a Sunderland shipbuilder; they had one son and five daughters. The son, Albert Ernest Doxford (1868-1937), played an important part in managing the business; in 1916 the *Shipbuilder* described Doxfords as 'one of the few large concerns that can still lay claim to have a purely family executive' {*Shipbuilder* (1916) II 163-4 }. Still head of the firm, Sir William Theodore Doxford died on 1 October 1916, less than three months after his wife; he left an estate valued at £153,946 gross.

JOE F CLARKE

Writings:

Presidential address *Transactions of the North East Coast Institution of Engineers and Shipbuilders* 3 (1886).

Presidential address *ibid* 4 (1887).

Address *Transactions of the Institution of Naval Architects* 29 (1888).

PP, RC on Labour (1892) C6894.

Sources:

Unpublished

Sunderland Public Library, Corder MSS.

Tyne and Wear Archives, papers of the Wear Shipbuilders Association.

BCe.

MCe.

PrC.

Joseph F Clarke, 'Labour Relations in Engineering and Shipbuilding on the North-East Coast ca 1850-1906' (Newcastle upon Tyne MA, 1967).

Published

Joseph F Clarke, 'Shipbuilding on the River Wear 1780-1870' in R W Sturgess (ed), *The Great Age of Industry in the North East* (1981).

David Dougan, *The History of North East Shipbuilding* (Allen & Unwin, 1968).

Shipbuilder 1916, II.

J W Smith and T S Holden, *Where Ships are Born* (Sunderland: Thomas Reed & Co, 1946).

Sunderland Echo 2 Oct 1916.

Transactions of the North East Coast Institution of Engineers and Shipbuilders 33 (1916-17).

WWMP.

WWW.

Sir Eric Drake CBE, chairman of the British Petroleum Co Ltd, 1970 (courtesy of British Petroleum Company plc).

DRAKE, Sir Arthur Eric Courtney

(1910-)

Petroleum company executive

Arthur Eric Courtney Drake was born in Rochester, Kent, on 29 November 1910, the eldest son of Dr Arthur William Courtney Drake, a surgeon, and his wife Ethel née Davidson. He was educated at Shrewsbury School and Pembroke College, Cambridge, where he read modern languages and law and where he was a prominent oarsman. A member of the Leander Club, he rowed in winning boats at Henley and was in the successful London Rowing Club crew which visited Australia for the Melbourne Centenary Celebrations in 1934. Meantime he qualified as a chartered accountant and gained the William Quilter prize of the Institute of Chartered Accountants of England and Wales.

After meeting Sir John Cadman (qv) on his return journey from Melbourne he joined the Anglo-Persian Oil Co (hereafter the Company but APOC until 1935, then the Anglo-Iranian Oil Co until 1955 and the British Petroleum Co thereafter) in 1935 as an accountant. In 1938 he was posted to Abadan. Postings to Kirmanshah and Bombay followed before he returned to Abadan where he received his first managerial appointment in 1942 as the refinery's commercial superintendent. In 1946-49 he was commercial manager of Iran and Iraq and acting manager in Baghdad. At this time he negotiated a wayleave through Syria for a pipeline from the Persian Gulf to the Mediterranean as well as a refining concession in Syria, but neither the pipeline nor the refinery was ever built.

Drake returned to head office briefly in 1949-50 before returning to Persia to act as principal assistant to the Chief Representative of the Company in Tehran. By the end of that year unexpectedly he was posted general manager in Iran and Iraq, the most prestigious overseas appointment at that time. It was a period of deteriorating relations between the Company and the Persian Government which culminated in the nationalisation of Persian Oil in May 1951 and, after a series of incidents and negotiating failures, the Company was obliged to cease operations. In the midst of these activities Drake found his position untenable following the passage of an anti-sabotage bill in the Persian Parliament and left Iran for Basra on 27 June 1951. Returning to London he was called to a meeting of the Cabinet on the crisis in Abadan in July. It had been a disappointing experience and left Drake with bitter memories.

Nevertheless, whatever the circumstances of his frustration, Drake was an ambitious, not to say, pugnacious personality and took the challenge in his stride. Recovering from his ordeal and receiving confidence from his management, he was sent to Australia on an important mission to negotiate with the Commonwealth and Western Australia Governments for an agreement to build a refinery at Kwinana, which he accomplished successfully in a shorter time than was expected. During 1952-54 he was the Company's Representative in North America where he obtained first-hand experience of the American oil industry and its leading personalities. Now with a far better appreciation of the international aspects of the oil business, he was well fitted for his next position.

This was as a general manager in head office in charge of the newly-formed Supply and Development Department, which was created from a merger of the previous Petroleum Supply and Central Planning Departments. Drake admitted to knowing little about the subject, but it was a vital appointment. The loss of crude oil production from Persia and refined products from Abadan created an enormous supply problem and though losses were made good from elsewhere, notably Kuwait, the Persian Gulf and Iraq, the supply system based on new refineries and different transportation patterns was not operationally efficient. It was necessary to develop an integrated strategy involving different crudes, various refineries, tanker runs and consumer needs in the most economical manner to maximise the returns for the least cost. It was a worldwide exercise requiring detailed statistical information, logical and practical planning and knowledgeable experience about market demands for a wide range of products. Within two years the Suez Crisis had put the team to the test of an emergency situation from which it emerged commendably adaptable. A generation of Company managers owed their subsequent senior appointments to the experience gained in this control of operations which was intellectually stimulating and commercially crucial as the margins of profitability were beginning to contract. During the Suez crisis Drake served as vice-president of the oil industry's committee to implement recommendations on the sharing out of available supplies. This was not only a multi-disciplinary undertaking, but one of international co-operation.

By now Drake's business interests were widening and in 1958 he was appointed a managing director and became a member of the Council of the Chamber of Shipping, becoming president in 1964. His shipping responsibilities in the Company increased and these were reflected in his membership of the General Committee of Lloyd's Register of Shipping since 1960, and the Ministry of Transport Shipping Advisory Panel, 1962-64.

Drake became deputy chairman of the Company in 1962. In 1969 he went to Washington in connection with American objections over the Company's acquisiton of Sinclair Oil Co assets which had been ruled illegal by the Antitrust Division of the Department of Justice. Drake

Sir Eric Drake chairman of BP discussing an area map of roads linking the drilling sites during his visit to BPs operations in Alaska, April 1969 (courtesy of British Petroleum Company plc).

challenged the Attorney-General, John Mitchell, as a result of which a satisfactory settlement was reached generally preserving the Company's position. On the retirement of Sir Maurice Bridgeman (qv), Drake succeeded him as chairman in 1969 and in 1971 became deeply involved in industry discussions with the Organisation of Petroleum Exporting Countries (OPEC), which had been formed in 1960 to protect the interests of the 'host' countries. In 1973 he was engaged in a controversial conflict with the Prime Minister, Edward Heath, when he refused, without a specific government directive empowering him so to do, to divert supplies of contracted oil shipments to the United Kingdom rather than their scheduled destinations elsewhere. Perhaps the highlight of Drake's time as chairman was the inauguration by the Queen on 3 November 1975 of production from the Forties Field, the first oil to be landed from the first major oil field discovered in the British sector of the North Sea.

As chairman of British Petroleum, Drake set himself four principal objectives: firstly, to decentralise managerial responsibilities so that each part of the operations was accountable for its affairs; secondly to end the association with Shell in the UK marketing company, Shell-Mex & BP; thirdly to diversify away from dependence on Middle East sources of crude oil; and fourthly to reduce the Burmah stockholding in British Petroleum. He was a forceful chairman. For his services in Persia he was made CBE in 1952. He was knighted in 1970.

Since retirement in 1975, Sir Eric has held a number of directorships including P&O and the Toronto-Dominion Bank. He has been a member of the Committee on Invisible Exports in 1969-75; of the governing body of Shrewsbury School, 1969; of the Committee of Management, Royal Naval Lifeboat Institution 1975; of the Court of City University, 1969 (life member); and of the City and Guilds Insignia Award Association, 1971-75. In addition he has been honorary Petroleum Adviser to the British Army, 1971; honorary member of the Honourable Company of Master Mariners, 1972; honorary Elder Brother of Trinity House, 1975; freeman of the City of London, 1974; honorary fellow of Pembroke College, 1976; chairman, Mary Rose Trust, 1979. He also served on the board of governors of Pangbourne Nautical College, 1958-69, and the Court of Governors, London School of Economics and Political Science, 1963-74. In 1971 he received the Hambro British Businessman of the Year award and an honorary DSc from Cranfield College. The following foreign honours have been bestowed on him; Commander, Ordre de la Couronne, Belgium, 1969; Knight Grand Cross of Order of Merit, Italy, 1970; Officier, Légion d'Honneur, France, 1972; Order of Homayoun, Iran, 1974; Commander, Ordre de Leopold, Belgium, 1975. He is also DL for Hampshire (1983-) and one of HM Lieutenants for the City of London.

Sir Eric's recreational activities have been dominated by sailing. He was married twice, firstly in 1935 to Rosemary Moore, by whom he had two daughters, and secondly in 1950 to Margaret Elizabeth Wilson, by whom he had two sons.

R W FERRIER

Sources:

Unpublished

BCe.

MCe.

Published

BP Shield International Nov 1975.

WW 1982.

Harley Drayton (courtesy of the BET Federation).

DRAYTON, Harold Charles Gilbert

(1901-1966)

Transport financier

Harold Charles Gilbert Drayton, later nicknamed 'Harley', was born at Streatham, London, on 19 November 1901, elder of the two sons of Bob Gilbert Drayton, a gardener with the London County Council, and his wife Annie née Keep. The two boys were very young when their mother died and they were thereafter mostly brought up in the Croydon home of Alexander Low, a Scottish sanitary inspector, one of whose daughters Harley Drayton later married.

At the age of thirteen and having read little more than the Bible, Drayton got his first job as an office boy with the Government Stocks & Other Securities Investment Co, London, one of the dozen investment companies run by Viscount St Davids (qv). In 1920 Government Securities bought British Electric Traction, then chiefly operating trams and electric light undertakings. Drayton's abilities were soon noticed by J S Austen, a solicitor and St Davids' close associate and chairman of BET, 1921-42. He befriended and encouraged Drayton. Austen and Drayton managed the St Davids investment group from 117 Old Broad Street and through it Drayton emerged as a powerful if shadowy figure. By 1933 he was a director of Government Securities and succeeded Austen (who became chairman) as manager in 1938. While Drayton's financial power was over-stated in the popular press of the time, his personal qualities were remarkable, especially his retentive memory and encyclopaedic knowledge of financial and company information.

Drayton became a director of some 40 companies, and by no means all were confined to transport. His group included Provincial Newspapers and Mitchell Cotts, while outside it he was a director of Eagle Star Insurance and from 1948 of the Midland Bank, of which another of his mentors, Alexander Roger (qv), was already a director. Drayton was a director of the Grand Union Canal from 1934 and of Ideal Building & Land Development from 1937. Among the smaller companies that he nursed to maturity was the engineering firm of Acrow.

Austen and St Davids had invested in South American railways, and in 1935 Drayton became a director of the Antofagasta (Chile) & Bolivia Railway, and of the associated Chilean Northern Railway and the Andes Trust, eventually becoming its chairman. As a director of the Buenos Aires & Pacific Railway, in 1943 he also joined the boards of the Central Argentine Railway and the Buenos Aires Great Southern Railway as part of the policy of greater co-ordination between Anglo-Argentine broad gauge railways. He was also chairman of the Costa Rica Railway. During the Second World War Drayton was one of the three British commissioners sent to the Argentine to start negotiations for the sale for over £150 million of the country's three principal railway companies to the Argentine Government.

Meantime J S Austen had developed BET into a holding company of national significance in road passenger transport, and in 1933 he secured a place for Drayton on the BET board. His impact was quickly felt when he began to diversify away from road transport undertakings, commencing with the purchase of Advance Laundries, prompting Austen to tell the shareholders 'we have taken in a little washing'. After Lord St Davids died in 1938 and Austen in 1942, Drayton became de facto head of the St Davids group. In 1946 Drayton succeeded R J Howley (qv) as chairman of BET. He remained in the chair until his death; though the running of the bus business was left to John Spencer Wills (qv).

While BET chairman, Drayton took two major decisions: he successfully resisted nationalisation of the buses and he backed independent television. Under the terms of the Transport Act, 1947, the newly-created British Transport Commission acquired the railway companies, the canals and all road hauliers working more than 25 miles from their base. To many people's surprise, the bus industry was not included in these clauses of the Act, but the Commission had the duty to prepare 'Area Schemes' for the public ownership of road passenger transport, and the ability to acquire operating companies in advance of the publication of such Schemes. This they quickly did, when BET's rival holding company, Thomas Tilling Ltd, agreed in September 1948 to sell the whole of its interests to the Commission. The Commission settled with Tillings for the sum of £24.8 million, and the City took note. By the summer of 1949 the Scottish holding company, Scottish Motor Traction Group also sold their inland transport investments to the Commission, as did the 'third force' in England and Wales, Red & White United Transport, and several individual companies of standing. The City did its sums, and waited for news of the sale of BET, encouraged by the sale to the Commission of a road haulage group, Transport Services Ltd, of which Drayton was also chairman. It seems to have escaped the financial press that the Act provided for compulsory purchase of road haulage companies only, and the pundits were, therefore, surprised when Drayton and his board resisted all advice and pressure to sell the bus interests. In July 1949 shareholders were told that these interests were making a better return on the company's investment than it could expect from the interest on the purchase price. This, however, was not the whole of the argument. When Drayton asked the shareholders to support the view of the board that nationalisation should be opposed in principle, he was perfectly sincere. He had played a great part in the City's money-making activities, but there is no doubt that he had a sincere belief in the virtues of the market and the positive contribution of its financial institutions to the prosperity of the nation, though this did not blind him to the value of statutory protection for bus operators. The shareholders backed him and BET was never nationalised. When the first Area Scheme was promulgated in the North-East, BET joined the Labour-controlled municipalities in opposing it, but the scheme faded away in due course after the change of Government in 1951.

After 1948 Drayton became interested in television and films. He became chairman of the British Lion Film Corporation, and in 1956 financed the development of commercial television, including Associated Rediffusion, which lost £6 million in its first two years but by 1962 made £7 million a year, which justified Drayton's characteristic persistence.

Drayton was a formidable personality: drawing on his pipe he would make quick decisions which he supported with obstinacy and courage. And he was a man whose interests were not bounded by the world of high finance. He deeply regretted the failure of the British Government to take part in the formation of the Common Market in 1955-57, and was treasurer of the United Kingdom Council of the European Movement. Politically a Liberal, Drayton was involved by Lord St Davids in the portfolio management of the Lloyd George Political Fund in the inter-war period, and is reputed to have made a great success of it. Drayton became president of the Free Trade Club in 1943 and unsuccessfully contested Bury St Edmunds as a Free Trade Liberal in the general election of 1945. Most of the provincial newspapers acquired by his holding company, United Newspapers, were traditionally Liberal free traders in editorial policy. United Newspapers acted closely with his printers, the Argus Press.

Harley Drayton inherited Plumpton Hall, south of Bury St Edmunds, from J S Austen, and at weekends became a countryman and a serious farmer: pampering his pigs and dispensing claret after his shooting parties, reading the lesson in the parish church and enjoying the country-squire life on his 700 acre estate. His links with East Anglia led him in due course to take an active part in the foundation of its university at Norwich. He was High Sheriff of Suffolk in 1957. He collected illuminated manuscripts and early maps, and had what may have been a unique collection of first editions of Daniel Defoe.

He married in 1926 Christine Collie Low. They had no children but the marriage was very happy and Drayton carried on much of his business at Plumpton and at his London home at 20 Kensington Palace Gardens. Harley Drayton died of lung cancer on 7 April 1966, leaving £2,121,321 gross.

JOHN HIBBS

Writings:

PP, RC on Press (1947-48) Cmd 7448.

Sources:

Unpublished

BCe.

MCe.

PrC.

Information from Sir John Spencer Wills.

Published

Commercial Motor 15 Apr 1966.

DNB.

Charles S Dunbar, *The Rise of Road Transport, 1919-1939* (I Allan, 1981).

Roger Fulford, *The Sixth Decade* (BET house history, pp, 1956).

Financial Times 9 Apr 1966.

Charles F Klapper, *Golden Age of Buses* (Routledge & Kegan Paul, 1978).

Anthony T S Sampson, *Anatomy of Britain* (Hodder & Stoughton, 1962).

—, *Anatomy of Britain Today* (Hodder & Stoughton, 1965).

Stock Exchange Yearbook, 1920-45.

WWW.

DREW, Julius Charles

(1856-1931)

Multiple store retailer

Julius Charles Drew was born at Pulloxhill near Ampthill on 4 April 1856. His father was Rev George Smith Drew, vicar of Pulloxhill, an Evangelical Anglican clergyman and Hulsean lecturer at Cambridge in 1877 and the son of George Drew, a Marylebone tea broker. His mother was Mary Peek, first cousin of Sir Henry W Peek Bt, MP (1825-98), head of Messrs Peek Bros & Co of Eastcheap, also in the tea trade.

After schooling in Bournemouth, Drew joined the firm of Peek & Winch, tea importers established in Liverpool by his mother's brother, Francis Peek. The firm sent him to China as a tea buyer.

After a few years in the tea importing business, Drew returned home and moved into retailing. In 1878 he opened a tea shop of his own in Liverpool. Evidently he was attracted by the growing demand for tea related to rising Victorian prosperity, which was then lifting the tea businesses of Richard Twining III (qv) and Arthur Brooke (qv). Five years later Drew took a partner, John Musker, and moved to London where his elder brother, William Francis Drew, practised as a barrister of the Inner Temple.

J C Drew's tea business expanded into groceries so promisingly that in March 1885 he and Musker formed the Home & Colonial Trading Association, Drew being the 'controller and chief shareholder' {Mathias (1967) 126}. Drew's legal adviser in launching the Home & Colonial was his brother-in-law William Capel Slaughter (qv), a solicitor who had recently qualified with Ashhurst, Morris, Crisp & Co, City solicitors, and now had a partnership of his own with William May.

At this point the business operated two types of shop: 'a few large, prestige stores stocking a wide variety of lines, and then a larger number of smaller specialist shops on the customary multiple shop lines, known as 'tea stores'' {*ibid*, 126}. While most branches were opened in the London area, Drew envisaged a national network of multiple shops and by 1888 had followed his original shop and headquarters at 268 Edgware Road with three other large stores, in Birmingham, Leeds and Islington (the other end of London) as well as nine smaller tea stores. Supplies of tea came through the Mincing Lane auctions and the contacts which Drew had developed in the East.

Then abruptly, five years after moving to London, Drew left the management of the Home & Colonial Trading Association. The firm in 1888 was converted to a private limited company, Home & Colonial Stores Ltd, with an authorised capital of £200,000, under the chairmanship and management of his brother-in-law, W C Slaughter. Drew remained a director and held a majority of the 150,000 ordinary £1 shares.

Julius Drew's achievement was remarkable. After only fifteen years in business he had accumulated sufficient personal wealth to retire in style. Now a wealthy rentier in his mid-thirties, Drew was clearly anxious to complement economic position with social status, a quest that would consume him and much of his fortune for the next forty years. He began by joining the ranks of gentleman landowners. He bought Culverdon Castle at Tunbridge Wells in 1890, then moved to Wadhurst Hall, a huge house just over the Sussex border, becoming a Sussex JP in 1900. Next he turned to his pedigree. His brother William produced a genealogical tree which showed them descending from the Norman Drews (or Drus or Drogo) of Broadhembury near Honiton in Devon. Julius therefore bought a farmhouse nearby and installed William in it. Then in an act of grandiose social display, he set about restoring the lost family estate. On what he conceived to be the land of his ancestors (an estate eventually totalling 1,500 acres) overlooking the steep gorge of the River Teign near Drewsteignton, Drew built a ponderous, solid granite (in some places six feet thick) castle. Imposing his preferences on the architect, Edward Lutyens (qv), Drew made his Castle Drogo a combination of medieval castle and Tudor home, but with twentieth century comforts. Started in 1911, with a budget of £60,000, it took nearly twenty years to build. As late as 1923 Drewe (he changed his name to its older form by deed poll in 1910) still recorded his seat as Wadhurst Hill, Sussex.

Julius Drew in 1890 married Frances Richardson, daughter of Thomas Richardson, a Buxton cotton manufacturer, Thomas Richardson; they had three sons, Adrian (1891-1917) killed in Flanders while serving in the Royal Field Artillery; Basil (1894-1974); and Cedric (1896-1971); and two daughters, Mary and Frances.

Julius Drew died on 10 November 1931, leaving an estate of £207,700 gross.

DAVID J JEREMY

Sources:

Unpublished

BCe.

MCe.

PrC.

Published

Colin Amery and Margaret Richardson (eds), *Lutyens. The Work of the English Architect Sir Edwin Lutyens* (Arts Council of Great Britain, 1981).

Burke's Landed Gentry 1906, 1937.

Kelly's Handbook to the Titled, Landed and Official Classes for 1924 (Kelly's Directories Ltd, 1923).

Peter Mathias, *Retailing Revolution. A History of Multiple Retailing in the Food Trade. Based upon the Allied Suppliers Group of Companies* (Longman, 1967).

Daniell O'Neill, *Lutyens: Country Houses* (Lund Humphries Publishers Ltd, 1980).

Michael Trinick, *Castle Drogo* (Exeter: National Trust, 1982).

WWMP.

DREYFUS, Henry

(1882-1944)

Chemical manufacturer

Henri (later Henry) Dreyfus came of French Alsatian Jewish origins and was born in January 1882 in Switzerland, the son of Abraham Dreyfus. Trained as a chemist, he held a doctorate of the University of Basle. In 1912, in conjunction with his elder brother, Camille, and a silk dyer, Alexander Clavel, he set up in Basle a company for the manufacture of cellulose acetate and other chemicals. Cellulose acetate, since its initial discovery in 1865, had been the subject of various patents for various uses: as a basis for cinematograph film, for paints and varnishes including 'dope' used for treating the outer skin of early aircraft, or for spinning into artificial silk. Dreyfus was amongst those who took out such patents though they were hotly contested, both then and later, on the ground that they lacked originality. In particular, they were rejected in Germany. Whatever Dreyfus's claims to originality as an inventor, the fact remained that at the outbreak of the First World War the sole sources of 'dope' available to the Allied powers were a firm in France and the Dreyfus plant in Switzerland. In 1915 the British War Office accepted a tender from the Dreyfus firm to supply dope; and in 1916 the Dreyfus brothers and Clavel came to Britain and, in conjunction with other capitalists, set up the British Cellulose & Chemical Manufacturing Co Ltd. Land was purchased at Spondon, near Derby, and work began on the erection of a factory to manufacture cellulose acetate dope and related chemical products. With the aid of tax concessions and loans from the Government, together with the financial involvement of a group of explosives manufacturers, production finally started in 1917. So too did trouble for the company in the form of complaints about further delays, about the government-supported monopoly which it had secured, and about some dubious share-pushing and speculation.

Dreyfus's name first came into the public eye in Britain in the course of 1918-19 when a House of Commons Select Committee followed by a special tribunal set up by the Government reported on the doings of the company in connection with what had come to be called 'The Dope Scandal'. However, the company survived, the adverse publicity died down, and in 1920 it was launched as a public company with the stated intention of making artificial silk by the cellulose acetate process. In the following year it began to market the yarn under the name of 'Celanese' and in 1923 the company changed its name to British Celanese Ltd. By 1927 Henry Dreyfus had become chairman and managing director. (His brother Camille, meanwhile, had moved into a comparable position in the Celanese Corporation of America which he had started in 1918, though also remaining on the board of the British company; a Canadian Celanese company was set up in 1926.) In the course of the 1920s and 1930s Henry Dreyfus built up the Spondon plant of British Celanese Ltd into a remarkable example of a vertically integrated chemical-textile concern, undertaking the basic chemical processes, the spinning of yarn, weaving, knitting and dyeing, and the manufacture of garments. A vigorous selling and advertising campaign ensured that 'Celanese' became a household name in Britain in the 1930s, especially in its use for women's underwear. Dreyfus was at pains to try to distinguish his product from viscose rayon. He was not ultimately successful in this but certainly in Britain (as in the USA and Canada) Celanese made remarkable strides in the rayon market generally; and his company dominated acetate yarn output in the inter-war years.

There seems little doubt that it was Henry Dreyfus himself, as both entrepreneur and technical expert, who gave to British Celanese the dynamic qualities which it exhibited at that time. But the price of his contribution was high. Autocratic and difficult to work with, his brash optimism, disregard of costs and extravagant pursuit of goals gave British Celanese a chaotic financial history and a disastrous profit record. The need to repay government loans together with the high development costs in the early 1920s saddled the company with a large proportion of preference capital and a heavy burden of debt on mortgage debentures. Outside interests were perforce brought in to provide finance but the

Dreyfus brothers between them managed to obtain a controlling interest and in 1927, to the accompaniment of speculation, public rows and threats of legal action, ousted the outsiders. Despite a substantial rise in sales and trading profits, however, preference dividends remained in arrears and no dividend was ever paid on the ordinary shares until 1944.

As if all this were not enough, the personal qualities which Henry Dreyfus brought to bear upon business life also included a pugnacious determination to defend his patents at all costs. But just as the Germans had rejected his original patents, so did others doubt the validity of later patents which he took out. A Belgian court decided against him in 1927. Undeterred, in 1931 he issued writs against Courtaulds and two other British companies for infringement of patents. Judgement was given against him in 1933 and it was upheld by the Court of Appeal and then by the House of Lords in 1935. Still undeterred, Dreyfus persisted in further litigation, this time alleging false evidence. Again he lost but prepared to go to appeal. By this time, 1937, an incensed body of shareholders calling themselves the British Celanese Shareholders Union had come into being. In October 1937 Dreyfus withdrew his appeal. Attempts were made to secure an understanding with Courtaulds; they led to merger negotiations but these were abandoned in 1940. British Celanese was finally taken over by Courtaulds in 1957.

Dreyfus in 1938 married Elizabeth Deborah Jenkinson, daughter of John Banks Jenkinson 'captain in the Rifle Brigade' {MCe}.

Henry Dreyfus died on 30 December 1944, depriving his company of an unusual though controversial entrepreneur. His will was proved at £2,499,492 gross. To die a millionaire and to have failed to pay any dividend to one's ordinary shareholders for two decades is in itself quite an achievement. He left everything to his brother Camille.

D C COLEMAN

Sources:

Unpublished

MCe.

PrC.

Published

Donald C Coleman, *Courtaulds. An Economic and Social History* (3 vols, Oxford: Clarendon Press, 1969-80).

—, 'War Demand and Industrial Supply: the "Dope Scandal", 1915-19' in Jay M Winter (ed), *War and Economic Development* (Cambridge: Cambridge University Press, 1975).

Economist, passim.

WWW.

DRUMMOND, Dugald

(1840-1912)

Railway engineer

Dugald Drummond was born at Ardrossan, Ayrshire, on 2 January 1840, the son of George Drummond, a permanent way inspector on the Bowling & Balloch Railway (subsequently the North British Railway) and Christina née Thomson. He was apprenticed with Forrest & Barr, general engineers and millwrights, Glasgow, then worked on the Bowling & Balloch line, followed by two years at the Canada Works, Birkenhead, of Peto, Brassey & Betts which built locomotives for domestic and overseas railways. One major influence upon Drummond's subsequent career as a locomotive engineer was William Stroudley (qv) with whom he worked at the Cowlairs depot, Glasgow, of the Edinburgh & Glasgow Railway (subsequently North British Railway) in 1864. Both had a disagreement with S W Johnson, the works manager, whose episcopalian allegiance irked Drummond, and they took employment at Inverness in the Highland Railway shops. Initially Drummond was appointed as foreman-erector but he became works manager in 1866. Stroudley went to the London, Brighton & South Coast Railway in 1869 taking the post of locomotive, carriage and wagon superintendent. He was soon joined by Drummond who became works manager. Although of opposite characters (Drummond was noisy and tough) there developed a famous professional friendship between the two engineers which was cemented at Brighton.

Drummond began his own independent career in 1875 when he returned to Cowlairs as the locomotive, carriage and wagon superintendent for the North British Railway. Straight away he introduced Stroudley practice by both standardising locomotive parts and, at least initially, closely following Brighton locomotive designs. Stroudley's influence continued on through Drummond's successors at Cowlairs and on the Caledonian Railway and was even felt on the Highland and the Glasgow & South Western Railway through Drummond's brother Peter. However Drummond also began to develop his own design style at Cowlairs, evidenced in 1876 by the construction of a 4-4-0 express engine which subsequently became his standard type. As with the transfer of Stroudley practice, this too was closely copied by his brother, by Matthew Holmes and W P Reid who followed Drummond on the North British, and by J Lambie and J F MacIntosh on the Caledonian.

In 1882 Drummond was appointed as the locomotive superintendent of the Caledonian Railway. He came with a reputation as a perfectionist in engineering detail but he soon showed that he had his own important ideas about the development capacity of the steam locomotive. These were revealed in his 6 feet 6 inches 4-4-0 class, built by Neilson & Co, which was one of the really outstanding locomotive designs of the late nineteenth century. Its cylinders anticipated Churchward's developments twenty years later, but their design features were not fully displayed in the 1880s in terms of economy and power, as they called for new handling methods by the footplate men. Drummond's influence at St Rollox went beyond locomotive design; he introduced on the Caledonian automatic continuous brakes, steam heating for carriages and gas lighting on passenger trains. Equally important as his development work on engines and rolling stock was his flair for production engineering in its widest sense. He realised important economies for the Caledonian by concentrating the company's locomotive shops at St Rollox, which involved a new layout and new machinery, and through changes in light engine and rolling stock movement. His major contributions to the company were recognised by substantial salary increases in 1884 and 1888. At St Rollox Drummond first came into contact with Robert Urie who was to be his own protégé. In the 1880s Urie was initially Drummond's chief draughtsman and then works manager.

Drummond left the Caledonian in 1890 following a proposal to act as the engineer for a syndicate which was going to build locomotives in Australia. When these arrangements fell through, he set up as a consulting engineer and opened with his son, George, the Glasgow Railway Engineering Co, Govan. Drummond hoped that this firm would receive orders from the railway companies which had previously employed him but he was a tough, if not rough, man and had bruised many of his past acquaintances. This was one reason for the limited success of his engineering enterprise. Another contributory factor may have been the depression of the early 1890s, following the Baring crisis. The works did build locomotives until 1901, mainly industrial engines, but thereafter concentrated on rolling stock parts, some in conjunction with Beardmores. George Drummond took over the management of the undertaking and it survived until 1958.

In 1895 Drummond took the post of locomotive superintendent for the London & South Western Railway at a salary of £1,500, which was increased to £2,000 a year later. His arrival at Nine Elms led to an immediate shake-up of the personnel followed by an influx of Scots, including Rober Urie as works manager. Drummond's now-established design style of inside cylinders with an 'American' wheel layout was repeated for his new employers and his crowning achievement was the T9 4-4-0 express class. At Nine Elms and for the first time in his career Drummond experimented. He had always favoured simple rather than compound engines, frowning on Webb's designs, but his first express engine for the London & South Western was a hybrid 4-2-2-0 'double single' which made its appearance in 1897. It suffered from a shortage of steam and slipping driving wheels, faults which were not rectified by a new boiler and cylinders. Obstinacy came more and more to the fore in Drummond's character and despite the lack of success he built five similar engines in 1901. The majority of his ideas were excellent in theory but often failed to achieve their potential in actual running while complicating locomotive maintenance. The most appreciated by the footplate men were his accurate steam reverser and balanced regulator.

Drummond tried to meet the problems of branch line working, the economics of which were being seriously affected from the turn of the century by road transport, in two ways. On the Plymouth branch in 1906 he introduced push-and-pull working and for the Fratton line in Portsmouth he revived American ideas of the 1860s, the self-contained steam rail-motor. His rail-motors were not a success but they were used by the Great Western Railway for trials.

All locomotive engineers by the 1900s faced the problem of designing engines that would cope with the increasing traffic. Drummond's particular problem was the elimination of double heading on the Honiton Bank for West Country express trains. He produced four classes of 4-6-0 locomotives, all of which apart from the T14s were outright failures as they would not steam and would not run freely. He redeemed his reputation with the D15 4-4-0 class which first appeared in 1912 and replaced the T14s on the most demanding express duties to Bournemouth and Southampton.

Equally as important as his design of locomotives for the London & South Western was Drummond's transfer of their railway workshops from Nine Elms to Eastleigh in 1910. These became the largest and most modern locomotive works in Great Britain and their location near Southampton was at a strategic point in the company's network. It was a repeat, but on a much grander scale, of Drummond's organisation and development work for the Caledonian.

Drummond's relationship with the footplate men was ambivalent. The Scots engineer had a very strong personality and most of the stories and legends that have grown up around him have their roots in his handling of drunkenness. Drummond's code at his Monday morning levees was straightforward: the first offence was dealt with by a reprimand and an order to sign the pledge; a second appearance resulted in dismissal. His disciplinary code was tempered by mercy; he opposed victimisation and often used a 'jury' consisting of an offender's peers. Drummond was strongly interested in the education and welfare of his men and consequently established classes at the works. However he was easily angered and had a volcanic temper. Working irregular hours, he could appear anywhere on the network of the London & South Western at any time, especially after 1899 when he had his own private inspection engine. He was against noise, regarding an engine blowing off as being unnecessary, while visible smoke which impaired cleanliness was in Drummond's view due to bad firing.

Drummond in 1886 became a member of the Institution of Mechanical Engineers while four years earlier he had been elected to membership of the Institution of Civil Engineers. He was also a member of the Association of Railway Locomotive Engineers and had served as a major in the Engineer and Railway Staffs Corps, Territorial Force.

In 1905 he took the title of chief mechanical engineer. His obstinacy and cantankerous nature got worse with age and may have contributed to his death. In November 1912 he received a scald, either on a locomotive footplate or as a result of a mustard bath; the leg turned gangrenous, was amputated and the resulting shock killed him. Dugald Drummond died on 7 November 1912.

PHILLIP L COTTRELL

DRUMMOND Dugald

Writings:

On the Heating of Carriages by Exhaust Steam on the Caledonian Railway (W Clowes & Sons, 1888).

Lectures Delivered to the Enginemen and Firemen of the London & South Western Railway Company on the Management of their Engines (6th ed, Locomotive Publishing Co, 1921).

Sources:

Unpublished

Scottish BCe.

Published

Donald L Bradley, *Locomotives of the London and South Western Railway* part I (Railway Correspondence & Travel Society, 1965).

Henry C Casserley, *London & South Western Locomotives* (I Allan, 1971).

Cuthbert Hamilton Ellis, *The South Western Railway* (Allen & Unwin, 1956).

—, *Twenty Locomotive Men* (I Allan, 1958).

—, *The London, Brighton and South Coast Railway* (I Allan, 1960).

Tony Fairclough and A Wills (eds), *Southern Steam Locomotive Survey, The Drummond Classes* (Truro: Bradford Barton, 1977).

James W Lowe, *British Steam Locomotive Builders* (Cambridge: Goose & Sons, 1975).

Minutes of Proceedings of the Institution of Civil Engineers 195 (1914).

Oswald S Nock, *The Caledonian Railway* (I Allan, 1962).

—, *The London and South Western Railway* (I Allan, 1965).

Proceedings of the Institution of Mechanical Engineers (1912) part 4.

Railway Times 16 Nov 1912.

Times 9 Nov 1912.

John N Westwood, *Locomotive Designers in the Age of Steam* (Sidgwick & Jackson, 1977).

Ronald A Williams, *The London and South Western Railway* II *Growth and Consolidation* (Newton Abbot: David & Charles, 1973).

Sir Arthur Duckham (courtesy of Babcock Woodall-Duckham).

DUCKHAM, Sir Arthur McDougall

(1879-1932)

Gas engineer and industrial statesman

Arthur McDougall Duckham was born at Greenwich in Kent on 8 July 1879, the second of the three sons of Frederick Eliot Duckham MICE, a civil engineer and his wife Maud Mary née McDougall. Each of the Duckham boys was to achieve prominence in their chosen fields: William, the eldest, ran a harbour works company; Arthur left an indelible mark on the gas and chemical industries of the world; and Alexander, the youngest, established an oil company whose domestic products were to become a household name.

Arthur Duckham was educated at Blackheath Proprietary School and left at seventeen to become an articled pupil under Frank Livesey, chief engineer to the South Metropolitan Gas Co. He and his (unrelated) colleague Sir George Livesey (qv), the chairman at South Metropolitan, together deeply influenced Duckham. Under their guidance, he studied furnace-work, coal carbonisation and chemical engineering in general. Duckham concluded that coal gas would become the foundation of future industrial growth. Imbued with this idea, he intensified his studies to cover all branches of furnace development and coal carbonisation, frequently spending his evenings studying engineering at King's College, London.

In 1899, Duckham was appointed an assistant superintendent of the South Metropolitan Gas Co based at the company's Old Kent Road works. Two years later, at just twenty-two years of age, he joined the Bournemouth Gas & Water Co as assistant engineer under Colonel Harold W Woodall, engineer and general manager, who became a lifelong friend.

During the latter part of the nineteenth century, several attempts had been made to perfect a design for a vertical gas-making retort in which coal, fed in at the top, would fall continuously by gravitation through a zone of heat to end up at the bottom as coke. The publication of the unsuccessful work of Settle and Padfield apparently triggered Duckham's particular interest in this problem. At the time Woodall and he were searching for ways to improve existing methods of gas manufacture. Duckham's solution was to keep the retort full and control the coal feed by the rate at which coke was extracted. Others had gone wrong, he surmised, by attempting to synchronise coal feed and coke extraction to try to preserve a constant void at the top of the retort. His was a simple enough solution, but one that proved a turning point in the development of gas making and in Duckham's career.

In 1903 Duckham formed a partnership with Woodall; they patented the continuous vertical retort and then started to sell their invention to the gas industry. Experimental units were built and the first commercial plant consisting of four 20 foot retorts, ordered by the Bournemouth Gas &

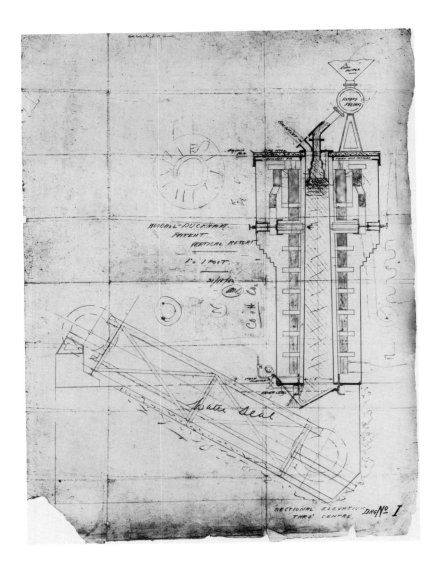

Woodall-Duckham patent vertical Retort (1903) (courtesy of Babcock Woodall-Duckham).

Water Co came into operation in 1906. That year the partners formed Woodall-Duckham Ltd to exploit the Woodall-Duckham system. They borrowed a modest capital and persuaded three companies to back the infant concern with supplies and services, providing generous credit in return for shares. Newton Chambers & Co Ltd of Sheffield supplied castings, Gibbons Bros of Dudley provided steelwork and erection services, while Thos Vale & Sons Ltd of Stourport contributed field construction services, mainly in the building of firebrick settings. These shareholders were subsequently bought out as the new company prospered. Later the partners acquired suitable offices in Westminster. Two of Duckham's earliest installations, at Nine Elms and Liverpool, were failures (because the gas failed to meet the candle-power standard) but a set of retorts installed at Poole in 1908 performed satisfactorily: after six years Duckhams's technology was fully operational.

In the years before the First World War, Duckham emerged as a dominant figure in the developing British gas industry. Six feet tall, weighing eighteen stone, he had great personal charm and the ability of inspiring others to renewed efforts without losing loyalty and friendship. Duckham's greatest strengths were those of the salesman, and the engineer. He spent long hours at the drawing board and yet was always available to others. His hints and nudges solved many a difficulty and associates invariably acknowledged his assistance. Two stories epitomise the vigour with which he approached his work. When a charge of coal in one of the retorts defied all attempts to move it, Duckham himself took the rod used to free it. The heat was so intense that his clothes began to smoulder, but Duckham, totally engrossed in what he was doing, worked on while a stoker sprayed him with water. His chest bore the scars of this incident for life. On another occasion, Duckham literally camped out for fourteen days in one gas works, with his wife smuggling in food and changes of clothing, in order to obtain guarantees and payment over an order for materials: had he stepped off the premises a writ for debt would have been served on him.

Duckham's success as an industrial organiser was widely recognised by the First World War. His company had no manufacturing facilities to turn over to war work in 1914 so personnel were deployed in the war effort. Woodall himself returned to his regiment. In 1915 Duckham became a member of the Munitions Inventions Department and was appointed Deputy Controller of the Department in November. He also sat on the committee on labour supplies for munitions work in September 1915. Singled out for advancement by Lloyd George, he took up the post of Deputy Director-General in charge of machine guns, rifles and other materials of this type in January 1916 and became chairman of the Advisory Committee to the Minister of Munitions the following September. In May 1917, he became a member of the Munitions Council for Aircraft, Tanks and Mechanical Transport and in November 1918 was appointed to the Munitions Demobilisation Board, an important government body responsible for the transition from war to peace and civilian production. In June 1917 he sat on the Committee on the British Empire's mineral resources, formed in response to the campaign drummed up by Billy Hughes (Australian Prime Minister) and others against German metallurgical combines in Britain (like the Merton Group). In June 1918, he was appointed Director-General in charge of design, production and inspection of aircraft. In February 1919, he was a member of the Air Council in charge of the whole aircraft supply of Great Britain and chairman of the War Cabinet Priorities Sub-Committee. His services to the nation were recognised in 1917 with a KCB. An associate recalled that in the war years

> Duckham seemed to be the Soul of Whitehall...(whose associates)...looked forward to his too infrequent visits. The deeper the gloom, the greater was his cheer; whatever trouble there was he was always willing and anxious to help. He made no carping criticisms of what had been done in the intervals — the line he took was to express astonishment that so much could have been accomplished. In that way, he certainly got the best possible out of

those with whom he had come into contact {*Institution of Chemical Engineers Quarterly Bulletin 28* (1932) 4}

After the war Woodall-Duckham's sales of the continuous vertical retort again gathered momentum. By the end of 1918, the number of installations either completed or in hand had risen to over a hundred and Duckham was already negotiating for licenses to be granted to French and German companies. The slump of the early 1920s left Duckham's company relatively untouched. Previously, designers but not contractors, the firm had worked from a very small capital base and a half-share in brickworks. However, judicious management permitted Woodall-Duckhams to buy in new materials in large quantities and at low prices. Part of the profits from this venture were passed on to clients, allowing the company to maintain its level of work while others were losing ground. The remainder of the profits went into expanding the business. A chemical plant division was formed to develop a new lead bath tar distillation process. Installations were built in some 70 gas works, coke oven works and tar treatment plants. This expansion led to Woodall-Duckham's involvement in by-product development, a field which it continued to dominate. By 1925 approximately half of all the coal carbonised in Great Britain was treated on the continuous vertical retort principle and three years later the Woodall-Duckham Co had a turnover of £1 million a year.

At his death, Duckham was chairman of Woodall-Duckham (1920) Ltd, Woodall-Duckham Vertical Retort & Oven Construction Co (1920) Ltd, British Furnaces Ltd, PECO Ltd, Stourbridge Refractories Co Ltd, Thermal Industrial & Chemical (TIC) Research Co Ltd; he was also a director of Alexander Duckham & Co Ltd, British Benzol & Coal Distillation, British Magnesite Calcining Co and Leatherhead Gas and Lighting Co. Duckham became a director of British Cyanides and remained on their board until April 1924.

Duckham was very active in his profession. He joined the Insititution of Civil Engineers in 1918 but felt that chemical engineers needed a professional body of their own. In 1922, he was appointed chairman of the committee formed to organise the Institution of Chemical Engineers. Subsequently, he became chairman of the provisional council and with the incorporation of the Institution the following December, Duckham was unanimously elected the founding president, an office he held until 1925. He held the office of president of the Society of British Gas Industries for two years and was vice-president of the British Commercial Gas Association. He was also elected an honorary member of the Institution of Gas Engineers. During this period, Duckham was a prolific and visionary technical writer and practically every publication of the period carried his views in one form or another.

Duckham emerged as a leader of the British business community in the 1920s: concerned about the problems facing both sides of industry, he gained the politicians' respect as a spokesman for business. Brought up as a Liberal, he moved over to Conservatism in later life. In 1919, he was appointed an industry representative on the Coal Industry Commission set up under Mr Justice (later Lord Justice) Sankey to examine ways of making the then heavily fragmented industry more economically efficient. Duckham submitted a minority report. He believed that an enormous amount of fuel was wasted, mainly through inefficient management techniques, and that the solution lay in state ownership of the nation's mineral rights and the working of coal mines under leases from a Ministry of Mines. Concerned by growing labour problems, he urged that workers should have a minimum standard wage and that their representatives should sit on his proposed area directorates. Duckham was a member of the Standing Committee on Fuel Economy from August 1926. In the 1920s too he chaired a War Office committee on the initiation, conduct and control of research, design and experimental work on guns, ammunition and projectiles: a committee which did important preliminary planning for rearmament.

At the request of the Australian Prime Minister, Bruce, the British Government in 1928 appointed Duckham to lead a commission of independent businessmen to advise on trade opportunities in Australia. The commission sailed in August, landed at the end of September and proceeded to visit every state, covering some 20,000 miles within the country. Their resulting report, issued in January 1929, highlighted the new country's vast resources, strongly advocated a firm trading partnership between the two countries, and recommended permitting higher levels of emigration to Australia. On their return, the four members of the Commission, under the auspices of the Empire Marketing Board, travelled widely throughout Great Britain, extolling the advantages of Australian markets. In the Birthday Honours of 1929, Duckham was created a GBE.

In February 1929, Duckham was appointed chairman of the Standing Committtee on Mineral Transport which drew unflattering comparisons between the type and size of wagons used in this country and of those on the continent of Europe. Later in 1929 Duckham became chairman of the Government's Advisory Committee on applications for assistance from public utility undertakings, under the Development (Loan Guarantees and Grants) Act of 1929, until February 1930. He also sat on the Unemployment Grant Committee in July 1929. Other business commitments, most arising from his dedication to improving Commonwealth trade through the Empire Marketing Board, forced him to relinquish this position. He was president of the British Export Society for 1930 and early in 1931 became deputy president of the Federation of British Industries. He was also chairman of the Empire Policy subcommittee of the FBI and led a Federation mission to Canada that year. At the time of his death he was president-elect of the FBI.

Arthur Duckham married in 1903 Maud (d 1969), the eldest daughter of the well-known impressionist painter A D Peppercorn. Among her sisters were two concert pianists, a concert violinist and a highly acclaimed painter. The Duckhams had two daughters and a son. From his wife Duckham caught an enthusiasm for the arts. In addition he was something of a gourmet and enjoyed golf, dancing, tennis and squash.

Sir Arthur Duckham died suddenly after his regular game of squash, on Sunday 14 February 1932. He left £78,786 gross.

DENNIS TEESDALE

DUCKHAM Sir Arthur McDougall

Writings:

letter on fuel conservation *Times* 5 Nov 1920.

letter on trusts and combines *ibid* 27 Oct 1923.

letter on fiscal policy *ibid* 4 Dec 1923.

letter on domestic heating *ibid* 18 Sept 1924.

'The Domestic Fuel Problem' in John Roberts (ed), *Mining Education* (Pitman & Sons, 1926).

'The British Chemical Industries: Manufacture of Gas, Coke and By-Products' *The Manchester Guardian Commercial* 5 Aug 1926.

Report of the British Economic Mission to Australia (issued by the Dominions Office, 7 Jan 1929).

letter on British investment in Australia *Times* 1 Apr 1929.

letter on iron and steel *ibid* 28 Dec 1931.

Atlantic Letters on World Affairs (Eyre & Spottiswood 1932).

Sources:

Unpublished

PRO War Office papers, WO 32/9928 (papers of the Duckham committee on initiation, conduct and control of research, design and experimental work on guns, ammunition and projectiles).

BCe.

PrC.

Published

T C Bridges and H H Tiltman, *Kings of Commerce* (G G Harrap & Co, 1928).

Burke's Peerage.

Charles Carpenter, 'A Tribute' (Woodall-Duckham Ltd 1932).

H E Milner, 'The W-D Story' *Intercom, The Woodall-Duckham Journal* 1967.

Proceedings of the Institution of Civil Engineers 1869. 1907–8, 1918.

'Sir Arthur Duckham GBE, KCB Memorial Tribute' (Woodall-Duckham Ltd 1932).

Times 15, 17 Feb 1932.

Transactions of the Institution of Chemical Engineers 3 (1925).

S G M Ure in *Quarterly Bulletin of the Institution of Chemical Engineers* 28 (Apr 1932).

Trevor I Williams, *A History of the British Gas Industry* (Oxford University Press, 1981).

Woodall-Duckham 1903-78 (Woodall-Duckham Ltd, 1978).

WWW.

DU CROS, Sir Arthur Philip

(1871-1955)

Tyre manufacturer

Arthur du Cros was born in Dublin on 26 January 1871, the third son of William Harvey du Cros (qv) and Annie née Roy. He was educated at one of Dublin's National schools, and at the age of fifteen entered the lower ranks of the Civil Service. Like his father, he was a keen amateur cyclist, and in 1889 he rode at the Queen's College, Belfast, sports using the new pneumatic tyres. In 1892 Arthur joined his father's firm, the Pneumatic Tyre & Booth's Cycle Agency Ltd, and became general manager. In 1896 he was made joint managing director with his father.

Arthur was a forceful businessman who played an energetic role in the development of Dunlop Rubber after 1900. During this period the tyre business was revolutionised by the development of the motor car. The Dunlop company moved from assembling tyre parts for cycles to manufacturing its own tyres, and making other rubber products. There was also considerable foreign expansion, including the establishment of a factory in Kobe, Japan, in 1909. Arthur was the main influence behind the company's policy of vertical and horizontal integration in these years. After 1909, in response to a sharp upward trend in world rubber prices, the Dunlop Board decided to acquire its own rubber estates. Arthur personally selected estates in Ceylon and Malaya for purchase by the company. By 1917 the company owned about 60,000 acres of rubber growing land, mostly in the Malay Peninsula. Before the First World War Arthur du Cros also initiated Dunlop's policy of acquiring its own cotton mills.

Arthur, therefore, deserves considerable credit for the growth of the Dunlop Rubber Co before 1914, and for laying some of the foundations on which its expansion in the inter-war period was to be based. Nevertheless, Arthur's policies had two major flaws, which had an adverse effect on the company's development and ultimately a disastrous effect on the du Cros influence within the firm. The first problem was that he tended to favour excessively the interests of the du Cros family, which were not always identical with those of Dunlop Rubber. A considerable amount of Dunlop funds, for example, were used to launch and support a taxi cab business, W & G du Cros, owned by two of Arthur's brothers, the benefits of which to the Dunlop company were minimal. Again, members of the du Cros family were placed in many of the senior managerial positions, even when their ability hardly merited the appointment. Such policies contributed to the firm's decline in competitiveness in the world tyre industry during the 1920s.

A second problem, both for Dunlop Rubber and the du Cros family, was Arthur's tendency to engage in financial and share manipulation, a policy which was increasingly inappropriate for the management of one of Britain's largest manufacturing companies. Before 1914 Arthur became

General view of Fort Dunlop from the air (taken from W H Beable Romance of Great Businesses*).*

closely allied with James White (qv), a financier with connections in the Lancashire cotton business. White was used by Arthur, in a series of unorthodox financial transactions, to finance the diversification into the cotton business, and during the war to fund the re-establishment of a Dunlop manufacturing company in the United States. During 1917 White and his associates acquired control of a block of Dunlop Rubber's ordinary shares from the Dunlop Pneumatic Tyre Co, (usually known as the 'Parent Tyre Company'), which since 1912 had been a holding company, largely owning the du Cros shares in Dunlop Rubber. White subsequently abandoned his alliance with Sir Arthur (he was made a baronet in 1916), and by the end of 1918 Sir Arthur had lost practically all his influence in Dunlop Rubber. In February 1919 Sir Arthur was made titular president of the company in succession to his father, and was given a consultatory agreement. Within two years White's speculative financial policies, the expense of the American factory, and the recession of 1920-21, combined to bring the company to the verge of bankruptcy. In August 1921 Dunlop Rubber announced a loss of £8 million on its year's trading. A subsequent special investigation of the circumstances of the firm's near crash was critical of the policies of Sir Arthur du Cros and James White but, during the chairmanship of Sir Eric Geddes (qv), it was agreed that the Investigation Report should not be published, and in return Sir Arthur du Cros's consultatory agreement was cancelled.

During the 1920s Sir Arthur du Cros adopted a policy of broadening the business of the Parent Tyre Co, whose name was changed to Parent Trust

& Finance Co in 1922, and general financial business was undertaken. Among other activities, Sir Arthur became a substantial shareholder in the financial interests of the financier Clarence Hatry (qv). The collapse of the Hatry Group in the autumn of 1929, and the subsequent trial of Clarence Hatry on fraud charges, left Parent Trust & Finance with losses in excess of £3 million. The business was wound up in July 1932, with a considerable loss to Sir Arthur du Cros's personal fortunes.

Before the collapse of Parent Trust & Finance Sir Arthur du Cros was a generous benefactor to many causes. He was an honorary member of the National Art Collections Fund and an Associate of the National Gallery of British Art. Among his gifts were £7,000 to the Royal Free Hospital, £6,000 towards the purchase of the first national airship, and £50,000 to the War Office during the First World War for the purchase of three motor ambulance convoys. Among his other varied activities, Sir Arthur du Cros was honorary colonel of the 8th Battalion Royal Warwickshire Regiment, a JP for Middlesex and a founder of the Junior Imperial League. He also had a parliamentary career as a Unionist, unsuccessfully fighting Bow and Bromley in 1906 before being elected MP for Hastings 1908-18, and Clapham 1918-22.

Sir Arthur du Cros married three times. By Maude née Godding (married 1895, divorced 1923), he had two sons and two daughters. He then married Florence née King in 1928, and after her death in 1951 he married, in the same year, Mary née Beaumont. She survived her husband.

Sir Arthur du Cros died on 28 October 1955, leaving an estate of £28,202 gross.

GEOFFREY JONES

Writings:

Wheels of Fortune (Chapman & Hall, 1938).

Sources:

Unpublished

Dunlop Rubber Co, London, archives.

Published

DNB.

Economist, 28 Sept 1929, 30 Jan 1932.

Geoffrey Jones, 'The Growth and Performance of British Multinational Firms before 1939: the Case of Dunlop' *Economic History Review* 2nd ser 37 (1984).

Hubert A Meredith, *The Drama of Money Making* (Sampson Low & Co, 1931).

Times 31 Oct 1955.

WWMP.

WWW.

DU CROS, William Harvey

(1846-1918)

Tyre manufacturer

William Harvey du Cros was born in Dublin into a family of Huguenot ancestry on 19 June 1846. He was educated at the King's Hospital, Dublin, between 1855 and 1860.

His first job was as a bookkeeper in a Quaker merchant's shop. In 1869 he was appointed assistant secretary to the Irish Commercial Travellers' Association. The origins of his subsequent career, however, lay in his interest in athletics rather than his early business experience. By his early thirties William Harvey had established a reputation as a leading amateur athlete in several sports, including cycling, and he became president of the Irish Cyclists' Association.

It was through this strong interest in cycling that, in 1889, William Harvey became aware of John Boyd Dunlop's (qv) pneumatic tyre patent. Du Cros took a prominent role in establishing the syndicate which was formed to exploit commercially the new tyre. He undoubtedly had a clear perception of the commercial opportunities of the invention in the booming cycle industry.

William Harvey du Cros became the dominant influence in the development of the tyre company. The firm survived the invalidation of Dunlop's master patent, and began a rapid expansion during the 1890s. William Harvey's sons were recruited into the business, and they played a key role in the firm's expansion outside Ireland. During the early 1890s Arthur (qv) was despatched to England, William and Fred to Belgium and France and Harvey Jr, Alfred and George to the United States and Canada. By 1893 the firm had shifted its main tyre assembly plant to Coventry, and established small subsidiary companies in France, Germany and the United States; then the American factory was sold in 1898. The 1890s saw the firm grow rapidly. In 1893 the capital stood at £75,000, and in 1896 a new £5 million company was launched, the Dunlop Pneumatic Tyre Co, with the aid of the speculator E T Hooley (qv). In the late 1890s the firm diversified from tyre assembly into tyre manufacturing, and in 1900 (rather later than certain Continental firms) the manufacture of car tyres began. Further product diversification came in 1910, with the production by Dunlop of its first aeroplane tyre and its first golf ball.

It is clear that during the 1900s William Harvey du Cros was a major influence in the company's affairs, although his exact role is difficult to distinguish from that of his sons, especially Arthur. During the 1910s Arthur assumed growing powers. In 1918 William Harvey was made first president of the Dunlop Rubber Co, a purely titular appointment. By the time of his death Dunlop Rubber had grown to be the fourteenth largest British manufacturing company, with an authorised capital of £6 million.

In addition to his position as a pioneer of the tyre industry, William

Harvey du Cros was also a JP for Sussex and Unionist MP for Hastings 1906-8. He was Chevalier of the Légion d'Honneur, and Knight of the Order of Isabella la Catolica.

William Harvey du Cros married twice, first to Annie, daughter of J Roy Esq of Queen's Co (she died in 1899); secondly, to Florence, daughter of William Gibbings, Esq, of Bow, Devon.

He died on 21 December 1918, leaving £42,143 gross.

GEOFFREY JONES

Sources:

Unpublished

Dunlop Rubber Co, London, archives.

PrC.

Published

Arthur du Cros, *Wheels of Fortune* (Chapman & Hall, 1938).

Geoffrey Jones, 'The Growth and Performance of British Multinational Firms before 1939: the Case of Dunlop' *Economic History Review* 2nd ser 37 (1984).

William W Woodruff, *The Rise of the British Rubber Industry during the 19th Century* (Liverpool University Press, 1958).

WWMP.

WWW.

DUDLEY, 1st Earl of Dudley
see WARD, William

DUDLEY, 3rd Earl of Dudley
see WARD, William Humble Eric

Sir Andrew R Duncan (taken from J C Carr and W Taplin History of the British Steel Industry *Oxford: Basil Blackwell, 1962).*

DUNCAN, Sir Andrew Rae

(1884-1952)

Industrial conciliator and statesman

Andrew Duncan was born at Irvine, Ayrshire, on 3 June 1884 the second son in the family of eight of George Duncan, a missionary and social worker, and his wife Jessie née Rae. He was educated at Irvine Royal Academy and Glasgow University where he graduated in 1903. After a brief interlude as a pupil teacher at the Ayr Academy, he turned to the law for his career. He joined the firm of Biggart, Lumsden in Glasgow, qualifying as a solicitor, taking a second degree at Glasgow (part-time LLB) and, in 1920, being called to the Bar.

By that stage, however, his career had taken a decided industrial and political turn, aided by the contacts of his senior partner, Sir Thomas Biggart, among the ship-building employers. Sir Thomas was a pioneer in the modern development of trade associations, and later leaders of a number of associations were among Duncan's youthful contemporaries. Duncan himself became secretary of the Shipbuilding Employers' Federation and in the First World War he moved to London with the SEF. Political leaders soon saw the merit of the patient, tactful and charming immigrant from the north, and he served on a number of wartime committees for the Government in the field of shipping and shipbuilding. Having in this way been brought to the notice of political leaders, he was appointed, on the morrow of the war, Coal Controller, with the task of supervising the transfer of the coal industry from state control to private ownership. Between 1920 and 1927, though he remained with the SEF as its vice-president, he served on various commissions of inquiry, in the coal industry in Britain and Nova Scotia, national health insurance, and the 1924 dock strike. These appointments were a testimony to one of his great qualities — his ability to see the other point of view, an indispensable trait in a good conciliator. In both his future major tasks, his brief was to persuade rather than order and in both he was nominally subject to the jurisdiction of a higher authority. He was rewarded for his public service with a knighthood in 1921. His own attempts to enter politics directly in these years were, however, unsuccessful: he was defeated as the Liberal candidate at Cathcart in 1922 and at Dundee in 1924. He did, however, maintain close links with both Liberal and Conservative politicians, and in 1926 Stanley Baldwin persuaded the SEF to release him permanently for public service in the reorganisation of electricity supply. This did not, however, reduce his influence over the developing plans for rationalisation in shipbuilding. He successfully insisted that his friend Sir James Lithgow should join the electricity board with him, and he was a major confidante of Montagu Norman (qv) in the subsequent developments in shipbuilding reorganisation. In January 1927, however, he became full-time chairman of the newly-formed, state-appointed Central Electricity Board at a salary of £7,000 per annum.

The generation of electrical power had been first started by private companies. It had also been taken up by municipalities. In neither case was the organisation large enough to achieve economies of scale: an undertaking transcending the confines of any one municipality could have produced more economically, but, given the variation in standards, amalgamation was not easy. Accordingly, under an Act of 1926, the Central Electricity Board was given the function of buying electricity from selected stations, installing new capacity in conjunction with existing undertakings, and transmitting the resulting power to a common standard throughout the entire country by a National Grid which it would construct, own and operate, and selling the electricity thus produced at cost to the distributing undertakings which remained in private or municipal ownership. It is not clear that stations were always selected purely on economic grounds; sometimes they were chosen because they were 'persuadable'. Higher authority, so-called, was vested in the Electricity Commissioners, survivors of an earlier piece of legislation, with powers to provide to the Board initial regional inter-connection plans and compulsorily to close down inefficient stations. There are two points to be noted about the Central Electricity Board of which Duncan was chairman between 1927 and 1935. It represented a middle way between full freedom for the initial undertaking, private or municipal, on the one hand, and total nationalisation, on the other. Duncan soon won the confidence of middle opinion and of many private industrialists by his skilful organising abilities and the Board attracted little of the opprobrium heaped on subsequent nationalised bodies. The CEB also enjoyed a high degree of independence, Ministers having no power of dismissal and rarely interfering. When, in 1931, most official salaries were cut, Duncan successfully insisted that the salaries of Board members be maintained. He used his unusual independence wisely: the National Grid began operating in 1933 and was constructed on time and within the budget. The new Board was able to concentrate generation on the most efficient stations and, within a decade, wholesale electricity prices in Britain were cut to almost a third of their former level: a remarkable economic achievement.

Having set one of Britain's first public corporations on a profitable and expansionary path, Duncan was looking for a more challenging post. His CEB chairmanship had already been accompanied by honours and widened experience: he was a director of the Bank of England (1929-40), a member of the Industrial Court (1931-32) and chairman of the Sea Fish Commission (1933-35). In 1934, he was pressured by the Government and the Bank of England to move to the newly-formed British Iron and Steel Federation, as chairman, and it was to the steel industry that he devoted the rest of his career. He remained a part-time member of the CEB until 1940, and was also a non-executive director of major British companies such as ICI, Dunlop, North British Locomotive and Royal Exchange Insurance.

As independent chairman of the British Iron and Steel Federation from the beginning of 1935, as in the electricity supply industry, he had to seek a middle way through negotiation. His weapons were his contacts in the world of Whitehall and the banks. Through Montagu Norman at the Bank of England, he could exert influence on the supply of bank finance to the steel industry, while he also worked closely with Sir George May (qv), chairman of the Import Duties Advisory Committee, which had recently granted tariff protection to the industry. Although the BISF had no formal powers of control over the iron and steel companies who were its members, Duncan was able to establish moral authority over the industry's firms, and exerted considerable influence on investment planning. The Federation genuinely became in the later 1930s an independent force, holding the ring between private, collective and public interests, rather than a mere talking shop. Under Duncan's leadership the industry made a start on the scrapping of old plants, and the restructuring and re-equipment of new ones. The emphasis in the later 1930s was perhaps too much on the restrictive aspects of rationalisation: an essential pre-requisite in these difficult years, but quite a contrast with Duncan's expansionist stance in a very different industry, electricity, and indeed, with his experience in the steel industry when demand conditions improved. His capacity for organisation and for seeing through difficult situations to an acceptable solution, shown clearly in these years, have, however, rarely been paralleled in industrial statesmanship. Duncan's service was recognised by the award of the GBE in 1938.

When war came, the BISF became the Iron and Steel Control, strengthening its hold over the industry for wartime production planning. Duncan, briefly, became a civil servant, at a considerable reduction in salary, though this was made up. At the beginning of 1940, however, he resigned this post and his other public offices to accept an invitation from Neville Chamberlain to become President of the Board of Trade, being elected unopposed as MP for the City of London constituency. That year he was sworn to the Privy Council. In the summer, Churchill's new Government made him Minister of Supply, a post (with a brief interlude back at the Board of Trade in 1941) he held until 1945. He preferred the Ministry of Supply, where the records show him as an efficient minister, angling for scarce resources as was inevitable in the period of wartime shortage. On the Conservatives' defeat in the post-war election he remained an opposition MP (nominally serving as an 'independent' until 1950) but decided to return to the BISF as chairman in 1945. Stewarts & Lloyds led some steelmen in an attempt to prevent his return, but the plan was thwarted by the alert intelligence of his devoted secretary, Miss Michie.

On his return to the BISF, Andrew Duncan was faced with a dual problem: the threat of nationalisation and the outbreak of the Korean war. Both issues demanded the same answer — an expansion of capacity. This expansion was accomplished through a series of five-year development plans which considerably raised the industry's output. In part, the plans were drawn up in concert with the industry; in part Andrew Duncan used his powers of persuasion to try and ensure that firms conformed. It was in a new Iron and Steel Board, as a counterpart to the Central Electricity Board, that Andrew Duncan saw an answer to nationalisation. Not that he succeeded in resisting nationalisation; the Labour Party was too resolved for that. But the structure of the steel industry was more complex than coal, gas or electricity, and nationalisation came only late in the day. Indeed Labour's new nationalised Steel Corporation had been in being for only a few months when the Conservatives, under Churchill, were returned to power in 1951. It was Andrew Duncan who persuaded Churchill to commit the new Government to denationalisation. It would have been difficult for Churchill to have refused what the party very much wanted, but the case was unusually well prepared. Andrew Duncan had served Churchill well in war, and had briefed him and vetted his speeches on steel, generally on a Saturday morning, in London or at Chartwell. Andrew Duncan, however, died before denationalisation could be accomplished. His successor in fact, though not in name, was Sir Ellis Hunter (qv). One evening Ellis Hunter found himself summoned to number 10 Downing Street; Churchill wished to welsh on the promise to denationalise; but Ellis Hunter, faithful still to his friend, Andrew Duncan, held Churchill to his commitment.

The critical question is whether Andrew Duncan succeeded in broadening the minds of the steel leaders. The answer is: only in part. For example, Guest, Keen & Nettlefolds purchased a large expanse of land near Newport, Gwent, as the site of a new works; but the company never proceeded with the project. On the eve of renationalisation, with the return of Labour to power in 1964, no company was prepared to contemplate a degree of rationalisation in the Scunthorpe area. In this sense Andrew Duncan failed.

Andrew Duncan was possessed of a rare objectivity of mind — a virtue in most walks of life, a fatal weakness in partisan politics. While passionately interested in the deeper issues of politics, he did not linger in Parliament, leaving in 1950. He sought rather to influence politicians from the frontier with industry. Perhaps that is why his qualities never fully realised their deserts.

He married Annie, daughter of Andrew Jordan, a Glasgow painter and decorator, in 1916; they had two sons. Sir Andrew Duncan died on 30 March 1952.

AUBREY JONES

Writings:

Report by the Advisory Committee for Coal and the Coal Industry on the Possibility of Affecting Economies in the Costs that Make up the Price of Coal to the Consumer (HMSO, 1923).

Report of the Royal Commission on Coal Mining Industry in Nova Scotia (Ottawa: F A Acland, 1926).

Report of the Royal Commission on Maritime Claims (Ottawa: F A Acland, 1927).

Report of the Royal Commission Respecting the Coal Mines of Nova Scotia, 1932 (Halifax: N S Ministry of Public Works & Mines, 1932).

Report of the Sea Fish Commission for the United Kingdom (HMSO, 1934).

Report of speech by Sir A Duncan in the House of Commons, Wednesday 17 November 1948 (British Iron & Steel Federation, 1948).

Sources:

Unpublished

PrC.

Personal knowledge.

Published

Roy H Campbell, *The Rise and Fall of Scottish Industry* (Edinburgh: MacDonald, 1981).

DNB.

Leslie Hannah, *Electricity before Nationalisation* (Macmillan, 1979).

Times 31 Mar, 4, 7, 16 Apr 1952.

John Vaizey, *The History of British Steel* (Weidenfeld & Nicolson, 1974) with additional notes from the British Steel Corporation.

WWW.

WWMP.

Sir Val Duncan (taken from D Avery Not on Queen Victoria's Birthday. The Story of the Rio Tinto Mines *Collins, 1974).*

DUNCAN, Sir John Norman Valette

(1913-1975)

Non ferrous mining executive

John Norman Valette (known as Val) Duncan was born at Pinner, Middlesex, on 18 July 1913, the eldest of four children of barrister Norman Duncan and his wife Gladys Marguerite née Valette. He was educated at Harrow School before proceeding to study law at Brasenose College, Oxford.

On graduating from Oxford Duncan joined Gray's Inn and in 1938 was called to the Bar. His legal career was cut short by the outbreak of the Second World War. In 1939 Duncan joined the Royal Engineers to specialise in the planning and supervison of major operations. He served successively on the staffs of Generals Eisenhower, Alexander and Montgomery before joining the team planning the invasion of France. Following the allied invasion Duncan was responsible for ensuring the free flow of men and materials through Holland and Belgium and for the liaison with the civil authorities of those countries on transportation matters. For his contribution to the war effort Duncan was awarded the

OBE in 1944. The Netherlands conferred on him the rank of commander, Order of Orange Nassau and he was awarded two Legion of Merit medals by the United States.

Having acquired a taste for high level organisation and management Duncan decided to stay in the army after the war ended. In 1946 he was appointed Assistant Secretary at the Control Office for Germany and Austria with the rank of colonel. Through this position Duncan's career took a decisive turn. His superior, with whom he worked closely, was Mark Turner, an experienced merchant banker then serving as Under Secretary at the Control Office. Turner formed a high regard for Duncan's organisational abilities and leadership qualities and with the aim of making a career in business he recommended that his protégé gain some top-flight commercial experience. In 1947, with this advice in mind, Duncan accepted an offer from Sir Arthur Street, deputy chairman of the new National Coal Board (NCB) and former deputy head of the Control Office, to join the NCB as assistant director of marketing.

Duncan remained with the NCB for little more than a year. In July 1948 he was invited by Mark Turner to join the Rio Tinto Co as commercial manager at a salary of £2,400 per annum. At the time Turner was acting as stop-gap managing director for the long-established overseas mining enterprise and was charged with the task of finding a permanent chief executive capable of solving the formidable problems which beset the company. Thus Duncan joined Rio Tinto as heir apparent. He took over the managing directorship in January 1951 at a salary of £4,000 per annum, allowing Turner, who remained a leading member of the Rio Tinto board and Duncan's closest colleague, to devote more of his time to merchant banking.

At the time of Duncan's recruitment, the Rio Tinto Co was at the lowest ebb in its long history. Since 1873 the firm had extracted huge quantities of sulphur and copper bearing pyritic ores from its mines in southern Spain and before 1930 it held an imposing record for high profitability and financial stability. All this, however, had been changed by the onset of the international depression, the Spanish Civil War, the vicissitudes of the Second World War and the autarkic economic policies of the Franco dictatorship. Duncan found the company's Spanish business firmly in the grip of the Francoist authorities with prices, wages, purchases and sales controlled to limit both managerial initiative and profitability. Virtually all senior executive time was devoted to the resolution of wearisome, bureaucratically-imposed problems and the financial health of the company was only maintained by dividends from holdings in the Northern Rhodesian copper belt acquired during the late 1920s. It was Val Duncan's task to extricate Rio Tinto from the stranglehold of the Spanish authorities and revitalise the ailing, dispirited enterprise.

In the course of the next few years Duncan justified Mark Turner's confidence in his ability to breath new life into the ageing Rio Tinto Co. Together, Duncan and Turner persuaded their colleagues and leading shareholders (the London and Paris Rothschilds who held about 10 per cent of the company's ordinary share capital) that Rio Tinto should aim to become a growth orientated, broadly-based natural resource company with operations concentrated in politically stable parts of the world, especially in the Commonwealth countries. In the late 1940s and early 1950s interests in a whole range of potential mines were secured: from tin and wolfram in Portugal to diamonds in South Africa and copper in Uganda. However, Rio Tinto's bid to diversify was hampered by the lack of proper organisation for the discovery or appraisal of mining prospects. Between 1952 and 1954, therefore, Duncan established a network of amply-funded exploration subsidiaries to search for mineral deposits that might be operated on a large scale in Canada, Africa and Australia.

Duncan's efforts during these years succeeded in engendering a positive sense of challenge and purpose within the Rio Tinto Co in spite of the continuing struggle for survival in Spain. It came as a great relief nonetheless when in 1954 the easing of Spanish economic difficulties allowed the opening of serious negotiations for the sale of the Rio Tinto mines to Spanish interests. The talks with the specially formed consortium proceeded remarkably smoothly, culminating in June 1954 in an agreement by which the Rio Tinto Co sold its Spanish assets in exchange for £7,667,000 in cash (payable over seven years) and a one-third share in the Spanish operating company to be formed to operate the mines. As a 'mark of appreciation' for the skilful and diplomatic way he had conducted the negotiations, Duncan's salary was raised to £9,000 per annum.

The sale of the Spanish mines released both human and financial resources for the task of rebuilding and reorientating the Rio Tinto Co. An intense period of exploration followed which sent Duncan and other Rio Tinto executives to all parts of the world to supervise exploration agreements and consider the mine development deals put to the company from time to time. The first tangible result of this activity came in 1955 with the purchase of a majority interest in the Algom group of uranium mines in the Elliot Lake district of Canada. The authorised share capital of the Rio Tinto Co was raised from £8 million to £12 million to accommodate the purchase and a loan capital of $200 million was raised against various supply contracts to fund the development of seven major mines. The company's position in the uranium industry was consolidated by the simultaneous acquisition of a controlling interest in the Mary Kathleen mine in Australia. By the end of the 1950s Rio Tinto was responsible for 15 per cent of the world's production of uranium oxide. A series of lesser advances had also been made in the past few years to give Rio Tinto an active involvement in the mining of emeralds, gold and nickel (all in Southern Rhodesia). More importantly, the company had gained control of two highly promising mineral prospects: the vast Hamersley iron ore deposits in Western Australia and the Palabora copper deposits in South Africa.

After a decade as managing director Val Duncan was evidently in a position to reflect that considerable strides had been made toward establishing Rio Tinto in the front rank of international mining houses. Yet the company had not attained the 'ideal' form pursued throughout the 1950s: it was not broadly based, it was still dependent on copper belt dividends for the bulk of its net profits and, in terms of financial power, it was dwarfed by the leading American mineral corporations. Moreover, the uranium industry was entering a deep depression, threatening the viability of the majority of Rio Tinto mines.

Recognising these facts, Duncan in the early 1960s considered a merger as a means of speeding the process of organisation building and reducing the financial dangers posed by the collapse of the uranium market. An ideal prospective partner was found in the London-based Consolidated Zinc Corporation. The operations of Consolidated Zinc were concentrated in Australia where the company owned valuable lead and zinc properties in the legendary Broken Hill district of New South Wales. Its compatibility with Rio Tinto was both strategic and structural. Strategically the leading directors of Consolidated Zinc wished to attain big company status through geographic diversification and the development of important new prospects, particularly the vast Weipa bauxite deposits in northern Queensland. Structurally, the company was about the same size as Rio Tinto with net profits running at a little over £1 million per annum and its major interests were in complementary rather than competing areas. Thus it was reasoned that merger would at a stroke produce a large and broadly-based concern with the financial and technological resources to undertake a range of very promising new ventures. Negotiations were initiated in 1961 and in July 1962 the two companies came together to form the Rio Tinto-Zinc Corporation (RTZ). Duncan was appointed managing director of the new concern, and in 1963, on the retirement of A M Baer, he became chairman and chief executive of RTZ.

Under Duncan's leadership RTZ rapidly rose to prominence in the world metal industries. In partnership with Kaiser Aluminum the firm built an integrated aluminium business in Australasia (Comalco Ltd). The Hamersley iron and Palabora copper projects were brought to fruition. Extensive exploration was continued, eventually yielding large-scale mines in Papua New Guinea (Bougainville copper), Canada (Lornex copper) and South West Africa (Rossing uranium). Meanwhile, the scale and the scope of the business was further expanded through the purchase of going concerns: Atlas Steels (high-grade, speciality steels) in Canada, Borax Holdings (chemicals) in the United States and Capper Pass (scrap metal refiners) and Pillar Holdings (aluminium fabricators) in the United Kingdom. By the early 1970s RTZ had achieved the geographically and geologically diverse pattern of operations long pursued by Val Duncan. In 1974 the group employed funds totalling £1,266 million (shareholders' equity £462 million) to generate sales of £1,165 million and a net profit of £143 million.

The success of RTZ in achieving prominent multinational status in the mineral industries cannot of course be explained simply in the terms of the leadership qualities of its chief executive. The growth and profitability of the group was dependent on many factors and the efforts of many individuals, and at the top Duncan worked closely with other senior directors, especially Mark Turner (deputy chairman) and Roy Wright (deputy chief executive) and Frank Byers (head of exploration). Nevertheless, it is evident that Duncan made a uniquely important contribution to advancing the fortunes of the enterprise. He was without question the principal architect of the strategy of promoting growth through involvement in a stream of large-scale, capital-intensive natural resource projects. Moreover, Duncan initiated many of the policies that made possible the realisation of ambitious strategic objectives. Potential financial limits to growth were overcome through the funding of massive projects with a high ratio of loan capital to equity. Multi-million dollar loans were raised by Duncan and his team throughout the world through the device of offering pre-negotiated long term supply contracts as collateral. Potential organisational and managerial limits to growth were overcome by the progressive devolution of responsibilities to a series of nationally-based companies, each charged with the goal of involving the RTZ group in substantial new projects. By the early 1970s RTZ had emerged as a fairly loosely-knit family of companies with the activities of the parent concern limited to providing group services and controlling major strategic or financial decisions and the appointment of top personnel.

Beyond the practical business sphere, corporate growth and the changing political climate in many mineral-rich countries brought problems which increasingly demanded a creative response from Val Duncan. Most importantly, nationalism in various guises promoted the charge that RTZ was stripping host nations of valuable resources for little national gain, causing the company's operations to be scrutinised by political leaders and the general public in many countries. Duncan, having endured the worst excesses of Spanish economic nationalism, was acutely aware of the dangers inherent in such situations. His response was to reduce the possibility of confrontation with host country Governments through the implementation, where feasible, of what he referred to as 'the RTZ code of good citizenship'. This involved working toward a high degree of local autonomy in decision-making, the employment of a high proportion of host country nationals in senior management, the ensuring of a majority for host country nationals on the boards of local companies, the payment without demur of justly imposed local taxes and royalties and the provison of opportunities for local investors (government or private) to acquire progressively a major stake, and in some cases a majority interest, in the equity of local companies. In operating according to the code, Duncan intended that the activities of RTZ should be seen by all concerned to lead to a just division of rewards between itself and host nations, thereby reducing the appeal of potentially dangerous nationalist economic propaganda.

Success in the emotive business of international mining inevitably brought Val Duncan into the public eye. The result was a progressive increase in his activities outside RTZ. In 1968 he was appointed by the Wilson Government as chairman of the Review Committee on Overseas Representation to report on the most cost-effective means of organising the diplomatic and associated services. In a provocative report the committee argued the case for a more commercially orientated and informed diplomatic service organised to concentrate resources in countries of principal economic interest to Britain. Numerous other opportunities also arose for Duncan to express his views on various subjects to influential groups. Before businessmen, political leaders and academics in many parts of the world and members of international organisations such as the United Nations, he argued strongly in favour of multinational corporations as agents of economic progress in developing societies, economic internationalism, British membership of the EEC and a strong and well-armed NATO alliance.

At a more practical level, Duncan's advice was sought on a regular basis by many organisations. He became a director of the Bank of England in 1969 and a director of British Petroleum in 1974. He served variously as the chairman of the Mermaid Theatre Trust, as a governor of the National Institute of Economic and Social Research, as a member of the Council of Voluntary Service Overseas, as a governor of Harrow School, as a member of the Council of the Overseas Mining Association and as chairman of the Commonwealth Mining and Metallurgical Institutions. Official recognition of his achievements in business and public life came with the granting of a knighthood in June 1968 and with his subsequent appointment as DL of Kent. Sir Val Duncan died suddenly on 19 December 1975 at the age of sixty two. His wife, Lorna Frances née Archer-Houblon, whom he had married in 1950, had died twelve years previously in 1963. The couple had no children. Sir Val left £654,590 gross.

CHARLES E HARVEY

Writings:

'Government Policy towards Private Investment Abroad' in H W Shawcross et al, *Overseas Investment or Economic Nationalism?* (Institute of Economic Affairs, Occasional Paper No 15, 1966).

PP, Report of The Review Committee on Overseas Representation 1968-69 (1969) Cmnd 4107 (chairman).

Britains's Role in the World Today (Institute of Directors Lecture: RTZ Pamphlet, 1969).

A Briton Looks at the Changing Australia (Institute of Directors Australian Division Lecture: RTZ Pamphlet, 1969).

Canada Today and Tomorrow (Address to the Empire Club Toronto: RTZ Pamphlet, 1970).

The Multinational Corporation as seen through British Eyes (Seminar on the Multinational Corporation, Council on Foreign Relations, New York: RTZ Pamphlet, 1972).

Stewardship (American Mining Congress, Industrial Minerals Convention Lecture: RTZ Pamphlet, 1972).

Is Democracy in Its Present Form Making the Efficient Working of the Capitalist System Impossible? (Royal Commonwealth Society Address: RTZ Pamphlet, 1973).

The Rio Tinto-Zinc Corporation (Statement to the United Nations Study Group on Multinational Corporations: RTZ Pamphlet, 1973).

Sources:

Unpublished

The Rio Tinto-Zinc Corporation Ltd, London company archives; including published Rio Tinto Co *Annual Report and Accounts* (1948-54 inclusive) and RTZ *Annual Report and Accounts* (1962-75 inclusive).

PrC.

Published

David Avery, *Not on Queen Victoria's Birthday: The Story of the Rio Tinto Mines* (Collins, 1974).

Daily Telegraph 22 Dec 1975.

Financial Times 20 Dec 1975.

G Foster, 'RTZ's Unparalleled Prospect' *Management Today* Sept 1970.

Forbes Inc, 'Val Duncan - Rio Tinto Zinc' *Forbes* Dec 1966.

Charles E Harvey, *The Rio Tinto Company: An Economic History of a Leading International Mining Concern 1873-1954* (Penzance: Alison Hodge, 1981).

Times 20 Dec 1975.

Richard West, *River of Tears: The Rise of the Rio Tinto-Zinc Mining Corporation* (Earth-Ireland Ltd, 1972).

WWW.

DUNLEATH, 1st Lord Dunleath
see MULHOLLAND, John

DUNLOP, John Boyd

(1840-1921)

Pneumatic tyre inventor and manufacturer

John Boyd Dunlop was born in Dreghorn, Ayrshire, on 5 February 1840, the son of John Dunlop, a farmer, and his wife Agnes née Boyd. He was

J B Dunlop (taken from W H Beable
Romance of Great Businesses
Heath Cranton 1926).

educated at the Irvine Academy before, much against his parents' wishes, he trained as a veterinary surgeon at the Royal (Dick) Veterinary College, Edinburgh. In 1867 he moved to Northern Ireland establishing a large veterinary practice in Belfast.

His career was a classic example of an inventor largely devoid of entrepreneurial skills. Although Dunlop's discovery, or rather re-discovery, of the pneumatic tyre was a critical development in the history of the rubber industry, his role in the foundation of the large British rubber manufacturing company which now bears his name was a limited one.

He developed a pneumatic tyre in 1888. During the 1860s the fitting of solid rubber tyres to vehicles, especially bicycles, had become fairly common. In the 1880s cycles increased in popularity, as a series of technical innovations made the machine easier to use and in 1885 J K Starley (qv) introduced the safety form of bicycle from which the most popular twentieth century design derived. Dunlop's invention, therefore, came at a commercially very opportune moment, although the impetus for his work seems to have lain in personal rather than business reasons. The traditional story, which is probably not apocryphal, is that Dunlop's young son asked his father for some device to make his solid-tyred bicycle run faster on Belfast's streets. Dunlop registered a patent for the pneumatic tyre in December 1888 and was granted a final patent in March 1889.

The commercial significance of the pneumatic tyre was soon recognised. In 1889 Dunlop entered into an agreement with a Belfast cycle firm, who manufactured cycles suitable to be fitted with Dunlop's home-made tyres and probably assembled some tyres themselves to Dunlop's specifications. Dunlop, however, felt unable to develop his invention further on his own, and late in 1889 he joined with Harvey du Cros (qv) and others in establishing the Pneumatic Tyre & Booth's Cycle Agency Co Ltd with an authorised and issued capital of £25,000 to exploit the new tyre commercially. Dunlop received £300 in cash and three thousand £1 shares in the new company. There was some resistance by cycle manufacturers to the new tyre, but its outstanding advantages over the solid rubber tyre soon assured its universal adoption.

Dunlop subsequently lost all influence in the company, as difficulties with his invention occurred. The major problem was that Dunlop had been unaware of an earlier pneumatic tyre patent taken out by Robert William Thompson in 1845. Thompson's patent was extremely detailed and thorough, and left the Dunlop patent with no novel features. Dunlop became aware of the Thompson patent in November 1890, and the English courts invalidated Dunlop's master patent two years later. Moreover, Dunlop's invention left many major problems unsolved. The Dunlop tyre was secured to the rim by sticking, which made access to the tube very difficult. In 1890 the Pneumatic Tyre Co purchased two patents, the Welch and the Bartlett patents, covering methods of attaching the tyre to the rims, and it was these patents which provided the technical platform for the company's subsequent growth. Nor did Dunlop have much to do with the adaptation of his tyre to motor cars in the later 1890s.

Dunlop resigned his directorship in the tyre company in March 1895. Ironically, however, when Harvey du Cros formed a new £5 million

DUNLOP John Boyd

company in England in 1896 to continue the tyre business, he recognised that Dunlop's name was associated in the public mind with the pneumatic tyre and launched the company as the Dunlop Pneumatic Tyre Co.

Dunlop was dissatisfied with his own share of the financial rewards his invention had generated, but he seems to have underestimated the efforts needed to adapt his idea to commercial use, and the capital required.

On resigning from the tyre company, Dunlop moved from Belfast to Dublin and became the chairman of Todd, Burns & Co, a large draper's shop in Dublin. His chairmanship of this store was his only major commercial activity in his later years.

He married in 1871, Margaret Stevenson, a saleswoman from Ballymena and daughter of a farmer, James Stevenson; the marriage produced a son

Joseph Duveen, pencil drawing by W Tittle (courtesy of the National Portrait Gallery).

DUVEEN, Joseph

1st Lord Duveen of Millbank

(1869-1939)

Art dealer

Joseph Duveen was born in Hull on 14 October 1869, the eldest of eight sons and four daughters of an immigrant Dutchman, Joel Joseph Duveen, and his English wife, Rosetta née Barnett, daughter of a Hull jeweller and goldsmith. Both his parents were Jewish.

His father, on leaving a post with a produce-importing firm, set up with very little capital a business importing Delft pottery and Chinese porcelain. In 1879, when young Joe was ten, he moved the family to London. Leasing shop premises at 181 Oxford Street, Joe's father expanded his business to include eighteenth century furniture, tapestries and objets d'art. When Joe's schooling at Brighton College ended, paternal pressure obliged him to give up his ambitions of going up to Oxford, and at the age of eighteen he began his training in the family firm.

With careful management, trade was prospering by this time, the shop attracting a wealthy, aristocratic clientèle, and Joel was exporting to his brother Henry in Boston and later New York, where Henry was developing contacts and opening up an important new market with wealthy American industrialists. In 1890 the two brothers formalised their partnership with the founding of the firm Duveen Brothers, and business flourished, later aided by the changing trend in taste away from the heavy Victorian style of furnishing and décor which accompanied the ascendancy of the new monarch, Edward VII.

Joe served a useful apprenticeship under his father and uncle, learning to curb his naturally ebullient and overbearing manner and developing charm and an ability to influence and persuade clients. Like his father he possessed a keen business sense, a willingness to work hard, and a discerning eye for quality and saleability.

Despite the solid success which so far had been achieved, Joe chafed at the limitations imposed on the firm by his more cautious father and uncle. His ambition was to increase the firm's prestige and profits by purchasing works of art of the highest value, and especially to break into the profitable but more hazardous picture market which his seniors had avoided owing to the risks accompanying the greater financial outlays.

In pursuing such ambitious projects, Joe was assisted by his uncle Henry and his father's waning influence due to ill-health. Even before his father's death in 1908 Joe negotiated the purchase of several major art collections, including those of Oscar Hainauer in 1906, of Rodolphe Kann in 1907, and shortly after Joel died, of Maurice Kann. The benefits of such large-scale purchases were immediate: valuable publicity on an international scale, and a vast stock of paintings, sculptures, furniture and works of art, including those of great masters, on which the firm was able to draw for many years. Moreover, Joe's marriage on 31 July 1899 to Elsie Salamon, the beautiful daughter of a New York tobacco merchant, facilitated his cultivation of social and business contacts and strengthened his internationalist outlook, especially his interest in America.

As his influence in the firm increased, his overriding concern became the development and consolidation of Duveen Brothers on an international level. He supervised personally the opening of galleries in the Place Vendôme, Paris, in 1908, and through this branch it became possible to develop a wider catchment area for buying and selling within Europe. New clients were attracted, notably Baron Adolphe de Rothschild, Dr Wilhelm Von Bode of Berlin's Kaiser Friedrich Museum, and Calouste Gulbenkian. This success further encouraged Joe Duveen to extend the new image he was creating for Duveen Brothers by promoting elegant, well-designed galleries in which to display important art treasures. To this end he designed and built in 1912 new premises in New York, at the junction of 5th Avenue and 56th Street, in order to take full advantage of the market developing among American industrial tycoons. The London business, which had been based at Bond Street since 1893, and closed in 1912 because of a heavy tax on overseas subsidiaries of English-registered companies, in 1919 entered new premises at 4 Grafton Street, Piccadilly, under the auspices of the American side of the business. This completed Joe's programme of building and expansion, and provided for Duveen Brothers a framework well-suited to supplying the American market from European sources.

Within this framework, Joe sought to strengthen his position in the firm, regardless of the family friction which his dictatorial ways and reluctance to share control provoked among his younger brothers. Following Joel's death, Henry and Joe worked well together, Henry remaining the firm's head and principal asset holder, and Joe holding a subsidiary stake but providing the driving force and leadership behind the expansion. On Henry's death in 1919, Joe purchased his share and subsequently bought out the remaining members of his family, by which time Duveen Brothers was placed among the few top firms monopolising the international art market, and its clients were amongst the wealthiest collectors in the world.

Credit for such an achievement was due in part to Joe's father and uncle for laying the groundwork and building up the firm from small beginnings. Perhaps Joe's willingness to take financial risks was a reflection of his confidence arising from the financial stability enjoyed by the firm. Indeed, Joel Duveen was knighted a few months before his death, and his estate at probate amounted to over £600,000. Henry, too, held the respect of wealthy, aristocratic and even royal clients, and his contacts were invaluable to the firm when its activities were extended. But it was Joe who had the vision, determination and ruthlessness necessary to take the firm to its peak and maintain it there until his death in 1939. Joe was an accomplished mentor, negotiator and salesman, and he exploited to the full the acquisitive aspirations of the very rich in America and Europe.

To encourage collectors to become clients of the House of Duveen, he used a variety of methods of persuasion with a high degree of success. His charm, infectious enthusiasm and flamboyance attracted some; others more hesitant succumbed to offers of long-term credit, long-term approval, and the occasional sale at cost price. Under an arrangement with Bernard Berenson (1865-1959), a leading expert in Italian art, entered into by Joe in 1911, Berenson authenticated paintings handled by Duveen Brothers and helped to secure new stock. Because Duveen and Berenson neither liked nor trusted each other they usually communicated through Duveen's assistant in Paris, Edward Fowles (1885-1971). Confidence in the infallibility of Berenson's authentications was deliberately fostered by Joe, since he recognised that among such wealthy clients, provenance of the work of a great artist rather than its price, was the most important criterion securing a sale. Berenson was also able to act as agent, arranging for the purchase of works of art by the firm, and on these he received a percentage of their profits on sales. Provenance in some of these cases is today held in doubt, and criticism has been levelled at the degree of over-restoration practised by the firm. But the success of the association, which terminated in 1937 following a dispute, can be gauged by the fact that Berenson reputedly earned more than £1.6 million over the twenty-six years of their collaboration.

The success of Duveen Brothers also relied heavily on Joe's ability to secure stock of the highest quality, against competition from other leading international dealers. Joe possessed a considerable knowledge of art treasures in private hands, and was prepared personally to travel long distances in order to make major purchases. Moreover the record-breaking prices which he was prepared to pay, both privately and at auction, enabled Joe to outbid rival dealers, and drew much public attention to the firm. Throughout his career he was successful in generating confidence among bankers and financiers, several of whom were clients and family friends, and this enabled him to obtain the credit to maintain the firm's purchasing power at a high level. He was always confident that he would find a purchaser for the finest works when their sale was backed by the Duveen name and a Berenson authentication. The payment of high prices, too, helped to maintain the market level, which was an important consideration.

Success for the firm depended upon Joe's personal involvement, and every year he travelled between Europe and New York, where after 1911 he spent the major part of his time closely monitoring progress on major deals. Such was his dedication that he continued to work actively and to maintain direct control right up to the time of his death, regardless of the cancer which afflicted him for the last five years of his life.

Nevertheless, in addition to Joe's personal qualities, external circumstances heavily contributed to the firm's success. Dealers rather than auction houses dominated the international art market at that time. American demand was strong with a shortage of European art for millionaire industrialists anxious to establish major collections. In 1909 the removal in America of the ad valorem import duty on paintings, sculptures and works of art over one hundred years old further encouraged that demand, as did a public bequest system granting tax concessions to individuals who undertook to leave works of art to museums on their death; and this bequest system also benefited Joe in preventing items sold to such individuals from reappearing on the market at less than a 'Duveen' price.

Inevitably there were obstacles to overcome. Perhaps the most serious was a clash with the American Customs over tax evasion on imports prior to the removal of the ad valorem duty, which led to the imposition of heavy fines following an out-of-court settlement in 1911. Law suits were a recurrent feature of Joe's life and may have explained why some of his closest friends were also lawyers.

But despite setbacks, the combination of Joe's dynamism, resourcefulness and skill as an entrepreneur, together with complementary market forces, turned the House of Duveen into one of the most prominent and successful businesses in the international art market at that time. The Duveen records show that over the course of thirty years, £100 million of European works of art were shipped to America, to be purchased by collectors of such calibre as Henry E Huntington, Henry Clay Frick, Andrew Mellon, Jules Bache, Joseph Widener and Samuel H Kress. As a result, 'Duveen' masters are now widely represented in major American national collections.

Joe's prominence in the art world, and the propaganda which he encouraged and enjoyed, influenced taste more widely than merely among his own clients. He was responsible for helping to stimulate demand for, and increase the values of, works of the British, Dutch and Italian schools, which largely succeeded the previously fashionable paintings of the nineteenth century French Salon, and the Barbizon and Hague schools.

Despite his very busy life, Joe found time to mount exhibitions in support of the work of contemporary British artists, and to supervise the building of the galleries which he donated to the British Museum, the Tate, the National Gallery and the National Portrait Gallery. He made many art benefactions, and endowed a chair in the History of Art at London University.

As a man who sought and enjoyed visible recognition of his personal success, he was rewarded with many overseas honours; and in Britain, for his services to art, he was created knight in 1919, baronet in 1927 and First Baron of Millbank in 1933. He was also a Trustee of the Wallace Collection in 1925-39, of the National Gallery, 1929-37, and of the National Portrait Gallery, 1933-39. These were controversial appointments, owing to his status as an art dealer, and his trusteeship of the National Gallery was terminated when Neville Chamberlain became Prime Minister in 1937.

Joseph Duveen died on 25 May 1939 in Claridges, the hotel which for many years had been his London headquarters, and was buried in the Willesden Jewish Cemetery. It is difficult to assess the wealth he accumulated in his lifetime since the value bound up in stock, together with money owed by clients, was high. But before he died, he paid his debts, including a loan of £1.2 million made by Parrs, the London bank, at the beginning of the century and renewed annually thereafter. A gross figure at probate in this country of £2,814 was left in trusts to his wife and only child, a daughter Dorothy. The joint successors to the House of Duveen were his nephew, Armand Lowengrau, and Edward Fowles, who had directed the Paris galleries since 1915.

JILL L GOSLING

Writings:

Thirty Years of British Art (*Studio*, special autumn number, 1930).

Sources:

Published

Samuel N Behrman, *Duveen* (2nd ed, Hamish Hamilton, 1972).

David Alan Brown, *Berenson and the Connoisseurship of Italian Painting* (Washington DC: National Gallery of Art, 1979).

William G Constable, *Art Collecting in the United States of America: An Outline of a History* (Thomas Nelson & Sons Ltd, 1964).

DNB.

James Henry Duveen, *Collections and Recollections: A Century and a Half of Art Deals* (Jarrolds, 1935).

Edward Fowles, *Memories of Duveen Brothers* (Times Books, 1976).

Colin Simpson, 'The Tainted Connoisseur' *Sunday Times* 3 Feb 1980.

Times 26, 27, 29 May, 2 June 1939.

WWW.

Col H C S Dyer (courtesy of Vickers Ltd).

DYER, Henry Clement Swinnerton

(1834-1898)

Employers' association organiser and armaments industry manager

Henry Clement Swinnerton Dyer was born on 30 December 1834, the second son of four sons and three daughters of Sir Thomas Swinnerton Dyer (1799-1880), Ninth Baronet of Brompton Hall, Middlesex, and Westcroft Park, Chobham, Surrey, a captain in the Royal Artillery, by his wife Mary Ann (d 1880), daughter of Col John Albeck Clement RA. Dyer was commissioned into the Royal Artillery at the age of seventeen, and served in both the Crimean War and the repression of the Indian Mutiny. His horse was shot from under him twice, at the siege of Sebastopol and the battle of Cawnpur, and he was named a Knight Commander of the Orders of the Crown of Italy, of Charles VII of Spain, and of the Rose of Brazil; he also held the Spanish Military Order of Merit. He became assistant superintendent of the Royal Small Arms Factory at Millbank in 1869 and then of the Royal Small Arms Factory at Enfield in 1872-75. He retired from the army in 1876 with the rank of colonel and became superintendent of the artillery works of Sir Joseph Whitworth & Co at Manchester. In 1883 Sir William Armstrong (qv) hired him to manage his new steel works at Elswick, Newcastle upon Tyne, which was specially concerned with the production of raw material and forgings for large guns. When in 1897 Armstrongs took over Whitworths, Dyer was a natural choice as managing director of the Manchester firm with which he had previously been associated. By the time of his death, Dyer had thus made the circuit of almost all the major gun producing establishments of the country, both public and private. Despite its evident success, his career is less distinctive in its own right than emblematic of the close connections between consumers and producers of armaments in Victorian Britain, as well as of the use of military men as managers in large industrial enterprises.

Dyer's real importance was as the architect of the Engineering Employers' Federation (EEF) and of its victory over the unions in the 1897-98 lockout. Previous attempts to form a permanent national organisation of engineering employers had foundered on divisions between the marine and inland producers, and on commercial rivalries among the marine districts themselves. Thus the marine firms held aloof from the Iron Trades Employers' Association (ITEA) formed at the initiative of Sir William Armstrong after the success of the Nine Hours strikes in 1872, and even his own firm failed to join. From the moment of his arrival at Armstrongs, Colonel Dyer seems to have devoted himself to the cause of wider cooperation among engineering employers; his experiences with firms scattered around the country may have enabled him to play such a unifying role. In 1884, during a protracted dispute over apprenticeship at Sunderland, Dyer was instrumental in creating a joint committee to coordinate employer activity on the three rivers of the North East Coast. This committee then affiliated to the ITEA, though the key initiatives towards a national employers' organisation would come only in the following decade.

The boom which began in 1889 touched off a wave of industrial conflict throughout Britain, as unions sought to regain ground lost to employers during the previous two decades of depression. The storm centre of this movement in engineering was the North East Coast, where nearly every year from 1889 to 1894 saw a major dispute over issues ranging from wages, hours and overtime to demarcation and apprenticeship ratios. As the largest and most aggressive employer in the district, and one which was experimenting with new methods of systematic management, Armstrongs was naturally at the fulcrum of these conflicts. The restrictive influence of trade unions was a major target of its directors' public statements in the early 1890s, and in 1894 Colonel Dyer wrote to Sidney Webb that, 'owing to the rapid succession of labour troubles in this district during the last few years', the firm had decided not to build a new plant for producing steel plates which it believed would otherwise have been profitable, and indeed had 'decided not to increase our works in any way or expend any more capital in developing them' {BLPES, Webb Trade Union Collection, EA 21, Folio 18. Memorandum from Colonel

Dyer to Sidney Webb (1894?)}. Armstrongs therefore led the way in developing new tactics of coordinated employers' action which became prominent on the North East Coast, such as the use of enquiry notes to prevent competing firms from hiring workers on strike and that of sympathetic lockouts in stages of 25 per cent in response to selective strikes against individual firms.

By the middle of the decade, the North East Coast employers under Dyer's leadership appear to have set their sights on the formation of a national employers' organisation. When in late 1895 the Amalgamated Society of Engineers (ASE) put forward demands for wage advances in several districts, Dyer (who had served as president of the abortive National Federation of Engineering and Shipbuilding Employers 1893-1894) proposed to the Glasgow employers that a communications network be established to ensure that any strikes would run concurrently. Even closer cooperation developed between the Clyde and Belfast firms, who adopted the tactic of a staged sympathetic lockout pioneered on the North East Coast. The successful conclusion of this dispute prompted Dyer to convene a meeting at Carlisle in November 1895, where he overcame the traditional rivalry between the Clyde and North East districts and laid the foundations of the EEF. The Federation, formed officially in April 1896, was a far more centralised and well financed organisation than its predecessor the ITEA, and took as its objective the coordination of employer resistance to union demands across the whole spectrum of contested issues from wages and hours to machine manning, payment systems and 'interference with foremen'.

At the outset, membership in the Federation was confined to the marine districts of Barrow, Belfast, the Clyde and the North East Coast, but Dyer soon set out to build the EEF into a truly national organisation. He was assisted in this project by the mounting tensions between employers and skilled workers over machine manning provoked by the diffusion from the mid-1890s onwards of American-model automatic and semi-automatic machine tools. A strike against the employment of handymen on machine tools at a Glasgow firm in August 1896 provoked the EEF to threaten the ASE with a staged national lockout of its members, and the Federation met in November of that year to coordinate resistance to union claims in the name of employers' property rights in the machines. In the context of increasing fears of foreign competition, these conflicts over mechanisation proved a powerful force for convincing engineering employers in a variety of districts that their common interests outweighed their traditional antagonisms. But it was not until the spring of 1897, when Armstrongs had taken over the leading Manchester firm of Whitworths, and installed Colonel Dyer as managing director and as secretary of the local branch of the ITEA, that the Federation was able to draw in any of the inland districts.

While in 1896 Dyer had privately expressed his willingness to concede control of certain machines to the ASE in exchange for a free hand with the rest, by the following year he had become convinced of the necessity for a decisive confrontation with the unions. Thus at a conference on the machine question in March 1897, Dyer and the other Federation leaders rejected compromise proposals from the ASE for the rating of machines, and the conference broke up with lockout threats still outstanding in a number of disputed cases. In the event, however, it was not the machine question but a revival of union demands for the eight-hour day which permitted Dyer to widen the scope of his organisation by means of a national lockout. A joint committee of engineering and shipbuilding unions had threatened to strike against all London firms which had not conceded the eight-hour day by July 1897, and the EEF responded to the latter's appeal for help with the threat of a national lockout. When the ASE men refused to withdraw their notices at the beginning of July, the Federation began to lock out its members in stages of 25 per cent per week.

Dyer had prepared the Federation well for this confrontation. Plans had been laid for a strike levy on member firms, for a Foremen's Mutual Benefit Society to detach supervisors from their allegiance to the unions, and for an ample supply of blacklegs. Using a delicate combination of diplomacy and force, Dyer was able to expand the firm's membership from 180 at the outset of the lockout to 702 at its close. Fears of foreign competition, hopes of mechanisation, and an intransigent defence of managerial prerogatives together formed an effective banner under which to rally employers from diverse sectors and districts, while a boycott exercised through the extensive subcontracting network maintained by Armstrongs and other large firms proved sufficient to coerce many holdouts into the Federation's camp. Dyer also won the support of public opinion by portraying the ASE as luddite enemies of progress and property in his statements to the press, and by tarring its 'new unionist' general secretary with a socialist brush.

Having alienated both the other craft societies and the largely unorganised handymen, the ASE found itself isolated and unable to prevent Armstrongs and other firms from continuing partial operations. With strike costs of £30,000 per week and a continuing accession of new firms to the Federation, the union was soon threatened with imminent bankruptcy and by the autumn was ready to sue for peace. Rejecting all attempts at mediation by the Board of Trade, Dyer and the Federation leaders drew up a draconian set of 'Terms of Settlement'. These gave employers the freedom to hire non-unionists; to institute piecework systems at prices agreed with the individual worker; to insist on up to 40 hours overtime per worker per month; to employ as many apprentices as they chose; and to place any suitable worker on any machine at a mutually agreed rate. After minor modifications these were accepted by the members of the ASE in January 1898.

During the course of the dispute, Dyer was widely accused of attempting to smash the ASE, and the first version of the Terms of Settlement, which appeared to threaten collective bargaining over wages, sparked off a fierce debate over the 'legitimate functions of trade unionism' {ASE (1898) passim} among intellectuals sympathetic to the labour movement. Dyer stoked such fears by his euphoric comments on a visit to the notorious Carnegie works at Homestead, Pennsylvania (where a private army of Pinkerton guards had been used to smash the American Ironworkers' Union in 1892), and by his avowal that the EEF was 'determined to obtain the freedom to manage their own affairs which has proved so beneficial to the American manufacturers' {letter to the *Times* 5 Sept 1897, reprinted in *ibid*, 74-75}. But he seems to have believed that unions were genuinely necessary to conduct negotiations between workers and management in large-scale enterprises, and aimed not to destroy them but rather to confine them within the narrow limits of what he believed to be their legitimate functions. The revised Terms of Settlement, while extracting an explicit recognition of managerial prerogatives in work organisation, conceded a certain role for collective bargaining in wage determination, and by virtue of a novel disputes procedure sought to make the union itself responsible for suppressing the local resistance of its members.

These Terms of Settlement and the disputes procedure that accompanied them survived with minor modifications until their repudiation by the ASE in 1914, and their principles were restored by a second lockout in 1922. But Colonel Dyer lived to see neither the successes nor the frailties of the regime he had done so much to establish. The exertions of the lockout seem to have overtaxed his already weak heart, and he died at his home at Appleby Lodge, Rusholme, Manchester, on 21 March 1898, leaving an estate of £143,890 gross. Colonel Dyer was succeeded as president of the EEF by his colleague at Armstrongs, Sir Andrew Noble (qv), and the Federation established a charitable fund in his memory.

Dyer was survived by his wife, Amelia Susan (d 1903), only daughter and heir of John Ward of Otterington Hall, Hampshire, and a stepdaughter of Admiral Russell Eliot. They had a son and a daughter, the son, Leonard Whitworth, becoming Fourteenth Baronet.

JONATHAN H ZEITLIN

Writings:

letter to the *Times* 5 Sept 1897.

Sources:

Unpublished

BLPES, Webb Collection, EA Vol 21, memo from Dyer to Sidney Webb.

PrC.

Jonathan H Zeitlin, 'Craft Regulation and the Division of Labour: Engineers and Compositors in Britain 1890-1914' (Warwick PhD, 1981).

Published

Army Lists, searched by the Royal Artillery Institution Librarian.

ASE, *Notes on the Engineering Trades Lock-Out* (1898).

Burke's Peerage 1980.

Hugh Clegg, Alan Fox and Alan F Thompson, *A History of British Trade Unions 1889-1910* (Oxford: Clarendon Press, 1964).

The Engineer 85 (25 Mar 1898).

Engineering 65 (25 Mar 1898).

'The Engineering Dispute: Some Plain Facts about It' *Cassiers Magazine* 13 (1897).

James B Jefferys, *The Story of the Engineers, 1800-1945* (Amalgamated Engineering Union, 1946).

Times 22 Mar 1898.

Eric Wigham, *The Power to Manage: A History of the Engineering Employers' Federation* (Macmillan, 1973).

Jonathan H Zeitlin, 'The Labour Struggles of British Engineering Employers, 1890-1922, in Howard Gospel and Craig Littler (eds), *Managerial Strategies and Industrial Relations* (Heinemann, 1983).

E

EADIE, Albert

(1862-1931)

Cycle manufacturer

Albert Eadie was born in Birmingham on 7 January 1862, the son of Richard Eadie, a rose engine turner, and his wife Selina née Newey. On leaving school in 1876 Albert Eadie started work at Perry & Co, Lancaster Street, Birmingham, where he rose to the positions of a 'traveller' and later sales manager of the Cycle Parts Department. The West Midlands, at this time, contained a multiplicity of small firms engaged in the new growth industry of cycle and cycle components manufacture. Eadie acquired his reputation as one of the most successful salesmen in this competitive environment.

In November 1891, Eadie left Perrys and joined the Redditch company of George Townsend & Co Ltd, which had its origins within the Redditch and district needle industry. The company, founded in 1855, had, by the time Eadie arrived, diversified; besides needles, a variety of springs,

Albert Eadie (courtesy of M Cannons).

bicycles and cycle parts were being produced at Townsend's Givry Works in Hunt End, near Redditch.

Eadie brought to the Townsends his experience, reputation and urgently-needed new capital. He also brought in Robert Walker Smith, previously the chief designer and assistant works manager at the Coventry cycle works of D Rudge & Co Ltd. Walker Smith provided not only his own engineering skills but a number of skilled workmen whose task was to supervise production in the Hunt End factory.

The team of Eadie and Walker Smith effectively took executive control and restructured the old Townsend company. In August 1892 the company's name was changed to the Eadie Manufacturing Co Ltd with Albert Eadie as managing director and Walker Smith as director. One of Eadie's first tasks was to sell off the needle interest and the right to manufacture needles under the Townsend trade mark passed to Alfred Shrimpton & Sons. The new business centred on cycle components, bicycles and light engineering. In 1892 the company produced a new range of models, named the Royal Enfield in celebration of a successful contract they had gained to supply gun parts for the Enfield Ordnance Works.

The 1890s were busy years for Eadie and Walker Smith as they developed and improved their cycles operation. The business was restructured in 1896 as the New Eadie Manufacturing Co, which manufactured bicycles, assembly parts for smaller bicycle builders and related cycle components based at a new factory in Union Street, Redditch. At the old Hunt End works, the New Enfield Co specialised in quality cycles bearing the Enfield and later Royal Enfield trademarks, the latter with the accompanying slogan 'made like a gun' as proof of pride in craftsmanship and serving as a reminder of the company's earlier connections with the Enfield Ordnance Works. As well as the two main companies, Eadie's other projects included companies making bicycle chains, bicycle spokes and general cycle acessories.

Albert Eadie also made technical improvements which were widely adopted in cycle design. In 1903, adapting from earlier designs by W Reilly and Mars, he patented a two-speed gear that 'had considerable popularity ... (and) ... was widely used for a number of years' {Caunter (1955) 48}. Perhaps the innovation for which Eadie's name became best known was the 'Eadie Coaster' which acted as an efficient back-pedalling brake. This was based on earlier patents, but Eadie popularised its use in the British cycle industry.

Eadie and Walker Smith in 1899 turned to manufacturing motor bicycles, under licence from De Dion, and this marked the beginning of what was later to become a long range of Royal Enfield motor cycles. Eadie also made an attempt at motor car production and in 1906 became chairman of the Enfield Autocar Co, though here he ran into immediate difficulties when Renault took action over a breach of French patents.

In 1907 the Eadie complex was split with the takeover of the Eadie Manufacturing Co by the Birmingham Small Arms Co. BSA took ownership of all Eadie's interests except for the Enfield Cycle Co and the Enfield Autocar Co. Eadie resigned from the Enfield Cycle Co while Robert Walker Smith stayed and guided the future development of the Royal Enfield. The deal between BSA and Eadie was more of an amalgamation than a simple takeover. Eadie became a member of the BSA board and the managing director of the BSA cycle and motor cycle department, marking the return of BSA to cycle manufacture two decades after earlier attempts had been abandoned. By 1909 BSA produced their first motor cycle at the Union Street factory in Redditch under Eadie's supervision. Eadie, together with Frank Baker and Charles Hyde, formed a small yet energetic team that rapidly developed BSA as a force in cycle and motor cycle production. By 1913 BSA was one of the largest manufacturers of cycles and motor-cycles in Great Britain. Within two years of joining BSA Eadie was acting managing director of the company. Though he held this position for only a year, he remained a director of the company until his death in 1931. In 1911 he became a director of Daimler.

While there had been a mass of companies dabbling in cycle and motor-cycle manufacture during the take-off of the industry in the two decades before the First World War, Eadie's contribution is significant in that he played a formative role in the development of both the Royal Enfield Co and the BSA cycle and motor cycle department. Eadie's involvement in the cycle industry was not only that of a businessman or an inventor, he was also an enthusiatic sportsman. He was a president of the Eadie Cycling Club, the Redditch and District Cycling Club, the Midland Cycling and Athletic Club and the Midland Roses Association. Eadie's main leisure pursuits of cycling, motoring and shooting reveal a close relationship between his business and sporting interests. In politics Eadie was a 'zealous' Unionist and a frequent campaigner in support of local Unionist politicians, including the East Worcestershire MP (Sir) Austin Chamberlain. Reflecting his early days as a salesman, perhaps, he became an honorary officer of the Redditch branch of the United Kingdom Commercial Travellers Association.

Eadie died on 17 April 1931 at Selsey, Sussex, after a long period of ill health, leaving £36,131 gross. A local obituary mourned the passing of 'one who from two to four decades ago was one of the most prominent figures in the industrial, political and social life of Redditch ...' {*Redditch Indicator* 25 Apr 1931}.

M J CANNONS

Sources:

Unpublished

University of Warwick, Modern Records Centre, BSA papers (MSS 19A).

BCe.

PrC.

W Solloway, 'The Townsend Story' (1966) (Copy in Redditch Public Library).

Published

Cyril Francis Caunter, *Handbook of the Collection Illustrating Cycles* Pt I (HMSO, 1955), Pt II (HMSO, 1958).

A B Demaus, *Fifty Years of the Bicycle in Worcestershire 1880-1930* (Tenbury Wells: the author, nd).

with Napiers: pig-farming never quite equalled that, even though he established the largest pig-breeding business in the UK. On the farm, however, he did pioneer the use of mechanical traction.

He was twice married and had two daughters. His first wife, whom he married in 1892, was Eleanor Rose Sharp, daughter of John Sharp, warehouseman, of Forest Hill; his second was Myra Caroline Martin daughter of John Martin, 'gentleman' {MCe}. S F Edge died at Eastbourne on 12 February 1940 leaving £399 gross.

W J READER

Writings:

My Motoring Reminiscences (G T Foulis & Co, 1934).

Sources:

Unpublished

MCe.

PrC.

Published

Roy A Church, 'Markets and Marketing in the British Motor Industry before 1914 with Some French Comparisons' *Journal of Transport History* 3rd ser 3 (1982).

DNB.

Kenneth Richardson, *The British Motor Industry 1896-1939. A Social and Economic History* (Macmillan, 1977).

Samuel B Saul, 'The Motor Industry in Britain to 1914' *Business History* 5 (1962).

Times 13 Feb 1940.

Charles Wilson and William J Reader, *Men and Machines. A History of D Napier & Son, Engineers, Ltd 1808-1958.* (Weidenfeld & Nicolson, 1958).

WWW.

Sir George Edwards (courtesy of Dr N Barfield).

EDWARDS, Sir George Robert

(1908–)

Aircraft manufacturer

George Robert Edwards was born in Walthamstow, Essex, on 9 July 1908, the son of Edwin George Edwards, a stationer, and Mary Elizabeth née Freeman, who died soon after the birth. George was educated at South West Essex Technical College and gained an external University of London BSc(Eng).

Upon graduation at the age of twenty he went into general engineering until he joined the design staff of Vickers (Aviation) Ltd at Weybridge Surrey in 1935. There he worked under R K Pierson on a great variety of aircraft, some having Barnes Wallis's geodetic structures, such as the Wellington, Warwick and Windsor. In 1940 he was promoted to experimental manager and in September 1945, upon the elevation of Pierson to chief engineer, became chief designer. Following the 1943 Brabazon recommendations, Vickers had studied the conversion of wartime types to civil use, and of these the most promising appeared to be the civil Wellington, the VC1 Viking. George Edwards led the team which took the basic Wellington wing and engines and the Warwick tail surfaces and developed a new stressed-skin passenger fuselage to go with them. He also led the sales campaign to make it a success by convincing the Government that interim craft as recommended by Brabazon were essential to capture the markets and hold them until the new types could appear. Though the Viking would have to meet the new International Civil Aviation Organisation standards, its development was pushed hard and the first flight took place on 22 June 1945. A production order followed and on 1 September 1946 the Viking flew its first commercial service for the new British European Airways (BEA). In all 163 were built, together with 263 Valetta and 163 Varsity military derivatives.

In the meantime Pierson had discussed with the Brabazon Committee a successor for the Viking. This became in 1945 the Brabazon IIB, in essence a pressurised turboprop replacement. The VC2 Viceroy, later renamed Viscount, became the design responsibility of Edwards in September 1945 after Pierson became chief engineer, and upon Pierson's death in 1948 Edwards took over full technical responsibility as well. Just forty years old, he had the drive and sound technical and sales sense to make a success of the project. It was he who selected the Rolls-Royce Dart engines for their ruggedness, who opted for the circular pressurised fuselage, and who lengthened the fuselage to counter the serious underestimates of capacity made by all concerned. If it had not been for Edwards's pertinacity inside and outside Vickers, the Viscount might well have gone to the scrapheap in 1947. It had started as a 24 seater, but went into service as a 53 seater with the gross weight up from 34,000 to 56,000 lb. In April 1953 the Viscount began regular commercial flights for BEA,

The Vickers Viscount (courtesy of Dr N Barfield).

and orders followed from more than 60 other airlines, the largest coming from the USA and Canada. In all 445 Viscounts were built, worth £177 million, of which £147 million came from overseas sales, by far the biggest and most successful civil programme Britain had ever won.

In the meantime Edwards also became responsible for the development of the Valiant four-jet, high-altitude nuclear bomber, which first flew on 18 May 1951 from the grass airfield at Wisley. Its construction introduced a number of new design and machining concepts including, for the first time, sculptured milling and glasscloth plastic bonding. On the whole the Valiant was built with the same philosophy as the Viscount; in Edwards's own words it was 'an unfunny aircraft' which could be delivered ahead of more sophisticated designs. A total of 107 were built at high rate, starting the RAF's V-bomber deterrent force and making all British tests with nuclear bombs. While the Viscount led to the larger and more complex, but not nearly so successful, Vanguard (only 43 sold), so the Valiant led to the Vickers V1000, the world's first large long-range jetliner, which never flew at all. The Government withdrew its support in 1955, about six months before it would have flown, leaving the majority of the world market to the American 707 and DC8. Edwards managed to salvage something in the VC10 and Super VC10 jets of the 1960s, though by this time the market could not be recovered.

A director of Vickers 1955–67, Sir George (he was knighted in 1957), found himself and his company increasingly hamstrung by politics. Within a year of the V1000's cancellation, in 1956, the British Overseas Airways Corporation asked for permission to order, for its transatlantic services, 30 Boeing 707s, as there was no suitable British aircraft available — both the major American aircraft manufacturers, Boeing and Douglas, had announced their new four-engined airliners in 1954, for which they received large orders; meantime Britain's lead in jet technology had been cut by the grounding of the Comet I's in 1954-55, after four fatal accidents. The Government hedged, but finally decided that BOAC might buy 15 if an equal number of a comparable British aircraft were ordered. After a year considering the de Havilland 118 (which was then withdrawn) the airline switched to Vickers and Sir George was asked to build the VC10 with exceptional short-field performance, even though this penalised it in other ways. During 1957 the design was evolved specifically to meet BOAC's needs and proved capable of meeting the rigorous demands of the

*BAC-Sud Aviation Concorde
(courtesy of Dr N Barfield).*

airline's Empire services. BOAC ordered 35 on 14 January 1958 for delivery from 1964. During those six years relations between Vickers and BOAC deteriorated, with BOAC attempting to cancel the order in what became a contest of economic estimates and political wills. Sir George defeated his opponents until 1964 when the banker Sir Giles Guthrie (qv) became chairman of BOAC under a new mandate and managed to phase out many Super VC10 purchases. While the airline publicly criticised the aircraft as uneconomic, its own annual reports showed it to be an outstanding economic proposition.

Sir George's burdens were vastly increased from 1958 with the fight over the single Ministry order for a new warplane, the technically very advanced TSR2 supersonic bomber and reconnaissance aircraft. He led the joint team of the Vickers-English Electric project, which was the catalyst of the creation of the British Aircraft Corporation (the merger of Vickers, English Electric and Bristols) in 1960. The new company then acquired Hunting aircraft at Luton, founded by Percy Hunting (qv), which produced the design for a twin-jet airliner, which subsequently evolved into the BAC One-Eleven. TSR2 was cancelled in 1965. By then Vickers had also spent £60 million of its own and £30 million of government funds in developing the VC10 and the BAC One-Eleven, and had embarked on the Concorde. The latter, the world's first supersonic transport, had its origins in 1955, but the rising costs of advanced technology and Britain's wish to enter the EEC made the Government stipulate that an international partner be found. When General André Puget became chairman of Sud Aviation in 1962, Sir George found an agreeable ally, and presciently placed subcontracts with Sud factories to initiate the physical process of co-operation. Throughout the interminable political arguments, Sir George was unquestionably the man who made it actually happen. Sir George became chairman and managing director of BAC in 1963; he retired from the managing directorship in 1972 and from the chairmanship at the end of 1975, two years before it was forcibly nationalised into British Aerospace. Thus he left the BAC before the predicted £1,000 million development cost of the 400,000 lb aircraft became a reality in service a month later. Edwards's one great fear during

Concorde development had been that the Americans would decide to build an aluminium competitor, which fortunately they did not. However he had also had central involvements in setting up the Anglo-French Jaguar and Anglo-German-Italian Tornado combat aircraft programmes. A measure of his success was the growth in BAC's turnover and profits: sales rose from £191.4 million in 1968 to £307.1 million in 1975; over the same years trading profit more than doubled, rising from £12 million to £26.9 million.

Sir George Edwards, a resolute lively man, sharp and friendly, was a combination of hardheaded businessman and technician with a slight East London accent, a man of enormous ability, enabling him to comprehend the whole of some of man's largest undertakings. He came into British aviation just as the technological revolution flowered in the 1930s, and he led the Vickers/BAC team from there through the advent of jets to the supersonic age, an era when international competition and government intervention had the effect of eroding national aviation projects and companies.

Edwards was a council member (1949) and president of the Royal Aeronautical Society (1957–58). His abilities were recognised by honours ranging from his MBE (1945), CBE (1952) and KBE (1957) to the pro-chancellorship of Surrey University (1966); fellowships of the Royal Aeronautical Society (1960) and the Royal Society (1968), the Institution of Mechanical Engineers (1976), and of the Institute of Aeronautics and Astronautics (USA); and seven honorary doctorates from English universities. He published a large number of papers in technical journals on both sides of the Atlantic. Among his many other awards were the George Taylor gold medal (1948), the Daniel Guggenheim medal (1952) and the British Gold Medal for Aeronautics (1959). His crowning honour was the Order of Merit, conferred in 1971.

He married in 1935 Marjorie Annie née Thurgood; they had one daughter.

ROBIN HIGHAM

Writings:

Presidential Address to Royal Aeronautical Society 28 February 1958 *Royal Aeronautical Society Journal* Apr 1958.

'Partnerships in Major Technological Projects' Seventh Maurice Lubbock Memorial Lecture (Oxford University Press, 1970).

'Technical Aspects of Supersonic Civil Aircraft' *Royal Society* 29 Mar 1973.

'Looking Ahead with Hindsight' Sixty-Second Wilbur and Orville Wright Memorial Lecture, Royal Aeronautical Society London, 6 December 1973 *Royal Aeronautical Society Journal* Apr 1974.

'The British Aerospace Industry – A National Asset' Second Christopher Hinton Lecture, The Fellowship of Engineering London, 29 November 1982.

Sources:

Unpublished

BCe.

MCe.

Information from Bill Gunston and Dr Norman Barfield.

Personal knowledge.

Published

The Aeroplane Directory 1961.

Aerospace June 1973.

Charles F Andrews, *Vickers Aircraft since 1908* (Putnam, 1969).

DNB.

Charles Gardner, *The British Aircraft Corporation: A History* (Batsford, 1981).

John D Scott, *Vickers: A History* (Weidenfeld & Nicolson, 1962).

WW 1982.

EDWARDS, James Coster

(1828-1896)

Tile and brick manufacturer

James Coster Edwards was born at Trefynant in Denbighshire in 1828, being christened at Llangollen parish church on 28 November. At this time his father, William Edwards, was employed as a clerk at some local coalmines. After an elementary education, J C Edwards began work as an apprentice to a draper in Wrexham, leaving to become a storekeeper at the New British Iron Co's works in Acrefair, Denbighshire. At the age of about thirty he was involved in an unsuccessul venture in operating a smelting works.

In about 1860 his father bought some coal works, and J C Edwards used the clay from the seams to make common bricks and earthenware, in a yard where he employed a man and two boys. He became the first to exploit fully the value of the red Ruabon marls and so helped to initiate the recovery of the local economy from the long recession caused by the decline of the iron industry in the 1820s. As the market for architectural and industrial ceramics developed, new works were established and by the time of its founder's death, the firm of J C Edwards employed nearly 1,000 men in four large factories. A works at Trefynant, bought in the 1860s, eventually covered six acres and made encaustic tiles and sanitary

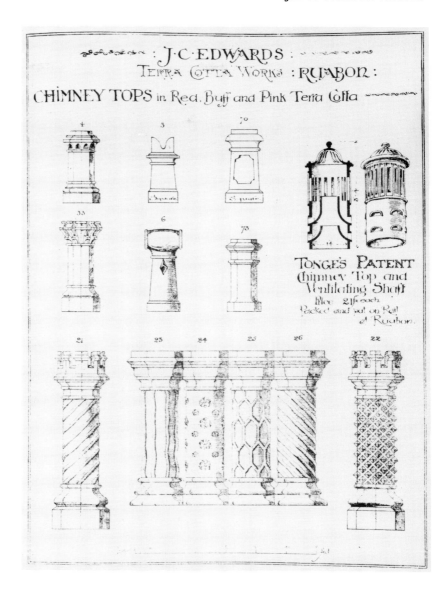

Designs of terracota chimney tops from a catalogue of patterns by J C Edwards c 1903.

pipes. In 1871 or the following year J C Edwards took over two kilns at Penybont sited by one of the richest clay reserves of the area. Initially used for the manufacture of roofing tiles and facing bricks, it was this clay that proved ideal for being pressed and fired into the red terracotta for which the business became famous. It was used in London and most of the provincial cities, but most widely in Birmingham, Leeds and the towns of south Lancashire and Cheshire. Among the most important contracts that J C Edwards supplied were the Prudential head office extension in 1897-1901 in Holborn, London, designed by Alfred Waterhouse (qv), and the exterior of the Assize Courts in Birmingham by Aston Webb and Ingress Bell in 1887-91. For more modest buildings, a range of copings, pier caps and other components was sold from catalogues. While J C Edwards is supposed to have designed some of the details himself, he also commissioned architects for designs: Douglas and Fordham, for example, were responsible for a range of chimney tops. The Penybont works was extended in response to growing demand, so that it incorporated 45 kilns and provided employment for 500 workers in 1896. In 1883 a new works was opened at Coppy, Rhos, for the manufacture of glazed and enamelled bricks. Pottery making was introduced in the fourth of J C Edwards' factories, at Plas Kynaston.

After about 1890, J C Edwards progressively withdrew from the management of his business, to pursue responsibilities as a landowner and as a figure within the county. He moved into Trevor Hall near Llangollen and purchased the adjacent West Tower Estate. He held office as a JP, DL and in 1892-93, as High Sheriff, in the county of Denbigh.

J C Edwards and his wife, Elizabeth, had five daughters and two sons.

In the spring of 1896 he went to Guernsey for a recuperative holiday, but died on 26 March at Government House. He was buried at Llantysilio church, near Llangollen. He left an estate proved at £54,904 gross. His sons, J C Edwards and E Lloyd Edwards, inherited the business but, reflecting changing architectural demands, terracotta was made on a decreasing scale in the Edwardian and inter-war periods, with flooring tiles and facing bricks making up the bulk of the production until the firm closed in the early 1960s.

MICHAEL STRATTON

Sources:

Unpublished

PrC.

Published

'Chimney Top Designs: Douglas and Fordham, Architects' *British Architect* 43 (1895).

'Contemporary Manufacturers and Art Workers: J C Edwards ' *Building News* 58 (1890).

'J C Edwards' *Bye-Gones Relating to Wales and the Border Counties* 13 (1895-96).

G C Lerry, 'The Industries of Denbighshire' *Denbighshire Historical Society Transactions* 1959.

Llangollen Advertiser 27 Mar, 3 Apr 1896.

'Visit to J C Edwards' Works' *Builder* 43 (1882).

Wrexham Advertiser 28 Mar 1896.

EDWARDS, Sir Ronald

(1910-1976)

Industrialist and promoter of management education

Sir Ronald Edwards (courtesy of Mrs Margaret Ackrill).

Ronald Edwards was born on 1 May 1910 in New Southgate, North London. His father Charles Edwards, who eventually became a foreman, was a gas fitter at the Southgate Gas Works; he had had little education, having run away from a disliked stepmother as a boy. Edwards's mother, born Alice Osborne, was a kindly but anxious woman, who worried over the health of her two surviving sons, Ronald and Clifford, and the uncertain digestion and temper of her husband.

Charles Edwards was determined that his sons should have a better education than his own, and he bullied but also coached Ronald through a scholarship from his elementary school to Southgate County School; the boy was not happy amongst the better-off and better-dressed schoolmates, and, afraid of teasing, only admitted to short sight and the need for glasses when he was thirteen. He surprised himself by reaching matriculation standard in the School Certificate, but there was no thought of his staying at school beyond the age of sixteen. He left, to become an office boy in his father's gasworks. His most favourable impression at school was of the manners and mores of some of the middle-class women teachers. At the end of the year, again on his father's initiative, Edwards left the gasworks to become a general clerk and office boy in a very small firm of accountants, Barker & Bell. That firm was taken over by a larger one, J Dix Lewis Caesar, and Edwards and his father were not pleased to find that Ronald was relegated to office boy. Edwards therefore remonstrated, and was taken under the wing of a senior partner as a junior audit clerk, and he also enrolled for a correspondence course which led to his becoming a certified accountant. His father paid for this course out of his post office savings. The premiums which would be required if he were to become an articled clerk, and then a chartered accountant, were quite out of the reach of his family. There was therefore, no question of his ever being a partner in the firm.

He did well in the office, becoming an expert on tax and tax avoidance which benefited his firm, and himself through a small rise in pay. He was not at ease socially with the articled clerks, and enrolled for a Bachelor of Commerce degree of the University of London spending his spare evenings attending lectures at the City of London College. Having passed the first examination, he decided to do the second, longer part of the course through correspondence, and after working late at the office in Cheapside, he stayed on, doing his correspondence essays. He gradually realised that the men who annotated them and sent them back to him were outstanding people. They included Professor Paish, Lionel (Lord) Robbins, and (Sir) Arnold Plant. Edwards wrote of the last '... he quite literally taught me to reason ... Learning to think was totally intoxicating.'

{unpublished memoirs} The outcome was a first class honours degree, and in 1935 an assistant lectureship at the London School of Economics, a place which ever after retained his affections. Under the guidance of Plant and Robbins, he began to use the tools of economic analysis to question some established tenets of accountancy, most often in the pages of *The Accountant*. This brought him some criticism, particularly from the head of his department in the LSE (Stanley Rowlands), but also increasing approbation from academic and other accountants. He was fortified in his stance by the friendship of Ronald Coase and Ronald Fowler, who were appointed to the LSE at the same time as himself, and like him, given full lectureships and permanent appointments in 1938. In 1936 he married Myrtle Violet Poplar, previously a secretary at Dix Lewis Caesar: their relationship proved a very happy one.

When the war began in 1939, Edwards continued to write and teach, but the LSE was evacuated to Cambridge where he joined it for part of each week. After being rejected by the Royal Navy because of unsuspected colour blindness, Edwards in May 1940 joined the newly-established Ministry of Aircraft Production, at a salary of £800 per annum, the sum he was earning by then at the LSE. A spell in Harrogate and London was followed by a year in Birmingham and Coventry in the aftermath of fierce air-raids on those cities, to re-establish disrupted factories and re-site others. He was helped in this by Myrtle, in the sort of ad hoc arrangement only manageable in an emergency. He saw the inside of many factories, and had the opportunity to review their efficiencies — and their accounts. The gap between well and badly run firms was great, and he made actual and mental notes about this. Subsequently he was recalled to London to help in the assignment of the 'labour budget' of manpower — that is, to assist in the management of the manpower allocated by the Cabinet to the Ministry of Aircraft Production, and to defend it against the demands of the other ministries. When the bulk of this work was over, he was put in charge of a section which sought to identify shortcomings in the range of British industries which were needed in wartime. His work concentrated on the watch and clock industries, training grounds for the skills essential to the production of measuring devices in aircraft. These industries had dwindled in pre-war Britain. Edwards' plans for them post-war drew high praise from Sir Stafford Cripps, led to the re-establishment of the industries with a temporary government subsidy as he recommended, and led to his own association with them. He became chairman of the British Clock and Watchmakers Association in 1946, and held that office until 1969.

In spite of financially tempting offers to remain in the civil service, Edwards returned to the LSE in 1946. He was unanimously appointed Sir Ernest Cassell Reader in Commerce with reference to Industrial Administration. A year later he established a seminar, in which he hoped to bring together men from the practical world of business, academics who were interested in how the cogs in the economy worked, and civil servants who in the course of the war had had to deal with many business enterprises. That this was such a novelty illustrates the very segregated nature of British public life which Edwards wanted to shake up. He also hoped that businessmen would learn from each other, and that the diffusion of ideas would in some measure encourage better practices in business at large. He had some opportunity to try his ideas of the way customers might react to prices, and how this in turn might lead to a better allocation of the nation's resources, through his membership of the Clow Committee, set up by the Government in 1948 to investigate the use of electricity by non-industrial users. This was an introduction to the newly nationalised electricity supply industry, and an appointment gained through his friendship with the Labour Minister for Fuel and Power, Hugh Gaitskell. Pre-war, he had run a seminar with him on pricing in public utilities. Now, the committee's recommendation which was largely Edwards's, was accepted in principle — it was for a higher price for electricity in the winter quarter, to limit consumption to something like the load which the overtaxed supply industry could produce and distribute — but it was modified in its implementation, so firm conclusions were difficult to draw.

Edwards did not get the chair of accountancy when it became vacant at the LSE but in 1949 he was made Professor of Economics with special reference to industrial organisation. He produced an excellent book called *Co-operative Industrial Research*, fired by what he saw of the contrast between well-directed and half-hearted efforts, and a smaller volume, *Industrial Research in Switzerland*, inspired by what he saw of the Swiss economy on his visits for the watch industry. His contacts with the world of business increased through his seminars, and he began a book, *Business Enterprise*, with Harry Townsend, a junior colleague at the LSE, which included some of the papers which were read at the seminars, besides his own, and Townsend's reflections.

Before it was finished, he again was drawn into an examination of the electricity industry. This time, the inquiry was into the organisation and efficiency of the whole industry. Sir Edwin Herbert (Lord Tangley) was its chairman, but Edwards was its driving force, and the unifier of the style and contents of its report. Most of what it recommended — a more commerical spirit in the industry, a better grip on pricing, a separate generating board — was accepted. Edwards imposed on it a unity and cheerfulness of style unusual in such a report. Percy (Lord) Mills was now Minister for Fuel and Power, and when Edwards included something on this and the other nationalised industries in a draft of his book, he sent it to Mills for comment. The outcome this time was Edwards's appointment as deputy chairman part-time, of the newly established Electricity Council, with the prospect of his being appointed chairman two years hence (ie 1960). At the Council, he was put on to wage negotiations, to which he was temperamentally unsuited, and to finance, where he was much more at home. He spent far more time going through the files and figures than he had allowed for, and did not establish personal relations with many people at the Council; also, his reputation was that of a critic of the industry, and a newcomer to it. His title of 'professor' was no recommendation, and in 1960 he did not get the chairmanship from a Minister unwilling to antagonise some doubting civil servants and a considerable body of Council opinion. Edwards took this manfully, got to know people better, was able to speak convincingly on behalf of the Council when the Government in 1961 produced a White Paper on the nationalised industries, and at the same time won the good opinion of civil servants as they became better acquainted with him, saw the wisdom of some of his views, and saw his basic concern for efficient, properly-costed nationalised industries. In 1962 he became chairman.

In this capacity, he was on good terms with both Labour and Conservative Ministers. This was the era of consensus, when the issues for nationalised industries turned on how they should be run, not whether they should exist. The Conservative Government in 1962 established the NEDC, which advocated an expansion of the electricity supply industry beyond its own intentions, in order to eliminate a possible bottleneck in anticipated national growth. The Labour Government of 1964 espoused the National Plan, which also called for an expansion of electricity supply. Edwards was from the outset wary of these additions, in spite of extrapolated trend lines. Fortunately, delays in the 100 per cent performance of larger generating sets, and then constructional delays in power stations meant that all the excess capacity which might have been available was not. Even so, it was hard to earn a sensible return on capital when so much of it was tied up in uncompleted projects, and higher prices to consumers might in the long run drive customers to other sources of fuel and so quite waste the industry's outlay. Governments were also concerned to restrain increases in the price of electricity in order to hold down demands for increased wages, which might make exports uncompetitive, and also fuel inflation.

In spite of all these pressures, the electricity supply industry during Edwards's chairmanship made a positive return on investment — but went into the red two years after he left it. His judgement of the longer term was correct. He was also constructive in the matter of wages and conditions of work. He was the driving force behind a remarkable series of agreements on status, productivity and pay, which had the effect of reducing the six or seven hours of overtime normally worked by manual workers in the industry to one or two a week. Pay temporarily dropped as hours dropped then caught up; labour efficiency increased; and new conditions of work — such as the right to visit a doctor or dentist in working hours — were introduced. In these things, one can see the result of Edwards's own awareness as a young man of social differentiation, his observations of the comparatively low pay in the industry during his membership of the negotiating committee in 1958-60, and also of his reflections on the 'Macmillan rebuke', an admonition delivered by the Prime Minister to the industry's negotiators in 1961, when they were endeavouring to avoid the major consequences of a strike by a comparatively minor infringement of the Government's wages policy. With R V Roberts, and some help from others, Edwards told the story in *Status, Productivity and Pay*, published in 1971. By the time it was published, much of what Edwards had sought to achieve was being undermined. Nevertheless, its rather circumspect and dull pages quietly tell a fascinating story.

Edwards left the Council in 1968. Before he went, he did his best to get agreement for the re-structuring of the industry — most notably to make the Generating Board subordinate to the Council, so that its overextended power station programme would be brought under its control. He persevered with this after he left, but to no avail. The same government policies — or lack of them — which had led to acceptance, even encouragement, of the Generating Board's plans, meant that his labours were fruitless. He was not concerned with the atomic programme because it was atomic, but because it was too large.

His next appointment was to be chairman of the Beecham Group, the large pharmaceutical and consumer product organisation. Its retiring chairman, H G Lazell (qv), knew that there were three very able young men in the highly prosperous company, any one of whom might, after a proving time of some seven years, become its chairman. In the meantime, he needed someone else to succeed him. But he did not want a conventional caretaker. He wanted a man with some drive, who, while consolidating the Group's more recently acquired subsidiaries, could banish the 'pills and powders' image of Beecham, and particularly through an ability to present a good case to Government, when need be, get more respect, and thence more of a hearing for the firm and the pharmaceutical industry. A number of pressures were involving Government with the industry, eg disquiet over the cost of drugs to the National Health Service, and the debate over the correct testing of drugs, an issue raised by the thalidomide tragedy of the 1960s. Edwards, with his sound views on finance, his long association with politicians and civil servants, his interest in applied research, and his age — fifty-eight — was exactly what Lazell wanted. What is more, he did exactly as Lazell hoped. Beecham remained the most consistently profitable company in the British economy since 1945. It was always in the top ten for profitability. Under Edwards it continued to acquire and consolidate, not only in the United States (eg Massingill) but also in Europe (Ligner). An address by Edwards in 1970, the 'Case for Competition', put the argument for a competitive though compassionate economy in a way which appealed to businessmen and Conservative politicians alike, and yet did not lose him the esteem of moderate Labour MPs. His speech on the pharmaceutical industry in 1974 was a reasoned plea on its behalf. What is truly noteworthy about both is that they are plain statements of the obvious; this is a rare quality in the speeches of businessmen and academics unless the speeches are also boring, and Edwards's were not.

Edwards's major disappointment in Beecham was the failure to merge Glaxo Ltd with his company. He wanted to do this in order to cope with the mounting cost of the development of pharmaceuticals. Big resources were needed if a British firm were to be strong enough to meet foreign competition. This move, contested by Glaxo, was disallowed by the Monopolies Commission in 1972. Edwards conclusion was that without it, Beecham would contine to grow, but not as fast as with it.

In 1975, when he was sixty-five, Edwards's retirement, long planned for that year, was announced. He had a number of minor but irksome maladies, including back trouble after a car accident, and a major difficulty with his sight. He had hereditary glaucoma, and while he was at the Electricity Council, an operation to reverse the damage in one eye had been unsuccessful. In 1972, he developed a minor heart condition, manageable in itself, but possibly able to cause fluctuations which would damage his sight. He therefore, rationally, had good reason to retire. His intention of continuing involvement in Beecham's affairs (he became its president) was curtailed; as at the Electricity Council, he found that, once he had vacated the chair, influence was not entirely welcome. After a holiday, and at last buying the bigger boat he had thought of intermittently for twenty years (he sailed a 16-foot Falcon in Weymouth Harbour), he felt better and restless; nevertheless when Lord Ryder of the National Enterprise Board asked him to become chairman of Britain's most troubled company, British Leyland, manufacturer of cars, trucks and buses, he declined. It became clear no one was prepared to take on such a challenge. It was also felt by business, trade unions and Government that it was important to the national economy that there should be a large British manufacturer of vehicles. The balance of payments deficit had been rectified more than once by the firm's exports and it employed 170,000 directly. On a second approach, Edwards, from a mixture of motives, agreed to take it on.

He got an agreement from Ryder that the management of British Leyland, and not Ryder or the NEB would deal with the vexed labour relations of the firm, and that, while the Government was prepared to put more than £2,000 million into the company, there should be no direct or indirect interference in its running. Instead, the relationship should be that of management to shareholders — ie reporting, with the sanction of sacking in the last resort. Ryder infringed both these principles, but Edwards established that this would not happen again. He also made the commendable resolution to shun publicity, until he had something worth saying. This was a marked contrast to the flamboyant style of (Lord) Stokes, the previous chairman. Edwards began work on his first annual address to the shareholders, explaining some of these things, and the measures he was taking to improve the quality of the products, on which sales would in the future depend.

Before he could deliver it, he died quite unexpectedly on 18 January 1976, not of the heart condition, but of a long-standing but undiagnosed disease of the liver. His ability to make something of British Leyland was scarcely put to the test, but his strong-willed successor, Sir Michael Edwards, used some of the same tactics and principles that he initiated.

Edwards had a highly complex character, and the variety of men and women who grieved over his death bore testimony to this. His family were devoted to him, and so were his secretaries. He had many good friends in other businesses, but also critics within those which he ran. This often happens with forceful leaders who are dictatorial in manner and temperament, but this was not Edwards's style. He had a creative mind, but preferred to work by time-consuming discussion and consensus. This, to him, meant that he could be friendly with those with whom he disagreed, but they did not always see it that way. Moreover, while patient with patient people, he could be peremptory with pretentious ones. He worked immensely long hours himself, and expected others to do the same when he called for facts and figures to establish a case. When he was writing something, or merely editing someone's draft, he went over and over the sentences. He also liked to be something of an enfant terrible in his younger days, and when he was older, he could not resist affronting some of his more radical colleagues in the LSE by adopting a brass tacks, no-nonsense philistine persona (in fact he loved classical music and ballet, and appreciated his wife's taste in art and décor). This led to a hostile piece in the *Observer* when, in 1966, it was suggested that Edwards might be Director of LSE. He backed away from the suggestion, but he was perhaps naively hurt by the reaction he had produced.

He liked the politics of consensus — and he did not think that consensus could cover more intervention in the economy than there was by 1974. His last major government inquiry, this time with himself as chairman, was into civil aviation (1967-69). He sought with considerable success to produce a report which would be acceptable to both major parties by injecting competition into airline operation, without the disruption of major denationalisation, and the risk then of re-nationalisation. It was also crisp and lively in style. Edwards was not a keen committee man. His favourite committee was the University Grants Committee, because it was run effectively with a minimum of references back. He did not become wealthy until he became chairman of Beecham (he eventually earned £41,000 per annum, made from profitable investments, and died worth £208,563), but when employees were being asked to accept only small increases at the Government's request he cut his own salary. It was an unusual gesture; he saw money as the reward for effort and endeavour. He made friends in unlikely places — his MAP chauffeur, thirty years on wrote to congratulate him when he was knighted in 1963; Bryher, the historical novelist, and daughter of Sir John Ellerman (qv), contributed airfares so that his wife could accompany him on his various fact-finding travels; an East End hawker, whose accounts he disentangled while at Dix Lewis Caeser, lent him money towards his first house, and impressed him with maxims about trading which Edwards still pressed into service at Beecham and when he became a director of ICI in 1969. Academics were sometimes wary of him — his field of interest, the behaviour of business, what made for its success, and for its failures, now a commonplace of many applied economists and others, was startling in its novelty, and did not lend itself readily to abstractions or model-making. He was above all a man who offered explanations which people in a number of disciplines and occupations could understand and accept, a rare quality in British public life.

MARGARET ACKRILL

Writings:

'The Nature and Measurement of Income' *The Accountant* 13 articles. 2 July-24 Sept 1938. Revised and reprinted in W Baxter (ed), *Studies in Accountancy* (1950, 1962, 1977).

Co-operative Industrial Research: A Study of the Economic Aspects of Research Associations Grant-aided by the Department of Scientific and Industrial Research (Pitman, 1950).

'Industrial Technologists and the Social Sciences' *Economica* Nov 1951.

(with Harry Townsend) *Business Enterprise. Its Growth and Organisation* (Macmillan, 1958).

(with idem) *Studies in Business Organisation* (Macmillan, 1961).

(with idem) *Business Growth* (Macmillan, 1966).

PP, British Air Transport in the Seventies. Report of the Committee of Inquiry into Civil Air Transport (1969) Cmnd 4018.

'The Case for Competition' *Journal of the Royal Society for the Encouragement of the Arts* 119 (1971).

EDWARDS Sir Ronald

A complete list of Sir Ronald's writings has been deposited in the *DBB* files.

Sources:

Unpublished

Electricity Council, archives.

Annual reports of the London School of Economics, the Electricity Council, the Beecham Group and British Leyland.

BCe.

MCe.

PrC.

Ronald Edwards's unpublished memoirs.

Correspondence in the possession of Lady Edwards, Clifford Edwards, and private papers housed by the Beecham Group.

Oral information from Lady Edwards and nearly 50 colleagues and friends (complete listing in *DBB* files). This entry is based on materials collected for a forthcoming biography of Sir Ronald.

Published

Ely Devons, *Planning in Practice: Essays in Aircraft Planning in Wartime* (Cambridge University Press, 1950).

W K Hancock and Margaret M Gowing, *British War Economy* (HMSO, 1949).

Leslie Hannah, *Engineers, Managers and Politicians* (Macmillan, 1982).

Douglas Jay, *Change and Fortune: A Political Record* (Hutchinson, 1980).

John Jewkes, *Ordeal by Planning* (Macmillan, 1948).

(Lord Richard) Marsh, *Off the Rails. An Autobiography* (Weidenfeld & Nicolson, 1978).

Reginald Maudling, *Memoirs* (Sidgwick & Jackson, 1978).

Times 20 Jan 1976.

WWW.

Sir William Palin Elderton (courtesy of the Equitable Life Assurance Society).

ELDERTON, Sir William Palin

(1877-1962)

Actuary and insurance company executive

William Palin Elderton was born at Fulham on 26 June 1877, one of eight children and the second son of William Alexander Elderton, an army tutor who had been a Cambridge wrangler, and Sarah Isabella née Lapidge. Among the other children were Thomas Howard, later Sir Thomas Elderton, KCIE, chairman of the Calcutta Port Trust, and Ethel Mary Elderton, later a distinguished statistician who for a long time worked closely with Professor Karl Pearson.

Elderton was educated at Merchant Taylors' School but seems to have developed slowly. The untimely death of his father prevented his going to Cambridge; instead he went straight from school to the staff of the Guardian Assurance Co in 1894 and qualified for the fellowship of the Institute of Actuaries in 1901. In 1908, he joined the Star Assurance Society under J D Watson, whom he succeeded as actuary on Watson's retirement in 1912. By this time, Elderton had established an international reputation in his profession and had given proof of that essentially practical outlook which, allied to his actuarial skills, made him so remarkable a figure for the following half-century.

In October 1913, he was invited to become actuary and manager of the Equitable Life Assurance Society, with which he remained connected for the rest of his life, retiring as chief executive in October 1942 but continuing as a non-executive director. For six years (1947-53) he was president of the Society and, as such, chairman of the board.

At the time of his appointment, the Equitable had drifted far from the pre-eminent position which it had enjoyed following its foundation in 1762 as the first life office to transact life assurance on scientific principles. Its early success led to fears about its size because company structure had not yet evolved to provide an adequate framework for the business. The Equitable was established as an unincorporated mutual society and at its zenith had almost 10,000 members. It was thought that the Society would be manageable if the total membership could be stabilised at not many more than 5,000 members, new entrants replacing the deaths. The well-intentioned measures designed to produce this, in fact led in due course to stagnation until the situation could be remedied in 1892. Though the control of the Society was modernised by the adoption of new articles of association in 1893, it had never completely recovered from the long period of stagnation. Indeed, Elderton's predecessor as actuary of the Equitable saw little prospect of ever achieving a sufficient flow of new business. Elderton, with energy and enthusiasm, revitalised the Society and transformed it into a modern, thriving life office. The total funds of the Society, standing at £4.6 million in 1869, increased from £5 million in 1914 to £14 million in 1943. This remarkable growth was largely due to

Elderton who, building on the company's unique history, developed business through the Society's existing connections and his own wider contacts; expanded staff and organisation; and managed the Society's resources with care and imagination.

Elderton was called to leadership in both professional and business organisations, becoming chairman of the Life Offices' Association (1927-28); chairman of the British Insurance Association (1937-38); president of the Institute of Actuaries (1932-34); president of the Insurance Institute of London (1935-36); president of the Chartered Insurance Institute (1942-43). He served on the Council of the Royal Statistical Society, 1921-45, with four short breaks, being a vice-president in 1926-27 and 1941-42. In 1931 he was elected a fellow of the Faculty of Actuaries in Scotland.

Throughout his business life, he contributed much to the profession through his books, papers and practical research on a wide range of topics concerning life assurance and statistics. These included three major papers on the valuation of life assurance business and a stream of articles concerning the study of mortality experiences and the construction of tables. His part in the foundation and development of the Continuous Mortality Investigation was a major achievement. In 1937, the Faculty of Actuaries and the Institute of Actuaries jointly presented to him a gold medal, a signal honour in recognition of his distinguished services to actuarial science. In 1938, the University of Oslo conferred on him the honorary degree of PhD.

He contributed much to statistics especially through his friendship with Karl and Egon Pearson. His book on *Frequency Curves and Correlations* was originally published in 1906 by the Institute of Actuaries; it served a wider, university circle, with subsequent editions in 1927, 1938 and 1953, the latest revised edition appearing in 1969. In his early years, he contributed to *Biometrika* and, in 1901, computed the first table of the χ^2 integral. Although Elderton was occupied with a busy professional life outside the statistical group at University College, London, his outside position was not without some importance to the group. When the Biometrika Trust was formed in 1935, he was invited to become the first chairman of the trustees and served until 1961.

During the First World War, Elderton served with Sir Alfred Watson as statistical adviser to the Ministry of Shipping and the value of his service was recognised by honours conferred by both Britain and France. He carried out similar duties in the Second World War, ultimately becoming chief statistical adviser to the Ministry of War Transport. He was created a knight in 1938, KBE in 1946.

In 1938, Elderton was appointed chairman of the White Fish Commission which led to the establishment of the White Fish Authority. For some years, too, he was chairman of the East India Railway Co, when it was concerned with the investment of the sinking-fund moneys for the benefit of annuity-holders. He was also a member of the Court of the Royal National Pension Fund for Nurses and was a governor of the City of London College.

He had an intense love of the countryside and enjoyed walking and sketching and painting. He was also interested in genealogy and contributed a paper to the Society of Genealogists. Elderton was a warm personality with a quick brain and an accurate memory. While he was far-sighted in business, he was also an efficient and sympathetic administrator which made him a well-loved leader of a team both in his office and in the various projects with which he was connected. All through his life, he had a ready interest in young people, keen to help them to make the best of their lives, however humble, encouraging them with humour and sagacity.

Elderton in 1920 married Enid Muriel, daughter of George Podmore, a schoolmaster; they had one son. Sir William Elderton died on 6 April 1962, leaving £61,865 gross.

MAURICE E OGBORN

Writings:

A much longer and more comprehensive list of Elderton's writings is in the *DBB* files. His most important were in contributions to learned journals, especially the *Journal of the Institute of Actuaries*. His books included:

Frequency Curves and Correlations (Institute of Actuaries, 1906).

(with Ethel Mary Elderton) *Primer of Statistics* (Adam & Charles Black, 1909).

(with Richard C Fippard) *The Construction of Mortality and Sickness Tables* (2nd edition, A & C Black, 1922).

(with Henry J P Oakley) *The Mortality of Annuitants, 1900-1920. Investigation and Tables* (Institute of Actuaries, 1924).

Shipping Problems, 1916-1921 (A & C Black, 1928).

Sources:

Unpublished

BCe.

MCe.

PrC.

Published

Biometrika 49 (1962).

Journal of the Institute of Actuaries 88 (1962).

Journal of the Royal Statistical Society 125 (1962).

Times 7, 11, 13, 26 Apr 1962.

Transactions of the Faculty of Actuaries 28 (1964).

WWW.

ELLERMAN, Sir John Reeves

(1862-1933)

Shipping magnate and financier

Sir John Ellerman with his son John in the early 1920s (courtesy of the Times Newspapers Ltd).

John Reeves Ellerman was born at 100 Anlaby Road, Hull. He was the son of Johann Herman Ellerman (née Ellermann), a corn merchant and shipbroker who had migrated from Hamburg to Hull in 1850. The senior Ellerman's family had always been Lutherans and had been employed as corn millers and merchants for generations. (Ellerman was widely assumed, both by Jews and anti-semites, to be Jewish but he had no Jewish ancestry.) Although one recent historian has claimed that the senior Ellerman had 'achieved considerable success' in business {Taylor (1976) 9}, and although he had been appointed the local Hanoverian honorary consul, Ellerman's father left only £600 when he died in November 1871, aged fifty-two, when his son was only nine years old.

Ellerman's mother, Anne Elizabeth Reeves, whom the father had married in 1854, came from somewhat more prosperous stock. She was the daughter of a local solicitor, Timothy Reeves, who left £20,000 when he died. Ellerman's mother survived her husband by many years, dying in April 1909. Ellerman was her only son; he had two sisters, one of whom survived until her one hundred and third year in 1959. Ellerman was nominally an Anglican throughout his life, although no account of his life has ever mentioned the least interest in religion on his part. 'He rarely attended a church', one biographer has remarked {private information}.

After his father's death, Ellerman was taken by his mother, for reasons which remain obscure, to live in Caen, France, where Ellerman acquired a keen interest in sports, especially in mountain climbing and swimming, and what his daughter described as a 'Continental view of life' {Bryher (1963) 97}. Ellerman here learned fluent French and always held the French in high regard.

Ellerman returned to England to attend, briefly, King Edward VI School in Birmingham, where his mother had moved. In later life Ellerman was quoted as saying 'If I had gone to public School I should never have got so far in business'{Taylor (1976) 9}. Ellerman lived away from home from the time he was fourteen onwards following — so his daughter reports — an argument with his mother over smoking in the drawing room. Apparently on the advice of his maternal grandfather, Ellerman articled himself to William Smedley, a Birmingham chartered accountant. When he was sixteen, his maternal grandfather died, and Ellerman inherited a legacy, part of which he lent to Smedley in return for the right to take an annual four months' holiday while still under articles. Ellerman spent this time mountain climbing in Switzerland and India.

It was during this period that Ellerman's superlative abilities at finance first became evident. Ellerman passed his accountancy examination with the highest possible marks, according to his daughter. After working briefly for a Birmingham accountancy firm, Ellerman moved to London where he gained employment with Quilter, Ball & Co, one of the capital's most eminent accountancy firms. Within two years he was offered a partnership by the firm's head, Sir Cuthbert Quilter.

At twenty-four, deciding that his abilities were such that they could no longer be shackled to a larger firm, Ellerman formed his own accountancy business, J Ellerman & Co, at 10 Moorgate. Thus began the most critical, and perhaps most obscure phase of Ellerman's career. It is clear that Ellerman prospered exceedingly during the next seven years. In 1890, he established the Brewery & Commercial Investment Trust, perhaps the earliest of his major financial undertakings, and one which he continued to head until his death. Like everything in his remarkable career, the Trust soon grew enormously, appreciating fourteen-fold in nine years. Significant non-shipping interests thus pre-dated Ellerman's shipping career, and played a major role throughout his entire life. At this time, he mixed freely with the younger London financial world, meeting many of those men who would collaborate with him during the next phase of his career, and rapidly acquired a reputation for outstanding ability. He opened a branch of his firm in Birmingham, and in partnership with Henry Osborn O'Hagan (qv), company promoter, then of the City of London Contract Corporation, controlled four trust companies by the time he was twenty-nine.

When Ellerman was twenty-nine, early in 1892, the great shipowner Frederick Leyland (qv) collapsed and died at Blackfriars Station, London. Ellerman now entered the shipping business for the first time. With O'Hagan and Christopher Furness (qv), another talented, self-made financier-turned-shipowner, Ellerman formed a syndicate which acquired and reorganised Leyland & Co. (In his autobiography, O'Hagan claimed an instrumental role in introducing Ellerman to the shipping world by securing the original election of Ellerman to the Leyland board while he was still only a large shareholder and a figure unknown to shipping interests.) Furness, originally chairman, was succeeded before the end of 1892 by Ellerman, who became chairman and managing director. The firm was reorganised as a public company with a capital of £800,000, a figure which was considered by many to be far higher than its actual valuation. The takeover of so eminent a firm (Leyland himself had acquired and renamed the Bibby Line, an even older and more famous company) by young unknowns was widely criticised in the financial press, who prophesied disaster. Instead, under Ellerman's leadership, the company grew and prospered, despite his inexperience as a shipping magnate, and Ellerman alone more and more came to dominate the firm. His daughter observed many years later that he 'had taken to shipping 'like a duck to water' {Bryher (1963) 26}. Ellerman soon eased out Furness from Leylands's board. 'Two Napoleons could not exist' {O'Hagan (1929) Vol 1 384}. In acquiring Leyland, Ellerman set a pattern which marked his career in shipping for the next quarter century. Ellerman's method was to purchase control of old-established shipping firms which, though still possessing a perfectly sound fleet and trading network, and much business goodwill, had entered into a period of entrepreneurial decline, often because of the incompetence of the heirs of the firm's founder. These firms dealt almost exclusively in merchant shipping rather than passenger transport. As his capital and wealth grew, Ellerman bought the entire capitals of these companies. Having secured them, he applied to them his unique financial and entrepreneurial skills, and added them to his growing empire. Ellerman's method was thus the very opposite of that of the ordinary 'asset stripper', for his aim was at all times to revitalise these lines and reorganise them as modern, profitable enterprises. While adding to his own wealth, Ellerman, it is fair to say, also saved hundreds of jobs and, in all likelihood, millions of pounds for the British shipping industry. Ellerman ought thus to be seen, as much as anything else, as the forerunner of the modern professionally-trained business manager, men often brought into a declining company for the same reasons and at the same point as Ellerman acquired his new shipping interests. Ellerman's place in the annals of modern British entrepreneurship is, if for no other reason, a significant one and decades ahead of its time.

Although there were other shareholders, Ellerman evidently secured the majority of Leyland shares soon after becoming chairman, for he ran the company virtually untramelled while enjoying a growing reputation for great wealth. Under Ellerman's lead, Leyland expanded with great success into the lucrative but crowded north Atlantic trade and paid an average dividend of 11 per cent over the next eight years. Ellerman modernised the Leyland fleet but did not immediately acquire other shipping companies. His first such venture occurred in 1900 when he took over the West India & Pacific Steamship Co, merging it in a reorganised and renamed Frederick Leyland & Co (1900). Ellerman was by now a full-time shipping magnate, having left his accountancy interests.

Ellerman first gained international attention in May 1901 when he sold most of Frederick Leyland & Co (1900) to J P Morgan, the American financial giant then at the height of his powers and bent on forming a transatlantic shipping combine, the International Mercantile Marine. Both the sale to American interests of a British shipping firm, and Ellerman's perspicacious handling of his end of these negotiations aroused widespread comment. Ellerman received a price (estimated at between £1 million and £2 million) which, it is alleged, was 50 per cent higher than the company's most recent valuation and, moreover, he received this sum in cash. Ellerman also remained as chairman of Frederick Leyland at Morgan's request. Ellerman compensated for the sale of most of Leyland by acquiring Papayanni & Co an old-established Liverpool shipping line, founded by a Greek migrant sixty years before, but like Leyland, faced with managerial crisis following the death of its principals. Ellerman acquired Papayanni in June 1901. With his purchase, Ellerman controlled 28 ships, compared with the 50 or more held before the Morgan sale. On the other hand, he was now certainly a multi-millionaire.

Ellerman then formed and floated a public company, his new shipping concern, renamed the London, Liverpool, & Ocean Shipping Co. Its directors, besides Ellerman, were Miles Mattinson, KC, a distinguished lawyer, MP, and company director, who remained a close confidant of Ellerman during the rest of his life, and Val Prinsep, Frederick Leyland's son-in-law who combined business acumen with eminence in the artistic world, being a Royal Academician. Like Mattinson, he remained Ellerman's close colleague and friend until his death in 1905 and his son, Throby, eventually became managing director of Ellermans. The new concern quickly acquired a 50 per cent interest in the City Line, a long-established Glasgow firm owned by the Smith family which, like the Papayannis, was in crisis following the death of its executives, for a price said to be £1 million. Still in 1901, Ellerman's company also acquired the Hall Line, yet another old firm whose principal, Robert Alexander of Liverpool, was in failing health and without heirs. Ellerman's interests at this time were mainly in the Mediterranean trade, a speciality augmented by still another acquisition at this time, the smaller Westcott & Laurance Line. Ellerman resigned his retained chairmanship of Frederick Leyland at the end of 1901 to devote himself solely to his own interests; at the same time he reorganised the board of the London, Liverpool, & Ocean Co, which now included, besides Ellerman, Mattinson and Prinsep, the brothers R A and F G Burt, all of whom would be associated with Ellerman for years to come. Also at this time, the former Leyland Line ships which Ellerman had retained were renamed the 'Ellerman Lines', and given the Liverpool-Portugal Western Mediterranean route, while Papayanni briefly continued to operate under its own name, eventually succumbing to the Ellerman Lines label.

During the latter part of the Boer War, Ellerman made his rapidly-expanding empire available for government troop and war supplies carriage. This gave Ellerman Lines the opportunity to break into the closely-regulated South African Shipping Conference, dominated by a few old firms like Union Castle — entering in the form of their Hall Line subsidiary. This route proved a long-lasting and major part of Ellerman's business. In 1903, Ellerman also re-entered the Atlantic trade (specifically, trade with Argentina and Uruguay) which Ellerman had surrendered to Morgan in 1901, and the Allan Line of Glasgow entered into an agreement with Ellerman's Hall Line to share this route. Ellerman encountered considerable difficulties on this route, which was subject to what one historian has described as 'cut throat competition' {Taylor (1976) 38}. Ellerman next reached out to the Indian trade and acquired another old and respected London-based firm, Bucknalls. In India, Ellerman specialised in transporting jute and other native products. Late in 1905 he negotiated a working agreement with still another established firm, the Glen Lines, and entered into trade with China and the Far East. Expansion into the East African coast and to the Persian Gulf followed before the outbreak of the war. Ellerman attempted to give some unity to his ever-growing empire by designing a new uniform for his employees and a new company pennant (a blue flag with the letters JRE in white) in use from October 1904: these would soon become renowned among the world's shipping lines.

Ellerman's rapid expansion quickly attracted considerable attention from the press and other sources. Ellerman's Boer War contributions, and what some sources have described, without any real evidence, as his growing presence behind the scenes in the Conservative party, brought him a baronetcy in 1905. (Ellerman chose as his motto 'Loyal jusqu'à la mort' and took the business-like title of 'Ellerman of Connaught Square'.) This was the only hereditary honour Ellerman ever received. He was also elected president of the British Chamber of Shipping in 1907, only fifteen years after he had entered the shipping trade.

Ellerman was far more than a shipowner; he was a profit maximising financier by training and inclination. His non-shipping interests were always substantial and probably were the source of at least one-third of his income. In 1914, for instance, the *Directory of Directors* recorded Ellerman as chairman of Ellerman Lines and director of Shaw, Savil & Albion, the shipowners, but as chairman or director of nine non-shipping companies, including six breweries: the field of his initial venture beyond accounting. Brewery shares always formed an extensive part of his portfolio. In 1902, according to James Taylor, he owned shares in 38 different breweries, and by 1918, more than 70. Ellerman seems to have been attracted to breweries for three reasons. Firstly, he customarily acquired extensive debenture shares (as he did throughout his range of investments) which gave him both greater control of the firm and a hold over its rock-solid property assets. Secondly, breweries generally yielded a higher rate of return than most other businesses. Thirdly, breweries often stood, like the shipping interests he acquired, on the downward slope of the entrepreneurial cycle, and were ripe for his attention and business abilities. Two such firms in which Ellerman served as chairman for many years were J W Cameron & Co of Hartlepool and Hoare & Co of Tower Bridge. In 1905, following the award of his baronetcy, Camerons invited Ellerman to become chairman, a position he held until his death. Hoare & Co had been founded in the fifteenth century; within one year of Ellerman's gaining control, it had earned its biggest profit in 435 years. Under Ellerman's control it expanded in a way which belied its age. In 1919 it acquired the Red Lion Brewery, which stood on the site of today's Waterloo Station, and in 1926 it acquired the City of London Brewery.

Ellerman also became a substantial figure in the British colliery business. He entered this field not to rehabilitate torpid firms, but to provide his ships with inexpensive and secure supplies of coal. He provided his shipping firms' chief coal bunkers around the world with top-quality British coal in huge quantities. He held shares in 22 collieries by the early 1920s, although he does not appear to have sat on the boards of any colliery companies listed in the *Directory of Directors*. (It is possible that many colliery firms were still private partnerships not listed in that guide.) Ellerman also held extensive and increasing non-shipping interests in newspapers, property, and general finance houses from this period.

By 1910 Ellerman was certainly the richest man in Britain. (It is likely — although the truth may never be known — that he achieved this position sometime between 1905 and 1910.) He had also already acquired a legendary reputation as a shadowy Croesus. While the size of his fortune at this time can only be estimated, it seems clear that he had already exceeded in wealth the other top British fortune-holders of the day, notably the Duke of Westminster (about £15 million), Sir Julius Wernher (qv), who left £12 million in 1912, Charles Morrison (qv) (who left £11 million in 1909), and perhaps Lords Iveagh and Leverhulme (qqv), who were probably in the same range. The war only added further to his standing. According to an obituary in 1916 Ellerman 'was quoted as saying that he was the richest man in England, being worth at that time £55 million' {*Morning Post* 18 July 1933}. If this remark is accurate — and it would be out of character for Ellerman to mislead — then Ellerman was certainly, in real terms, the richest man in British history down to the present time, and had added to his fortune at a rate exceeding that of any man in Britain. He was also the only Englishman who could be compared with the American centi-millionaires of the day like Rockefeller and Mellon. As with his American counterparts, Ellerman's wealth was already a household fact to the man-in-the-street. When Robert MacAlmon married Ellerman's daughter in 1919, he mentioned his wife's connections to a friend, the writer Wyndham Lewis. In his autobiography MacAlmon records the awe-struck silence which greeted his revelation: Lewis immediately turned his thoughts, it seems, to how Ellerman might help Britain's struggling writers and artists. Children in Eastbourne, where Ellerman owned a seafront mansion, were often brought to see the home of the richest man in England.

Ellerman was an advisor on shipping to the British Government during the First World War, and placed his ships at the Government's disposal. Mainly for his activities during wartime — which chiefly occurred behind the scenes — Ellerman was made a Companion of Honour in 1921, an order usually reserved for cultural figures and senior politicians, and a singular award for a businessman. The war generally proved a profitable, though, naturally, disruptive time for Ellerman. He expanded his North Atlantic trade, added part of the interests of the Watson Steamship Co to his group, and began a rice milling concern in Burma. Towards the end of 1916 came the last and greatest of his shipping takeovers. Ellerman then purchased Thomas Wilson Sons & Co of his native Hull, the largest private shipping company in the world, from the Second Lord Nunburnholme and his relatives, who were anxious to leave the shipping field which had made the family's fortune in the previous century. Ellerman's price was about £4.1 million. The firm was renamed Ellerman's Wilson Lines, and its shareholder's funds, which stood at £5.3 million at the end of 1916, rose under Ellerman's stewardship, to £8 million by the end of 1920. The Wilson Line had lost 26 ships from enemy action when Ellerman purchased the company, and Ellerman was well-aware of the closeness of the war's outcome. On Armistice Day 1918, Ellerman told his daughter — in an apparent reference to Albert Ballin — that 'The man who holds a similar position to myself in Germany has just committed suicide. I want you always to remember (that) the War has been a very close thing' {Bryher (1976) 190}.

Apart from the vicissitudes of his far-flung business empire in wartime, Ellerman was also extremely vulnerable, in the xenophobic hysteria of the time, as a second-generation German with a German surname and vast but mysterious business interests. Yet Ellerman was able to avoid most, but not all press criticism of his position, largely by owning a major slice of Fleet Street. In 1904 he became the largest shareholder in the *Financial Times*. He became a major shareholder in the *Daily Mail* and its associated newpapers at about the same time, and, with Lord Northcliffe (qv) whom he greatly admired, bought into the *Times* in 1912, becoming its third largest shareholder. During the war he bought the well-known weekly magazines, the *Sphere*, the *Tatler*, and the *Illustrated London News* among others. According to one of the few press attacks against Ellerman published during the war the *Times* 'ignored him as a war shipping profiteer, although it published cruelly unjust attacks on Sir Walter Runciman. That was simply an accidental coincidence' {*Daily Chronicle*, 30 April 1917}. This article also claimed that at the time Ellerman controlled one-eighth of Britain's significant shipping tonnage, totalling nearly 1.5 million tons, that the value of the shipping interests under his control exceeded £35 million, that Ellerman paid more income tax in 1916-17 than anyone in Britain, and that his annual income was about £3 million. Whatever the truth of the matter, Ellerman did escape the gaze of Fleet Street to a remarkable extent. After the war, he gradually divested himself of his newpaper interests, at great profit, beginning with the *Financial Times* in 1919 and his *Times* holdings in 1922. Ellerman was, of course, no newspaperman, and never attempted, as Beaverbrook did at this time, to use a previously acquired financial fortune to become a major press lord.

During the 1920s Ellerman became heavily involved in the London property market as a major purchaser, perhaps, indeed, the most ambitious London property buyer up to that time. Although Ellerman had acquired the freehold of his City office premises in 1915, his London property ventures began in earnest in 1920 when he purchased a portion of the Covent Garden Estate, including the Drury Lane Theatre, and formed a new concern, the Ellerman Property Trust, to supervise his property transactions. In the late 1920s he bought three chunks of central London which put him on nearly the same footing as the largest London property magnates like Lord Portman and even the Duke of Westminster. In 1925 he purchased 21 acres of prime Marylebone land from Lord Howard de Walden, reputedly for £3 million. Included in this area was Great Portland Street. In 1929 he purchased nearly 14 acres of Chelsea, including over 500 house properties, from the Cadogan and Hans Place Estates. In the same year he purchased from Lord Iveagh's trustees 82 acres of freehold land in South Kensington, originally belonging to Lord Kensington, with 1,150 houses and 200 blocks of flats. This he quickly resold to Metropolitan Ground Rents for over £900,000 and a 30 per cent profit. Ellerman also owned many smaller properties all over London, buying prime and promising sites as they came on the market. As with all other facets of Ellerman's business life, he paid individual attention to each transaction, and prided himself on his profound knowledge of the minutiae of the property market. During the last phase of his life, Ellerman was plainly one of the largest London landowners and, indeed, although he owned no agricultural land at all, was probably one of the biggest landlords in Britain in terms of rental income. Again, as with every other phase of Ellerman's career, in his property dealings he was in no sense a destructive or ruthless profit-seeker, and cannot be compared with the notorious property developers of post-war London. He had apparently turned to London property because of the security it provided in his overall portfolio.

Ellerman was also actively interested in a large number of other financial trusts and companies which were privately traded and hence not listed in the *Directory of Directors*. Their individual nature remains obscure although they probably included family trusts. In Ellerman's will he listed the 'trust companies managed by me' as including Moorgate Trust, Audley Trust, Audley British Investment Trust, F W Cook Investment Trust and the Ellerman Property Trusts. Industrial concerns there listed by Ellerman included J W Jameson Ltd, Bieckert's Brewery Co, and the River Plate Electricity Co. Earlier in his career he had been chairman of Milwaukee & Chicago Breweries Ltd, vice-chairman of William Gray & Co (1918) Ltd, a shipbuilding firm, and a director of Wilsons and of North-East Railway Shipping Co Ltd.

Meanwhile the backbone of Ellerman's career, his shipping interests, faced a new and infinitely less promising world when peace dawned in 1918. Ellerman's subsidiary concerns had lost nearly one hundred ships; all costs had greatly risen and world trade had greatly declined. Yet Ellerman's shipping concerns faced the future in considerably better form than many of its rivals. Apart from possessing a genius at the helm and the vast reserves of capital Ellerman commanded, his shipping firms were entirely free from debentures and mortgages, while Ellerman personally owned all ordinary and most preference shares in his firms. Ellerman naturally had a keen eye for such genuine growth areas as there were, and some expansion in Ellerman's shipping interests did occur during the 1920s, especially in the South and East African markets and in the Persian Gulf and Indian routes. Although Ellerman's shipping interests had declined in value from their wartime peak, Ellerman was still by far the richest man in the country, and of his shipping interests in this period it may be said that he weathered the storm and restored normality as well as anyone could. As a result of his mistrust of the Labour Party, which came to office in May 1929, he predicted a sharp economic decline and rearranged his portfolio to a certain extent just before the Depression actually came, although he did not, as was sometimes said, truly forsee it or its dimensions. It is probably true to say that the size of his fortune, remarkable as it was, had declined from its First World War peak. Nevertheless, it is difficult to point to any seriously mistaken business judgement in his entire career.

Ellerman had been in declining health for some time and, suffering a mild stroke in early 1933, he died at the Hotel Royale in Dieppe, on 16 July 1933, at the age of seventy-one. Despite the fact that his death occurred just after the nadir of the greatest depression in history, Ellerman left the extraordinary sum of £36,685,000, by far the largest British fortune left up to that time or indeed left down to the death of the second Sir John Ellerman (qv) in 1973 (Ellerman made no attempt to avoid death duties). Some idea of the unique status of the size of Ellerman's fortune in the annals of British entrepreneurs and wealth-holders may be gleaned by a number of relevant comparisons. Ellerman left nearly three times the fortune left by Britain's second wealthiest man Edward Guinness, Lord Iveagh the brewer, whose estate totalled £13.5 million in 1927. Ellerman by himself was wealthier than any of Britain's three wealthiest families — the Wills (qv), the Coats, or the English Rothschilds (qv) — were collectively; each of these families had produced ten or more millionaire wealth-leavers over several generations. Ellerman left about 30 per cent of all the wealth passing by probate in Britain in 1933, when nearly 400,000 adults were deceased in Great Britain. Among modern British businessmen, only Lord Nuffield (qv), and probably Lord Nuffield alone, can be mentioned in the same breath as Ellerman. But Nuffield (who gave away more than £30 million and left £3.5 million) earned his fortune in a novel area of manufacturing, which made centi-millionaires out of car makers like Ford, Dodge and Citroen in other societies. Starting without means or connections, Ellerman made his money in traditional fields where Britain had been predominant for centuries and its business dynasties successful for generations.

It is difficult to account for Ellerman's enormous fortune. Some contemporaries pointed to his parsimony; most of his obituaries claimed that he spent only 3.5 per cent of his income, and reinvested the rest without fail. Although little is known of his charitable activities, it is likely that he gave away very little, and certainly very little which brought him into the public eye. One obituary claimed that he 'gave generously to charity' in the Boer War {*Daily Mail* 18 July 1933}, while during the First World War he purchased St John's Lodge in Regents Park and established it as a home for disabled officers at a cost of £30,000 per annum.

Ellerman's will, drafted in July 1930, is extremely lengthy but a model of its kind; so much so that probate was granted on the largest estate in British history in the remarkable period of only five weeks (the average estate normally required about three months). Ellerman's executors were Frederick George Burt, secretary of Ellerman Lines, Sir Miles Mattinson, and the younger John Ellerman upon reaching twenty-one years and six months. According to this will, £6 million had been retained in liquid form to pay death duties. Within two years, Ellerman Lines were to be divided between his shipping and non-shipping interests. Small bequests (no more than £12,500 to each) were left to distant relatives, while charitable bequests totalled about £6,000. Ellerman's daughter received £800,000; his widow, £100,000, their house, and £36,000 per annum. The great bulk of Ellerman's estate went to his son, who thus received, after death duties, more than £20 million, and succeeded, aged twenty-three, to his father's place probably as the richest man in England.

The organisational framework of Ellerman's empire remained broadly similar throughout much of his career. In 1914, he served as chairman of nine companies listed in that year's *Directory of Directors*: Ellerman Lines, Brewery & Commercial Investment Trust, Debenture Securities Investment Trust, Flint & Co, J W Cameron, Lion Breweries, London General Investment Trust, Milwaukee & Chicago Breweries, and the United Discount and Securities Co. All of these were directly and personally controlled by Ellerman. At the time, Ellerman sat on only two boards of directors of companies of which he did not serve as chairman: the New Westminster Brewery and Shaw, Savill & Albion Lines. Significantly, Ellerman never sat on the boards of any companies, no matter how important or economically significant, over which he could not exert a primary degree of control. Despite his preeminent wealth, Ellerman had no interest in becoming a British J P Morgan, in attempting to dominate the commanding heights of the British economy by control over its banks, heavy industry, or transport network. This same pattern of command continued throughout Ellerman's career, and his directorates remained much as they were in 1914 until his death. By 1929 Ellerman sat on no boards of companies of which he was not chairman, and then chaired only nine companies, all remaining from 1914.

Ellerman's method of entrepreneurship consisted of gaining and holding the closest possible degree of control of the companies in which he was involved. He almost invariably held all or most of both the ordinary and preference shares of his key companies, although his total portfolio holding was very wide. He invariably chose to expand and develop by the most commercially sound method, avoiding anything which smacked of speculation or overextension of his resources. He was especially partial to gaining control of a company by holding debentures in it, which gave him ultimate control of that company's properties by means of fixed interest repayments. To all his undertakings Ellerman gave his total and full attention, backed by his superb memory and his professional knowledge of accountancy and finance. In essence, Ellerman was perhaps the first, and probably the most successful professional management entrepreneur, making a career of taking old but sound firms and restoring them to efficient and dynamic performance by expert means, which were at all times both scrupulous and sound. In this, Ellerman was decades ahead of his time, and his career plainly implies that the British economy had room for many Ellermans. Ellerman cornered the market in his fields of endeavour by being the ablest entrepreneur of his day. Especially toward the end of his life, Ellerman kept a good deal of his assets in highly liquid form as bank deposits. He was reputed to be the largest single depositor in the London banks, and to keep as much as £10 million in this form. (One reason for this was the special concern he had for smooth succession, and the ready payment of estate duties, upon his death.)

Much about Ellerman's career, when compared to those of other successful British entrepreneurs of his time, was anomalous or even unique, and considerable insight into his success may be gained by making this explicit. Unlike most British entrepreneurs, Ellerman was a genuine loner, probably the most striking and complete lone wolf in British business history, the purest approach to disembodied business intellect ever seen in Britain. He owed nothing to family, friends, or business associates apart from the very small circle of colleagues like O'Hagan to whom he almost certainly owed less and less as his career progressed. He was not the product of a major public school or a university. His lack of any family ties whatever in the business world immediately marks him as very different from the majority of successful nineteenth century businessmen, who almost invariably rose through the family firm. Similarly, Ellerman had no communal, religious, or sectional attachments or loyalties, again unlike many successful British businessmen. As will be shown, he scrupulously avoided entering society or the landed gentry. Although his relations with his shipping staff and men were genuinely good, Ellerman avoided labour-intensive industry, and especially avoided fields where he might have to direct his labour in a personal manner.

He rose primarily in the City of London and in the world of commerce and finance, sectors of the British economy inherently more lucrative than manufacturing and industry. According to his obituary, he 'had only one interest in his life. That was his work. His work was his hobby and his hobby was his work. He enjoyed acquiring some enterprise and building it up into a success, just as a great doctor gets deep satisfaction from curing a difficult or unusual disease' {*Daily Mail* 18 July 1933}. In her autobiography, Ellerman's daughter remarked of her father,

> I was always more interested in money, I think, than my father. He was a mathematician and his interests were in abstractions. I have seldom known anyone more remote from the things of this world. The success or failure of an equation meant a great deal to him, its rewards to himself very little. He

possessed the detachment that lifts finance into an art, creates "risk capital"
and is one of the nation's most valuable assets {Bryher (1963) 106}.

Ellerman's positive traits were less striking. He was a professionally-
trained and highly competent accountant, and strikingly able to use his
professional knowledge to his independent advantage. The contrast in this
regard between Ellerman, trained with the chartered accountants of
Birmingham and London, and the rough-hewn shipowners whom he
succeeded, trained in the school of hard knocks, was surely immense.
Ellerman, according to all accounts of his character, had a phenomenal
memory, and prided himself upon knowing details of all of his businesses
and the whereabouts of all of his ships. His interest in business life never
flagged, even when he was an old man, and he never delegated or
transferred the responsibility for the direction of his undertakings.

Ellerman never entered, nor sought to enter, British 'society'. The value
system and life-style of the aristocracy and squirearchy were utterly alien
to him. He owned no agricultural land, no castles or stately homes,
dividing his time between his mansion at South Audley Street, London, a
seafront house in Eastbourne, and hotels on the continent, especially in
France. As part of a business deal, Ellerman had in 1918 acquired
Longhaven House and Slains Castle in Aberdeenshire from the Errol
family. Ellerman never visited these uncharacteristic holdings, selling
them within three years. Although he acquired a baronetcy when only
forty-three, he neither sought nor received the high rank in the peerage
which could unquestionably have been his, as it came to so many lesser
businessmen in this period. Although a keen Conservative, Ellerman's
political interests and influences were always indirect. It is inconceiveable,
for instance, that he could ever have sought any elected office. He held, in
fact, no offices, positions, or posts of high degree of any sort, and must
have declined any such offers made to him. The usual accoutrements of
wealth and status in modern Britain — membership of a gentleman's club
or a growing fondness for the turf and the card table — were equally
unknown to him. 'No legends had gathered round his name', the *Daily
Mail* concluded in its obituary. 'He was the Silent Ford — the Invisible
Rockefeller. He had no public life. He had hardly ever been
photographed'.

Ellerman had few hobbies. Those of his youth, mountaineering and
vigorous physical activity, gave way to some golf, but his only physical
activity in later life was walking. Ellerman was fond of travel, and
travelled around the world. He lived for several months each year on the
Continent and elsewhere, and his daughter's autobiography recalls her
childhood trips to Egypt, Italy and France. Ellerman would remain in
constant touch with his London headquarters on these trips. Ellerman also
maintained a lifelong interest in art. He was no philistine, and acquired a
collection of contemporary French paintings of some note. His City office
was known for the excellence of its decorations. He was fond of French
cooking and an expert in the subject. In appearance Ellerman was often
said to bear a close resemblance to King Edward VII in maturity: a
bearded, portly figure. There are few photographs or paintings of him; the
best portrait, by Sir Luke Fildes, has brilliantly caught Ellerman's

paradoxical and seemingly impossible combination of perception and detachment.

Ellerman's private life was as mysterious as much of the rest of his career. The available standard reference sources disagree, for example, on his date of marriage, *Kelly's Handbook* stating that this occurred in 1898, *Burke's Peerage* that it took place in October 1908. There is no English marriage certificate to be found at either date and the precise date and place of Ellerman's marriage remains unknown. His wife Hannah, daughter of George Glover, is a somewhat shadowy figure who, it seems, led a primarily domestic life. She died in September 1939, aged seventy-one. It is known that Ellerman had two children by her. The elder, a daughter, was born at Margate in September 1894. Her given name on her birth certificate was Annie Winifred Glover; there is a dash in the space indicating the name of the father. She died in Switzerland in 1982. The younger Ellerman's son and heir, the second John Reeves Ellerman was born in London on 21 December 1909. Both were unusual and interesting personalities.

Ellerman's daughter lived at Eastbourne during much of her youth. She disliked the private school to which she was sent, and soon developed the traits of individuality, independence, and courage which marked her entire life, demonstrating as well great intelligence and unusual memory. Informed sources agree that, had she been a man, she would inevitably have succeeded her father and carried on in his singularly successful manner. Instead she became a novelist and poet of some note, writing many books under the pseudonym 'Bryher'. She knew many notable European writers and from the mid-1920s she lived in Switzerland. During the 1930s she played a courageous role in assisting several hundred German Jews, including the philosopher Walter Benjamin, as well as non-Jewish opponents of Hitler to escape from Nazi Germany. Her autobiography, *The Heart to Artemis*, published in 1963, provides one of the most useful sources about Ellerman's life, especially his childhood.

In 1920 while in New York, Annie Ellerman married a wandering young American bohemian poet and publisher, Robert MacAlmon (1896-1956), who lived in Paris during much of the 1920s where he was a friend and confidant of Ernest Hemingway, James Joyce, Gertrude Stein and other experimental writers and artists. A source more likely to be hostile to Ellerman and his way of life is difficult to imagine, and in MacAlmon's autobiography, *Being Geniuses Together* (1938), we have one of the few and certainly the most devastating portrait of Ellerman at home, based upon MacAlmon's residence in Ellerman's South Audley Street mansion for several months shortly after his marriage. At the mansion — described by MacAlmon as a 'stuffy old museum' — conversation was restrained 'so that servants would not overhear', and the walls and hallways were crammed with the most banal paintings and statuary. The Ellerman family, according to MacAlmon, led 'a frighteningly anti-social and lonely life, with their few "friends" or acquaintances, business associates, or, more accurately, employees of Sir John'. Ellerman was 'jealous of [his wife's] friendships'... planning his family's life to the minutest detail'. His son, then aged eleven, was 'taken wherever he went by his parents, a governess or a tutor, in either the Rolls-Royce or the Lanchester'. 'As regards finance', MacAlmon concludes, '[he was] ... a genius, but in many other respects he was a perfect case of arrested development, suffering innumerable childish fears' {MacAlmon (1938) 1-4}. Ellerman was also vengeful toward those businessmen who had crossed him, recorded MacAlmon, who quotes him telling his daughter, 'Dolly, that man once did something against me. I waited fifteen years, but he had to leave England. Now I will let him return' {*ibid* 59}.

In fairness, the portrait left by MacAlmon — who was divorced by Annie in 1927 (she married Kenneth MacPherson, an artist, the same year) — may well be biased and exaggerated; Ellerman, it seems, did manage to converse with MacAlmon about poetry and art without embarassment to either; Ellerman, indeed, left MacAlmon £500 in his will, despite his daughter's divorce. Others who knew Ellerman well have also seen other more redeeming facets to his personality. He was according to these sources ' a typical Victorian gentleman, charming and polite', 'extraordinarily perceptive and thoughtful'; the 'favourite guest' of waiters, and 'when finding he was in error and some junior clerk was correct, he would apologise unreservedly and openly' {information from James Taylor}. His guarded private life was the natural product of his wealth and fame and flowed as well from an equally natural desire to protect his children from interlopers, while his preference for solitude and privacy had been part of his character from early youth. Acquaintances of Ellerman, no matter how sincere, would inevitably expect him to demonstrate a personal generosity toward themselves commensurate with his wealth. Certainly the very considerable degree of independence he allowed his daughter, and the acceptance he gave, apparently without quarrel, to her unknown husband, is evidence that MacAlmon's depiction is unduly harsh.

Ellerman can thus not in fairness be compared with the genuinely paranoid, anti-social and destructive multi-millionaires who have so commonly appeared in the United States. If any comparison suggests itself, it is to a grand master chess champion who, while appearing solitary and eccentric to others, creates masterpieces by means of continuing ratiocination against a lifelong series of opponents. It is often argued whether chess is a game, an art, or a science; in Ellerman's case, he made business life into all three. 'Ellerman had the reputation of always learning from his mistakes', an employee recalled. 'His success... stemmed from his practice of reviewing his decisions and remedying the bad ones. He never cried over spilled milk' {private information}.

So much of Ellerman's business life was carried on by him alone that the searching and detailed account of his career which it evidently deserves may well now be impossible, but surely no one can fail to be supremely impressed by Ellerman's achievement, perhaps the greatest tour de force in British business history, or fail to perceive that Ellerman's methods genuinely have much to teach a later generation of business historians, and even businessmen, in a way which is true of few if any of his contemporaries. At the end of the day, however, the historian is forced to conclude that the known facts of Ellerman's career and of his approach to business entrepreneurship are probably insufficient to explain his extraordinary and singular success. Some special quality or qualities, evidently possessed by Ellerman, must be adduced to account for his achievements; their nature may well elude the historian forever. Ellerman has many serious claims to being regarded as the greatest entrepreneur in the whole history of British capitalism; his standing as the most sui generis of leading British entrepreneurs is beyond dispute.

WILLIAM D RUBINSTEIN

Sources:

Unpublished

James Taylor, Blundellsands, Lancashire, holds the Ellerman Lines and associated company papers.

BCe.

PrC; Will.

Published

Bryher (Annie Winifred Ellerman), *The Heart to Artemis* (Collins, 1963).

Burke's Peerage.

Daily Chronicle 30 Apr 1917.

Daily Express 17, 18, 19 July 1933.

Daily Mail 17, 18, 19 July 1933.

Directory of Directors 1892.

DNB.

Kelly's Handbook.

Robert MacAlmon, *Being Geniuses Together* (Secker & Warburg, 1938).

Morning Post 17, 18, 19 July 1933.

Henry Osborne O'Hagan, *Leaves from My Life* (2 vols, John Lane, 1929).

William D Rubinstein, *Men of Property* (Croom Helm, 1981).

James Taylor, *Ellermans. A Wealth of Shipping* (Wilton House Gentry, 1976).

Times 17, 18, 19 July 1933.

WWW.

ELLERMAN, Sir John Reeves

(1909-1973)

Shipowner and financier

The second John Reeves Ellerman was born in Folkestone on 21 December 1909, the only son and heir of the first Sir John R Ellerman Bt (qv) the shipowner and financier, and his wife Hannah née Glover. At the time of his son's birth, the senior Ellerman was forty-seven years old, and was entering the zenith of his unique business career. As the younger Ellerman was the only son and only close male relative of the wealthiest man in Britain his upbringing was bound both to present special problems and to be fraught with the material for psychological and personal trauma. The younger Ellerman's ability to cope with this was in itself a personal triumph and a personal tribute, both to himself and his father.

The younger Ellerman was educated at St Bede's Preparatory School at Eastbourne and spent two years at Malvern School (despite his father's misgivings about public schools) before finishing his education in Switzerland. Although an extremely intelligent and serious man, he did not proceed to university but read for the Bar at the Inner Temple, and then joined his father's staff at the Moorgate headquarters.

In December 1933, at the age of twenty-three, and long before he was really ready for the mantle, the younger Ellerman suddenly inherited the bulk of his father's fortune and formal control of his vast shipping, financial and property empire. Although the senior Ellerman had built up a highly competent managerial team, which was able to shoulder a considerable share of the burden which devolved upon it, the future of the Ellerman realm crucially depended upon the quality of the new heir. Although the younger Ellerman was not, and never pretended to be, in the same class as his father (few men were) he discharged his duties in a highly competent manner and was, according to those who knew him well, capable of mastering the intricacies of the business world in a highly professional way. Ellerman Lines adapted in a competent if conservative way to the constantly changing conditions of the next four decades, with their unexampled combination of dangers and setbacks for British commerce, including heavy wartime losses. Ellerman Lines modernised and expanded its fleet, especially after the mid-1950s, without introducing any startling departures, although there was a greater emphasis on passenger traffic and, from the 1960s, on new-design cargo ships, containerisation and computerisation, as well as a new emphasis on the South African and Australian markets. Ellerman Lines remained divided into its older individual components, and was not managerially rationalised until after the younger Ellerman's death in 1973. It avoided as well any departures into bulk petrol carrying or into any new transport fields, sticking mainly to the paths laid down by its founder. The reputation of Ellerman Lines in this period was as a conservative but wellbank's staff. Further afield, he was a governor of St Edward's School, Oxford, and one of the three honorary members of the Oxford Society, playing a notable part in raising funds for the restoration of Oxford's historical buildings. He was treasurer of St Dunstans and a member of the National Marriage Guidance Council. Essentially a modest man, he did not flaunt his charitable activities.

His recreations he listed as reading, golf and motoring. In 1958 he retired as deputy chairman of Barclays, but remained on the board.

Ellerton in 1918 married Dorothy Catherine, daughter of William John Green, a Hornsey timber buyer. They had two sons.

When he died on 20 August 1962 the *Economist* recorded that he 'was a master banker and a most human person. He had no arcane professionalism about him'. Sir Frederick Ellerton left an estate of £68,908 gross.

P E SMART

Writings:

'Is Retail Banking Desirable?'

Sources:

Unpublished

BCe.

MCe.

PrC.

Published

DNB.

Economist 25 Aug 1962.

Times 21, 22 Aug 1962.

Anthony W Tuke, 'Sir Cecil Ellerton' *The Spread Eagle* Sept 1962.

— and R J H Gillman, *Barclays Bank Limited, 1926-1969* (Barclays Bank, 1972).

WWW.

Sir John Elliot on his 1st day as chairman of London Transport, 1 October 1953 (courtesy of London Transport).

ELLIOT, Sir John

(1898-)

Railway manager

John Elliot (Blumenfeld) was born in East Battersea, London, on 6 May 1898, the younger son of Ralph David Blumenfeld, editor of the *Daily Express* 1904-32, and Theresa 'Daisy' née Blumfield (his second cousin). Educated at Marlborough, where he was 'happy all day long', he went to Sandhurst and was commissioned in the 3rd Hussars in 1917. He served with them in France, being involved with the rest of Gough's Fifth Army in the great German attack of 21 March 1918, an anniversary that he never failed to remember.

He resigned his commission in 1921, when adjutant at Aldershot, not having the private income then required for a peace-time cavalry officer. After a year with the *New York Times* he joined the London *Evening Standard*. In 1923 he assumed the surname Elliot (his second Christian name). He left the *Standard* in 1924 on a disagreement with the proprietor, Lord Beaverbrook (qv), and in 1925 joined the Southern Railway, reporting directly to Sir Herbert Walker (qv), the outstanding railway general manager of his generation. At first Elliot was public relations assistant, then, from 1926, he became assistant for public relations and advertising. In both spheres he began, with Walker's support but not always his full comprehension, a process of presenting the rapidly modernising and electrifying Southern to the public as an up-to-date concern, projecting an image of enterprise through the press and also new signs, rebuilt stations, named locomotives, and lively publicity. Elliot became development assistant to the traffic manager in 1930, assistant traffic manager in 1933, and assistant general manager in 1937. During this period he was much concerned not only with the working of the railway itself but also with the Southern's interests in the railway-associated provincial bus companies and civil aviation, its development of continental traffic, promotion of business from the USA, and preparations for the coming war.

In 1939 Elliot became deputy general manager to Eustace Missenden (qv). He succeeded Missenden as general manager in July 1947 and thus became 'chief regional officer' of the Southern Region of British Railways on 1 January 1948. Early in 1949 he visited Australia to report on the efficiency of the Victorian Railways, but declined an offer to stay as their chairman. On 1 January 1950 he was 'translated' from Waterloo to Euston. The LMS Railway had never fully welded its constituents together as the Southern had largely succeeded in doing, and the London Midland Region was British Railways' problem child. It was not in good heart or in good repair when Elliot arrived, and he set out to master its complexities, especially on the freight side, and to get some overdue maintenance done. Like the well-trained regimental officer that he was, he went much among

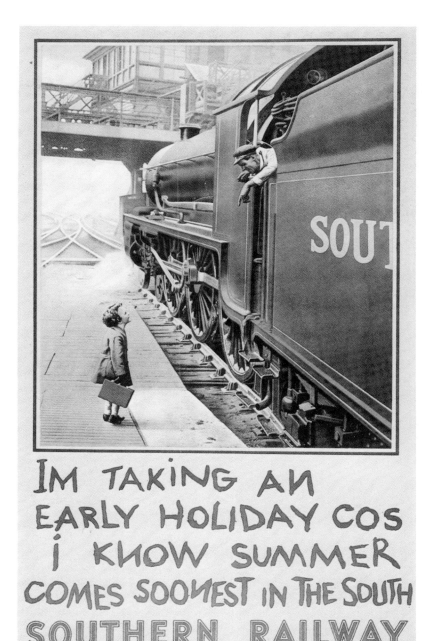

IM TAKING AN
EARLY HOLIDAY COS
i KNOW SUMMER
COMES SOONEST IN THE SOUTH
SOUTHERN RAILWAY

A reproduction of a 1939 Southern Railway Poster, based on their famous picture of the 1920s, promoting the use of railways for holiday travel (courtesy of the National Railway Museum, York).

the rank and file, holding open meetings for staff with 'no holds barred'; but his time at Euston was short, for at the end of March 1951 he was appointed to succeed Missenden as chairman of the Railway Executive.

His position at Marylebone, as head of British Railways, was difficult. As a relative junior, not regarded by all as a 'real' railwayman, he had to deal with strong and independently-minded colleagues; the Western Region maintained its tradition of considering inferior all practices that differed from those of the late Great Western Railway; and there was a chronic state of exasperation, on both sides, in the relations between the Railway Executive and its overlord and banker, the British Transport Commission, under Lord Hurcomb (qv). Things were not much better between the regions and Railway Executive headquarters. Elliot decided at once that a new atmosphere of confidence must be created. In his short time as Railway Executive chairman he strongly backed plans for electrification of the Eastern Region lines from Liverpool Street and Fenchurch Street; here his Southern Railway background enabled him to see quickly that these areas showed all the symptoms that had led to success south of the Thames. But there were strikes, and the railways' finances did not improve.

The Conservative Government, returned to power in October 1951, decided, as part of its reorganisation of the British Transport Commission's structure under the Transport Act, 1953, to abolish the Railway Executive, specifically providing that no one should be appointed as the chief executive of the railways. Elliot's job thus came to an end, and in October 1953 he became chairman of the London Transport Executive. At 55 Broadway, Westminster, he threw himself heartily into the task of running the organisation created by Lord Ashfield (qv) and advocating more investment in it, especially its Victoria line, while consistently maintaining close and loyal relations with the BTC's new chairman, Sir Brian Robertson (qv). It was a grief to him that he had to deal with a seven-week busmen's strike in 1958, but he conducted it so that, in the reluctantly admiring opinion of a trade-union leader, in no dispute had the management's position been so clearly put to the staff and the public. In 1959 Robertson offered Elliot the chairmanship of the Pullman Car Co and of Thomas Cook & Son, to which he moved. He held these appointments until 1963 and 1967 respectively. He was chairman of Willing & Co, advertising contractors, from 1959 to 1970 and of London & Provincial Poster group from 1965 to 1971, and he was on the boards of the Colonial Development Corporation from 1959 to 1966 and of the Tilling Group from 1959 to 1970.

Elliot showed considerable skill in all his appointments in reading public opinion and going out to meet it half-way — something that the traditional type of railway manager had done only intermittently, if at all. In the detail of management he chose rather to put his trust in the advice of professionally-trained colleagues than to seek to understand their special skills; indeed, his staff were often surprised and sometimes alarmed by the casual way he treated statistical information in speeches and interviews. But he had an invaluable 'hunch' for the essence, if not the detail, of a financial or technical problem; and he devoted much time to personal relations.

Whilst favourable to innovation, he had at the same time a keen sense of historic influences. He was a student of the French Revolutionary and Napoleonic periods and of modern military history, as his writings reveal. He sustained life-long loyalty to his school, Marlborough, to his regiment, the 3rd Hussars, and to Essex county cricket.

Elliot became a member of the Institute of Transport in 1938 and was its president in 1953-54. He was awarded the US Medal of Freedom and the Légion d'Honneur, and he was knighted in 1954.

He married in 1924 Elizabeth Marjorie, daughter of Dr A S Cobbledick, eye surgeon, of London; they had a son and a daughter.

MICHAEL ROBBINS

Writings:

'An Account of Stewardship' *Journal of the Institute of Transport* 25 (1953).

The Way of the Tumbrils. Paris during the Revolution and Today (Max Reinhardt, 1958).

'The Early Days of the Southern Railway' *Journal of Transport History* 4 (1960).

Where Our Fathers Died (*Daily Telegraph*, 1964).

On and off the Rails (Allen & Unwin, 1982).

Sources:

Unpublished

Board minutes, Southern Railway, 1925-47; Railway Executive, 1948-53; London Transport Executive, 1953-9.

BCe.

MCe.

Personal knowledge: the author, as secretary of London Transport Executive, was closely associated with Sir John Elliot, 1953-59.

Published

Michael R Bonavia, *The Birth of British Rail* (Allen & Unwin, 1979).

—, *Railway Policy between the Wars* (Manchester: Manchester University Press, 1981).

Charles F Klapper, *Sir Herbert Walker's Southern Railway* (Allan, 1973).

WW 1983.

Norman Elliott (courtesy of the Electricity Council).

ELLIOTT, Sir Norman Randall
(1903-)

Electricity industry manager

Norman Randall Elliott was born in West Ham, Essex, on 19 July 1903 the son of William Randall Elliott and his wife Catherine née Dunsmore. His father, W R Elliott, had been a star pupil of Sylvanus Thompson the mathematician and worked with Marconi (qv) on the first long-distance wireless telegraphy from Bournemouth to the Isle of Wight. He lacked ambition (feeling that a mathematician's best work is done before the age of twenty-five) and became the engineer and manager of the East Ham Electricity and Tramways department, a post he retained from 1901 to 1942. Bertrand Russell persuaded him that his son should be educated at home by his parents and a tutor and should then go to university later than usual. Norman was then given a liberal allowance of £400 per annum to complete the education of his choice at St Catharine's College, Cambridge. He gained an exhibition to read parts 1 and 2 of the mechanical sciences tripos, and switched to Law for his third year: a rather unusual combination, whch stood him in good stead in his future career as a generalist manager. He was called to the Bar in 1932, and then opted for a career in his father's field, with the Yorkshire Electric Power Co. He became deputy chief engineer of Ilford Corporation Electricity Department in 1936. He successfully applied for the chief's job at Gravesend in 1939, moving to a similar post at Wimbledon in 1944. He was, however, diverted from the latter by war service, dealing with electricity supplies for liberated towns and forward positions in France and Germany, under temporary commission as a lieutenant-colonel in the Royal Engineers, and later as a full colonel and deputy director of works, 21st Army Group. He received a military OBE in 1946.

The same year he became general manager and chief engineer of the London & Home Counties Joint Electricity Authority. When the electricity supply industry was nationalised in 1948, he was a natural choice as founder chairman of the South Eastern Electricity Board. He was determined to make a success of nationalisation, and with his deputy chairman W T Skinner, a good engineer and austere puritan, he set out to achieve this. He also served on the central authorities of the supply industry (first the British Electricity Authority, subsequently the Electricity Council) between 1950 and 1962. Walter Citrine (qv), the central authority chairman, found him a persistent opponent of augmented centralisation, and the Ministry felt him to be 'charming, able, but lazy' {Ministry of Power, Archives}. The image of relaxed eccentricity was one he deliberately cultivated: for example, by wearing pointedly odd socks! His softly-spoken, donnish personality made him well-liked by his colleagues, and his contributions to policy discussions were generally felt to be shrewd, sometimes self-indulgent. He sometimes made assertions insufficiently backed by research (for example on costs work on projectiles and plates which remained in use until the Second World War; in the early 1890s he became a director.

Ellis's problems as managing director were increasingly diverse. Innovation and new product development, above all else, squeezed profits in the 1870s, when a nadir was reached with only £7,000 profit and no dividend in 1879. Not until the late 1870s could the ore mines in Spain be adequately exploited, owing to the Carlist rising before 1876. Coal prices were depressed and mines brought labour problems with a major strike of six weeks in 1876. But the 1880s brought a new direction of development. Henry Pochin's son in law, Charles McLaren (qv), and Ellis's son Charles, both barristers, joined the board in 1883 and 1884, respectively.

Demand for shipping increased and the company was in a powerful position to exploit it, with a further new forging plant set up in 1886 and enlarged furnace capacity and a 10,000 ton Whitworth armour plate press available by 1896. A high proportion of all steel produced was being utilised in shipbuilding in Britain, and John Brown Ltd, Vickers and Cammell all took the step of vertical integration, seeking direct control of shipbuilding outlets. It was an industry which bought steel plate relatively cheaply, with a superiority rooted in the massive expansion of output of steel capacity between 1860 and 1880. Ellis chose the route of specialisation, maintaining a leading role in the production of armour plate and very heavy forgings, and retaining a key position in naval ordnance.

The firm specialised by the 1890s in the production of a wide range of shipping parts, including the well known compound armour plates, boiler material, flues, tubes, engine shafting and general forgings, beams, angles, steel propeller blades, as well as tyres, axles, railway springs, buffers, tools, foundry and forge pig iron, crucible cast steel, dealing with Governments and private buyers on a colossal scale. Capital investment to anticipate future development was a perennial problem. In 1897 Ellis reported they

> 'had added plant for armour in the last year to meet higher government specifications and used part of the profit of that year to cover that expenditure, and part to add extensions to the machinery of other departments. The past year had been one of the greatest anxiety with regard to the armour plate trade he had known since he became connected with the place forty-three years ago {ibid, cutting 28}.

At the start of the year, the Admiralty had been pleased with the quality of the Harvey plate they had been receiving, but thought John Brown Ltd and other firms could improve it. As a result they, and the other two armour plate makers of Sheffield, had to try. John Brown Ltd succeeded in a few months, hoping for at least twelve months of orders. Then, while they experimented, Krupps & Co made a very superior plate and the Government demanded that they equalled its performance. John Browns were forced to lay out very large sums of money to produce a rival plate and secure a patent. In return they expected to get very large orders, as naval building was expanding quickly. In 1897-98 some £30,000 was spent on new outlay in producing improved armour plates. Concurrently the firm's collieries continued to cause problems, for although they had raised one million tons of coal and had not made a loss, they had not made a reasonable profit either. Foreign competition was a mounting concern, and created major pressures in the search for control of outlets for the products of the works.

In June 1899 John Brown Ltd purchased outright the shares of the Clydebank Engineering & Shipbuilding Co, Glasgow. There were already strong links as the Atlas Works had been providing the armour for a Japanese battleship being built there and for other ships. It was a foreword linkage to secure safe outlets for the products of the Sheffield firm, and followed close upon a decision not to buy a shipyard owned by Earles Shipbuilding Co of Hull. A site of 80 acres, capable of producing everything from a luxury yacht to a tramp steamer was obtained, with new machine shops, 11 shipbuilding berths in two yards, and a large dock between for fitting out.

John Brown's expansion continued by purchase or merger. Devonshire Ellis was now aided by Charles McLaren, the deputy chairman since 1897. The Atlas Works were extended in 1901, when 130 houses in Kenninghall Street were pulled down. In November 1902 Thomas Firth & Sons Ltd amalgamated with John Brown by exchange of shares, bringing in a private limited company adjacent in its premises to the Atlas Works, with a capital in excess of £300,000. By that date John Brown Ltd's authorised capital of £2.5 million comprised £1,750,000 in £1 ordinary shares and £750,000 in 5 per cent cumulative preference shares of £10 each; of these, 500,000 ordinary shares were fully paid, 1,160,000 ordinary shares had 15s paid up and 50,000 preference shares were fully paid.

By 1904 the Atlas Works extended to 34 acres, employing 2,600 men on site, while the Rotherham collieries employed a further 5,400 men. The Sheffield weekly wage bill amounted to £10,000. The Atlas Works had 43 furnaces, which consumed 400 tons of coal and 100 tons of coke a day, 10 hydraulic presses, including one of 10,000 tons power, 33 steam hammers, 94 travelling cranes and 307 machine tools, producing about 100,000 tons of output per annum with a turnover of £3 million. Even in old age Devonshire Ellis continued his regular habit of a daily inspection of all these developments.

On the Clyde 8,000 men were employed, again with about £10,000 a week paid in wages. Most firms producing capital goods experienced sharp fluctuations in demand for their products, and the new shipbuilding enterprises were no exception. Between 1901 and 1907, the earliest period for which figures are available, net profits fluctuated widely between £14,126 a year (in 1905) and £137,011 (in 1907), and the rate of return on capital value moved with corresponding volatility between 1.87 per cent in 1905 and 17.04 per cent in 1907.

Ellis spent the last years of his life attending the launching of ship after ship on Clydebank, though he missed that of the Cunarder *Lusitania*, the world's largest passenger liner in 1907. He resigned as managing director on reaching the age of eighty in 1904, but continued as chairman until his death.

One measure of his success was the profitability of the firm in its last years. Dividends averaged 12 per cent in the seven years to 1904, while 8.33 per cent merited an apology in 1904. By then the company was building a series of Cunard liners, of which the *Caronia* was at that time the largest yet attempted in Great Britain. The Atlas Works was being overhauled, and Firths were setting up manufacturing facilities in Russia, at the Salamander works in Riga to supply shells. The aim was to defeat the tariff barrier, and it was the beginning of an extensive network of overseas selling agencies.

Ellis's technical achievements were considerable, though again it is difficult to distinguish between his own early efforts and the later policy of employing good people. As Sir Henry Bessemer said in 1889

> The most intelligent of all the steelmen in Sheffield were in the works of John Brown & Co, and their practical man Mr J Ellis, was actually the first man in Sheffield to come to the conclusion that the new process was worth looking at {ibid, cutting 79}.

In 1889 Ellis received the gold medal of the Iron and Steel Institute and became the president of the Institute in 1901. He was also elected to the Institution of Civil Engineers in 1884. His contribution should perhaps be judged in terms of persistent pressure towards improvements in the manufacturing process, rather than in terms of the individual innovations with which he is associated, which ranged from engineering to steel processing developments. In business he appeared to combine tough individualism and a capacity to work with others which assisted in the gradual emergence of specialisation of managerial functions within the company by the 1880s.

In later life he served as a JP for twelve years. For ten years he was chairman of the South Yorkshire Coal Owners Association, 'the period covering some of the keenest struggles of the great industry' {ibid, cutting 40}, though he lamented that it was generally impossible to get the owners to maintain agreements for long. Undoubtedly his technical experience made possible the setting up of the heavier rolling mills at John Brown in 1863, which decreased the extent of blistering in plates and reduced the number of bars or plates required for the finished products. In his long association with the firm, Ellis presided over a massive expansion not only in its size, but in its technological development and organisational change, so that after the merger with Thomas Firth in 1902, John Brown Ltd competed with Vickers for the place of the largest enterprise in Sheffield, and both competed and cooperated in overseas ventures with them, including the naval yards in Spain.

John Devonshire Ellis was a 'rare specimen of a man who devoted the whole of his life to the interests of one great concern' {ibid, cutting 75} to such an extent that it is difficult to separate his personality from that of the enterprise. He was reputed to take only two days' holiday a year. An early riser, he caught the Worksop-Sheffield train daily to arrive in his office at 9.0 am precisely, and left at 4.0 or 5.0 pm each afternoon. His chief hobby was growing chrysanthemums. Politically he was a Conservative, and an able public speaker. Anglican by religion, he regularly attended the Priory Church at Worksop.

He married Elizabeth, daughter of Edward Bourne, a farmer of Childs Ercall, Shropshire, in 1848, and lived first at Thurnscoe Hall, Rotherham and later at Sparken near Worksop. They had five sons and one daughter.

He died on 11 November 1906 leaving £60,756 gross.

PAUL NUNN

ELLIS John Devonshire

Sources:

Unpublished

Sheffield City Library, 'Newspaper cuttings relating to Sheffield' Vol 36 (1890-1914).

MCe.

PrC.

Kenneth C Barraclough, 'The Development of the Early Steelmaking Processes—An Essay on the History of Technology' (Sheffield PhD, 1981).

Published

Sir Henry Bessemer, *Sir Henry Bessemer FRS: An Autobiography. With a Concluding Chapter by His Son, Henry Bessemer* (Offices of *Engineering*, 1905).

Duncan L Burn, *The Economic History of Steelmaking 1867–1939: A Study in Competition* (Cambridge: Cambridge University Press, 1940).

DNB.

The Engineer 16 Nov 1906.

Engineering 16 Nov 1906.

Charlotte J Erickson, *British Industrialists. Steel and Hosiery, 1850–1950* (Cambridge: Cambridge University Press, 1959).

Firth Brown (np, 1953).

Firth Brown Centenary, 100 Years in Steel 1837-1937 (pp, Rubys, 1938).

Sir Allan J Grant, *Steel and Ships, the History of John Brown's* (Michael Joseph, 1950).

Robert J Harrison, *An Economic History of Modern Spain* (Manchester: Manchester University Press, 1978).

JISI 1906.

John Brown and Company Ltd, 1864-1924 (pp, np, 1924).

M Lewis and R Lloyd-Jones, 'Industrial Structure and Firm Growth. The Sheffield Iron and Steel Industry, 1880-1900' *Business History* 25 (1983).

Donald N McCloskey, *Economic Maturity and Entrepreneurial Decline: British Iron and Steel 1870–1913* (Cambridge, Massachusetts: Harvard University Press, 1973).

Men of the Period, England (Biographical Publishing Co, 1896).

Sir Eric Mensforth, *Family Engineers* (Ward Lock, 1981).

Minutes of the Proceedings of the Institution of Civil Engineers 118 (1894).

Peter L Payne, 'Iron and Steel Manufacture' in Derek H Aldcroft (ed), *The Development of British Industry and Foreign Competition 1875-1914* (Allen & Unwin, 1968).

Sidney Pollard and Paul Robertson, *The British Shipbuilding Industry 1870-1914* (Cambridge, Massachusetts: Harvard University Press, 1979).

Clive Trebilcock, 'British Armaments and European Industrialisation 1890-1914' *Economic History Review* 2nd ser 26 (1973).

Kenneth Warren, 'The Sheffield Rail Trade, 1861-1930: An Episode in the Locational History of the British Steel Industry' *Transactions of the Institute of British Geographers* 34 (1964).

ELLIS, Richard Adam

(1850-1945)

City estate agent and land surveyor

Richard Adam Ellis, portrait in chalk by D Freeborn Martin, 1938, in the possession of the Richard Ellis partnership.

Richard Adam Ellis was born in Edmonton, London, on 30 May 1850, the second son of Edward Ellis, an architect and his wife Agnes née Adam. Edward's brother, Edward Brookes Ellis, joined their father's practice and became a leading architect of City offices. Educated at Bruce Castle School in Tottenham, Richard Adam Ellis was in 1875 taken into the City auctioneers' and surveyors' business of his uncle Richard Ellis (1800-85), whose father, also Richard Ellis (ca 1769-1846), had built up the business on that founded by his uncle William Ellis (1744-1808), who had come to London in 1760, from Steeple Ashton, Wiltshire, to be apprenticed as an 'upholder'.

Richard Adam Ellis inherited the business in 1885 at a time when the firm was developing the large estates of South London, notably Denmark Hill, Champion Hill, Tulse Hill and Camberwell, often financing the speculative builders who were replacing large Victorian villas with streets of suburban housing. At that time also, the surveyors' profession was becoming codified; Richard Adam Ellis became a member of the Surveyors' Institution in 1882, the year after it received its royal charter, and a fellow the following year. In 1892 he became a liveryman of the Clothworkers' Company, for which he acted in property transactions.

He continued to develop South London. In 1906-7 he put together the land for King's College Hospital, and sold off the Sanders Estate in Denmark Hill, Herne Hill and Ruskin Park. In the City of London, his clients included Twinings (qv), Cayzer Irvine, the Kleinworts (qv) and the Oppenheimers. In 1908, on the constitution of the Port of London Authority, Ellis arranged the purchase of a large piece of land between Seething Lane and Trinity Square, upon which the PLA headquarters was built to the design of Sir Edwin Cooper.

Ellis was friendly with Sir Alfred Savill, senior partner in another family firm of estate agents based in Lincoln's Inn, but with interests mainly in North London and the provinces to balance those of Ellis in the south. Late in 1920 the two partnerships were merged, advertising as Messrs Alfred Savill & Sons and Messrs Richard Ellis & Son (Lincoln's Inn and Fenchurch Street). One of the Savill sons entered the Ellis office as an assistant. But in 1921 Ellis was invited to revalue the City of London Real Property Co for Sir William Burton; this proved so successful that Richard Ellis thereafter acted for CLRP, and the brief association with Savill was severed. In 1925 the partnership was strengthened still further in the City with the addition of John Flatt, previously City valuer.

Richard Elis was involved with many of the largest City property deals in the inter-war period, notably for the sale of the East India House site, for the building of Lloyds, and in 1930 for the development of a site in Leadenhall Street, for the building of Cunard House.

In 1936 Ellis was elected master of the Clothworkers' Company, but at the age of eighty-six was excused service. He still visited the office, and delighted in the name of 'King of Fenchurch Street': he was, indeed, much annoyed on one visit to find a board of a rival firm on a Fenchurch Street building, and demanded it be taken down. He retired formally in 1938.

He lived for fifty years at Greenwoods, Stock, Essex, in which county he was a JP from 1907. He married in 1878 Emma, daughter of William Booker of Edmonton; she died in 1937. They had two sons and two daughters; the elder son, Hugh, died of typhoid in India in 1902, and the younger son, Rae Adam, died of wounds in October 1918.

In the obituary recorded by his profession it was noted that

> During his business life he showed great foresight in redevelopment schemes in the City and outside and, what is perhaps the greater merit, inspired the confidence of those concerned to bring them to successful fruition. There are probably few, if any, properties in and around Fenchurch Street, Leadenhall Street, Mincing Lane and the produce market area which at some time or another have not passed through Mr Ellis' hands for sale, purchase or other purpose. Nothing but the best satisfied him, either in character, architecture, landscape gardening or professional work {*Journal of the Chartered Surveyors' Institution* (Nov 1945) 234}.

Richard Adam Ellis died at the age of ninety-five on 26 September 1945, leaving £64,024 gross.

DAVID H E WAINWRIGHT

Sources:

Unpublished

BCe.

MCe.

PrC.

Published

Journal of the Chartered Surveyors' Institution Nov 1945.

Kelly's Directory 1945.

F M L Thompson, *Chartered Surveyors. The Growth of a Profession* (Routledge & Kegan Paul, 1968).

David Wainwright, *Richard Ellis, 1773-1973* (Hutchinson Benham for Richard Ellis, 1973).

William H Ellis (courtesy of Dr Paul Nunn).

ELLIS, Sir William Henry
(1860-1945)

Iron and Steel manufacturer

William Henry Ellis was born at Thurnscoe Hall near Rotherham on 20 August 1860, the fourth son of John Devonshire Ellis (qv), a founding partner in the firm of John Brown, and his wife Elizabeth Parsons née Bourne. He attended Uppingham School and the College of Science in Leeds (later Leeds University). From November 1878 he served a technical apprenticeship with Tannett, Walker & Co of Leeds, so that his education 'exemplified what has come to be regarded in Britain as an excellent type of training, combining academic and practical or industrial phases' {Erickson (1959) 44}.

His first responsible job was the erecting of a vertical blowing engine at a copper smelting works in Serbia. This involved taking the plant about one thousand miles from Galatz up the Danube, transporting it twenty miles over mountains and through forests on bullock carts before erection. For two years he worked as a foreman in the Leeds works before returning to John Brown & Co Ltd's Atlas Works in Sheffield in October 1885 to take charge of the construction of a 4,000 ton hydraulic forging press, a pair of hydraulic pumping engines and two overhead travelling cranes. By October 1887 this was finished, and he became under manager of the foundry department.

His elder brother Charles (d 1937) read history at Cambridge and became a barrister before returning to the board of John Brown Ltd in 1884. Specialising in legal and commercial problems he entered the top level of management twenty two years before William who joined the John Brown Ltd board in 1906, the year of his father's death. William had shown a marked talent for technical, commercial and administrative work. In his first period at John Brown Ltd he concentrated upon technical improvements, and was manager of the forging department for many years. He became one of the very few sons of leaders of the first generation steel firms who took an active part in the management of the firm rather than being a figurehead. For much of his working life such responsibilities continued to be shared with his brother, Charles, who was managing director 1892-1915 and 1919-28.

By 1907 John Brown Ltd was at the centre of a complex of interlocking shareholdings and directorates. Apart from the ownership of the Clydebank Shipbuilding & Engineering Co, the company had exchanged shares with the neighbouring firm of Thomas Firth & Sons Ltd in 1902. It bought the Trent Iron Works at Scunthorpe in 1907, and by acquisition of a large block of shares, held a controlling interest in Harland & Wolff Ltd. This firm provided a further outlet for forgings and castings, although no change was undertaken in the management of the two companies. Additional fuel supplies were ensured by the purchase of Dalton Main Collieries in 1909 as the older mines at Aldwarke and Car House became exhausted. John Brown Ltd's shipyards specialising in naval building at Ferrol and Cathagena in Spain began a joint enterprise with Vickers in 1899, and the Coventry Ordnance Works were further developed.

It was an era of strategic decision-making in the firm. Pig iron production ceased at the Atlas Works by 1911 as the cost-advantages of other sites became apparent. The firm depended ever more upon maintaining outlets for heavy engineering products, and it was the search for control of raw material supply and outlets which 'drove Sheffield to the sea' {Sheffield City Library, newspaper cuttings 36 (1907) cuttings 97-100}. Such developments required persistent re-investment, and large amounts from each year's gross profits tended to be re-invested in these years; for example in 1907 £50,000 out of a net profit of £234,237 was ploughed back. The most conspicuous products of the company were now the Cunarders and battleships of Clyde Bank. Typical was the *Lusitania*, 'the greatest floating hotel in the world' {ibid}, which neared completion in June 1907. Most of its heavy iron and steel fittings were built at the Atlas Works under the supervision of William Henry Ellis, as were those for the stream of battleships flowing from Clydebank and the enlarged facilities at Scotstown. Thus the 1907 *Inflexible* cost £1.75 million, and was capable of greater speed and had greater fire power than earlier warships. The importance of such trade is illustrated by the stream of increasingly prominent British and foreign politicians and military men who attended the Cutlers' Company feasts in the years before 1914, and by the honours which were heaped upon the leading figures in the industry; for example the firm's chairman, Charles McLaren (qv), became Lord Aberconway in 1911.

Ellis played a key part in the decision to establish the Firth Brown research laboratories in 1908 which served both enterprises, and which were to be important in the key discovery of stainless steel in 1913 and 'Staybrite' corrosion resistant steels in 1923. These developments, and the production of the largest hollow rolled forgings ever produced (17 feet 8 inches diameter; wall thickness, 5 inches) represented some of the major contributions of the two companies to technological progress. The forgings were used in the National Physical Laboratory Wind Tunnel, of which Ellis was a director in the 1920s. Such research laboratories were unusual in the steel industry in 1908; but the scepticism of contemporaries was overcome by the rapidity of useful results which were applied in effective innovation, not only in the local supplies of stainless steel to the cutlery trades, but in a range of applications. During the First World War most of the production was used in aero-engine valves.

Until 1914 William Henry Ellis continued to be primarily involved in the management of the Atlas Works; a new 6,000-ton forging press had been completed in 1911 and in 1912-13, despite railway and coal strikes, record outputs were achieved. He oversaw the dismantling of all the old Bessemer steel plants, which had been among the country's largest, and the Atlas Works finally ceased production of steel rail. All puddling disappeared and iron everywhere gave way to steel. The company produced 2.5 million tons of coal in South Yorkshire while its share capital and plant was valued at £5 million. The year 1914 was the jubilee of the company, which now employed 55,000 men in its own works and those of its dependent companies. Demand for shipping and armaments boomed, and in July 1915 the works at Sheffield and Clydebank were placed under government control after the Munitions of War Act. Charles Ellis was asked to serve in the Ministry of Munitions, and Lord Pirie (qv), the chairman of Harland and Wolff, joined the board until 1918.

William Henry Ellis remained very active in Sheffield. In 1915 a new power station was erected, the East Forge was established, and a new rolling mill was commissioned. In September electric arc furnaces for steel smelting were installed, enlarged versions of the arc furnace in use at Firths since 1907. By 1917 a new forging press and hammer shop were also in use. Manpower shortages necessitated the employment of vast numbers of women and girls, and the productivity of the associated Firth Shell Works and National Shell Factory at Templeborough were pushed to new heights. Demands on the company peaked by 1917 and it was essential to reorganise management and productive facilities. William Ellis chaired the Sheffield management committee while other directors controlled coalmining and shipbuilding interests. In 1918 the steel foundry was moved to Scunthorpe while Firths expanded their Siemens capacity onto the old Atlas Foundry site. The company also secured a controlling interest in the Carnforth Iron Co to ensure the supply of hematite ore.

War also brought public responsibility. William Ellis was Master Cutler 1914-18, after holding other offices in the Cutlers' Company. Problems existed early in the war in controlling exports of manufactures to countries friendly to Germany, and the Master Cutler was forced to act in a committee which granted export licences when controls were hastily applied in July 1915. At one point such certificates were being issued at the rate of 250 a day, and totalled over 200,000 before the war's end. No administrative machinery had been available for this purpose, and the ancient Cutlers' Company was mobilised to prevent exports of goods containing tungsten, molybdenum, or both. It was a task requiring specialised expertise and efficient administration. The Master Cutler was also involved in provision of the four million cut-throat razors for the conscript forces and fund raising for the wounded. For this work William Ellis was made GBE in 1918.

After the war Sir Charles Ellis (knighted 1918) and Sir Thomas Bell (qv) were re-appointed to the board of John Brown Ltd in 1919 and Sir William

Ellis and Bell became joint managing directors with Sir Charles Ellis. Sir William Ellis continued to control the Atlas Works as managing director from 1919 to 1931.

Like other naval ordnance and steel enterprises, the company's future was clouded in 1918. A five week coal strike revealed one future problem, but the complete end to armament work was bound to cause serious difficulties. There was an immediate search for new outlets with new machine shops and tyre rolling. A link with Cravens Railway Carriage & Wagon Co (Darnall) in 1918-21, which would provide an automatic outlet for tyres, axles and springs, made a modest preparation for the future. The Coventry Ordnance Works, which had concentrated on naval guns, was sold off, and became absorbed in the newly formed English Electrical Co. The boom of 1918-20 postponed the difficulties a little, but labour problems and high costs loomed. Moulders, coal miners and the railwaymen all took strike action in 1919-20. American and German competition heightened in steel and shipping. In shipbuilding in particular production costs in Britain were far higher than elsewhere, and a liner which had cost £500,000 in 1914 cost £1.5 million by 1920.

Company profits held for a few years, with a dividend of 5 per cent in 1921-22. Output at the Atlas Works fell dramatically by this year, to a third of that of earlier years. Battleship orders were cancelled, and manpower losses were inevitable. The company sought to diversify its output further, starting a new tyre mill and spring shops. In subsequent years output at the Atlas Works remained at a lower level, with only a very modest recovery of employment and output in 1924-25. The coal dispute in 1925, and the eventual General Strike in 1926 deprived the works of fuel, and high-priced foreign coal was used in an attempt to deliver promised production, but shipbuilding remained restricted not only by deficient demand, but because of shortages of steel and engineering products. Financially the 1920s were years of very large losses for all the armaments and shipbuilding companies.

By June 1930 a capital reorganisation was undertaken, with a meeting of debenture holders. Debenture holdings were reconstructed, with a new redemption scheme involving a cumulative sinking fund commencing in 1935 and calculated to redeem debentures by 31 December 1965. The debentures' life had been short initially, but by the late 1920s debenture holders were unprepared to renew them, and new debenture purchasers could not be found as by 1929 no dividend had been paid on ordinary shares for two years.

With advice from accountants Sir Gilbert Garnsey (qv) and William Mackinnon, the capital of the company was reorganised. Uncalled capital on ordinary shares was called up, preference shares were subdivided into £1 shares, and a non cumulative preferential dividend of 7 per cent and the right for five years to convert one half of each holding into ordinary shares at par was instituted. The capital of the company was reduced, with share capital fixed at £2,375,000, by writing off 8s on each £1 preference share, and 14s on each of the issued ordinary shares. The scheme was approved by the members and sanctioned in August 1930.

Ellis's last years with the company involved substantial rationalisation and the eventual merger with Thomas Firth & Sons in 1930. The Atlas and Scunthorpe Works were transferred to Firths and John Brown & Co Ltd acquired in return for a large block of Firth shares. It was a merger between complementary enterprises with differing specialisms. John Brown Ltd always specialised in heavy forgings and armour plate, while Firths produced projectiles, special steel products and high-class tools as well as forgings. At managerial level the merger was not difficult as personnel were already interwoven, and at lower levels too there were close links, including research and development, marketing, and joint worker recreation and other facilities. In effect John Brown & Co Ltd, which continued to operate mines and build ships, became the parent company of the new Thomas Firth & John Brown Ltd, holding almost all the shares in the purely steel section of the business. There followed a successful marriage after the difficult and unprofitable years of the 1920s. By 1931 Ellis had already begun the development of large hollow forged boiler drums which were used in power station building, an expanding field in the next decade.

Throughout his long life William Ellis remained active in a wide range of activities. In Sheffield he was a JP, member of the Sheffield Infirmary board, one of the Town Trustees and the Church Burgesses, a trustee of the Savings Bank and a member of the University Council. He was a member of the Disposals Board and of the Overseas Committee of the Board of Trade in 1920. In 1924-25 he was president of the Iron and Steel Institute and in 1925-26 a member of the Privy Council Committee of the Department of Scientific and Industrial Research. A governor of Imperial College and a member of the National Physical Laboratory, he was also on the Cambridge Appointments Committee. In 1925 he became president of the Institution of Civil Engineers, and in 1928 presided over the engineering section of the British Association meeting in Glasgow. In 1918 he received an honorary D Eng from Sheffield University, and was also made a Commander of the Order of the Crown of Italy.

Living at Weetwood in Ecclesall, he, like his father and son, enjoyed gardening. An Anglican and a keen organist, he was fond of playing in cathedrals and churches and donated an organ to his old school Uppingham (of which he was a trustee). Unlike his father, he was an incessant traveller and 'Apart from business activities, what may well have been nearest to Ellis' heart were mountains and hills' {*Alpine Journal* 55 (Nov 1945) 208-210}. A keen and intrepid mountaineer, he joined the Alpine Club in 1905, attending the fiftieth jubilee celebrations in 1907. Though he travelled in Europe, the Near East, North and South America and Australia, he spent most summers in the Alps doing the classic climbs. Of small stature and light build he kept fit until an advanced age, running daily round his garden and spending weekends on the Derbyshire hills. He climbed Helvellyn every year in later life, including his last. At seventy he climbed the Matterhorn and on his seventy-fifth birthday, the Jungfrau. In 1938 he established a £4,000 fund 'to help sick or disabled guides and their families' in Switzerland and was made an honorary member of the Swiss Alpine Club.

Politically a Conservative and a member of the Carlton Club, he took little part in politics. He married in 1889 Lucy Rimington (d 1938) the daughter of Francis William Tetley, a director of Joshua Tetley & Son of Leeds; they had two sons and two daughters. He died on 4 July 1945 in Sheffield, leaving £149,301 gross.

PAUL NUNN

Sources:

Unpublished

Sheffield City Library, 'Newspaper cuttings relating to Sheffield'.

MCe.

PrC.

Published

Alpine Journal 55 (Nov 1945).

Duncan L Burn, *The Economic History of Steelmaking, 1867-1939. A Study in Competition* (Cambridge: Cambridge University Press, 1940).

DNB.

Lawrence du Garde Peach, *The Company of Cutlers in Hallamshire in the County of York 1906-56* (Sheffield: Pawson & Brailsford, 1960).

Engineer 13 July 1945.

Engineering 13 July 1945.

Charlotte J Erickson, *British Industrialists. Steel and Hosiery 1850-1950* (Cambridge: Cambridge University Press, 1959).

Firth Brown, *100 Years in Steel* (Sheffield: T Firth & J Brown, 1937).

—, *Thos Firth and John Brown Ltd* (Sheffield: Firth Brown, 1954).

Sir Allan J Grant, *Steel and Ships. The History of John Brown's* (Michael Joseph, 1950).

Sidney Pollard and Paul Robertson, *The British Shipbuilding Industry 1870-1914* (Cambridge, Massachusetts: Harvard University Press, 1979).

WWW.

ENGELBACH, Charles Richard Fox

(1876-1943)

Motor vehicle manufacturer

Charles Richard Fox Engelbach was born in Kensington, London, on 20 May 1876, the son of Lewis Engelbach, a clerk in the War Office whose family had Huguenot origins, and his wife Jessie née Bryan. He attended Sandringham School, Southport, Lancashire. At the age of sixteen, and with a £1,000 gift from his godfather, he became a premium apprentice

C R F Engelbach (courtesy of Mr Peter J Engelbach).

with Armstrong, Whitworth in Newcastle upon Tyne, where he specialised in the manufacture of naval gun turrets.

Poor eyesight prevented him from joining the Boer War and about this time he declined an offer of a professional singing career with the D'Oyly Carte Company. Engelbach first became involved in the motor industry in 1900 when Armstrong, Whitworth, were making the Rootes Venables paraffin-engined car at their factory at Scotswood on Tyne. He was later appointed works manager, and held that post during the period of the production there of cars with Wilson & Pilcher gearboxes, between 1904 and 1906. He then built for them a special factory for the production of the more advanced 30 hp Armstrong, Whitworth cars which were highly regarded for their quality of design and manufacture. The Armstrong directors turned down his proposal to mass produce motor-cars at a rate of 6,000 per annun and it was therefore left to William Morris (qv) to market the Morris Oxford in 1913 as the first British equivalent of the Ford Model T. Engelbach continued with the production of 30 hp Armstrong, Whitworth cars, and smaller models of that make, until 1914 when he was called up for service in the RNVR, of which he had been an enthusiastic member in the Tyneside Division since its formation in 1905.

Appointed at the rank of lieutenant commander, he was 'brought ashore' after a year to take over the 4.7 inch Howitzer department of the Coventry Ordnance Works, where he remained for the duration of the war. For his services to munitions production, he was awarded the OBE. He then worked for a short time as general manager of a component supplier in London. His experience with car production together with his knowledge of quantity production of munitions led to his selection by the re-constituted Austin board at the shareholders meeting as works director for the Austin Motor Co's plant at Longbridge, near Birmingham, in 1921. Ernest L Payton, the financier, was also brought in and his influence, together with that of Engelbach brought the company back on to a sound footing after it had been in the hands of a receiver.

Engelbach was regarded by his contemporaries as one of the finest production engineers in Britain, an opinion supported by his reorganisation of the entire Longbridge factory which he carried out during the winter of 1925-26, when he brought to his new situation both ideas and staff from Coventry. He employed the series production line method in his reorganisation. Each main component was machined, and the parts were assembled under one superintendent in the same shop. Assembled components were conveyed to the appropriate point in the chassis erecting track along which the car was moving. Engelbach established a system of payment by results to replace less cost-effective overtime and this raised productivity; increased effort on the part of assembly line workers being directly rewarded by bonus payments.

As a result of his complete reorganisation, output at the Austin factory was increased by 52 per cent, production costs were reduced by 38 per cent, at the same time total labour charges increased by 65 per cent with a doubling of average individual wages and company profits. Car production had been 16,429 in 1925, but dramatically rose to 37,520 in 1927. When Engelbach and Payton came in 1921, Austin's had a debt of over £2.3 million. By 1927 the reorganisation created a net profit of over £400,000.

Engelbach continued to control the production side of the Austin Motor Co until his eyesight deteriorated to such an extent by early 1938 that sometimes he had to be guided around the factory. He was forced to retire on 1 March of that year, to be replaced by Leonard Lord (qv) from Morris. He retained his seat on the Austin board, however, until his death. Part of Engelbach's skill lay in his ability to 'put a team together and work it together' {C P G Engelbach, 9 Feb 1984}. On his departure, notices appeared round the factory reading 'O Lord give us Engelbach' {ibid}.

Engelbach was also a director of Birmid Industries Ltd, a former president of the Birmingham and District Engineering Employers' Association and a member of the permanent board of the Allied Employers' Federation, president of the Institute of Automobile Engineers, and general council member of the Allied Employers' National Federation. In the 1930s he served on the Government Shadow Factory Committee responsible for organising shadow factories. In 1928, Engelbach presented a long paper on his work to the Institute of Automobile Engineers. He and Herbert Austin were quick to appreciate the value of broadcasting as a medium for putting forward new ideas; they spoke together on BBC radio about the work of a motor car factory for thirty minutes in January, 1933.

Outside business he was a freemason, belonging to the Federation Lodge in which he held the office of Provincial Grand Warden; president of the Austin Branch of the British Legion; and patron of the Birmingham Western Area Boy Scouts. He found recreation in yachting and golfing.

Engelbach in 1902 married Florence née Neumegen, by whom he had two sons. His wife had been born and brought up in Spain, her family being in the sherry business, and had trained as a portrait painter in Paris and London; later she turned to flower painting and had some of her work hung in major art galleries, including the Tate and the Royal Academy. Engelbach died on 19 February 1943 leaving £110,733 gross.

ROBERT J WYATT

Writings:

'Some Notes on Reorganising a Works to Increase Production' *Proceedings of Institute of Automobile Engineers* 23 (1927-28).

'Engineering' *Listener* 9 (1 Feb 1933).

'Problems in Manufacture' *Proceedings of the Institute of Automobile Engineers* 28 (1933-34).

Sources:

Unpublished

BCe.

PrC.

Information from Mr C P G Engelbach (younger son of C R F Engelbach).

Published

Austin Magazine Apr 1943.

Birmingham Mail 19 Feb 1943.

Roy A Church, *Herbert Austin: The British Motor Car Industry to 1941* (Europa, 1979).

J A Ireland, 'The Armstrong Whitworth Car' *Close-Up* No 19 (1960).

Robert J Irving, 'New Industries for Old: Some Investment Decisions of Armstrong Whitworth 1900-14' *Business History* 17 (1975).

Kenneth Richardson, *The British Motor Industry, 1896-1939* (Macmillan, 1977).

Robert J Wyatt, *The Austin 1905-1952* (Newton Abbot: David & Charles, 1982).

WWW (Florence Engelbach).

ENGLISH, John

(1789–1878)

Needle manufacturer

John English II was born in 1789, one of the five children of John English I, needlemaker, and his wife Elizabeth. The Feckenham (Worcestershire) needlemaking business which, until the 1920s bore their name, had been founded by John II's grandfather Job English in 1756. The business was moderately prosperous by the time that John II took over in about 1823. Family capital had been ploughed back and expansion had taken place during the period 1786-92.

When John II took over the firm, the needle trade was organised on an external contract basis. Initially John I had put out the job of scouring and had rented needle pointing places at watermills owned by other needlemakers, hiring additional power as required, but he built his own watermill towards the end of the eighteenth century; the 'softworkers' who guttered the needle eyes and soft straightened them worked in their own homes. The needles were then hardened and tempered. This process, too, was often contracted out but John English I built up his own hardening shop. The needles were then put out again for hammer straightening (by women) and this process was followed by a further scouring and polishing on a handturned stone and, finally, packing in paper for sale.

John English II expanded the business in the 1820s and early 1830s but stagnation set in and penetration of the London market through their showroom at Gracechurch Street proved difficult owing to strong brand loyalty existing in the trade. In 1837 English wrote 'I have legitimately conducted my business keeping within the limits of my own capital and ... fortunately (or perhaps in the present circumstances, unfortunately) I have no creditors.'

John English's needles were exported to Turkey, India (1830 onwards), South America, the USA and (from 1843) Australia. He visited the USA in 1839 in an attempt to resuscitate the flagging US needle trade but shortly afterwards arranged with J Pratt to act as selling representative for the USA and by the 1860s Pratt was sole agent there.

John English II married Mary Jelfs. They had two children, a son Thomas who joined his father in the business, and a daughter Sara, who married J J W Gutch, manager of the London showroom. Thomas took over the management of the needle business in 1845, his father increasingly suffering from gout, but he began to exhibit signs of mental instability and in 1853 was confined to an asylum. John II resumed control for the remainder of the 1850s and 1860s but his style of management was less vigorous as he was confined to bed with gout more frequently.

Total sales grew from £3,694 in 1858 to £10,344 in 1866, peaking at £13,189 in 1870 but being so heavily dependent on outworkers it was difficult to respond swiftly enough to increased demand and in 1873 the firm purchased a steampowered factory, Eagle Mill, Studley.

John English II retired from the business finally in 1872, transferring his share of the assets to his grandsons Alfred and Arthur Henry Gutch. The firm was badly affected during the depression of the 1880s, sales falling to £3,153 in 1884, and in 1892 the firm became a private limited company with a capital of £7,500. In the mid-1920s the firm was wholly acquired by Henry Milward & Sons.

John English II invested in land as his father had done and by 1860 his rental of over £700 per annum exceeded his returns from needlemaking. His investment portfolio grew as he purchased government stocks as well as shares in banks. He advanced money to the Pratt brothers and lent sums on mortgage to friends. After his retirement he retreated to his country estate at Feckenham. He was involved in local church affairs besides the management of Feckenham Free School. He was probably worth £40,000 on his retirement in 1872. He died on 27 January 1878 in his eighty-ninth year, leaving under £2,000 gross.

JENNIFER TANN

Sources:

Unpublished

Redditch Public Library, Gutch papers.

PrC.

S R H Jones, 'John English & Co, Feckenham: A Study of Enterprise in the West Midlands Needle Industry in the Eighteenth and Nineteenth Centuries' (London PhD, 1980).

Published

H I Dutton and S R H Jones, 'Invention and Innovation in the British Pin Industry, 1790-1850' *Business History Review* 57 (1983).

S R H Jones, 'Hall, English & Co, 1813-41: A Study of Entrepreneurial Response in the Gloucester Pin Industry' *Business History* 18 (1976).

B C G Nokes, 'John English of Feckenham, Needle Manufacturer' *ibid* 11 (1969).

Redditch Indicator 2 Feb 1878.

ENO, James Crossley

(1820-1915)

Manufacturing chemist

James Crossley Eno was born in 1820 at 3 Barrack Square, Newcastle upon Tyne, where his parents James and Elizabeth Eno kept a general shop. Nothing is known about his early education, but he served an apprenticeship with a druggist in The Side, a busy commercial street near to the River Tyne. His master was probably Joseph Garnett, an eccentric bachelor philanthropist. In 1846 Eno was appointed dispenser at the Old Infirmary at a salary of £60 year. He seems to have made himself generally useful, performing dental work when not dispensing prescriptions.

After Eno acquired the chemist and druggist business of John Burrell at 57 Groat Market (later renumbered as No 5) in 1852, he began the typical life of a commercially alert druggist. He continued his dentistry, sold human and animal medicines, and launched three products under his own label: a tooth enamel for do-it-yourself fillings, a hair restorer, and a treated linseed oil for poultices.

Having thus tested his business ability, he began to make the Fruit Salt with which his name is still associated. It was a mixture of tartaric and citric acids with sodium bicarbonate, which produced an effervescing drink when stirred into water. The bicarbonate was a product of the Tyneside alkali industry. Fruit Salt was not a primary chemical manufacture for no new substance was formed; the scale of the common pharmaceutical techniques of weighing, mixing, sieving and bottling could be extended as need arose. For the next twenty years, though, the scale remained appropriate to a one-man business and he continued to describe himself as dispensing chemist and surgeon dentist. Eno pushed his product by giving free samples to the ship captains who tied up at Newcastle Quay, thus ensuring that his name travelled round the world.

It is difficult to assess Eno's originality. It has been suggested that he got the idea from a favourite Infirmary prescription used by a polymath, Dr Dennis Embleton, but Eno was in business before Embleton began to visit the Infirmary. Similarly, the effervescing granules of Edward Bishop were not introduced into pharmacy until 1857, and then only with the object of making unpleasant medicines palatable. Prescriptions of a similar nature were probably common knowledge in 1853, and Eno's success was due to commercial enterprise rather than scientific insight. Some later advertisements refer to J C Eno's 'patent' but this seems to be a misuse of terms, or confusion with the term 'patent medicines', for which there was a growing demand in the nineteenth century as the careers of Beecham and Holloway (qqv) demonstrated.

In 1876 Eno left the practice of retail pharmacy and dentistry for the large-scale manufacture of his Fruit Salt in London. He acquired Woodhall, a large house and grounds in Dulwich, and a factory site in Pomeroy Street, New Cross. He then began to compose his characteristic advertisements, the concentrated texts of which he always wrote himself. In a period when proprietary remedies were flaunted with exorbitant bombast, Eno restricted his claims to success in cases of biliousness, feverishness, sleeplessness, headache, disorderly stomach, and 'sudden changes in the weather'. Supporting statements appeared from army officers in Egypt and India, and tea planters in Assam. Not that Eno was unduly modest, for at the age of seventy he testified that taking his own medicine had saved his life in a recent bout of fever, and he claimed that the wise provision of Eno's Fruit Salt had helped to win the Afghan War. Over every advertisement, however, there hung an aura of moral earnestness, with little homilies on such virtues as duty, honesty and steadfastness. In the 1880s Eno added another product, 'Vegetable Moto', an example of a large class of laxative pills based on aloes, gamboge or scammony. It did not have the appeal of the Fruit Salt.

When a new Infirmary building was planned in Newcastle in 1899, Eno promised to make good the difference between what was needed and what had been raised. This amounted to £8,500, and other gifts brought his total contribution to over £10,000. He died in London on 11 May 1915 at the age of ninety-five, leaving £1,611,607 gross.

W A CAMPBELL

Writings:

A Treatise on the Stomach and Its Trials (F Newbury & Son, 1874).

Sources:

Unpublished

PrC.

Published

A Birthday and Some Memories, 1868-1928 (J C Eno Ltd, 1928).

Newcastle Council Reports 1900.

Newcastle Weekly Chronicle 22 May 1915.

University of Durham College Medical Gazette 7 (1907).

Ward's North of England Directory 1852.

ERCOLANI, Lucian Randolph

(1888-1976)

Furniture manufacturer

Lucian R Ercolani (courtesy of Hew Reid).

Lucian Ercolani was born in St Angelo in Vado in Tuscany, Italy, on 8 May 1888, the eldest son of Abdon Ercolani, a picture frame maker. With the birth of the other children (one sister, three brothers), the family moved to Florence but Lucian stayed in St Angelo with his grandmother until the age of seven, when he rejoined his parents. Abdon Ercolani was an unusual man in the Italy of his day, not only was he a picture frame maker attaining the highest standards of craftsmanship whose work is still on show in many of the national galleries of Europe, but he was also a Protestant evangelist. When his preaching activities created problems for him in Italy, he and his family emigrated to England in 1898, under the aegis and sponsorship of the Salvation Army.

Lucian Ercolani was educated at schools in Italy and London but left at the age of fourteen to start work for the Salvation Army as a messenger boy at 6s a week in 1903. He entered the Salvation Army joinery workshops in 1905. Meantime, he continued his studies as a student of drawing and design, five nights a week for five years at the Shoreditch Technical Institute. Towards the end of this period he worked through the night to finish a drawing of a jewellery cabinet. This was seen the next evening by the editor of the *Cabinetmaker* who was visiting the Institute; he published the design in his trade magazine and as a result in 1910 Lucian was appointed designer for Frederick Parker Ltd of High Wycombe, manufacturers of high-quality bespoke furniture. He remained in this position until 1913 when he resigned to join Ebenezer Gomme (qv) of High Wycombe as the designer of domestic furniture.

In 1920 Lucian was approached by a consortium comprising Messrs Rich & Peters, twine merchants, and Messrs Harding & Ironmonger, merchant bankers, who urged him to start up on his own account as a manufacturer. He agreed. The company of Furniture Industries Ltd was formed and with the initial paid-up capital of £10,000 a 17 acre site in High Wycombe was purchased. Ercolani, whose savings amounted to only £300, subscribed none of the capital, but it was a provision of the initial agreement that he had the option to purchase a 52 per cent share holding at any time in the future. Production started in this new business in 1920 with two machinists, two cabinetmakers, and two polishers.

Business prospered and in 1931 Lucian Ercolani was personally invited to take over the long-established furniture manufacturer, Walter Skull Ltd. He secured control of Furniture Industries by making it a subsidiary of Walter Skull Ltd in which his personal holding was 12,000 shares compared to his partners' 8,000.

During the Second World War, Ercolani switched from furniture making to producing a vast quantity of small wooden items needed for the war effort; for example by 1944 they had manufactured 36 million tent pegs, which were one of more than a hundred kinds of military articles the firm produced. The end of the war in Europe gave Ercol (as the firm was now known) the opportunity to take a fresh look at furniture production. In the 1920s Lucian Ercolani had visited America and had been particularly impressed by 'Shaker Furniture' with its simplicity, clarity of design and fitness for purpose. As the leading designer cum producer of domestic furniture in High Wycombe in the 1920s and 1930s, Ercolani had suffered terribly from plagiarism, having to accept that within three months of producing a new range of furniture, he would be copied by other firms in the town. In 1944 Ercol were invited to produce 200,000 Windsor chairs for the Ministry of Supply at 10s 6d each. Ercolani managed to purchase 20,000 cubic feet of English elm for the seats of the chairs, and with the help of the Forest Products Research Laboratory successfully kiln dried this neglected timber species. Out of these circumstances late in 1944, grew the design-led production of furniture, upon which the firm's fortunes were so effectively established.

The firm had some 300 employees in 1947 and 750 in 1960; most of them had worked for Ercols since their apprenticeship. In 1950 Lucian Ercolani divided his holdings within the family (though he never retired) and his son Lucian became chairman and, with his younger son Barry, joint managing director.

Lucian Ercolani was made a fellow of the Royal Society of Arts and a fellow of the Society of Industrial Artists in 1933; he received the OBE in 1963.

Ercolani left the Salvation Army in 1909 and joined the Baptist Church. In 1915, in Walthamstow Baptist Church, he married Eva May Brett, daughter of George Brett, a retired police officer, of London. They had two sons and one daughter. Lucian Ercolani died on 9 June 1976 leaving £99,558 gross.

HEW REID

Writings:

A Furniture Maker (Benn Ltd, 1975).

Sources:

Unpublished

MCe.

PrC.

Information from the Ercolani family.

Published

Leonard J Mayes, *The History of Chairmaking in High Wycombe* (Routledge & Kegan Paul, 1960).

Times 12 June 1976.

Sierd Sint Eriks (courtesy of Mullard Ltd).

ERIKS, Sierd Sint

(1900-1966)

Electronics industrialist

Sierd Sint Eriks was born at Oosterzee in Holland on 26 September 1900, the third son of Jan Eriks, manager of a large agricultural co-operative which was responsible for marketing the products of the farmers in the area, and his wife Janna née Klijnsna.

After a particularly happy childhood and adolescence, in which family discipline and a keen interest in outdoor pursuits were dominant features, he laid the foundations for his future career by studying economics at Rotterdam Commercial High School. Eriks was a young man of great personal and physical charm, outstanding characteristics which he was to retain throughout his life. A big man, well over six feet in height and proportionately broad, his head was large, his forehead high, all features which gave him an outstanding presence in any society.

Joining the sales organisation of Philips Gloeilampenfabrieken NV in Eindhoven during the summer of 1924, he was placed in charge of the small section dealing with the sale of Christmas Tree lamps. Early in 1925 he was transferred to the department concerned with the export of radio valves and X-ray tubes. After a brief spell with the Philips agent in Portugal towards the end of 1925, he spent the next four years in Australia and New Zealand where he was instrumental in laying the foundations of the Philips business throughout Australasia.

Recalled to Europe in 1929, he was appointed general manager of the Mullard Wireless Service Co which, with its associated manufacturing organisation, the Mullard Radio Valve Co, had been acquired by Philips some years previously. Scorning almost all social activities, which he grew to regard as a waste of time, Eriks was to devote almost the whole of the rest of his life to the interest of the Mullard firm, its business, its factories and, in particular, its staff.

The company had been established by Stanley Mullard (qv) in 1920, primarily to manufacture high power transmitting valves for the Royal Navy. With the advent of broadcasting in 1922-23 the company began to expand to meet the demand for receiving valves but the technical advances of the mid-1920s exposed the little company's need of scientific research facilities and led to the take-over by Philips. In turn, this led to the resignation of Stanley Mullard from the day-to-day management of the company and to his replacement towards the end of 1929 by S S Eriks.

Eriks soon showed himself to be a shrewd and capable manager, slow to make up his mind while he considered every detail but quite determined when the decision was taken. Although he was in essence a 'Philips man' and was serving as their representative in charge of their UK-based subsidiary, his own strength of character and the political circumstances of the time were such that he was able to establish a substantial degree of independence from Dutch control without in any way prejudicing the closest co-operation on technical matters between the Mullard staff and those of the Philips laboratories in Eindhoven.

One of Eriks's outstanding traits was his capacity for foresight and the manner in which he applied it throughout his life in planning long-term policies and practical developments. Quite deliberately he trained himself to keep his mind continually focussed three to four years ahead and to develop his industrial plans in accordance with his considered judgement of the probable trends.

Taking over as general manager of Mullard in 1930 at a time of increasing industrial depression, Eriks became deeply impressed by the misery caused by unemployment, particularly in the North. By the mid-1930s he considered that war with Germany was almost inevitable and he foresaw the possibility that the UK would be cut-off from the European continent and that England would thereby lose the support of the Philips factories and laboratories in Holland. As an insurance, he therefore began in 1936 to plan for the opening of a factory at Blackburn in Lancashire with the joint aims of relieving unemployment in the area and of ensuring the continuity of production in the event of war.

In planning the factory, Eriks insisted that it be capable of undertaking every phase of radio valve manufacture from the basic raw materials to the finished product, a philosophy unique among valve manufacturers at the time which, in the event, rendered the company completely independent of external supplies and which enabled new or modified designs to be put rapidly into production. Thanks to Eriks's foresight, Mullards' Blackburn factory was destined to become by far the most important source of radio valves for the allied forces throughout the war.

Isolated from all contact with the Philips research laboratories in Eindhoven after 1940, Eriks also became convinced of the need to establish a major electronics research laboratory in this country. Although the project was opposed by the Philips directorate from their war-time headquarters in America, Eriks persisted in his plans which were eventually to mature at Salfords, near Reigate in Surrey, as one of the most important high-technology research laboratories in the country.

The electronics developments which occurred during the Second World War greatly emphasised the importance of a close association between government research establishments, the universities and industry. Eriks believed that the continuation of this close association was vital in the post-war era and, largely with this aim in view, the Mullard company sponsored the establishment of three specialised laboratories: the Mullard Space Science Laboratory in association with London University, the Mullard Radio Astronomy Laboratory at Cambridge, and the Mullard Cryomagnetic Laboratory at Oxford. All proceeded to make important scientific contributions in their respective fields.

In the post-war era, Eriks led his company through a long period of change and expansion. The re-opening of the BBC Television Service, suspended during the war, gave rise to a tremendous demand for special valves and for television picture tubes. Mullards was especially important as a manufacturer of valves and tubes for radio and television receivers in the 1950s, supplying 70 per cent of the receiver manufacturers' needs, partly because it persuaded Pilkingtons 'to manufacture pressed glass parts on a large scale, which had the effect of almost halving the price of bulbs for television tubes over the period 1950 to 1955'. {PP, HC 1956-57 (16) XVI, 92} Between 1935 and 1954 electronic valve production in Britain rose from 10 million per annum to 54 million and in 1954 Mullard had 58.5 per cent of the market, four times the share of its nearest rival. Mullard's profits on capital employed ranged between 46.6 and 52.6 per cent on valves and 17.7 and 37.8 per cent on tubes, in 1951-54: more than the other manufacturers. To manufacture television tubes a special factory (the most modern of its type in Europe) was established in 1954 at Simonstone, also in Lancashire.

Towards the end of his career, Eriks faced his greatest challenge with the invention of the transistor. Only very gradually did it become clear that the transistor and semi-conductor techniques would eventually lead to the replacement of the valve for all but a very few specialised and high-power purposes and that the valve industry as Eriks had known it throughout his career would, in due course, almost disappear. Characteristically, Eriks prepared for the changes he foresaw by establishing a special factory for the manufacture of transistors in Southampton in 1957 but, such was the slow pace of the fundamental developments involved that he was to retire (in 1964) and die (in 1966) before the valve, as he had known it, was displaced by the transistor and, subsequently, by integrated circuitry and micro-electronic techniques.

Apart from his primary responsibilities to the Mullard Co, Eriks held a number of important posts in allied and industrial organisations. He was appointed chairman of Philips Electronic & Associated Industries in 1955 and he took a leading part in the affairs of both the British Valve Manufacturers' Association and the Semiconductor Manufacturers' Association.

With his broad outlook and vast experience, Eriks enjoyed the friendship and respect of all the leading figures in the industry, one of whom subsequently wrote: 'Over a long period I had business relationships with Eriks involving many millions of pounds. I found him a man of tremendous integrity whose word was always his bond. I learned to value his word more than any legal document' {*Times* 1 Oct 1966}.

Eriks was awarded the OBE in 1948 in recognition of his services throughout the Second World War and, being still a Dutch subject, he was awarded an honorary KBE in 1961 'in recognition of his valuable services to British interests' {*The Announcer* Sept 1961}. In his native country he was appointed a vice-president of the Netherlands Chamber of Commerce and created an Officer of the Order of Orange Nassau.

Eriks was an intensely reserved man with few, if any, close personal friends of either sex. Having no interest in any form of social activity, he customarily worked extremely long hours; his life was his business, his business his life. He was far from being unapproachable but he found informality difficult, familiarity impossible and if few of his associates could claim to know him well, none could do so on a personal basis. He married in 1942 Margaret Isabel Duncanson, daughter of Robert Duncanson a master builder. Few of his colleagues were surprised when the marriage proved a failure; there were no children.

Sierd Sint Eriks died on 27 September 1966, leaving £80,914 gross.

G R M GARRATT

Sources

Unpublished

MCe.

PrC; Will.

Information from Jack Akerman, M G Mason, Miss Hilda Perkins (Eriks's secretary) and F J Philips.

Published

The Announcer Sept 1961.

The Pianomaker Oct 1966.

PP, HC 1956-57 (16) XVI, Monopolies Commission Report on the Supply of Electronic Valves and Cathode Ray Tubes.

Times 28 Sept, 1 Oct 1966 (appreciation by Sir Jules Thorn).

WWW.

ERLANGER

see **D'ERLANGER, Sir Gerard John Regis Leo** *and* **D'ERLANGER, Leo Frederic Alfred**

ESSENDON, 1st Lord Essendon

see **LEWIS, Frederick William**

EVANS, Sir John

(1823-1908)

Paper manufacturer

John Evans was born at Britwell Court, Buckinghamshire, on 17 November 1823, the second of the four sons of Rev Arthur Evans and his wife Anne, the sister of John Dickinson, the Hertfordshire paper manufacturer. He was educated by his father, who became the headmaster of Market Bosworth Grammar School in Lincolnshire in 1828. Although John wanted to go to Oxford University, his mother arranged for him to enter her brother's firm.

John Evans started work in the accounts office at Nash Mills in 1840; by 1845 he was earning £200 per annum. John Dickinson did not really treat him as a member of the family, and disapproved of Evans's marriage to his daughter, Harriet Ann, in September 1850, although he gave his formal consent. Soon after his marriage, John Evans, together with Dickinson's other son-in-law, the barrister Frank Pratt Barlow, was admitted as a partner in the firm. This was one of the largest paper manufacturing concerns in the country: by 1854 the mills, offices and workmen's cottages were valued for insurance at nearly £140,000. It is not known whether Evans or Barlow was given any share in the capital, nor what their salaries were.

Evans's role in the business, particularly after John Dickinson retired in 1857, was to supervise the production and basic services of the mills. Until at least 1876 he kept all the firm's cash books himself. One of his main concerns was to ensure the abundant supply of water essential to paper manufacture and, at that time, a major source of energy for the mills as well.

Under his direction the business grew steadily, if unspectacularly. For many years, following John Dickinson's death in 1869, the firm was burdened by the payment of a total of £100,000 under the provisions of his will; much of this went to his son, John Dickinson II, who had shown little interest in his father's business. Despite this handicap, capital was found to extend Apsley Mill, which by 1876 was turning out three million envelopes a week, to install new machinery and to lease additional mills. The most important innovation during these years was the participation of the firm in the experiments Thomas Routledge (qv) was conducting in the use of esparto grass as a substitute for rags as the raw material for paper-making.

By the late 1870s Evans was responsible for seven mills containing 14 paper-machines in Hertfordshire, a mill at Manchester preparing pulp for paper manufacture, a box-making house at Belfast, a stationery factory at 65 Old Bailey, and a share in Routledge's esparto mill in Sunderland. However the decade 1876-86 was bad for the paper-trade and in 1880 Evans, who considered himself primarily a paper-maker, had to admit that the firm's profits relied on the manufacture of stationery rather than the manufacture of paper. By 1885 it was decided to close some mills and develop others, and Evans chose to retire, leaving the work of concentration and conversion to the younger partners. The firm became a private limited liability company in March 1886, with a capitalisation of £500,000. This figure was considered too high in the trade, in the light of the likely profits of the company, and indeed the first year of trading showed a profit of only £2,000 on a turnover of £260,000.

John Evans's experience in supervising the production of perhaps the largest paper-making business in the country helped him to become one of the leading figures in the paper trade for many years. He was the founder and first president of the Paper Makers' Association and the more informal Paper-Makers' Club. One of the objects for which he organised the Association was to lobby the Government to remove the duty on paper of 11s 2d a pound; it was at last repealed in 1861, thanks not only to the efforts of Evans and his colleagues, but to those who saw the tax on paper as a tax on knowledge. In the 1860s Evans led the unsuccessful attempts of the trade to persuade the Government to retain import duties on paper coming from countries which charged export duties on rags for paper-making.

In his day, Evans was probably best known for his important work in several fields of learning. Among the institutions of which he was at one time president were the Numismatic Society, the Geological Society, the Anthropological Institute and the Institute of Chemical Industry. He was for many years treasurer of the Royal Society, and a trustee of the British Museum. He also found time to take a very active part in local affairs, serving for several years as a chairman of quarter sessions and of Hertfordshire County Council; he was High Sheriff of Hertfordshire in

1881. He was a staunch Tory but not a party man, distrusting all politicians, but especially Gladstone. Evans was made a KCB in 1892.

By his first wife he had five children; one of them was the eminent archaeologist Arthur Evans; another Lewis, entered the firm of John Dickinson in 1871, becoming a partner in 1881. When Harriet died, John Evans married his cousin, Fanny, daughter of Joseph Phelps, a merchant. After her death in 1890, he married in 1892 Maria Lathbury, an archaeologist and daughter of Charles Crawford Lathbury, 'gentleman' {MCe}; they had one daughter, the distinguished historian Joan Evans. He died on 31 May 1908, leaving £147,347 gross.

CHRISTINE SHAW

Writings:

For a list of Sir John Evans's writings see L Fower, *Sir John Evans, KCB, 1823-1908: Biographie et Bibliographie* (Chalon-sur-Saone, 1909). Evans does not seem to have published or lectured on paper-making.

Sources:

Unpublished

Information supplied from material in Dickinson Robinson Group archives by A W Clarke.

MCe.

PrC.

Published

The Dickinson Centenary Supplement to the *Hertfordshire, Hemel Hempstead Gazette and West Herts Advertiser* 16 Apr 1904.

DNB.

Joan Evans, *Time and Chance, the Story of Arthur Evans and his Forebears* (Longmans & Co, 1943).

—, *The Endless Web: John Dickinson & Co Ltd 1804-1954* (Cape, 1955).

Lewis Evans, *The Firm of John Dickinson and Company Limited, with an Appendix on Ancient Paper Making* (1896).

Hertfordshire, Hemel Hempstead Gazette and West Herts Advertiser 6 June 1908.

Times 1 June, 31 July 1908.

WWW.

William Evans (taken from Owen Vernon Jones William Evans*).*

EVANS, William

(1864-1934)

Grocer and mineral water manufacturer

William Evans was born, at Trellwyn Farm, near Fishguard, Pembrokeshire, in the rural districts to the west of the South Wales coalfield, on 24 August 1864, the oldest of the 14 children of Thomas Evans and his wife Moira. At the age of six, William was enrolled in school, at Jabez Chapel and for six years he made the daily six-mile return journey in furtherance of a sound elementary education. However with six other children to support, William's parents had little option but to send him, at the age of twelve, to Haverfordwest to start an apprenticeship with James Rees, a grocer. William also managed to deliver milk for his uncle who lived in the town. With his apprenticeship completed, William, at sixteen, moved to Aberbeeg in Monmouthshire, where he worked for three years as a junior at Alderman William Thomas's grocery store; he then secured the managership of the Porth branch of Messrs Peglers' grocery stores.

In 1883, when William arrived in Porth, the confirmation of the Rhondda Valleys as Britain's foremost coal mining district still lay a little in the future, and although his immediate impressions were far from favourable, he soon began to appreciate the economic potential which existed for the grocery trade. The population of the Rhondda had doubled, to 55,632, in the decade to 1881, and by the new century it was over 113,000, reaching its peak of 167,900 in 1924. In 1885 William left Peglers to enter into partnership with his former employer, William Thomas, an association which lasted a mere two years, but long enough to see the birth of the firm's title 'Thomas & Evans' and to give William a crucial start in his business life. In 1888 when the partnership was finally dissolved and Thomas, who had supplied the bulk of the original capital, had been repaid his £238, plus profits of £720, William, at the age of twenty-four became an independent grocer, in a shop with an established clientele.

His marriage in 1887 to Annie Jane Evans, the daughter of a Porth butcher and neighbour, provided a strong basis for the extension of William's business as he developed an ambitious approach to the business of selling food and drink to the rapidly growing mining communities. He quickly appreciated that the average coal-miner's family would spend a major part of its expanding wage packet on food and he introduced an ever widening range of products into his business. In addition, he ensured that the extent of his market was maximised by directing employees to travel up both the Rhondda Fawr and Rhondda Fach in pursuit of trade.

William's business activities expanded in the 1890s. In 1890 he commenced the baking of his own bread when the Hannah Street Bakery was opened in Porth; between 1893 and 1895 three branch shops were

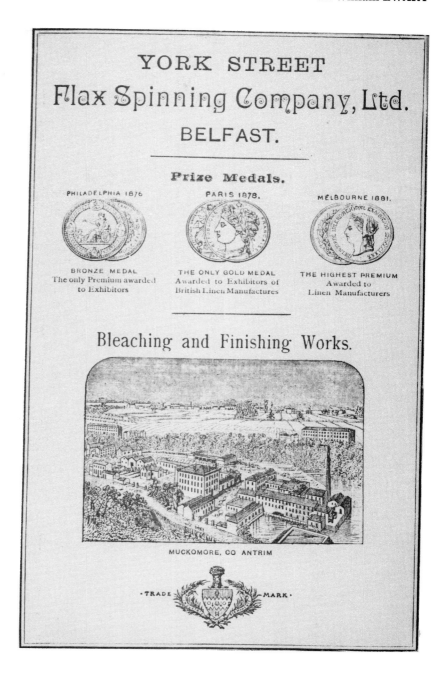

YORK STREET
Flax Spinning Company, Ltd.
BELFAST.

Prize Medals.

PHILADELPHIA 1876   PARIS 1878.   MELBOURNE 1881.

BRONZE MEDAL
The only Premium awarded
to Exhibitors

THE ONLY GOLD MEDAL
Awarded to Exhibitors of
British Linen Manufactures

THE HIGHEST PREMIUM
Awarded to
Linen Manufacturers

Bleaching and Finishing Works.

MUCKOMORE, CO ANTRIM

· TRADE ·   · MARK ·

Advertisement for York Street Flax Spinning Co Ltd taken from The Home and Foreign Trade Directory *1892.*

from preparing the flax to marketing it. This enabled the firm to keep the prices of its finished products lower than those of single sector firms and therefore to outsell them.

By the early 1880s, however, even Messrs Ewart & Sons was beginning to feel the effects of recession. Thus, to reduce the personal financial risks of failure William had the firm incorporated as a limited liability company in 1883. Despite this the Ewart family still retained all the profits of the firm, for the shareholders were William and six of his sons.

By 1889, when the third William died, the firm employed between 5,000 and 6,000 hands, 3,700 of whom worked in the spinning and weaving section. It operated 33,500 spindles and 2,000 powerlooms. The annual wage bill for the firm was over £150,000 and it had branch houses in many of the leading trading centres of the world including London, Manchester, Paris and New York.

Ewart held office in many of the linen trade organisations in Belfast including the Flax Supply Association, the Linen Merchants' Association and the Irish Linen Traders' Association. He was also president of the Belfast Chamber of Commerce for a period and in 1859-60 he was Lord Mayor of Belfast.

Outside business the third William Ewart was very active in church and public affairs. He made time for these activities by delegating authority for the running of the firm to his sons, six of whom were involved in its management both at home and overseas (the seventh son opted for being a policeman instead). Sir William was a staunch member of the Church of Ireland. He took a leading part in the endowment and erection of seven churches and held office in many church societies including the Young Men's Christian Association, the Protestant Orphans Society and the Belfast Sailors' Home. He was an active promoter of popular education and almost completely paid for the building of St Mary's National Schools in Belfast. In politics he was a Conservative and represented North Belfast in parliament from 1878 until his death. He was created a baronet in 1887.

He married Isabella, daughter of the late Lavers Mathewson, Esq of Newton Stewart, County Tyrone, in 1840 and they had fourteen children of whom nine (seven sons and two daughters) survived him. At his death on 1 August 1889 he left an estate valued at £313,127.

EMILY BOYLE

Sources:

Unpublished

MCe.

PrC.

Emily Boyle, 'The Economic Development of the Irish Linen Industry, 1825-1913' (Queen's University, Belfast PhD, 1979).

Published

Belfast Newsletter and Northern Whig 5 Aug 1889.

The Home and Foreign Trade Directory (Belfast: Wm Strain & Co, 1892).

Harold C Lawlor, 'Rise of the Linen Merchants — The Ewarts of Belfast' *Fibres and Fabrics Journal* 10 (Apr 1943).

PP, Factory Inspectors' Report (1871) C 348.

WWMP.

FAIRBAIRN, Sir Andrew

(1828-1901)

Textile machinery manufacturer

Andrew Fairbairn was born at Anderston, Glasgow, on 5 March 1828, the only son of Peter Fairbairn, a partner in the Anderston Foundry, and his wife Margaret née Kennedy. Disappointed with the results of his partnership, Peter Fairbairn left to join his older brother (later Sir) William in Manchester for a few months, before starting the Wellington Foundry, Leeds in 1828, where he made woollen machinery in which wood was replaced with metal as far as possible. Andrew was sent first of all to a private tutor in Geneva and then to Glasgow High School. He entered Christ's College, Cambridge but soon transferred to Peterhouse, graduating as thirty-seventh wrangler in 1850. From Cambridge he went to the Inner Temple and was called to the Bar in 1852. After three years on the Northern Circuit and West Riding Sessions he left the law and prepared to take his place in the family business.

First he went to America, and then to Hanover to study German, becoming the firm's representative in Europe. Early in the 1850s the business became a partnership, including Peter (knighted when he was mayor of Leeds in 1858 on the occasion of Queen Victoria's visit to open the new town hall) and Andrew Fairbairn, and Thomas Greenwood (qv) and John Batley who left in the mid-1850s to start their own engineering and machine-tool business nearby in Armley. On the death of Sir Peter Fairbairn in 1861 Andrew took over, and ran the business on his own for two years before admitting two partners, T S Kennedy, a cousin on his mother's side, and J W Naylor, who had joined the firm in 1843 and was effectively managing director under Andrew Fairbairn's chairmanship. Naylor was formally appointed managing director in 1882 when Kennedy retired: the business was incorporated with A S Macpherson (indentured to Peter Fairbairn in 1849) taking Kennedy's place. As Fairbairn, Naylor & Macpherson the company continued to grow steadily, despite the collapse of the Leeds flax spinning trade. New machinery was developed for preparing hemp, jute, ramie and silk waste as well as machinery for spinning rope and twine.

During the Crimean War Fairbairns made machine tools for the manufacture of ordnance, supplying the Enfield and Elswick works with machines for making Armstrong cannon. After the war they continued to produce machine tools for ordnance and locomotive manufacturers. In 1867 the business employed 2,000 hands and was the biggest employer in the Leeds engineering sector, with a third more workers than either Butler's Kirkstall Forge or Kitson's Airedale and Monkbridge Foundries, whilst Greenwood & Batley employed less than a thousand. Exports of machinery for spinning coarse fibres to India and the Philippines increased, as did the home trade in rope and twine spinning machinery (strong linen twine being used in sewing machines in the new boot factories).

At the turn of the century negotiations began to unite Fairbairns with their major rival in Leeds, Samuel Lawson of the Hope Foundry, and with Combe, Barbour & Combe of the Falls Foundry, Belfast, creating a near monopoly of manufacture of flax spinning machinery (with a special interest in exports to India and South America). The new company was incorporated on 11 July 1900 (authorised share capital £800,000) with Sir Andrew and A S Macpherson amongst the six directors, and Sir Andrew (he was knighted in 1868) as the first chairman, a post he held until his death. Fairbairns provided 46 per cent (£85,852) of the buildings and land of the group.

In Sir Andrew's absence from business a reliable group of managers ran the family firm. After he entered Parliament in 1880 the board was strengthened by the addition of the works manager and other senior staff including T G Mylchreest. Eventually the original triumvirate died in rapid succession, Naylor in 1899, Sir Andrew in 1901 and Macpherson in 1902, leaving Mylchreest to represent Fairbairns on the new company board.

The textile machines developed under Sir Andrew won major awards at the international exhibitions in London (1862) and Philadelphia (1876). The labour force rose from 1,400 in 1861 to 2,400 in 1876 when the Wellington Foundry occupied 32,000 square yards.

In local politics Andrew Fairbairn was a rarity, a Liberal Anglican. Like his father, Andrew Fairbairn became Mayor of Leeds. The following year, 1867, he was re-elected, and in 1868 received the Prince of Wales for the opening of the National Exhibition of Works of Art, being knighted soon after. He resigned the mayoralty to stand for parliament as an Independent Liberal at Leeds, only to come fourth out of the five candidates. His politics were independent; even though he was an Anglican, he favoured disestablishment of the Church in Ireland (but not in England).

Sir Andrew, deeply interested in education, supported a public library which was opened in 1869 and was elected first chairman of the School Board in 1871. Under his leadership surveys were carried out, sites bought and 24 elementary schools built with 1,300 places. With Lord Frederick Cavendish he was instrumental in founding the Yorkshire College in 1874, which, with the older School of Medicine, became a constituent of the Victoria (later Leeds) University in 1897. He was a life-governor and honorary secretary of the university and a keen supporter of technical education, especially in engineering. He retired from the School Board in 1878, following disagreements over finance when others took a much narrower view of education than he did; he then began a new phase of his political life.

He left the family mansion in Leeds and moved to Knaresborough, where he contested the 1874 election in the Liberal interest. The Tories had been prepared well and a former MP, Basil Woodd, regained the seat comfortably. Fairbairn's support for Gladstone's disestablishment of the Church of Ireland and the 1872 Licensing Act told against him. In 1878 he again moved, close to York, and built Askham Grange and a school for the village of Askham Bryan. In that year he was appointed to the Royal Commission (Engineering and Agricultural Section) of the Paris Exhibition 'with a special regard for the interests of Leeds'. He also became a director of the Great Northern Railway (his managing director was then appointed to the board of the lesser Lancashire & Yorkshire Railway). Because of his railway interests he presided over the committee which organised the first International Railway Congress in Brussels in 1885; he was vice-president of the congress and was awarded the Order of Leopold. In 1889 he presided over the First Section of the Paris International Railway Congress and was made Commander of the Légion d'Honneur. In 1895 he chaired the English section of the congress in London.

In 1880 Sir Andrew was elected as a Liberal MP for the East Division of the West Riding; after the redistribution of seats he stood for the Otley part of his old constituency and was elected in 1885. He voted against Home Rule in June 1886 and in the ensuing election in July he stood as a Unionist and was defeated. He attempted to return to parliament, standing at Pudsey in 1895, but was defeated.

He became High Sheriff of Yorkshire in 1892 and was a JP for both Leeds and the West Riding. He served as a captain in the Yorkshire Hussars and as a major of the 7th West Yorkshire Rifle Volunteers. Sir Andrew was president of the Leeds Centre of the St John's Ambulance Brigade, becoming a Knight of Grace of the Order of St John of Jerusalem, and vice-chairman of the Royal Albert Asylum at Lancaster. He was also chairman of the company that built the Leeds Grand Theatre in 1878.

In 1862 he married Clara Fredericia, daughter of Sir John Lambton Lorraine, Bt, of Kirk Hale, Northumberland. They had no children. In her later years Lady Fairbairn's health was poor, so that they spent part of the year in Yorkshire, part in their London home in Portland Place and most of the winter at the Villa Trois Fontaines, Biarritz where in May 1901 Sir Andrew fell ill. He was escorted by his doctor back to London and died there on 28 May 1901, leaving an estate proved at £349,612 gross.

EDWARD CONNELL

Sources:

Unpublished

Leeds City Archives: Fairbairn Lawson papers; Leeds Education Committee, School Board Reports 1873-1903; Hepper Estate Valuation Books vol 270.

PrC.

Published

British Association for the Advancement of Science, Leeds Meeting, 1927, General Handbook (Leeds, 1927).

Deacon's Court Guide, Yorkshire West Riding (C W Deacon & Co, 1900).

Industries of West Yorkshire part 1, 1887 (Historical Publishing Co, 1887).

Railway News 8 June 1901.

Richard V Taylor, *Leeds Worthies, The Biographia Leodiensis; or, Biographical Sketches of the Worthies of Leeds and Neighbourhood ...* (Simpkin, Marshall & Co, 1865-67).

M A Travis, 'The Work of the Leeds School Board, 1870-1903' *University of Leeds Institute of Education Research and Studies* 8 (1953).

VCH Yorkshire.

WWMP.

WWW.

Yorkshire Post 1 June 1901, 8-17 July 1926 'Tercentenary Supplement'.

FAIREY, Sir Charles Richard

(1887-1956)

Aircraft manufacturer

Charles Richard Fairey was born in Hendon, Middlesex, on 5 May 1887, the son of Richard Fairey, a mercantile clerk and Frances née Jackson. His father later became a London timber merchant and importer, but suffered a business failure and died in 1898 just after making a fresh start, leaving the family poor. Fairey had to leave Merchant Taylor's School, and after some schooling elsewhere, enrolled at fifteen as a non-paying premium apprentice at the Jandus Electric Co of Holloway, studying in the evenings at the City & Guilds (Finsbury Technical) College. Upon passing his final examinations in electrical engineering (first class honours), he took charge of installing the electic lighting in docks and warehouses at Heysham, Lancashire. Independent and self-confident, he was dismisssed a few months later for reasons now unknown. But he quickly obtained the appointment of assistant to the manager and analytical chemist of the Finchley Power Station and gave evening lectures at the Tottenham Polytechnic and Finchley Technical College. He lived at home, and pursued an interest in model aeroplanes, winning national prizes for model aeroplane design in 1910 and 1911. He contacted the department store A W Gamage & Co, Holborn, and sold them the rights to his designs for £300 plus royalties on sales. Fairey contracted to build the models in quantity and deliver them at 5s 6d each, plus case and packing.

Already in 1909 he had helped to build a full-size aeroplane at what would become Hendon aerodrome. In 1911 he met Captain J W Dunne, whose patents he had unwittingly infringed with his model; Dunne merely required that acknowledgment be given in the instructions booklet. Then he offered Fairey a job. Despite the objections of his family, Fairey accepted. At Eastchurch he moved at once into the thick of things as manager of the Blair-Atholl Aeroplane Syndicate, supervising the construction of Dunne's flying machines, learning the need to reduce structural weight, and meeting the bright Cambridge undergraduates who were building a glider there. More importantly, he met the Short brothers (qv) and in 1913 joined them first as chief stressman, then as works manager, and finally as chief engineer. He was not happy with the move of the company to Rochester and in 1914 tried to join the RNAS, but was told by the Director of the Air Department, Commodore Murray Sueter, that he was more valuable as an aircraft constructor. Fairey set up his own firm, The Fairey Aviation Co Ltd, in 1915, with the help of his Cambridge friends, who put up about £15,000; of Short Bros who gave him his first contract, for a dozen of their aeroplanes; and of Sueter, who gave him an Admiralty order for aircraft. Though not an easy taskmaster in an industry which had its ups and downs, Fairey inspired loyalty and many employees remained with the company throughout its life.

During the remainder of the First World War the company built Shorts and Sopwith aircraft to Admiralty orders, and at the same time began to develop its own designs. Especially important was the development of flaps, for which Fairey received both a patent (and in 1936, the Wakefield gold medal of the Royal Aeronautical Society). As his aircraft were mostly seaplanes or operated off ships, wing flaps were much needed.

The Fairey Aviation Co like the aeronautical industry in general, had a difficult time in the years immediately after the war. In 1919, there was a brief trial, soon abandoned, of motor-car body building. Production of the Fairey III, first produced in 1917, was continued at a new, permanent factory at Harlington, near London. Other Fairey aircraft, the Fawn and the Flycatcher, though successful as designs, received only small orders. The company went into voluntary liquidation in 1921, and was reformed. However, by 1925, more than half of all British military aircraft were Fairey designs. His leadership in aircraft design was confirmed by the Fairey Fox, a fighter bomber whose prototype was at first turned down by the Air Ministry. Fairey went ahead with the development of the aircraft, at a cost of £20,000, using an American Curtiss D-12 engine, and produced an aeroplane capable of flying 50 mph faster than any other aeroplane of its type in the RAF. After a demonstration flight the chief of air staff, Sir Hugh Trenchard, immediately ordered a squadron of Foxes.

The profits of the Fairey Aviation Co in 1919-26 averaged £113,000 a year; for the year to 31 March 1927, they were £125,363; the following year £160,192. In 1927 the company had changed its name to The Fairey Aircraft Holding Co Ltd, but in 1929 was converted into a public company under its old name. 300,000 10s ordinary shares and 300,000 £1 8 per cent first mortgage debentures were offered to the public; the remaining 700,000 ordinary shares of the £1 million authorised share capital were assigned to the Fairey Aircraft Holdings Co, together with £325,000 cash, as the purchase price of the private company. Fairey himself held £106,250 of the £150,000 income stock of the Holdings Co. As well as the factory in Middlesex, the company had 125 acres of land and foreshore at Hamble near Southampton, with a small factory and seaplane testing station. The Middlesex works has recently been equipped 'to enable aircraft to be constructed in metal to meet the requirements of the Air Ministry' {Times *Prospectuses* (1929) 301}. Over 1,500 workers were employed by the company, which had assets of £615,486 and £430,000 of orders in hand at the end of 1928. Five types of Fairey aircraft were in service with the RAF in 1929, and many aeroplanes had been sold abroad to foreign Governments, including the Australian, Irish, Argentine, Chilean, Dutch, Portuguese and Japanese. Fairey himself was to be managing director for at least five years, 'and to give to the Company the benefit of any inventions made by him during that period relating to aeroplanes, seaplanes, flying-boats or other flying machines' {*ibid* 302}. In 1931 he founded the Avions Fairey Co in Belgium, which sold many aircraft based on the Fox to the Belgian Government.

Fairey continued to produce new aircraft designs in the 1930s. One of the more important was the Swordfish. In 1933 the SR I prototype was destroyed in a flat spin, but Fairey pressed on and in seven months produced a second, which in 1935 went into production as the Swordfish, and lumbered through operations until 1945. It was followed by further aircraft for the newly independent (1937) Fleet Air Arm, notably the Albacore, the Firefly and the Barracuda, and after the Second World War by the Gannet turboprop.

Fairey spent the war in government service, first helping organise increased output in the air industry, and then in the USA, where he was sent in August 1940 with the British Air Mission to Washington as a production expert. He rose to be Director General of the BAM in 1942. His work in the USA was invaluable. He was at once made the British representative on the Joint Aircraft Committee, an immensely powerful four-man body which determined priorities. For his work he was elected an honorary fellow of the American Institute of Aeronautical Sciences, and in May 1944 he was formally knighted, though the honour had been announced in 1942. In the meantime he had suffered a series of heart ailments, was forced to resign from the BAM on 30 April 1945, and spent three months in hospital in Boston.

The company, meanwhile, had to manage without him. The war caused cancellations and spread management thin, as they controlled some 25 enterprises, including manufacturing Halifaxes in a shadow factory and major repair contracts, as well as making their own naval aircraft. Difficulties arose as engines and sub-contracted parts failed to arrive on schedule. In December 1942 the new Minister for Aircraft Production, Sir Stafford Cripps, singled out the Fairey Co as his first trouble-shooting job.

A government-appointed managing director was sent in, and the situation was very uncomfortable, for Short Bros had already been nationalised. But the board remained basically the same from 1934 to 1957. What did happen was that for the first time in British industry, American-style project management was imposed to see new designs into production.

Upon his return to the UK Fairey became joint managing director with his friend Sir Clive Baillieu (qv), who had been brought in to act as joint chairman in January 1944. Though the company suffered from a lack of senior technical designers, it produced the turboprop Gannet, helicopters and the Fairey Delta 2 research aircraft, which in early 1956 became the first machine in the world to do over 1,000 mph in level flight. It was a fitting capstone to Sir Richard's supervision of his company.

Fairey was chairman of the Society of British Aircraft Constructors, 1922-24, a member of the research council of the Royal Aeronautical Society, 1922-26, and its president, 1930-31 and 1932-33. He was a fellow of the City and Guilds Institute, a vice-president of the Institute of Directors and an honorary vice-president of the Anglo-Belgian Union. As well as his wartime knighthood, he received an MBE from the British Government in 1920; he was also a Commandeur de l'Ordre de la Couronne (a Belgian order), and in 1947 was awarded the Medal of Freedom with Silver Palm by the US Government for 'exceptional meritorious services in the field of scientific research and development'. {*DNB*}

Away from aviation Fairey's main recreation was yacht-racing and design. He originally took up yachting for relaxation, having been ordered to rest by doctors in 1927 after years of overwork. No doubt this additional interest in the sea was responsible in part for his abiding concern with anti-submarine warfare and for his contributions in that field, just as his electrical training led him eventually into guided missiles. He became Commodore of the Royal London Yacht Club in 1935 and served on the council of the Yacht Racing Association (now the Royal Yachting Association).

Fairey married twice. He divorced his first wife, Queenie née Markey, whom he had married in 1915; they had one son. His second marriage in 1934, was to Esther, daughter of Stephen Whitney, a retired bank manager; they had a son and a daughter. One of his sons, Richard, joined the company after the war and rose to be general manager and a director until his death in 1960. Sir Richard Fairey died on 30 September 1956 in a London nursing home, leaving an estate proved at £883,646 gross.

ROBIN HIGHAM

Sources:

Unpublished

BCe.

MCe.

PrC.

Published

Centenary Journal, Royal Aeronautical Society, 1866-1966 (Royal Aeronautical Society, 1966).

DNB.

Geoffrey W Hall, 'Sir Richard Fairey' *Journal of the Royal Aeronautical Society* June 1959 (Hall was Fairey's stepson).

H A Taylor, *Fairey Aircraft Since 1915* (Putnam, 1974).

Times 1 Oct 1956.

Times, *Prospectuses* 77 (1929).

WWW.

FALK, Herman Eugen

(1820-1898)

Salt manufacturer

H E Falk (courtesy of the Salt Museum, Northwich, Cheshire).

Herman Eugen Falk was born in Danzig on 20 November 1820, the fourth of five children of David Wilhelm Falk (1773-1848), and his second wife Julianne Charlotte née Rickert. His bourgeois forbears had been members of the Lutheran establishment and variously involved in the municipal affairs of Danzig, a Prussian port and an entrepôt for Eastern European trade. Following a liberal education, Falk migrated to Liverpool about 1839, setting up as a general merchant in partnership with his older brother, Robert Julius Falk (1810-77). The firm traded worldwide in timber, grain, iron, cotton, manufactured goods and Cheshire salt. A staple British export, salt was an essential ingredient in food preservation and the glass and chemical industries. Between 1841 and 1844 Robert Falk Senior & Co acquired various rock salt and brine works. At Meadowbank, Winsford, in the Weaver valley, the younger brother exploited the deepest workable rock salt, though his enterprise was crippled through natural disaster and undercapitalisation. The Falks also signed unadvisedly ambitious railway contracts to supply sleepers, and had to be rescued financially by Dempsey, Frost & Co during 1845-46. Following this setback Herman Falk retreated to the forests of New Brunswick, Canada.

On his return to the Winsford salt trade two years later, he joined the price-fixing ring known as the Rock Salt Co, revived during the slump of 1847 and led by John Thompson. Having gained an intimate acquaintance with European markets, he began about 1849 to sell cargoes surreptitiously. The association commenced legal actions in the course of which Falk was arrested for debt and contemplated fleeing abroad. In 1850

Furnival's large salt works at Wharton, Winsford. c 1830 (courtesy of the Salt Museum, Northwich, Cheshire).

he agreed to abandon the salt trade, but did not, though expelled from Meadowbank. However, following a 'treaty of peace' of 1853 {Manchester Central Library, Falk papers, agreement by H E Falk, 25 May 1853}, he secretly reacquired Meadowbank works where he manufactured salt continuously from the boom year 1856 until the crisis of 1888. He also expanded his Liverpool agencies, especially in the coal trade.

Pushing and energetic, he outpaced numerous domestic and foreign rivals, manufacturing nearly 7 per cent of Cheshire's tonnage by 1877. He claimed to study the 'salt formations of the whole globe' {The Salt Museums, Northwich, report on Cheshire Salt Districts Compensation Bill, 1881, query 3,993}, a typical Falk exaggeration, but at least three of his journeys, those of 1874, 1876 and 1879-80, inspired memoirs, somewhat tendentious, on the salt trade of the United States, India and East Asia. The overproduction of Cheshire salt remained a problem throughout his life and he devoted much time to the quest for new markets. In 1845 he was among the first merchants to ship to Calcutta after the opening of Bengal to British salt. Following the business crisis of 1857 he persuaded major proprietors in 1858 to establish the Salt Chamber of Commerce of Cheshire and Worcestershire, which sought new markets, monitored tariffs, studied treaties, and lobbied the authorities to facilitate salt exports, especially to the Empire. The chamber disseminated statistics, complementing Falk's salt circulars, issued since 1843, and its policy statements were recognised as Falk upon Falk, particularly during his twenty years of presidency. Falk attended negotiations for the seminal Anglo-French commercial treaty of 1860. To counteract a temporary recession during a period of general prosperity, he convened about 1864 a new salt trade committee, underpinned by a brokers' association, to tackle the problems of overproduction and reckless competition. Following practices at least as old as 1764, this syndicate regulated wages, prices and production. But, during recession, restrained only by gentlemen's agreements, members fought for orders at any price. Alternatively, when prosperous, the labour-intensive trade attracted undercapitalised operators, particularly Weaver boat owners. Falk excluded this proletarian element from the association, holding it responsible for the industry's 25 per cent overproduction.

Falk believed that any legislative interference with this safest, healthiest of industries would ruin the trade which supported 30,000 people. In February 1877, when a Royal Commission investigated noxious vapours from salt works, offensive to landscape and lungs, he blamed factors beyond his control such as poor coal and stokers' refusal to work his own patent furnaces. {*PP* (1878) C2159-I, 294-300} Despite his opposition, legislation was passed in 1881 to extend the alkali inspectorate's powers to include saltworks. On the question of land subsidence in the salt districts, though offering helpful information for an inquiry in 1873, Falk denied individual responsibility, the dereliction of 'those gruesome regions' {*Sunday Chronicle* 5 Sept 1886} resulting from natural causes and centuries of exploitation for the common good. However, the misleading nature of his evidence in 1881 to the committee studying a compensation bill (promoted by property owners and local boards) and his influence with the Winsford ratepayers (who refused to share parliamentary costs), delayed legislation until 1891.

Falk complained that improving workers' wages encouraged bad workmanship and truculence rather than gratitude. He facetiously referred to his men as 'our masters'{*PP, HC* (1878) C 2159-I, 298}. In 1868 when most proprietors capitulated to strikers, Falk stood firm upon economic grounds for the industry's own good. He obtained from the Prussian consul and German pastor in Liverpool 80 Germans, eager to earn their passage to America, who for a short period accepted unregulated hours at one-third less wages than Englishmen. The saltmaster continued to employ foreigners and when Germans in turn 'conspired' with 'rebellious spirit' {*PP, HC* 1888 (305) XI, 154, 158} Falk, following negotiations with the labour association, recruited docile Poles or Hungarians, despite opposition from his radical Oxford graduate son, Herman John (who was to marry Rachel Toynbee in 1878). He regarded immigrant labour, about one-third of his own workforce of 250-350, as a satisfactory permanent solution for the problems of the industry. But Falk's practice was not adopted elsewhere. He sought to counter the 'gross materialism' of his workers' continual wage demands by a policy of paternalism, hoping to substitute 'contemplation of the arts and sciences' {*Daily Post* 10 June 1872} for the cash nexus. In pursuit of his object a school and housing were hastily erected to his own design. He sponsored a friendly society. In 1885 the medical officer of health, admittedly seeking a little sensation, reported critically on the foreign workers' living conditions. Falk replied that he could not reform 'the inherent dirtiness of the race, just ... as you find in the Irish population' {*PP, HC* 1888 (305) XI, 32} and reminded the authorities that they had congratulated him for carrying out all their sanitary recommendations. Vilified in the newspapers as 'a Cheshire salt hell' {*Sunday Chronicle* 5 Sept 1886} the colony was investigated in 1888 by the Select Committee on emigration and immigration. Nevertheless the press campaign fuelled resentment among the native-born unemployed towards Falk's foreign workers.

Falk supported investment in transport, including the Cheshire Lines railway with its branch to Meadowbank in 1870. His introduction to the

River Weaver in 1863 of iron steam barges, constructed in his own shipyard, and his promotion in 1864 of the Weaver & Mersey Carrying Co, undercut the freightage and loosened the stranglehold of independent Weaver boat owners. He was the first salt manufacturer chosen as trustee of the Weaver navigation.

Between 1884 and 1888 beset by a ruinous recession and challenge from Teesside brine, Falk formulated a scheme, based on proposals of Manchester businessmen in the early 1870s for the acquisition of all manufactories and proven salt lands by one company 'to control the make as well as the market ... in order to lay the giant bully competition' {Manchester Central Library, Falk papers, scheme for a Salt union, June 1884, 3}. The creation of such amalgamations was the tendency of the age, a new device, made easier by limited liability. He promised generous compensation to those salt proprietors willing to join the scheme as well as the prospect of dividends rising from 21 to 30 per cent. It was not his intention to offer shares in the new venture to the public. Falk's monopolistic dream was not realised. Semi-retired to his model farm, Catsclough (a longstanding passion) and hailed as the father of the salt trade, Falk, nearing seventy, determined not to serve as the industry's commercial statesman. However, in 1887-88 he uttered a call to arms, reported by the national press, which persuaded London financiers through the intermediation of Robert Fowler, a Westminster solicitor, to float a public company incorporating most of the salt proprietors. Falk continued to protest the necessity for an absolute monopoly. When thwarted in this, he threatened to withdraw from the supporters' list and refused to join the board (though his elder son, Herman John, did). Economists warned that the enterprise was doomed to failure. Eventually the syndicate was formed which purchased the majority of British salt firms for £3,464,519, well above market value, paying extravagant prices to the more obdurate, for immediate resale with commission to a limited company. Registered on 6 October 1888 with £4 million capital, Salt Union Ltd sold shares, at a premium, to some 4,000 enthusiastic investors, mainly in Cheshire. The 'great Salt Trust' {*Times* 15 Sept 1888} controlled 91 per cent of output, reduced production, raised prices and declared a 10 per cent dividend during its first year. But competition at home and abroad, transport and coal strikes, crippling legal disputes, overcapitalisation and an undemanding board had resulted, by 1896, in tumbling prices, profits and dividends. Nevertheless the Salt Union survived until absorbed in 1937 into ICI. Inspired, though not created by Falk, this derelict combine fared hardly any better than earlier salt associations in managing the salt industry. Salt Union Ltd provided a graphic example for the promoters of similar schemes in other industries of the penalties of inadequate planning and anachronistic management methods.

Falk attended services of the Established Church but eschewed civic or party political involvement, save in the cause of improving the salt trade.

In 1844 Falk married Elizabeth daughter of John Thompson, until his death in 1842 a painter, plumber and glazier in Wavertree and formerly a glass dealer in Liverpool. Elizabeth's sister was already married to Falk's brother Robert. There was one daughter of this union. Following Elizabeth's death in 1851 Falk married in 1854, Anne, daughter of Charles

Garside Hadfield of Bootle, merchant, by whom he had two sons and three daughters. In 1894 late in life he married, in London, Alice, daughter of an engineer, Walmsley Stanley. In his will of 1897 he bequeathed his whole personal estate to Alice, apparently owning no realty, and characteristically desired his relations not to wear mourning, at least not longer than six months. Falk died on 19 January 1898. His probate valuation put his effects at only £16,949 gross.

DAVID IREDALE

Writings:

PP, *HC* 1873 (185) LIII Landslips in the Salt Districts.

Salt in India; Notes Taken on a Tour in November and December 1874 (Northwich : 1875).

Salt in North America : Notes taken on a Tour in the Autumn of 1876 (Northwich : 1877).

PP, RC Noxious Vapours (1878) C2159, C2159-1.

PP, *HC* 1878-9 (123) IV Noxious Gases.

A Winter Tour through India, Burmah and the Straits (Longmans & Co, 1880).

Salt in India, (no 2): Notes Taken on a Tour, Winter 1879-80 (Northwich: *Guardian*, 1880).

PP, *HC* 1888 (305) XI SC Emigration and Immigration (Foreigners).

PP, *HC* 1890-1 (206) XI SC Brine Pumping (Compensation for Subsidence).

Sources:

Unpublished

Cheshire CRO, The Castle, Chester, Falk records including those from Chambers of Northwich, solicitors DCN 13-19; Salt Union Ltd archive DIC/SU 1-14.

Manchester Central Library, Archives Department, St. Peter's Square, Manchester, Falk papers.

John Rylands Library, Manchester University, Salt Chamber of Cheshire and Worcestershire, annual reports, 1858-89.

The Salt Museum, Northwich, Cheshire, Stammbaum der Danziger Familie Falk von der Gegenwart auf das 15te Jahrhundert, 1886 (original belonging to Mr A Andersson, Alabama, USA); Cheshire Salt Districts Compensation Bill, report of Select Committee of House of Commons, 1881.

Published

Albert F Calvert, *History of the Salt Union* (Effingham Wilson, 1913).

—, *Salt and the Salt Industry* (Pitman's Common Commodities & Industries, 1919).

W H Chaloner, 'William Furnival, H E Falk and the Salt Chamber of Commerce, 1815-1889; Some Chapters in the Economic History of Cheshire' *Transactions of the Historic Society of Lancashire and Cheshire* 112 (1960).

Chester Chronicle 9 June 1888.

Daily Post (Liverpool) 10 June 1872.

Economist 13 Oct 1888, 18 Nov 1901.

William Furnival, *A Statement of Facts* (1833).

Julia M Holmes, 'Father of the Salt Trade' *Cheshire Round* 1 (1967).

David A Iredale, 'The Rise and Fall of the Marshalls of Northwich, Salt Proprietors : A Saga of the Industrial Era in Cheshire, 1720-1917' *Transactions of the Historic Society of Lancashire and Cheshire* 117 (1966).

Henry W. Macrosty, *The Trust Movement in British Industry: A Study of Business Organisation* (Longmans, 1907).

Northwich Guardian 20 Aug, 7 Sep 1892.

Mary Rochester, *Herman Eugen Falk* (Chester : Cheshire Libraries and Museums, A Salt Museum publication, 1982).

The Sunday Chronicle (Manchester) 5, 12 Sep 1886.

Times 15, 24 Sep, 12 Oct 1888, 20 Jan 1898.

The Umpire 3, 10 Mar 1889.

Thomas Ward, *Notes of the Cheshire Salt Districts Compensation Bill* (Northwich : *Guardian* Office, 1881).

FARINGDON, Lord
see HENDERSON, Alexander

FARLEY, Reuben

(1826-1899)

Ironfounder and coalmaster

Reuben Farley was born in West Bromwich, Staffordshire, on 27 January 1826, the eighth of ten children of the mining engineer Thomas Farley (1781-1830) and Elizabeth (1792-1885), daughter of John Llewelyn. Like other future local leaders, Farley was a day pupil at the local Borwicks Heath Academy and an active member of the West Bromwich Institution for the Advancement of Knowledge. This schooling helped Farley to give speeches that were erudite as well as fluent and to display 'intellectual abilities of no mean order' {Jewell (1893) 16}.

Having been apprenticed to a local mining surveyor on leaving school, Farley took over the Dunkirk Colliery when he was twenty-one. He later added at least one other pit in association with his first wife's family. Farley also owned some brickworks. His principal involvement in unincorporated firms, however, lay in ironfounding. By 1861, in partnership with his sister's husband, George Taylor, Farley was able to purchase the local Summit Foundry, which became the core of the firm of Taylor & Farley. Twenty years later Farley bought his late brother-in-law's share and became sole proprietor.

During the later nineteenth century, as Black Country ironfounding expanded in the wake of the decline of the basic iron industry, the company grew rapidly and became 'one of the largest of its kind in South Staffordshire' {*West Bromwich Chronicle* 20 Nov 1896}. Taylor & Farley's rolls and other mill and forge machines were well known throughout the major iron and steel districts, and the firm won a medal at the 1897 Brussels Exhibition.

Farley remained the active head of Taylor & Farley, which occupied much of his time. Nevertheless, his experience and connections were much valued in boardrooms, and Farley played a leading role in several of the large limited companies which became significant, though still atypical, features of the area's economy from the 1870s. Farley was both a leading shareholder and chairman in two private corporations — Fellows, Morton & Clayton, a large canal carrier which his brother-in-law Joshua Fellows had founded, and Edwin Danks & Co, an important local maker of boilers and boats. Farley was also influential in two public companies which encountered major technical and financial problems while pioneering large-scale, deep-shaft mining on the south eastern side of the Black Country. A promoter and director of the Sandwell Park Colliery Co, Farley later became disaffected. He was an active chairman, however, of the Hamstead Colliery Co and represented the firm at regional meetings of coalmasters.

Through these commitments, together with his chairmanship of the South Staffordshire Ironfounders Association, his involvement in other employers' organisations and his personal ties to key businessmen in the district, Farley became 'one of the leading figures in the industrial life of the Black Country' {*Birmingham Daily Mail* 13 Mar 1899}. Moreover, although he made no claims to national prominence, Farley was an original member of the Iron and Steel Institute. Nor was he a cipher in the field of labour relations. Here many of Farley's attitudes were stern. No friend to 'grandmotherly legislation' {Staffordshire RO D888/1 27 May 1897}, he condemned the eight-hour day as 'interference with the liberty of the subject' {*Birmingham Daily Post* 3 Feb 1891}. Farley also criticised union organisers for alienating employers from workmen. Still, though embattled at Hamstead, Farley evidently experienced little labour trouble in his own firm, where he provided excursions and pensions.

Farley was perceived locally as a 'self-made man' whose position was 'entirely due to his meritorious conduct, integrity, and ability' {*Free Press* 24 Mar 1883}. Yet while the probate value of his estate, £167,735 represented a significant improvement on his father's social position, Farley's early acquisitions suggest that, like many upwardly mobile Victorian businessmen, he started his career with substantial assets in hand. Futhermore, Farley was less a brilliant innovator or manager than someone adept at pooling capital with other businessmen. Farley was an exacting negotiator who nonetheless won goodwill through his 'genial disposition and courteous bearing' {*Birmingham Daily Mail* 13 Mar 1899}.

Business success allowed Farley to collect paintings and to travel. Late in life he also acquired and improved a substantial house in West

Bromwich, where he was determined to continue to reside. If Farley deliberately eschewed 'gentrification' his sons grasped it eagerly. They were educated at Uppingham, and in two cases, at Cambridge; the eldest had an estate in Huntingdonshire, while the two younger sons lived in rural Warwickshire. Nevertheless the latter became actively involved in Taylor & Farley after 1918.

Reuben Farley's principal significance, however, lies neither in his impressive business success nor in his foundation of a partially landed family. For Farley was a classic example of the many Victorian businessmen who were active and influential leaders in the public affairs of industrial towns.

Farley's contributions were modest in the relatively contentious fields of religion and partisan politics, where his early enthusiasms waned. At first an active Wesleyan, Farley converted to Anglicanism by the 1860s. He remained devout, served as a churchwarden and led the 'Church Party' in the first School Board election in West Bromwich in 1871. Yet Farley subsequently avoided sectarian disputes: he refused to stand for re-election to the School Board, remained friendly with many Nonconformists and continued to patronise Dissenting as well as Anglican causes. In politics Farley was a keen Liberal early in his adult life. By 1868 however, he had distanced himself from the 'advanced' Liberals of the neighbourhood, whose enthusiasm for religious controversy and protection of trade unions was increasing. Farley, desiring 'less of Party and more of Patriotism' {Speech on Parliament}, was an inactive Liberal Unionist from 1886. Many fellow townsmen had urged him to stand for parliament when West Bromwich acquired its own seat a year earlier. However, like many other Victorian businessmen heavily involved with local affairs, Farley declined the opportunity.

Instead, he channelled his formidable energies into the municipal and philanthropic betterment of his native town. A firm believer in the Black Country's belated but vigorous version of the 'civic gospel' found elsewhere in cities such as Birmingham, Farley felt obliged to 'make the lives of the people brighter and happier' {*Weekly News* 25 Apr 1896}. He thought that civic improvement would also assist prosperity and would prevent both business irresponsibility and excessive demands by working men. In addition, Farley no doubt aspired to the social prominence he achieved as 'the foremost figure in the public life of the town' {*Free Press* 17 Mar 1899}.

Farley was a county magistrate from 1879, and one of the first borough JPs of West Bromwich. An active Poor Law guardian in the 1850s and 1860s, Farley, like many leading businessmen, later abandoned that particularly troubled sphere of local administration in order to concentrate on municipal affairs. He served for eight years as chairman of the West Bromwich Improvement Commissioners, took a leading role in their provision of local amenities, and defeated Joseph Chamberlain (qv) in a battle for control of the town's gas supply. When West Bromwich was incorporated in 1882 Farley's was the only name suggested for the mayor's chair. He filled it four more times and received particular credit for discouraging partisanship in council affairs. Throughout his local government career Farley proved especially adept at promoting prestigious projects — such as municipal utilities and civic buildings —

through which the Black Country's local authorities compensated for their patchy record in providing basic services such as sanitation.

Voluntary societies as diverse as the Rifle Volunteers, friendly societies, a choral society and West Bromwich Albion Football Club found Farley an active officer and major contributor. For a quarter-century he attended almost every committee meeting of the West Bromwich Building Society, and he bequeathed £1,000 to the district hospital, on whose 'weekly board' he had served for thirty-one years. Farley also assisted co-ordination between philanthropy and local government, notably by promoting technical education. Having developed a close relationship with the Fifth Earl of Dartmouth, Farley played a key role in Lord Dartmouth's gift to the town of its major park. Farley himself gave West Bromwich both a recreation ground and a museum. Such facilities, he thought, would allow 'all classes and sections of the community' to meet 'on common neutral ground' {*Free Press* 8 May 1886}.

Farley did not escape criticism, especially from those sections of the lower middle class and working class which argued that his projects pressed too hard on small ratepayers. Yet he learned to compromise, thus enabling his own plans to prevail, albeit in modified form. Moreover, Farley remained personally popular, even among his opponents, for his generosity, honesty and tactfulness — and as a symbol of the town's rapid economic and social progress during his lifetime. West Bromwich made Farley its first freeman in 1896 and erected a clock tower in his honour a year later. At Farley's death the mayor, a former critic, ordered public mourning; 'thousands of humbler citizens' {*West Bromwich Chronicle* 15 Mar 1899} attended the funeral.

A successful entrepreneur and an effective business leader, Farley was especially influential as a civic dignitary. By concentrating on relatively uncontroversial 'improvements' Farley typified the increasingly conciliatory and progressive leadership of the late nineteenth century Black Country elites.

Having confined his activities primarily to his home locality, Farley helped to complement the regional emphasis of wealthier and more cosmopolitan colleagues such as Sir Alfred Hickman (qv). Farley's unusually protracted and diverse public service only exaggerated a general, if by the 1890s a declining, tendency for prosperous Victorian businessmen to exert themselves in the public affairs of the localities from which they drew their substantial profits. Men like Farley had especially great impact in medium-sized towns, such as those in the Black Country, where civic life was poorly developed until the later nineteenth century. Their interventions helped replace the disputed edicts of earlier nineteenth century local leaders with the less absolute but more accepted decisions of the quasi-democratic 1890s.

Each of Farley's wives — Hannah Duce (m 1867; d 1876), Elizabeth Haines (m 1879; d 1885) and Harriette Fellows (m 1887; d 1938) — came from an important Black Country business family. His last spouse bore him five children; the youngest was born when Farley was seventy. Farley died in West Bromwich on 11 March 1899, having attended a public meeting less than a fortnight earlier.

RICHARD TRAINOR

Writings:

Speeches in the possession of Mr R D Farley.

PP, HC 1895 (253) VIII, Appendix to Second Report SC Distress from Want of Employment.

'A Sketch of the Rise and Progress of West Bromwich in the Queen's Reign. With Some Personal Reminiscences' *Free Press* (West Bromwich) 2, 9, 23, 30 July 1897.

Sources:

Unpublished

Lichfield Joint RO, Will of Thomas Farley (1830).

PRO, BT31/14999/29283 Fellows, Morton & Clayton Ltd.

Staffordshire RO, D876 Hamstead Colliery Co Ltd; D888 South Staffordshire Ironmasters Association MS; D1117 Sandwell Park Colliery Co Ltd MS.

West Bromwich Central Library, papers of West Bromwich Institution for the Advancement of Knowledge.

West Bromwich Central Library and West Bromwich Town Hall, West Bromwich Improvement Commissioners MS; West Bromwich Borough and County Borough MS.

C Reg: Edwin Danks & Co (Oldbury) Ltd (48,829).

PrC: Will.

Interview with Mr R D Farley, 10 Apr 1982, and his letters to author, 22 Nov, 4 Dec 1983.

Richard H Trainor, 'Authority and Social Structure in an Industrialised Area: A Study of Three Black Country Towns, 1840-1890' (Oxford D Phil, 1981).

Published

George C Allen, *The Industrial Development of Birmingham and the Black Country 1860-1927* (George Allen & Unwin, 1929).

Birmingham Daily Mail 13 Mar 1899.

Birmingham Daily Post 3 Feb 1891.

Burke's Landed Gentry 1937.

Derek Fraser, *Power and Authority in the Victorian City* (Oxford: Basil Blackwell, 1979).

Free Press 24 Mar, 14 July 1883, 9 Aug, 20 Sep 1884, 8 May 1886, 27 Oct 1893, 17, 24 Mar 1899.

John A Garrard, 'The Middle Classes and Nineteenth Century National and Local Politics' in Garrard *et al* (eds), *The Middle Class in Politics* (Farnborough: Saxon House, 1978).

Frederick W Hackwood, *A History of West Bromwich* (Birmingham: *Birmingham News,* 1895).

Ernest P Hennock, *Fit and Proper Persons; Ideal and Reality in Nineteenth Century Urban Government* (Edward Arnold, 1973).

Robert Hunt, *Memoirs of the Geological Survey of Great Britain ... Mineral Statistics ... for 1853 and 1854* (Longmans, 1855).

Jewell's Annual and Year Book of Useful Information on West Bromwich for the Year 1894 (West Bromwich: E C Jewell, 1893).

Journal of the Iron and Steel Institute 55 (1899).

Kelly's Official Handbook to the Titled Landed and Official Classes 1940, 1955.

Frederick B Ludlow, *County Biographies: Staffordshire 1901* (Birmingham: J & G Hammond, 1901).

Ryland's Iron, Steel, Tin-Plate, Coal, Engineering, & Allied Trades Directory 1890, 1920, 1940, 1942.

Staffordshire Advertiser 18 Mar 1899.

Richard H Trainor, 'Peers on an Industrial Frontier: The Earls of Dartmouth and of Dudley in the Black Country, c1810 to 1914' in D Cannadine (ed), *Patricians, Power and Politics in Nineteeth-Century Towns* (Leicester: Leicester University Press, 1982).

VCH Staffordshire 2.

Wednesbury Herald 18 Mar 1899.

Weekly News (Oldbury) 25 Apr 1896, 18 Mar 1899.

West Bromwich Chronicle 20 Nov 1896, 29 Oct 1897, 15 Mar 1899.

West Bromwich Midland Chronicle & Free Press 12 Mar 1943, 14 Jan, 13, 20 Oct 1944, 1 Feb 1946.

Sir Samuel Fay in 1918 taken from George Dow Great Central *3 (Locomotive Publishing Co, 1965).*

FAY, Sir Samuel

(1856-1953)

Railway manager

Samuel Fay (in later life he chose to be known always as 'Sam') was born at Hamble, Hampshire, on 30 December 1856, the second son of Joshua Fay, a 'gardener' {BCe} of Huguenot origin, and his wife Ann née Philpot. He went to Blenheim House School, Fareham, and entered the service of the London & South Western Railway in 1872, serving as a clerk at various country stations and then at Kingston-on-Thames. In 1881, with two other railwaymen, he started the *South Western Gazette* (few British railways then had house magazines), and two years later he published a brief and spirited history of the company, *A Royal Road*. In 1885 he became chief clerk to the superintendent of the line, and six years later assistant storekeeper. His chance arrived when he was appointed manager of the Midland & South Western Junction Railway in 1892, on a five-year contract at a salary of £300 with commission based on net revenue.

This company's line was a rural one 60 miles long, from Andoversford, Gloucestershire, to Andover, Hampshire. It had been bankrupt for over seven years. Fay had great difficulty to start with in finding money to keep the traffic moving. But he was resourceful, attentive to detail, and dauntlessly energetic. The receiver was dismissed in 1893 and Fay succeeded him, until the company was declared solvent in 1897. In 1894-98 its traffic increased by 73 per cent, its expenditure by 18 per cent. That was largely Fay's doing. He fully appreciated the potential of the railway as a route from the North to Southampton and developed its through services, greatly facilitated by the construction of the Marlborough & Grafton Railway, opened in 1898, carrying its traffic clear of the Great Western.

His powers now thoroughly demonstrated, in 1899 he returned to the London & South Western as superintendent of the line. In that capacity he visited the United States twice, but the full benefit of his experience there did not accrue to his employers, for on 1 January 1902 he left their service to become general manager of the Great Central Railway, at a salary of £3,000 per annum.

Though not bankrupt, the Great Central was financially in very low water, hopelessly overspent by the building of its London extension. Fay had already shown what he could do for an impecunious minor railway company. He now tried to do the same for a large one in a similar position. He exploited all its advantages as a through route from the North to the South and South-West by a steady development of cross-country services. They were announced by continuously-maintained publicity, a matter that

Lancashire boilers in Immingham power house taken from George Dow Great Central 3 *(Locomotive Publishing Co, 1965).*

630-hp engines in Immingham power house taken from George Dow Great Central 3 (Locomotive Publishing Co, 1965).

much interested Fay himself. No British railway manager of his time (except Albert Stanley (qv) of the London underground) had the same feeling for public relations. It permeated all the company's business; *Per Rail*, the comprehensive guide to the freight services issued in 1913, was just as carefully prepared as the glossy posters designed to attract passengers.

The company had to fight hard for all its traffic. This Fay enjoyed too. His manners were aggressive, sometimes overbearing. Yet though his relations with the Great Northern were uneasy, the two sought a fusion in 1907, extended to include the Great Eastern also. The plan was vetoed by parliament. Had it succeeded, Fay was to have been general manager of the combined company. The Great Central's own expansion culminated in the completion of its new port at Immingham, brought into use from 1910 onwards. That had been planned before Fay's arrival; but the execution of the task owed much to him, as was very properly recognised when the King knighted him on the dock side in 1912. If Fay did not succeed in making the Great Central profitable, he did everything he could to see that the company attracted business, and retained it.

Fay played his part in the national management of railways during the First World War. In 1917 he went to the War Office as Director of Movements, and a year later he became Director-General of Movements and Railways, with membership of the Army Council, and with general rank.

At the amalgamation which brought the Great Central into the London & North Eastern Co in 1923 Fay retired from railway service, his company voting him a pension of £3,000. He was chairman of Beyer Peacock & Co Ltd, the Manchester locomotive builders, 1923-33, and a director of two railways in Argentina.

He married in 1883 in All Saints Church, Kingston-on-Thames, Frances Ann, daughter of Charles Farbrother, an upholsterer; they had six children.

Sir Sam Fay died at Awbridge, Hampshire on 30 May 1953 leaving £3,614.

JACK SIMMONS

Writings:

A Royal Road: Being the History of the London & South Western Railway, from 1825 to the Present Time (Kingston-on-Thames: W Drewett, 1883).

Report of the Railways Commission (Wellington, New Zealand: W A G Skinner, 1925).

The War Office at War (Hutchinson, 1937).

Sources:

Unpublished

BCe.

MCe.

PrC.

Published

'The Directorate of Movements and Railways' *Railway Magazine* 44 (1919).

DNB.

George Dow, *Great Central* (3 vols, Locomotive Publishing Co, 1959-65) 3.

Richard L Hills and David Patrick, *Beyer Peacock* (Glossop: Transport Publishing Co, 1982).

Colin G Maggs, *The Midland & South Western Junction Railway* (Newton Abbot: David & Charles, 1967).

Edwin A Pratt, *British Railways and the Great War* (2 vols, Selwyn & Blount, 1921).

Times 1 June 1953.

WWW.

FEDDEN, Sir Alfred Hubert Roy

(1885-1973)

Aero-engine designer and manufacturer

Alfred Hubert Roy Fedden (usually known as Roy) was born in Bristol on 6 June 1885, the youngest son of Henry and Mary Elizabeth Fedden; his father was a leading figure in the sugar trade. After Clifton College he refused a place at Sandhurst. His father had bought one of the first motor cars in Britain, which was constantly breaking down, and Fedden became intrigued by the challenge of improving it. He attended Bristol Merchant Venturers Technical College, and served a premium (£50) apprenticeship at the Bristol Motor Co, where he insisted on learning practical engineering from forging to finishing. In 1906 he joined the drawing office of Brazil Straker & Co, the British engineering group whose Fishponds works manufactured steam wagons and motor buses, on the strength of his own two-seater car, for which he had also designed the engine. This was the beginning of success with light, sound designs in which he competed in road races, and which aroused his interest in aviation. Fedden became works manager and chief engineer of Brazil Straker in 1909, and in this capacity (following a year in South Africa recuperating from a bad football injury in 1911), he visited France in 1912 and 1913, seeking without success a licence to manufacture Clerget rotary engines. In 1914 he became technical director of the company, and a member of the board. Shortly thereafter, on a visit to the Mercedes plant in Stuttgart he stumbled into their secret aero-engine factory and was highly impressed.

The Royal Navy, which had turned him down for a commission in 1903, now thrust him into aeronautics. The RNAS sent him 300 crated Curtiss OX-5 engines for examination and rebuilding. He worked them over at once and their time between overhauls rose from five hours to two hundred. This gave him such a reputation that the whole firm was requisitioned for engine work. Not long after his became the only works apart from those of Rolls Royce to be allowed to make their engines. An agreement made at the time with Rolls Royce barred Fedden from developing an in-line water-cooled engine for ten years, so in 1917 he decided to enter the competition to the produce a 300 hp air-cooled radial for the RNAS. His design lost when the Minister, Lord Weir (qv), insisted that the contract go to the disastrous ABC Dragonfly, which was a failure. Fedden then decided, with Weir's encouragement and in his own perspicacious way for which he became irritatingly famous, that the future needed higher horsepowered engines of far greater reliability. Consequently he designed the Jupiter, which after the Paris Air Show of 1921 was eventually licensed in 17 different countries and flew in 262 different types of aircraft; for each one Fedden received 0.5 per cent royalty, which soon made him a very rich man.

Meanwhile, at the end of the war the old Brazil Straker firm had been sold off in bits, leaving Fedden and his design team with the nascent

Writings:

(with Emile Garcke) *Factory Accounts: Their Principles and Practice* (Crosby, Lockwood & Son, 1887) (six other editions, the 4th of which, 1893, was reprinted by Arno Press, 1976).

(with Emile Garcke) *Summary of the Factory and Workshop Acts, 1878-1891, for the Use of Manufacturers and Managers* (Crosby, Lockwood & Co, 1893).

'The New Accountancy' *Incorporated Accountants Journal* May 1907.

'The Accountancy of Tomorrow' *ibid* Dec 1910.

'Cost Accountancy: Its Evolution and Its Trend' *Accountant* 28 June 1919.

'Some Principles Governing the Ascertainment of Cost' *Incorporated Accountants Journal* Nov 1919.

'Cost Accounting and Rationed National Expenditure' *Cost Accountant* Dec 1921.

'Industrial Economics in Relation to the Bearing on National Welfare of the Ascertainment of Cost' *Accountant* 11 Feb 1922.

'Accountancy in Relation to Cost and Market Prices' *ibid* 3 Nov 1923.

Industrial Economics in Relation to the Bearing on National Welfare of the Ascertainment of Cost (Norwich: London & Norwich Press, 1923).

'Accountancy as an Aid to the Solution of Social Problems' *Incorporated Accountants Journal* Aug 1925.

Sources:

Unpublished

MCe.

PrC.

Published

The Accountant 2 Jan 1926.

Jack Kitchen and Robert H Parker, *Accounting Thought and Education: Six English Pioneers* (Institute of Chartered Accountants in England and Wales, 1980).

D Solomons, 'The Historical Development of Costing' in D Solomons (ed), *Studies in Cost Analysis* (Sweet & Maxwell, 1968).

WWW.

FENTON, Sir Myles

(1830-1918)

Railway manager

Sir Miles Fenton (courtesy of the National Railway Museum).

Myles Fenton was born at Kendal on 5 September 1830, the son of Myles Fenton and educated locally. At the age of fifteen he joined the Kendal & Windermere Railway as a junior clerk, and thus embarked on a career which encompassed more than half a century. Fenton's comparatively rapid rise in railway management — he became general manager of the Metropolitan Railway at the age of thirty-two — owed something at least to a readiness to move far and often in search of promotion. In the space of ten years he worked in the passenger superintendent's department of the East Lancashire and in the general manager's office of the Eastern Counties, acted as assistant to the divisional superintendent of the Manchester, Sheffield & Lincolnshire at Hull, was chief assistant to the goods manager of the London & South Western Railway, and manager of the Rochdale Canal — all before he was twenty-five years old. In 1856 he took up his first major appointment, returning to the East Lancashire as secretary, and when the company merged with the Lancashire & Yorkshire in 1859 he became assistant manager of the enlarged concern.

Fenton travelled south again in 1862 to take up the post of operating superintendent on the Metropolitan Railway, and in the following year was appointed general manager, with a salary of £800 a year plus bonus (raised to £1,200 in 1869). The Metropolitan, London's first underground railway, faced a serious crisis when the Great Western suddenly terminated its contract to work the line, and Fenton was asked to introduce and maintain a complete train service at short notice. He responded to this challenge with his customary enthusiasm and skill. Profitable operation followed, but future viability was threatened by the actions of unscrupulous contractors. By the time Sir Edward Watkin (qv) became chairman in 1872, the company was in danger of financial collapse. However, Fenton quickly established a close working relationship with Watkin, and together they pulled the company round. Watkin clearly had a high regard for his chief executive, and when his position on the South Eastern was threatened by a boardroom revolt in 1878-79, he asked Fenton to move across London to assist him. Fenton served as general manager of this much larger company from 1880 to 1896. He worked hard to improve the company's deplorable operating record, reviving both Continental and suburban services, and proved to be a skilful negotiator in the inevitable battles with competitors such as the London, Chatham & Dover and the London, Brighton & South Coast.

In 1899 Fenton had the distinction of being the first railway general manager to receive a knighthood while still in office. However, this honour owed more to his political affiliations — like Watkin he turned to the Unionist cause with enthusiasm and was recommended by the

Marquis of Salisbury — than to any exceptional services to the travelling public. Nevertheless, he was undoubtedly a competent manager whose contribution to the fortunes of his companies was frequently hidden by Watkin's shadow. He retired in 1896, shortly after Watkin, but agreed to act as a consulting director to the South Eastern, a task he also performed for the South Eastern & Chatham (a merger of the South Eastern and London, Chatham & Dover) from 1899. He was also a director of the Central Bahia Railway of Brazil and an associate member of the Institution of Civil Engineers.

Fenton married Charlotte Jane, daughter of G Oakes. He died at his home, Redstone Hall, near Redhill, on 14 March 1918 at the age of eighty-seven, leaving an estate proved at £3,420.

T R GOURVISH

Writings:

British Railways and Their Capabilities for Home Defence (Aldershot: Gale & Polden, 1888).

Sources:

Unpublished

PrC.

Published

Theodore C Barker and Michael Robbins, *A History of London Transport* (2 vols, George Allen & Unwin, 1963–74) I.

Railway Gazette 22 Mar 1918.

Railway News 16 Mar 1918.

WWW.

FENWICK, John James

(1846-1905)

Department store proprietor and manager

John James Fenwick was born in Richmond, North Yorkshire on 31 July 1846, the son of John Fenwick, a tallow chandler, and Mary née Cooper. To reduce the burden of a large family at home, he was sent to live with his paternal grandparents on their farm at Feldom in Swaledale and for some time went to school at Reeth. At the age of eleven (after the death of his grandfather) he returned to Richmond, and attended the Corporation school until the age of fifteen. He was then apprenticed to a draper in Stockton, whom he served for seven years, after which time his master is said to have recognised his ability and advised him to seek his fortune in Newcastle upon Tyne. In 1868, therefore, he became an assistant at the Newcastle drapers Moses & Brown in Mosley Street. Setting his sights higher, he moved in the following year to the more exclusive firm of Charles Bragg & Co of Pilgrim Street, who described themselves as silk mercers. By hard work, a determination to please and a genuine interest in materials and fashion he prospered, and was promoted to buyer and then manager at a salary of £350 a year and a share of the profits which averaged another £250. As a sideline he took up selling insurance and in 1877 he was offered the full-time Newcastle agency for the National Provident Institution, but turned it down because he planned eventually to set up in business on his own. The decision to do so came fortuitously in 1882 when he was dismissed by Braggs, apparently because of his insurance activities. He subsequently sued his former employers and won damages of £1,000 for breach of agreement, a sum which was useful in assisting the expansion of his business; more importantly, the case brought publicity and business for his new shop. He was to see the closure of Braggs in 1889.

With foresight, Fenwick chose to set up shop at 5 Northumberland Street, then almost entirely a prestigious residential street, describing himself as a mantle maker and furrier. He used the local press for advertising, something the better class of shop did not do, but imparted an impression of Parisian elegance which attracted attention. He visited his customers in their homes throughout the region and drummed up trade, rapidly building up a reputation for fashionable dresses. In 1884 he was able to move to larger premises at 39 Northumberland Street, with an option on 37 which he took up in 1885. He had the old houses remodelled, with an architect-designed shop front with large windows which caused a sensation with its few, well-displayed, elegant gowns. Working very long hours, he aimed at distinction and high fashion. He now went to Paris as well as London for new ideas and adopted Modiste, Newcastle as his telegraphic address.

A number of new ventures were tried. In 1887 he took a collection of his fashions to the Riviera to offer to the English community. A branch was

Having lost his seat in parliament in the 1918 election he resumed his part in the full-time running of the company. In 1924, on the death of Sir James Reckitt, Ferens became joint chairman with Arthur Reckitt, and sole chairman in 1927 when Arthur Reckitt died. Ferens continued to go to the office every day, until he was eighty-three years old. There was an urgent need in the 1920s for new products to be developed and marketed, as those products which still provided the bulk of the company's profits and sales, such as washing blue and grate polish, were beginning to become outmoded. The most successful of the new products were bathcubes, Karpol car polish and Windolene window cleaner. The older directors, including Ferens, were at times anxious about the diversion of attention from the established 'bread and butter' lines to these new ventures, but fortunately for Reckitts, their doubts were overcome. More effort than ever had to be put into the branches and subsidiaries abroad, as the imposition of prohibitive tariffs in one country after another made it necessary, against the will of the board, to run down the export trade from Hull in favour of increasing production abroad in Europe, Australia and the USA.

An ardent teetotaller, Ferens was one the leading spirits behind long negotiations by the Reckitts board to buy a public house, the *Bird-in-Hand*, situated virtually under the boardroom windows. The owners, aware of the desire of Ferens and his fellow directors to have done with this perpetual reminder of the dangers of drink, held out for fourteen years, finally agreeing to sell for £7,500 in 1923; Reckitts' orginal offer in 1909 had been £500.

In 1873 Ferens married Esther Ellen Field (Ettie) (d 1922) the daughter of William Field, a wholesale grocer and general merchant in Hull. They had met through the Brunswick Chapel, which Ferens had joined on first going to Hull. The marriage was childless, but they had an adopted son.

Ferens died on 9 May 1930 leaving £293,852 gross. Estranged from his adopted son, he left the bulk of his fortune to charity. One of the principal beneficiaries was Hull University College. Ferens specifically requested his trustees, so far as possible, to keep the shares in Reckitts which provided the income for his bequests.

MONA S BLACK

Sources:

Unpublished

BCe.

MCe.

PrC.

Mona S Black, 'An Outline Investigation into the Life and Work of Thomas Robinson Ferens (1847-1930)' (Dissertation toward the Diploma in Social Studies, University of Hull, 1974).

Published

Thomas W Bamford, *The University of Hull. The First Fifty Years* (Oxford University Press, 1978).

Desmond Chapman-Huston, *Sir James Reckitt, a Memoir* (Faber & Gwyer, 1927).

Basil N Reckitt, *The History of Reckitts and Sons Limited* (A Brown & Sons, 1951).

Times 10, 28 May 1930.

WWMP.

WWW.

FERGUSON, Henry George

(1884-1960)

Manufacturer of tractors and agricultural implements

Harry Ferguson (courtesy of Massey-Ferguson Ltd).

Henry George Ferguson was born in Growell, County Down, Ireland, on 4 November 1884. He was always known as Harry, which was a family name. He was the fourth of eleven children, three girls and eight boys, born to James Ferguson, a farmer, and his wife Mary née Bell.

Harry's schooling was limited. He disliked farm work and was also unable to accept his father's religious dogmatism. When he was eighteen he left to work in his brother's motor and cycle repair shop in Belfast. There he displayed his remarkable mechanical aptitude. He attended evening classes at the Belfast Technical College. He also became interested in aviation and in 1910 built and flew the first aeroplane to fly in Ireland. He established his own motor car and farm implement business in Belfast in 1911, still (1982) in existence as Thompson-Reid, Ltd.

During the First World War Ferguson was asked by the Irish Board of Agriculture to supervise the use of tractors in food production. This experience showed him the need for a tractor suitable for small farms and gave him the concept of his unit principle: that is, a linkage that enabled interchangeable implements to be controlled by the driver of the tractor. He saw Henry Ford and the Fordson tractor as the instruments to realise this ambition, but his first approaches to Ford were fruitless. In 1925 Ferguson and two American brothers named George and Eber Sherman of Evansville, Indiana, formed Ferguson-Sherman, Inc to market ploughs for use with the Fordson, but the Depression and the discontinuance of Fordson production in the United States in 1928 wrecked their business.

Harry Ferguson pictured in the early 1950s at the wheel of one of his famous TE 20 'little grey Fergies' (courtesy of Massey-Ferguson Ltd).

Ferguson then returned to Belfast, and turned his attention to tractor, rather than implement design. By the early 1930s he considered his unit system complete and came to an agreement with the David Brown Co of Huddersfield. A new company, David Brown Tractors, was formed to manufacture his tractors, which were sold by another new company, Harry Ferguson Ltd, Huddersfield. This was Ferguson's preferred business arrangement. He would provide the ideas and designs and do the selling (he was an excellent salesman), and someone else would do the manufacturing. The sales company ran into difficulties, and the two firms merged to form Ferguson-Brown Ltd, in 1937. This association lasted only three years — Harry Ferguson was always difficult to work with — but it had lasting consequences in that David Brown became a major manufacturer of tractors and agricultural implements. Some 1,250 tractors were produced before the arrangement was terminated; they were the first production tractors in the world to incorporate a three-point linkage and hydraulic lift with draft control system.

In 1938 Ferguson at last enlisted the interest of Henry Ford, and the two men reached a verbal 'handshake' agreement whereby the Ford Motor Co would build tractors of Ferguson's design, using his patents. They would be sold in the United States through a company named Harry Ferguson, Inc. (He was not a modest man.) Production began in the USA in June 1939; 306,221 9N and 2N tractors were produced in 1939-47. This was a personal enthusiasm of Henry Ford, not shared by other officials in his

In 1958, three of the Coventry-made tractors became the first vehicles ever to reach the South Pole overland. Except for minor modifications to the electrical system and the fitting of snow tracks, they were identical with regular production models (courtesy of Massey-Ferguson Ltd).

company. Ford of Britain made little effort to overcome wartime government restrictions which prevented them from converting from Fordson to Ferguson tractors in the middle of the war. After Henry Ford's grandson, Henry Ford II, became head of the company in 1947, he cancelled the unwritten agreement with Ferguson, who then proceeded to manufacture his own tractors in the USA at Detroit in October 1948, with the TO-20 Model. He sued the Ford Motor Co for violation of the antitrust laws and infringement of patents and in 1952 received settlement of £9.2 million, the largest amount that had ever been won by a plaintiff in a patent action.

Meanwhile he resumed activity in Britain, where Harry Ferguson Ltd, Coventry was organised to sell tractors built by the Standard Motor Co. Ferguson demonstrated his considerable powers of persuasion by inducing Sir Stafford Cripps to release the necessary steel at that time of acute post-war shortages. This enterprise was highly successful. The 'Little Fergie' (very similar in design to the 9N) dominated the British tractor market — 517,651 were produced, 1946-56 — but there was constant friction between Ferguson and Standard Motors (latterly under Alick Dick (qv)). In 1953 Ferguson merged both his British and his American companies with the Canadian firm of Massey-Harris, which needed a good tractor for its line of agricultural implements and the entry into the US that Harry Ferguson, Inc could provide. Ferguson received $15 million in stock, making him the largest shareholder in the combined firm of Massey-Harris-Ferguson; he became chairman of the company.

Harry Ferguson stayed in the organisation just about a year, before disputes about costing procedures and planned engineering changes to Ferguson products led to his resignation. He then concentrated on Ferguson Research Ltd, created in 1950 to design an automobile with four-wheel drive, each wheel driven independently, four-wheel steering, and independent suspension. He wanted to improve the safety of road vehicles by eliminating skidding due to spinning or locking of the driving wheels. The technical problems were extremely complex, and although a few prototypes were built, Ferguson was unable to get any British motor manufacturer to attempt production.

Ferguson was a small, spare, energetic man. In his later years, he crusaded for a price-reducing economy. He fervently believed, as he told Franklin D Roosevelt, that 'the right way to get rid of poverty and to raise the standard of living everywhere is not to spread more money about but to produce more wealth by cost-reducing methods and so bring down prices' {*DNB*}. He instilled this vision into many of those who worked with him; as one of his staff put it, 'we were not employees: we were converts. Joining the Ferguson organisation was like joining the Church'{*ibid*}. He also believed that world food production could be greatly increased by the mechanisation of small farms, and he did much to make such mechanisation possible.

Ferguson married Mary Adelaide, daughter of Adam Watson of Dronmore in 1913. They had one daughter, Betty. He died at his home near Stow-on-the-Wold, on 25 October 1960, leaving an estate proved at £598,899 gross.

JOHN B RAE

Sources:

Unpublished

PrC.

Published

DNB.

George B R Fielden, *Invention, Innovation and Design* First Harry Ferguson Memorial Lecture (Belfast: The Queen's University of Belfast, 1970).

Colin Fraser, *Harry Ferguson. Inventor and Pioneer* (John Murray, 1972).

Allan Nevins and Frank Hill, *Ford: Decline and Rebirth: 1933-62* (New York: Charles Scribner's Sons).

Edward P Neufeld, *A Global Corporation, a History of the International Development of Massey-Ferguson Limited* (Toronto: University of Toronto Press, 1969).

John B Rae, *Harry Ferguson and Henry Ford* (Belfast: Ulster Historical Foundation, 1980).

Times 26 Oct 1960.

WWW.

FERRANTI

see **DE FERRANTI, Gerard Vincent Sebastian** *and* **DE FERRANTI, Sebastian Ziani**

FFRENCH, Charles Austin Thomas Robert John Joseph

6th Lord ffrench of Castle ffrench

(1868-1955)

Railway contractor and financier

Charles Austin Thomas Robert John Joseph ffrench was born at Birchgrove, Roscommon, on 20 June 1868, the elder son of the Hon Martin Joseph ffrench (1813-93), by his second cousin, Catherine Mary Ann O'Shaughnessy. His father, who succeeded as Fifth Lord ffrench in 1892, was resident magistrate at Cashel in Tipperary, 1846-82. The second baron had shot himself in 1814 following the insolvency of his ffrench Bank, and left his affairs so entangled that his will was not proved until 1915: there were therefore no great estates carried with the title, to which ffrench succeeded in November 1893. Two of his sisters became nuns, and he was educated at the Roman Catholic school of Clongowes Wood College and at Trinity College, Dublin.

He settled at Graaf Reinet in Cape Colony, moved to Johannesburg around 1896, and according to his friend Leo Amery, later spent a good many years in Rhodesia. There he befriended George Pauling (1854-1919), the rumbustious Rhodesian Minister of Mines and Public Works in 1894-96, who was a railway contractor in partnership with Cecil Rhodes' nefarious confidential agent, Rutherfoord Harris (1856-1920). In 1907 they appointed ffrench as their agent in China, and in the next seven years he negotiated railway contracts, such as for the Fakumen in Manchuria, 1907-8, the Canton-Hankow line, 1908-9, the Chinchow-Aigun, 1909-11, the Canton-Chungking-Lanchow, 1911-12 and the Yangtse-Singyifu, 1913-14. All of these schemes were thwarted, either by Russian and Japanese political jealousy, or because of the exclusive British diplomatic support in China given to the Hongkong & Shanghai Bank until the loan made by Birch Crisp (qv) in 1912. As a result, Pauling spent almost £60,000 in China from 1898 to 1914 without securing any return.

ffrench, who visited President Taft in Washington and P A Stolypin in St Petersburg during 1911, was responsible for attempts in 1915-16 to ease the Russian Government's wartime supply bottlenecks by building a railway from the ice-free port of Murmansk to Petrozavodsk. Paulings used Austrian prisoners-of-war as labour, but withdrew after obstruction by the Russian war ministry.

In 1918 ffrench became first chairman of a new issuing house, BST Ltd. The company (whose initials denoted British Stockbrokers' Trust) was part of the wartime corporatist movement led by Dudley Docker, Sir Vincent Caillard (qqv) and other 'productioneers': it was an institution as innovatory in intention as the British Trade Corporation, the export bank formed in 1917 to further economic imperialism and to break the big German banks' international power, of which Lord Faringdon (qv) was Governor.

BST was a revolt by provincial brokers who had long resented the way in which new capital issues were offered to them for subscription. Despite the provincial centres being the wealth-producing areas of the country, the London issuing houses, so BST's promoters complained, usually gave them only a few hours to decide whether to participate in any imminent issue, thus preventing them from investigating its soundness. BST was instead framed as an issuing house which would provide provincial investors with sound shares on fair terms: it declared itself opposed to the 'high-handed and overbearing attitude' of the London Stock Exchange, a body inimical to 'the interests of the investing public, the provincial brokers and the country generally'. BST also assailed City orthodoxy by disavowing the practice whereby foreign loans issued in London contained no stipulation that a proportion of the proceeds must be spent on contracts placed in Britain. For over a decade, leading manufacturers had advocated a system of 'tied loans' to ensure that British capital was spent on British goods, and had inveighed against the use of British capital by German business interests. This resentment was reflected in BST's envenomed references to British investors 'being made the tools and servants of German economic penetration' by those 'issuing houses of German origin [which had hitherto] commanded the situation' {*Economist* 9 Feb 1918}. Although BST was backed by provincial brokers, the provincial Stock Exchange Committees were not directly involved in its formation, and indeed the Liverpool committee was hostile to it.

The City hierarchy swiftly retaliated against this challenge to tradition. The Committee of the London Stock Exchange decreed, with effect from 1 February 1918, that BST was a 'combination of stockbrokers' whose operations were only fit for stockbrokers 'in their individual capacity', and therefore, that any provincial broker who was a shareholder in BST would forfeit his rights, under Rule 189 of the Stock Exchange, to have his orders executed by London stockbrokers at half the scales of brokerage charged to ordinary clients {*Economist* 19 Jan 1918}. BST circumvented this attack on its supporters' profit-margins by forming subsidiary companies in the five main provincial investment areas. Starting in the Midlands, BST (Birmingham) Ltd was formed in May 1918, followed by the Mersey Investment Trust in July 1918, BST (North of England) Ltd in December 1918, BST (Edinburgh) Ltd in April 1919 and BST (Manchester) Ltd in August 1919. These companies acted as feeders to the parent BST, and could be used by provincial stockbrokers without fear of persecution by the London Stock Exchange: it was thus hoped to mobilise and unify the investment power of each region into a force which the City could not afford to ignore. As well as chairing BST, ffrench was a director of the five subsidiaries, and was thrilled at the prospect of juggling millions. Of other board members, BST's managing director, Edgar Crammond, was a former secretary of the Liverpool Stock Exchange, whilst Sir Edmund Wyldbore-Smith represented Dudley Docker.

BST, with issued capital of £170,600 until January 1920, and of £488,000 thereafter, paid dividends of 6 per cent for 1918-19, 10 per cent for 1919-20 and 7 per cent for 1920-21. The group's performance mirrored that of the national economy, so that, for example, BST (Birmingham) paid 7 per cent in 1918-19, 19 per cent during the boom of 1919-20 when there were many new industrial issues, and 5 per cent during the depression of 1920-22. Another subsidiary, BST (South America) was registered in 1921, and the group was reorganised in May 1924, when a new company, the British Shareholders Trust, was capitalised at £550,000. The change of name signified an attempt to quieten the antagonism which had been aroused in 1918 by the phrase 'Stockbrokers Trust', and after 1924, BST sought acceptance in the City alongside other, less controversial, investment trusts which had recently been formed. The Trust, which by this date had made many large industrial issues and was among the most active of domestic issuing houses, thus followed many other bold wartime reconstruction plans in being tempered during the early 1920s. For reasons which are unclear, ffrench was replaced as chairman in November 1924 by Wyldbore-Smith, and BST's successive chairmen after 1926, Sir Follett Holt and Sir Pierce Lacy, were also close associates of Docker.

After leaving BST, ffrench continued for some years as a director of Card Clothing & Belting Ltd, Charles Morgan & Co Ltd, and Shanks Ltd. He became acting chairman in 1926 and chairman in 1927 of Sakhalin Oilfields Ltd, a company formed in 1912 and with issued capital of £251,702. It owned 50 petroleum claims in Siberia: but all of these had been nationalised by the Soviets, and its registered office was in High Street, East Finchley. Subsequently ffrench retired to his ancestral home, Castle ffrench at Ballinasloe, County Galway.

Described in 1913 as 'a cadaverous long-nosed Jesuit, treacherous and

George Findlay Jr's career at first followed that of his father and elder brother James. He left Halifax Grammar School in 1843 and worked at first as a mason on the Halifax branch of the Manchester & Leeds Railway. In 1845 he was engaged under the contractor Thomas Brassey, assisting his brother in the construction of bridges on the Shugborough-Armitage section of the Trent Valley Railway. He then spent a short period in 1847 working as a mason in London, first with Messrs Bransome & Gwyther on the construction of the London & North Western Railway's locomotive sheds at Camden, and next with Messrs Grissel & Peto on the rebuilding of the Houses of Parliament. He then returned to Brassey, and between 1847 and 1849 was engaged on contracts on the North Staffordshire Railway. Brassey subsequently appointed Findlay chief inspector of mining and brickwork for the construction of the Walton Tunnel on the Birkenhead, Lancashire & Cheshire Junction Railway.

In 1850 Brassey commenced construction of the Shrewsbury & Hereford Railway, appointing Findlay as his engineer for the contract. After the partial opening of the railway in 1852 Brassey also undertook its operation, and Findlay, in a decisive turning point in his career, was offered and accepted the post of traffic manager. Under Brassey's policy of delegated management Findlay was given complete control of the operation of the Shrewsbury & Hereford, and he quickly demonstrated his capabilities; under the terms of rental agreements which guaranteed shareholders first 4 per cent and then 4.5 per cent on their investment, and a share of further profits, dividends rose to 6 per cent before the end of Brassey's lease.

The strategic position of the Shrewsbury & Hereford Railway brought Findlay into close relations with other railway companies and gave him personal and professional contacts which were later to stand him in good stead. He also became directly involved in the opening up of mid-Wales to railways. In 1861 Brassey contracted to work the Knighton Railway, a branch from the Shrewsbury & Hereford line at Craven Arms whose ultimate objective was South-West Wales, and Findlay was also appointed traffic manager of that undertaking. In the same year Findlay entered into an arrangement with Thomas Savin, who followed Brassey's example by contracting for the construction and subsequent operation of much of what was later to become the Cambrian Railways system. Findlay became general manager of two of these lines, the Oswestry & Newtown and Llanidloes & Newtown railways, but through working arrangements and Savin's influence his responsibilities extended much further through the nascent Cambrian network. At the same time he retained his traffic managership of the Knighton, and, until 30 June 1862, of the Shrewsbury & Hereford. The latter company was leased jointly by the London & North Western Railway and the Great Western and West Midland railways from 1 July 1862, and Findlay was appointed by the LNWR as its district superintendent for Shrewsbury and South Wales.

In the shadowy railway politics of mid-Wales and the Marches in the early 1860s Findlay's dual responsibilities for the LNWR and for Savin were at first complementary, as the Cambrian group of companies looked primarily to the LNWR for support against the incursions of the Great Western into their territory. However, by the time the Cambrian Railways company was created by amalgamation in July 1864, Savin was working or constructing a network of railways reaching northwards around Cardigan

Bay toward the Lleyn peninsula, a potential alternative port 'for Ireland, and southwards to the mining valleys of South Wales. This involved the possibility of conflict with other LNWR interests; in addition, Savin had built up much of his influence by his willingness to accept securities rather than cash in payment for contracts, and his financial position became increasingly exposed as his contractual liabilities extended to more difficult sections of line. Findlay's connection with Savin thus became less easy to reconcile with his LNWR responsibilities, and in 1864 he was moved to Euston to take up the post of chief goods manager under William Cawkwell, the company's general manager. His predecessor, Charles Mason, became assistant general manager, and Findlay's appointment at the age of thirty-nine to so important a post in Britain's leading railway company was a clear indication of his standing as a manager.

Cawkwell himself took up a seat on the board of directors of the LNWR with effect from 1 March 1874 and relinquished the general managership. Richard Moon (qv), the chairman of the company, announcing this at a general meeting, referred to the 'mythical opinion' that the general manager should be responsible for the entire working of the system, a task which he described as 'practically impossible' {*Railway News* 28 Feb 1874}. Under new management arrangements Cawkwell was given a special remuneration of £1,000 per annum, and he, the chairman and two other directors assumed special management responsibilities on behalf of the board. Findlay succeeded Cawkwell as the company's chief executive officer, though with the title of chief traffic manager in deference to Cawkwell's position and the views expressed by Moon. Findlay's salary in his new post was £2,500 per annum; his successor as general goods manager was on a salary of £1,500. In 1880, with Cawkwell taking a less active role, Findlay was given the title of general manager, and when Sir Richard Moon retired in 1891 Findlay was himself offered the chairmanship. However, he declined, preferring to remain on as general manager, and on the recommendation of the new chairman, Lord Stalbridge, was awarded a knighthood in the Birthday Honours in 1892, an honour he briefly enjoyed for a year later he was dead.

Findlay was also the author of *The Working and Management of an English Railway*, which went through six editions between 1889 and 1899. Practical rather then theoretical, the book expressed Findlay's own approach to management; and his stress on delegation, on the clear definition of duties and responsibilities, and on the systematic conduct of business was reflected in contemporary assessments of his management style. The organisational structure of the LNWR as he left it and as he described it in his book was in essence largely as he had found it, with the general manager heading a professional management staff of company secretary, chief goods manager, superintendent of the line, chief engineer and chief mechanical engineer, with a divisional and district line management structure. The system of officers' conferences which fed into the cycle of board meetings was inherited from Huish's management reforms of the 1850s, and the varying demarcation between the roles of leading board members and senior professional managers of Huish's period was also evidenced by Findlay's own career with the LNWR.

The scale of the undertaking which Findlay had to manage, however, its employees, an attitude with which he inspired his juniors. Although Sir Clavering saw the need for diversification after the war, his ventures into pharmaceuticals and scientific instruments only provided the foundations for later development.

Apart from his business activities, Sir Clavering farmed 400 acres at Stutton Hall, Suffolk, giving him first-hand knowledge of the customers' side of the fertiliser business. A lifelong supporter of the Conservative party, he was elected as MP for Woodbridge in 1929. He resigned in 1931 due to pressure of work; he unsuccessfully contested the Ipswich seat in 1945. He served the community in Suffolk, becoming High Sheriff for the county in 1942, a chairman of the Orwell bench in 1948, and DL of the county in 1958. Fison was a keen shot and salmon fisher, and an outstanding tennis player, playing at Wimbledon in 1914 and 1920. In 1922 he married Evelyn Alice Mary daughter of Francis Lawrence Bland, a banker of Ipswich; they had two daughters.

MICHAEL MOSS

Writings:

'Britain's Fields are Still Under-Fertilised' *Times Review of Industry* May 1958.

Sources:

Unpublished

Fisons Ltd, Report and Accounts for the Year ended 30 June 1962.

BCe.

MCe.

Sir Clavering Fison, 'Development and Organisation of Fisons Limited' (Edwards Seminar Paper 204, 26 Feb 1957).

Published

Fisons Journal May 1958.

PP, HC 1958-9 (267) XVI, Monopolies Commission Report on the Supply of Chemical Fertilisers.

WWMP.

WW 1982.

FITZWILLIAM, William Thomas Spencer Wentworth

6th Irish and 4th English Earl Fitzwilliam

(1815-1902)

Coalowner

William Thomas Spencer Wentworth Fitzwilliam was born at Milton, Northamptonshire, on 12 October 1815, the second son of the Fifth Earl Fitzwilliam and Mary, daughter of the First Baron Dundas. He was educated at Eton and Trinity College, Cambridge, graduating MA in 1837. After his elder brother died in 1835 he succeeded to the title of Viscount Milton. His father was active both as a politician (in the hereditary Whig interest) and in cultural affairs, being an FRS, an FSA, and president of the British Association. The Fifth Earl enjoyed excellent relations with his colliers and took a great interest in the development of the collieries and their management structure.

Fitzwilliam inherited a colliery empire in South Yorkshire and was one of the few landowners in that area who also worked their own coal, although various outlying areas were let to independent coalmasters. On inheriting the family estates of about 115,800 acres after his father's death in 1857, Fitzwilliam owned seven collieries; during the 1860s production was concentrated from three. 'He spared no expense to furnish his collieries with the most approved appliances for reducing to a minimum damages incurred by the miners, and they on their part regarded him as one of their best friends'. {*Yorkshire Post* 21 Feb 1902} At the time he took over the collieries a considerable proportion of the coal produced was for virtually guaranteed sales: in 1853, for example, some 76 per cent of colliery income came from sales to the associated coke ovens and ironworks and to the Great Northern Railway. Fitzwilliam himself believed in negotiating through neither masters' associations nor trade unions, preferring to deal direct with his own colliers — writing publicly (from Coolatin) in 1893

> I have always refused to belong to any association or federation which might fetter me in my dealings with my workmen; and I wish to secure for them the same absolute freedom to be or not to be members of any association or federation they think best ... There cannot be a more false or dangerous doctrine than the belief that the interests of employer and employed are opposed to each other's. {John Goodchild loan MSS, printed circular}

By 1901, the year prior to his death, Fitzwilliam employed 1,063 men in and about his three collieries. He was a model employer in a variety of ways: he provided schools, good quality cottages with ample (and to the collier remunerative) land, almshouses, churches, village facilities, pensions and relief, and took an active interest in the affairs of the local miners' permanent relief fund. An obituary notice confirms what appears to have been the real situation, that 'Relations with his workpeople were [almost] invariably of the pleasantest kind' {*Yorkshire Post* 21 Feb 1902}. A personal acquaintance praised his truth, enthusiasm rectitude and boundless knowledge and simplicity.

As Lord Milton, he served as Whig MP for Malton (a family seat) in 1837-41 and 1846-47 and for County Wicklow (where the family had a house), 1847-57. Ever an ardent politician, he took an active part in the political life of the West Riding, his principal house being at Wentworth Woodhouse near Rotherham, and he served from 1857 until 1892 as its Lord Lieutenant. In 1886 he became a Unionist. He was an ADC to Queen Victoria. He was an enthusiastic fox hunter. In 1838, he married Lady Frances Harriet Douglas, eldest daughter of the Seventeenth Earl of Morton; they had eight sons, one of whom died in infancy.

Fitzwilliam died on 20 February 1902 at Wentworth Woodhouse at the age of eighty-six. His will was proved at £2,881,619 gross.

JOHN GOODCHILD

Sources:

Unpublished

City of Wakefield M D Archives, Goodchild Loan MSS.

PrC.

Published

Complete Peerage.

Graham Mee, *Aristocratic Enterprise: The Fitzwilliam Industrial Undertakings 1795-1857* (Glasgow: Blackie, 1975).

WWMP.

WWW.

Yorkshire Post 21 Feb 1902.

FLAVEL, Sidney Smith

(1846-1931)

Kitchen range and stove manufacturer

Sidney Smith Flavel was born at Leamington, Warwickshire, on 26 October 1846, the eldest son of Sidney Flavel (1819-92) 'Ironmonger' {BCe} and Elizabeth née Smith (daughter of Alderman John Smith of Coventry). His grandfather was William Flavel (1779-1844), who in 1803 had opened in Leamington, at that time a village with a population of 300, a branch of the ironworks which he had established in Coventry. For a firm specialising in the manufacture of grates and kitchen ranges the growth of Leamington (it had reached 13,000 by 1840) provided a local market, which was augmented by canal and, later, rail connections. The Eagle Foundry was built by William on the south bank of the Warwick-Napton Canal in 1833, to replace earlier, inner town sites. William, who laid the foundation of the firm's prosperity with his 'Patent Kitchener' (in fact he failed to take a patent on this design), was succeeded by Sidney Sr. The capacity of the works was increased by the installation of a new steam engine in 1856, and by 1860 it employed about 100 workers.

Sidney Flavel Jr was educated at Warwick School and Maidenhead College. His first inclination was towards holy orders but after he left school he spent three years at the Horseley Works, Tipton, learning the foundry business. He began work in his father's Eagle Foundry at 30s a week in 1867, the year Sidney Sr bought out his partners. Sidney Jr was taken into partnership about 1868. Further extensions were made to the works, and during the 1880s the firm's first gas, as opposed to solid fuel, stove was developed. In this the firm was following a general trend, made possible by the application of the Bunsen burner principle and probably stimulated by the provision by gas companies of ample daytime district pressure to permit the use of cooking and heating apparatus.

On his father's death in 1892 Sidney Flavel Jr became sole proprietor and in 1902 he converted the firm into a private limited company, at the same time absorbing the rival Imperial Stove Co, formed by three ex-employees as the Old Town Foundry in the 1860s. Flavel's eldest son, another Sidney (b 1879), was joint managing director, but he died in 1904 as the result of a motor accident at Warwick. His youngest son, Percival William, became a director in 1911, and managing director and majority shareholder in 1916, but he did not become chairman until his father's death in 1931. Considerable development took place at Flavels between the wars: iron founding was transferred to the Imperial Works in 1921 and new cupolas were erected in 1924 when other improvements were also made, including erection of a continuous casting plant (modernised in 1937). It was not, however, until the 1930s, after Flavel's death, that recognisably 'modern' models entered the product range, in the shape of the 'Kabineat' (1934, revised 1936) and the 'Type 37'. The finish on these models was made possible by the development of Flavels' own porcelain-enamelling plant. An important new product was added in 1928, in the form of the 'Metro' gascoke fire grate, built and distributed by Flavels to a design evolved by the South Metropolitan Gas Co.

Sidney Flavel's long chairmanship was combined with extensive participation in local government, politics and religious life. He was six times mayor of the borough of Leamington, an original member of Warwickshire County Council, for twenty years a member of the county magistracy, chairman of Kenilworth Petty Sessions and Leamington Watch Committee, vicar's warden of All Saints, Leamington for over forty years, and associated with Leamington Conservative Club and many other organisations in the town. He was also a freemason. He was an early and enthusiastic supporter of the National Society for the Prevention of Cruelty to Children, and was first chairman of its South Warwickshire branch. Flavel married on 5 October 1876 Gertrude, the third daughter of Henry Robinson of Borehamwood; there were three sons (the second, Gilbert Henry, made his career in the navy) and a daughter. He died on 16 March 1931, leaving an estate proved at £68,553.

Following the death of Percival Flavel in 1939, the firm was sold to the Whitehead Industrial Trust who subsequently sold the business to Glynwed.

RICHARD STOREY

Sources:

Unpublished

BCe.

PrC.

Personal information from the late S W B Flavel.

Published

How We Build (Leamington: Sidney Flavel & Co Ltd, 1937).

Leamington Spa Courier 12 Aug 1910.

Royal Leamington Spa Courier 20 Mar 1931.

E G Stewart, *Town Gas, Its Manufacture and Distribution* (HMSO, 1958).

Alexander Fleck, 1957, portrait by Lawrence Gowing (courtesy of the National Portrait Gallery).

FLECK, Alexander

Lord Fleck of Saltcoats

(1889-1968)

Chairman of chemical manufacturing company

Alexander Fleck was born in Glasgow on 11 November 1889, the only son of Robert Fleck, a coal merchant, and Agnes Hendry, daughter of James Duncan, a coal clerk. He was educated at Saltcoats Public School and Hillhead High School, but his family were unable to pay for him to attend school beyond the age of fourteen. He had already determined on a scientific career, and in order to pursue this took a job as a laboratory assistant at Glasgow University. There he attracted the attention of Professor Frederick Soddy, and became his assistant. By studying first at evening classes and then as a daytime student Fleck managed to obtain an honours degree in chemistry at the age of twenty-two. In 1911 he joined the staff of Glasgow University working with Soddy on the chemistry of the radioactive elements, until in 1913 he joined the staff of the Glasgow Radium Committee, researching into cancer. In 1916 he was awarded a DSc for a thesis on the chemistry of radio elements.

Fleck moved to industry in 1917, becoming chief chemist of the Castner Kellner Co at Wallsend-on-Tyne. Here, those qualities as a scientist and as a man which were to distinguish him throughout his career — insatiable curiosity, a desire to see and try things for himself, a warm and approachable attitude to all those who worked around him — soon made their mark. He became works manager in 1919. Fleck did not find this transition to management difficult: 'It was as easy as getting up in the morning' {Sampson (1962) 462}. He won the respect of the workmen by, for example, investigating a dispute about the working conditions of the process men in the sodium plant by spending a week on shift-work doing a process worker's job.

Castner, Kellner had become linked with Brunner, Mond in 1916. Brunner Mond increased their holding to a controlling interest in 1920 and hence the merger of Brunner Mond with three other chemical manufacturers to form Imperial Chemical Industries in 1926 brought Fleck into the service of ICI.

When ICI decided to concentrate production of sodium cyanide at new works on the south site at Billingham, and to close Wallsend and two other works that had been manufacturing cyanide, Fleck was responsible for the planning and operation of the new works named the Cassel works. He became manager of the Alkali Division of the ICI subsidiary of Synthetic Ammonia & Nitrates Ltd, later re-named as ICI (Fertilizer and Synthetic Products) Ltd, holding this position during 1927-31; in 1929 he was appointed a delegate director of this subsidiary.

Fleck's abilities, energy and enthusiasm brought him further rapid promotion. In 1931 ICI decided to form a large new division incorporating all the works of the United Alkali Co including their pyrites mines in Spain, the Castner Kellner Alkali Co, the Cassel Works at Billingham, and Chance & Hunt at Oldbury. The new division was named ICI (General Chemicals) Ltd, and Fleck was appointed managing director. The rationalisation called for by the amalgamation of works producing a large number of chemicals in different parts of the country was carried out by Fleck with skill and vigour. Under his direction the General Chemicals Division became one of the most important and profitable in ICI.

In 1937 Fleck returned to Teesside, this time as chairman of the Billingham Division. At the time of his appointment, ICI had finally come to terms with the fact that the massive capital investment they had made in fertiliser manufacture at Billingham would never realise the hopes that had been placed in it in 1926 as a future major bastion of ICI production and profit. A 1935 report pointed out that the factory, one of the major centres for chemical manufacture in the world, had changed from 'a fertiliser factory, with Industrial side-lines, to an Industrial Chemical factory, with a small Fertiliser interest' {Reader (1975) 160}. In 1937, the year of Fleck's appointment as chairman, £5.11 million was written off the value of the fertiliser plant. Hopes for the future at Billingham now centred on processes for producing oil from coal. The oil-from-coal plant was opened at Billingham in October 1935 and the first petrol was produced in February 1936. However, it was soon clear that coal was unsuitable raw material for this process, both technically and economically, and it was replaced by creosote. Still the results were disappointing, and it was only its value during wartime — when disappointing returns were of less consequence than a domestic source of petrol not dependent on imported oil — that gave the plant renewed significance (though there were those that said the plant produced just enough fuel to keep sufficient fighters flying to protect the plant).

It was not so much this plant that made Billingham a site of great importance for war production and a prime target for German air raids; Billingham also had plant for producing many chemicals indispensable in war, particularly hydrogen and hydrogen compounds. So vulnerable did the site seem that plans and preparations were made before the war for duplicate plants for some of the more important products to be built in other areas. Fleck was responsible throughout the war for keeping this vital industrial complex running, despite the damage from air raids — over 100 high explosive bombs fell on Billingham in these years. Fleck's energy and personal warmth, his ability to sympathise with and talk readily to staff at all levels came into their own during these difficult years. His daily meetings with his directors and works managers 'were an inspiration to all to keep the factory in operation, whatever the difficulties' {DNB}. From 1939 to 1942 he was also a delegate director of ICI (Plastics) Ltd, and from 1941 to 1944 a delegate director of ICI (Dyestuffs) Ltd. He was appointed to the main board of ICI in 1944 but did not relinquish the chairmanship of Billingham until the end of the war.

On the main board, Fleck had special responsibility for the Billingham Division and for Central Agricultural Control, which dealt with the marketing of ICI's agricultural products. He was also given responsibility for the major new chemical plant complex at Wilton across the Tees from

Billingham. £25 million had been earmarked for investment on this site by the end of 1947. The scheme included two plants of the now expanding Plastics Division, a large chlorine plant, and a cracking plant for producing 'heavy organics', chemical raw materials from oil, which started up in 1951. The Wilton works were the largest investment ICI had made since the unsuccessful scheme to establish a major fertiliser plant at Billingham in the late 1920s and early 1930s. From 1947 to 1951 Fleck was also chairman of Scottish Agricultural Industries Ltd, a holding company, in which ICI had a controlling interest, which brought together some of the leading Scottish fertiliser firms. He was appointed a deputy-chairman of ICI in 1951 and in 1953 was elected chairman.

ICI had expanded rapidly since the war. By 1954 the volume of production had doubled since 1946, while the workforce had increased by only 17 per cent; yet ICI employed 112,000 in the United Kingdom alone. In 1953 ICI made a trading profit of £52.1 million on consolidated sales of £281.9 million; in 1954 sales rose to £352.1 million, with a trading profit of £71.6 million. Sales continued to rise throughout the 1950s, though less steeply towards the end of the decade; profits did not keep pace: in 1959 sales of £508.5 million brought profits of £79.75 million. But 1959 also saw the peak spending, £60.4 million, of the post-war capital programme. There had been a steady change in the pattern of operations, with a larger proportion of turnover and profits coming from new products. In 1957 products not manufactured before the war accounted for a quarter of home sales and a third of export sales. ICI's increased interests in synthetic fibres led to the formation of a new Fibres Group in 1954. The synthetic fibre Terylene did particularly well in the 1950s, as did the paints Dulux and Dulite.

As chairman, Fleck travelled constantly, visiting ICI establishments both in the UK (where ICI had over 100 plants by 1957) and abroad. His desire to see things for himself whenever possible, his continuing close interest in people at all levels of the firm and his personal warmth and charm made the chairman a familiar figure to many employees. His concern for them found practical expression too. He was a firm supporter of the profit-sharing scheme introduced during his first year as chairman, not because he saw it as an incentive to increased productivity, but because he hoped that it would promote better understanding between managers, workers and stockholders. (His suggestion back in 1942 that the principle of the staff grade scheme be extended to cover all of ICI established personnel, and his conviction that the differences in hours and conditions between staff and 'payroll' were indefensible had marked him as a 'dangerous revolutionary' {Reader (1975) 299} in the eyes of at least one ICI director in earlier years.)

Fleck, in contrast to the authoritarian, paternalistic figures who had founded ICI (Harry McGowan and Alfred Mond (qqv)), was recognisably a modern professional manager, both in his technical training and in his liberal attitude to labour relations. He was always ready to be convinced by argument, but was quick to spot weaknesses or prejudices in a person's reasoning and had no hesitation in presenting his own opinions forcefully on such occasions. He would evaluate technical and commercial objections to a proposal, and if he considered such objections were surmountable he would remind those concerned that it was their function to propose

known locally for distributing £1 and a hundred-weight of coal every Christmas to all the old-age pensioners in Sandbach.

In 1896 Edwin Foden married Elizabeth Alice Devonport; they had three children, Florence Mary (b 1897), Dorothy (b 1898) and Dennis (b 1900). Elizabeth Foden, the daughter of a potteries glassware worker, died in 1912 and Edwin Foden in 1929 married again, his second wife, Mary Cooke, coming from a Cheshire farming family. The sole child of this union was Edwin Peter Foden (b 1930), who still manages the business his father founded, now (1983) the only surviving independent lorry firm in Britain. Edwin Foden died on 23 December 1950, leaving an estate proved at £97,396.

William Foden married Ellen Arden Davies, the daughter of Thomas Davies a hotel keeper; they had three children, William (b 1894), Reginald George (b 1900) and James Edward (b 1901). William Foden died on 2 June 1964 leaving an estate proved at £25,301.

C GULVIN

Sources:

Unpublished

BCe.

PrC.

Information from E P Foden and J E Foden.

Published

Crewe Chronicle 30 Dec 1950.

Pat Kennett, *ERF* (Cambridge: Patrick Stephens, 1978).

—, *The Foden Story* (Cambridge: Patrick Stephens, 1978).

Portrait of a Pioneer (Sandbach: ERF Ltd, 1970?).

Sandbach Chronicle 12 June 1964.

Patrick J Foley ca 1880 (courtesy of Pearl Assurance plc).

FOLEY, Patrick James

(1836-1914)

Manager of assurance company

Patrick James Foley was born in Leeds in March 1836, although he always liked to regard himself as a son of Ireland. Because of distressing conditions his parents emigrated from Sligo, on the West coast of Ireland, to Leeds in the 1830s. Catholic schools in Leeds and, for a period, Prescot (near Liverpool) provided his education.

On leaving school he worked as a clerk at a foundry near Leeds. After a period in Liverpool he moved to the East End of London, and in his early twenties was making a success of a job with a friendly society. At this stage he became convinced of the need to offer the poor an opportunity, by means of small weekly payments collected from their homes, to provide for funeral expenses and thus avoid the ignominy of being buried without dignity on the cheapest possible terms by the parish.

Life assurance in its present form had been established at the end of the eighteenth century but it was too expensive for the poor. Their needs were inadequately met by burial clubs and sick-benefit societies, which frequently served only local communities and were on no solid financial basis. The need for provision for burial expenses was recognised as early as 1807, when a bill for establishing 'A Fund and Assurance Office for investing the savings of the Poor' was debated but rejected. Industrialisation and the growth of the railways resulted in extensive population movements, which rendered the small local burial clubs even more ineffectual in meeting the needs of the poor. To meet these needs, friendly societies, aiming to provide for funeral expenses, multiplied in the 1840s and 1850s. Following the Companies Act of 1844 the British Industrial Life Assurance Co was formed in 1852, and others followed. All differed from the established life assurance offices of the day inasmuch as they collected small weekly premiums from the homes of the policyholders. One of Foley's main beliefs was that life assurance while necessary for the well-to-do, was indispensable to the poor. But he developed grave doubts about the integrity of a senior official of the friendly society that employed him, and consequently severed his connection with them.

In the late 1850s, Foley and some friends became connected with a loan-club (The Pearl Loan Co) that met in the *Royal Oak*, a public-house near Commercial Road in Whitechapel. This loan club developed into the Pearl Life Assurance Association and Sick Benefit Society, registered as a friendly society in 1862; Patrick James Foley was one of the four members signing the rules. Two years later, in July 1864, Foley and his associates filed a memorandum of association of Pearl Life Assurance, Loan & Investment Co Ltd, with an authorised capital of £25,000 (£350 paid up).

The company, which was the 1419th to be registered, had seven directors who each subscribed £50 for 100 shares; their occupations included builder, carpenter, writing-master and cabinet-maker. Foley, described as an accountant, was appointed manager in addition to being a director.

His salary at the time is not known, but two years later it was increased to £2 5s a week. This salary was augmented by fees for new business obtained, for during the first few years the directors canvassed the dockland area of London during the day (when they were reputed to wear green peaked caps embroidered with the name Pearl), and in the evening wrote policies and made up the books. Some twenty years later Foley occasionally accompanied agents on their rounds, and in the 1930s there were policyholders who remembered the tall top-hatted, frock-coated figure who in years gone by had collected premiums with elegance and charm. From 1875 directors were precluded by the Friendly Societies Act from acting as collectors, but the tradition of working directors who knew the business has been maintained, and for over a hundred years all Pearl directors (after the first seven) have been recruited from the staff — a practice which is unusual, if not unique, for life assurance offices.

The year 1864 was not an auspicious time to start a company transacting industrial life assurance. There were others already in the field and the Government that year started a Post Office life assurance scheme. In 1870 the rate of failure of newly-established offices resulted in the passing of the Life Assurance Companies Act, the earliest legislation of this type which, inter alia, required a deposit of £20,000 with the Accountant General of the Court of Chancery before commencing business.

Of the seven original directors John Keene was appointed chairman, and one room in his house, Denmark House, in Commercial Road, was the headquarters. Foley was appointed manager, but in 1870 the business was moved to 39 City Road, where Foley made his home. Although at first business was obtained solely from the London area, especially the East End, in a short while agents were appointed in many towns throughout the country. In 1874 the title of the company was changed to Pearl Life Assurance Co Ltd and the following year it began underwriting ordinary life assurance. The first policy for £500 sum assured was issued to P J Foley at a half-yearly premium of £18 4s 2d.

Business continued to increase rapidly and in 1877 the new policy issues exceeded 2,000 a week. The company leased larger premises in Adelaide House, London Bridge, which remained the site of their head office until they moved to the present head office in High Holborn, the foundation stone for which was laid by Foley in 1912. Adelaide House was a prestigious building — according to the chairman of the AGM in 1878 'the position, one of the best in the City of London is worth at least £500 as an advertisement only' — but later proved inadequate to house the head office staff, which had risen from one in 1864 to 300 in 1900, and overflow accommodation was obtained in nearby buildings.

In addition to being one of the first directors, Foley was also the manager of the company, and later managing director until he became president in 1908, a position he retained until his death in 1914. Foley is always regarded as the founder of the Pearl and he is credited with the remarkable growth that took place during his fifty years with the company. Nearly all this expansion was self-generated, apart from an

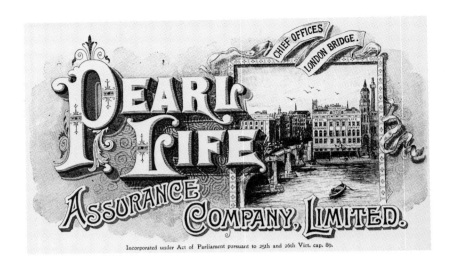

Chief offices of Pearl Life Assurance Company Limited, at London Bridge (courtesy of Pearl Assurance plc).

amalgamation in 1910 with the London, Edinburgh & Glasgow Assurance Co Ltd, which had assets of £1,025,238.

In 1871 Pearl's premium income was £7,121 and Pearl were fifty-third out of 55 life offices, but by 1913 the premium income was £2,752,895 and the company was third out of 78. During the same period the accumulated funds increased from £1,092 to £8,317,943 with nearly 5 million policies on the books. The authorised share capital rose from £25,000 (£350 paid up) to £1,500,000 (£440,050 paid up), all of which was new money, not bonus issues.

Although one of the first soundly-based industrial assurance offices in London, the Pearl never claimed to be the largest insurance company. Others were well established before 1864, and it was not until 1919, after Foley's death, that the Pearl wrote insurance business other than life. Nevertheless, the growth from very small beginnings prompted the *Insurance Mail* in July 1906 to write: 'P J Foley is one of the very few men who founded a life office and lived to see it annually receive an income of over a million sterling'.

Foley was not a great innovator but he was an enthusiast. His contribution to the success of the Pearl, apart from enthusiasm and hard work, was his ability to select and inspire the agency staff. He travelled the UK, personally interviewing superintendents and staff before appointment. In the first four years the company had established agents in the main cities in the UK and the staff employed had risen from one to 57; in the next forty years the workforce rose to 10,000. The apparent harmony on the board that lasted during Foley's lifetime was perhaps due to his dominating personality.

Preoccupation with the Pearl did not mean that he ignored the rest of the industry. The practice of many agents on transferring from one office to another was to persuade policyholders to lapse the policy with office A and effect a new one with office B. Although of short-term financial benefit to the agent, this was detrimental to policyholders and offices alike

Companies House, London, Company Reports.

Guildhall Library, London, Company Reports.

Middlesex RO, London Metropolitan District Railway.

PRO, Kew: Great Western RAIL 250; London Chatham & Dover RAIL 415; Hull Barnsley & West Riding RAIL 312; Didcot Newbury & Southampton RAIL 156; Banbury & Cheltenham Direct RAIL 18; Regent's Canal City and Docks Rly RAIL 860; dissolved companies, BT 31.

MCe.

PrC.

Information from Dr J M Sanderson.

Published

Aberdeen Free Press 6 Apr 1904.

Philip S Bagwell, 'Rivalry and the Working Union of the South Eastern and London, Chatham & Dover Railways' *Journal of Transport History* 2 (1955-56).

Theodore C Barker and Michael Robbins, *A History of London Transport* (2 vols, George Allen & Unwin, 1963–74) I.

Catalogue of an Exhibition of Pictures from the Collection of the late J Staats Forbes (Brighton: Museums and Fine Art Galleries, 1908).

DNB.

Engineer 8 Apr 1904.

Terence R Gourvish, 'The Performance of British Railway Management after 1860: The Railways of Watkin and Forbes' *Business History* 20 (1978).

John Marshall, *A Biographical Dictionary of Railway Engineers* (Newton Abbot: David & Charles, 1978).

Railway Times 9 Apr 1904.

Ernest Thesiger, *Practically True* (William Heinemann, 1927).

FORBES, Sir William de Guise

(1856-1936)

Railway manager

William de Guise Forbes was born in Dublin, on 21 June 1856; his father, William Forbes, was general manager of the Midland & Great Western Railway. He was educated at Dulwich College, London, and on the

FORBES Sir William de Guise

Sir William Forbes (courtesy of the National Railway Museum).

Continent, where he acquired an exceptional command of French and German. In 1873 he joined the London, Chatham & Dover Railway, whose chairman and general manager was his uncle, J S Forbes (qv). At first he worked in the goods department; later he transferred to the accountant's office and was travelling auditor for a time. In 1889, he became Continental manager, and during his tenure of that post Victoria Station became the chief gateway for Continental travellers, rather than Charing Cross, which belonged to the rival South Eastern Railway. Shortly afterwards, Forbes was promoted to be traffic manager. Following the working union between the LCD and SER in 1899, Forbes was appointed assistant general manager, but on 30 May of that year, moved to the London, Brighton & South Coast Railway as general manager designate. In due course, he took over from J F S Gooday, and retained his position until the grouping of railways following the First World War. On the formation of the Southern Railway on 1 January 1923, he became one of three joint general managers, but retired six months later.

While at the LCD, Forbes worked always under the shadow of his uncle. During more than twenty years with the LBSC, on the other hand, he gave ample proof of his own business ability. By 1908, his company's share of Victoria Station had been rebuilt. Pullman services were

London Brighton and South Coast Railway, Crystal Palace electrification 1911, 6600 v AC (courtesy of the National Railway Museum).

developed on the lines to Eastbourne, Worthing and especially to Brighton, where the 'Southern Belle' was a notable success. Faster and more comfortable cross-channel steamers came into service. Through services were arranged between Liverpool, Manchester and other centres to Brighton and Eastbourne. Most important of all, a start was made in 1903 on a programme of electrification. Since 1899 there had existed a threat that a new company might be formed to build an electrified line from London to Brighton. Moreover, suburban traffic was declining, as a result of competition from buses and trams. The line from Victoria to London Bridge was the first to be converted. Electric trains came into service there on 1 December 1909 and won back a good share of the lost traffic. It was decided to electrify the whole of the suburban network by 1916. The war would have caused difficulties anyway, but what made it quite impossible to continue with the plan was the fact that the main contractor was the German firm, AEG. There is little doubt that, but for the war, the LBSC would have become the first completely electrified railway in Great Britain.

The company's income and dividends provide a measure of Forbes's achievement as general manager. In round figures, the company's gross revenue rose from £3 million in 1899 to £7 million in 1922. At the end of his regime, the dividend on ordinary stock stood at 6.5 per cent — virtually unchanged as compared with 1899, when it had been 6.25 per cent.

Outside his company, Forbes served as chairman of the General Managers Conference at the Railway Clearing House. He was knighted in 1915, and was also admitted to the Légion d'Honneur, the Order of Leopold (Belgium) and the Order of Dannebrog (Denmark).

In 1902, Forbes married Louise Tronche, of Souillac, France. They had one son. Forbes died on 14 February 1936, leaving an estate proved at £34,538.

HENRY PARRIS

Sources:

Unpublished

PRO, Kew, RAIL 1100/290, 292.

PrC.

Published

Chapman F Dendy Marshall, *History of the Southern Railway* revised R W Kidner (Ian Allan, 1963).

George T Moody, *Southern Electric 1909-79* (5th edn, Ian Allan, 1979).

Railway & Travel Monthly 3 (1911), 9 (1915).

John H Turner, *The London, Brighton & South Coast Railway* vol 3 *Completion and Maturity* (Batsford, 1979).

Times 15, 17 Feb 1936.

WWW.

Sir William B Forwood, portrait in oil by R E Morrison ca 1919 (courtesy of Merseyside County Art Galleries).

FORWOOD, Sir William Bower

(1840-1928)

Liverpool merchant

William Bower Forwood was born at Edge Hill, Liverpool, on 21 January 1840, the second son of Thomas Brittain Forwood and Charlotte, daughter of William Bower, a well-known cotton broker. The Forwood family were from Kent. William's grandfather George Forwood came to Liverpool where he became a successful produce broker and wrote in favour of the repeal of the Corn Laws. Thomas was a partner in the merchanting and shipping firm of Leech, Harrison & Forwood; cotton was one of their principal commodities. He was the vice-president of the Chamber of Commerce and chairman of the Traffic Committee of the Mersey Docks & Harbour Board. After retiring from his business he worked as a magistrate, and for the restoration of Chester Cathedral.

William attended Liverpool Collegiate School, and then the Pestalozzi School of Dr Heidenmeier, at Worksop, Nottinghamshire, which gave him his broad and advanced outlook. Fresh air, exercise and the study of science and practical subjects were essential parts of the curriculum. Thomas refused to let William read mathematics at Cambridge on the grounds that it would ruin his son's taste for business. William later deplored the cultural narrowness of his home life, describing it as 'quiet and uninteresting, happy because we knew no other'. William described his father as an 'excellent correspondent ... with a love and a capacity for hard work'. To William, hard work was clearly the key to real success. His own early business life he described as 'hard work and late hours' {Forwood (1910) 21}.

Leaving school in 1856 or 1857 William worked for a leading local firm of brokers, Salisbury, Turner & Earle. A cruise round the world undertaken to recuperate from an illness, gave him a variety of adventures, and some experience of seamanship; he taught himself navigation. Returning home in November 1859 he entered the family business, being admitted a partner in 1862. The firm was then playing a key role in the national economy, since his brother Arthur (later Sir Arthur Forwood, Bt, MP and Tory boss of Liverpool City Council) had recently returned from the USA where, sensing the imminence of civil war, he had bought vast quantities of cotton. William had also made a voyage to the USA by steamer; he was suspected of conveying dispatches and money to the Southern States and arrested in New York; he returned home via Canada.

In 1862 Thomas Forwood retired. Arthur, though only twenty-six and William now ran the business in dynamic style. The firm became steamship owners, putting steamers into the West Indian trade in opposition to Alfred Holt (qv) (who later withdrew to concentrate on the Far East), as well as blockade-running to the Confederate States. Defying crushing opposition, they compelled their competitors to join them in the formation of a large company, the West Indian & Pacific Steamship Co, of which Leech, Harrison and Forwood were managers. The capital was fixed at £1 million (afterward increased to £1.25 million). The fleet consisted in 1878 of 14 ships, the largest of which was registered at 1,699 tons. The firm worked with small capital and depended heavily on the confidence of its bankers, Leyland & Bullins.

After nine years, Arthur's growing political aspirations necessitated the sale of the shipping interests, which was not unprofitable. Arthur took charge of a new company, Atlas, which ran steamers between New York and the West Indies. The problem of reclamations in the cotton trade took William to the USA again, where he learned of the practice of cotton banking, that is, holding large stocks against which sales are made for future delivery. The firm introduced this practice to the UK and occupied the field alone for some years, making large profits. Just before 1870 a house was opened in Bombay. In 1871 branches were opened in New York and New Orleans. The firm also found the capital for the banana industry and a railway in Costa Rica.

Despite increasing prosperity, William still described his twenty-five years in business as a time of strenuous hard work. In 1890 he retired from the business to devote his time to public work, much of which was, in fact, largely of a commercial character. Writing in 1910, he regretted this step. But it is doubtful if he could have made so distinctive a contribution to the life of Merseyside had he stayed in the business.

His public life began when he joined the Council of the Chamber of Commerce in 1867. In 1870 he became vice-president and the next year president, the youngest ever. He was also elected a fellow of the Statistical Society in that year. Together with other merchants he helped to shape the Merchant Shipping Bill and the Bankruptcy Bill via the Chamber's Commercial Law Committee. He was president of the American Chamber of Commerce in 1872. When friction occurred between brokers and merchants, he was a leading spirit in the successful endeavour to bring all branches of the trade together in a new association, the United Cotton Association, of which he was first chairman, in 1877. That same year he was also president of the International Cotton Convention held in Liverpool, as a result of which false packing was largely stamped out.

To a merchant, efficient and cheap communications are of prime importance. When in 1872 a merger of the London & North Western Railway with the Lancashire & Yorkshire Railway was mooted, there was widespread fear of increased charges. All the towns in Lancashire and Yorkshire joined with Liverpool in opposing the scheme in parliament and William was elected chairman of the Joint Committee. The bill was thrown out and a Railway Commission to try allegations of unfair charges was formed.

In 1880 at the annual meeting for the election of Dock Board members William Forwood led the great challenge of the Liverpool Chamber of Commerce to the policy of the Port Authority, the Mersey Docks and Harbour Board. He charged the Board, on the Chamber's behalf, with levying exorbitant dock dues and yet failing to provide adequate facilities for shippers, pointed out areas of the Board's administration where economies could be achieved, even profits made and urged the funding of the Board's debt. He was convinced, too, that a paid chairman should be

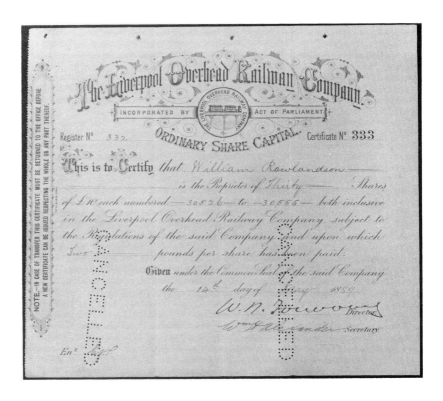

Share certificate of the Liverpool Overhead Railway Company (courtesy of Merseyside County Council).

appointed, 'someone we can get at every day, like the General Manager of a railway'. The trade of Liverpool, he alleged, was fading away, passing to rival ports, 'before our very eyes' {Merseyside County Archives, Mersey Docks & Harbour Board, 4/37, p20}. The success of the port had lead to complacent conservatism which infected every fresh recruit to the board.

His warnings were not heeded. It was not till after the First World War that the office of general manager acquired full executive power, although the secretary bore the title of general manager from 1894. The Manchester Ship Canal scheme rose largely out of protest against the high dues. Forwood was Liverpool's leading spokesman in opposition to the Manchester Ship Canal, amassing the statistics for the commercial case. He endured thirty hours of cross-examination all told. He admitted the gross overcharging of the railway companies, having headed many deputations to the London & North Western Railway about this issue in vain. He suggested to the Dock Board that it should buy the Bridgewater Canal and secure a competitive route.

Forwood's involvement in the overhead railway was part of his concern for better communications. The crowded state of the streets around the docks made movement slow not only for merchants and shipowners but for crews of ships, stevedores and master porters. The Dock Board had obtained parliamentary powers to build a railway along the line of docks, but hesitated to take action. Forwood headed a deputation of those who felt that this dilatory attitude was hampering the port's trade, and offered to find the capital for the Board. It agreed. Parliament approved of the

John, William Herbert and Alfred) joined the firm in 1874. In an agreement dated 1886, there were ten Fosters mentioned as having an active interest in the firm, the four principals besides William all being his sons. In dynastic terms, as well as in terms of earlier financial power, William's role in the firm's history was therefore very dominant, as was frequently reflected in the tone of his letters to his father and brothers. William married first in 1848, Emma Elizabeth, the daughter of Swithin Anderton, a local worsted manufacturer. Emma died in 1865. His second marriage, in 1867, to Mary Ellen Hornby of Flotmanby, near Filey, East Yorkshire, daughter of Thomas Hornby, yielded a further six children to add to the six by his first marriage. As an illustration of nineteenth century vertical social mobility, the marriages of William's children are worth noting. Robert John was married twice, first to the daughter of Lord Bateman and on her death to the daughter of Frederick Fawkes of Farnley Hall near Otley. Herbert married the daughter of Lord Bruce and three of William's daughters married into the landed gentry: the Fletcher-Twemlowe's of Betley Court, Shropshire; the Fentons of Littley Court, Herefordshire and the Bowles-Shakespeares of Langley Priory, Leicestershire.

The ability of William's children to transcend socially their father's humble origins was rooted in the huge wealth generated by the growth of worsted, alpaca and mohair productions at Black Dykes Mill (now known as Black Dyke Mills and famous as the home of the brass band of that name, founded originally by John Foster Sr). The firm was relatively unusual in the worsted industry which was characterised by being horizontally organised into firms specialising in wool combing, or spinning, or weaving. All three processes were vertically integrated at Black Dyke Mills, but in addition, between 1835 when the first mill building was created to spin yarn and the partnership deed of 1891, the firm was described as acting as merchants and bankers, soapmakers, chemical dyestuffs, coke and coaltar manufacturers, dyers and finishers, colliery owners, brick and tile manufacturers, farmers, builders and contractors. These diverse activities had all been added during William's active participation in the firm between 1834 and 1882, when he retired.

The firm's growth as a textile producer, which remained its predominant function throughout, can be traced in various ways. The number of spindles operated grew from 3,036 in 1837-44 to 35,398 in 1862. After a brief period of uncertainty, steady growth was resumed after 1879 to reach a peak of 51,368 spindles in 1889. The number of power looms rose annually from 61 in 1842, shortly after the firm began to turn over from handloom weaving, to 744 in 1855, reducing to 634 in 1860, but then jumping to 892 in 1861. Again, as in weaving, the market disturbances associated with the American Civil War brought a check to growth but by 1870 the pre-war level in the number of looms had been regained and by 1875 this reached 962. The subsequent slow fall in total numbers to 745 in 1890 was more than offset by an increasing proportion which were of greater width. The wool combing section began with 6 combing machines in 1852, rising slowly to a peak of 57 in 1880, thence falling to 42 after 1886. Incomplete evidence only enables one to chart the annual growth of capital employed from the mere £11,185 of 1834 to £1,463,165 in 1867, when the surviving financial records cease. There are no surviving records of the output of tops, yarn or cloth. The firm was principally noted for its speciality production of cloth made from cotton warps clothed with alpaca or mohair wefts (as witness the incorporation of the head of an alpaca into the family crest) and in this line of production it was on a par with the great firm founded by Titus Salt (qv), with whom the Fosters colluded at times in fixing the price of raw material.

William Foster, in addition to his manifold textile and related activities was active in the railway world as a director of the West Riding & Grimsby line, the sale of which, including Wakefield Station, he negotiated with the Great Northern. Failing to get the latter company or the Lancashire & Yorkshire to link Bradford with Halifax via Thornton (as close to Queensbury as topographically possible) he formed and became chairman of the Bradford & Thornton Railway Co (1870) in which the Great Northern held half the shares. In 1872 he became a director of the Lancashire & Yorkshire Railway Co and chairman of a new company to build a line from Bradford via Thornton to Keighley.

From the family seat of Hornby Castle near Lancaster (which his father purchased in 1862 for £205,000 and to which William retired in 1882), William Foster held 10,841 acres in Lancashire and 1,884 more in the West Riding; in 1879 these estates had a gross annual value of £9,098. Foster was a JP for Bradford, the West Riding and Lancashire; vice-president of the Bradford Chamber of Commerce and a founder of the Bective Movement of 1881 to promote the weaving of ladies' clothing made from British wool. He served as High Sheriff of Lancashire in 1881 and as Deputy Lord Lieutenant of Yorkshire. A Liberal in politics he was invited to stand as parliamentary candidate for North West Lancashire in 1880 but declined on the grounds of the ill health that had pursued him throughout the period covered by his diaries (1865-76), for he was frequently ill and in constant pain as a result of a fistula which, treated by the application of nitric acid, necessitated cutting away part of his consequently damaged bowel in 1873. It is important to record that this dominant, and very successful businessman with so many interests was thus chronically ill and, given the evidence of his diaries, inclined to melancholy and pessimism.

He appears not to have been associated with any major technological innovation, but rather to have attained his dominant position in the firm and position of eminence in the local industry by assiduous attention to technological and commercial matters during the massive physical growth of the mills attained wholly within his lifetime.

A prominent freemason, William Foster was also an active member of the Church of England, financing substantially the extensive additions to Holy Trinity Church, Queensbury, which his father had helped to endow in 1843. He was active musically as a member of the committee which organised the Bradford Subscription Concerts and also in the furthering of local education, acting for twenty-five years as trustee and manager of the Queensbury National Schools.

William Foster died, only two years after his retirement, in 1884, leaving £1,280,000.

E M SIGSWORTH

in the *Nineteenth Century* in June 1877. His reputation in financial matters was not good. The discreet Charles Manby glanced at his rapacity in 1863; Edward Watkin (qv) attacked it more openly in 1872. He purchased two estates in Ross-shire, totalling 57,000 acres, in 1865-67 and was a cantankerous director of the Dingwall & Skye Railway, which crossed his land, until he met with humiliation in 1873. His personal estate when he died totalled £179,330, his pictures fetching £66,000 at Christies. He had some admirable qualities. In the 1850s he showed touching and repeated kindness to the fallen George Hudson at Boulogne. He could keep private feelings separate from public controversy; Sir Lintorn Simmons became and remained his friend. His admiration for Brunel (though he never approved of the broad gauge) lasted all his life. When the Maidenhead bridge had to be widened he reconstructed it with great sensibility. His own works were sometimes elegant: the Pimlico bridge almost the only one erected by a railway in London that adorned it; the Albert Edward Bridge at Coalbrookdale (still standing) a most graceful single span; and the masonry approach works to the Forth Bridge are magnificent.

Fowler also undertook much work of other kinds. He was intermittently engaged on Irish railway problems in 1856-72, and he advised the Egyptian Government on engineering matters in 1871-79. He contributed amply to the work of his profession, serving as president of the Institution of Civil Engineers in 1866-67. His presidential address dealt mainly with engineering education. He was made KCMG in 1885 and a baronet in 1890. He married in 1850 Elizabeth, daughter of James Broadbent of Manchester; they had four sons. Sir John Fowler died at Bournemouth on 20 November 1898.

JACK SIMMONS

Writings:

'On the improvements in the River Tees', in Sir William G Armstrong, *The Industrial Resources of the District of ... the Tyne, Wear, and Tees* (Longman & Co, 1864).

Address ... on Election as President of the Institution of Civil Engineers, Session 1865-66 (William Clowes & Sons, 1866).

India. Report on the Best Width for the Proposed Narrow Gauge Railways for India, and Their Applicability to the Indus Valley (Spottiswoode, 1870).

'The Central African Railway', appended to Alvan S Southworth, *Four Thousand Miles of African Travel* (Sampson, Low & Co, 1875).

Egypt and Equatorial Africa (T Kell, 1876).

Nineteenth Century June 1877.

Lecture on Egypt (Spottiswoode, 1880).

Dredgers and Dredging on the Tees (1884).

(with Benjamin Baker) 'Forth Bridge' *Nineteenth Century* 1889.

Sources:

Unpublished

Lincolnshire RO, Stubbs 1/7.

Published

Theodore C Barker and Michael Robbins, *A History of London Transport* (2 vols, George Allen & Unwin 1963–74).

DNB.

George Dow, *Great Central* (3 vols, Locomotive Publishing Co, 1959-65).

G S Emmerson, *John Scott Russell* (1877).

Engineer 86 (1898).

Engineering 66 (1898).

Thomas Mackay, *The Life of Sir John Fowler* (J Murray, 1900).

Proceedings of the Institution of Civil Engineers 135 (1898-99).

John Thomas, *The Skye Railway* (Newton Abbott: David Charles, 1977).

W Westhofen, *The Forth Bridge* (*Engineering* Offices, 1890).

WWW.

FOWLER, Robert Henry

(1851-1919)

Agricultural machinery manufacturer

R H Fowler (courtesy of the Institute of Agricultural History and Museum of English Rural Life, University of Reading).

Robert Henry Fowler was born at Melksham, Wiltshire, on 6 February 1851 of Quaker parents. His father, Henry Fowler, was a prominent London timber merchant trading from St Saviour's Dock at Southwark; his mother was Ann Ford née Barclay (1822-1913), daughter of Robert Barclay, of Leyton, Essex, a banker. His uncle, John Fowler, was embarking in 1850 upon a noteworthy business career that culminated with the opening of the Steam Plough Works at Leeds in 1862. Robert Henry, or Harry as he was known, was apprenticed to a firm of London solicitors and patent agents, Wilson, Bristowe & Carpmael, and duly qualified as a solicitor. However in 1876 he was induced to join the Leeds concern by another uncle, Robert Fowler.

John Fowler had died in 1864, having laid the technical and commercial basis for the firm's future development, and the running of the concern, still styled John Fowler & Co, then passed to Robert Fowler. In the mid-1870s Fowlers were still supreme among UK steam-plough makers, and also made traction engines and railway locomotives. Overseas markets had been developed to complement a still buoyant home trade. Harry rapidly acquired an interest in the firm's products, especially ploughing engines, and displayed skills both in works administration and selling. During 1879-81 he made his first world tour, fostering new markets in the Far East, particularly in Hawaii, where he started a prosperous trade by persuading King Kalakaua to accept a set of Fowler ploughing tackle as settlement of a poker debt. In 1881 Harry Fowler was made general manager at Leeds, which soon led to clashes with other senior staff, caused by his autocratic style of management. However, an ailing Robert Fowler found himself relying more and more on his nephew to run the whole concern. There was certainly little doubt over Harry's commitment to the business, as prior to 1886 he received neither salary or commission, nor had he been admitted to the partnership.

Fowlers' home and export trade, along with that of other agricultural steam engineers, slumped badly in the mid-1880s. Annual sales fell to about £30,000 and only ten sets of ploughing tackle were dispatched in 1885. One immediate reaction was to convert the firm in August 1886 into a private limited company, styled John Fowler & Co (Leeds) Ltd, with a nominal capital of £680,000, a debenture issue of £150,000 and with Robert Fowler as chairman and managing director. The firm's short-term prospects must have looked bleak and there was serious talk of abandoning ploughing engine production altogether. When Harry Fowler became managing director in 1888, following his uncle's death, such ideas were forthrightly dismissed. Harry was convinced that the firm's future continued to lie in ploughing engine production, backed up by traction engines and light railway machinery, and he spent the next thirty years assiduously justifying this belief to such an extent that 'Fowlers' and 'steam ploughing' became virtually synonymous worldwide. In many ways the sheer extent of Harry Fowler's success was ultimately to the firm's detriment. It was committed to worldwide sales of highly sophisticated and expensive pieces of steam engineering with no alternative products in reserve, and with minimal interest in the rising power of the internal combustion engine. However until the bubble burst, the firm's prosperity grew and grew under Fowler's committed leadership.

Another reaction to the slump of the mid-1880s was to extend traction engine production to include road rollers, a product Fowlers had previously agreed to leave to Aveling & Porter, and to expand into electrical engineering, though the latter was abandoned in the 1890s. By 1891 annual sales had recovered to reach £275,000, yielding a net profit of £19,400, and in 1910 they peaked at £485,700 with a profit of £98,600. The major areas of growth were Germany and Austria-Hungary, which, despite the problem of German tariff barriers, took 40 per cent of Fowlers' total output by 1913. Harry Fowler favoured the formation of an overseas branch network rather than relying on agencies alone, and by 1913 Fowlers had branches and agencies covering Germany, Austria-Hungary, France, Italy, Poland, Rumania, Russia, Turkey, China, Australasia, South

Africa, the Philippines, India, Cuba, Hawaii, Peru, the Argentine, Egypt and British East Africa. Only the Canadian and US markets proved impossible to penetrate. A South African farm, started in 1904, and eventually comprising 22,000 acres, proved to be a failure and was closed in 1913.

At Leeds, Fowler was an advocate of the piece-work system, while in 1904 he introduced profit-sharing schemes for selected members of the workforce of about 1,500. He was keenly interested in factory buildings and plant and visited the USA in 1901 to study American designs and methods. In September, 1905, Fowler became chairman of the company; subsequently he pursued a policy of dividend restraint, paying a maximum of only 10 per cent a year, in order to build up substantial reserves.

The bubble burst in 1914. The outbreak of the First World War destroyed most of the firm's European business almost overnight, and greatly hampered other export sales. Fowlers' Magdeburg branch was closed by a decree of the German Government on 3 July 1916 and its assets, valued at £173,401, sold off to a rival firm, R Wolf AG, leaving outstanding debts of £102,314. Government orders and ample reserves kept Fowlers in business. Fowler's appointment as a food consultant to the British Government led to large orders for sets of steam ploughing and agricultural traction engines for the home market. In addition the British and Russian Governments ordered hundreds of military road locomotives and traction wagons, though the Russian orders were never paid for, because of the Revolution. But by the late 1910s Harry Fowler was decidedly pessimistic over the firm's future. He felt that the loss of the European market was probably irretrievable, and he realised that internal combustion was now a strong competitor to agricultural steam power, especially in the products of North American manufacturers. Large sums of capital would be needed to modernise the Leeds works to meet this challenge. Whether Fowler would have succeeded remains uncertain, as he died in 1919. His son and successor, Charles Henry Fowler, certainly failed to meet it.

Harry Fowler was a single-minded autocrat with a strong belief in his firm's products, but like several other business leaders of his generation, such as T L Aveling (qv), he was blinkered by over-reliance on steam power. His style of management brought results, but was not always well-liked as can be seen from references in the anonymous 1880s poem, 'The Wages of Leeds':

> Where the young ploughboy rules alone supreme,
> With arrogance a Sultan might beseem.
> How many workmen at this tyrant's whim have
> In a moment been discharged by him?'

Fowler's excessive devotion to his firm meant that he took little part in political or public life. He was a Conservative and a freemason, as well as a member of the executive committee of the Engineering Employers' Federation.

Fowler married Amy Isabel Eryes, a member of the Church of England; consequently he resigned from the Society of Friends, though he was buried at the Friend's Meeting House at Wanstead. They had one son,

rather than by bureaucracy. All the companies that joined Tillings did so freely; there were no take-overs.

Fraser thought diversification in itself was ineffective without co-ordination, inspiration and a buoyant attitude. He described himself as a 'positive expansionist and natural optimist' {Fraser (1963) 166} and his spirit of optimism and belief in the necessity of motivating all staff, from boardroom to shopfloor, with a sense of personal involvement and commitment, suffused the thinking and organisation of Tillings. As chairman of Tillings he proclaimed on behalf of the company 'We believe that man's capacity, properly encouraged, knows no bounds and finds no barrier insurmountable. I have often repeated the statement that ultimate success depends upon the individual. I stick to it' {*Economist* 18 Apr 1964}. If workers were only interested in getting, rather than earning money, Fraser was inclined to lay the blame at the door of their managers. In the boardroom, Fraser claimed he never had to put any issue to the vote on a board he chaired, but he provided leadership, stating his own position for discussion by his colleagues, rather than simply allowing a consensus to emerge. Geoffrey Eley, who succeeded Fraser as chairman after his death, described him as the main architect of Tillings.

Such a forceful and positive personality inevitably made enemies as well as friends. Energy and the will to win shaded into the desire to dominate. In the City he was a controversial figure; he had great respect for its traditions, which he defended in print, but was something of a natural rebel. However, his personal warmth, gaiety and gift for friendship, his sensitivity to the feelings of others, his genuine gift for leadership and for creating an atmosphere of enthusiasm and success helped to temper the more formidable or overpowering aspects of his character.

Wishing to undertake some public work, but thinking that the duties of an MP would be too demanding, Fraser served as a Conservative member of Chelsea Borough Council, 1945-50, and chaired the Finance and General Purposes committee. He was a liveryman of the Fishmongers' Company, and a member of the committees of several clubs, including the St James' and the Garrick (he liked the companionship, variety and anonymity of club life). In his later years he built up a collection of abstract paintings, and became a trustee of the Tate Gallery.

Fraser's natural optimism (complemented by his ardent faith as a Christian Scientist) was reflected in his attitude to his personal finances. As a young man he spent all his income, thinking that a full social life was as valuable an investment for someone making his way in the City without the benefit of family or public school connections, as any other. After the Second World War, when the City was still disrupted and there was little business to be done, his personal financial position was quite precarious; his remedy was to capitalise his pension contributions, and then surrender his insurance policies to wipe out his overdrafts, feeling he should let the future look after itself; security, he argued, damps initiative. It was only in his later years that he possessed any number of stocks and shares. His estate was proved at £136,983.

In 1931 he married Cynthia Elizabeth, daughter of Francis Walter; their very happy marriage produced one daughter (who was killed just before the date set for her wedding) and two sons. Business provided all the fun, stimulation and interest Fraser wished for, but he never allowed it to encroach on his family life. He died at his London home on 3 January 1965.

CHRISTINE SHAW

Writings:

The Whole World Needs the City (City of London Society, nd).

tribute to Sir Frederick Heaton *Times* 5 May 1949.

'Issuing Houses and the Raising of Long-Term Capital in London' in *The Pattern and Finance of Foreign Trade* (International Banking Summer School, 2nd School 1949) (Europa Publications, 1949).

'The Challenge of Today' *Sunday Times* 22 Oct 1950.

'True Values' *ibid* 11 May 1952.

'A Message from the Chairman' *TT Topics* 1 (1962).

All to the Good (Heinemann, 1963) (autobiography).

obituaries of Graham Thompson and Lord Brabazon of Tara *TT Topics* 7 (1964).

Sources:

Unpublished

BCe.

MCe.

PrC.

Sir Kenneth Hague, 'The Development and Organisation of Babcock & Wilcox Ltd' (Edwards seminar paper 203, 18 Nov 1958).

P H D Ryder, 'The Development and Organisation of Thomas Tilling Limited' (Edwards seminar paper 303, 27 Nov 1962).

Information from R W Clouston of Babcock International Ltd.

Published

J W Beyen, *Money in a Maelstrom* (Macmillan, 1951).

Economist 26 Apr 1952, 25 Apr 1953, 26 Apr 1954, 16 Apr 1955, 21 Apr 1956, 12, 26 Apr 1958, 25 Apr 1959, 23 Apr 1960, 29 Apr 1961, 13 Apr 1963, 18 Apr 1964, 17 Apr 1965.

Statist 11 Mar 1950, 21 Apr, 19 May 1951, 21 Mar 1953, 8 May 1954, 30 Apr, 14 May 1955, 28 Apr, 12 May 1956, 4, 11 May 1957, 4 Jan, 10 May 1958, 9, 16 May 1959.

Times 4, 6 Jan 1965.

Times *Prospectuses* 113 (1953).

TT Topics (Thomas Tilling Ltd house magazine) 1962-65.

WWW.

FRASER, William Milligan

1st Lord Strathalmond of Pumpherston

(1888-1970)

Petroleum entrepreneur

William Fraser, Lord Strathalmond of Pumpherston, CBE, LLD, (courtesy of British Petroleum Company plc).

William Milligan Fraser was born in Glasgow on 3 November 1888, one of the four sons and four daughters of William Milligan Fraser (1852-1915) and Janet née Loch. His father was associated with the Scottish shale oil industry for some thirty-five years as manager of the Uphall Oil Co and later as founder and chairman of the Pumpherston Oil Co, which incorporated other shale oil undertakings. Fraser was educated at the Glasgow Academy and the Royal Technical College, Glasgow.

At the age of twenty-one in 1909 he joined his father's company at 4s a week. He became a director of the Pumpherston Oil Co and its associated concerns in 1913 and on the death of his father in 1915 he succeeded him as managing director. Before the First World War he had already visited the United States to inform himself about mining and oil developments there, and he returned in 1918 as chairman of the Inter-Allied Petroleum Conference Specifications Commission. For his war-time services he was created a CBE. His early experience in the Scottish shale oil industry of which he was such an important member and about which he knew so much, proved to be a practical apprenticeship of the most enduring kind. He was early exposed to a range of managerial problems, technical difficulties, labour relations and financial considerations which, with his remarkable natural talents, provided the experience upon which his later business life depended.

In 1918, with the shale oil industry facing increasing competition from crude oil, Fraser established a joint selling organisation for the various companies comprising the Scottish industry. In 1919 he went further and formed Scottish Oils Ltd, in which all the producing, refining and marketing interests of the Scottish shale oil industries were associated and which was later in the year absorbed by the Anglo-Persian Oil Co. The financial position of the shale oil industry had deteriorated and it was only in combination with an oil company that it had any chance of survival. Even so, severe labour unrest continued to be felt until the industry was reorganised and established on a firmer basis with the construction of a new refinery at Grangemouth in 1924, and the rationalisation of the other older and uneconomical plants. Fraser was to the fore in these activities, defending and encouraging traditional interests but bringing them into line with more recent methods, conditions and practices. Respected for his experience in the shale oil industry, he was able to modernise and reconcile it with the objectives of the Anglo-Persian Oil Co, thus prolonging its existence till the changing of national policy by the elimination of subsidies in 1966 finally made its demise inevitable.

For the Anglo-Persian Oil Co the acquisition of the Scottish shale oil industry was useful, but, more important, it became a base for its commercial operations in Scotland from which it could develop marketing and refining operations. This was Fraser's particular responsibility, and in 1923 he was appointed a managing director of the company, at the same time as Sir John Cadman (qv). They developed and maintained a strong affection and respect for each other's qualities and abilities over a long time. After Cadman became chairman in 1927 he persuaded Fraser, with considerable difficulty, for he was deeply attached to his Scottish environment and connections, to live in London and become his deputy in 1928. It became an admirable complementary partnership. Cadman had diplomatic and administrative gifts no less than his technical understanding; Fraser was an intensely practical manager with an eye for detail and a shrewd commercial sense, who though less recognised internationally than Cadman, was not a stranger to the international oil industry. He had the quiet determination of the Scot, often mistaken for unimaginative dourness, but essentially a methodical matter-of-fact approach to matters, almost mundane, which are essential to the maintenance of an effective business.

Fraser grew in stature, and during the years 1928-34 was involved in the decisive negotiations between the company and Royal Dutch-Shell, which terminated their commercial feuding in the United Kingdom and elsewhere by the formation of the Consolidated Petroleum Co, in which the two groups shared certain Eastern and African marketing interests, and that of Shell-Mex and BP in which their UK interests were associated. He played a leading role in formulating the 'As Is' proposals for a rationalisation of marketing and producing interests, principally of the Anglo-Persian Oil Co, Royal Dutch-Shell and the Standard Oil Co (NJ) in association with some other major oil companies. These proposals helped, to some extent, to stabilise supplies of petroleum products in relation to demand in the 1930s, after over-production and the falling demand occasioned by the Depression in the late 1920s. He was involved as chief negotiator under Cadman in Persia in April 1933 for a new concession after Riza Shah had cancelled the D'Arcy Concession in November 1932. He was a director of the Iraq Petroleum Co, active in the negotiations and preparations which resulted in production commencing in Iraq in 1936, and was also involved in the negotiations by which the company eventually, with Gulf Oil Corporation, acquired a joint concession in Kuwait in 1934. Thus by the mid-1930s, at a time when Cadman was becoming less involved in the day-to-day workings of the company of which he was chairman, Fraser was not only the anchor-man, but exercising greater responsibility and showing more authority.

It was not necessarily accepted that he would follow Cadman as chairman, but in the circumstances of war and the death of Cadman in 1941, Fraser did succeed him, continuing to guide the company through the turmoil of hostilities into the uncertainties of peace. He took part in the talks in Washington for an Anglo-American Oil Treaty in 1944, and was acutely aware of the dangers which his company faced in the post-war commercial competition, with inadequate marketing facilities and marked concessionary pressure for increased production — and revenue — in a world of increasing oil production from new sources. It was presumed at

Mrs Freake was particularly interested in music and the stage and their house in Cromwell Road contained a private theatre, where innumerable musical and theatrical events were performed (usually in aid of charity) before fashionable audiences which frequently included members of the Royal Family.

By the 1860s Freake was withdrawing from the day-to-day conduct of the business (which increasingly devolved on James Waller) in order to devote himself more to public life and good works. However, an attempt to enter Parliament as the Conservative MP for Chelsea in 1868 did not succeed. His good works ranged from the presentation of small cash prizes for architectural drawing, engineering and botany at King's College, London, where from 1869 Freake was a member of the Council, to the building of the Metropolitan Police Orphanage and the erection of a block of model dwellings for 108 families in Chelsea. At Twickenham, where he was an extensive landowner following his purchase of the Copt Hall and Fulwell Park Estates, he presented the local inhabitants with a new town hall (1877) and a free library (1882).

When not living in Cromwell Road, Freake divided his residence between Fulwell Park and his house at Bank Grove, Kingston-upon-Thames. In later life he suffered from gout and often sought relaxation at Brighton or Broadstairs.

His career culminated in a baronetcy given him in 1882, chiefly in recognition of his erection at his own expense of the National Training School for Music in 1874-75. (This building, beside the Albert Hall, is now the Royal College of Organists.) The Prince of Wales was closely interested in the School and in the opinion of Gladstone's political secretary had 'persistently and somewhat questionably (if not 'fishily') pressed Freake's name on the Prime Minister'. {Bahlman (1972) I, 254} (An earlier offer of a mere knighthood from Disraeli had been declined.)

Freake died suddenly at his town house in South Kensington on 6 October 1884 and was buried in Brompton Cemetery. With his death the business virtually came to an end, his oldest surviving son, Tom, who inherited the title, being more interested in yacht racing and the Casino at Monte Carlo. In 1886 Freake's outstanding commitments on the Smith's Charity Estate were taken over by another local building firm, C A Daw & Son, led by William Adams Daw (qv), which also bought Freake's plant and equipment.

J GREENACOMBE

Sources:

Unpublished

Estate records particularly those of the Grosvenor Estate, the Smith's Charity Estate and the Alexander Estate.

Greater London RO, Middlesex Deeds Register.

King's College, London, Archives.

PRO, death duty registers.

University of Manchester, Crawford MSS.

Victoria and Albert Museum Library, diary of Sir Henry Cole.

Diaries and papers in private hands.

Published

Dudley W R Bahlman (ed), *The Diary of Sir Edward Walter Hamilton, 1880-1885* (Oxford: Clarendon Press, 1972).

Builder 18 Apr 1857.

Lady's Pictorial 11 Oct 1884.

Francis H W Sheppard (ed), *Survey of London, Vol 38: The Museums Area of South Kensington and Westminster* (Athlone Press, 1975).

—, *Survey of London, Vol 40: The Grosvenor Estate in Mayfair Part II* (Athlone Press, 1980).

—, *Survey of London, Vol 41: Southern Kensington; Brompton* (Athlone Press, 1983).

Surrey Comet 11 Oct 1884.

Times 9 Apr 1857, 30 Oct, 20 Nov 1868, 9 Oct 1884.

Dr Edwin Freshfield (courtesy of Mrs J Slinn).

FRESHFIELD, Edwin

(1832-1918)

Solicitor to the Bank of England

Edwin Freshfield was born at Bank Buildings, in the City of London on 26 November 1832, the second son of James William Freshfield (1801-57), a partner in the firm of Freshfield & Son, members of which had acted as solicitors to the Bank of England since the early eighteenth century. Edwin's mother, Mary Ann Dawes also came from a legal family — her father was Thomas Dawes, a well-known City solicitor whose clients included the Phoenix Assurance Co and Rothschilds. Unusually for a solicitor at that time, Freshfield was educated at Winchester and Trinity College, Cambridge where he graduated in 1854. At Cambridge he coxed the university boat which was stroked by the young McNaughton, later a distinguished judge. After leaving Cambridge Edwin Freshfield spent some months in 1854 travelling abroad, at first in Europe and then in the Middle East where his return journey was delayed by the outbreak of the Crimean War.

Back in England, he served his articles with the family firm at Bank Buildings then in charge of his uncles, Charles and Henry Freshfield. In 1858 he was admitted to the profession and to the partnership, then known as Freshfields & Newman and comprising five partners. The appointment as solicitor to the Bank of England, which was in those days a personal one, was held by Henry and Charles Freshfield, but when Charles retired, Edwin and his elder brother, William Dawes were made joint holders of the appointment, in 1869. Edwin Freshfield's professional life spanned more than sixty years in the City. Besides the Bank of England, the firm's commercial clients included shipping companies such as the Peninsular & Oriental Steam Navigation Co, mining companies and banks, both at home and overseas, and old colonial companies such as the Hudson's Bay.

Edwin succeeded to the appointment held by his father and grandfather, as solicitor to Lloyd's. In the late 1860s the appointment, which had not previously been unduly onerous, brought Freshfield considerable problems. When the Committee of Lloyds found that it had insufficient powers to penalise members, Freshfield advised a revision of the institution's by-laws. But before any action could be taken a serious dispute developed between Lloyd's and one of its members, a Liverpool underwriter, Forwood, who was also a wealthy ship-owner and managing director of the West Indian & Pacific Steamship Co. The disagreement centred on the question of Forwood's honesty which Lloyd's Committee decided, without seeing the man, was suspect and the Committee proceeded to forbid him entrance. When Freshfield pointed out that the Committee only had powers to forbid entrance to an insolvent member, which Forwood was not, the Committee passed a resolution with retrospective effect enabling it to make the ban. Forwood's successful challenge to the Committee in the Courts made clear the need for reform, which came in the shape of the Lloyd's Act of 1871. The Act incorporated Lloyd's and gave it a proper system of by-laws including the institution of elaborate procedures for the expulsion of members. In June 1871, Edwin Freshfield was appointed an honorary member of Lloyd's although shortly afterwards, for no recorded reason, he ceased to act for the Corporation.

On behalf of the Bank of England Freshfield was involved in extensive litigation between 1887 and 1891 in the leading case of *Vagliano Brothers v The Bank of England*. Similarly for the Bank the firm was concerned with the work following the rescue of Barings in 1890. In the 1890s Freshfields' profits were about £15,000 a year.

Freshfield, through his marriage in 1861 to Zoe Charlotte Hanson, daughter of John F Hanson the Levant Company's representative in Smyrna, acquired property in Smyrna and visited it regularly. Through his connections with the Middle East, City merchants who had originally come from that part of the world, such as members of the influential Ralli family, became clients of the firm. His interest in matters Greek and Eastern also led Freshfield into a correspondence with W E Gladstone (who was coincidentally a client of the firm, although not personally of Edwin).

As well as his professional involvement in the City's business and commercial life, Freshfield took a leading part in the City's civic life as treasurer to the Commission of Lieutenancy for the City and commander of the Honourable Artillery Company with which his family had long been associated. Freshfield was a prominent figure in City institutions being, at various times, Master of the Vintners' Company, of the Clothworkers' Company and of the Needlemaker's Company. For some years he also acted in a professional capacity for a number of the City livery companies in protracted litigation over lands in Ireland. He was active in the City of London Conservative Association and the City Law Club.

Apart from these wide-ranging interests Freshfield was a distinguished scholar and antiquarian. His three-volume treatise on the laws of the later Roman Empire gained an LLD from Cambridge in 1884. He was a collector of books of liturgiology and photographs of Byzantine architecture and lectured authoritatively on both subjects. He helped to revive the Order of St John of Jerusalem in England, becoming one of its Knights of Justice. He was a fellow of Winchester College, 1888-95. For many years his London home was in Russell Square and his country house, The Mint, was in Chipstead in Surrey. In his eighty-sixth year and still an active senior partner of the firm, he died, on 1 September 1918 leaving £24,019 gross. His only son Edwin Hanson Freshfield was, until 1921, a partner in the firm which today as Freshfields continues to be a leading City firm advising, among its many clients, the Bank of England.

JUDY SLINN

Sources:

Published

Judy A Slinn, *A History of Freshfields* (pp, 1984).

Times 2, 4 Sept 1918.

Venn, *Alumni Cantabrigienses*.

Main Fry Factories in the centre of Bristol (courtesy of Cadbury Ltd).

seven more factories were opened in Bristol, erected on the site of slum tenements in the heart of the city.

Although it was not until the death of his uncle Francis Fry in 1886 that actual control of the business passed to Joseph Storrs Fry II and his cousin Francis, Joseph had taken effective control before then. The rapidly growing population, rising living standards, and the decline in the national consumption of alcohol all contributed to expansion in the market for Fry's products. By the time Frys became a private limited company in January 1896, with an authorised capital of £1 million, there were 4,500 employees. The surviving company archives do not provide evidence of Joseph Storrs Fry's contribution to the business, but a comparison with the performance of Frys' main rival, Cadburys, during the years in which he was the leading figure in the firm, suggests a lack of dynamism, a failure to grasp available opportunities. Thus while Frys continued to build new factories (four of them under Joseph Storrs Fry's chairmanship) in the cramped centre of Bristol, Cadburys and Rowntrees moved to fresh sites, where they built large factories which were among the most modern of their day. There is no evidence that Frys tried to meet the marketing opportunity to develop a high-grade British milk chocolate to end the dominance of Swiss imports, as Cadburys did with their Dairy Milk,

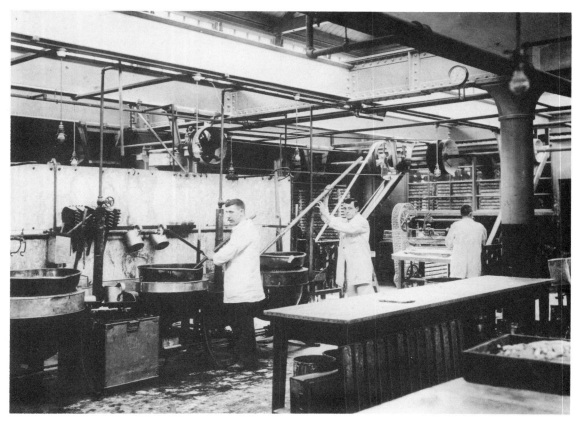

Sugar Boiling, 1908 (courtesy of Cadbury Ltd).

launched in 1905. Frys' sales (including exports) increased from £143,750 in 1870 to £761,969 in 1890, and £1,326,312 in 1900; in that year Cadburys' sales were £1,226,552 (their sales in 1870 had been £54,790, in 1890 £515,371). In 1910 Cadburys' sales exceeded those of Frys — £1,670,221 against £1,642,715 — and in 1913, the year of Joseph Storrs Fry's death, were £2,210,990 against Frys' £1,866,000. Furthermore Frys profitability was declining; their average annual profits for the eight years 1906-13 were £160,000; Cadburys average annual profits for the same period were £320,000. Joseph Storrs Fry must bear a large measure of the responsibility for this loss of impetus; he lacked the foresight and vigour of his competitors George Cadbury and Joseph Rowntree (qqv).

One aspect of the business which did engage his full interest and attention was the welfare and conduct of the workforce. Joseph had introduced a simple daily religious service conducted by himself or his cousin, in 1854. Employees were recommended to involve themselves solely in their work; encouraged to be kind and helpful to others, to be quiet during hours of work, and on no account to wander from department to department. Those found singing, eating the firm's goods, entering beer shops outside working hours, or acting with any impropriety were subject to the firm's and family's strict censure. In a memorandum to employees dated 1872 Joseph Fry wrote: 'As all have to live by the business it is the interest of everyone to try and promote its success. If it does not succeed, employment must fail. Therefore try to be industrious and punctual and not to waste time, or money or goods. Want is the end of waste' {in Fry archives}.

Joseph Fry, a gentle, reflective, kindly man, reserved in manner, had a singularly uneventful private life. He never married, living with his widowed mother until she died when he was sixty, after which he returned to live in the rooms his parents had occupied at the time of his birth. A convinced Quaker, he spoke at meetings and in due course became acknowledged as a minister for the Society of Friends and a leading preacher at the Friars, Bristol. He regularly attended the London Yearly Meeting of the Society of Friends and was for several years clerk to the meeting, the highest office of the Society. He took an active interest in Sunday Schools, played a prominent part in the founding of the Friends First Day Sunday Association in 1847 and was secretary to the Bristol committee for forty years. He became chairman and treasurer of the Bristol hospital in 1892 and was elected president in 1908. He joined the YMCA in 1871 and became president of the Bristol branch in 1877, but became disillusioned with what he came to see as the undue weight given to improving recreational facilities at the expense of the more traditional evangelical Christian activities. Like all Friends Joseph Fry was opposed to war, and was active in the peace movement; he supported total abstinence and social purity movements and worked for the abolition of the opium trade and vivisection by making charitable donations and attending and chairing meetings. In 1909 he became an Honorary Freeman of Bristol, and in 1912 was awarded an honorary LLD by Bristol University.

Joseph Storrs Fry II remained chairman of the business until his death on 7 July 1913, when he was eighty-six years old and had become blind. His estate was proved at £1,332,525. His death, followed by the First World War which brought the whole chocolate industry almost to a standstill, with imports severely restricted and exports impossible, left J S Fry & Sons unable to cope with the competition of Cadburys. After the death in 1919 of Francis Fry, an amalgamation was arranged and the financial interests of J S Fry & Sons were merged with those of Cadbury Bros. The British Cocoa & Chocolate Co was formed to hold the ordinary shares of Cadburys and Frys, although both companies continued to trade under their own names. Soon afterwards, in 1921, the decision was taken to transfer the entire Fry business out of Bristol to Smerdale at Keynsham. Lack of space in which to expand, the difficulty in transporting goods between the eight factories and 16 subsidiary factories in other parts of the congested city led to the decision to move, a decision which, if it had been taken earlier, might have altered the later history of J S Fry & Sons.

GILLIAN WAGNER

FRY Joseph Storrs

Sources:

Unpublished

Cadbury Schweppes PLC, Bournville, archives, 'History of J S Fry and Sons' (typescript).

J S Fry & Sons, Keynsham, nr Bristol, archives.

PrC.

Information supplied by Basil Murray.

Published

The Annual Monitor 1914.

DNB.

The Friend 1860.

Joseph Fry, *History of the Fry Family* (pp, 1926).

Times 8 July 1913.

'To work for Frys a hundred years ago' *Somerdale Magazine* 1969.

'Two hundred years of Advertising' *The Quiver* 1926.

FULLER, George Pargiter

(1833-1927)

Rubber manufacturer

George Pargiter Fuller was born in Baynton, near Edington, Wiltshire, on 8 January 1833, the scion of a leading county family in Wiltshire and second son of John Bird Fuller (1801-1872), of Neston Park, Wiltshire, a DL and JP who could trace his family back to one of Cromwell's generals. His mother was Sophia Harriet, daughter of John Hanning, of Dillington Park, Ilminster, Somerset.

George was educated at Ilminster Grammar School, Winchester and then Christ Church, Oxford, where he graduated in 1855 and gained a cricket blue in 1854-55. After Oxford he read for the Bar at the Inner Temple.

From 1862 he was a captain in the Royal Wiltshire Yeomanry, retiring as a major in 1888. He married in January 1864 Emily Georgina Jane, second daughter of Sir Michael Hicks-Beach, Eighth Baronet. They had five sons, John (b 1864), William (b 1865), Henry (b 1870), Robert and Edward (b 1878), as well as one daughter, Georgina (b 1863), later Lady Hobhouse.

On his father's death in 1872 George Fuller inherited Neston Park, the country home built shortly after 1790 and enlarged in 1840. He augmented his landowning in the country by purchasing Great Chalfield, a noted mediaeval manor a few miles to the south of Neston Park, from Sir George Burrard's widow. G P Fuller was a progressive agriculturalist. He owned one of the first steam-powered hay-drying machines, had cart horse feeders automated from a grandfather clock and owned a horse-drawn flail hedge cutter. His agricultural interests extended overseas and he bought a tea plantation in Ceylon called Abbotsleigh.

In 1872 George had become a partner in a brewery in Chiswick which his grandfather had rescued and although he was never actively involved, his third son, Henry, became the first chairman of the company, now known as Fuller, Smith & Turner. It was therefore with little knowledge of manufacturing but with considerable experience of estate management and strong connections, locally and nationally, that George Fuller entered the industrial business world in the 1890s.

In response from urgent appeals from the managing director of Avon India Rubber Co of Melksham, a public company incorporated in 1894, George Fuller, concerned at the serious unemployment in Melksham, rescued the company from financial disaster by introducing fresh capital. In 1895 he joined the board, becoming chairman in 1898. His fourth son, Robert Fleetwood Fuller a trained electrical engineer, and gold medallist from Faraday House, in 1896 joined the company as assistant to the managing director at a salary of £100 a year. This began a lifetime of service to the company by Robert and an ever increasing interest by the family. With fresh capital, they turned to the production of car tyres and in the ten years 1900-10 sales increased fourfold. In 1901 a new pneumatic tyre shop was erected and in 1903, 29 beaded-edge motor-tyre moulds were installed. In 1906 the first advertisement for Avon motor tyres appeared in *Autocar*. The directors, with some courage and vision, regularly reinvested most of the profits in the business. In 1908, taking advantage of the Companies Act of that year, Avon again became a private limited company, which brought its control more closely into the hands of the Fuller family. Houses for the workpeople were built as well as new shops, and the big chimney which became a local landmark. By this time Avon had become a going concern able to provide regular and increasing employment and pay five times as much in wages as in its first year. At that time Robert Fuller (then Major Fuller) was joint managing director, a post he held until 1931, with F T Swanborough (who died in 1915). In 1908 the first depot was opened in London. By 1914 the Melksham factory had attracted the attention of the *Times* which devoted a full-page article to the works. By this date the company specialised in the production of motor cycle tyres, and manufactured golf balls, and had opened an office in Paris.

In 1915 the Sirdar Rubber Works at Bradford-on-Avon was taken over, adding some 300 more workers and a most useful plant to the company's growing resources. New solid tyre shops and stores were finished at Melksham at about the same time. In November 1917 the capital of the company was increased from £50,000 to £275,000 by the creation of

45,000 £5 ordinary shares. In that month the Avon works were visited by King George V, accompanied by Queen Mary. At the end of 1919, with men returning from war service, the number employed at Melksham doubled to 1,300 and output increased rapidly with demand always ahead of supply. In 1920 magnificent ferro-concrete shops came into use at Melksham. The post-war depression was weathered with unimpaired vitality. In 1922 the number of depots increased to twelve by the opening of a new depot at Cardiff. By 1929, after G P Fuller's death, the number of employees had increased from the original 24 in 1890 to 1,500, some evidence of the driving force given to the company by father and son.

George Fuller took a prominent part in local government and from 1870 until 1878 was chairman of the Board of County Affairs. He was appointed High Sheriff for Wiltshire in 1878 and was also a JP. By this time, Fuller was a leading Liberal in Wiltshire and in 1876 he joined with other Liberals in founding the *Wiltshire Times* to co-ordinate Liberal opinions in the county. In 1880 he unsuccessfully contested the parliamentary seat for Wiltshire North but was elected MP (Liberal and Home Rule) for West Wiltshire in 1885. He held the seat until defeated in 1895 by Colonel Chaloner, later Lord Gisborough.

George P Fuller died on 2 April 1927, leaving £431,011 gross.

Major Robert Fuller, who had been deputy chairman since 1926, took over as chairman on his father's death and held this office until appointed president, in recognition of his long and valuable service with the company, shortly before his death on 9 September 1955. By this time the workforce numbered 3,500. The chairmanship of the company passed to his son-in-law, C M Floyd, three generations of the family thus contributing to the growth and success of Avon.

SIDNEY FLAVEL

Sources:

Unpublished

MCe.

PrC.

Published

Foster, *Alumni Oxonienses*.

Robert P Fuller, *The Chairman's Memories* (Avon Rubber Co, 1947).

A Romance of Rubber: The Avon Tyre and Rubber Works 1886-1927 (Avon Rubber Co, 1927).

Times 22 June 1914, 10 Nov 1917, 4 Apr 1927, 12 Sept 1955.

VCH Wiltshire 4.

Wiltshire Gazette 7 Apr 1927, 15 Sept 1955.

Wiltshire Times 17 Sept 1955.

WWMP.

WWW.

Christopher Furness (taken from C Jones, Pioneer Shipowners, Liverpool: 'The Journal of Commerce and Shipping Telegraph', Charles Birchall & Sons Ltd, 1934).

FURNESS, Christopher

1st Lord Furness of Grantley

(1852-1912)

Entrepreneur in shipping, coal, iron and steel

Christopher Furness was born at West Hartlepool on 23 April 1852, the seventh son of John Furness and Averill, daughter of John Wilson of Naisbet Hall, County Durham. For a time John Furness worked as a coal trimmer on the developing railway line of the town, but in 1850 he established a grocery and provisioning business in Lynn Street. Under the direction of his sons, principally the eldest, Thomas (b 1836), the firm developed into one of the largest of its kind in the North East. Thomas Furness & Co, as it came to be known, carried on the business of import and export wholesale merchants, ships chandlers and coal factors. John Furness died in 1885 leaving an estate sworn at £460.

After being educated at Anderson's School, Christopher joined the family firm and in 1870 was sent to Sweden as a buyer. During the blockade of the Elbe by the French fleet, Furness gained a corner on the grain market and secured an estimated profit of between £50,000 and £60,000 for the firm. He became a partner in the company two years later.

In the mid-1870s, T Furness & Co acquired several large provisioning contracts, the fulfillment of which required the importation of foodstuffs from the USA and the Continent. Initially, the firm chartered ships for this purpose, but in 1877 it purchased several sailing brigs from William Gray (qv). Christopher's interest gravitated toward these shipping operations, which the other partners viewed as too risky, so that in 1882 he bought the ships and with a capital of £100,000 established the Furness Line as a private concern.

The following year Furness acquired an interest in the shipbuilding yard of Edward Withy & Co of West Hartlepool. He later became the largest shareholder of the firm, and having made a considerable fortune in speculative shipbuilding during the boom of the late 1880s, amalgamated the two companies under the style of Furness, Withy & Co Ltd in 1891. At this time, Furness owned 18 steamers outright and held interests in 21 other ships and seven regular lines.

During this early stage of his career, Furness's vessels traded chiefly on the North Sea and the Atlantic. In the 1890s, the latter route expanded considerably and Furness formed several new lines. In conjunction with J P Morgan, Furness, Withy established the Chesapeake & Ohio Steamship Co Ltd to trade between Liverpool, London and Virginia. Five years later, Furness, Walter Glynn and J R Ellerman (qv) formed the Wilson & Furness-Leyland Line to operate combined passenger and cargo services between Boston, New York and London. In 1898, Furness entered the Canadian trade by purchasing a bankrupt Canadian company and by promoting the Manchester Liners to trade to Halifax, Nova Scotia. To support this growth on the Atlantic routes, Furness, Withy acquired the British Maritime Trust Ltd, which specialised in chartering tonnage to regular lines.

After 1895, Furness became interested in the coal, engineering and steel industries of the North East, while enlarging his shipbuilding holdings. In so doing, he took advantage of the favourable financial conditions of the last few years of the nineteenth century to amalgamate and promote a number of firms over which he presided as chairman, while holding less than a controlling interest. Operationally, a sustained programme of shipbuilding precipitated this development. In some cases, shortages of shipbuilding components and the desire to recover suppliers' profits created his interest in acquiring control of his sources of supply.

In 1896, Furness gained control of the marine engineering firm of English, Westgarth & Co, of Middlesbrough. To reduce competition, he amalgamated the company with two others in 1900 and became chairman of the combination. Richardsons, Westgarth, as it was named, supplied engines for most of the ships built at Furness's yards and expanded its product range to include hot-blast engines, electrical machinery, turbines and diesel engines.

Furness entered the steel trade in 1898 by purchasing an interest in the South Durham Steel & Iron Co Ltd, whose output consisted largely of ship plates. In association with William (later Sir William) Cresswell Gray, he converted the firm into a public company two years later. In 1899, Furness promoted the Weardale Steel, Coal & Coke Co Ltd which had extensive coal-mining operations and small plate-making capacity. The firm abandoned plate manufacture in the face of severe competition from imports and in 1900 purchased the capital of the Cargo Fleet Iron Co. The directors intended to transform the obsolete works into the first integrated iron and steel plant on Teesside to manufacture plates. Since this policy threatened the interests of the South Durham, a share exchange was concluded whereby Cargo Fleet acquired the capital of that firm and agreed to produce angles, joists and rails. As their individual manufacturing policies ceased to conflict, the ownership and control of the three companies became dispersed after 1905.

After acquiring the Middleton Yard of E Withy & Co, Furness, Withy purchased Irvine's Shipbuilding & Dry Dock Co Ltd in 1896. Both shipyards constructed mainly tramp vessels. In association with J S Barwick, in 1901 Furness acquired the Northumberland Shipbuilding Co Ltd, which built the same class of tonnage to a standard 7,000 ton design.

Furness, Withy became interested in R Stephenson & Co Ltd, but this firm encountered difficulties modernising its facilities and failed in 1908. Palmer's Shipbuilding & Iron purchased the yard in 1912, Furness having acquired a substantial interest in this latter company in 1898.

After the turn of the century Furness did not significantly expand further in the heavy industries, but concentrated instead upon shipping. Following the creation of the International Merchantile Marine by J P Morgan in 1902, Furness and Alfred Jones (qv) attempted to organise a British counter combination to contest the North Atlantic passenger trade. The £20 million combine was to acquire Cunard, Elder Dempster, the Royal Mail Steam Packet and some of Furness's lines. Lacking the support of the Canadian Government and being unable to secure the confidence of the parties involved, the scheme collapsed and Cunard won assistance from the British Government to build the *Mauretania* and the *Lusitania*. The frustration of these plans produced a marked alteration in the policies of Furness, Withy & Co. The firm abandoned the passenger trade and concentrated upon cargo carrying, while taking steps to diversify its interests away from the Atlantic.

Between 1903 and 1910, Furness expanded his coal, clay and ore carrying operations and developed a network of coastal lines. During a period of depressed freight rates between 1907 and 1910, this growth assumed a concentrated form. In 1907, Furness, Withy purchased the fleets of the British Maritime Trust and the Chesapeake company in order to reduce running costs and to rationalise operations. The firm also took advantage of low ship values to buy four smaller fleets and transferred the vessels to its ore and clay trades. In 1909, Furness entered the Argentinian frozen meat trade by acquiring an established company that possessed contracts with shippers and expanded its activities. The following year Furness, Withy consolidated its position in the trade by purchasing a controlling interest in Houlder Brothers Ltd.

With the improvement in freight rates during 1910, Furness gradually regained his former position on the Atlantic by acquiring four established lines trading to America, while increasing antitrust agitation prevented the rival IMM from pursuing a policy of buying out competitors. Furness also began arranging a combination of firms operating on the Great Lakes which was completed by the formation of the Canada Steamships Line in 1914. With these developments Furness, Withy abandoned its policy of concentration and increasingly assumed the form of a holding company. By 1912, the firm held interests in 307 ships of 1.4 million tons deadweight, or about 10 per cent of the British merchant marine. At the outbreak of war in 1914, Furness, Withy was interested in close to 450 vessels.

In promoting the growth of his interests, Furness pursued a number of distinct policies. During slumps he purchased companies with ageing works at reduced prices, injected the capital necessary for the modernisation of their facilities and restored them to a competitive state. Similarly, he acquired ailing shipping lines that possessed established trading rights, and financed the construction of new tonnage. In other instances, Furness promoted entirely new industrial undertakings based on newly-invented productive processes and developed new shipping routes with the assistance of subsidies or by securing exclusive carrying contracts with shippers. The success of these ventures depended on careful timing and access to capital.

Furness raised the funds necessary for expansion in a variety of ways, depending on the cost of money, the state of the stock market and the availability of retained earnings. He increased the capital of Furness, Withy from time to time in order to finance acquisitions and often personally underwrote these issues. Between 1891 and 1912, the capital of the firm rose from £700,000 to £3.5 million. An interesting feature of the changes in the capital structure of the company was the increases in gearing prior to booms. This policy augmented the profits available for ordinary dividends and for retention in the business. Up to 1914, retained earnings amounted to 58 per cent of the reported profits, but this source of funds was not sufficient to support all available opportunities for expansion. Consequently, Furness arranged share exchanges, deferred payment schemes and pledged the assets of recently-acquired firms as security for loans which were repaid out of the earnings of the new subsidiary. Because of the reluctance of banks to provide loans to the firm without his personal guarantee, Furness committed his own funds and assets to specific projects. After 1910, banks became more ready to support and Furness, Withy was able to negiotate medium-term loans independently of its founder and to act as a guarantor for loans arranged on behalf of its subsidiaries.

Although operational considerations determined the direction of the growth of Furness's enterprises, financial conditions exerted a direct influence upon the structural forms that developed. Expansion that took place during slumps caused ownership and control to become concentrated, while booms precipitated structural dispersal through stock market flotations and schemes involving joint financing. Despite these oscillations, where the pattern of ownership permitted, the head office of Furness, Withy gradually assumed responsibility for directing shipping operations in order to reduce running costs and to co-ordinate the activities of its subsidiaries. The head office did not, however, establish staff departments, but instead allocated service functions to specially-qualified branch offices and subsidiaries. With the exception of some of the shipbuilding firms, the interests in the heavy industrial sector were not subject to the direct control of Furness, Withy. Throughout the lifetime of its founder, the Furness group remained a collection of single- and multi-function units and concurrently exhibited the characteristics of both centralised and decentralised structures. Apart from the partial development of a head office, the structural changes that the group underwent do not reveal a comprehensive design intended to accommodate and integrate further growth, but rather resembled organisational adjustments made in response to short-term trends.

The degree of the operational integration of Furness's diverse interests varied condiderably. The shipping, shipbuilding and engineering companies were closely associated, while the steel firms supplied the shipyards with material, but because of the large output of their mills outside markets remained very important. The coal firms controlled by Furness were also integrally related to his other interests and export orders for fuel helped to provide employment for the growing number of collieries owned by Furness, Withy. In making purchases Furness's companies gave each other preference at market prices. Nevertheless, smooth operational co-operation depended upon the temperaments of the managers involved, the mutual interests of the firms and the strength of Furness's personal and financial influence.

Furness held a majority of the capital of Furness, Withy until 1907, and thereafter remained the largest shareholder. At all times he was intimately involved in the affairs of the company. He conducted most important negotiations personally and was closely consulted when appointments were made throughout the group. Furness made all major decisions on matters of policy while being closely advised by his nephew, S W Furness, who succeeded him as chairman of Furness, Withy in 1912, and F W Lewis (later Lord Essendon (qv)). In the later years, Furness delegated more responsibility to others in order to preserve the managerial stability of the firm at the senior level after his death.

The principal officials of the Furness Group received their training in Furness, Withy and rose through the ranks. Members of the family followed the same course. Because Furness's son, Marmaduke (qv), showed no interest in the business during his father's lifetime, the sons of his brother Stephen became the managerial cadre that succeeded the original management of the firm. Technical experts with established reputations, such as Benjamin Talbot (qv) of Cargo Fleet, were recruited from outside, while others in the shipbuilding and engineering trades stayed with the firms that Furness acquired.

One of Furness's most noteworthy interests was the commercialisation of new technical inventions. He ordered the *Eavestone*, the first motorship built in Britain and his yacht, the *Emerald*, the first turbine vessel to cross the Atlantic. The reconstruction of the works of Cargo Fleet was the most technically complex project associated with Furness, incorporating as it did the most modern equipment available and employing Talbot's new continuous steelmaking process. Even the construction of Furness's hunting lodge, Cundall Manor, became an experiment in the use of steel and stressed metal.

Despite the number of his business commitments, Furness pursued an active political career. After holding a variety of local offices, he defeated William Gray to become the Liberal MP for Hartlepool in 1891. He was defeated on the Home Rule issue by the Unionist candidate, Thomas Richardson, in 1896. In the election of 1900, Furness was re-elected for Hartlepool and returned in 1906 unopposed. Furness won the seat again in 1910, but was unseated on petition because of the irregular practices of one of his agents. One month later he was raised to the peerage, having been knighted in 1895. A radical Liberal, Furness favoured registration reform, 'one man one vote', the abolition of the hereditary principle of the House of Lords and supported Lloyd George's budget of 1909.

Furness's written works include *The American Invasion*, which describes his visit to the United States in 1901 and discusses the reasons for the competitive superiority of that country. *Co-partnership in Coalmining* and *Industrial Peace and Efficiency* explore the facets of co-partnership and provide details of the profit-sharing plans introduced at the Wingate Collieries and Irvine's shipyards in 1908. The latter agreement was terminated after only one year because of union opposition, and was denounced by Keir Hardie. In his maiden speech in the Lords, Furness called for a parliamentary commission to investigate the wider application of co-partnership.

Although Furness allowed trusted subordinates to exert their own authority and was responsive to the suggestions of his advisors, he exhibited many of the attributes of an authoritarian personality, especially when he was doubtful of the capacity of individual managers. Projects such as the reconstruction of Cargo Fleet and the Atlantic Combine, reflect the scope of his commercial vision and his willingness to take great risks, while his concern for the relation of capital and labour is indicative of the breadth with which he viewed commercial activity. At the same time, Furness devoted great attention to detail and showed impatience with those not of his turn of mind. The diversions he permitted himself included yachting and hunting.

Furness died at Grantley Hall on 11 November 1912, after a lengthy illness during which he was attended by a United Methodist minister, leaving an estate of £1,844,305. His landed property, which amounted to over 30,000 acres, and the greater part of his estate Furness left to his son Marmaduke (b 1883 and later 1st Viscount Furness), the only child from his marriage in 1876 to Jane, daughter of Henry Suggitt, a builder. He left his shares in Furness, Withy & Co in trust to guarantee their retention by the family.

GORDON BOYCE

Writings:

The American Invasion (West Hartlepool: A Slaton, 1902).

Industrial Peace and Efficiency (West Hartlepool: A Slaton, 1908).

Co-operation in Coalmining (West Hartlepool: A Slaton, 1909).

Sources:

Unpublished

British Steel Corporation, Northern Regional Records Centre, Middlesbrough, Cargo Fleet Iron Co, South Durham Steel & Iron Co archives.

Furness, Withy & Co Ltd, Fenchurch Street, London, archives of Furness, Withy & Co, British Maritime Trust, Houlder Bros.

Manchester Liners Ltd, Manchester Liners House, Manchester, archives.

National Maritime Museum, Greenwich, archives.

C Reg: Furness, Withy & Co (34,810).

BCe.

MCe.

PrC.

Interview with Miss E Mary Furness and Frank Furness.

Published

DNB.

Dod's Parliamentary Companion 1895.

Fairplay 1892-1912.

A J Henderson, *Under the Furness Flag* (C Birchall & Son, 1951).

Syren and Shipping 1899-1912.

Times 24 Oct, 16 Nov 1908, 7, 12 Jan, 15 Dec 1909, 23, 29, 30 Apr, 2, 3, 4, May 1910, 11 Nov 1912.

W C Willis, *The South Durham Steel and Iron Co Ltd* (Portsmouth: Eyre & Spottiswoode, 1969).

WWMP.

WWW.

FURNESS, Marmaduke

1st Viscount Furness of Grantley

(1883-1940)

Shipbuilder and steel manufacturer

Marmaduke Furness was born at Hartlepool on 29 October 1883, the only son of Christopher Furness, First Baron Furness (qv), and Jane née Suggitt. Details of his education and early life are scarce, but it is clear that although Marmaduke was elected to the boards of a number of the shipping firms established by his father, including Furness, Withy & Co Ltd (1907) and Manchester Liners Ltd (1906), he played no active role in their affairs before 1914. Personal differences between father and son are thought to account for the latter's lack of interest in business.

When the First Lord Furness died in 1912, he was succeeded as chairman of Furness, Withy & Co by Stephen Wilson Furness (knighted 1914), a nephew who for many years had acted as the chief executive of the Furness Group and one of two close advisors to its founder. Shortly after Sir Stephen was killed accidentally in 1914, Marmaduke approached Frederick W Lewis, later Lord Essendon (qv), who was the other senior advisor to the First Lord Furness, and expressed a desire to participate actively in the business. Thus, with no executive experience to qualify him for the position, Marmaduke became chairman of Furness, Withy & Co in 1914, with Lewis acting as deputy chairman.

Despite his lack of training and his inexperience, Marmaduke quickly became conversant with the affairs of the Group; he 'developed a remarkable shrewdness and ability, and displayed great energy in the conduct of the business', according to Lewis {Memorandum 11 Aug 1919}. During the war, Marmaduke exhibited particular interest in the operations of Furness, Withy's coal, steel and shipbuilding subsidiaries. Having disposed of the greater part of its shipbuilding interests in 1916 and 1917, Furness, Withy formed a new subsidiary in 1917, the Furness Shipbuilding Co Ltd, to construct a new shipyard at Haverton Hill on the River Tees. In response to the national emergency created by the U-boat successes in the spring of 1917, Marmaduke became the driving force behind the new company's development. He secured government assistance in recruiting the labour and requisitioning the equipment for the new facility, which was fitted out to build ships of standard design. The keel of the yard's first vessel was laid only five months after the ground had been broken on the new site. However, Marmaduke was created First Viscount Furness in 1918, not for his work at Haverton Hill, but as a reward for acting as an advisor to the American shipbuilding industry at the request of the British Government.

Soon after the conclusion of the war, the heavy cost of the Haverton Hill yard caused differences concerning the future policy of the Furness Group and the general conduct of the business to arise between Marmaduke and Lewis, who had been largely absent from Furness, Withy on account of his duties at the Board of Shipping during the hostilities. Consequently, in 1919 Lewis arranged for the shipping subsidiaries to purchase the Furness family's 30 per cent interest in the ordinary capital of Furness, Withy & Co. Lewis met part of the £10 million price by transferring the shipyard and the Group's other industrial investments to Marmaduke.

Furness Shipbuilding Co Ltd had an authorised capital of £650,000, increased in 1919 to £3 million, although only £650,000 was ever issued during Furness's lifetime. It was a private company and no financial details, other than those concerning the company's share capital, were made public.

Under the direction of Furness and Benjamin Talbot (qv), managing director of Cargo Fleet Iron Co Ltd, Furness, Withy's former steel interests expanded rapidly immediately after the war. In order to secure supplies of iron ore and pig iron for Cargo Fleet and South Durham Steel & Iron, the East Coast Steel Corporation, a private company which had been formed in 1917, acquired Cochrane & Co in 1918 and the following year purchased the Seaton Carew Iron Co Ltd. As was the case with Furness Shipbuilding, no financial information concerning East Coast Steel was released to the public, except for details of the capital. In 1922, issued capital stood at £1.8 million (the authorised capital was £5 million). By 1924 the authorised capital was reduced to £4,322,814 and the issued capital to £1,122,479, and remained at these levels until the company was wound up voluntarily in November 1930.

This followed the merger in 1928 of Cargo Fleet and South Durham. They had also acquired extensive ore properties in Northamptonshire during and immediately after the war. The merger finally realised one of the ambitions that had eluded the First Lord Furness. In an exchange of shares, South Durham Steel & Iron acquired about 92 per cent of the £1 million shares of Cargo Fleet, acquiring most of the remaining shares in the next few years. South Durham's own share capital increased from £650,000 to £1.25 million. At a time when proposals were being made to rationalise the steel industry by creating regional combinations, a plan to amalgamate the South Durham group with Dorman Long & Co Ltd was put forward in 1933, but ultimately the scheme came to nothing. One major obstacle was the attitude of Furness to the proposed merger; he wanted special treatment and a high price for his large shareholding.

Apart from Furness Shipbuilding, Cargo Fleet and South Durham, after 1919 Furness also held seats on the boards of Broomhill Collieries Ltd, Richardsons, Westgarth & Co Ltd, the Easington Coal Co Ltd, Weardale Steel, Coal & Coke Co Ltd, and the North East Banking Co Ltd.

Marmaduke Furness married firstly, in 1904, Ada (d 1921), daughter of George Hogg, a marine underwriter of Seaton Carew, County Durham; they had a son, Christopher, who was killed in action in France in 1940 and received a posthumous VC, and a daughter, Averill (d 1936). His second marriage was in 1926, to Thelma Converse, daughter of Harry Hays Morgan, the American Consul-General at Buenos Aires; their son, William Anthony, succeeded Furness as Second Viscount. Following a divorce from Thelma in 1933, Furness married Enid Cavendish, daughter of Charles Lindeman, an Australian winegrower, and widow of Brigadier-General Frederick Cavendish. Furness died on 6 October 1940 leaving an estate valued at £3,653,930.

GORDON BOYCE

Sources:

Unpublished

British Steel Corporation, Northern Regional Records Centre, Middlesbrough, Cargo Fleet Iron Co, South Durham Steel & Iron Co, archives.

Furness, Withy & Co Ltd, Fenchurch Street, London, archives.

Manchester Liners Ltd, Manchester Liners House, Manchester, directors' minutes.

Memorandum of 11 Aug 1919 photocopy, in possession of author.

BCe.

MCe.

PrC.

Information from Grant Miln, director of Smith's Dock Co Ltd, and Dr Jonathan Boswell.

Interviews with the Second Viscount Furness, Miss E Mary Furness and Frank Furness.

Published

Burke's Peerage and Baronetage.

DD.

Lady Thelma Furness and Gloria Vanderbilt, *Double Exposure. A Twin Autobiography* (Frederick Muller Ltd, 1959).

The Shipbuilder June 1920.

Stock Exchange Official Information 1919, 1920, 1928.

Stock Exchange Official Year-Book 1939.

Stock Exchange Year-Book 1918-30.

WWW.

FYFFE, Edward Wathen

(1853-1935)

Importer of bananas

Edward Wathen Fyffe taken at Box, near Stroud ca 1911 (courtesy of Dr P N Davies).

Edward Wathen Fyffe was born in Woodchester, Gloucestershire, on 31 December 1853, the younger son of Ebenezer Wathen Fyffe and Martha Wathen née Dunn. Sometime in the early 1850s Ebenezer acquired control of the family tea businesses established in the eighteenth century, and in due course the firm took the title of E W Fyffe, Son & Co. About 1865 Ebenezer bought a house at Box, near Minchinhampton, where Edward spent much of his teens. Edward first tried his hand at farming, but two unsuccessful attempts convinced him that he should join his father in the tea trade. As a first step he undertook a trip to Ceylon. This provided useful experience as well as personal contacts with the growers, and on his return he appears to have been well content to join the family firm as a wholesale tea dealer.

Ebenezer died in 1882 and, thereafter, Edward was in sole charge of the company (his elder brother was ordained). His activities were profitable enough to enable him to marry, and in 1884 he married Ida Stanton Brown, the daughter of Samuel Burton Brown, a Baptist minister from West Hackney. Their two children, both girls, were born in September 1885 and October 1886. The nearness of the two births led to a weakening of the mother's health and she developed a form of tuberculosis. This was regarded as being so serious that her husband was advised to take her to the Canary Islands.

making precision grinding machines), whose British agency was retained by the parent company.

F P Burnage, son-in-law of Charles Churchill, became the new chairman and Gabriel the new managing director of Charles Churchill & Co. In December 1934 Gabriel restored the firm's manufacturing base by purchasing complete control of the Redman firm which he had been nursing since he became its chairman in 1927. The Churchill-Redman Co's production line at Halifax, under A K McCall, a Gabriel appointee, had been modernised in the late 1920s and its turnover climbed from £21,000 in 1927 to £42,000 in 1935 and then to £141,773 in 1939, with profits before tax rising from £2,367 in 1935 to £23,415 in 1939. Employment grew from 30 in 1927 to 300 in 1939. The basic technology still originated in the USA. In September 1937 Gabriel despatched McCall on a tour of major machine tool manufacturers in America, including Cone Automatic Co and Cleveland Hobbing Co. At Springfield, Vermont, McCall negotiated a manufacturing licence for Jones & Lamson's Fay automatic lathe and nine months later the first Fay lathe left the Churchill-Redman works in Parkinson Lane, Halifax.

Still, neither Churchill-Redman, nor the British machine tool industry as a whole, met effective demand. This grew with the expansion of the motor industry in the early 1930s — the Ford Motor Co placed the first of its many orders with Churchill-Redman in 1931 and Gabriel set up a new machine tool headquarters at South Yardley in the Midlands' motor manufacturing region in 1938. Demand for machine tools was augmented by rearmament after 1936 and then by the outbreak of war in 1939.

For much of the Second World War Gabriel served as Controller of Machine Tools, in charge of the Ministry of Supply's programme for mobilising the industry which had to meet 83 per cent of home demand, the rest coming from the USA under 'cash and carry' and Lend-Lease arrangements. The Machine Tool Control imposed specialisation of production on the industry's firms, laid down standardised specifications, fixed prices and ensured that every machine tool firm ran day and night until military and civilian needs were met. Targets were reached in November 1943 and machine tools then came off the Lend-Lease list. A year later Gabriel was released from the Ministry of Supply, partly because of severe back trouble, and returned to Churchills to plan postwar reconstruction. His own manufacturing firm, Churchill-Redman, turned out 2,000 machine tools during the war and at its height had a workforce of 412, over half of whom were women.

Peacetime released the pent-up civilian demand for machine tools while currency controls restricted American imports. In mid-1945 Churchill-Redman had a backlog of orders worth well over £250,000, representing 433 machine tools of which over 80 per cent were for export. Gabriel expected the British motor car industry, and to a lesser extent the agricultural machinery industry, to generate the bulk of fresh demand and he set about expanding Churchill's total machine tool capacity in well-tried ways.

Firstly in February 1945 he visited the USA to negotiate arrangements under which Churchills would manufacture hobbing and gear shaving machines, required by the motor industry particularly. Capacity was then increased by purchasing the Longfield Foundry in Halifax, for high-

Churchill Blaydon works (courtesy of Mr Ralph Gabriel).

quality castings, and by leasing from Vickers, Armstrong part of the extensive Admiralty Works in Scotswood Road, Newcastle upon Tyne. Here government surplus Churchill Fay and Conomatic lathes were reconditioned and then in 1948 the new gear cutters, Churchill-Cleveland Rigid hobbers and Churchill-Redman Red Ring gear shaving machines, were produced. Simultaneously, at Halifax, Gabriel launched a third initiative, the search for technical improvements in machine tool performance. Higher cutting speeds and faster times in sizing work pieces, setting up work and transferring it to another machine were the objectives which led the firm's engineers to develop a new heavy-duty copying lathe, forerunner of the CR P5 range of fully automatic, multi-tool and profiling lathes. Another result of Halifax R & D was a lathe with an automatic feed and delivery, which heralded an automatic machine tool production line. Gabriel's last major post-war initiative was the reorganisation of Churchill's management structure. Full board authority was delegated to an executive board and three advisory boards representing manufacturing, wholesaling and retailing interests.

The growth in machine tool demand, stemming from the expansion in motor car manufacture, was reflected in Churchill-Redman turnover which rose from just over £200,000 in 1946 and 1947 to £900,000 in 1953 and over £1 million in 1955. To meet the demand new capacity and new products were sought in the mid-1950s. The Scotswood operation, under Ralph Gabriel, the chairman's son, moved to a purpose-built and wholly-owned factory at Blaydon on the other side of the Tyne in 1957. The previous year the Scotswood Division was hived off from Churchill-

Redman and formed into a new company, Churchill Gear Machines Ltd; the Halifax Division then became Churchill Redman Ltd. At Blaydon this new subsidiary made machine tools for the motor industry, ranging from gear hobbing and shaving machines to the Grob spline and gear forming machine and the Vertimax vertical spindle production lathe, invented in the war by James Anderson, a Glasgow garage proprietor in charge of a government shadow factory.

Anderson's company was one of a number of innovative firms in the industry which Gabriel brought into the Churchill Group in the 1950s and early 1960s. Others included E T (Gauges) Ltd for special tooling (in 1959) and Dorsett Marine Ltd which made glass fibre boats (in 1961). Other firms were acquired for the additional capacity they offered: Denhams Engineering Co Ltd of Halifax, purchased in 1960; Henry Milnes Ltd of Bradford, purchased in 1961; and Herbert Hunt Ltd, drill manufacturers of Manchester, which was moved to Halifax. Gabriel preferred to run these acquisitions as separate operating companies, to which he added a selling firm, Charles H Churchill Ltd, in 1962, because he believed that this satisfied the realities of geographical dispersion and pride in work among the skilled craftsmen who formed the bulk of the Churchill workforce. It also made it easier to trace sources of profits and losses. Signalling the Churchill Group's reliance on the motor industry, the firm's headquarters were moved in 1950 from Lambeth in London to Coventry Road, Birmingham, though J B Gabriel kept his chairman's office at Caxton Street, London, until 1960. The parent company's capital was increased to £1.26 million in 1955. A decade later the Churchill Group was one of the largest in the machine tool industry, with group sales of £14 million and employing 2,000. However when in 1965 Tube Investments made an offer for all Churchill shares (of which less than half belonged to the Churchill and Gabriel families), Beresford Gabriel decided to negotiate rather than resist the offer, in view of rising German and Japanese competition and the concomitant needs drastically to increase investment and to cut labour costs. When TI took over the Churchill Group in 1966, Beresford Gabriel retired, having been a leading figure in the British machine tool industry since the 1930s.

One major criticism that can be levelled against Gabriel is that he too closely allied the fortunes of his firm with American manufacturers. When he overcame import problems by a policy of extending manufacturing licences, he found that American conditions limited his freedom to export. Thus in 1950-59 Churchills exported 15 per cent of their products, compared to the British machine tool industry's proportion of 26 per cent.

Beresford Gabriel belonged to both the Institution of Mechanical Engineers (associate, 1919; member 1952) and of the Institution of Civil Engineers (associate, 1914). In 1949-51 he served as president of the Machine Tool Trades Association. Early in life Beresford Gabriel enjoyed rowing and later took up golf. Raised as a Methodist, he later attended the Church of England, but could not always agree with Anglican doctrines. Politically, he regarded socialism as a false paradise.

He married in 1914 Elfrida Ianthe Mary Griffith Clarke, daughter of Edward Clarke, a merchant. They had three sons, the youngest of whom, Ralph, read engineering at Cambridge, served in the REME in the Second World War and afterwards joined the management of the Churchill

Group, becoming managing director of Charles Churchill & Co Ltd in 1958 and deputy chairman in 1963. Their eldest son became a solicitor and their second son a farmer. J B S Gabriel died at Kenilworth on 7 July 1979 leaving £80,971 gross, which did not accurately reflect his lifetime's wealth accumulation.

DAVID J JEREMY

Writings:

Foreword to L T C Rolt, *Tools for the Job. A Short History of Machine Tools* (B T Batsford Ltd, 1965).

Sources:

Unpublished

Institution of Civil Engineers, London, library indexes.

Institution of Mechanical Engineers, London, library indexes.

BCe.

MCe.

PrC.

'The Churchill-Redman Story' (typescript in possession of Churchill-TI, Blaydon, Newcastle upon Tyne, dated 7 Feb 1961).

Information from Ralph Gabriel and John McG Davies.

Published

Derek H Aldcroft, 'The Performance of the British Machine-Tool Industry in the Interwar Years' *Business History Review* 40 (1966).

Churchill TI (Blaydon on Tyne: Churchill TI, nd but ca 1965).

Daily Telegraph 19 July 1979.

Terence R Gourvish, 'Mechanical Engineering' in Neil K Buxton and Derek H Aldcroft (eds), *British Industry between the Wars: Instability and Industrial Developments, 1919-1939* (Scolar Press, 1979).

The Machine Tool Trades Association (Inc), *Report on the Future of the British Machine Tool Industry* 30 Aug 1945.

PEP, 'The Machine Tool Industry' *Planning* 15 (1948).

Lionel T C Rolt, *Charles Churchill 1865-1965* (Birmingham: Charles Churchill Co Ltd, 1965).

—, *Tools for the Job. A Short History of Machine Tools* (B T Batsford Ltd, 1965).

Samuel B Saul, 'The Machine Tool Industry in Britain to 1914' *Business History* 10 (1968).

GAINFORD, 1st Lord Gainford
see PEASE, Joseph Albert

GALLAHER, Thomas

(1840-1927)

Tobacco manufacturer

Thomas Gallagher (or Gallaher, he dropped the second 'g' in his name during the 1870s) was born in Templemoyle, County Londonderry on 27 April 1840, the third son in a Protestant family of nine children. His father, also named Thomas, was a substantial farmer and proprietor of several successful corn mills. The younger Thomas was educated privately and it would seem briefly, for at an early age he helped in the family business. In later life he recalled 'at twelve and a half I was gaffer in charge of some fifty men. I managed them then without trouble and it has been the same ever since' {*Northern Whig* 23 Apr 1923}. Unwilling to accept a subsidiary role within the family corn mills, Thomas for a time considered careers in law and the army. He rejected both, deciding instead to establish himself independently.

Following an apprenticeship with Osborne & Allen, general merchants of Londonderry, where he learnt the techniques of tobacco manufacture, in 1857, with £200 borrowed from his mother at 5 per cent interest, he established his own firm in the city. It was an opportune moment, for from the early 1850s per capita tobacco consumption in Ireland rose rapidly, doubling by 1900. By a mixture of energy and hard work — in later life he claimed to have worked seventeen hours a day — he earned a reputation for producing a pipe tobacco far superior to the adulterated product common in Ireland and managed to build a small export trade to Britain. In 1863, in co-operation with his brother-in-law, he transferred business to Belfast, which offered a rapidly expanding market and better port facilities. The firm prospered and in 1873 Thomas married Robina Mitchell by whom he was to have five daughters and a son (the latter did not survive him). By this time the firm was marketing snuff and tobacco throughout Ireland and beginning to replace hand-operated methods of production with power-driven machinery. In 1881 a five-storey factory employing 600 was constructed in York Street, Belfast and during the next decade, following regular visits by Thomas to the USA, the firm vertically integrated by the acquisition of plantations and stemming factories in Kentucky and Virginia, which Gallaher personally supervised. In 1888 premises were established in London employing 200 and in February 1896 the business became a limited liability company with a capital of £1 million. The same year a new factory was built on its present site in Belfast. By this time Gallahers was the largest tobacco firm in Ireland and, at least in terms of the number of travellers it employed, 16, third in the United Kingdom.

In 1898 Thomas's position in the industry was recognised when he became chairman of the National Association of Tobacco Manufacturers. Yet, perhaps surprisingly, he refused to join the Imperial Tobacco Co founded in 1901 to combat American competition. Later he alleged that this was because he would not be 'cribbed, confined or combined by any ring' {*Irish News* 4 May 1927} but his decision was also influenced by the fact that Gallaher's interests were still predominantly Irish and Imperial was very much seen as a British organisation. Furthermore, Thomas did not relish the prospect of playing second fiddle to the Wills family (whose firm also remained outside the 1898 National Association). Nevertheless the decision had no adverse affects, though Gallahers had to beat off a challenge from 'Buck' Duke's American Tobacco Co by producing (under the 'Park Drive' brand) machine-made cigarettes which Thomas had originally despised. During the years before the First World War the firm's output increased in line with total UK production and expanded its markets in Britain, the Empire, the USA and Scandinavia.

During the 1920s the company experienced difficulties partly because of the losses to its Southern Irish market during the boycott of 1920-22. The firm found it difficult to recover its trade after partition in 1923 as the Free State Government imposed prohibitive dues on the importation of manufactured tobacco. Additionally there was competition from English companies in what was, in the 1920s, a stagnant UK market. Annual net profits (pre income tax) which averaged £195,373 for the five years 1924-28, plunged to their lowest level in 1925 when they stood at £144,442. Furthermore by this time Gallaher, who suffered from heart trouble in his later years, took a smaller role in the running of the firm and John Gallaher Michaels, a nephew, became managing director in 1921. The new management, however, proved reluctant to restructure the business by introducing new products and sales methods. In particular it was insufficiently quick to accelerate the movement from pipe tobacco to cigarettes at a time of rapidly changing public tastes: the result was that the firm's market share fell. Even so net profits in 1927 nearly recovered to their 1924 level, at almost £215,000. New entrepreneurial talent and capital appeared only after Thomas's death when the company became public in 1928. Trustees for the Gallaher family sold their holdings for £2 million to the Constructive Finance & Investment Co a consortium established by the merchant banker Edward de Stein. Stein himself became chairman, though some family interest in the firm was maintained through the presence on the board of John Michaels. The move proved a turning point in the firm's fortunes and its share of the tobacco market, particularly in cigarettes, increased throughout the 1930s. In 1932, to forestall a takeover by American Tobacco the new board entered into an arrangement with Imperial whereby the latter acquired 51 per cent of

Gallaher's ordinary shares, but agreed to leave 'the management of the business to go on undisturbed and unhampered' {*PP, HC* 1960-61 (218), 59}.

Gallaher's interests were not confined to tobacco. He was an ardent tariff reformer, becoming vice-president of the Tariff Reform League and a member of Joseph Chamberlain's (qv) Tariff Reform Committee. He was a JP for County Antrim and a life governor and benefactor of the Royal Victoria Hospital, Belfast. As chairman of the Belfast Steamship Co he co-operated with William A Pirrie (qv) in building up the Liverpool cross-channel service. It was in this capacity that in 1907 he came into conflict with James Larkin who had been sent from Liverpool to organise the dock labourers into trade unions. This Gallaher firmly resisted, refusing either to recognise the union or to meet Larkin. The dispute intensified when the company sent to Liverpool for replacements for striking workers, which drew from Larkin, never one to mince words, the comment that Gallaher was an 'obscene scoundrel' who 'valued neither country, nor God, nor creed' {Larkin (1968) 24}. This conflict escalated into the most widespread and prolonged industrial struggle that Ireland had ever experienced, involving most of the workers employed in the unloading and transport of goods in the port and the city of Belfast. At one stage in the dispute the Royal Irish Constabulary, angry at the unpaid overtime required of them to protect strike breakers, mutinied and were replaced by the military. In the end after two deaths and more wounded, the employers were successful. Workers returned to the Belfast Steamship Co and 'expressed their sorrow for what had happened' {*ibid*, 32-3}.

Thomas Gallaher was not, and never claimed to be, a technical innovator. In later life he attributed his success to hard work and an ability to grasp market opportunities. 'There is no royal road to fortune. You must work ... there isn't luck anywhere. It's opportunity. You have to train your mind to grasp its particular message and your hand to make capital out of it' {*Belfast Telegraph* 4 May 1927}. It is obvious, as his dealings with Larkin showed, that he had a pronounced streak of ruthlessness. As an employer, whether in the tobacco industry or the docks, he had little time for trade unionism — 'Do not argue' was one of the mottoes displayed in his York Street factory. He was not, however, without benevolence to his employees and was the first employer in the tobacco industry to reduce the working week from fifty-four to forty-seven hours. But perhaps his greatest achievement was to create, in Belfast, a non-sectarian workforce, something requiring both moral and physical courage. On one occasion Gallaher managed to keep a potential agitator out of the factory only by acquiring a pistol and personally threatening to shoot him.

Thomas Gallagher died on 3 May 1927 at his home in Greencastle, near Belfast aged eighty-seven. In his will he bequeathed, largely to his family and its trustees, £230,204 gross in Northern Ireland and £273,750 in England, a total of £503,954, though as indicated above, the total family holdings in the company assets were well in excess of this figure.

DAVID S JOHNSON

GALLAHER Thomas

Sources:

Unpublished

Northern Ireland PRO, wills 1927/276.

PrC.

Private communication from Michael Jenkins, Assistant Public Relations Manager, Gallaher Ltd, Kingsway, London, 1981.

Published

Bernard W E Alford, *W D and H O Wills and the Development of the UK Tobacco Industry 1786-1965* (Methuen, 1973).

Belfast Newsletter 4 May 1927.

Belfast Telegraph 4 May 1927.

Maurice Corina, *Trusts in Tobacco* (Michael Joseph, 1975).

Gallaher Ltd, *Gallaher Ltd and Subsidiary Companies 1857-1956* (Gallaher, 1956).

The Industries of Ireland: Part I Belfast and the Towns of the North (Historical Publishing Co, 1891).

Interview with Thomas Gallaher, *Northern Whig* 23 Apr 1923.

Irish News 4 May 1927.

Irish Times 4 May 1927.

David S Johnson, 'The Belfast Boycott 1920-22' in J M Goldstrom and L A Clarkson (eds), *Irish Population, Economy and Society. Essays in Honour of the Late Professor K H Connell* (Oxford: Clarendon, 1982).

Emmet Larkin, *James Larkin. Irish Labour Leader 1876-1947* (Mentor, 1968).

Northern Whig 4 May 1927.

PP, HC 1960-61 (218) Monopolies Commission Report on the Supply of Cigarettes and Tobacco and of Cigarette and Tobacco Machinery.

Edward J Riordan, *Modern Irish Trade and Industry* (Methuen, 1920).

Arthur E Tanner, *Tobacco* (Pitman, 1912).

Times *Prospectuses* 77 (1929).

Robert M Young, *Belfast and the Province of Ulster in the Twentieth Century* (Brighton: Pike, 1909).

WWW.

Gamages, Holborn (taken from W H Beable, Romance of Great Businesses*).*

other shop-keepers could not match. With the spread down the social scale of all kinds of outdoor activities, Gamage's became known for its sports and camping equipment, becoming supplier to many schools and clubs and being appointed the official Boy Scouts' outfitters. When motor cars were beginning to reach a wider public than their aristocratic pioneers, Gamage opened a department selling 'Everything for the Automobilist', including a Gamage motor car; and Albert Gamage himself became a member of the Royal Automobile Club. He was president of many athletic clubs, a donor of challenge shields and cups to workmen's clubs. It was this specialisation in sports that led, in 1907, to the purchase of Benetfinks of Cheapside.

Gamages differed from other London department stores in that it had initially developed by supplying the needs of male customers working in the City, Fleet Street and Holborn, and had expanded further by becoming a 'people's popular emporium' catering for their families as well. In contrast, the main thrust of the expanding West End stores was towards attracting women customers with fashionable merchandise displayed in elegant surroundings. On 12 July 1904 Gamage took the whole front page of the *Daily Mail* (the first advertiser to do so) announcing further extensions to the 'People's Popular Emporium', which already had more than two acres of floor space for the display of goods, and twice as much again for offices, stock-rooms, staff rooms, kitchens and canteens, and the mail order department. Everything that Gamages sold (and they claimed to sell *everything*) could be ordered by post — except ammunition and explosives which could only be bought on the premises. By 1930 annual sales exceeded £1 million and there were over 2,000 employees in the Holborn buildings.

By the 1920s Albert Gamage, while still over-seeing the store, had bought Grange Farm, Chartridge, Hertfordshire, and was spending much of his time there. He married in 1888 the daughter of J G Murdoch. They had two sons and one daughter.

Gamage died on 5 April 1930, leaving £28,766 gross. Although in life never a showman in the sense of promoting himself, Albert Walter Gamage was laid in state in his Motoring Department, with members of staff mounting guard day and night at the catafalque. His son Eric, already managing director, became chairman. The firm, as a department store, closed in 1972 when its Holborn buildings were pulled down.

ALISON ADBURGHAM

Sources:

Unpublished

BCe.

PrC.

Published

William Henry Beable, *Romance of Great Businesses* (Heath Cranton Ltd, 1926).

Thomas C Bridges and Hubert H Tiltman, *Kings of Commerce* (GG Harrap & Co, 1928).

Gamages Christmas Bazaar, 1913 (Newton Abbot: David & Charles, 1974). Introduction by Alison Adburgham.

Mr Gamage's Great Toy Bazaar, 1902-1906 (Denys Ingram Publishers, 1982). Introduction by Charlotte Parry-Crooke.

Guardian 5 Feb 1972.

Sunday Telegraph 19 Mar 1972.

Times 15 Mar 1972.

WWW.

Sir David Gamble (taken from E Gaskell Lancashire Leaders. Social and Political *The Queenhithe Printing and Publishing Co Ltd).*

GAMBLE, Sir David

(1823-1907)

Chemical manufacturer

David Gamble was born in Dublin on 3 February 1823, the only son of Josias Christopher Gamble and his wife Hannah née Gower, the daughter of Henry Gower, a Dublin solicitor. Josias Gamble, a native of Enniskillen in the north of Ireland and a graduate of Glasgow University (MA 1797), after a short period as Presbyterian minister at Enniskillen (1799-1804) reportedly started to make bleaching powder in County Monaghan. He was certainly manufacturing chemicals in Dublin in 1806. In 1828 the family moved to England where Josias became junior partner to James Muspratt, another Dublin chemical manufacturer who pioneered the Leblanc soda-making process in Liverpool in 1822 in order to supply the growing soap industry in the area. Driven out of that borough because of public outcry at his factory's pollution of the atmosphere, Muspratt had moved a dozen miles to St Helens, then a small town of only about 6,000 inhabitants without effective local government, and it was here that Gamble joined him. When Muspratt moved on yet again two years later, Gamble took on other partners (and eventually the Crosfields of Warrington) until such time as his son was of age to join him in his own, much smaller, business close to the original premises.

David Gamble was educated at a private school nearby, Cowley Hill academy run by Francis Morley, himself soon to become a successful chemical manufacturer in the district; then at University College, London, in the session 1839-40; and finally, perhaps influenced by Thomas Graham who had moved from the Andersonian to the chair of chemistry at UCL, at the Andersonian College, Glasgow (subsequently Glasgow Royal Technical College). Unlike most business men, therefore, David Gamble had benefited from having a father with an academic, as well as a long practical training, and had himself received a good grounding in chemistry. He eventually built up a good library in the subject, including works in French. He joined his father at the new works in 1843, trading as J C Gamble & Son. His father, then in his mid-sixties and ailing, died early in 1848 leaving him in control, though he was still not yet twenty-five years of age.

He had married at the beginning of the previous year Elizabeth Haddock, the daughter of Thomas Haddock, a prominent local coalowner. They had 11 children, all of whom survived; but many years were to elapse before the four older sons (born in 1848, 1852, 1856 and 1858) could join him in the active management of the firm. It nevertheless flourished under David's capable direction, the works by 1865 being of the same rateable value as the larger factory in which his father had been an original partner and which had itself grown fourfold during the previous twenty years. J C Gamble & Son then decomposed about 25 tons of salt per day, had gone into the manufacture of potassium chlorate and had also developed a thriving business in magnesium sulphate (Epsom salts). In recognition of his position in the local business community he was made a director of Parr's Bank when it was formed into a limited company in 1865. In November of that year he 'was requested to examine the customers' accounts at St Helens from time to time, with the exception of those of the alkali manufacturers' and to report thereon {National Westminster Bank, Parr's Banking Co, directors' minutes}. Although he was paid £150 a year 'for St Helens duty' from 1883, he was not a frequent attender at directors' meetings. He remained on the board of Parrs until his death.

Although the chemical industry grew more rapidly from the 1840s at Widnes on the River Mersey than at St Helens, partly because of the former's transport cost advantages, J C Gamble & Son continued to flourish and to show resourcefulness, as, for instance, when Walter Weldon was brought from London to develop his manganese recovery process; but with the development of the competing Solvay ammonia soda process, the home market was threatened by Brunner, Mond & Co, and a flourishing export trade which the Leblanc makers had built up, particularly to the United States, was also put in jeopardy. Gamble, who had already joined with some of his fellow chemical manufacturers in 1867 to form the Tharsis Sulphur & Copper Co to ensure their sulphur supplies, and was also involved in 1883 in the setting up of the Lancashire Bleaching Powder Manufacturers Association in an attempt to limit output in that branch of their industry in order to maintain overall profitability in the face of the new Solvay competition, was not reluctant, with four of his sons, to take the ultimate step, the merging of the individual Leblanc businesses in the United Alkali Co Ltd in 1891. That his company was then valued at £320,00, £131,000 more than the next largest chemical concern in St Helens, is a good measure of his business success.

Gamble joined the Royal Agricultural Society in 1850, acquired land in the vicinity of his works and during the 1860s built himself a fine, well-situated house a mile to the north of St Helens. Apart from a few interests in Liverpool, where he kept a steam yacht and was a member (and in 1882 commodore) of the Mersey Yacht Club — and where he helped to establish the University College — all his outside activities seem to have been devoted to the town where he lived and worked. He supported the first St Helens Improvement Act in 1845, was named as one of the original Improvement Commissioners, serving as their chairman, 1856-62. When the town was incorporated in 1868, he became its first mayor, being re-elected for a second term and serving again in that office in 1882-83 and 1886-87. A lifelong free trader (he contributed 10 per cent of his early earnings to the Anti-Corn Law League), he stood for Parliament as a Liberal when the town first obtained independent representation in 1885 but was narrowly defeated. His main interest, apart from the Church of England and its schools, to both of which he contributed generously, was the Volunteer movement in which he was the leading spirit in the district, serving as lieutenant colonel from 1860 to 1887 and providing the local Volunteer Hall. In 1889 nearly 900 of his fellow townspeople subscribed over £1,000 in his honour, 900 guineas of which were spent upon a portrait painted by Sir Hubert Herkomer which hangs in St Helens Town

Hall. In 1893 he gave £25,000 for the building of a technical institute and library in the town centre 'for the purpose of assisting our people to make themselves equal or superior to those countries where technical education has been an institution for a great number of years' {Barker and Harris (1954) 463}.

For his many public services Gamble was made a CB in 1887, a baronet in 1897 and a KCB in 1904. He died on 4 February 1907 leaving an estate valued at £388,265 gross.

T C BARKER

Writings:

The Descendants of John Haddock (np, 1897).

Sources:

Unpublished

Glasgow University Archives.

National Westminster Bank Ltd, London, archives, records of Parr's Banking Co Ltd.

University College, London, absentees book 1839-40 and register of students.

MCe.

PrC.

Published

Theodore C Barker and John R Harris, *A Merseyside Town in the Industrial Revolution* (Liverpool: Liverpool University Press, 1954).

Chemical Trade Journal 1 Mar 1890.

Dublin Directories.

Ernest Gaskell, *Lancashire Leaders: Social and Political* (Queenhithe Printing & Publishing Co Ltd, nd).

William J Reader, *Imperial Chemical Industries. A History* (2 vols, Oxford University Press, 1970-75) 1.

St Helens Newspaper 6 June 1885, 8 Feb 1907.

Times 10 May 1907.

WWW.

GARCKE, Emile Oscar

(1856-1930)

Electrical power promoter and accountant

Emile Oscar Garcke, born in Germany in 1856, came to Britain as a young man and became naturalised in 1880. Three years later he was appointed secretary of the Brush Electrical Engineering Co and by 1893 he had become the firm's managing director and chairman. In the 1890s he emerged as one of the City's leading experts in electrical promotions, a status which he sustained to his death. In 1896 he established *Garcke's Manual of Electrical Undertakings*, the industry's annual authority which continued publication until 1960. He was elected a member of the Institution of Electrical Engineers in 1889, founded the Tramways and Light Railways Association, and became a fellow of the Royal Statistical Society and a member of the Institute of Actuaries. His journalistic promotion of the electrical industry included an entry in the *Encyclopedia Britannica* and a series of articles for the *Times* in 1907.

Though actively involved in electricity supply companies and firms engaged in electrical engineering, it was for the promotion of the electric tram that Garcke was particularly known. Electric trams carried more passengers more quickly than their horse drawn counterparts. They also could take advantage of cheap off-peak daytime generating capacity in the early stages of electrical development when electricity was principally used for public and domestic lighting. On 26 October 1896, the British Electric Traction Co (BET) was registered, with Emile Garcke as a managing director, in order to take advantage of the opportunities for electrified tramways initially in Britain and later overseas. The BET was Garcke's brainchild. He recognised that there were two potential obstacles to the company's expansion; first, the cost and pitfalls of applying a new technology; second, the political and legal constraints imposed by the attitudes of municipal authorities to the private conduct of utilities and the legislation governing electrical and tramway undertakings. The BET's early boards were constructed with both factors in mind. Supplementing Garcke's expertise on the technical side as fellow managing directors were J S Raworth and W L Madgen, who ranked among the most experienced electrical engineer industrialists of the day. Complementary expertise was provided by politically pugnacious directors with experience of Government. The first chairman was Sir Charles Rivers Wilson, a former Treasury official and private secretary to Disraeli, an ex-member of the Council of the Suez Canal, and the chairman of the Grand Trunk Railway of Canada. He enticed onto the board Sir Charles Fremantle, an old associate from the Treasury who had also served on the board of the Suez Canal Co and was Deputy Master of the Mint. Conservative Party politicians of robust anti-socialist views, such as Arnold Foster and Lord Rathmore, added their mettle to this array of talents.

For the BET to prosper it was essential for it to operate as an efficient and effective organisation. As joint author, with John Manger Fells (qv), of *Factory Accounts, Their Principles and Practice*, the first systematic statement of cost accounting for a British audience, published in 1887, he had demonstrated his theoretical command of the most modern management methods. This mastery was applied in structuring the control and reporting relationship between the BET and its 80-odd subsidiaries in which the BET was a holding company of a distinctly modern type. Its small head office staff was divided into seven specialist departments whose work was coordinated by a committee of management comprising the three managing directors. The BET provided expert counsel on the establishment of new subsidiary tramway companies and monitored the progress of established undertakings, though day-to-day operations were the concern of local management. The accounts of subsidiaries were kept strictly separate. Garcke himself summarised the structure as one of, 'independence and autonomy of the separate companies in regard to their own affairs but solidarity of all in regard to general questions of principle and policy'. {Fulford (1946) 33}

Garcke's earliest tramway schemes were at Hartlepool, Kidderminster, Oldham, and Stoke on Trent; by 1899 there were nearly 40 tramway undertakings in the group and by 1901 the BET had 124 miles of electric tramway running. However, healthy dividends in the first half dozen years were followed by a suspension of dividend from 1907, the poor trading results being blamed upon the antagonism of local authorities and competition from the motor bus. Eventually, in 1915 the company's capital of £5 million was written down by almost £1 million and the payment of modest dividends resumed. By this time the BET had begun also to operate motor buses, an activity which expanded as the tramway services contracted. Emile Garcke conceived of buses as feeders to the tramway network and it was his son, Sidney (qv), who joined his father on the board of BET, who insisted upon the development of bus operating subsidiaries in their own right. Sidney later remarked: 'I have spent a lot of time taking up the tramways my father laid'. {Klapper (1961) 241}

The second half of the 1890s was an inauspicious moment for launching an electrical combine. Enthusiasm for municipal ownership of utilities was running high in local councils and the services provided by many private companies were the butt of much abuse. The BET's attempts to promote subsidiaries provoked hostility from local authorities and the company was styled the 'Octopus' or the 'Oligarcke' in the municipal press. Garcke, Rivers Wilson, and their sympathisers entered vigorously into the controversy over the legitimate limits of municipal economic enterprise at the turn of the century. Indeed, it was at the meetings of the Electrical Trades Section of the London Chamber of Commerce, a forum established by Garcke, that the early initiatives to launch a propaganda counter offensive to the rising tide of 'municipal socialism' were taken.

Garcke was no newcomer to the political controversies surrounding electricity and electric traction. In the mid-1880s he had served as the honorary secretary to Lord Thurlow's Electric Lighting Act Committee which sought to amend the terms of the 1882 Act and give greater incentives to private companies to initiate undertakings. Furthermore, he had represented the London Chamber of Commerce at the Board of Trade conference of 1895 which resulted in the formulation of the Light Railways Act of 1896. This effectively curtailed the veto powers of local authorities over private tramway promotions and under which many BET schemes proceeded.

Garcke took an active interest in the electrical industry until the end of his life and it was not until 1929, his seventy-third year, that he relinquished executive duties with BET. The services of a personal secretary of exceptional ability, John Spencer Wills (qv), later himself chairman of BET, provided invaluable assistance towards the end of his career. In later life, however, he found time to devote to other interests, notably philosophy and the promotion of industrial harmony. He enjoyed philosophical discussions with a group of friends in Maidenhead and in 1929 he published a volume entitled *Individual Understanding: A Layman's Approach to Practical Philosophy*. The same year saw his appointment as chairman of the Industrial Copartnership Association. His enthusiasm for the reconciliation of capital and labour led him to fund personally a new headquarters for the organisation and doubtless it was a kindred combination of desire to promote understanding and knowledge and humane concern for the needy which led him to donate £25 per annum to the London School of Economics in its early years.

Garcke married Alice, daughter of John Withers, a brush manufacturer, in 1882.

Emile Garcke died on 14 November 1930, at Pinkney's Green, Berkshire, leaving a widow and his son, Sidney. His estate was valued at £167,150 gross.

RICHARD ROBERTS

Writings:

(with John M Fells) *Factory Accounts, Their Principles and Practice: a Handbook for Accountants and Manufacturers, with Appendices etc* (Crosby, Lockwood & Co, 1887). Further editions: 1888, 1889, 1893, 1902, 1911, 1922, and summarised edition, 1893.

'Discussion on "The Treatment, Regulation, and Control of Electric Supply by the Legislature and the Board of Trade" by Major P Cardew' *Journal of the Institution of Electrical Engineers* 19 (1890).

'Discussion on "Generation of Electrical Energy for Tramways" by J S Raworth' *Journal of the Institution of Electrical Engineers* 26 (1897).

'Discussion on "The Electrical Power Bills of 1900: before and after" by W L Magden' *Journal of the Institution of Electrical Engineers* 30 (1900-1901).

The Limitations of Municipal Enterprise: Being a Paper Read before the National Liberal Club Political and Economic Circle, on 24 October 1900 (P S King & Co, 1900).

PP, HC-HL 1900 (305) VII and 1903 (270) VII Joint SC on Municipal Trading 1900.

The Progress of Electrical Enterprise: Reprints of Articles from the Electrical Supplement of the Times on the British Electrical Industries (Electrical Press, 1907).

Board 1920-30. He was also chairman of the Iron and Steel Industrial Research Council and a member of the Department of Overseas Trade's Advisory Council. Gardner became an increasingly influential member of the Summers Board, which in the post-war boom of 1920 bought the Shelton Iron Steel & Coal Co, Buckley Colliery and Talk-o'-th'-Hill Colliery. He won a considerable reputation for his experience in iron, steel, coal and chemicals, and in 1930 was recruited by the Bank of England as the Governor's Industrial Adviser and as managing director of the Bank's wholly-owned subsidiary, the Securities Management Trust, at an annual salary of £12,000.

SMT was formed by the Bank in November 1929 to act as their medium for industrial development and as their intermediary in obtaining rationalisation in steel, cotton, shipbuilding and other depressed basic industries. It held the Bank's interests in such concerns as the Scottish firm of Beardmore or the International Power & Paper Co of Newfoundland formed after the financial crisis brought on Armstrong, Whitworth by the mismanagement of their Newfoundland investments by Sir Glynn West (qv). Also in 1930 Gardner became a director of the Bankers' Industrial Development Corporation launched, with 25 per cent participation by the Bank of England, as a finance company to encourage rationalisation and reorganisation. The work of SMT and BIDC has received much attention from both contemporaries and historians as the Bank of England's first serious involvement in national industrial policy and as their response to what Austen Chamberlain called 'that school of thought and activity represented by Lord Melchett (qv) and described in the cant of the day as Rationalizers' {PRO, FO 371/13459, minute of 26 Jan 1929, f 12}. The purpose of the rationalisation movement, which had only gained strength around 1927 with the evident failure of the return to the gold standard as a panacea for industrial decline, was to improve national productive efficiency by reducing wasteful competition and writing off surplus capacity. The BIDC was however more than a reaction to the cant of the rationalisers: it was also, crucially, intended as belated proof that the City held a constructive concern about the state of British industry and thus aimed to forestall direct interference by the Labour Government of 1929-31.

Perhaps Gardner's most signal service for BIDC was to prepare his 'Confidential Report on the Structure of the Iron and Steel Industry of Great Britain, Including Plans for Rationalisation' (1931). This was the blueprint for steel rationalisation that Montagu Norman (qv) and the BIDC tried unsuccessfully to implement in the 1930s. Gardner proposed large vertical regional amalgamations based on best-practice technology and large-scale operations; but his scheme was a technical expert's pipedream, as cursory as it was radical, and badly deficient in prescribing means to this ends. In the first year to April 1931, BIDC launched capital issues for both the National Shipbuilders Security Co (which was acquiring surplus shipbuilding capacity and closing it down) and the Lancashire Cotton Corporation (which was trying to rationalise one of the declining basic industries of the country), but in financial terms both issues were difficult and unsatisfactory. The bad past results of the depressed basic industries had destroyed their credit. In future, Gardner tried to raise money by other means, as for example £500,000 loaned to

Stewarts & Lloyds in 1932 to finance their new Corby steelworks. Initially Gardner was apprehensive in 1930-32 lest the effect of giving tariff protection to the steel industry would be to relieve the economic pressure on the steelmakers and thus to delay the enforcement of rationalisation. He was active in trying to devise schemes to avert this, as for example when he proposed forming BID Steel Finance Corporation in July 1932. He urged that in return for protection, steel manufacturers should be obliged (by legislation if necessary) to pay a levy on all steel ingots produced, the proceeds to be used by BIDSFC as the interest and sinking fund on large capital issues made to reorganise the industry. BIDSFC would then have gradually placed these issues on the market. For Gardner this proposal had the double merit that while it exerted compulsion on the steelmakers, it yet ultimately left the industry under untrammelled private control. It was however rejected by the other members of the BIDC.

The impact of SMT and BIDC was circumscribed by the Bank of England's caution, the clearing banks' mutual jealousy and manufacturers' proud suspicions of one another. 'He is in a very strong position ... for he is not personally dependent in any way upon them or upon his associates', the Prime Minister was told of Gardner, 'he is quite fearless' {PRO Prem 1/224, Sir Horace Wilson to Neville Chamberlain, 25 June 1937}; but in reality his achievements were limited. Gardner became a director of Credit for Industry Ltd in March 1934, was nominated by the Bank of England to the Voting Control Committee of Beardmores in April 1936, and was chairman of T & T Assets Ltd (1935-36), Armstrong Whitworth Securities, Armstrong Whitworth Engineers and the New Jarrow Steel Co. He was also a director of Special Areas Reconstruction Ltd formed, with Bank of England support, to sponsor new small industries in especially depressed areas (including those hit by rationalisation closures); its achievements were nugatory.

Gardner, who was chairman of the London Iron & Steel Exchange in 1936-37, resigned from all his appointments associated with the Bank of England in January 1938 to become chairman of the Society of British Aircraft Constructors. He was presented with £5,000 by the Bank on his retirement. 'The British aircraft industry has provided itself with an ambassador, already skilled in solving industrial difficulties, to serve as principal negotiator between the industry and the Government, and to help industry in laying long-term plans', the *Times* declared on 13 January 1938, 'an industrialist who is not an aircraft manufacturer and who might interpret the industry's views to the Air Ministry without personal bias . . . [will] be invaluable in the drawing together of customer and producer'. Gardner was at the heart of pre-war aerial rearmament, serving in 1938-39 on the Air Council Committee on Supply and on the Air Minister's Industrial Advisory Council. He became a member of the Civil Aviation Planning Committee on its formation in 1939. Following the outbreak of war he sat on the Air Supply Board in 1939-41 and the National Production Advisory Council in 1942-43. He was on the Joint Central Advisory Committee on the Production Executive, and from 1942 chaired the Ministry of Aircraft Production's Production Efficiency Board. One of his particular responsibilites, following the heavy German night bombing of 1940, was to arrange the dispersal of aircraft plants all over Britain, scattering both plant and labour, so that the dislocation of production would be minimal after a direct hit. Bruce-Gardner (as he was now known) relinquished all these appointments in 1943 to become Controller of Labour Allocation and Supply at the Ministry of Aircraft Production.

In the autumn of 1944 Hugh Dalton, President of the Board of Trade, following recommendations from Ernest Bevin, the Minister of Labour, and Sir Stafford Cripps, the Minister of Aircraft Production, appointed Bruce-Gardner as Chief Executive for Industrial Reconversion from war to peace. Gardner had 'direct access ... at all hours' to Dalton, who regarded him as 'an able and thrustful business man of good standing' who 'rendered most valuable service during the difficult period of the switchover'. Dalton 'found him easy to work with and ... liked his energy and his sense of humour'; 'he had a wide outlook ... was very quick to see points and take decisions, and he was authoritative, but not pompous, towards other industrialists' {Dalton (1957) 430}.

Bruce-Gardner relinquished his post as Chief Executive for Industrial Reconversion in 1946, although acting as the Board of Trade's Industrial Adviser during 1947, and returned to private industry. He was a director of Guest, Keen & Nettlefolds for twelve years to 1958, and also joined the boards of the Consett Iron Co, Crompton-Parkinson and other steel companies. He became chairman of Scunthorpe Rod Mill after its board reconstruction in 1953. He was deputy chairman of the Steel Co of Wales, chairman of John Lysaght and chairman from 1953 of the British Iron & Steel Corporation following the Conservative Government's denationalisation of the sector. He was president of the Iron and Steel Institute 1955-56 and president of the Iron and Steel Research Association.

A member of the Institution of Mechanical Engineers, he was knighted in January 1938 and at the recommendation of the Ministry of Aircraft Production was created a baronet in 1945. He received honorary life memberships of the American Society of Metals and of the American Institute of Mining & Metallurgical Engineers.

Gardner married in 1911, at Lewisham, Gertrude Amy, daughter of Charles Rivington Shill; they had two sons and a daughter. Latterly he lived at Abingdon in Berkshire, where he died on 1 October 1960 leaving £419,335. His elder son Douglas (born 1917), was later deputy chairman of Guest, Keen & Nettlefolds and chairman of the Iron and Steel Institute 1966-67.

R P T DAVENPORT-HINES

Sources:

Unpublished

Bank of England, Securities Management Trust papers of Sir Charles Bruce-Gardner.

BLPES, papers of Lord Dalton.

PRO, papers of Board of Trade, Foreign Office, Ministry of Aircraft Production and Premier's Office papers.

Scottish RO, Edinburgh, papers of Sir Arthur Steel-Maitland.

PrC.

Information from Dr Stephen Tolliday and Sir Douglas Bruce-Gardner.

Published

Ian D Colvin, 'The Germans in England 1915' *National Review* (1915).

Edward H J N Dalton, *The Fateful Years* (Muller, 1957).

Richard S Sayers, *The Bank of England 1891-1944* (3 vols, Cambridge: Cambridge University Press, 1976).

WWW.

GARFORTH, Sir William Edward

(1845-1921)

Colliery manager

William Edward Garforth was born at Dukinfield, Cheshire, on 30 December 1845, the second son of William Garforth, a Cheshire ironmaster and Sarah née Hall, and the grandson of the mineral agent John Garforth who had founded the Dukinfield ironworks in 1825 and won leading bridge contracts such as that for the Menai tubular bridge. William was educated at C P Mason's school at Denmark Hill, near London and was subsequently trained as a mining engineer in Lord Stamford's survey office and at his father's colliery and works. For some time he worked in the family ironworks, which incorporated local colliery interests which he managed. In 1879, for reasons which are unclear, he left Dukinfield and was appointed manager of the West Riding Colliery at Altofts, near Normanton in Yorkshire at a salary of £500 a year.

In his early days with the firm of Pope & Pearson at West Riding Colliery, Higsons of Manchester were consulting engineers for the firm, and despite sinkings being made into deeper and more gassy seams, Higsons advised the continuing use of naked candles. In 1886 the almost inevitable happened, when an explosion occurred and 21 lives were lost. The firm then employed over 1,100 men (a number which rose to 1,796 by 1911) and Garforth began to improve the ventilation of the collieries subsequent to the explosion both by sinking new air shafts and by introducing underground machinery worked by compressed air. He was himself a considerable inventor.

they needed to assess the progress of their investment. Garnsey argued that company balance sheets, which were traditionally confined to the financial affairs of each separate legal entity, should be supplemented by sufficient additional information to enable users of accounts to assess the position of the entire group of companies controlled by the holding company. These views attracted a great deal of attention, both immediately and over the next few years. For example, during the months of May and June 1925, the *Times* published a series of letters debating the case for and against the publication of group accounts. Surprisingly Garnsey was not invited to give evidence to the Company Law Amendment (Greene) Committee of 1926, though views were sought from a number of other leading accountants, including Francis D'Arcy Cooper (qv) who was a powerful adversary of Garnsey on the question of group accounts. The evidence presented to the Greene Committee shows that, in general, the business community was not yet ready to abandon its preference for secrecy in financial affairs, and company accounts which concealed more than they disclosed continued to be regarded as acceptable. Garnsey's ideas stood the test of time, however, and the essential ingredients of the group accounting requirements imposed by the Companies Act of 1948, can be traced back to his lecture. Garnsey published a number of accounting works, including a revised version of the 1922 lecture which became a standard work on the subject of holding companies' accounts, and he was in heavy demand as a speaker throughout the 1920s and early 1930s.

Sir Gilbert Garnsey was chairman of the London Members Committee of the ICAEW, 1923-26, and a member of the Institute's Council from 1928 until he died. He possessed a pleasant and genial disposition, and was very popular with his colleagues and even his opponents. In his youth he was a good footballer, and obtained money for his articles by playing for Aston Villa's second team; later he played both golf and tennis. As a freemason, he was a Past-Master of the Chartered Accountants' Lodge.

He married in 1915 Miriam Garnsey née Howles, BSc, daughter of John Howles, a cotton mill manager. When he died suddenly on 26 June 1932 at the age of forty-nine, he was survived by his wife, and their son and daughter. He left an estate valued at £151,466 gross.

J R EDWARDS

Writings:

'A Few Notes on Shipping Accounts' *The Accountant* 7, 14 Mar 1914.

'Holding Companies and Their Published Accounts' *ibid* 6, 13 Jan 1923.

Holding Companies and Their Published Accounts (Gee & Co, 1923 and 1931).

Comments on a Paper by Sir Henry Bunbury Entitled 'Control of Expenditure within Government Departments' *The Accountant* 9 Feb 1924.

'Insurance Company Accounts, Suggested New Form of Accounts with Explanatory Notes' *ibid* 3 Jan 1925.

'Holding Companies and Their Published Accounts' *ibid* 20 Feb 1926.

'Some Notes on Goodwill as an Item in the Value of Business' *ibid*.

'Limitations of a Balance Sheet' *ibid* 20 Oct 1928.

(with Judge T E Haydon) (eds), *Secretary's Manual on the Law and Practice of Joint Stock Companies with Forms and Precedents* (21st edition, Jordan & Sons, 1930). 1930).

Sources:

Unpublished

BCe.

MCe.

PrC.

Published

The Accountant 2 July 1932, reproduced in Robert H Parker (ed), *British Accountants: A Biographical Sourcebook* (New York: Arno Press, 1980).

Edwin Green and Michael Moss, *A Business of National Importance: The Royal Mail Shipping Group, 1902-37* (Methuen & Co, 1982).

History of the Ministry of Munitions (8 vols, HMSO, 1918-22) 3, part 1.

Susan Howson and Donald Winch, *The Economic Advisory Council 1930-39* (Cambridge: Cambridge University Press, 1977).

The Incorporated Accountants' Journal July 1932.

Edgar Jones, *Accounting and the British Economy 1840-1980: The Evolution of Ernst and Whinney* (Batsford, 1981).

Jack Kitchen, 'The Accounts of British Holding Company Groups: Developments and Attitudes to Disclosure in the Early Years' *Accounting and Business Research* Spring 1972.

Sheila Marriner, 'The Ministry of Munitions 1915-19 and Government Accounting Procedures' *Accounting and Business Research* Special Accounting History Issue, 1980.

Times 28 June 1932.

WWW.

Sir Richard Garton (taken from Manbre & Garton Ltd 1855–1955).

GARTON, Sir Richard Charles

(1857-1934)

Brewer

Richard Charles Garton was born in Bedminster on 8 October 1857, the eldest of five sons of William Garton (1832-1905), brewer, of Roselands, Woolston, Hampshire and his wife, Ellen, daughter of Thomas Miller Littleton. William Garton pioneered the production of saccharum or invert sugar at Southampton in 1855. His company, Garton, Hill, using the patent of Charles Garton, William's brother, rapidly developed its brewing sugar business to an output of 100 tons per week and in 1882 built a factory at Battersea, London. Gartons also developed extensive brewing interests in the Southampton area.

Richard Garton was educated at Owens College, Manchester, and then studied at Marburg University, Germany, where he specialised in biochemistry with a particular interest in fermentation. In these years the basis of the modern science of fermentation was being laid, developing on from the work of Pasteur and others. Garton became one of the leading figures in England on the subject. Garton's expertise made him the natural successor, alongside his brother Charles, as head of Garton & Co about 1904. Garton was invited to join the board of Watney Combe Reid in 1902. Cosmo Bonsor (qv) was then chairman but Garton's flair for business quickly marked him out as his successor. Other board members were Colonel Oswald P Serocold, Richard Combe, and C H Babington. Garton helped to guide the company through the traumas of the years 1900-20 when a sharp setback in trade, and financing difficulties, compounded a dramatic decline in licensed property values. As a result it became necessary to reduce Watney's capital from £9 million to £6 million in 1906 by writing 75 per cent off deferred ordinary stock. The First World War initially threatened even worse conditions, but healthy price rises allowed by the Government, and a much more realistic attitude to capacity and production (under Garton's guidance part of the Mortlake breweries were converted to produce unrationed honey sugar to offset the jam shortage) allowed Watney's to recover profitability sharply by the end of the war. The post-war boom encouraged the company to invest in new maltings and to give more attention to the chemistry of brewing in which Garton specialised. With the improvement in trade the company was able to write up the capital to its original value in the period 1922-25. Garton played an important role in brewing industry politics at this time. Along with Sir William Waters Butler (qv) and Edgar Lubbock, he was a leading advocate of public house improvement and a staunch defender of the liquor trade against prohibitionists and state ownership advocates alike. He maintained that continued private ownership of 'the trade' was by no means incompatible with the wider social responsibility of brewers

Garton, Sons & Co Ltd, factory at Battersea (taken from Manbre & Garton Ltd 1855–1955).

and retailers to discourage the abuse of alcohol. The bridge between private profit and social responsibility was the improved public house.

In 1924 Garton's sugar interests were registered as Garton & Sons Ltd with an authorised share capital of £500,000. In 1926 Richard Garton and his brother Charles discussed with Albert Eustace Berry (qv), of Manbré Sugar & Malt Ltd, a plan to fuse interests. What began as a proposal for an

Manbre & Garton Ltd, Hammersmith (taken from Manbre & Garton Ltd 1855–1955)

amalgamation ended up as a sale when Gartons was sold to the Manbré group for £2,300,000, with Sir Richard Garton as chairman and Berry as managing director.

Garton briefly flirted with politics, contesting Battersea unsuccessfully for the Conservatives in 1900. He was High Sheriff of Surrey in 1913, and Lord of the Manor of Hastehill. He had houses at Haslemere in Surrey and Loch Buie on the Isle of Mull. His other major interest was Cancer Research, which he supported actively until his death. His contribution of £20,000 allowed the setting up of the British Empire Cancer Campaign in 1923, and he became its founding secretary and treasurer. He was also honorary treasurer of King's College of Household and Social Science at London University. His interests included racehorse breeding and collecting eighteenth century drinking glasses. Garton was knighted in 1908, and created a GBE for his war services in 1918. He married in 1883 Nellie, daughter of Andrew Durrant of Bishops Hall, Chelmsford, and had two daughters. Lady Garton died in 1925.

With the retirement in 1928 of Sir Cosmo Bonsor, chairman for thirty years, Garton succeeded to the position. From this date, Garton and Oswald P Serocold were in effective charge. At the end of 1932 Garton made way for Serocold but he remained on the board as deputy chairman. He also devoted a part of his retirement to Manbré Garton & Co, and never relinquished the directorships of his two companies. He died on 22 April 1934, leaving £2,641,364 gross.

TOM CORRAN

Sources:

Unpublished

BCe.

PrC.

Published

Brewers Journal 15 May 1934.

Brewing Trade Review May 1934.

Burke's Landed Gentry 1965.

Financial Times 25 Apr 1934.

Arthur C Fox-Davies, *Armorial Families* (Hurst & Blackett, 1929).

John L Garbutt, *Manbré & Garton Limited, 1855-1955. A Hundred Years of Progress* (pp, 1955).

Hurford Janes, *The Red Barrel, A History of Watney Mann* (John Murray, 1963).

Walter P Serocold, *The Story of Watneys* (Watney, Combe, Reid & Co, 1949).

Jeanne Stoddart, *Manbré: A Hundred Years of Sugar Refining in Hammersmith 1874-1974* (Fulham & Hammersmith Historical Society, 1974).

Times 25 Apr 1934.

WWW.

GARTSIDE, Thomas Edmund

(1857-1941)

Cotton spinner

Thomas Edmund Gartside (courtesy of Mr Edmund Gartside).

Thomas Edmund Gartside was born at Royton, about two miles north of Oldham, Lancashire, on 9 February 1857, the only son of Alice Gartside and an unknown father. He was educated at Royton Wesleyan School, leaving at the age of about ten, and then attended evening classes at the local Temperance Seminary, concentrating on book-keeping and arithmetic.

He started work when twelve years old, as a check boy with the Royton Industrial Co-operative Society at their new shop on Middleton Road, earning 6s for a sixty-nine hour week. After two years he moved into the cotton industry which dominated the Lancashire region, beginning as a warehouse boy at the Moms Mill (later the Belgian Mill), Luzley Brook, and then successively becoming an office boy in the Belgian Mills and junior clerk in the office of the newly operational Royton Spinning Co. Inspired by the current massive expansion of the spinning industry in Oldham, this mill company had been floated in 1871 as one of the joint-stock limited liability cotton companies then spreading in Lancashire — permitted under the mid-nineteenth century Companies Acts and appropriate to the initially small scale of firm and factory within the industry. It started its 50,000 spindle mill (then the typical size of new mills) in 1873, at the beginning of Lancashire's greatest joint-stock boom of the nineteenth century. Tommy (as he was known) stayed with the Royton Spinning Co for five years, until 1878. On reaching his majority he shrewdly sought legal and administrative experience, by clerking for a local solicitor, John Francis Mellor, for two years, and then by working as assistant clerk for the Oldham Poor Law Guardians for eight years.

He returned to the cotton industry in 1889 when he was appointed secretary of his old firm, which now had a second mill, of 20,000 spindles, built adjacent to their first one in High Barn Street, Royton. With the Royton Spinning Co for the next five years, Gartside learned the business of mill management. He was also part-time secretary of the Royton Industrial Co-operative Society, 1876-95.

Shiloh Mill, Royton (courtesy of Mr Edmund Gartside).

In 1894 Tommy Gartside was invited to become secretary and general manager of Shiloh Spinning Co Ltd (he had been a director since 1891). One of the first wave of mill-building Oldham 'limiteds' launched at the height of the 1873-75 flotation boom, Shiloh had a capital of £30,000 in £5 shares of which 1,552 shares at 7s paid up were held by 291 shareholders. The nominal share capital was doubled in 1881. By 1891 Shiloh had two mills in operation at Holden Fold: No 1 of 26,460 mule spindles employed 100 people and No 1a (completed 1888) of 9,144 mule spindles, both spinning American and Indian cotton into coarse yarns which were sold to East Lancashire manufacturers of household textiles. But the company's profits were falling below expectations. It paid dividends of between 1.5 and 6.5 per cent in 1882, 1883 and 1885, then paid none until (probably) 1897. Between 1884 and 1893 its financial record was one of the worst of Oldham's limited mills, with its debit balance trebling in the decade 1885-94. In the flotation boom of 1889-92 new and much larger mills, of 100,000 spindles, were being built, pressuring Shiloh's position even further — locally, the first of the 1890s giants was the Holly mill built in 1890-92 with 72,660 spindles.

Gartside successfully liquidated the debit balance between 1895 and 1897, aided by the improvement in trade of 1897. He trebled the company's total capital by increasing the proportion of loan capital to 76 per cent of the total by 1902, so enabling the company to pay high dividends to shareholders (who received 10 per cent annually, 1904-26) and a fixed interest to the loan holders. This performance may have been aided by the installation of Platt's mules (the firm's original, less productive, mules were supplied by Asa Lees) from 1901 and by economies in bulk cotton purchasing, but not by any increase in labour productivity since, each hand operated 334 spindles in 1889 and 338 in 1939, spinning low counts (between Nos 8 and 36). Some economies of scale came from the construction of a second much larger mill, initially of 74,748 spindles but augmented to 101,460 with the addition of another storey in 1905. Gartside consolidated his position at Shiloh on becoming managing director in 1903 and chairman in 1907.

The widespread ownership of shares in the Oldham mill companies gave men like Tommy Gartside and John Bunting (qv), whose success in promoting and running companies was cumulatively proven, the chance to build up networks of part-ownership, or even outright control of an empire of companies. With Shiloh paying good dividends, Gartside began to extend his activities to other coarse spinning mills in Royton, creating a group of interests in the Edwardian mill-building boom of 1904-5. On behalf of a Royton syndicate in 1904 he purchased the Highfield Mill (25,764 spindles) for £7,725 and became chairman of the reinvigorated mill, renamed Park Mill. The board of the Vine Mill Co (Royton) Ltd (formed 1897), of which Gartside became a member in 1897, in 1905 promoted another company, the Grape Mill Co Ltd with a capital of £70,000 in £5 shares issued to Vine shareholders. Tommy Gartside became director and its deputy chairman. By 1919, when Lancashire's cotton spindleage was close to its all-time high of 61 million (1917), Tommy Gartside was the chairman of eight Royton spinning companies whose mills had a combined spindleage of nearly 929,000 — nearly half those in Royton and about 1.5 per cent of Lancashire's spindles.

During the inter-war period Gartside's empire, which rested on the manufacture of coarse yarns, faced the problems of prolonged recession. Overseas, especially American and Far Eastern, markets in low count yarns collapsed in 1921. Gartside, like other spinners who survived, resorted to a variety of devices to preserve his companies. The capitals of the Shiloh, Holly, Vine and Park companies were reconstructed in 1920-21 partly in order to remove the burden of loan capital, though the reconstruction of Grape Mill Co Ltd in 1925 was so generous to existing shareholders as to gain notice in the *Financial Times*. Short-time working was practiced extensively and the industry's standard wage lists were progressively reduced between May 1920 and 1932. However, Gartside, now nearly seventy and unfettered by indebtedness to any banks, rejected the prevailing policy of restraining capital investment. Using his carefully garnered reserves (which were typically concealed in his companies' balance sheets), he made two bold moves in search of markets. He converted Park Mill (Royton) Ltd's No 2 mill to condenser spinning in order to produce coloured soft yarns for linings, and succeeded in building up a large trade. Secondly, he persuaded the board of Shiloh Mills Ltd (its name was changed in 1920) in 1926 to build another, larger mill (the Elk), of 107,240 spindles. Equipped by Platts, it cost £250,000, gave employment to 400 people and opened in 1927; spinning soft twist for hosiery, it proved to be profitable for three decades. Through nearly all his mills Gartside declined, as did most Lancashire spinners, to adopt American spinning technology, especially the ring spindle, by which he might have lowered some overhead costs. Of the 1,022,920 spindles in his empire of eight companies in 1935 — which represented 2.17 per cent of Lancashire's spindles — only 101,340 were rings. To be fair though, rings could not produce certain qualities of yarn, like the soft twist then appropriate for hosiery.

Gartside kept his mills going by taking a fiercely independent line. He refused to join the Cotton Yarn Association, formed in 1926 by local spinners in order to raise yarn prices, and held out until the Depression when it became clear that undercutting would destroy his own profits. Gartside then negotiated the Royton coarse count price agreement with the other major mill group headed by Will Cheetham (1869-1942), in 1933-34. Likewise he bitterly opposed the Government's rationalisation schemes implemented by the Lancashire Cotton Corporation and designed to overcome the industry's basic problems of overcapacity, obsolescence and over-specialisation. While Lancashire spindles were reduced by 25 per cent, 1923-35, and those in Royton by 22 per cent, Gartside's mill spindleage increased by 14 per cent. Gartside's stubbornly independent spirit, though not always his achievement in surviving commercially, characterised the mass of medium-sized Lancashire spinners who long resisted merger with the industry's large combinations both in the nineteenth and the twentieth centuries. Under Gartside Shiloh dividends averaged 8.65 per cent per annum 1902-41 (they were passed in eight half years, 1929-32 and 1934-35) which was one quarter above the average annual dividend paid by Oldham's limited spinning companies during that period. In 1933 the trade press reported 'Shiloh Mills Ltd, Holden Fold, Royton, Oldham, are definitely the outstanding example of the limited liability movement in the cotton industry of Lancashire' {*Textile Weekly* 23 June 1933}.

Outside the eight spinning companies of which he was chairman, Tommy Gartside was a director of four more, including the Willow Bank and Durban spinning companies; he was also director of Messrs John Hepworth & Co, yarn agents, and of the London & Lancashire Insurance Co (local board). At his death he was on the boards of companies owning upwards of 2 million spindles, or 5.1 per cent of Lancashire's spindleage in 1939.

Within the cotton industry he belonged to the Oldham Master Cotton Spinner's Association (vice-president, 1923-38) and to the Federation of Master Cotton Spinners' Associations; he also took 'a keen interest in the International Federation of Master Cotton Spinners' and Manufacturers' Associations, having attended several congresses in America, Switzerland and Egypt' {*Oldham Standard* 11 Jan 1941}. For a long-time he was a member of the Manchester Royal Exchange.

A Liberal, Gartside was a member of Royton District Council 1906-15 and chairman for a period; in 1913 he was appointed a Lancashire JP. He served as churchwarden at St Paul's Parish Church, Royton, from 1908 until his death.

GARTSIDE Thomas Edmund

T E Gartside in August 1883 married Harriet Travis (d 1937) at Prestwich Parish Church; they had two sons and two daughters, who were educated at Oldham Hulme Grammar School. Tommy Gartside, still chairman of his eight companies, died on 8 January 1941 after a brief illness. He left £237,497 gross. His younger son, James Brewer Gartside (1897-1964), took over the main responsibility for running the various businesses which Tommy Gartside had built up, and what remains of his empire is now merged into one business under the management of the third generation of Gartsides, though by 1984 it had contracted to two mills with 20,800 spindles, and with a significant part of its turnover no longer in traditional spinning.

DAVID J JEREMY

Writings:

To the Electors of Haygate Ward (address printed for author at the time of the Royton District Council Election, 1 Apr 1912).

Sources:

Unpublished

BCe.

MCe.

PrC.

Information from Edmund T Gartside (grandson) and Dr D A Farnie.

Published

Douglas A Farnie, *The English Cotton Industry and the World Market, 1815-1896* (Oxford: Clarendon Press, 1979).

—, 'The Emergence of Victorian Oldham as the Centre of the Cotton Spinning Industry' *Saddleworth Historical Society Bulletin* 12 (1982).

Financial Times 4 Mar 1925.

M W Kirby, 'The Lancashire Cotton Industry in the Inter-War Years: A Study in Organisational Change' *Business History* 16 (1974).

Manchester Guardian 11 Jan 1941.

Brian R Mitchell and Phyllis Deanne, *Abstract of British Historical Statistics* (Cambridge: Cambridge University Press, 1962).

Oldham Chronicle 11 Jan 1941.

Oldham Standard 11 Jan 1941.

J H Porter, 'Cotton and Wool Textiles' in Neil K Buxton and Derek H Aldcroft (eds), *British Industry between the Wars. Instability and Industrial Development 1919-1939* (Scolar, 1979).

The Shiloh Story 1874-1974 (Royton: Shiloh Spinners Ltd, 1974).

Textile Weekly 23 June 1933.

GASKELL, Holbrook

(1813-1909)

Chemical manufacturer

Holbrook Gaskell (courtesy of Mr John Cantrell).

Holbrook Gaskell was born on 5 March 1813 at Wavertree, Lancashire, the oldest son of cousins, Roger Gaskell and Ann née Hunter. Based in Liverpool, his father managed the commercial offshoot of a Warrington sailcloth firm, a business in which the Gaskell family had been prominent traders and manufacturers during the eighteenth century. Gaskell began his education at a private school in Norton, near Sheffield, run by a Unitarian minister. At the age of fourteen, he became apprenticed to Yates & Cox, Liverpool iron merchants and nail makers, where his duties were mainly clerical.

On attaining his majority, Gaskell began looking for alternative openings since there was little prospect of obtaining a partnership with his employers. He considered reading for the Bar and a more adventurous scheme of settling in the East Indies. While still undecided about his future course, he was introduced to the young Scots engineer, James Nasmyth, who was looking for a partner to undertake the supervision of commercial and financial operations, at the Bridgewater Foundry, Patricroft, near Manchester. Gaskell joined Nasmyth in October 1836 and remained with the firm until June 1850 when ill-health forced an early retirement. Partly as a result of his sound business management, Nasmyth Gaskell & Co became one of Britain's leading engineering firms producing machine tools, steam engines, locomotives, foundry equipment and the famous steam hammers.

By June 1855, Gaskell's health was sufficiently restored for him to enter into a second partnership with the industrial chemist, Henry Deacon, a former apprentice of Nasmyth's firm. For a brief period, Gaskell supported his new partner's plans to manufacture soda by the ammonia soda process, but soon forced him to return to the conventional Leblanc methods and during the 1860s, Gaskell Deacon & Co became one of the largest and most successful Leblanc works in Widnes. Gaskell's responsibilities were similar to those he had accepted at Patricroft and he continued his active involvement until the 1870s. In November 1890, the works he had helped to establish became one of the factories of the United Alkali Co and in recognition of his services to the chemical industry Gaskell was appointed to a vice-presidency.

Gaskell had wide interests outside his work: he supported various radical Liberal causes such as the extension of the franchise; he partially endowed the chair of botany at University College, Liverpool with nearly £6,000; and he served as a magistrate. He was also one of the proprietors of the *Liverpool Daily and Weekly Post and Echo*.

Gaskell married in 1841 Frances Ann Bellhouse, daughter of Henry Bellhouse; their sons Holbrook, James Bellhouse and Frank all became partners in Gaskell Deacon & Co. Holbrook Gaskell died at the age of ninety-six on 8 March 1909 at Woolton, near Liverpool. He left an estate valued at £449,769 gross.

JOHN CANTRELL

Sources:

Unpublished

Eccles Central Library, Nasmyth collection, Gaskell letters and miscellaneous materials including 'In Memoriam Holbrook Gaskell 1813-1909, a privately printed collection of obituaries, funeral and memorial sermons.

MCe.

PrC.

Published

John A Cantrell, 'James Nasmyth and the Bridgewater Foundry: Partners and Partnerships' *Business History* 23 (1981).

R Dickinson, 'James Nasmyth and the Liverpool Iron Trade' *Transactions of the Historic Society of Lancashire and Cheshire* 108 (1956).

D W F Hardie, *A History of the Chemical Industry in Widnes* (ICI, 1950).

— and R Dickinson, 'Gaskell Deacon 1853-1953' *ICI Ltd, General Chemical Division News* Aug 1953.

Albert E Musson and Eric Robinson, *Science and Technology in the Industrial Revolution* (Manchester: Manchester University Press, 1969).

Samuel Smiles, *Industrial Biography* (John Murray, 1863).

— (ed), *James Nasmyth. An Autobiography* (James Murray, 1883).

GATES, Ernest Henry

(1873-1925)

Worsted manufacturer

Ernest Henry Gates was born in Dorking, Surrey, on 22 November 1873, the son of William Gates, a bricklayer and his wife Elizabeth née Gent.

Sir Eric Geddes (taken from C Addison, Politics from Within *vol II).*

GEDDES, Sir Eric Campbell

(1875-1937)

Transport company executive and industrialist

Eric Campbell Geddes was born in India, at Agra, on 26 September 1875. He was eldest son of an established Scottish civil engineer, Acland Campbell Geddes (1831-1908), who from the 1850s to the 1880s was deeply involved in the survey and construction of Indian railways, and his wife Christina Helena Macleod née Anderson, daughter of Rev Dr Alexander Anderson. His mother organised the first School of Medicine for Women at Edinburgh jointly with her sister and sister-in-law Elizabeth Garrett Anderson (the first woman to practice medicine or be elected as a mayor in England).

Although born in India, Geddes spent most of his early life in Britain and from the beginning of his schooling at Edinburgh Academy in 1886, he showed a rebellious streak which, attributed by his brother Auckland (qv) to a 'Highland-rebel' make-up, defied all authority that sought to curb it. Between 1886 and 1892 he attended four reputable schools in Britain, each of which he was required to leave, and in flat defiance of family intentions for his future, in 1893 he left for America. Here a hardening process commenced which transformed the cheerful, intelligent but troublesome and irresponsible boy into a great organiser and big thinker who by his middle life was ready to play a major part in national affairs.

Two-and-a-half grim and variegated years in America, where Geddes worked as a typewriter salesman, office-boy, steelworks labourer, lumberman, station agent, assistant yardmaster, car tracer, bartender and theatrical publicity agent were a prelude to a longer period of employment in India where he married Alice Gwendolen Stokes in 1900. She was the daughter of Rev Arthur Stokes who ran a school for boys at Mussourie and was a member of a prominent Dublin family. Geddes's work in India was initially in the area of estate development with the firm of Carew & Co, an old business that after the Mutiny had received grants in the Nepalese Terai of large tracts of forest land which Eric, with railroad and logging experience, might profitably develop. The work involved preparing land for producing crops, mainly sugar cane. In connection with jungle clearance, however, Geddes needed to organise the laying of many miles of light railway which were effectively extensions of the Powayan Steam Tramway, a railway some 40 miles in length controlled by Carew & Co. Of this he became manager. In 1899 the line was inspected with a view to purchase by an official of the Rohilkund & Kumaon Railway. Impressed by Geddes's capacity for organisation, the official offered Geddes an appointment with the Rohilkund & Kumaon as assistant traffic superintendent at Bareilly. Geddes accepted, became acting superintendent in 1900 and in 1901, superintendent. When in 1904 the railway was called upon to effect the speedy concentration of a considerable force of arms, the efficiency with which this was done so impressed Lord Kitchener, the Commander-in-Chief, that he requested that the responsible official be presented to him. Geddes had made a contact which would be renewed in 1914.

Due to the ill-health of his wife, however, Geddes was by 1904 seeking opportunities outside India and in that year a family friend, Sir George Gibb (qv), offered him an opening as claims agent of the North Eastern Railway in England, of which company Gibb was general manager. Although the opening was, in truth, a relatively modest one, Geddes was being offered the chance to join an organisation in which selected young men were carefully groomed for high office and in his contact with Geddes, Gibb had been impressed by the young man's uncommon energy and adaptability. Geddes seized the chance, moved his wife to Yorkshire where she produced three sons in 1907, 1908 and 1912, and himself enjoyed a meteoric rise in the service of the NER. Promoted commercial agent in 1905, chief goods manager in 1907, Geddes in 1911 was offered the chief executive post on the London & South Western Railway. He used this offer to secure for himself the post of deputy general manager of the NER with a clear undertaking as to future salary and succession to the post of general manager upon the retirement of the incumbent, Sir Alexander Butterworth (qv).

Geddes's rise to top management in Britain's most efficient and financially strong railway by the age of thirty-six was a tremendous feat. He impressed at this time as a 'sort of elemental force possessing physical courage and fondness for outdoor pursuits owing nothing to books but blessed with the knack of assembling the relevant facts about any problem and then deciding firmly the action to be taken' {Bell (1951) 37}. Within the NER managerial cadre, though, his personality caused some difficulty and deterioration of the team spirit upon which Gibb had placed great emphasis during his period as general manager.

The First World War effected a fundamental change in Geddes's career, thrusting him from provincial obscurity to national eminence. Fretting from the start of hostilities to share fully in the war effort, Geddes by December 1914 had raised two Pioneer Battalions from the company's employees. More significantly, however, over Christmas 1914 he was reintroduced by Sir George Gibb, now on the Army Council, to Lord Kitchener and subsequently to the Minister of Munitions, David Lloyd George, with a view to full-time service. Kitchener initially tried to arrange for Geddes to study railway transport in France, and when this failed due to military resistance, attempted unsuccessfully to make him general manager of Vickers to solve a worsening production crisis. Uninfluenced by the prejudices of military and civil corps towards outsiders and convinced of the contribution hustling, improvising, creative businessmen could give the war effort, Lloyd George put Geddes to work in the Ministry of Munitions. Of Geddes, Lloyd George wrote, 'He had the make of one of their powerful locomotives. That is the impression he gave me when one morning he rolled into my room. He struck me immediately as a man of exceptional force and capacity ... and ... he turned out to be one of the most remarkable men which the State called to its aid in this anxious hour for Britain and her Empire' {Lloyd George (1933) I, 249}. Appointed Deputy Director-General of Munitions Supply, man to work for, nor was he always personally considerate. {Tennyson (1957) 175}

He had however high integrity in personal dealings and business, and was a dynamic industrial leader; in Britain he pioneered American concepts of mass production and time and motion study.

In 1924, with some reluctance, Geddes also became chairman of Imperial Airways. This was formed in that year following the Report of Sir Herbert Hambling's committee on Civil Air Transport Subsidies which had criticised the government policy of subsidising four separate and competing companies. Frederick Szarvasy (qv) of the British Foreign & Colonial Corporation, who had been indispensable in saving and reconstructing Dunlop Rubber, helped to settle the financial terms whereby the Daimler Hire, Instone Airline, Handley Page Transport and British Marine Air Navigation companies united as Imperial Airways, with issued capital of £500,000, and a government subsidy originally agreed at £137,000 per annum for the first four years of operations, gradually decreasing to £32,000 in the tenth and final year. Szarvasy and the Government only prevailed on Geddes to take the job on the condition that the accountant Sir George Beharrell joined IA's board. Beharrell had previously worked with Geddes on the North Eastern Railway, Ministry of Munitions, Admiralty, Ministry of Transport, the Geddes 'axe' committee and Dunlop Rubber (where he succeeded Geddes as chairman in 1937). Geddes later brought another Dunlop director and accountant, Sir Hardman Lever, onto the IA board, to the later annoyance of his successor as chairman of IA, John Reith (qv).

IA's operations began badly, with a bitter dispute in April and May 1924 by pilots over their pay and conditions. The board were 'too secretive in dealing with the men' and 'never learned the value of either good labour or good business relations': Geddes himself treated the pilots like 'the engine drivers he had known on the old North Eastern Railway' {Higham (1960) 80}. After the intervention of the newly-appointed air superintendent, Herbert Brackley (qv), the pilots resumed work. IA began by concentrating on developing its European services, but suffered sharp competition from the national airlines of Belgium, the Netherlands and Scandinavia, as well as the heavily state-subsidised German monopoly, and strongly-backed French operators. The Air Ministry would not pay the necessary commercial subsidies for Europe recommended by the Hambling committee, and after IA had lost over £24,000 in 1926 through this policy, it embarked on a new policy of creating routes linking outposts of the British Empire. In 1926 IA took over the RAF's Cairo-Basra route, and in 1927 their Cairo-Bagdad desert route. Following an official statement by Sir Samuel Hoare, the Air Minister, in 1928 that IA's mission would henceforth be imperially-orientated, it extended its connections to Karachi and Delhi (1929), Cape Town (1932), Singapore (1933) and Australia (1934). These long international routes required negotiations of flying rights over foreign countries, and Geddes as an ex-Cabinet Minister was charged with these negotiations, which provided the origins of the Law of the Air and their five freedoms. By 1934 IA's European mileage was minimal, and indeed they had tried to relinquish all European services.

The mileage flown by British civil aircraft on regular routes rose from 699,990 in 1924 to 1,166,000 in 1929; in the same period passengers increased from 10,321 to 28,484, and cargo from 350,700 to 994,300 ton miles. In 1928 the basis of the government subsidy was altered, with the Government taking a £25,000 shareholding and committing itself to £2.76 million over eleven years instead of £806,000 over six years as under the older agreement. IA had 22 fatal accidents in its first sixteen years, with 108 lives lost and 39 injured.

Geddes ran IA secretively in order 'to protect it against KLM, a most annoying competitor' {ibid, 84}. KLM was faster and more efficient than IA on eastern routes, and the British deficiency was not wholly explained by IA's obligation to carry and deliver the imperial mail. The Post Office was certainly niggardly in its support of IA, and the Empire Air Mail Scheme of 1934 was not fully adopted in Geddes's lifetime. IA was also obliged to buy its aircraft at high cost, since its orders were always small, and machines had therefore to be hand-built. Quantity orders only began in 1934 with Empire flying-boats and Ensigns for the Empire Air Mail Scheme fleet. There was no development of experimental civil prototypes until 1939. Geddes's policy was 'the minimum of political interference with the maximum cooperation from the Air Ministry' {ibid, 83}, but by 1934 he 'was operating one of the longest and most expensive and slowest air routes in the world' {Hyde (1976) 314}. He was by no means happy in the job, and in 1928 was to have been succeeded by a former director of Vickers, Lord Chetwynd; but after gaffes by the latter on a trip to India, Geddes was obliged to remain in the chair.

Geddes was president of the Institute of Transport in 1919-20; of the Federation of British Industries, 1923-24; president of the Association of Trade Protection Societies of the United Kingdom, 1923; and gave evidence to the Royal Commission on the Private Manufacture of and Trade in Arms, 1935-36. He was knighted in 1916, created KCB and GBE in 1917, and GCB in 1919. He was sworn to the Privy Council in 1917, received an honorary degree from Sheffield University in 1920, and the Junior Institution of Engineers' Gustave Canet medal in 1922.

He was chairman of both Dunlop Rubber and Imperial Airways at the time of his sudden death on 22 June 1937. After cremation his ashes were scattered by air over the English Channel. He left £112,894 gross. In appearance he was robust, rubicund and by temperament impatient.

Punctuality was his passion. He lived in his later life at Hassocks near Brighton. Leaving by motor at exactly 8 am, returning again at 7 pm, he spent three hours daily in these journeys. At 7.30 pm he sat down to dinner. At 8.15 he rose up again. His way of life conformed to the teachings of the Shorter Catechism. He was looked on as the strong silent man of real power and influence. In his home a telephone was on a pay-box system {Beaverbrook (1956) xvii}.

R J IRVING and R P T DAVENPORT-HINES

Writings:

PP, Committee on National Expenditure Reports (1922) Cmd 1581, 1582, 1589.

letter on public works loans and British materials *Times* 28 May 1923.

letter on allocation of British share of Boxer indemnity *ibid* 5 Dec 1924.

letter on Dunlop Rubber Co *ibid* 11 May 1931.

Mass Production: The Revolution which Changes Everything (Harmondsworth: Pelican, 1931).

letter on rubber restrictions *Times* 22 May 1933.

letter on German reparations 'until the pips squeak' *ibid* 15 Dec 1933.

PP, RC on Private Manufacture of and Trade in Arms (1936) Cmd 5292.

Sources:

Unpublished

British Library, papers of Earl Balfour especially Add ms 49709.

Dunlop Rubber Archives.

HLRO, papers of Bonar Law and David Lloyd George.

National Maritime Museum, Greenwich, papers of Dame Katherine Furse.

PRO, papers of Admiralty, Cabinet Office, Foreign Office, Ministry of Munitions, Ministry of Transport and North Eastern Railway.

RAF Museum, Hendon, Imperial Airways archives.

University of Warwick Modern Records Centre, papers of Sir Guy Granet.

PrC.

Information from Sir Reay Geddes, Geoffrey Jones, Michael Robbins, Arthur J Quinn Harkin.

Published

Lord Beaverbrook, *Men and Power* (Hutchinson, 1956).

R Bell, *Twenty Five Years of the North Eastern Railway 1898-1922* (Railway Gazette, 1951).

Burke's Peerage 1954.

DNB.

Economist 4 Feb, 16 Dec 1922, 5, 12 Jan, 14 June 1924.

Auckland C Geddes, *The Forging of a Family* (Faber, 1952).

David Lloyd George, *War Memoirs* (6 vols, Nicholson & Watson, 1933-36).

Robin Higham, *Britain's Imperial Air Routes 1918 to 1939* (G T Foulis, 1960).

Harford Montgomery Hyde, *British Air Policy between the Wars* (Heinemann, 1976).

Robert J Irving, *The North-Eastern Railway Company 1870-1914* (Leicester: Leicester University Press, 1976).

Peter Kline, 'Eric Geddes and the Experiment with Businessmen in Government 1915-22', in Kenneth D Brown (ed), *Essays in Anti-Labour History* (Macmillan, 1974).

Arthur J Marder, *From Dreadnought to Scapa Flow* (6 vols, Cape, 1961-70) 4, 5.

Kenneth O Morgan, *Lloyd George* (Weidenfeld, 1975).

Charles L Mowat, *Britain Between the Wars, 1918-40* (Methuen, 1964).

Sir Ronald Storrs, *Dunlop in War and Peace* (Hutchinson, ca 1946).

Sir Charles B L Tennyson, *Stars and Markets* (Chatto & Windus, 1957).

WWW.

GEE, Henry Simpson

(1842-1924)

Shoe retailer

Henry Simpson Gee was born at Lowerhead Row, Leeds on 6 April 1842, the eldest son of George Walker Gee, linen draper, and his wife Ellen née Simpson. He was educated privately at Grange School, Thorpe Arch, near Leeds.

After work-experience in his father's business he entered the successful leather tanning and dressing business of Stead & Simpson in 1863. Founded in 1834 by Edmund Stead, and Henry's uncle Edward Simpson at Upperhead Row, Leeds, by 1863 it occupied new, enlarged premises at Sheepscar, employing ca 600. Increased demand for ready-made footwear had prompted a diversification of interests, and Gee's career was to be centred on this new, ultimately dominant, side of the firm's activities. In 1864 he moved to Leicester to take charge of the company's new boot factories in Cank Street, and at Daventry.

Within a few years the founders began to relinquish control to their two nephews. Richard Fawcett, Stead's nephew, had taken charge of the Leeds leather warehouse upon Gee's move south: both were made partners. Clear business acumen now enabled Gee progressively to establish, then consolidate, his control over company trading and policy. He was the principal architect of the company's second generation of development and growth, which witnessed its emergence as a pioneer and leading exponent of the national retail chain-shop techniques the footwear industry did so much to nurture in the decades prior to the First World War. Systematically, the Leeds leather processing function was contracted, initially to provide capital to develop the more lucrative East Midlands footwear manufacturing activities. A considerable increase in productive capacity, based upon factory extensions and new technology, was undertaken so that by 1884 the Leicester factory made nearly 30,000 pairs a week. When the factory was destroyed by fire two years later, the insurance settlement amounted to £36,000. Thus, whilst employment at Leeds had fallen to ca 250, in the East Midlands (now including a new Northampton factory) there were over 1,750 employees.

Ultimately more important, however, was Gee's further diversification into retailing activities. Originally viewed as a means of absorbing excess manufacturing capacity, the first shops were merely expected to break even. In 1886, however, Gee initiated a programme of branch shop expansion in England's principal towns and by 1889 had 100 shops trading. That year the business was converted into a private limited company, Stead & Simpson Ltd, the assets of the existing partnership being purchased by the new company for £268,000. With his headquarters in Leicester, Gee became the chairman and remained in office until his death. He aimed at giving priority to the retail function but at first as much capital was expended upon the considerable and lucrative manufacturing business and export trade which survived into the interwar period. The Leeds leather business, however, was finally closed in 1892, the capital being liberated for further extension of the retail chain.

In addition to his ability to initiate successful marketing policies in the face of economic change within the industry, Gee's achievement also rested upon the judicious shifts made in the internal management of the firm. Both Fawcett and Simpson retired in 1889 but from the retirement of Stead in 1878, new partners and later the directors were drawn almost entirely from the ranks of the Midlands shoe industry rather than the leather trade. Chief amongst these was Gee's ex-Leicester manager, J Griffin Ward, a partner from 1878 and joint managing director with his brother John, 1889-97. Also on the original board of Stead & Simpson Ltd were David W Bell, the firm's chief footwear export agent, and Edward (later Sir Edward) Wood, a prominent Leicester shoe factor and a close friend of Gee. Wood was the chairman of Freeman, Hardy & Willis: Gee now joined the board of this company, later serving as its deputy-chairman, thus inaugurating a close and abiding link between the two firms.

However, Gee's business interests spread far beyond Leicester and the footwear industry. Besides his numerous directorships, they included the chairmanship of the Bugworth Colliery Co, and of Richard Hornsby & Son Ltd, Grantham, the agricultural implement makers. Gee clearly enjoyed a reputation amongst contemporaries for being one of the most astute businessmen in the industrial Midlands. Unlike most in footwear manufacturing he emerged as 'a merchant prince': the myopic, parochial business outlook which pervaded much of the nineteenth century shoe industry, did not cloud any part of Gee's expansive business personality. One obituary placed him in

the front rank as a commercial magnate ... [a man] who held more directorships than any other local [Leicestershire] man ... His financial interests were very wide: he was possibly the richest Leicester man ever ... {*Shoe Trade Journal* 25 July 1924}.

Such an assessment is underpinned by his prominence within the Midlands banking community. He was elected to the board of the Leicestershire Banking Co Ltd in 1878, becoming its chairman twelve years later. Between February and August 1900, he both initiated and conducted negotiations with Edward Holden (qv), managing director of the London City & Midland Bank Ltd (later the Midland Bank Ltd), which led to the Leicestershire's amalgamation with the Midland. In August 1900, he was elected a director of the London City & Midland, a post he retained until his death.

Heavy business commitments ensured that Gee played but a peripheral role in local life and politics. In 1878-81 he served as a Liberal town councillor for the North St Margaret's Ward, Leicester. Politically moderate at this time, he later supported the Unionist cause. In 1889, he became a JP for both the City and County of Leicester. A strong advocate of vocational education, he was the chairman of the Technical Schools Committee for some years. He was also the chairman of the Leicester Horse Tramway Co from its inception in 1874 until 1886, when it was municipalised, at which time he acted as the company's chief negotiator in the sale. He was president of the Leicester Chamber of Commerce, and the Leicestershire Trade Protection Society. He became identified with many of the town's charitable works, being both chairman and treasurer of the board of governors of Leicester Royal Infirmary. Although from a prominent Wesleyan Methodist background, be became a devout Anglican in adulthood: he worshipped at St John the Baptist Parish Church, Leicester.

Gee married Emily Francis, daughter of Dr Gorham of Tonbridge, in 1870: she died some time before him. They had four sons and two daughters, one of whom married Dr Astley V Clarke, a prominent local physician and promoter of university education in Leicester. Gee's sons all subsequently joined the board of directors of Stead & Simpson: Harry Percy in 1898 (managing director 1910, and chairman 1924), George C G in 1902, Charles D and Ernest E G in 1925.

Henry Simpson Gee died at home, Knighton Firth (a substantial residence with six acres of ground set in Leicester's premier suburb Knighton) after a short illness on 20 July 1924 aged eighty-three. He left an estate valued at £685,462 gross. The £20,000 he left for the Simpson Gee Endowment Fund to finance the Leicester, Leicestershire, and Rutland College (later Leicester University) was the single largest bequest made under the will.

KEITH BROOKER

Sources:

Unpublished

Midland Bank Archives: Leicester Banking Co Board Minutes (k 9-14); E H Holden's Midland Bank Diaries.

C Reg: Stead & Simpson (29,468).

BCe.

MCe.

DCe.

PrC; Will.

Published

Leicester Mercury 21 July 1923.

Shoe and Leather News 24 July 1924.

Shoe Trade Journal 25 July 1924.

Stead & Simpson Centenary 1834-1934: 100 years in the Boot and Shoe Trade (Leicester: pp, 1934).

Times 30 Sept 1924.

VCH Leicestershire.

GESTETNER, David

(1854-1939)

Office machinery manufacturer

David Gestetner was born in Csorna, Hungary, in March 1854, the son of Selig Gestetner. Leaving school at the age of thirteen, he was apprenticed to an uncle who made sausages in a shop in Sapron. In 1871 he moved to Vienna to become the apprentice of another uncle, a stockbroker, but after a financial crisis in Vienna in 1873 emigrated to the USA, travelling steerage. On his way to Chicago, where he was to stay with a friend, Gestetner had his pocket picked in New York. He was given a loan by a charity run by Hungarian immigrants, and found a job selling Japanese paper kites: he noted how the long strong fibres of the paper from which the kites were made gave unexpected strength to the material. Making his way to Chicago, he spent two years trying to run a laundry business before returning to Vienna to go into business with yet another uncle, a glue and gelatine manufacturer. Gestetner entered into partnership with his uncle, making and selling equipment for hectographs, a copying process using pads of gelatine. This business was not successful, the partnership was dissolved in 1879, and Gestetner moved once more, this time to London. There he became an assistant in Fairholme & Co, stationers in Shoe Lane.

GESTETNER David

Photograph of David Gestetner operating an 1893 automatic flat-bed cyclostyle (courtesy of Gestetner Holdings Ltd).

His first patent, taken out in London in that year, was for a development of the hectograph process. Soon, however, he was developing other ways to facilitate office copying. In 1880 he patented a board with a series of fine wires on one side, on which waxed paper could be placed to be written on with a blunt metal stylus. It is possible that the consideration of a more effective instrument with which to cut the stencil on such a surface led to Gestetner's most important invention, the cyclostyle, a pen with a sharp toothed wheel at its tip, patented in 1881. While this gave more effective perforation of the stencil, allowing a freer passage of the ink through it, it was not until Gestetner combined his new pen with a new kind of stencil from Japanese paper, easily perforated but held together by long, strong fibres, that the success and superiority of his process was assured. A

Sources:

Unpublished

Gestetner Holdings Ltd, Tottenham, London, archives.

MCe.

PrC.

Published

H V Culpan, 'The House of Gestetner' *Gestetner 70th Anniversary Celebrations Souvenir Brochure* (Gestetner, 1951).

Cyclostyle: The Story of a Little Wheel that Started a Big Revolution (Gestetner, nd).

1854-1934 (Gestetner, 1934).

D Gestetner (Gestetner, 1954).

Gestetner's Bulletin Nov 1933.

Gestetner Gazette 4 (1968).

Outlook (house magazine of Gestetner British selling organisation) Summer 1969.

W B Proudfoot, *The Origin of Stencil Duplicating* (Hutchinson, 1972).

Times *Prospectuses* 77 (1929).

Times 21, 26 Apr 1956.

S A Ghalib (courtesy of Mr S A Ghalib).

GHALIB, Selchouk Ahmed

(1913-)

Engineer and manager of nuclear power station construction company

Selchouk Ahmed Ghalib was born in Nicosia, Cyprus, on 17 December 1913, the son of Dr Ali Ghalib, a general practitioner, and his wife Shifa née Ziai. He was educated at Victoria College, Egypt and entered University College, London, in 1932 to read electrical engineering, specialising in electro-communications. In 1935 he obtained a first class honours BSc (Eng) degree and also the college diploma.

He joined Metropolitan-Vickers, Manchester as a college apprentice in 1935. During his practical training he took an interest in the development and application of the then-novel metadyne (a rotary power amplifier) to electric traction and in 1937 he joined the traction department of the company. With war looming, Metropolitan-Vickers saw the potential of the metadyne application to precision high-power servo systems and proposed such a system to the Admiralty; they asked the company to develop a remote power control system for the automatic stabilisation of one of their pom-pom gun mountings against ship motions (roll, pitch, yaw), and for the automatic following of the target position predictor. The precision required necessitated the development of a tight servo system of relatively high frequency for masses weighing many tons and inevitably having some backlash into the main geared drive. The degree of precision could only be achieved by the use of electronic control in the metadyne circuit. The initial stages of the development were completed by the outbreak of war and the performance of the system was satisfactorily demonstrated on an 8-barrel gun. This novel system brought together both Ghalib's academic training in electronic circuitry and his practical training in metadyne applications. He engineered the complete control system from a conceptual design produced by the company's research department.

After satisfactory trials, the Admiralty decided to fit the system initially to all the pom-pom guns in the Royal Navy. Because of the accuracy of the system it was no longer necessary to build 8-barrel guns; 4-barrel guns were sufficient and saved space and weight in the ship. Within Metropolitan-Vickers, Ghalib was given the task of setting up an engineering organisation to produce the necessary designs for the large-scale manufacture of the control system. Starting from scratch he built up a new department of some 100 designers. The same electronic control system was also applied to hydraulically-driven (Variable Speed Gear) guns, and eventually to all gun mountings in the Royal Navy, from pom-poms to the biggest armament (15 inch guns). Radar aerial mountings were fitted with this control system, using the electric metadyne drive. To ensure continuity of supplies of the equipment during the air raids, other companies were brought in at home and in Canada to manufacture to his department's designs. The accuracy of the system was continuously improved and the gun could follow the predictor with the accuracy of 1/60th of a degree. Towards the end of the war a similar system was also applied to the Centurion tank to stabilise the gun with the tank in motion. This was a particularly difficult technical problem due to the mechanical resonance of the gun-barrel, but was solved satisfactorily by tuned circuitry. It opened up new possibilities for battle tactics. As a result of these successful wartime developments, the company asked Ghalib in 1945 to set up a new section to develop the application of electronic control systems to industrial electric drives for many diverse applications, such as steel, paper and linoleum mills, machine tools, profiling, arc welding, turbines and generators, lifts, sorting, etc. The section soon grew to about 150 strong.

In the early 1950s, the possibility of generating electricity from nuclear power was being considered and Metropolitan-Vickers, together with another of the Associated Electrical Industries group of companies, British Thomson-Houston, formed a nuclear power company in 1954 with boilermakers John Thompson. It was called the AEI-John Thompson Nuclear Energy Co, and Ghalib was asked to set up the necessary team to work with the newly-formed United Kingdom Atomic Energy Authority on the design and construction of nuclear power stations. He spent three months learning reactor physics at the Atomic Energy Research Establishment at Harwell and three months delving into the design and construction of the early nuclear reactors producing plutonium for weapons and electricity for civil purposes. Returning to base and again starting from scratch, he built up a team of some 750 people incorporating the diverse engineering and scientific disciplines necessary for the design and construction of complete nuclear power stations. In 1956 his company was successful in obtaining one of the first two commercial nuclear power stations orders, Berkeley, against fierce opposition from the other nuclear consortia. In 1960 the AEI-John Thompson Co merged with the Nuclear Power Plant Co, to form The Nuclear Power Group (TNPG); Ghalib was appointed deputy general manager and became managing director in 1966.

TNPG were arguably the most successful of the consortia set up to construct nuclear power stations in Britain. Dungeness 'A', the third station to be built by TNPG, had the lowest generating costs (including capital charges). For the Oldbury station, on their own initiative, Ghalib's company pioneered in the early 1960s a novel design of pressure vessel — the pre-stressed concrete pressure vessel — which contained the whole of the primary circuit, replacing the steel pressure vessels used previously. This was perhaps the most important single development as it raised the safety of gas cooled reactors to a very high level. Since then the British Generating Boards have specified concrete pressure vessels for all their gas cooled reactors.

Orders for the advanced gas cooled reactor stations at Hinkeley Point 'B' and Hunterston 'B', were placed with TNPG in 1967. They were commissioned, late, in 1976, but still well ahead of those begun by other consortia. A measure of the confidence the Generating Boards had in TNPG and Ghalib's leadership was the award to TNPG of a complete contract by the South of Scotland Electricity Board in 1971 for the construction of a 2000 MW oil-fired station at Inverkip. In 1969 the Government decided to transfer the Atomic Energy Authority's Fast Reactor team and the Prototype Fast Reactor construction to one of the consortia; under Ghalib's guidance TNPG's negotiations were successful and all the key staff of the Fast Reactor team joined TNPG, which then completed the PFR at Dounreay. In 1970, after a few years of painstaking discussions and negotiations, Ghalib reached an agreement with the German firm Kraftwerk Union, a daughter company of Siemens, and the strongest of continental reactor companies, to set up as equal shareholders, a multinational reactor company for the design, development and exploitation of the Fast Reactor in the long term and of the light water reactors and gas cooled reactors in the short term. The proposed multinational company would have been sufficiently strong to compete against the American companies. The plans had to be abandoned in 1972 when the British Government announced its intentions to create a single British reactor company. No alternative plan comparable in its broad concept to that proposed by KWU/TNPG to set up a strong European company has yet emerged.

Ghalib was elected president of the British Nuclear Forum and served in 1969-71. In collaboration with his European colleagues in Foratom, he founded the Gas Breeder Reactor Association with headquarters in Brussels under the leadership of TNPG. Its membership at one time reached 14 manufacturing companies and electric utilities from eight different countries. At the invitation of the CBI, Ghalib was chairman of the Nuclear Committee of the Union des Industries de la Communauté Européenne, 1973-75.

In 1975 the British Government set up a single reactor company, called the National Nuclear Corporation, which absorbed TNPG. Having worked for forty years in industry, Ghalib retired but became a consultant to the South of Scotland Electricity Board and to other organisations with nuclear interests. In 1976, he was awarded the CBE, and — again at the invitation of the CBI — he became a member of the Universities, Polytechnics and Industry Committee. In 1978 he was made a Fellow of Engineering. He married in 1934 Dorothy Adelaide Poulton and has one son.

STEPHANIE ZARACH

Writings:

'Industry's Contribution to Nuclear Power' *Financial Times Survey* 9 Apr 1956.

'Equipment for the Control of the Reactor' *Journal of British Nuclear Energy Conference* 2 (Apr 1957).

'Nuclear Power Plants' *Financial Times* 1 July 1957.

'Development of the Magnox Reactor — Calder Hall to Oldbury' Parliamentary and Scientific Committee 24 July 1962.

'The Future of Atomic Power' *Memoirs and Proceedings of the Manchester Literary and Philosophical Society* 106 (1963-64).

'Advantages of the Magnox Reactor to Spanish Industry and Economy' *Anglo-Spanish Nuclear Power Symposium* 1 (Risley, ENG, UKAEA 1965) paper no 1.

PP, HC 1966–67 (381) XIX SC on Science and Technology. 'UK Nuclear Reactor Programme'.

PP, HC 1968–69 (401) XXII SC on Science and Technology. 'Reorganisation of the Nuclear Power Industry'.

'Steam Generating Heavy Water Reactor' International Atomic Energy Agency. SM-126/30 (1970).

British Patents:

1947 (637,128; 637,129; 649,219)

1948 (656,304)

1949 (663,776; 672,687)

1950 (665,319; 690,035)

1952 (719,250)

1956 (844,606).

Two views of Rosyth Naval Base on the Firth of Forth (taken from G Harrison, Alexander Gibb. The Story of an Engineer).

clock. The outbreak of war in August 1914 increased the pressure on Gibb to complete. He virtually did so when the emergency entrance was opened on 16 February 1916, on time and three months before the Battle of Jutland, after which the repair facilities at Rosyth were keenly tested. Yet Gibb did not know whether the contract was a profitable one until, after the war, in 1922, the Admiralty Arbitrator settled his claims. The total cost to the Admiralty for the Rosyth Dockyard was £6,959,000, following the Arbitrator's final award of 6 March 1923.

The completion of the bulk of the Rosyth contract and then the death of his father in October 1916 determined Gibb to participate more directly in the war effort. Through his uncle Sir George S Gibb he met Sir Eric Geddes (qv), then Director General of Transportation, British Armies in France, and in January 1917 was gazetted lieutenant colonel with the Royal Engineers and Chief Engineer, Ports Construction, to the British Armies in France and Belgium: with responsibility for the reconstruction of Belgian ports and railway junctions which the retreating Germans were expected to destroy. Next he was involved in measures to defeat the German U-Boat campaign, Geddes appointing him Civil Engineer-in-Chief to the Admiralty. Gibb developed a scheme for constructing a series of towers across the Channel but before this could be implemented the war ended. Geddes, now Minister of Transport, made him Director General of Civil Engineering in the new Ministry and here Gibb stayed, working on projects for a Severn Barrage and a Channel Tunnel, until 1921, when Geddes retired also. For his war services Gibb was appointed CB and KBE in 1918 and GBE in 1920.

In 1921 Sir Alexander Gibb decided to set up as a consulting civil engineer, attracted by the nature of the work (which was more creative and carried a higher professional status than that of the contractor) and the general prospects for large engineering contracts following the Trade Facilities Act of 1921. This empowered the Government to support development schemes at home or in the Empire. From his first office, two rooms in Victoria Street, Westminster, he moved to Queen Anne's Lodge, Westminster on 22 May 1922 and launched the firm under the title Sir Alexander Gibb & Partners. Gibb perceived that both the organisation and resources of consulting engineering firms, such as that in which he trained, required drastic modification in order to match new levels of technical knowledge. It would no longer be sufficient for senior partners to delegate wholesale to juniors on site, and no one or two partners could hope to keep pace with the rapid changes in engineering techniques and materials. Gibb changed the structure of the consulting engineering partnership by welding the senior partners into a closely-knit team relying, as needed, on the expertise of specialists in the newer branches of engineering. In the first ten years Gibb had just two partners, Rustat Blake, a contemporary of Gibb under Wolfe Barry, who had done outstanding work on railways in India and Australia; and John Ferguson, who came from Formans & McCall, the Glasgow railway engineers with whom Gibb worked during his pupilage. Gibb's personal assistant was Hugh Beaver (qv) and a Gibb nephew joined as a pupil in 1925. Beaver became a partner in 1932 as did Leopold (later Sir Leopold) Savile. Over the years other staff were recruited from Formans & McCall. Equally important were the specialist consultants to whom Gibb turned, men like Charles Merz (qv), William McLellan, consulting electrical engineers, and Ralph (later Sir Ralph) Freeman a senior partner in Freeman, Fox & Partners. By 1939 there were six partners — Gibb, Blake, Savile, Beaver, Guthrie Brown and Angus (later Sir Angus) Paton, Gibb's nephew — and a staff of about 200.

Between the wars Gibb and his partners undertook the design and supervision of a wide range of work; in the UK it included the Aquarium for the Zoological Society; first designs of Barking Power Station for the County of London Electric Supply Co Ltd; a survey of the foundations of

St Paul's Cathedral, part of the larger structural project in which Basil Mott (qv) was also involved; consultancy work for two Scottish hydroelectric schemes, the West Highland project (which was never constructed) and the Galloway Power Scheme promoted by the Power & Traction Co, which was completed in 1936 (all of these contracts involving electrical engineering came via Gibb's friends, Merz and McLellan); the Kincardine road bridge across the Forth (opened 1936); and the Guinness Brewery at Park Royal, London.

Abroad the firm was responsible for supervision of the hydroelectric development, construction of the town site and paper mills at Corner Brook, Newfoundland, for the Newfoundland Power & Paper Co Ltd (a project heavily supported by the British Government under the Trade Facilities Act and completed in 1925); a survey, with recommendations for long-term development, of the technical facilities and administration of the national ports of Canada (made in 1931-32 and implemented after 1935); dealing with the silting problem at the port of Rangoon (which Gibb solved when, using a hydraulic tidal model in University College, London, he discovered that silting would start to diminish in 1936); the Singapore Naval base, completed in 1938; and the Captain Cook Dock at Sydney. In addition Gibb was adviser to various foreign Governments including Colombia, Persia and Turkey as well as Canada, a capacity in which his incisive mind readily dealt with red tape.

After the outbreak of war in September 1939 Sir Alexander Gibb & Partners became agents and consultants to the Ministry of Supply, for whom they supervised the construction of ordnance and chemical factories; and the Ministry of Aircraft Production, for whom they organised an underground factory for aeroplane engines at Corsham and another near Kidderminster. In 1944 the firm joined with five others and 26 contractors to produce the Mulberry harbour which facilitated the Normandy landings. By this time Sir Alexander was suffering from failing health. After 1940 he eased off — having travelled 280,000 miles and visited 60 countries by 1939. In 1942 he bought a house at Hartley Wintney in north Hampshire and retired there in 1945.

He received numerous honours, all of which he listed in his *Who's Who* entry; besides his knighthood, the highest were commander of the Order of the Crown of Belgium (for his First World War Services); membership of the Royal Company of Archers (Queen's bodyguard for Scotland); election to FRS (1936); the presidency of the Institution of Civil Engineers (1936-37); and an honorary LLD from Edinburgh University. Raised in the established church of Scotland (his uncle John became a professor of church history at Cambridge), Alexander devoted much time to his masonic activities, becoming Junior Grand Warden of the Grand Lodge of Scotland. He listed his recreations as shooting, fishing and hunting and had a fondness for history which was manifest in his very considerable biography of Thomas Telford and his BBC lecture of 1937.

The facts of Alexander Gibb's career cannot be separated from his qualities as a man — quick judgment, immense energy, humour, love of his native Scotland, utter loyalty to those he admired, a way of picking the man to trust and backing him to the limit, impatience of sham; nor from the family life, hospitality and country sports which always meant so much to him.

Gibb in 1900 married Norah Isobel Monteith (d 1940), younger daughter of Fleet Surgeon Lowry John Monteith, RN; they had three sons, the eldest of whom, Alistair, succeeded as senior partner after 1945 but died following an accident in 1955. Sir Alexander Gibb died at Hartley Wintney on 21 January 1958, aged eighty-five. He left £79,191 gross.

DAVID J JEREMY

Writings:

Report of the Light Railways (Investigation) Committee (HMSO, 1921).

Presidential address *Institution of Chemical Engineers* 1928.

National Ports Survey, 1931-32. Report by Sir Alexander Gibb (Ottawa, F A Acland, 1932).

Presidential address *Junior Institution of Engineers* 1932.

The Story of Telford. The Rise of Civil Engineering (Alexander Maclehose & Co, 1935).

Presidential address *Institute of Welding* 1935.

Presidential address *Proceedings of the Institution of Civil Engineers* 1936.

The Confessions of an Engineer (BBC, 1937).

Presidential address *Institute of Transport* 1937.

Presidential address *Institute of Engineers in Charge* 1939.

Sources:

Unpublished

PrC.

Information from Sir Angus Paton.

Published

DNB.

Godfrey Harrison, *Alexander Gibb. The Story of an Engineer* (Geoffrey Bles, 1950).

— and A J S Pippard, 'Sir Alexander Gibb' *Biographical Memoirs of Fellows of the Royal Society* 5 (1959).

PP, HC 1923 (33) XV Navy Appropriation Account, 1921-22.

Times 22 Jan 1958.

WWW.

Claude Gibb ca 1956 (courtesy of UKAEA).

GIBB, Sir Claude Dixon

(1898-1959)

Heavy electrical equipment manufacturer

Claude Dixon Gibb was born at Alberton, South Australia, on 29 June 1898, the third child of John Gilbert Gibb, a carrier of Port Adelaide, and his wife Caroline Elizabeth née Dixon. He attended Alberton Primary School and Lefevre High School, becoming a scholarship student at the South Australian School of Mines. After a course in mechanical and electrical engineering he gained some practical experience as an electrician for the Adelaide Cement Co and then, at the age of nineteen, joined the Australian Flying Corps as an air mechanic. He later qualified as a pilot and served in France.

After the First World War he returned to Australia, enrolling as an undergraduate at the University of Adelaide and later becoming a senior research assistant to the professor of engineering, Robert (later Sir Robert) Chapman. Gibb gained a diploma in mechanical and electrical engineering in 1922 and the bachelor's and master's degrees in engineering in 1923 and 1927 respectively. He decided to reinforce his academic training with broad practical experience in England before settling into an engineering career in Australia and through the Messrs C A Parsons' resident engineer in Australia he gained a student apprenticeship with the firm at Newcastle upon Tyne — at £2 14s a week. A thesis he submitted to the University of Adelaide early in 1924 gave him the additional support of an Angas engineering scholarship.

He rapidly gained a varied experience of practical work in heavy engineering, beginning his training in the turbine erecting shops at Heaton, in Newcastle, on 3 March 1924 and proceeding to the blade and other shops. After a few months he went to London joining the outside erection staff then working on the installation of 20 MW and 40 MW sets for the Barking 'A' power station. Due to the illness of the resident engineer Gibb found himself in charge when an accident occurred in December 1925. His handling of the investigation bought him to the notice of Sir Charles Parsons (qv), the chairman, who brought him back to Heaton. As manager of the steam test house he reorganised the testing organisation and facilities in order to accommodate the increased size of machines, and went on investigative missions to several power stations in the London area with a view to improving their performance. He held a similar brief in the company's design and drawing offices as assistant to A Q Carnegie the technical director. In June 1929 Sir Charles Parsons made Gibb a director with the title of chief engineer — 'unusually rapid promotion for a relatively young man' {Bowden (1960-61) 32}. After the death of Sir Charles Parsons in 1931, he succeeded Carnegie as technical director at Heaton Works and over the next decade was preoccupied with the challenge of raising the output of steam turbines. By 1933 the Parsons' technical team had succeeded in producing lighter turbine blades by rolling them in a hollow form. Offering this new technology, Gibb personally negotiated and won, against fierce opposition, the contract for two 50 MW turbo-generators for an extension to the Bunnerong Power Station in Sydney, New South Wales. Running at 3,000 rpm (twice the speed of similar turbines in the late 1920s), the success of these machines 'undoubtedly led the way to the general adoption of the large output high speed machine.' {*ibid*}

Early in 1938 Gibb was appointed general manager of C A Parsons & Co Ltd and before war intervened he implemented two major changes in production. On the electrical side he installed new impregnating plant, capable of varnishing, under vacuum and pressure, the end windings of all the largest stators then envisaged. On the mechanical side he reorganised the blade shops and negotiated to supply many land and marine turbine builders with strip or segmental blading ready for assembly. In this market he first met Vice Admiral Sir Harold A Brown (1878-1968), Engineer-in-Chief of the Fleet. After war broke out in 1939 Brown, now retired from the Navy and Director General of Munitions Production at the Ministry of Supply, secured Gibb's transfer to the Ministry, first as his own assistant. Gibb later became Director General of Weapons and Instruments Production (1941), Director General of Armoured Fighting Vehicles (1943) and chairman of the Tank Board (1944).

Gibb's wartime impact was greatest in tank production. In 1943 he galvanised the Directorate of Tank Design into action and the result was the Centurion, a medium tank built by Vickers Armstrong which went into production just as the war ended — it played an important part in the Korean War and overseas sales of Centurions, 1945-60, earned the UK economy over £130 million. Just prior to D-Day in 1944, Gibb successfully implemented a crash programme to fit Sherman tanks with the British 17 pounder gun, thereby enabling them to match the 88 mm gun fitted to German tanks. For these wartime services he was knighted in June 1945.

Throughout the war Gibb preserved his interest in Parsons and in 1944 he was appointed a joint managing director. Planning for the post-war situation, in which he (correctly) assumed that a backlog of orders for generating plant and a rising demand for electricity would expand the market for heavy electrical generating equipment, he began re-equipping the heavy machine shops at the Heaton Works. On returning as chairman and managing director of C A Parsons & Co Ltd, Sir Claude set about modernising the company's plant broadly with the purpose of building much larger generating sets. A new core building shop, measuring 315 feet by 60 feet and equipped with a 200 ton main crane, was built in nine months in 1946-47; the iron foundry was reconstructed with its capacity castings doubling in weight, up to 40 tons; new pipe shops followed in 1949-50; a six-storey design and research building was constructed in the early 1950s; and new buildings housing turbine blade and condenser construction and an apprentice training school were also added. To finance this investment, in 1947 C A Parsons & Co Ltd was converted into a public company with its capital raised from £450,000 to £2 million, which was increased again to £5 million in 1953 and £10 million in 1956.

At the same time Sir Claude oversaw the expansion of the production facilities of A Reyrolle & Co Ltd, large and specialised manufacturers of switchgear and associated equipment located at Hebburn, also on the Tyne. Reyrolle owned 60 per cent of C A Parsons & Co's capital and Gibb joined the Reyrolle board in 1944, became deputy chairman in 1945 and chairman in 1949 (until 1958). With these two complementary manufacturers of heavy electrical generating equipment behind him, Gibb was well positioned to seize the market opportunities that opened at home and abroad in the post-war world.

At home the conservatism of headquarters engineers in the Central Electricity Board and its successor, after nationalisation in 1948, the British Electricity Authority, at first led to the placing of orders for the relatively small generating sets of 30 MW and 60 MW and the manufacturers supported this in order to develop volume production. When Sir Josiah Eccles (qv) became deputy chairman of the Authority in 1954 and immediately brought F H S Brown (qv) in as generation design engineer the situation changed. Early in 1955 Brown was proposing '200 MW sets as the major element in the forward programmes for 1960-62' {Hannah (1982) 112}. By late 1957 Eccles and Brown proposed a 550 MW 'cross compound set' such as was common in America. Along with English Electric and AEI, Parsons were the only British manufacturers capable of supplying the turbines for these large sets. Yet Gibb in the early 1950s defected from the turbine manufacturers price ring — in order to secure more orders, on which to employ his new fixed capital investment at Heaton, and also to obtain a larger market share closer to a monopoly position.

While the home market for large sets remained problematic, Gibb turned to Canada where post-war industrial expansion created the demand for power and where there was a readiness to follow the American pursuit of scale economies. Against stiff opposition Parsons won the contract for the first of four 100 MW turbo generators for a new steam power station (named after Richard L Hearn) to be built by Ontario Hydro on the shores of Lake Ontario. Sir Claude, whose links with the Canadian engineers went back to 1932 when he had toured North America, visited Toronto in 1949 to negotiate the tender and by 1950, after other visits, he secured the contracts for the remaining three generators. Despite a major accident all four sets were in operation by winter 1953-54. When the Hydro system was extended Parsons won two more contracts, one for four 200 MW turbo generators in 1956 and one for two 300 MW generators in 1957. Parsons' reputation was by now so high in their field that they were approached by the Tennessee Valley Authority which wanted to install a 500 MW set. Despite the opposition of both European and American contractors, Parsons won this contract also, though in the midst of negotiations Sir Claude died. Some measure of the growth of the company under his chairmanship is indicated by the increase in total output of the generators installed by Parsons: in 1945 this totalled 247 MW; in 1959 it totalled 1,590 MW.

Gibb was first among the heads of the largest British electrical firms to advocate the application of atomic energy for the generation of electric power. As a member of the Technical Committee set up in 1946 reporting to Lord Portal the new Controller of Production of Atomic Energy, Gibb developed a warm admiration for both John Cockroft, the nuclear scientist in charge of the Council's Research Group at Harwell and Christopher

Hinton (qv), the engineer in charge of its Industrial Group at Risley. In 1946 Parson undertook the design and manufacture of the dc electro magnet and vacuum chamber for the Harwell 800 ton cyclotron. Next they supported Risley. The first initiative with industry in nuclear power

was taken by Hinton in 1947 when Risley was anxious to forge ahead with pressurised gas cooled reactors to produce power. Hinton asked Sir Claude Gibb for help from Parolle, the Reyrolle Parsons design subsidiary, and Gibb responded with his usual warmth; he would ensure that the firm did not undertake anything else likely to interfere with it {Gowing (1974) II, 185}.

Thereafter Parsons engineers worked closely with the Ministry of Supply: on the Pippa (a pilot natural uranium reactor — the least complex reactor — producing both power and plutonium) design study at Harwell in 1952 and with the Calder Hall team at Risley. When the first nuclear station (a dual purpose one, for power and plutonium production) was built at Calder Hall in Cumbria in 1954-56, Parsons supplied the turbo-alternators and the gas circulatory blowers.

For the specialised electrical equipment manufacturers like Parsons the problem in contracting for nuclear power stations was that they lacked a general ability. The newly-formed UK Atomic Energy Authority in 1954 therefore suggested that the turbo alternator manufacturers should join with the boilermakers to negotiate licences with the UKAEA for sharing in the design and construction of turnkey nuclear power stations. Sir Claude responded quickly and within eight weeks had formed the Nuclear Power-Plant Co Ltd a consortium of eight companies: A Reyrolle & Co Ltd; Sir Robert McAlpine & Sons Ltd; Clarke, Chapman & Co Ltd; Head, Wrightson & Co Ltd; Whessoe Ltd; Strachan & Henshaw Ltd; and Alexander Findlay & Co Ltd; besides Parsons. The NPPC won the contract (worth about £40 million) for the Bradwell nuclear power station, one of the first Magnox designs — a gas cooled reactor in which the nuclear fuel was encased in magnesium alloy cans. Gibb triumphantly announced in 1958 that the design and construction experience gathered from Calder Hall 'would enable savings of many millions of pounds to be made on each nuclear station built' {Gibb (1958) 82}. In fact the capital cost of Bradwell exceeded estimates by the remarkably low level of 10-20 per cent. However, in contrast to conventional projects which were only a few months late, the first four nuclear power stations overran their construction times by two or more years and completion of Bradwell, due in 1960, delayed until 1962. The high hopes of nuclear advocates like Sir Claude Gibb were not immediately realised: 'the overall cost per kWh of electricity generated in the first two Magnox stations (Bradwell and Berkeley) in their early years was nearly two-and-half times that of the best coal-fired stations which the CEGB were then commissioning. This added financial losses of £20 million (3 per cent of the industry's turnover) annually to electricity costs' {Hannah (1982) 243}, but by the time Sir Christopher Hinton began to lead the nuclear retreat in the 1960s Gibb was dead.

In his first enthusiasm for nuclear power Gibb in 1957 decided to establish a Nuclear Research Centre (opened 1959) at Heaton. In 1957, too, he secured a supply of nuclear graphite (needed as a moderator material, for the nuclear programme to be expanded): with the consent of the UK Atomic Energy Authority he formed a joint company (The Anglo-Great Lakes Corporation Ltd) with the Great Lakes Carbon Corporation of America to build a plant for the production of 10,000 tons of nuclear graphite and 5,000 tons of commercial-grade graphite per annum. The agreement was signed in February 1957 and by June 1958 the factory was in production — an astonishing speed which, characteristically, Gibb achieved by his own 'personal drive and direction in the whole period of negotiation and construction' {Hinton (1959) 92}.

It is a moot point whether Gibb's commitment to nuclear power served the best interests of C A Parsons Ltd and the heavy electrical engineering industry. While more manpower and talent were shifted into the company's nuclear energy equipment contracts the conventional side ran into technical problems, with massive turbine failure in its 500 MW sets. Simultaneously in the 1960s Britain's share of the world's conventional turbine market fell relative to that of America.

Sir Claude Gibb's achievements were recognised professionally, industrially and nationally. Elected an FRS in 1946, he served on the council of the Royal Society in 1955-57 and was vice president, 1956-57. A vice-president of the Institution of Mechanical Engineers, 1945-51, he received its Hawksley medal (twice), its Parsons memorial medal and, most coveted, its James Watt international medal. He was president of the engineering section of the British Association in 1957; chairman of the council of the International Electrical Association, of the Athlone Fellowship committee, and of the committee on the organisation of government research expenditure; a member of the Ridley committee on the use of coal, gas and electricity; of the Board of Trade's informal advisory group on exports, and of the council of King's College, Newcastle upon Tyne. He received honorary degrees from London and Durham and besides his knighthood was appointed KBE, in 1956.

In 1925 he married Margaret Bate (d 1969), daughter of William Harris, an ironmonger of Totnes; they met while he was on leave in England during the war. They had no children. Sir Claude Gibb suffered a severe heart attack in 1948 and two more in 1953. He died as the result of a fourth one at Newark, New Jersey, airport on 15 January 1959 and left £294,162 gross.

DAVID J JEREMY

Writings:

(with R W Chapman) 'The Stresses in Floors of Elevated Cylindrical Tanks' *Journal of the Institution of Engineers of Australia* 4 (1923).

'Post-war Land Turbine Development' *Proceedings of the Institution of Mechanical Engineers* 120 (1931).

'The Evolution of Design' *ibid* 127 (1933).

'Steam Turbines, Their Manufacture and Some Applications' *Proceedings of the Cleveland Institution of Engineers* No 5 (1935).

'Steam Turbines' *Journal of Cambridge University Engineering Society* 11 (1935).

'The Influence of Operating Experience on the Design and Construction of Turbines and Alternators' *Journal of the Institution of Engineers of Australia* 8 (1936).

'Looking Both Ways' *Journal of the Institution of Production Engineers* 27 (1946).

Britain's Energy: A New Conception (Greenock: Telegraph Print Works, 1949).

'Planning for Production Efficiency' *Transactions of the Manchester Association of Engineers* 1951.

'Report on Investigation into the Failure of Two 100 MW Turbo Generators' *Proceedings of the Institution of Mechanical Engineers* 169 (1955).

'Some Engineering Problems in Connection with the Industrial Application of Nuclear Energy' *Ibid* 171 (1957).

'The Development of Nuclear Energy for Electricity Supply Overseas' *Proceedings of the Tenth British Electrical Power Convention, Brighton, 1958* (Northampton: Lea & Co Ltd, 1958).

A more complete list of Gibb's writings, with 11 more titles of a less technical nature and published after 1945, is included in Hinton (1959), below.

Sources:

Unpublished

MCe.

PrC.

Published

A T Bowden, 'Sir Claude D Gibb — Engineer' *Transactions of the North East Coast Institution of Engineers and Shipbuilders* 77 (1960-61).

DNB.

Margaret Gowing, *Independence and Deterrence: Britain and Atomic Energy, 1945-1952* (2 vols, Macmillan, 1974).

Leslie Hannah, *Engineers, Managers and Politicians. The First Fifteen Years of Nationalised Electricity Supply in Britain* (Macmillan, 1982).

Sir Christopher Hinton, 'Sir Claude D Gibb' *Memoirs of Fellows of the Royal Society* 5 (1959).

John D Scott, *Vickers. A History* (Weidenfeld & Nicolson, 1962).

Stock Exchange Official Year-Book 1939, 1946, 1947, 1958, 1959.

WWW.

Sir George Gibb (courtesy of the National Railway Museum).

GIBB, Sir George Stegmann

(1850-1925)

Railway manager

George Stegmann Gibb was born in Aberdeen on 30 April 1850, the youngest son of the seven children of Alexander Gibb (1806-67), a civil engineer, and his wife Margaret née Smith, daughter of a Balmoral architect. He was educated locally at Aberdeen Grammar School before entering a solicitor's office as an articled clerk, qualifying as an LLB of London University. He began his career in legal work in commercial offices in London between 1872 and 1877. Next he became an assistant in the solicitor's office of the Great Western Railway for three years. Between 1880 and 1882 he practiced on his own account, also in London. In 1882 he was appointed solicitor to the North Eastern Railway at a salary of £2,000 a year and by 1891 had established himself as an able assistant and adviser to the general manager, Henry Tennant (qv), whom he succeeded in 1891 at an annual salary of £3,000.

Gibb inherited the management of the North Eastern at a time when diminishing returns were causing general concern in the industry. Over the next fifteen years he responded aggressively to the problem, changing the North Eastern from a relatively successful if somewhat staid railway into an exemplar of advanced managerial practice. He took a firm stand against some of the more conservative elements in the railway world, signifying his disdain for them by wearing a tweed suit in the office. Among his early and most enduring reforms was the establishment of a traffic apprenticeship scheme involving the recruitment of bright young men from the universities and business world, such as R L Wedgwood (qv) and E C Geddes (qv), and their rapid promotion into responsible positions in the traffic department. Concerned by escalating operating costs at a time when charges were controlled by legislation, he also set in motion a detailed appraisal of operating methods, organisation, and information systems and between 1900 and 1902 radically altered the company's approach in all three areas. The decline in operating efficiency was reversed and the North Eastern established firmly as the pacesetter in the railway world. Under his innovating management the company became the first main line railway to electrify a part of its system and developed its relatively progressive relations with the Amalgamated Society of Railway Servants to a situation of formal collective bargaining. His management in the 1890s was characterised also by some positive thought and action on the company's relationships with the ports of the North East coast and on traffic working on Tyneside where a heavy programme of investment was commenced in 1893.

Gibb's outstanding service as general manager ended in December 1905 when, following the board of directors' refusal to grant him a managing directorship (they awarded him instead £5,000 and a complimentary resolution), he became deputy chairman and managing director of the Underground Electric Railway Co of London and chairman and managing director of one of its operating units, the Metropolitan & District Railway.

At this time, UERL was in serious financial straits and Gibb's success in managing the North Eastern's urban passenger traffic, his progressive record on management techniques and finally his knowledge of London transport problems, through his service on the Royal Commission on London Transport between 1903 and 1905 (for which he was knighted), made him just the person UERL needed to revive its fortunes. An annual salary of £8,000 (£3,000 more than the North Eastern was by then paying him) secured his acceptance and on 1 January 1906 he moved to London. Having lost his services as general manager, the North Eastern promptly elected him to their board.

Gibb left the North Eastern a profitable, efficient company well positioned to benefit from the upswing in trade of 1906-14 and superbly resourced with young managers capable of running the railway for another generation. He joined an organisation close to bankruptcy and whose business strategy in key areas was founded on a mistaken comparison between British and American transport conditions. His reaction was to commission a searching examination of its business. Having failed in 1906 to persuade the London County Council to take it over in return for financial assistance, he pushed ahead with changes in pricing policy, closer integration of the activities of the different operating units, and restriction of competition with other London transport operators. Supported by an injection of youthful managerial talent from the North Eastern, including Frank Pick (qv), and from the USA, the UERL companies under Gibb's managership made financial progress and bankruptcy was avoided. His public image at this time was of a courtly official of great capacity and considerable charm.

The task of ensuring the survival of UERL was a colossal one and notwithstanding the success which Gibb had in achieving this, in May 1910 he exchanged his onerous responsibilities for the company, as well as his directorship of the North Eastern, for the chairmanship of the Government's newly-formed Road Board at the considerably reduced annual salary of £3,000. The reasons for the change have never been established fully, but although the move was in salary terms a reduction, in Civil Service terms the pay was very high (the head of the Civil Service received at that time £2,500) and was necessary, the Treasury was told, to get 'a good man'. At Gibb's insistence the job brought with it also a guarantee of ten years' service.

Gibb's chairmanship of the Board aroused controversy in Parliament and amongst the road lobby for much of the Board's existence. Its establishment had been sanctioned by Parliament in 1909 because of dissatisfaction with the failure of existing authorities to develop an effective road system. The new body was given powers to finance improvements to existing roads and to build new ones. Over 90 per cent of the monies disbursed in its lifetime were for the former purpose. While this solved the dust problem, the concentration on improvement rather than development, and the fact that the Board was essentially a 'one man show' whose policy was that of its chairman, a former railway magnate, led to the feeling that the railway interest had captured the Board and were preventing the building of new roads that would compete with railways. Whatever the truth (the Board's activities have never been assessed impartially), the Board was unpopular also because of its lack of direct accountability to Parliament and the Treasury's dislike of its financial foundations which, by allocating the proceeds of specific taxes to its funds, flew in the face of established practice. With the creation in 1919 of the Ministry of Transport, therefore, the Board lapsed, largely unlamented.

Although remaining Road Board chairman throughout the First World War, Gibb, who had served in 1901 on the War Office Committee on Reorganisation, was inevitably required for war service. He served on the Army Council and as a member and chairman of the Government Arbitration Board (Committee on Production) in 1915-18. By 1918, however, developing proposals for legislative reorganisation of the railways were alarming railway circles, and in November 1918 the North Eastern board decided to ask Gibb to advise them on their relationships with Government and on the 'grouping'. From 1 January 1919 he was back on the payroll (at an initial fee of £3,000 a year) and the advisory relationship lasted until 1922 when the final shape of the industry emerged. A short period as chairman of the Oriental Telephone Co completed his business life.

Gibb's rejuvenation of the North Eastern and his leading involvement in the railway reform movement around 1900 has left him an assured place in transport history as a prime mover in the development and implementation of improved methods of operational control in the industry. The virile organisation he built up proved an excellent training ground for some outstanding young railway administrators and the management techniques he adopted pointed the way Edwardian railway management in Britain needed to move to retain its edge. His concept of a traffic apprenticeship scheme is carried on to this day and after his death in 1925 he left behind an affectionate and grateful group of men who owed to his vision their first real chance in business life and who in the inter-war years emerged in many cases at the heads of their respective callings.

Gibb in 1881 married Dorothea Garrett Smith, nineteen year-old daughter of James William Smith, an artist. They had four sons and one daughter. Sir George Gibb died on 17 December 1925, leaving £46,501 gross.

R J IRVING

Writings:

PP, RC London Traffic (1903).

Sources:

Unpublished

PRO, Kew, Records of the North Eastern Railway Company, 1854-1923 RAIL 527. Records of the Road Board 1910-19, TI-11257; T27-216.

MCe.

PrC.

Published

Theodore C Barker and Michael Robbins, *A History of London Transport* (2 vols, George Allen & Unwin Ltd, 1963-74) 2.

R Bell, *Twenty Five Years of the North Eastern Railway, 1898-1922* (Railway Gazette, 1951).

C H Ellis, 'The Lewin Papers Concerning Sir George Gibb' *Journal of Transport History* 5 (1962).

Godfrey Harrison, *Alexander Gibb, the Story of an Engineer* (Geoffrey Bles, 1950).

Robert J Irving, *The North Eastern Railway Company 1870-1914: An Economic History* (Leicester: Leicester University Press, 1976).

R Jeffreys, *The Kings Highway* (Batchworth Press, 1949).

WWW.

GIBBONS, Edward Stanley

(1840-1913)

Stamp dealer and publisher

Edward Stanley Gibbons was born in Plymouth on 21 June 1840, the younger son of William Gibbons, a pharmaceutical chemist, and his wife Elizabeth née Langridge. Educated at Halloran's Collegiate Establishment in the town, he took a boy's interest in stamp collecting when the hobby spread in the early 1850s, a Victorian penny postage and the first postage stamps having been introduced in Britain in the year of Gibbon's birth. Gibbons left school in 1855 and took up a junior clerkship in the Naval Bank in Plymouth, intending to enter the banking profession, but the unexpected death of his elder brother William required his presence in the family business. The chemist's shop was sufficiently quiet for him to develop his interest in stamps which he was beginning to buy and sell even in his teens. His father, realising his son's business acumen, set aside a desk for Stanley's use and on that desk, virtually, the firm of Stanley Gibbons was founded.

Within three years his little business had prospered so much that Stanley took over a room above the shop for the infant firm of E Stanley

Gibbons, and then, before long, further dignity was achieved by the addition of a spurious comma, Stanley, Gibbons & Co. Two or three years later, about the year 1862, the death of his father made Stanley, now in his early twenties, the proprietor of the firm. He thereupon disposed of the pharmacy and devoted himself entirely to stamp trading.

Soon after this, in 1863, the classic and romantic incident occurred which gave rise in due course to the firm's trade mark. A couple of sailors, having noticed stamps in the window, came in and asked if he bought stamps. Receiving an affirmative answer, they told him they had some on board ship and would produce them. They returned the next day with a sack which they had won in a raffle in Cape Town, and which they emptied on to a table. It contained thousands of 'Cape Triangulars' for which they were glad to receive £5; Gibbons himself later estimated that he had made a profit of £500 on the deal.

By now he was importing stamps from all over the world. In 1865 he produced his first monthly price list, the fore-runner of the long-famous *Gibbons Catalogue*, which now (1983) is published in 22 parts. By 1870 he had made further ventures and had published his first albums, the *Improved* and the *V R*. Two years later he moved from Treville Street (the home was over the shop) to 8 Lockyer Street, and after another two years from Plymouth to London, where he took a house on Clapham Common. This proved inconvenient for business so he moved in 1876 to 8 Gower Street, where he remained for the rest of his active business life. During this time he declined offers from philatelists who desired to join him, even though their coming would have introduced substantial new capital into the firm.

By 1890, at the comparatively early age of fifty, he had accumulated a respectable fortune and decided to retire to his Thames-side villa and enjoy the chance of world-wide travel. A number of well-known collectors were interested in purchasing the business, and eventually in July 1890 Charles J Phillips, who had been a spare time dealer, offered to buy the entire business, stock, goodwill and trading name, for £25,000. The business was turned into a private limited company (with a capital of £20,000), with Phillips as managing director, while Gibbons himself was chairman. In the same month, the new company issued the first-ever house organ, *Stanley Gibbons Monthly Journal* (the comma had now been dropped).

From then onwards, all the developments were the work of the new firm rather than of Gibbons himself; the move to 391 Strand took place in 1893. In the next decade, Gibbons enjoyed to the full his penchant for travel, circling the world three times, visiting India half a dozen times, and spending many months in France and North Africa, and writing entertaining accounts of his journeys for the *Monthly Journal*. He naturally took the opportunity of buying for the firm, and on one occasion bought the complete stock of a provisional stamp at a post office in Wadi Halfa.

From his boyhood, Gibbons had a wide range of interests. At his first Plymouth home he formed 'The Amateur Colosseum of Science and Arts', complete with curios, library, and 'philosophical apparatus', and before he left Plymouth at the age of thirty-four had been president of the Plymouth Literary Association.

Gibbons never married. He died on 17 February 1913 (a year before his firm received the accolade of Royal Warrant Holder from George V), and left £13,172 gross.

O A BECKERLEGGE

Writings:
Numerous articles in *Stanley Gibbons Monthly Journal.*

Sources:

Unpublished

BCe.

PrC.

Published

The Stanley Gibbons Centenary (Gibbons, 1956).

GIBBS, Henry Hucks

1st Lord Aldenham

(1819-1907)

Merchant and merchant banker

Henry H Gibbs (courtesy of W M Mathew).

Henry Hucks Gibbs was born in Powis Place, Bloomsbury, London, on 31 August 1819, the eldest son of George Henry Gibbs (1785-1843) and his wife Caroline née Crawley (1794-1850), and the grandson of Dorothea Barnett Hucks (1760-1820) and Antony Gibbs (1756-1815), the founder of the merchant house of Antony Gibbs & Sons. The Gibbs were of Devon origin. The Hucks family, into which Antony Gibbs married in the 1780s, stood on the margins of the aristocracy and was the source of a landed inheritance in Hertfordshire and Oxfordshire for George Henry Gibbs on the death of his mother in 1820. Of this, Clifton Hampden manor in Oxfordshire passed to Henry in the 1840s, Aldenham House and Burston manor in Hertfordshire following in 1850.

impression gained overall is one of great personal confidence, nourished by social rank, City success, and intellectual authority. This no doubt contributed significantly to his behaviour in business, especially on the daunting strategic decisions taken between the 1860s and 1880s. At the very height of his firm's participation in the guano trade, and at a time when a Peruvian commissioner was suspiciously scrutinising his accounts in London, he summoned his uncle William from his Somerset retreat, placed the house under his direct charge, and took his family off on an eighteen-week European tour. When chastised by William for the duration of his absence, he defended himself in little more than a dozen lines. As for the commissioner, if he needed information on any point, 'let him dirty his fingers himself. We wash our hands of it' {*ibid*, 24 Oct 1857}. In old age, in an exchange with an uncooperative Sir Philip Currie, Permanent Under-Secretary of State at the Foreign Office, concerning British railway interests in Chile, Gibbs expressed the hope that 'the FO will not forget that my House really does know all that can be known about the West Coast of S America'. {Blakemore (1974) 132} A breathtaking dismissiveness was revealed in a parliamentary debate on elementary education in 1891 when Gibbs made some assertions about school finances in a Hertfordshire parish. Asked to specify the place, he replied: 'I will not give the name, and then I cannot be contradicted'. {*PD* 3rd ser 352, Col 20} Such public arrogance, however, was countered by a notable measure of private charm and amiability. This is clear from the tone and content of much of his private correspondence. He also carried unusual qualities of determination into his advanced years. Eager to prove that decrepitude had not yet set in, he ran at a stream near Aldenham House on his seventieth birthday and leapt safely to the other side. When he attempted the same feat at eighty, however, his old body failed him and he landed in the water.

Henry Hucks Gibbs was elevated to a barony in 1896. He married in 1845 Louisa Anne Adams (1818-97), granddaughter of William Cockayne, Sixth Viscount Cullen. They had five sons and a daughter. It was at Aldenham House, the old Hucks inheritance from which he took his title, that he died, aged eighty-eight, on 13 September 1907, leaving £668,211 gross.

WILLIAM M MATHEW

Writings:

The Game of Ombre (pp, 1874).

Letters in Bonamy Price *Chapters on Practical Economy* (Kegan Paul, 1878).

Letter to the Marquess of Salisbury on the Depreciation of Silver (pp, 1876).

The Double Standard (Effingham Wilson, 1881).

with Henry R Grenfell, *The Bimetallic Controversy* (Effingham Wilson, 1886).

Pedigree of the Family of Gibbs (pp, 1890).

A Colloquy on Currency (Effingham Wilson, 1893).

GIBBS Henry Hucks

Sources:

Unpublished

Guildhall Library, London, Antony Gibbs & Sons Ltd, family and business archives.

MCe.

PrC.

Correspondence with present Lord Aldenham, 1981-83.

William M Mathew, 'Anglo-Peruvian Commercial and Financial Relations, 1820-1865' (London PhD, 1964).

Published

Harold Blakemore, *British Nitrates and Chilean Politics, 1886-1896: Balmaceda and North* (Athlone Press, 1974).

Sir John Clapham, *The Bank of England. A History* (Cambridge: Cambridge University Press, 1944).

DNB.

Robert Greenhill and Rory Miller, 'The Peruvian Government and the Nitrate Trade, 1873-1879' *Journal of Latin American Studies* 5 (1973).

Robert Greenhill, 'Merchants and Latin American Trades' in D C M Platt (ed), *Business Imperialism, 1840-1930* (Oxford: Clarendon Press, 1977).

—, 'The Nitrate and Iodine Trades, 1880-1914' in *ibid.*

Samuel Dana Horton, *The Silver Pound and England's Monetary Policy Since the Restoration* (Macmillan, 1887).

David Joslin, *A Century of Banking in Latin America* (Oxford University Press, 1963).

Thomas W Keeble, *Commercial Relations between British Overseas Territories and South America, 1806-1914* (Athlone Press, 1970).

William M Mathew, *The House of Gibbs and the Peruvian Guano Monopoly* (Royal Historical Society, 1981).

Wilfred Maude, *Antony Gibbs & Sons Limited, Merchants and Bankers, 1808-1958* (pp, 1958).

PD 3rd ser 352 (1 July 1891), 4th ser 1 (25, 20 Feb, 9 Mar 1892).

Bonamy Price, *Chapters on Practical Political Economy* [Appendix including correspondence with H H Gibbs] (Kegan Paul, 1878).

Richard S Sayers, *The Bank of England, 1891-1944* (3 vols, Cambridge: Cambridge University Press, 1976).

Times 14 Sept 1907.

Charles Welch, *Modern History of the City of London* (Blades & Co, 1896).

WWMP.

WWW.

554

Herbert C Gibbs (courtesy of Lord Aldenham).

GIBBS, Herbert Cokayne

1st Lord Hunsdon

(1854-1935)

Merchant banker

Herbert Cokayne Gibbs was born at Frognal, Hampstead, London, on 14 May 1854, fourth son of Henry Hucks Gibbs (qv), later First Baron Aldenham, and Louisa Anne, daughter of William Adams. He was educated at Winchester, 1868-72, and then Trinity College, Cambridge (BA 1877). He joined the family merchant bank of Antony Gibbs & Sons in 1879, and after representing them in South America in 1880-81, was admitted as a partner in 1882. The firm had been transformed in the mid-nineteenth century from a minor London commission house into one of the richest merchant banks in the City by the Peruvian guano monopoly which it had held. It had, however, substantial interests elsewhere, especially in Australia. When Herbert Gibbs joined the firm its chief South American interest, for which he was increasingly responsible from the 1890s, was Chilean nitrates. During the First World War he represented Antony Gibbs & Sons in dealings with the Ministry of Munitions' Explosives Supply Department, and was instrumental in obtaining hundreds of thousands of tons of soda nitrate worth several million pounds. The firm's commission was voluntarily waived.

After the First World War the Chilean nitrate producers were hit by heavy competition from Germany, the USA and Yugoslav companies such as Baburizza Lukinovic. The Chilean Nitrate Producers' Association was slow to react to changed conditions, and maintained unrealistically high prices which led to the accumulation of large surplus stocks by November 1920. In January 1921, as the crisis advanced, the Chilean producers asked the Gibbs firm to organise a nitrate pool, of which Herbert Gibbs was selected as chairman. His firm's losses in the slump were known to be large: it was reported in May that they and the firm of Weir together held 700,000 out of almost 1 million tons of nitrate lying unsold in Europe, while a further 1.4 million tons of prepared nitrate were stored in Chile. Gibbs had actually contracted to sell all the nitrate they held save 18,000 tons, but the consumers had declared they were unable to accept delivery and had thrown it back on the pool. Gibbs had bought their large stocks at a price of 17s 6d per quintal, but by June 1921 the price was cut to 14s with reductions staggered to 9s 3d by May 1922. This represented a loss of several million pounds to the firm, which led it to reduce its commitment to the Chilean nitrate trade. Matters were further complicated by the anti-British intrigues of the Stickstoff Syndicate masterminded by the German financier Hugo Stinnes. The unemployment and suffering caused in Chile by the suspension of nitrate production was another disturbing, and politically threatening, element in the crisis.

Herbert Gibbs went to Chile on behalf of the Nitrate Pool in September 1921, and negotiated an agreement signed on 11 October whereby the Association of Nitrate Producers paid compensation of £1.5 million to the London and other buyers. Of this sum the Gibbs firm received 92 per cent, or £1,377,180. By that time the Chilean nitrate industry seemed 'a dead horse' {*South Pacific Mail* of Valparaiso, 13 Oct 1921}, and in 1922 the Gibbs's nitrate interests were separated from their other business and absorbed into the Cia Exportadora de Salitre de Chile. Whereas Gibbs had previously provided all their own finance for the nitrate business, they henceforth participated with Baring, Rothschild and Schroder. In 1928 Gibbs's nitrate subsidiary was absorbed by the newly-formed Chilean Nitrate of Soda Distributors Co, a sales corporation embracing the whole industry formed at the instigation of the Chilean Minister of Finance. However, in July 1930, prompted by fear of domination by the Guggenheim interests of the USA, the Chilean Government passed the Cosach Law making a government monopoly of nitrate and iodine. In this new Cosach organisation, Chileans held 37 per cent of the stock, the USA 35 per cent and the British (chiefly Gibbs) 24 per cent. Cosach was scandalously ill-managed, and its collapse in late 1931 would have bankrupted the Anglo-South American Bank, and would have started a panic in London, but for the intervention of the Bank of England and all the clearing banks except Lloyds. It was widely felt that the Cosach crisis could not have developed in such acute form if Gibbs had chosen to retain leadership in Chilean nitrate: politically it seemed 'a great pity that the definite identity of Great Britain in the Chilean nitrate industry should have been lost' {PRO FO 371/15080, despatch 297 of Sir Henry Chilton, 20 Nov 1931}.

Herbert Gibbs was involved in all this and attended almost daily at his City office until 1933. He paid only two visits in over fifty years to the continent where his firm transacted so much of their business; and although it is true that other partners, such as his cousin Brien Cokayne (1864-1932), Governor of the Bank of England 1918-20 (afterwards created Lord Cullen of Ashbourne), spent longer periods in South America, such absentee British capitalism resulted in business stagnation and political unpopularity. 'We shall begin to get a move on when directors are forced by law to travel annually to parts of the world in which their companies are interested', one diplomat wrote privately, 'national feeling here is rising against foreign companies ... whose directors are too old or have not the time to spare to come out and study the requirements of the country' {PRO FO 371/12737, Sir Malcolm Robertson to F W Goodenough, 1928}.

In the 1880s Herbert Gibbs was a director of the Anglo-American Brush Electric Light Corporation, and was for fifty years a director or chairman of the Rio de Janeiro City Improvement Co. He was on the board of the Pan de Azucar Nitrate Co until 1926, and chaired the London board of the Australian Mutual Provident Society.

He became a Commissioner of the Public Works Loans Board in 1884, rising to deputy-chairman in 1905 and chairman in 1921. Some 65 Labour MPs unsuccessfully voted in the House of Commons in 1930 for his removal from this Board as revenge for a speech in 1926 in which Gibbs averred 'while the miners were our enemies, we should not feed them' {*Times* 24 May 1935}. Gibbs was made an Income Tax Commissioner in

president of University College, Swansea in 1920 and apart from a brief interlude remained president until 1929. His name is perpetuated in Neuadd Gilbertson, a hall of residence.

In spite of his many activities Gilbertson was a quiet man who preferred to remain in the background and to avoid publicity as much as possible. Against medical advice he continued to be active during the 1920s not only in industry but in leisure pursuits. He was a self-taught but extremely capable cabinet maker and water-colourist. One of his leisure interests, about which his daughter Mary spoke enthusiastically, was to undertake long journeys by motor car in Europe at a time when motoring holidays were something of a pioneering adventure. On one of these he contracted diphtheria in Roumania and returned to Britain to die on 8 October 1929. He left £40,031 gross.

GRAEME M HOLMES

Sources:

Unpublished

PRO, W Gilbertson & Co company file, BT31/31031/21848.

University College, Swansea archives.

University of Warwick, Modern Records Centre, FBI records.

BCe.

MCe.

PrC.

Personal family notes of Arthur G Gilbertson.

Information from Arthur G Gilbertson and Mrs Hugh Vivian (née Mary Gilbertson).

Published

Edward H Brooke, *Chronology of the Tinplate Works of Great Britain* (Cardiff: William Lewis, 1949).

Cambria Daily Leader 24 Apr 1896, 23 June 1920, 9, 10 Oct 1929.

James C Carr and Walter Taplin, *History of the British Steel Industry* (Oxford: Basil Blackwell, 1962).

John H Davies, *History of Pontardawe and District* (Llandybie: Christopher Davies, 1967).

David W Dykes, 'The University College of Swansea' in W G V Balchin (ed), *Swansea and its Region* (University College, Swansea, on behalf of the British Association for the Advancement of Science, 1971).

Iron and Coal Trades Review 28 Mar 1913, 25 Sept 1914, 15 Nov 1915, 11 Oct 1929.

Walter E Minchinton, *The British Tinplate Industry, a History* (Oxford: Clarendon Press, 1957).

John Murray, Jr, *The Magdalen College Record* (pp, 1909).

GILCHRIST, Percy Carlisle

(1851-1935)

Consultant metallurgist

P C Gilchrist (from F W Harbord, 'The Thomas-Gilchrist basic process, 1879-1937', Journal of the Iron & Steel Institute vol 136 (1937).

Percy Carlisle Gilchrist was born in Lyme Regis, Dorset, on 27 December 1851, the elder son of Alexander Gilchrist, a barrister who died aged thirty-five, and his wife Anne née Burrows. Percy attended Felsted School, Essex, and, from 1868 to 1871, the Royal School of Mines in London where he gained the associateship in both mining and metallurgy and in 1870 was awarded the School's Murchison medal. In 1874 or 1875 he was employed as chemist at a works at Cwm Avon near Port Talbot in Glamorganshire: what he was doing in the intervening period is not known, but at that time a year's interval between graduation and the start of professional employment was not uncommon because of the low demand for trained metallurgists. In the autumn of 1876 Gilchrist moved to become analytical chemist to the Blaenavon Co's iron and steel works situated in Monmouthshire, near the head of one of the valleys east of Merthyr Tydfil. A few months later he reluctantly agreed to the requests of his cousin, Sidney Gilchrist Thomas (qv), that he should carry out the experimental work necessary to test and develop Thomas's ideas on dephosphorisation. Thus there occurred the partnership between the two men, Gilchrist finding the opportunities and means to conduct small-scale investigations in addition to his normal duties. The Blaenavon general manager, E P Martin, had to be admitted into the secret but, fortunately, became a helpful ally. In the autumn of 1878, following the publication of Thomas's seminal paper to the Iron and Steel Institute, the two cousins received a fresh offer of development aid, this time from Bolckow, Vaughan & Co in Cleveland; as a result Gilchrist moved to the Middlesbrough district where, during the next few years, he took a leading part in all the work done to make 'basic steelmaking' a reality.

Although he assisted Thomas in the preparation of several papers, he seems to have been content to leave to his cousin the marketing and business side of the invention. Nonetheless, as Thomas's health rapidly failed, Percy Gilchrist had some of the business thrust upon him. In 1882 he became managing director of the company, the Basic & Dephosphorizing Patents Co Ltd, set up by the patentees with interests in the process (Thomas, George James Snelus and Edward Riley) together with Thomas and Gilchrist's sponsors Bolckow, Vaughan & Co, to exploit the techniques for their mutual benefit. When, in 1894, the life of the significant patent expired, the company was wound up. At that time Bolckow, Vaughan's representative stated that 'the capital was £13 and there was only 6d a share called up ... On our share we received over £30,000.' {comment by Col J G S Davies, British Steel Corp, Bolckow, Vaughan & Co annual report (1894) 21}

Gilchrist was an original shareholder, and for some time from late 1882 alternate director with Thomas, in the North-Eastern Steel Co, created to build works in Middlesbrough to make rails and other products from the new 'basic' steel. Both A J Dorman (qv) and his partner A de Lande Long were original shareholders in this company, and Dorman was chairman from 1882 to 1884: it represented his first participation in steelmaking. In 1903 the North-Eastern Steel Co was taken over by Dorman, Long & Co.

Gilchrist during the 1880s worked hard to promote basic steelmaking by both converter and open-hearth furnace; he collated information from plants working the processes in various countries and did all he could to obtain British acceptance of basic steel by important engineering users and institutions such as the Admiralty and Lloyd's Register. He was instrumental in the appointment of Maximilian Mannaberg (qv) as manager of the new basic open-hearth steel plant owned by the Cliff family at Frodingham in North Lincolnshire.

In 1891 he was elected FRS and in the same year became a vice-president of the Iron and Steel Institute; later, in 1916, he was elected an honorary (life) vice-president. He was a member of several other bodies: the Institutions of Civil and Mechanical Engineers, the Society of Chemical Industry, and the Royal Society of Arts. The French Government appointed him Chevalier of the Légion d'Honneur.

In 1887 Gilchrist married Nora, daughter of Captain Fitzmaurice, RN: they had a son and daughter. By 1901 he had largely retired, and during the later years of his life he was an invalid. He died on 15 December 1935.

J K ALMOND

Sources:

Unpublished

British Steel Corporation, Northern Regional Records Centre, Middlesbrough, Bolckow, Vaughan & Co Ltd annual reports for 1893 and 1894, North-Eastern Steel Co Ltd papers.

BCe.

Published

H C H Carpenter, 'Percy Carlyle Gilchrist' *Memoirs of Fellows of the Royal Society* 2 (1936-38).

Reese Edwards, 'Percy Carlyle Gilchrist, FRS' *British Steelmaker* 17, no 11 (Nov 1951).

'Percy Carlisle Gilchrist' *Journal of the Iron & Steel Institute* 134 (1936).

Lilian Gilchrist Thompson, *Sidney Gilchrist Thomas. An Invention and Its Consequences* (Faber and Faber, 1940).

WWW.

Ronald B Gillett (courtesy of Gillett Brothers Discount Company plc).

GILLETT, Ronald Brodie

(1902-1965)

City discount house chairman

Ronald Brodie Gillett was born in London on 5 August 1902. The Gilletts had been bankers, originally in Oxfordshire, since at least 1820. Ronald Gillett's grandfather — George Gillett — was one of two brothers, who founded the discount house of Gillett Brothers & Co in 1867 and his father — Sir George Masterman Gillett, at one time chairman of the discount house — was a Labour MP who held ministerial office under Ramsay MacDonald. His mother was Edith Mary née Dixon. Ronald Gillett was educated at Bootham, the Quaker school, in York. On leaving school, he was for a short time in Barclays Bank, which in 1919 had absorbed Gilletts' other banking interests at Banbury and Oxford. He joined the discount house in 1922. He became company secretary in 1929, a director ten years later, and from 1946 until his death in 1965 he was chairman. He was also chairman of the London Discount Market Association from 1963 until early 1965.

It was Ronald Gillett's view that the discount market, of which he became one of the most senior members, performed a uniquely valuable function as an adjunct to the banking system and he was devoted both to his own house and to the market of which it formed part. He was likewise fascinated by the history of the techniques and traditions of bill-broking in the City of London. Although his approach to the market was to value its traditions, he was no mere traditionalist in any obvious sense. Indeed, he was perhaps the market's most original and articulate mind. Always he gave to its operations careful, continuing, and questioning thought, which no doubt owed something to his Dissenting background. He was constantly looking for ways in which the market could develop further and he — and his house — after the Second World War had much to do with the resurgence of the business in commercial bills, which were in fact the original reason for the market's existence. But he likewise wished to add to knowledge of his market and was active in educating a wider public in an understanding of the discount market (whether it was to university seminars, at the LSE or Hull, to visitors to his own discount house, or to courses in the City). It was during his chairmanship, too, that his house produced their famous book (subsequently translated into several foreign languages and running into four editions), *The Bill on London*, quickly to become a standard work. He was interested in the development of new money markets in countries like Canada and Australia and, more actively, his firm provided expertise to (and had a small capital interest in) discount houses in Johannesburg, South Africa, and Salisbury, Rhodesia. He was described as

a committed, competitive, enterprising discount broker who believed thoroughly in what he was doing and how he was doing it, and whose ideas carried too much of his own stamp to be universally accepted. {*Times* 24 Nov 1965}

He was also deeply serious, a man of decision as in the restructuring of his firm after the Second World War, when it became a public company with increased capital and an infusion of new management. Ronald Gillett died on 23 November 1965, leaving £41,157 gross. He was survived by his wife Hjordis Ottilia née Arvidson, whom he had married in 1936. They had no children.

J S G WILSON

Sources:

Unpublished

BCe.

PrC.

Gillett Brothers Discount Co Ltd, London, archives.

Published

'City Faces: Ronald Gillett' *Guardian* 24 Oct 1964.

Richard S Sayers, *Gilletts in the London Money Market, 1867-1967* (Oxford: Clarendon Press, 1968).

Audrey M Taylor, *Gilletts — Bankers at Banbury and Oxford* (Oxford: Clarendon Press, 1964).

Times 24 Nov 1965.

GILPIN, Sir Edmund Henry

(1876-1950)

Food machinery manufacturer

Edmund Henry (Harry as he was known) Gilpin was born in Nottingham on 4 February 1876 the youngest, and only boy in a family of four children. His father, Edmund Octavius Gilpin, was a stockbroker, married to Margaret Ann née Binns, both Quakers. Gilpin was educated at

GILPIN Sir Edmund Henry

E H Gilpin (courtesy of Mr Antony C Gilpin).

Ackworth School, near Pontefract, Yorkshire, but had to leave in 1891, at the age of fifteen, as a result of the failure of his father's firm.

He entered, straight from school, the employ of Joseph Baker & Sons, a small family business, with offices in City Road, London, and works in Willesden, dealing mainly in bakers' sundries of all kinds and shop fittings. Its annual turnover was then about £45,000. He started in the shipping office at a weekly wage of 10s but was soon 'moved up to the freer air of the showroom and began to learn the arts and crafts of salesmanship' {'Memories' (1945) 3}.

Joseph Baker, the Canadian founder of the firm, was by then increasingly entrusting the management to his four sons, one of whom, Joseph Allen Baker (chairman, 1902-18), had a profound influence on the young Gilpin. J A Baker was a devout Quaker, adult school leader, member of the LCC, and from 1905, Liberal MP for Finsbury, with a special concern for international peace (a concern carried on vigorously to this day by his youngest son, Lord (Philip) Noel-Baker); he was also the father-in-law of John (later Sir John) Braithwaite (qv) of the Quaker stockbroking firm. Baker watched keenly over Gilpin's career, and it was undoubtedly under his influence that Gilpin developed his own interests in adult education, politics and industrial relations. These concerns had deep and continuing roots in the two men's Quakerism, although Gilpin's active association with the Society of Friends diminished during and after the First World War as he was unable to accept its total commitment to pacifism. During that war, in addition to his business responsibilities, Gilpin served as chairman of the British Committee in Aid of the Italian Wounded, which sponsored the First British Red Cross Unit for Italy. This was a successor of the original contingent of the Friends' Ambulance Unit in Belgium and France and included a strong Quaker element. The Baker family, notably Allan and Philip, were prominent in the Unit, which was headed by the historian G M Trevelyan. For this service, Gilpin was awarded the Cross of Officer of the Crown of Italy (together with licence to wear this, issued by H M King George V).

Gilpin travelled as a salesman from 1893; meanwhile the engineering side of the business was expanding and diversifying and its turnover greatly increasing, so that, by the turn of the century, it had become the most important manufacturer of machinery for the food industry in the United Kingdom. In 1898, Baker gave him the challenging assignment of opening up markets in India, Burma, Malaya, Java, China and Japan, returning via Canada and the United States. 'Don't be downhearted if you don't get immediate results. We don't expect them' he was told {*ibid*, 6}. The trip lasted almost eighteen months and, in fact, after a difficult start, he eventually obtained some important orders, including equipment for biscuit factories in Burma and Japan, the latter taking three months of negotiation. There were many more orders from these countries in subsequent years and Gilpin became the firm's greatest salesman with unrivalled knowledge of overseas markets. When he re-visited Japan twenty-five years later, he found that the biscuit plant had successfully survived the great earthquake of 1923.

In 1902, the firm became a limited company with an authorised share capital of £200,000 (£180,000 issued), making its first issue of preference shares to the public. Gilpin and two colleagues 'went into open revolt' {*ibid*, 10} when it appeared that they were to be given no opportunity to take up any of the ordinary shares and, after much argument, they were allowed to buy a small number each year out of their salaries. This episode foreshadowed his subsequent public espousal of the causes of co-partnership and profit-sharing in industry. He became a director of the company in 1912, being given responsibility for the general direction of the business in both biscuit and chocolate manufacturing machinery.

With the outbreak of the First World War, and after some Quakerly hesitation, the company turned to the manufacture of munitions, notably the machining of shell forgings. Gilpin was also instrumental in persuading the War Office to replace the use of small field ovens by automatic bread machinery and ovens, erected in base bakeries, thus releasing thousands of men for other duties. Production was arranged jointly with one of Baker's main competitors, Perkins Engineers (formerly Werner, Pfleiderer & Perkins) of Peterborough, with the combined plant bearing the nameplate 'The Baker Perkins Standard Army Bread Plant'. Nearly all the bakery machinery ordered by the Government was made by these two firms. This proved to be the first step towards the eventual amalgamation of the two companies. Gilpin played a leading part in the protracted negotiations leading up to that amalgamation, which took place in 1920, the name of Baker Perkins Ltd being adopted three years later. In 1920 the authorised share capital was £400,000, though issued share capital, reserves, profit and loans amounted to £733,550. In the dramatic inter-war expansion of the firm, Gilpin's central role was strengthened by F C Ihlee of Perkins Engineers who had shared in working out the terms of the amalgamation and its implementation.

Gilpin's negotiating skill was also called on in 1919 to assist in the acquisition of the Werner & Pfleiderer factory in Saginaw, Michigan, thus adding production capacity to the company's existing sales organisation in the United States, Baker Perkins Inc. Similarly, in the inter-war years, he was involved in the market-sharing and pricing arrangements which Baker Perkins made with Savy Jeanjean & Cie, France, and Werner & Pfleiderer, Cannstatt, Germany. He also took part in establishing Baker Perkins in 1928 as the sole sales agency for the Forgrove Machinery Co Ltd, makers of wrapping machinery. He later became a director of Forgrove and was largely responsible for bringing it into the Baker Perkins Group in 1943. At the time of Gilpin's death in 1950, the annual turnover of Baker Perkins had risen to about £15 million.

Gilpin's excellent relations with Baker Perkins' customers enabled him to assist some of them in the development and expansion of their activities. For example, he advised Rowntrees on investing in Ryvita and also assisted them in an enquiry into the possibility of acquiring a subsidiary in the United States. He was far-sighted in recognising the potential of new processes, not least in 1929 in the initial stages of the development of Clarence Birdseye's invention of the quick-freezing of food products. He envisaged Baker Perkins securing the rights to build the necessary equipment both in the United States and in Britain. But his great efforts came to naught when the General Foods Co and Lever Brothers moved onto the scene. He regarded this as his 'worst failure', although from his 'Memoirs' it seems that his main mistake was to have put undue trust in some of those involved.

Generations of the Baker family, from the founder onwards, have attached great importance to good labour relations, and the firm has always had an outstanding record in this respect. Gilpin fitted easily into this progressive atmosphere. The philosophy he developed was expressed in an address on industrial relations in the post-war world which he delivered in 1946 to the Industrial Co-partnership Association, of which he became chairman shortly afterwards. He advocated representative works councils with access to full knowledge of the business of the company concerned; training for management, not least personnel management; and the setting up of a Royal Commission with wide terms of reference to consider the whole position of trade unions, to establish a Worker's Charter, and to advise generally on industrial relations. It was disappointing for Gilpin that his company did not introduce a profit-sharing scheme until 1947: this covered all regular employees who were over twenty-one and had been in the company's employment continuously for at least two years.

His extensive knowledge and experience in business and industrial relations brought Gilpin into the highest circles of the Liberal Party. He had unsuccessfully contested Finsbury, J A Baker's old seat, in 1922, and had then, in spite of favourable prospects, given up the candidature as he felt that the time and effort it would involve would conflict with his duty to Baker Perkins. He became active, however, in the organisation of the annual Liberal Summer Schools, and it was the latter's committee, in co-operation with Lloyd George, that took the initiative in setting up the Liberal Industrial Inquiry which, in 1928, published the Liberal Yellow Book, *Britain's Industrial Future*. Gilpin and his old friend, Benjamin Seebohm Rowntree (qv), were on the thirteen-member Executive Committee of the Inquiry, the chairman of which was another old friend, Walter Layton. Among the members, who included Lloyd George and J M Keynes (qv), Gilpin and Rowntree probably had the greatest experience in business and industrial relations, and they had a considerable hand in drafting the chapters on these subjects in the Yellow Book. Gilpin was chairman of the the executive of the Liberal Party Organisation, 1943-46, and became a member of the Liberal Council in 1949. He was also a vice-president and trustee of the National Liberal Club. Outside his business career, he probably looked back with the greatest satisfaction to his participation in the Liberal Industrial Inquiry.

From 1931, Gilpin was a member of the Export Credits Advisory Council of the Board of Trade, also becoming chairman of the Food Machinery Industrial and Export Group in 1949. In addition, he was a member of the council of the British Engineers Association. In 1946, he led a goodwill trade mission in Canada. This received recognition in the knighthood conferred on him in 1949.

Through extensive reading, Gilpin more than made up for the interruption of his formal education. Literary and Biblical quotations came easily to him, and he was a formidable orator of Churchillian style. He had a wealth of anecdotes, which he told in the appropriate dialects, and was a witty after-dinner speaker. In this capacity, he shone especially at the dinners of the Omar Khayyam Club, a society whose rather select membership included many leading authors and artists. Gilpin was always happy to bring friends like Keynes as guests to the Club's dinners. His recreational activities, which he took very seriously, included golf, billiards and bridge.

It was appropriate that Gilpin should endow a Gilpin elocution prize at his old school, Ackworth, of which he was the president of the Old Scholars Association, 1929-30. His oratory probably afforded him some compensation for his early dream of becoming an actor which had been frustrated by the family's financial difficulties and more particularly by the puritanical attitude of most Quakers to the arts at that time.

Gilpin was a director of the *Nation* along with Keynes, Layton and others, from 1923. After this was merged with the *New Statesman* he became a director of the *New Statesman and Nation* in 1947. Its editor, Kingsley Martin, wrote of him:

> He belonged to that increasingly rare type of Quaker business man who maintains his liberal and humanitarian outlook ... Though he was chairman of the Liberal Party Executive ... he cared primarily for the recovery of England and was prepared to co-operate with the Labour Government ... He was a man of great kindness and tolerance; he was tolerant even of the Socialist policies put forward in the journal of which he was a director {*New Statesman* 29 July 1950}.

Sir Harry Gilpin died in London on 24 July 1950, leaving £73,845 gross. He was survived by his wife, Olive Elizabeth née Capper, daughter of Samuel James Capper, whom he had married in 1901, and two sons, Bernard and Antony Capper.

ANTONY C GILPIN

Writings:

Anonymous contributions to *Britain's Industrial Future, Being the Report of the Liberal Industrial Inquiry* (Benn, 1928).

Industrial Relations in the Post-war World (Industrial Co-Partnership Association, 1946).

Intensive Investigations of Canadian Market by UK Engineering Mission *Board of Trade Journal* 12 Feb 1949.

'Fair Shares' *Spectator* 28 Apr 1950.

Sources:

Unpublished

BCe.

MCe.

PrC.

E H Gilpin, 'Memories of Fifty Four Years' (in Baker Perkins Ltd archives, unpublished typescript, 1945).

Information from Sir Ivor Baker.

Published

British Baker 28 July 1950.

Exports to Canada Report of the UK Engineering Mission, 1948 (HMSO, 1949).

The Friend 4 Aug 1950.

Irish Times 25 July 1950.

Manchester Guardian 25 July 1950.

Alexander Muir, *The History of Baker Perkins* (Heffer, 1968).

News Chronicle 25 July 1950.

The New Statesman and Nation 29 July 1950.

PD, HC, 5th ser 481, Cols 253–96 (21 Nov 1950).

Peterborough Citizen and Advertiser 28 July 1950.

The Record of the First British Red Cross Unit for Italy (pp, nd).

Times 25 July 1950.

WWW.

GIROUARD, Sir Edouard Percy Cranwill

(1867-1932)

Armaments manufacturer

Percy Girouard (courtesy of Mr Mark Girouard).

Edouard Percy Cranwill Girouard was born at Montreal on 26 January 1867, son of Desiré Girouard (1836-1911) and his second wife Essie (d 1879), daughter of Joseph Cranwill, a doctor from Cork. His father was a Canadian lawyer and politician, who was a Justice of the Supreme Court from 1895 and Deputy Governor General of Canada from 1910. Girouard was educated privately and at the Royal Military College at Kingston, Ontario, before becoming an engineer with the Canadian Pacific Railway in 1886. He was commissioned in the Royal Engineers in 1888, and was a railway traffic manager in 1890-95 at the Royal Ordnance Factories at Woolwich, near London, whose director-general was then Sir William Anderson (qv). In 1896 Girouard was sent to Egypt to accompany Kitchener's expedition to recover Dongola province in the Sudan. He helped to build the railway which was laid as Kitchener slowly advanced, receiving the DSO and other decorations for his work. Girouard, as director of Sudan Railways, was responsible for constructing the Sudan Military Railway on which work began in January 1897. 'He possessed rare good looks, bubbling high spirits, and that happy transatlantic ability to express himself crisply and tartly without causing offence ... Kitchener ... could never be angry for long with Girouard, who was the reigning favourite, privileged and indispensable' {Magnus (1958) 104}.

In 1898 Kitchener secured Girouard's appointment as president of the Egyptian Railway and Telegraph Administration, but on the outbreak of the Boer War in 1899 he was made railway director of the South African Field Force, with the rank of lieutenant-colonel. Girouard, with his magnificent command of detail and contagious feeling of personal invincibility, was highly efficient in organising the railways for the military campaign, despite his monocle 'the size of a Cathedral rose window' which gave him 'the air of the stage ass of burlesque' {Curtis (1951) 120, 140}. He was created KCMG in 1900. After the signature of peace, he was Commissioner of Railways in the Transvaal and Orange River Colony in 1902-4.

He returned to England in 1904 and sought a Liberal parliamentary candidature. 'The fact that he is a Canadian and has the whole French Canadian nation behind him and regarding him as the most distinguished man they have produced — excepting Laurier perhaps — is a factor of some importance in a struggle in which free trade is said to spell Little Englandism and anti-imperialism', the Liberal Chief Whip was advised {BM Add 46062, J Lawson Walton to Herbert Gladstone 28 October 1904}; but nothing came of the scheme, perhaps because Girouard lacked financial means.

After acting briefly as staff officer to the chief army engineer at Chatham, Girouard was made assistant quartermaster general for Western Command, based at Chester, in 1906. He was described at this time as 'A singularly ugly man with raucous voice and an assertive manner, harsh and vulgar, speaking of everyone by the [wrong] Christian name ... but of undeniable ability ... speaks much of his wife and wears an eyeglass [which] still further distorts [his] forbidding face' {NSWL, diary of G E Morrison 16 October 1905}. In 1907 Girouard was made a fellow of the Royal Colonial Institute and High Commissioner of Northern Nigeria, and was promoted Governor of the Protectorate in April 1908. He 'did more railway development in that colony probably than any other Governor has ever done in any British possession' {PRO FO 371/7242, A Edgecumbe to Sir Arthur Grant-Duff, 27 April 1922}, and took considerable, if controversial, interest in the systems of land tenure and land taxation.

He then became Governor and Commander-in-Chief of the East African Protectorate in July 1909. Despite acknowledging the need to develop African institutions and to maintain the authority of the chiefs, his proposals for African land, labour and taxation favoured the settlers. He forced the Masai to move, and made informal promises to settlers about new land allocations, while denying to the Colonial Office that he was doing either. 'Our governor is not playing fair; his mind and ambitions lead him into intrigues and bluffing' wrote one European in 1911 {Mungeam (1966) 263}. His handling of Masai land policy became regarded by the Colonial Office as both inefficient and deceitful, and his resignation was obtained in July 1912.

He had already made soundings about leaving government service to become a director of the Newcastle armourers, Armstrong, Whitworth, and joined their board forthwith. There were deep managerial and board weaknesses in the company which it was hoped to remedy by recruiting senior civil servants as directors. Sir George Murray, former head of the Treasury, and two former Secretaries of the Committee of Imperial Defence, Lord Sydenham and Sir Charles Ottley, joined Armstrongs' board around the same time as Girouard as part of an attempt to emphasise the company's quasi-official position in national defence. The company ranked as the third largest manufacturing employer in Britain, with 25,000 men in 1906. Girouard was put in charge of their Elswick works, which were riven with favouritism and ill-feeling, and required considerable changes of personnel and practices. He was little suited to the work, as one of his co-directors confided: 'He is a man with a super-abundance of driving-power, but I ... distrust his judgement; and his experience (for our purposes) is practically nil' {TWRO Rendel papers, box 166, Sir George Murray to Lord Rendel, 14 May 1912}. He was also given responsibility for Armstrongs' Canadian interests, and was made president of Armstrong Whitworth of Canada in 1914.

After the outbreak of war in August 1914, Girouard was loth to see the role of the big armament firms diminished by orders going to non-specialist engineering companies such as that of H S B Brindley (qv). 'It is not to our interest as munitions manufacturers to extend the scope of work nor is it ordinarily practicable to get good work from Companies who know little about the production of munitions', he wrote to Kitchener on 2 September 1914, although reluctantly conceding that in the current crisis 'armament manufacturers would patriotically place their experience at the disposal of the Government to organise the ordinary steel and machine works' to produce munitions {PRO 30/57/73}. By 20 March 1915 he was lamenting to Kitchener, 'the geese who can lay the golden eggs, *the armament companies*, are ... being slowly reduced to impotence' {PRO 30/57/73}. Despite these narrow views, he was appointed at Kitchener's instigation in March 1915 to the War Office's Armaments Output Committee where he shared with G M Booth (qv) responsibility for increasing munitions production.

Following the formation of the Ministry of Munitions in May 1915, Girouard was made its paramount Director General of Munitions Supply. From the outset his political chiefs were unimpressed with his personality, finding him too 'anxious to get things into his own hands and ... more concerned with his title and functions than with the business in hand' {BLO, Addison diary 27 May 1915}. They suspected him of favouring the erection of National Munitions Factories because they would not compete with Vickers and Armstrongs after the war; when he pushed the cause of technical experts within the Ministry, 'the princely salaries proposed by Girouard' for 'his numerous friends whom he has got in' were equally suspect {ibid 21 July 1915}. 'Girouard is no manager and spends too much time fussing about instead of sitting down and seeing that all the departments are doing their work', the deputy Minister noted, 'we are all struck with his very narrow outlook' {ibid 16 July 1915}. This inefficiency, coupled with 'his seemingly limitless officiousness' {Adams (1978) 47} led Lloyd George, the Minister of Munitions, to dismiss Girouard summarily on 22 July.

Note-heading of Glikstens (courtesy of Mr E Erdman).

The post-war pattern of the timber trade proved to be completely different from anything hitherto encountered. Wartime demand had left stocks at a low ebb, controls still existed and purchases of hardwoods from dollar areas were forbidden, and there was competition from alternative materials. As regards hardwoods, with UK forests depleted and no dollars to buy from the USA and Canada, the firm's main pre-war source of supply, Albert turned to West Africa, to the Gold Coast. Negotiations undertaken by a representative of the firm, were begun in 1946. After considerable bargaining Gliksten (West Africa) Ltd was incorporated in the Gold Coast Colony (now Ghana) — owning an option over 2,000 square miles of hardwood-bearing forest in the Gold Coast and Ashanti. The development entailed the reorganisation and mechanisation of the Stratford yards. The Belize interests were also brought completely up to date, giving the firm another important timber source. Exports of timber became a profitable part of Glikstens' business both from Ghana and British Honduras and to handle this trade a new company, Gliksten Export Sales Ltd, was formed in 1956. At home, after the war, Gliksten Doors Ltd was established and led the way in the introduction of the modern flush door: compared to existing doors they were free of all mouldings and edges which collect dust. In 1946, the Gliksten Group acquired the general joinery manufacturing firm of W Marsden & Co in Hull, and quickly adapted the factory to turn out modern flush doors.

Besides timber interests in Canada, sawmills and woodyards in Stratford, and directorships of many companies, Albert and his family derived a considerable income from property — the result of Reuben's shrewd investments in the West End of London. Albert devoted all his energies to his business and was not closely involved in public life (his name never appeared in *Who's Who*) or in the national organisation of the industry. In 1931-32, though, together with his brother Stanley, he purchased Charlton Football Club outright. The brothers reputedly put over £100,000 into the club as it rose from the Third Division in 1935, to the Second in the following year, and to the First in 1937.

Albert was a tall, handsome figure (six feet five inches in height) and is remembered as a hard-headed businessman, who was also extremely generous to those working for him when in need. Though he inherited a very sound business, he left it considerably expanded. He is said to have attacked the problem of colonial development with imagination and strove to benefit the countries in which he operated, giving promising colleagues a good deal of initiative in foreign ventures. He divided his time between homes at Beaconsfield, in Buckinghamshire, Belize, and the Gold Coast, but increasingly he made his home in Belize. He died there suddenly on 22 December 1951, leaving a considerable estate valued at £1,391,453 gross (duty paid, £1,111,782). He had married a French woman during the war: there were no children.

GEOFFREY TWEEDALE

Sources:

Unpublished

BCe.

PrC.

Private information from Edward Erdman and R E Groves.

Published

Edward L Erdman, *People and Property* (Batsford, 1982).

Stock Exchange Year-Book.

Times 24 Dec 1951, 30 May 1952.

GLUCKSTEIN, Montague

(1854-1922)

Caterer and food manufacturer

Montague Gluckstein was born on 18 July 1854 at St Giles in the Fields, Middlesex, the son of Samuel Gluckstein, a tobacconist, and Hannah née Joseph. Samuel Gluckstein (1821-1873) was a key figure in the complex and large family of which Montague was a member. Samuel arrived in London from Europe in 1841, married four years later, and worked in the typically Jewish tobacco trade as a cigar dealer in Whitechapel in the East End of

London. In this business Samuel was joined by a number of close relatives and by Barnett Salmon (1829-1897). The friendship and business relationship between the two men was sealed by Barnett's marriage to Samuel's daughter Helena in 1863. Shortly before Samuel's death, however, a family disagreement led his two oldest sons, Isidore and Montague, to form a family fund based on a complete pooling of resources and with the motto 'Union Fait La Force'. Involved in this practical expression of an ideal, which survives to this day, were Montague, Isidore and Joseph Gluckstein, Barnett Salmon, Julius Koppenhagen and Samuel Joseph. All were either sons or sons-in-law of Samuel Gluckstein.

After an education at the Foundation School, St Mary's, Whitechapel, Montague joined the family tobacco business, Salmon & Gluckstein, which was expanding rapidly with the aid of adventurous advertising and price-cutting tactics. Montague was on the selling side, acting as a traveller when not engaged in the factory. It was his experience at exhibitions 'that first brought home to [him] the dreary and standstill catering methods of that time' {Beable (1926) 83}. Having discussed the possibility of starting a new catering business with his brothers, who were agreeable providing the family name was not associated with anything so mundane, Montague secured the catering rights for the Newcastle Jubilee Exhibition of 1887. Joseph Lyons (qv), a distant relative, who was at that time running a stall at an exhibition at Liverpool, was brought into the partnership to act as ambassador and to negotiate with the exhibition authorities. Recalled Montague, 'our Newcastle venture made good — out of that humble but very important trio, tea, bread and butter of the best kind sold at a reasonable price, the foundation was laid of what was afterwards to be the largest catering business in the world' {ibid 85}.

Other catering contracts followed in Glasgow, Paris, and London. In 1894 the first Lyons tea-shop was established at 213 Piccadilly, and the idea of a cup of tea for 2d with other items at correspondingly low prices was rapidly followed by the opening of six or seven other establishments in various parts of London. In 1894 J Lyons & Co Ltd was registered, £70,000 (comprising £35,000 in cash and £35,000 in ordinary shares) being paid for the old business.

Expansion thereafter was rapid. In 1904 the tobacco side of the business, which had a capital of £600,000, was sold to the Imperial Tobacco Co, enabling the family partners to concentrate their energies on catering and food manufacturing. A completely new type of popular restaurant was planned — the corner house — the first of which, in Coventry Street, London, was started in 1909. Similar establishments, which also led the way in providing music for their patrons and abolishing tipping were soon opened in other areas of London. In 1896 the Trocadero Music Hall was acquired and, after some early problems in raising sufficient capital, later converted into the Trocadero Restaurant to provide high-class cuisine, again, at a popular price. Lyons was also heavily involved in more prestigious catering and was responsible for providing meals at Windsor Castle, the Daily Mail Banquet in 1921 at Olympia, and the British Empire Exhibition at Wembley in 1924. The partners opened hotels — the Strand Palace, the Regent Palace, the Royal Palace, and the Cumberland; operated bakeries from their Cadby Hall site in Kensington; began tea packing at Greenford, Middlesex; and started a highly successful business in packaged cake for sale through their own catering outlets and through a growing number of retail agents. But in these early stages of the company's history it was the teashop chain which attracted the most attention. By applying the multiple trading methods they had learned in the tobacco business, and by reaping substantial economies of scale, Lyons were able to offer remarkably good value in modest surroundings. The Lyons teashop, decorated in distinctive style with a white and gold fascia, was on its way to becoming a national institution.

By 1913 authorised capital had risen to £1,300,000 and at Montague Gluckstein's death stood at £5,325,000, with a controlling interest in W H & F J Horniman & Co Ltd, Black & Green Ltd, and the Drysdale Manufacturing Co Ltd. Montague played a leading part in inspiring this growth. Most of the firm's most important ideas stemmed from him and his great skill and knowledge in the property market was a considerable asset in both the tobacco and catering trades. However, he was a reserved and modest man, and, in 1917, the year Sir Joseph Lyons died, it was only with difficulty that he was persuaded to accept the chairmanship of the company. He held outside directorships such as the Westminster Electric Supply Corporation, the Guardian Eastern Assurance Co, and the Pall Mall Electric Co and it is possible that at one stage he might have developed a fuller business life outside catering. But in the 1890s he became involved in a law action concerning the promotion of a company based on the Olympia property. Harsh words were said in court about Montague's part in the affair. The effect on him was deeply wounding and he reduced his outside activities to concentrate his energies with even greater force on Lyons. We know little about his private or social life, and the writers of his obituary notices in 1922 hid behind references to 'the modest magnate'.

Montague Gluckstein in 1884 married Matilda Franks, daughter of Samuel H Franks, a cigar merchant; they had two sons and one daughter. At his death on 7 October 1922 Gluckstein left £67,986 gross.

DAVID J RICHARDSON

Sources:

Unpublished

BCe.

MCe.

PrC.

David J Richardson, 'The History of the Catering Industry, with Special Reference to the Development of J Lyons & Co Ltd to 1939' (Kent PhD, 1970).

Published

Stephen Aris, *The Jews in Business* (Cape, 1970).

William H Beable, *Romance of Great Businesses* (Heath Cranton Ltd, 1926).

Paul H Emden, *Jews of Britain* (Sampson & Low, 1944).

Jewish Chronicle 13 Oct 1922.

WWW.

Sir W Glyn-Jones (taken from Addison's Politics from Within *vol I).*

GLYN-JONES, Sir William Samuel

(1869-1927)

Trade association organiser and promoter of resale price maintenance

William Samuel Glyn-Jones was born in Worcester on 29 January 1869, the eldest son of George Griffith-Jones. He was educated at Merthyr Tydfil Grammar School. Having served an apprenticeship in Aberdare, where his father was Registrar of Marriages, he qualified as a pharmacist in 1891, and for a few years owned a pharmacy in Poplar in the East End of London. He studied law, was called to the Bar at the Middle Temple in 1904, and practised for a short period before entering parliament in 1910.

Glyn-Jones's contributions to professional and trade associations in pharmacy were numerous and substantial. Among his many achievements were the founding of the Chemists' Defence Association in 1900, and the inclusion in the National Health Insurance Act, 1911, of a clause reserving the supply of medicines to pharmacists.

In the business sphere, Glyn-Jones was best known for the development of resale price maintenance in proprietary medicines and other goods handled by retail chemists. In 1895 he began publishing the monthly *Anti-Cutting Record*, in which he advocated his cure for the extensive price-cutting which afflicted the trade. In the following year he founded the Proprietary Articles Trade Association (PATA), of which he remained secretary for thirty years. The PATA organised the collective withholding of its manufacturer-members' proprietary articles from price-cutting retailers. By the 1920s, under Glyn-Jones's leadership, it had become a pillar of the chemists' trade. His energy, persuasiveness and negotiating skills were major ingredients in the expansion of PATA, achieved in the face of the public hostility of critics such as Jesse Boot and Thomas Beecham (qqv). He skilfully dealt with knotty problems (such as dividends paid by co-operative retail societies, the distributors' margins on price-protected brands, and retailers' buying groups which circumvented the wholesalers) without jeopardising the allegiance of the manufacturers, wholesalers and retailers who supported and financed the PATA. His work in and for the PATA, as well as his other activities for the profession and its retail trade branch, was much appreciated by his fellow pharmacists during his lifetime.

Glyn-Jones's guidance and support were often given to other organisations of retailers trying to introduce or reinforce price maintenance in their own branches of trade. He himself hoped for a 'united organisation of shop-keepers' {*Chemist and Druggist* 19 June 1897} to strengthen and extend the sway of price maintenance and to resist adverse legislation. But in this he made no headway. Nevertheless, at the end of his life he registered a further success in the field he had made his own. He resigned as registrar and secretary of the Pharmaceutical Society (which he became in 1918) in 1926 in order to help Canadian pharmacists establish and organise their own PATA. He died soon after the new organisation had been launched. However, an adverse report of an official enquiry led to its termination shortly afterwards.

A Liberal, after unsuccessfully contesting Stepney in January 1910, he was elected in December 1910, holding the Stepney seat until 1918. He became Parliamentary Private Secretary to Dr Addison, Minister of Munitions in 1916 and Minister of Reconstruction in 1917. He was knighted in 1919.

Glyn-Jones was a member and office bearer of St George's Presbyterian Church, Palmers Green, North London. He married in 1894, Mary, daughter of John Evans of Tower Hill, Llanybyther, Carmathen; they had two sons and two daughters. Sir William Glyn-Jones died on 9 September 1927, leaving £3,198 gross.

BASIL S YAMEY

Writings:

The Law Relating to Poisons and Pharmacy (Butterworths, 1909).

Sources:

Unpublished

MCe.

PrC.

Published

F W Adams, 'William Samuel Glyn-Jones, 1869-1927' *The Pharmaceutical Journal* 202 (1969).

The Chemist and Druggist 13 Apr 1918, 17 Sept 1927, 31 Jan 1948.

Pharmaceutical Journal 1 Feb 1969.

Pharmaceutical Journal and Pharmacist 17 Sept 1927.

Times 10 Sept 1927.

WWMP.

WWW.

Basil S Yamey, *The Economics of Resale Price Maintenance* (Pitman, 1954).

Frederick Godber ('A Shell photograph').

GODBER, Frederick

(1888-1976)

Petroleum executive

Frederick Godber was born in Camberwell, South London, on 6 November 1888, the only son of Edward Godber, a carpenter, and his wife Marion née Peach. At the age of sixteen — in 1904 — he joined the Asiatic Petroleum Co as a clerk in its secretarial department. He was paid 10s a week. Records indicate that he made a favourable impression on his supervisor — 'a rather peppery tempered Dutchman' {*Shell Magazine* interview (1961) 92} for at Christmas he received a bonus of 17s 6d. The Asiatic Petroleum Co, later to become Shell Petroleum Co, was the joint marketing company of the Shell Transport & Trading Co and Royal Dutch Petroleum Co prior to the merger of the two companies in 1907. Godber moved up quickly within the company, gaining experience in both the 'Steamers' and 'Oil' departments before being appointed head of the newly-formed 'American' department in 1912, with two juniors to supervise. Although compulsory conscription was introduced in 1916, Godber was excused on grounds of vital civilian work. Meanwhile Godber in 1914 had married Violet Ethel Beatrice Lovesay, the daughter of George Albert Lovesay, a traveller.

Hitherto, however, Godber's experience had been with the marketing 'downstream' side of the business and in 1919 it was decided that he should spend two years in the USA travelling and learning about oil exploration and production: the 'upstream' side. However, his intended tour was halted at St Louis, where he became involved in work at the Roxanna Petroleum Corporation. In 1921, on the date he was originally scheduled to return to England, he was appointed president of the Corporation which was a subsidiary of the now Royal Dutch/Shell group of companies engaged in concessions and exploration. In 1922 Godber was appointed a director of Shell Union Oil. He stayed until recalled to London in 1928, when he was appointed a director of the Shell Transport & Trading Co. It is from this date that his personality and abilities begin to make a major impression on company activities.

Surviving papers reflect a man of great ability, tremendous drive and efficiency — although somewhat lacking in humour, firing off brisk instructions to staff at a considerable rate. He was a man with a very personal style of management, who took great pains to know his staff at all but the lowest levels. Throughout the depression years Godber received an enormous number of letters from those seeking employment. It is a reflection of his personality that so many felt able to approach, by then, a managing director in the personal way indicated by the papers. Indeed his private life was to become bound even more closely with that of the company — his two daughters (his only children) married the sons of two fellow managing directors, Andrew Agnew and Archibald Debenham. In 1934 he was appointed managing director of Shell Transport & Trading Co and from 1937 to 1946 he was chairman of Shell Union Oil Corporation, United States.

In 1938 the Government formed the Petroleum Board, its aim being to help maintain the supply of petroleum products in wartime. Although it worked closely with the Government through the Oil Control Board, a sub-committee of the War Cabinet and the Petroleum Division of the Ministry of Fuel and Power, the Petroleum Board sought to maintain the commercial nature of its separation as far as possible. Andrew Agnew came out of retirement to become chairman of the Petroleum Board and a member of the Oil Control Board. Godber was appointed chairman of the Overseas Supply Committee: an offshoot of the Petroleum Board, which was responsible for the purchase or award under the Lend-Lease Petroleum Products System. In 1942 he was knighted by George VI for his contribution to the war effort.

The culmination of his career came, however, in 1946 when he succeeded Lord Bearsted as chairman of Shell Transport & Trading Co. As chairman Godber involved himself in helping post-war recovery, not only in Britain but throughout Europe. He took a keen personal interest in the Group's staff and fostered a spirit of international friendship throughout the worldwide Shell community. By 1950 post-war trade improved as gasoline rationing ended in most European countries. The Shell Transport & Trading annual report for that year stated that Shell's basic policy was to 'render efficient and essential service to the public'. {Shell T&T Annual report 1950, 7} The first supertanker in which total engine power was transmitted through a single propellor, Shell's *Velutina*, was launched by HRH Princess Margaret in April 1950.

World demand for energy grew and by 1955 energy consumption was 45 per cent higher than in 1946 but when supply was threatened by the 1956 Suez Canal crisis and the sequestration of Shell Group properties by the Egyptian Government, Godber responded by ordering a fleet of Super Tankers (Very Large Crude Carriers: VLCC) for transporting vast quantities of oil around the Cape or on longer world routes.

Sir Frederick Godber was also instrumental in the construction of Shell Centre, a building commenced in 1957 and designed to house under one roof Shell Transport & Trading Co and appropriate service companies. Godber retired in 1961, shortly before the official opening of the building; by this time the company was a multinational giant. The net income of the Shell Transport & Trading Co was approximately £18,830,697 in 1959 having grown from a recorded £319,775 in 1903.

Godber had a number of interests outside Shell. In 1946 he became chairman of the 'Help Holland Council' an organisation committed to the post-war rebuilding of the Netherlands, work for which he was made a Grand Officer in the Order of Orange Nassau. Godber's business acumen was further recognised in 1953 when he was appointed chairman of the Commonwealth Development Finance Co Ltd, a post which he retained until 1968.

From 1954 onwards Godber was fêted with numerous awards and honours in recognition of his distinguished business career and services. In 1954 he was made an honorary Bencher of the Middle Temple whilst in 1956 he was made Baron Godber of Mayfield (taking the name from the village where he had lived for some time), the first time that a Shell Transport & Trading Co chairman had received a peerage. In 1957 he received the Cadman medal for services to the oil industry and in 1958 was appointed a trustee of the newly-formed Churchill College Trust Fund. The Leathersellers Company elected him as an honorary liveryman in 1962 whilst the Institute of Petroleum created him an honorary fellow in 1965.

Frederick Godber died on 10 April 1976, leaving £929,125 gross. He was survived by his wife and two daughters.

VERONICA RADY

Sources:

Unpublished

Shell Group, London archives, including Shell Transport & Trading annual reports.

BCe.

MCe.

Published

Shell Magazine 1961.

The Shell World (House Journal for Shell International Petroleum Co).

WWW.

Sir George Goldie 1898, portrait by Sir Hubert von Herkomer (courtesy of the National Portrait Gallery).

GOLDIE, Sir George Dashwood Taubman-

(1846-1925)

West Africa trader

George Dashwood Goldie-Taubman was born into the Manxian gentry at the Nunnery, Isle of Man, on 20 May 1846. He was the fourth and youngest son of John Taubman Goldie-Taubman, lieutenant-colonel in the Scots Guards and Speaker of the House of Keys by his second wife, Caroline, daughter of John Eykin Hovingdon of Hemingford, Cambridgeshire. As he later said, 'I had the good fortune to lose both my parents before they could have any influence upon me' {Wellington and Gwynn (1934) 103}. Educated at the Royal Military College, Woolwich, he passed his final examination for the Royal Engineers when blind-drunk in 1865: but his military career ended when he bolted to Egypt, without sending in his papers, after inheriting some money in 1867. There he lived in the desert for three years with an Arab girl, but after her death of consumption, returned to England in 1870. He next eloped with the family governess, Matilda Catherine Elliot, with whom he was besieged in Paris for four months during the Franco-Prussian War. In 1871 they were able to return to England, and were married at St Marylebone Church in July, subsequently producing a son (Valentine, born 1875) and daughter. Despite many candid infidelities, Goldie remained devoted to his wife: her death in 1898 drove him to take his first holiday (in the Andes) for over twenty years.

In 1875 his eldest brother bought the small and almost insolvent firm of Holland, Jacques which had traded with the Niger region since 1869. Goldie was given charge of its fortunes, and formed the Central African Trading Co Ltd in May 1876 (becoming its main owner with 1,135 shares). This new company next bought Holland, Jacques as the first step towards merging the many small, economically irrational Niger trading firms; and it was only afterwards that Goldie first visited the region, 'largely to escape from private entanglements', in 1877 {*ibid*, 93}. He made small progress until November 1879 when the Central and West African trading companies joined with various other firms to found the United Africa Co, nominally capitalised at £250,000. Apparently Goldie, despite his inexperience, was the animating force behind the merger, and the company's unusually autocratic articles of association bear his mark: directors, such as himself, were irremovable for seven years regardless of shareholders' voting, for example.

UAC bought the assets and rights of all British trading firms in the Niger region. Competition ceased, all resources were pooled, the palm-oil trade steadily expanded, and Goldie ('My dream, as a child, was to colour the map red') henceforth pursued 'a definite plan ... played out like a game of chess' to establish a British administration in the area {*ibid*, 28, 93}. To counter increasing French competition, a new National African Co was formed in June 1882 with nominal capital of £1 million and issued capital (heavily watered) of £316,675. Its stated objectives of governing the region in which it traded, and of excluding competitors by political means, were advanced by the decision of Gladstone's Cabinet, after much vacillation, in November 1883, that a British protectorate should take responsibility for the Cameroons, the Oil Rivers and the Niger, subject to no charge falling on Government funds and with the proviso that another expensive colonial Government should not be created. Goldie thus became the quasi-official instrument of British policy in West Africa.

In October 1884 he succeeded in buying out the last of his French rivals (for £60,000 paid in National Africa shares) and his company became the sole trader in the Niger basin. This deal was clinched a fortnight before the opening of the Berlin Conference (1884-85) which heralded Germany's scramble for African colonies. Goldie accompanied Lord Salisbury to Berlin, and National Africa's trading monopoly on the Niger ensured that British predominance in the area was confirmed by the Conference. Goldie's services at Berlin were rewarded with the KCMG in June 1887, and secured goodwill for the campaign, which had run since 1881, for a royal charter. After some official hesitation, this was granted in July 1886, and his company was henceforth known as the Royal Niger Co Chartered & Ltd. The charter gave the company wide administrative duties in the territories where it traded, confirmed the Niger basin as a British protectorate and 'delegated almost unlimited power in any region the Company could gain by treaties' {Perham and Bell (1963) 30}. It also strengthened the company in opposing the French and German Governments' projects to widen their spheres of influence in West Africa.

Goldie served as political administrator and deputy governor of the Royal Niger Co until 1895, when he succeeded the figurehead Lord Aberdare as Governor, but it was always his 'one-man show' {Wellington and Gwynn (1934) 25}. Despite its charter, the company suffered from renewed German and French competition which continued until Goldie secured territorial conventions with their representatives in 1893 and 1898 respectively. Mercantile activity by the African Association of Liverpool shipowners was only eliminated when Royal Niger bought all the Association's Nigerian assets in June 1893 in a deal which required the creation of another £50,330 shares, raising Royal Niger's issued capital to £493,680. Goldie also had to pacify native uprisings and suppress slave-raiding emirs, the Brass attack on Akassa in 1895 and the Nupe and Ilorin campaigns of 1897 being chief examples. In battle Goldie always attacked in a phalanx: 'I would be in the centre directing operations' he said, 'I enjoyed this part most of all' {ibid, 98}.

The company's financial performance improved with the granting of the charter, and unlike the later chartered companies of Rhodes and McKinnon in South and East Africa, Royal Niger became a dividend-paying concern. Dividends had been passed in 1885-87, but resumed in 1888 (when gross trading profits were £58,680 and turnover was £340,000) at 2.5 per cent. Throughout 1889-92, 6 per cent was paid annually, whilst trading profits fluctuated between £66,363 (1890) and £43,167 (1892); in the period 1893-98 dividends varied between 3.5 per cent in 1895 and 9 per cent for 1897. Reserves rose from £5,000 first allotted in 1894 to a total of £74,000 in 1897.

In 1898 Lord Salisbury's Cabinet, wanting détente with France and fearful lest Goldie's activities should annoy the French, entered negotiations to transfer Royal Niger's political powers over 382,000 square miles of Africa to the British Crown. Negotiations with Goldie were complex and rancorous, but an act passed in July 1899, with effect from 1 January 1900, gave the company £865,000 in compensation for its ceded territories. Goldie was succeeded as governor by his friend, Lord Scarbrough, and severed formal connections with the company (except during 1914-18 when he was honorary adviser). As the Niger Co, it retained its commercial power, and was bought in 1920 for over £8 million by Lever Brothers in a deal which injured the commercial prospects of both parties and which Goldie opposed.

It was Goldie's achievement in 1879-99 to lay the basis for delivering 20 million Africans from slave-raiding with singularly little bloodshed or destruction. His policy of 'indirect rule', in which imperial and tribal authorities co-operated in maintaining order through existent tribal institutions, was subsequently developed by his friend and employee, Frederick (later Lord) Lugard, into 'the most comprehensive, coherent and renowned system of administration in our colonial history'. {Perham (1960) 138} 'If in the last years he over-reached his resources; if Company rule was in parts anaemic and disjunctive; if it was harsh to the native traders and monopolist to the European, the responsibility lay squarely upon the Government which authorised a private agency to carry out a public enterprise'. {*ibid*, 18-19}

Goldie visited China during the Boxer rising of 1900, declined the offer of an Australian governorship in 1901, as also an approach from the Brazilian Government to administer the upper Amazon. In 1903 he was offered the governorship of Bombay, 'but he asked for a Peerage in addition and this request was not complied with' {Bodleian, Selborne papers, J S Sandars to Lord Selborne, 21 Sept 1903}. In 1904 he visited Rhodesia to advise the British South African company on organisation; he also sat on the Royal Commissions on the military preparations for the Boer war (1902-3) and on the disposal of Boer war stores (1905-6). On the former body he and Lord Esher led criticisms of the War Office's inefficiency, and the Conservative Government considered appointing him Secretary for War until warned by Joseph Chamberlain (qv) that Goldie 'is unsuited for office at home', perhaps because of his sex life {Bodleian, Selborne papers, Arthur Balfour to Lord Selborne, 23 Sept 1903}. Not obtaining further government employment, Goldie was an alderman of London County Council 1908-19 (chairing its finance committee), president (1905-8) and foreign secretary (1911-21) of the Royal Geographic Society, and president of the National Defence Association 1905-14 and 1915-20.

He received honorary degrees from Oxford and Cambridge, became a Privy Councillor in July 1898, was elected to the Athenaeum under Rule II in 1900, and was made FRS in 1902. After years of stoic suffering, he died of emphysema on 20 August 1925 in a small hotel bedroom off Piccadilly, leaving £73,293 gross.

Goldie was brilliant but tortured. Money was not his motive in business; he believed 'no man in a civilised community has any power worth exercising' {Perham (1956) 571}, and he despised fame characteristically explaining that he refused to have Nigeria called Goldesia 'because in 100,000 years [it] will have been wiped out by geological formations which we do not even dream of' {Wellington and Gwynn (1934) 99}. 'He believed passionately in the civilising influence of material prosperity; in efficiency; in almost every detail that accompanies material developments'. {ibid, 122} A militant aetheist, he was a cultural rebel who admired Huxley, Darwin, Shelley, Ibsen, Kipling and Wagner (whom he once joined in a practical joke). He pursued his recreations — reading, yachting and sex — immoderately. 'An extremely amused and amusing man', according to one woman, 'he combined uncontrollable passions, ruthlessness, indifference to individuals, contempt for sentimentality in any form, with the excitability and sensitiveness of a child; and a child's peculiar capacity for anger and pain' {ibid, 113}. Proud, mocking, masterful in big matters but petty in small ones, he engendered fanatical loyalty in subordinates and had almost hypnotic power over his few friends. Inconsolably miserable in his youth, always driven by violent nervous forces, he gave to Britain the riparian riches of Nigeria.

R P T DAVENPORT-HINES

Writings:

'The Hausa Association', pamphlet reprinted from *Imperial and Asiastic Quarterly Review* (Woking: 1895).

'The West African Liquor Trade: Statement to the Native Races and Liquor Traffic Committee' (1895).

'Britain's Priority on the Middle Niger' *New Review* June 1897.

'The Future of the Niger Territories' (London Chamber of Commerce pamphlet, 1897).

Introduction to Seymour Vandeleur, *Campaigning on the Upper Nile and Niger* (1898).

letter on Anglo-French rivalry over Lake Tchad *Times* 21 Dec 1893.

letter criticising cost and construction of Uganda railway *ibid* 20 Jan 1902.

letter on death of Cecil Rhodes *ibid* 28 Mar 1902.

letter on *Sergent Malamine* arbitration *ibid* 14 Aug 1902.

letter on North Borneo Company *ibid* 22 Aug 1902.

letter on London electric power *ibid* 6 July 1905.

'Twenty Five Years' Geographical Progress: an Address at York to the British Association for the Advancement of Science' *Geographical Journal* 28 (Oct 1906).

letter on geography and diplomatic entrance exams *Times* 20 Nov 1906.

'Geographical Ideals: an address delivered 22 November 1906' *Geographical Journal* 29 (Jan 1907).

letter on British expedition to Mount Everest *Times* 18 Mar 1907.

letter on national defence *ibid* 26 Dec 1907.

GOLDIE Sir George Dashwood Taubman-

Presidential Address to Geography Section of British Association in *Report of 76th Meeting of British Association at York in August 1906* (John Murray, 1907).

(attrib) 'Military Geography' *Journal of Royal United Services Institute* 52 (1908).

'Roche Abbey', 'A Dream: to Dorothy Ashton on her 15th Birthday', 'To a Wild Daffodil', three poems printed in Duchess of Wellington and Stephen Gwynn, *Sir George Goldie* (1934).

Sources:

Unpublished

Bodleian Library, Oxford, papers of 2nd Earl of Selborne.

PRO, Kew, Colonial Office and Foreign Office papers.

Rhodes House, Oxford, papers of Lord Lugard and Niger Co.

MCe.

PrC.

Published

Sibyl E Crowe, *The Berlin West Africa Conference 1884-1885* (Longmans, Green & Co, 1942).

DNB.

John E Flint, *Sir George Goldie and the Making of Nigeria* (Oxford University Press, 1960).

Geographical Journal (Dec 1925).

Isle of Man Examiner 28 Aug 1925.

Manchester Guardian 24 Aug 1925.

Dame Margery Perham, *Lugard, the Years of Adventure 1858-98* (Collins, 1956).

—, *Lugard, the Years of Authority 1898-1945* (Collins, 1960).

Dame Margery Perham and Mary Bell (eds), *Diaries of Lord Lugard* (4 vols, Faber & Faber, 1963).

Andrew Porter, 'The Hansa Association: Sir George Goldie, the Bishop of Dover and the Niger in the 1890s' *Journal of Imperial and Commonwealth History* 7 (1979).

PP, RC War in South Africa (1904) Cd 1789, 1790, 1791, 1792.

PP, RC on War Stores in South Africa (1906) Cd 3127, 3128, 3129, 3130, 3131.

Times 17 Jan 1899, 1 Jan 1900, 22 May 1906, 19 Nov 1907, 15 Apr, 22 Aug 1925, 16 Dec 1931.

Duchess of Wellington (Dorothy Wellesley) and Stephen Gwynn, *Sir George Goldie, Founder of Nigeria* (Macmillan, 1934).

Charles H Wilson, *History of Unilever* (2 vols, Cassell, 1954).

WWW.

GOLDSMID-STERN-SALOMONS
see SALOMONS, Sir David L

Victor Gollancz (courtesy of Victor Gollancz Publicity Department).

GOLLANCZ, Sir Victor

(1893-1967)

Publisher

Victor Gollancz was born in London on 9 April 1893, the only son of Alexander Gollancz and his wife Helena (Nellie) née Michaelson, a family of Polish origin with a long rabbinical heritage. Two uncles, Hermann and Israel, were knighted for academic achievements; Alex had a small jewellery business. Gollancz's childhood was marked by rebellion against his father's unquestioning Jewish orthodoxy and political conservatism. Educated at St Paul's School, Gollancz was a classics scholar of New College, Oxford, 1912-14. His army service included a period of secondment to Repton School (1916-18) from which he was dismissed for stirring up political dissension among staff and pupils.

When he entered publishing in 1921 with Benn Brothers Ltd, Gollancz had already found his vocation as a political educator. In 1923 he became managing director of a new general publishing company, Ernest Benn Ltd. Personality clashes with Sir Ernest Benn (qv) led to Gollancz's departure in 1927 to set up Victor Gollancz Ltd. His acknowledged brilliance as a publisher made the raising of finance easy. Although 40,000 £1 ordinary shares were subscribed, only 6s per share was called on and his working capital was initially therefore only £12,000. Gollancz was paid a salary and also had allotted to him 100,000 1s founder's shares which gave him absolute voting control.

Trading began in April 1928. By the end of 1928 64 books had been published and a 7.5 per cent dividend declared; 1929 yielded a 50 per cent dividend. Within a few years Gollancz was recognised as the most exciting general publisher in London. The firm's dramatic success on such small capital had almost everything to do with Gollancz's own fusion of talents. He had remarkable drive, energy and belief in his own judgement. A rebel by nature, he delighted in shocking the publishing establishment by his bold advertising and his innovations (with Stanley Morison) in typography and jacket design. He was shrewd in business and never permitted the firm's resources to be overstretched. Most important of all, he made authors believe in his commitment to their work and transformed into big sellers many who had been previously unknown or had had modest sales with other publishers. By 1932 his bestselling authors (many of whom had followed him from Benn) included Phyllis Bentley, A J Cronin, Dorothy L Sayers and R C Sherriff.

On the secure financial base of a profitable general list, Gollancz was soon able to begin the political publishing which he saw as the chief raison d'etre of his firm. The Liberal of youth and early adulthood had become a socialist and in 1936 he founded the Left Book Club (LBC), modelled on the Book Society and Collin's Crime Club. Run with Gollancz's usual energy and flair for improvisation, the LBC (subsidised by the firm) quickly became an important political force in the movement for a Popular Front against Fascism. By April 1939 its membership was almost 60,000 and in the region of two million books, half a million pamphlets and 15 million leaflets had been distributed under its auspices. Communists were vitally important in the organisation of the LBC and Gollancz — though never a party member and instinctively anti-totalitarian — was led to compromise with them to an extent that he later regretted over the political slant of the club's publications. With the Nazi-Soviet Pact in August 1939 the membership split and the LBC began a decline that eventually led to its demise in 1948.

During the Second World War Gollancz's main energies were devoted to trying to bring about reconciliation within the ranks of the left in order to assist the war effort, and working with The National Campaign for Rescue from Nazi Terror to secure government help for victims of Nazi persecution. Overwork (he slept little and wrote late at night, early in the morning and at weekends) and emotional distress led to a long and serious nervous breakdown in 1943. Once the war was over, he dedicated himself to combating the view that all Germans were guilty and launched Save Europe Now in 1945 to assist suffering Germans materially and fight against the policy of revenge. A convinced Judaeo-Christian (though a member of no religious group), he gave much assistance to Christian Action; with the outbreak of hostilities between Israel and the Arabs, he founded the Jewish Society for Human Service to help Arabs suffering from the effects of war.

During the 1950s Gollancz became a convinced pacifist. His main crusade was as chairman of the National Campaign for the Abolition of Capital Punishment, though he was also a prime mover in the foundation of War on Want. For the rest of his life he continued to take an interest in and assist a wide range of charitable and progressive causes, notably including prison reform and nuclear disarmament. Throughout his life, he gave generously to individuals and charities. As time went on, though — disillusioned with politics — he spent more and more time on metaphysical and religious reading, reflection, discussion and writing and on his lifelong passion for serious music.

Although the depth of his commitment to moral crusades and his writing activities occasionally distracted him, he was his firm's effective head until he suffered a stroke in autumn 1966. His style was always autocratic, his temper short and he disliked criticism. Yet his enthusiasm was infectious, his kindness to those in need legendary and his flair and

sales volume utility furniture, the design of which relied on the line and natural beauty of the timber.

HEW REID

Sources:

Unpublished

BCe.

MCe.

PrC.

D L Gomme, 'Development and Organisation of a Furniture Factory' (Edwards Seminar Paper No 221, 25 Feb 1958).

Published

L J Mayes, *The History of Chair Making in High Wycombe* (Routledge & Kegan Paul, 1960).

John L Oliver, *The Development and Structure of the Furniture Industry* (Oxford: Pergamon Press, 1966).

GOOCH, Sir Daniel

(1816-1889)

Railway engineer and executive

Sir Daniel Gooch, 1872, portrait by F Grant (courtesy of the National Portrait Gallery).

Daniel Gooch was born in the village of Bedlington in the coal-mining district of Northumberland, close to the major centres of steam locomotive innovation, on 24 August 1816. He was the sixth child and third son of John Gooch (1763-1833) and his wife Anna (1783-1863). His father was the cashier/bookkeeper at the Bedlington ironworks, where Daniel's maternal grandfather, Thomas Longridge, had been a partner and where Thomas' nephew, Michael Longridge, had become manager (1809) and then managing partner, and also a partner between 1823 and 1842 with Robert Stephenson in the locomotive works at Forth Street, Newcastle.

Although ten children were born to Daniel's parents, sufficient means were available to employ a servant, to educate Daniel at local private schools between the ages of four and fourteen and to make an allowance over to him during the early years of his career — even after his father's death in 1833. The Gooch family had many relatives and friends in the engineering industry, including the Longridges, the Stephensons and the Hawks, in whose works from the age of fifteen, despite poor health, Daniel gained a wide practical training that ranged from locomotive construction to marine engineering. In February 1831 his father took up a position at Samuel Homfray's iron works at Tredegar, South Wales. The family settled there and Daniel began his professional career in the foundry at the works. In January 1834 he moved to the Vulcan Foundry at Newton-le-Willows, Lancashire, which had just been established by Robert Stephenson and Charles Tayleur. After a bout of ill health, which forced him to give up work in the early part of the following September, he found employment at £1 a week at the Dundee Foundry under James Stirling. He stayed there throughout 1835. By the age of twenty he was ready for his first entrepreneurial venture: as a partner with Robert Shafto Hawks in a proposed locomotive works at Gateshead. Arguments within the partnership caused him to leave in March 1837 and led to the scheme's abandonment. Having given up a position with Robert Stephenson at Newcastle to go to Gateshead, Gooch turned to his eldest brother Thomas, who, as joint principal engineer with Robert Stephenson of the Manchester & Leeds Railway, was able to find him work. But before long, Isambard Kingdom Brunel, the engineer of the Great Western Railway, selected Daniel as the company's first locomotive superintendent. He joined the GWR on 18 August 1837, one week before his twenty-first birthday, at a salary of £300 a year. Apart from a brief interlude in 1864-65, he was to be directly associated with the company for the rest of his life.

Gooch proved to be one of the outstanding locomotive engineers of the period, combining an inventive capacity to solve complex technical problems with an awareness of financial and organisational considerations. He designed (1843) a variant on the usual (Stephenson) locomotive valve-gear, the Gooch link motion, which was used for a long time by the company; he developed probably the first dynamometer car (1848) — for estimating train resistances under various conditions; and he succeeded, where others had failed, in designing for the Metropolitan Railway (1862) a locomotive for working in tunnels that condensed its own steam. But his initial brief was to make Brunel's inappropriate broad gauge engines work. With Brunel's agreement he soon began to devise his own modifications to locomotives, introducing the principles of standard designs and interchangeable parts. Plans and templates were supplied to outside makers who were required to meet Gooch's exacting standards. But after the opening of the company's works at Swindon in 1843 — the planning, tooling and overall management of which were largely his responsibility — Gooch and Brunel were able in 1846 to convince the board that better locomotives could be built at Swindon than outside by suppliers. Gooch's locomotives were acclaimed for their fitness for purpose and reliability. Indeed, although the advocates of the broad gauge lost their case before the Gauge Commission of 1846, Gooch's theoretical arguments and practical demonstration of the power and economy under certain conditions of his broad gauge locomotives were very effective. Also in 1846 he set up an information system to monitor the costs of coal and oil used in locomotive running, using the data to compare the consumption of one engineman with another and thus to promote a spirit of competition and emulation among the men in his charge.

In the following years, having protected his Swindon workforce (numbering 1,800 in 1848) from the depression of the late 1840s, Gooch proved to be adept at persuading the board to insulate the company as far as possible from the vagaries of the market. As a result a rising proportion of rolling stock and rails (from 1861) as well as locomotives and tenders was manufactured internally. This strategy, however, exposed Gooch to the criticism of hostile directors, in particular those who joined the board after the amalgamations with the South Wales and West Midlands railways in 1863 — the largest of the company's mergers before 1914 and the cause of much organisational stress. The new chairman, Richard Potter (Beatrice Webb's father), introduced a system of director committees to shadow the various departments, including Gooch's. The object was to achieve better financial control and accountability. Soon Gooch was attacked for the high 'real' costs of manufacture at Swindon, including the rail mill; high locomotive running expenses compared with other railways (including the West Midland); and the value to the company of coal supplied from its own colliery in South Wales. Gooch was deeply offended by these attacks which came from men whom he despised as ungentlemenly, foot-loose entrepreneurs and speculators. He believed that they would abuse their positions as directors to benefit their own businesses (for example, colleries in South Wales) having undermined the policies that he stood for. He responded through cogently-argued papers in which he stressed the advantages of company control in terms of guaranteed quality and regularity of supply, as well as low first cost. He nonetheless decided to resign and took with him his youngest brother William, the manager of the locomotive works at Swindon since 1857. Although he had suggested to Potter that William might be his successor, his advice was ignored and Joseph Armstrong, who was in charge of the company's Wolverhampton works, was appointed. After twenty-seven years of service as an officer, Gooch left the GWR on 7 September 1864: he was never again to hold a salaried position.

By the time of his resignation he had ample income from other sources, having enjoyed the freedom to pursue rewarding professional and entrepreneurial activities outside (although often related to) the GWR. His salary was in any case substantial, reaching £1,000 a year in 1846 and £1,500 from 1851 until his resignation. It was augmented by the premiums paid by pupils (from 1839); consultancy fees (for example from the Geelong & Melbourne Railway); and payments for contracting to work other lines (such as the South Devon).

In addition there were the profits from various other enterprises in which Gooch invested, in particular the Ruabon Coal Co in North Wales, in which he invested £20,000 in 1856 and was its chairman. As the Ruabon Co entered an agreement with the GWR to supply a large fixed quantity of coal annually, those GWR directors and shareholders with other coal interests were naturally aggrieved and there followed the first skirmish with Potter and his friends. Although Gooch was vindicated by the GWR and by the Court of Chancery, the episode left behind in certain quarters the belief that his business ethics were not altogether above reproach. In

1860 he bought the Hirwaun colliery and three years later, in readiness for his departure from the GWR and also to secure a position for his eldest son Harry, Gooch joined Joseph Whitworth (qv), a major supplier of tools to the Swindon works, in forming a firm to manufacture guns.

Also in 1860 he began an association that drew together his talents in engineering, organisation and finance, and led to public acclaim and a baronetcy. He became a director of the Great Eastern Steamship Co (he was chairman between 1864 and 1880) and supervised the *Great Eastern's* fitting-out in succession to his friend Brunel who had died in 1859. In 1864 he joined the board of the Telegraph, Construction & Maintenance Co. This took the entire responsibility a year later, under contract to the Atlantic Telegraph Co, to lay an Atlantic cable. The *Great Eastern* was chartered for the task and Gooch supervised the necessary adaption. The attempt failed. To raise the capital for the second, successful expedition in 1866, the Anglo-American Telegraph Co was floated with Gooch as its chairman. Being on the boards of the three interested companies, he was able to coordinate the entire enterprise and, as in 1865, sailed with the *Great Eastern*, and was not merely at the London office. His contribution to the laying of the first Atlantic cable was rewarded with a baronetcy in November 1866. His interest in telegraphic communication did not falter, and in all probability the returns from his substantial investments in the industry made a large contribution to his fortune. For example, as chairman of the Telegraph, Construction & Maintenance Co between 1867 and his death in 1889 he regularly announced dividends of 20 per cent on ordinary shares. When he died he was a director of five firms that were involved in cable production or cable laying — together their paid-up capital exceeded £9.1 million.

While he was still the GWR's locomotive superintendent, Gooch was selected to stand as a Conservative for Cricklade, a constituency that included New Swindon. His success at the general election of 1865 was possibly an act of defiance by the company's employees against an unpopular board of directors, for at the time he was no longer an officer and could not expect to exert 'paternalistic' leverage on voters. On his return from the first cable-laying expedition he was asked to succeed Potter as chairman of the GWR. He was elected on 2 November 1865 with a fee of £1,000 a year. Along with J S Forbes and Edward Watkin (qqv), he was the only contemporary chairman of a major railway to have pursued a career in the industry. The company then had a paid-up capital in excess of £40.5 million, a labour force of around 20,000 and within a decade had the largest network in the country and the second largest level of receipts.

However, the national financial crisis of 1866 threatened the existence of the company and led Gooch to appeal, unsuccessfully, for assistance from the Government. Tight money conditions made the company vulnerable because in the previous three years the floating debt had expanded rapidly to finance maturing capital obligations and to meet the requirements of ambitious investment plans. Under Gooch major capital projects, such as the conversion of the gauge from broad to narrow, were postponed and drastic cuts in working expenditure, which reduced the quality of train services and adversely affected the company's public image, were ordered. Despite these stringent measures it was still necessary to appropriate current revenue to satisfy capital obligations and therefore, because

still involved in the intricate final domestic amalgamations. Protracted negotiations immediately after the war associated the Colonial Bank with the Anglo-Egyptian Bank and the National Bank of South Africa. In 1925 the three banks were merged, Barclays becoming Barclays Bank (Dominion Colonial & Overseas).

Goodenough's conception, modest in comparison with today's international banks, was revolutionary in its time. He persisted despite much informed criticism and the powerful opposition of Montagu Norman (qv), Governor of the Bank of England. Criticism was not unreasonable; Norman and others thought that Barclays would be overstretched in the very troubled times that clearly lay ahead. Goodenough was not, however, to be deterred, even by Norman's refusal of an account at the Bank. His achievement fell short of his ambitions: Barclays Bank DCO, as it was renamed in 1954, was to operate substantially only in Africa, the Mediterranean and the West Indies, but its success within its geographical limits was to make Barclays the first, for many years the only, British bank to combine domestic business with a wide branch network overseas.

In his new colonial bank Goodenough's two dominant interests, his bank and the British Empire, found fulfilment. He was to serve the Empire in other ways too. For example, he was for twelve years a member of the India Council; likewise he established in 1930 the Dominion Students Hall Trust, which provided a hall of residence for Dominion students in London. He took an active interest in the Institute of Bankers, of which he was a vice-president; he was a governor of the Charterhouse Foundation and of the school; and his services to Oxford University, especially as chairman of the Bodleian appeal, were recognised in his honorary DCL in 1933, a distinction giving particular pleasure to a man who always regretted that he had not himself been to Oxford.

He was keenly interested in agriculture, which he defended at a time when it was widely neglected. He was devoted to the Filkins estate in Oxfordshire, which had in earlier years belonged to his family, and which he was proud to have regained and restored.

He continued as chairman and presiding genius of the parent bank and its principal subsidiary until his death in 1934; it was to one of the most distinguished bankers of his day that the City then paid tribute. To a remarkable degree he had combined enterprise with a profoundly conservative respect for traditional banking principles. He disapproved of what he regarded as the over-hasty return to the Gold Standard in 1925. Having earlier foreseen the dangers, and the impracticability, of 'making Germany pay' after 1918 — 'typical politicians' talk' — he was prominent among the bankers who soon resumed the extension of credit to the German banks.

Goodenough was a formidable personality, a commanding figure in person and a stern disciplinarian in business. The integrity that informed all his dealings was part of an essentially kindly disposition which his business associates and many of his staff remembered warmly, as did children, with whom he was particularly at ease.

He married in 1898 Maeve Nacnamara, daughter of Charles Macnamara FRCS, a military surgeon. They had five children. His eldest son, William Macnamara Goodenough (qv), also became chairman of Barclays Bank.

GOODENOUGH Frederick Crauford

Frederick C Goodenough died on 1 September 1934, leaving £120,580 gross.

P E SMART

Writings:

Address (on Indian Currency) Delivered to the Liverpool & District Bankers' Institute — December 6, 1920 (Blades, East & Blades, 1920).

The Reparations Problem (1922).

Some Aspects of the Problem of the Inter-Allied Debts and Reparation Payments (Blades, East & Blades, 1922).

Anglo-American Financial Co-operation (New York, 1923).

Three Addresses ... in the United States of America, April-May 1923 (New York: New York Trust Co, 1923).

International Finance (Blades, East & Blades, 1925).

The Gold Standard (Blades, East & Blades, 1926).

A Brief Review of Post-War Finance in Great Britain (Blades, East & Blades, 1927).

Currency (Blades, East & Blades, 1931).

Sources:

Unpublished

MCe.

PrC.

SSRC Elites data.

Published

DNB.

Anthony W Tuke and P W Matthews, *History of Barclays Ltd* (Blades, East & Blades Ltd, 1926).

— and R J H Gillman, *Barclays Bank Limited, 1926-1969* (Barclays Bank, 1972).

WWW.

Sir William Goodenough (taken from
The DCO Story *by Sir Julian*
Crossley and John Blandford).

GOODENOUGH, Sir William Macnamara

(1899-1951)

Clearing banker

William Macnamara Goodenough was born at Fulham, London, on 10 March 1899, the eldest son of Frederick Crauford Goodenough (qv) by his wife Maeve, fifth daughter of Nottidge Charles Macnamara, FRCS. He was educated at Wellington College, where he was captain of cricket and rackets and head of the school. After active service in France in 1918 — he was commissioned in the Coldstream Guards — he went up to Christ Church, Oxford, as a history scholar, and obtained a second class in 1922.

After university he joined Barclays Bank, of which his father had been chairman since 1917. After serving as local director in Oxford and Birmingham, he became a director of the bank in 1929, a vice-chairman in 1934, and deputy chairman in 1936.

In 1933 he became a director of Barclays Bank (Dominion, Colonial & Overseas), the overseas bank which his father had created in 1925. In 1937 he became deputy chairman, and in 1943 its chairman, but four years later, when he was elected chairman of the parent bank on the death of Edwin Fisher, he relinquished the overseas chair. Four years later again, ill health enforced his premature retirement early in 1951, and his death followed within two months. During his period in office Barclays Ltd's deposits increased from £822 million in December 1943 to £1,288 million in December 1952.

His early death denied him the opportunity of utilising fully his remarkable administrative ability within the bank and the group of which it was the centre; these had been his primary interest since university, particularly the overseas bank, for which he shared his father's enthusiasm. But his shortened career had been notably full, encompassing much besides the bank. Not least was the Dominion Students Hall Trust, which his father had founded to provide a hall of residence, London House, for overseas students. Goodenough became its chairman of governors; after the war he set up a sister trust to provide similar facilities for women and married students. Their hall of residence was named William Goodenough House.

His years in the bank at Oxford, following his time at Christ Church, gave him a lasting affection for the University and the county, in which the family had their home at Filkins Hall. He was only thirty-five when he became chairman of the Oxfordshire County Council; he was later to be DL of the county. In 1931 Lord Grey of Fallodon, chancellor of the University, appointed him a curator of the University Chest, and he played a notable part in the reform of the University's financial administration. No less notable was his encouragement and drive in the newly formed Oxford Society. His services to the University, of which he became Deputy Steward, were recognised in 1951 by the offer of the honorary degree of DCL, but his death prevented him from receiving it.

In Oxford too lay the foundation of his long and fruitful association with Lord Nuffield (qv), who chose him to chair his trusts for the Oxford Medical School, and subsequently to be chairman also of, inter alia, the Nuffield Provincial Hospitals Trust and the Nuffield Fund for the Forces of the Crown. The culmination of the association was the Nuffield Foundation, of which Goodenough was the first chairman.

In 1942, following his successful handling of the medical aspects of the Nuffield activities, he was appointed chairman of the Inter-Departmental Committee on medical schools, which reported, with considerable effect, in 1944. In the same period, back in the banking area, he was chairman of the executive committee of the Export Credits Guarantee Department.

During the war he was active in a sphere particularly close to his heart, when he served on the committee formed by the Ministry of Agriculture and Fisheries to work on post-war agricultural education. At his home he had initiated extensive farming operations, and he was long and closely associated with the National Farmers Union; he was also prominent in the foundation of the Association of Agriculture.

He appreciated all aspects of country life: he listed his recreations as shooting and hunting — he was master of the Christ Church beagles in his university days, and later he was joint master of the Vale of the White Horse (Cricklade) Hunt.

His directorships included Mercantile & General Reinsurance Ltd, Westminster Chambers Association Ltd, and Foundling Estates Ltd; and he was a member of the Council of Foreign Bondholders.

His remarkable talent with people can perhaps be inferred from this record of diverse public activity. He was regularly in demand when there was disputation in one or other of the bodies with which he was associated, or, on occasion, in a troubled government department; seldom was he unable to reconcile the disputants. His warm personality is remembered by all who knew him, including the many very junior members of the bank staffs, whom he never failed to recognise.

In recognition of his public service he was created a baronet in 1943. In 1947 he was elected an honorary student of Christ Church, and in 1949 he received the honorary degree of Doctor of Laws of Manchester University. He was for many years a governor of Wellington College.

He married in 1924 Dorothea Louisa, eldest daughter of the Venerable the Honorable Kenneth Francis Gibbs, Archdeacon of St Albans, son of the First Lord Aldenham (qv). There were four sons and one daughter. Sir William died at his home at Filkins on 23 May 1951, being succeeded by his eldest son, Richard Edmund. His estate was valued at £147,887 gross.

P E SMART

Writings:

Report of the Inter-Departmental Committee on Medical Schools (HMSO, 1944).

Sources:

Unpublished

BCe.

MCe.

PrC.

Published

DNB.

Anthony W Tuke and R J H Gillman, *Barclays Bank Limited, 1926-1969* (Barclays Bank, 1972).

WWW.

GOODMAN, Frederick Buck

(1847-1931)

Birmingham merchant

Frederick Buck Goodman was born in Edgbaston, Birmingham, on 4 March 1847, the eldest son of John Dent Goodman (1816-1900), partner in the general merchant firm of Scholefield, Sons & Goodman, and his wife Mary Martha née Buck. The firm started around 1780, though there is evidence of even earlier activities. The Scholefields in the firm were Joshua, the first MP for the borough of Birmingham in 1832, and his two sons, one of whom, William, was mayor of Birmingham and succeeded as MP in 1847. The elder Goodman was apprenticed to the firm in 1831, became a partner in 1842 and gradually took over control as Parliamentary activities occupied his colleague. He was one of the promoters of the Birmingham Small Arms Co and its chairman from 1861 until 1900. He was also a director and later chairman of the London City & Midland Bank from 1880 to 1900. Goodman Sr was also interested in the gun-making firm of J R Cooper & Co, and was an acknowledged expert on the trade, writing on it for various publications.

Frederick B Goodman was educated in Harborne and at Keir House in Wimbledon, and then spent a year in Paris in 1864. He entered the family business as an apprentice in 1865. A surviving note-book traces his progress and salary (rising from £20 in his first year to £100 in 1868-69) and the business and moral behaviour of his contemporaries in the firm, until he became a partner in 1872.

Prior to that he made his first major business trip to Canada, the United States and the West Indies in 1869-70, accompanied for part of the time by his father. A faded press-copy letter book of this trip and of a subsequent one in 1872-73 gives a tantalising glimpse of the hardware merchant trade in the United States during what was one of the major booms of the nineteenth century. The letters relay some flavour of the extent of business and the precariousness of life, and give an insight into the way a young salesman was trained on the job. One order from Chicago for over 3,000 breech and muzzle loading guns is dated December 1872 and many were supplied by J R Cooper & Co.

The young Goodman made several more trips abroad for the firm, revisiting the United States in 1885 and 1901, and also going to Australia, New Zealand and South Africa. During the 'Great Depression' of the late nineteenth century, the firm seems to have remained stable rather than spectacularly prosperous. An analysis of the business for the years 1879-1881 and 1888-96 indicates an average turnover of £121,080 in the first three years, rising to £139,717 by 1888-90 and falling back to £113,544 in 1891-93. John Dent Goodman became less active in the business after a long illness in 1886, and Frederick continued to run it with his brothers C J and Edward Martin Goodman.

F B Goodman became increasingly active outside the firm. In 1875 he was appointed as one of the Guardians of the Standard of Wrought Plate in the Birmingham Assay Office. He was elected one of the five Wardens in 1906. He was also a major figure in the Birmingham Chamber of Commerce and was largely responsible, along with H C Field, for an almost complete reconstruction of the Chamber during his chairmanship between 1898 and 1904. During that time membership was more than doubled, a full-time secretary was appointed and the Chamber commenced a journal and several commercial publications. Goodman laid the basis for the active involvement of the Birmingham Chamber in national political issues in the years before the First World War.

Goodman was a Conservative, as was his father, and was chairman of the Edgbaston Ward Conservative Association from 1883 to 1890. He became a JP in 1880, and was appointed an Income Tax Commissioner in 1900. He was also involved with several charities including the Institution for the Blind, the Birmingham Eye Hospital and was a trustee of the General Provident Institution and of Lench's Trust. A member of the Church of England, he was honorary secretary of the Church Extension Fund for fourteen years from 1885. In 1873 he married Annie Mary Wilkinson, daughter of Charles Thomas Wilkinson, Vicar of St Andrews, Plymouth and Archdeacon of Totnes, Devon. They had no children.

In 1912 Frederick Goodman retired from active business on the conversion of the firm into a private limited company. He died on 8 June 1931, aged eighty-four. Goodman is not remembered as a particularly dynamic entrepreneur, but was able to sustain the firm through a difficult period. His major public contribution was undoubtedly his work on the Chamber of Commerce. In his will he left £55,397 gross.

ROY HAY

Sources:

Unpublished

Scholefield, Goodman Collection. Large case of documents, previously on deposit in the University of Birmingham Library. Currently in the hands of Scholefield, Goodman & Sons. I am indebted to Mr Colin Wilson for permission to consult these documents.

BCe.

MCe.

PrC.

Published

Birmingham Despatch 9 June 1931.

Birmingham Faces and Places Mar 1889.

Birmingham Gazette 10 June 1931.

Birmingham Mail 9 June 1931.

Birmingham Post 9, 10, 12 June 1931.

Edgbastonia no 122, July 1891, no 316, Sept 1907.

Roy Hay, 'The British Business Community, Social Insurance and the German Example' in W J Mommsen (ed), *The Emergence of the Welfare State in Britain and Germany, 1850-1950* (Croom Helm, 1981).

W T Pike (ed), *Birmingham at the Opening of the 20th Century: Contemporary Biographies* (Brighton: 1900).

'Scholefield, Goodman & Sons, Gun List for 1905', with an introduction by D W Bailey, in *Journal of the Historical Firearms Society of South Africa* 9 (1981).

GORDON, Harry Panmure

(1837-1902)

Stockbroker

Harry Panmure Gordon was born in Killiechassie, Perthshire in 1837, the only son of Harry George Gordon, a well-known City figure who was a director of the Union Bank of London. He was educated at Harrow, Oxford University, and Bonn University. In 1856 he secured a commission in the 10th Hussars, in which he served for four years. His father went bankrupt, according to one version partly as a result of his son's spendthriftness. Panmure Gordon thereupon resigned his commission and went to China, joining the trading firm of Lindsay & Co in Shanghai. Shortly after his arrival the Taiping rebellion broke out, giving him the chance to organise and command the Shanghai Mounted Volunteers. In 1865 he returned to England and, as a junior partner in the firm of J & A Scrimgeour, became a member that year of the London Stock Exchange. In 1876 he established his own stockbroking firm.

The firm of Panmure Gordon was best known in the late-Victorian and Edwardian era for its ability to place sizeable foreign loans with considerable speed. Not surprisingly, in view of its founder's personal background, it made a speciality of placing loans for Far Eastern Governments and railways, starting in 1885 with the Chinese Imperial Government gold loan. Panmure Gordon in this sphere maintained close links with the Hong Kong & Shanghai Bank, especially its London manager, Sir Ewan Cameron. Other foreign loans that Panmure Gordon arranged were for Malaga & Gibralter Rail in 1883, the Imperial Ottoman Ice Co in 1886, the Netherlands, India, Sumatra Tobacco Co in 1889, and the San Francisco Brewery in 1890. Brewery issues, both home and abroad, were in fact another speciality of the firm, earning Panmure Gordon the tag of the 'Boss Brewery Broker'. Between 1887 and 1900 he arranged some 20 brewery issues, including in 1890 Ind Coope and Newcastle Breweries as well as San Francisco. On most of these loans and issues Panmure Gordon took an underwriting commission of 2 to 3 per cent, together with an overriding commission of between a quarter and a half per cent. He generally had little difficulty in raising the desired funds, to judge by the phrase 'no allotment' that usually appeared in the firm's underwriting books. One company promoter with whom he was much associated was H Osborne O'Hagan (qv), for instance in 1886 placing on O'Hagan's behalf £330,000 worth of shares of Henry Clay & Bock Co and then in 1900, in liaison with the broking firm James Capel, raising over £7 million for Associated Portland Cement, though in that latter case running into difficulties. However, the most famous domestic issue with which Panmure Gordon was involved was the spectacularly over-subscribed Lipton one of 1898. The issue earned him the rather misleading reputation of being the inventor of the industrial preference share, but what was distinctive was the extremely lucrative tactic of issuing the £1 ordinary shares at a five shillings premium, thereby, according to Panmure Gordon himself, putting an extra £250,000 into Lipton's pocket. In this instance there was no underwriting, but Lipton presumably saw that his broker did not suffer.

Panmure Gordon's lifestyle made him a legend in his own time. His homes in Brighton, Carlton House Terrace, and near Rickmansworth were all lavish affairs in which he entertained freely; his penchant in the early morning was to drive a four-in-hand into the City; he was reckoned to have the best private collection of carriages in the world; his sartorial tastes were such that he possessed over a thousand neckties alone; and in *Who's Who* he listed his hobbies as salmon fishing, breeding collies, and running his estate. All this cost money (once computed by him at around £2,000 a month) but provided invaluable publicity, especially important in the context of the Stock Exchange's ban from 1885 on its member's advertising. The brains of the firm were usually attributed to Willie Koch, a naturalised Belgian who became a partner in 1889, but it was Panmure Gordon himself who provided the push and also the indispensable contacts. In O'Hagan's admiring words, not only did he have 'a perfect flair for getting himself talked about', but also he 'gained the entrée to all the banks and to the great financial and commercial firms, and took care to get into close touch with everyone who visited this country for any financial purpose' {O'Hagan (1929) I, 368}. Panmure Gordon was never short of energy: a clerk later recalled how his 'restless temperament showed itself in staccato phrases, constantly repeated, accompanied by a gesture of the hands, like a player throwing out a card in bridge' {Fletcher, *Evening News* 23 Apr 1934}. In 1892 he wrote a not unthoughtful account of a visit to the United States, *The Land of the Almighty Dollar*. Late in life he married Carrie, daughter of Thomas Beverley Hall of Beverley, York and South Australia, a much younger woman, producing no children and some acrimony. He died on 2 September 1902 at Nauheim, leaving £86,714 gross. On the first Saturday afterwards the Stock Exchange closed its doors, in a unique tribute to one of its members.

DAVID KYNASTON

Writings:

The Land of the Almighty Dollar (F Warne & Co, 1892).

Sources:

Unpublished

PrC.

Published

Financial News 3 Sept 1902.

Henry Osborne O'Hagan, *Leaves from My Life* (2 vols, John Lane, 1929).

J W Fletcher, 'Portrait of a Victorian Business Man' *Evening News* 23-24 Apr 1934.

Alec Waugh, *The Lipton Story* (Cassell, 1951).

B H D MacDermot, *Panmure Gordon 1876-1976* (pp, 1976).

WWW.

GORDON-SMITH, Sir Allan

(1881-1951)

Clock and instrument manufacturer

Sir Allan Gordon-Smith (courtesy of Smiths Industries plc).

Allan Gordon-Smith was born in Clapham on 3 January 1881, the fifth child and third son of Samuel Smith, and his wife Annie. His grandfather was Samuel Smith I, who founded the family business in Newington Causeway, London in 1851.

Allan Gordon-Smith (or AGS as he was to be known), was educated at Christ's College, Finchley, where he excelled at games and athletics. He later played rugby for the Harlequins and also distinguished himself as a runner. In 1898 at the age of seventeen he entered the Ecole d'Horologerie, at Bienne, in Switzerland, for a three-year course. The following year, the family business was registered as a private limited company and as his presence was needed at this time of development, he returned from Switzerland. In 1901, AGS became manager of the expanding business, firstly at 68 Piccadilly, and in 1902 at No 9 Strand. Two years later he formed a Motor Accessory Department at No 9 Strand. This became the manufacturing side of the business for which AGS was primarily responsible. Hitherto, the firm had been mainly concerned with clocks and jewellery, but in this year, he sold the first car speedometer (designed by one of his employees, P O Dorer), for installation in King Edward VII's 18/28 hp Mercedes. From this start, he built up a considerable manufacturing business covering automotive, aviation, marine and industrial products. By 1912 the firm had a turnover of £100,000.

S Smith & Sons (Motor Accessories) Ltd became a public company in July 1914, with AGS appointed managing director. At this date the firm employed 100 people. Shortly afterwards, a five-acre site was acquired at Cricklewood, in order to cope with the production of war contracts. These included essential instruments and associated equipment, much supplied in large contracts for the governments of France, Russia and Italy.

By 1917, the company had become interested in aviation matters with the acquisition of rights to an airspeed indicator, from Holcomb Clift its inventor. The Air Ministry also asked Smiths to produce KLG plugs, under licence. Smiths suffered during the recession of the early 1920s, but under the guidance of AGS were in a position towards the end of that decade to consider further expansion. He also worked for the revival of the British clock making industry, and to this end formed in 1928 the All British Escapement Co Ltd. In 1931 the firm's first synchronous electric clock was produced, and also large quantities of clock movements with British-made escapements.

By 1936 the Smiths Desynn System of remote indication became standard equipment on practically every British-built aircraft, and AGS headed a team of eight executives which visited the USA also in 1936 for a comprehensive survey of American techniques in aviation instrumentation. Among other things he acquired a licence from Bendix for the production in Britain of aviation instruments, including the altimeter (rate of climb indicator). Between 1929 and 1939 the Smiths' labour force grew from 1,700 to 8,000.

In 1937 AGS was appointed a DL of the County of Middlesex, and the following year, concerned with events in Europe, he gave a luncheon at the Trocadero Restaurant, London, for the purpose of inaugurating a country-wide Territorial Army recruiting drive. Plans were also made for the dispersal of vital production from the vulnerable London area.

He received a knighthood in the Birthday Honours of 1939. With the declaration of war, he handed over responsibility for the company to his son Ralph, and went to the Ministry of Aircraft Production as Controller of Construction and Regional Services. For this work he was awarded the KBE in 1941. Sir Allan was appointed to the Aircraft Supply Council in 1943. The previous year he was a signatory of the National Policy for British Industry statement.

Having assumed the chairmanship of the company in 1945, he immediately laid plans for the expansion of the business. As a director of EMI Ltd from April 1951, he formed a joint company, Radiomobile Ltd, in 1946 to manufacture and market car radios. Another joint venture, Anglo-Celtic Watch Co Ltd, with Vickers and Ingersol, undertook the manufacture of watches in South Wales, whilst the mass production of clocks started at Wishaw, near Glasgow.

Subsidiaries were established in Canada and Australia and at this time also, important new marine products were introduced. In 1947, following considerable research, the new all-electric Automatic Pilot, SEP1 (developed at the firm's Cheltenham works by F W Meredith), was introduced, which was to have such a significant impact on the aviation industry. By 1949 the business employed 12,500 people and in 1950-51 profit before tax was £1.5 million.

Sir Allan was a Freeman of the City of London, a fellow of the livery of the Worshipful Company of Clockmakers, a fellow of the British Horological Institute, a fellow of the Royal Society of Arts, president of the British Clock & Watch Manufacturers Association and a fellow of the National Jewellers Association. His great sporting interest was horse racing and at the time of his death he had 22 horses in training, and was a Steward at Goodwood. His horse *Fearless Fox* won the Ascot Gold Vase and the Goodwood Cup in 1931 (he also had a greyhound which won the Waterloo Cup). In 1950, his horse *Cloncarrig* narrowly failed to win the Grand National. In addition, he was keen on shooting, fishing and snooker, and was a very keen competitor.

Gordon-Smith in 1904 married Hilda Beatrice daughter of Edward Jarvis Cave. They had one son and three daughters. Sir Allan Gordon-Smith died on 12 February 1951 leaving £60,260 gross.

J A HOLLOWAY

Sources:

Unpublished

Smiths Industries PLC, London, company papers.

PrC.

Published

WWW.

GOSSAGE, William

(1799-1877)

Soap manufacturer

William Gossage was born in the Lincolnshire village of Burgh-in-the-Marsh in 1799. The youngest of thirteen children, he left school at the age of twelve and was apprenticed to his uncle, a druggist in Chesterfield. This training gave him a good practical knowledge of chemistry while the theoretical side was acquired through private study of published works. While at Chesterfield he showed the first signs of inventive ability, when he patented a portable alarm to waken his French tutor for early morning lessons.

Having completed his apprenticeship, Gossage moved to Leamington in 1823 and set himself up as a druggist producing Leamington Salts, among other chemicals. By 1831 he had moved to Stoke Prior, Worcestershire, to form a partnership with Jonathan Farndon as salt and alkali manufacturers using the extensive salt deposits nearby. The firm was reorganised as the British Alkali Co before 1835 and produced a wide range of chemicals including salt, soda, soap and bleaching powder. Like other soda manufacturers using the Leblanc process they received protests from surrounding landlords because the first stage of the process, when sulphuric acid and salt reacted together, released clouds of muriatic acid gas (hydrogen chloride) into the atmosphere. If the increasing demand for soda were to be met then this problem had to be elimanated. Gossage soon took up the challenge.

Next to the Stoke Prior works he found a derelict windmill, packed it with gorse, brushwood and coke and then passed water and muriatic acid gas in at the top. Because of the large surface area of contact between the gas and the sheets of water percolating through the windmill, nearly all the gas (being very soluble) was absorbed by the water by the time the droplets reached the bottom of the windmill. Gossage patented his acid tower in 1836, though it was not until the Alkali Works Act of 1863, which stipulated that at least 95 per cent of the muriatic acid gas produced had to be 'condensed', that the acid tower became universally adopted.

Another problem for the soda manufacturer using the Leblanc process was the loss of expensive sulphur (originally contained in the sulphuric acid) which was dumped as alkali waste. Besides the environmental consequences, this was undesirable because sulphur was an expensive raw material. Gossage realised this from his own experience and by 1837 had patented a method of reclaiming this sulphur. However it proved very inefficient in large-scale operation and Gossage spent over thirty years and about £20,000 trying to perfect an efficient method.

Gossage also engaged in other activities in the chemical industry. In 1841 he partnered Edward Benson in the British White Lead Co in Birmingham — white lead being used increasingly as a pigment. When this company collapsed in 1842, Gossage developed an interest in copper and zinc smelting, becoming an associate of Henry Vivian (later Sir Henry Vivian, MP) in Neath, South Wales. By 1847 Gossage was working with James Young on paraffin refining at the Ardwick Bridge works of Tennant & Co. But after returning to Stoke Prior for a short period, Gossage moved to Widnes, Cheshire in 1850 taking some of his employees from Stoke Prior with him.

Widnes had considerable advantages as far as chemical manufacture was concerned with sources of coal at Wigan and St Helens, limestone in North Wales and Derbyshire, and salt at Northwich and the surrounding area. Gossage chose a site in Widnes partly on the Mersey but with a larger frontage on the St Helens Canal. During his first four years there Gossage involved himself in alkali manufacture and copper smelting, simultaneously maintaining his other chemical interests, with his works, laboratory and house all in close proximity.

An early result of his Widnes activities was a new and cheap method (patented in 1853) for producing caustic soda (sodium hydroxide) which established caustic soda as an industrial chemical. Particularly needed for soapmaking, the method was adopted extensively in Merseyside, a major soap manufacturing area. Gossage's patent coincided with Gladstone's removal of the duty on soap (about 3d per pound of soap) and opened the way to more efficient batch processing (hitherto vats had to be sealed in the absence of an excise officer). But there was another restriction on the production of soap: curtailed supplies of Russian tallow as a result of the Crimean War. Gradually tallow was replaced by vegetable oils such as palm oil, and as the trading routes developed out of the expanding port of Liverpool so larger quantities of these oils were imported for soap manufacture. To Gossage its manufacture became increasingly interesting.

One result of his research was filled or silicated soap which changed the direction of his manufacturing activities. He developed filled soap by adding sodium silicate to soap made from palm oil (or tallow or resin) thereby both greatly increasing the soap's detergent power and reducing its cost (from 6d to 2d). Gossage saw the potential and in 1855 formed the company William Gossage & Sons Ltd with his sons Alfred and Frederick.

He converted his alkali works to soap production and abandoned copper smelting. Next he developed another type of soap, mottled (or marbled) soap, which he patented in 1857. It contained coloured impurities (due to iron compounds) which spread through the soap to give the appearance of veins, an appearance that William Gossage exploited to the full. William Gossage & Sons Ltd quickly acquired an international reputation. At the International Exhibition in London in 1862 the silicated soap received a prize medal. Mottled soap was marketed widely and, as with silicated soap, was produced for other soap manufacturers to sell. Between 1862 and 1887 it is reputed that over 200,000 tons of mottled soap were produced, much of it for export to Africa, India and China. This trade of William Gossage & Sons Ltd represented about 50 per cent of the United Kingdom's total soap exports.

Outside business Gossage was prominent in the development of Widnes, serving as chairman of the Local Board, in 1865, and as a JP and gave £500 towards the cost of building a local hospital. He was also a Wesleyan Methodist.

Gossage died at Bowdon, Cheshire, on 9 April 1877, leaving under £160,000. The company continued to expand under the direction of his sons Alfred and Frederick and T S Timmins.

PETER N REED

Writings:

A History of the Soda Manufacture (Liverpool: McCorquodale, 1861).

'On the Theory of the Manufacture of Soda' *Chemical News* 6 (1862).

'Note Historique sur la Fabrication de la Soude en Angleterre' *Cuyper, Revue Universelle* 12 (1862).

'Method of Assaying Rough Soda (Black Ash) for the Use of Soda Manufacturers' *Chemical News* 7 (1863).

'On the Soda Manufacture' *British Association Report* 40 (1870).

PP, HC 1862 (486) XIV, SC on Injury from Noxious Vapours.

British Patents:

1823 (4,753)

1828 (5,595)

1836 (7,046; 7,105; 7,267)

1837 (7,284; 7,416)

1838 (7,636; 7,693)

1843 (9,591)

1845 (10,976)

1850 (13,177; 13,424)

1852 (691)

1853 (1,232)

1854 (422, 762, 1,176, 1,707)

1855 (826, 908, 1,963)

1856 (252, 996, 1,293, 1,947, 2,100, 2,435, 2,630, 2,982)

1857 (41, 107, 518, 1,120, 2,379, 2,569, 2,878)

1858 (2,070, 2,336)

1859 (488, 594, 799, 1,099, 1,101, 1,329, 1,889, 2,612)

1860 (392, 1,086, 2,330)

1861 (2,059)

1862 (742, 1,371, 2,050)

1863 (2,259)

1869 (3,295, 3,700)

1870 (1,176)

1871 (2,868)

1872 (1,442)

Sources:

Unpublished

Hereford and Worcester RO, papers.

PrC.

Published

D J Adam, 'William Gossage 1799-1877' *Education in Chemistry* Mar 1977.

J Fenwick Allen, *Some Founders of the Chemical Industry* (Birmingham: Sherratt & Hughes, 1903).

George E Diggle, *A History of Widnes* (Widnes: Corporation of Widnes, 1961).

A E Dingle, 'The Monster Nuisance of All: Landowners, Alkali Manufacturers and Air Pollution, 1828-64' *Economic History Review* 2nd ser 35 (1982).

David W F Hardie, *A History of the Chemical Industry in Widnes* (Widnes: ICI, General Chemicals Division, 1950).

—, 'Chemical Pioneers: 15 William Gossage' *Chemical Age* 79 (1958).

Peter N Reed, 'Acid Towers and Weldon Stills in Leblanc Widnes' *Journal of the North Western Society for Industrial Archaeology and History* 2 (1977).

—, 'William Gossage and the Widnes Soap Industry' *ibid* 3 (1982).

Charles Wilson, *The History of Unilever: A Study in Economic Growth and Social Change* (2 vols, Cassell, 1954).

Sir Guy Granet (courtesy of the National Railway Museum).

GRANET, Sir William Guy

(1867-1943)

Railway manager

William Guy Granet was born at Genoa on 13 October 1867. He was the second son of William Augustus Granet (1818-78), merchant and banker of Genoa, and his wife Adelaide Julia, daughter of E Le Mesurier. Guy's grandfather, W A Granet (d 1854), was a French emigré who escaped from Toulon to Malta around 1793 and became commissary general in the British Army.

Guy Granet was educated at Rugby (1882-84) and Balliol College, Oxford, where he obtained a second class in modern history in 1889 and was a captain of the college boat. He spent four years in his father's business before being called to the Bar as a member of Lincoln's Inn in 1893. He practised on the Northern circuit, and frequently appeared as a junior with H H Asquith. When the Railway Companies Association was reconstituted in 1900, Granet became its first salaried secretary, succeeding Sir Henry Oakley (qv). In 1905, he became assistant general manager of the Midland Railway, taking over from John Mathieson as general manager in the following year. It was a surprising appointment. Almost forty years later, the *Railway Gazette* wrote in its obituary notice: 'We know no other instance of a man entering the railway service later in life than usual ... [and] having so successful a career.' The paper went on to quote the comment of a chief officer on the LNWR on hearing the news in 1905: 'Well, we have nothing to fear now!' {*Railway Gazette* 15 Oct 1943}. Such complacency proved to be ill-founded. Granet initiated an overhaul of the Midland administrative structure from top to bottom with the twin objects of increasing the company's turnover whilst keeping working expenses to a minimum. He set up a new system of traffic control to eradicate the chronic congestion caused by freight traffic, whereby many of the Midland's main arteries were in serious danger of strangulation. Once this had been achieved, it became possible to improve the punctuality of the main line passenger trains, which had been far from satisfactory. This was crucial for the Midland, which faced fierce competition for passenger traffic over many of its principal routes.

In the railway world generally, Granet played an important role in the development of industrial relations. The country was threatened with its first general railway strike in 1907. Lloyd George, as President of the Board of Trade, intervened and Granet acted as secretary to the employers' committee during the ensuing negotiations. One result of the settlement was the creation of a system of Conciliation Boards, supplemented by arbitration. During the national strike of 1911, the leading companies authorised Granet, with Sir Gilbert Claughton, to negotiate on their behalf. Like most railway leaders, Granet saw the conciliation system as an alternative to union recognition. That was, nevertheless, the destination to which it led. Granet took part, on behalf of the General Managers' Committee, in discussions with Aslef and the NUR which led to the first war bonus in February, 1915 — the first direct negotiations between railway companies and union officers. In January 1926 he became chairman of the Railway Companies Association and held that office through the General Strike.

The Midland's net income, after payment of interest, rose from £3,877,491 in 1905 to £4,829,473 in 1913. Over the same period, the dividend on ordinary stock increased from 5.375 per cent to 6.5 per cent. From 1 January 1914, Granet's salary was £6,000 per annum — which was in line with the general pattern in the industry.

In June 1915, Granet became Director of Railway Transport in the Ministry of Munitions, and shortly after, Controller of Import Restrictions. He moved to the War Office in October 1916 as Deputy Director-General of Movements and Railways. In this post, he worked closely with Sir Eric Geddes (qv), who wrote: 'Our chief difficulty, I think, will be to get things 'through' the War Office; once a paper gets there, it passes the wit of man to get it out again, and it is only by knowing the ropes and knowing where the snags are, and how either to get round them or knock them out of the way, that one can get anything done at all' {University of Warwick, Modern Records Centre, Granet Papers 191/3/3/49: Geddes to Granet, 19 Oct 1916}. From March 1917 until March 1918, and again from February 1919, he was Director-General of Movements and Railways, with a seat on the Army Council. In 1918, he served as chairman of the British and Allied Provisions Commission, and as representative of the Ministry of Food in Canada and the USA.

Granet in 1918 resigned his post as general manager of the Midland Railway and joined the board. Four years later he became its chairman. The process of grouping had already begun and on the formation of the London, Midland & Scottish Railway in 1923, he became its deputy chairman, succeeding to the chair a year later. He brought in Josiah Stamp (qv) to re-structure the company and resigned the chairmanship in his favour in 1927. Granet remained on the board, however, until his death.

He had a wide range of business interests, including many outside railways. When in April, 1930, the Bankers Industrial Development Corporation was formed to co-ordinate the financial aid given to rationalisation schemes, he became deputy to the chairman, Montagu Norman (qv), Governor of the Bank of England. In addition, he was deputy chairman of the Forth Bridge Railway Co, a member of the London Committee of the Ottoman Bank, and at various times a director of Associated Electrical Industries, British Thomson-Houston, Carpet Trades Ltd, the Central Argentine Railway, the Investment Trust Corporation, the Leopoldina Railway, Lloyds Bank, London Electricity Supply Co, Provident Accident & Guarantee Insurance, Provident Mutual Life Assurance, the Times Publishing Co, and the Whitechapel & Bow Railway.

Of special importance was his partnership in Higginson & Co, merchant bankers, which he joined in 1919. It was this involvement which led to a seat on the board of British Thomson-Houston. In that capacity, he was closely concerned in the merger with Metrovick which resulted in the formation of Associated Electrical Industries, and in due course Granet joined the board of the new company. Higginson & Co was the London house of Lee, Higginson of Boston, Massachusetts, who acted in the USA on behalf of Ivar Kreuger, the Swedish millionaire. They lent him large sums on the security of his match monopolies and sponsored immense flotations on his behalf. When Kreuger shot himself in 1932, the American firm was dragged down by his fall. Granet felt a degree of responsibility, but his offers to resign from the boards of Lloyds Bank and Times Publishing were refused. His standing in the business world, even after the Kreuger crash, is indicated by a cable in which Sir Felix Pole (qv), chairman of AEI, in 1934 called upon the American corporation, General Electric, to reduce its holding in the British company to less than 50 per cent: 'Would urge you to do this through Guy Granet and his powerful associates. Suggest you should let him have block of 300,000 forthwith' {Jones and Marriott (1970) 168}.

He served on the Royal Commission on the Civil Service, 1911-14, and was one of three members who submitted a minority report. In 1921-22, he was a member of the Geddes Committee on National Economy, and chairman of the South African Railways Commission in 1933. He was knighted in 1911 and created GBE in 1923.

In 1892, Granet married Florence Julia Gully (1872-1949), second daughter of William C Gully, who subsequently became Speaker of the House of Commons and 1st Viscount Selby. They had one daughter. Granet died on 11 October 1943, leaving £54,360 gross.

HENRY PARRIS

Writings:

Report of the Railway and Harbour Affairs Commission (1934) (Pretoria: The Government Printer, 1934).

Sources:

Unpublished

PRO, RAIL 1057/3383 and 1110/33.

University of Warwick, Modern Records Centre, Granet Papers.

MCe.

PrC.

Published

Geoffrey Alderman, *The Railway Interest* (Leicester: Leicester University Press, 1973).

Philip S Bagwell, *The Railwaymen — the History of the National Union of Railwaymen* (2 vols, Allen & Unwin, 1963-82).

Eric G Barnes, *The Midland Main Line, 1875-1922* (Allen & Unwin, 1969).

Birmingham Post 13 Oct 1943.

Burke's Peerage 1939.

DNB.

Terry R Gourvish, 'A British Business Elite: the Chief Executive Managers of the Railway Industry, 1850-1922' *Business History Review* 47 (1973).

Robert Jones and Oliver J D Marriott, *Anatomy of a Merger. A History of GEC, AEI, and English Electric* (Cape, 1970).

Modern Transport 23 Oct 1943.

Railway Gazette 15, 22 Oct 1943.

Times 14 June 1915, 15, 22 Oct 1943.

Alymer Vallance, *Very Private Enterprise: An Anatomy of Fraud and High Finance* (Thames & Hudson, 1955).

Vanity Fair 11 Nov 1908.

WWW.

GRANT (GOTTHEIMER), Albert (Abraham) Zachariah

(1831-1899)

Company promoter

Albert Zachariah Grant (born Abraham Gottheimer) as he was known for most of his life, was born in Dublin on 18 November 1831, the son of Bernard Gottheimer, an impoverished Jewish pedlar from Central Europe. Subsequently the family fortunes improved when Albert's father became a partner in a foreign 'fancy' business in Newgate Street, London. Albert was educated in London and Paris, became a clerk, and later a traveller in wines. In 1856 he married Emily Isabella, the daughter of Skeffington Robinson of London and Epsom.

In April 1859 Grant made his public entry into the institutions of the London capital market with the formation of the Mercantile Discount Co. His style of conducting financial transactions was established during the brief life of this house which failed during the 'leather' crisis of 1860-61. One of its customers subsequently alleged that:

Mr Gottheimer was willing to discount my promissory note of £3,000 for one week for the premium of £100, provided I gave him as collateral a bill of

623

mortgage on one of my small steamers, which he pledged his word of honour not to register in the Custom House until the promissory note came to maturity. He further kindly promised that should it not be convenient to me to take up the petit billet at the expiration of the time, he would renew on the same terms, and continue to do so, provided I invested £1000 or £1200 in shares of the Mercantile Discount, which was paying, he said, 15 per annum. {Xenos (1869) 65}

After being involved with finance paper during the upswing of the minor cycle which peaked in 1860, Grant became a major company promoter during the feverish credit boom of 1862-66. His first creation was the Crédit Foncier, of which, like the Mercantile Discount before, he was the general manager. This finance company was formed in February 1864, its shares being issued by the Mercantile Credit Association, the manager of which, Henry John Barker, had been associated with Grant in the short-lived Mercantile Discount. The capital of the new company was largely subscribed by London merchants but its board had a strong Irish flavour. A month later the Crédit Mobilier was put before the public; it was the identical twin of the Crédit Foncier, having the same board and the same general manager, Albert Grant. Initially it had no link with the more prestigious French institution whose name it shared but in the difficult conditions of 1866 and possibly to bolster its position, the London concern announced that it had entered into 'intimate relations' {*Bankers Magazine* (1866) 193} with the Parisian investment bank, now also in similar straits. Grant's two finance companies operated independently for only six months in 1864 before being amalgamated as the Crédit Foncier & Mobilier of England. Grant signed its memorandum of association and took initially 1,000 shares.

Throughout the 1860s boom the Crédit Foncier & Mobilier retained close links with the Mercantile Credit Association, which was reformed in May 1864 as the Imperial Mercantile Credit Association, following its merger with the Imperial Financial Co. Between 1864 and 1866 the Crédit Foncier & Mobilier undertook 11 major promotions of which four were in conjunction with the Imperial Mercantile. Nearly all of the flotations in which Grant had a hand in the 1860s led to legal disputes involving allegations of fraud. Over the Humber Ironworks & Shipbuilding Co, there were disputes with the company's vendors, difficulties with the London Stock Exchange, and complaints from the finance company's shareholders who had bought shares of the shipbuilding concern.

The Imperial Land Co of Marseilles provides one of the clearest examples of Grant's techniques of company promotion in the 1860s. As managing director of the Crédit Foncier & Mobilier, Grant acquired the future assets of the embryonic land company at Marseilles for £444,604; however they were ultimately transferred to the land company for £1,109,323 but with J Masterman acting as the apparent vendor. The difference of £664,719 was absorbed in two ways: the direct costs of promoting the company and, second, commissions to various persons involved. The finance company received £331,719 of which £59,000 was spent on advertising, printing and stationery, while the co-sponsors of the issue, the National Bank and the Agra & Mastermans Bank, each received £5,000 as a promotion commission. Commissions totalling £89,000 went to directors of the Crédit Foncier & Mobilier while H Lewis and F

Mackenna, directors of the National Bank, also both received £15,000. 'Various other sums were given away, and it appeared that Mr Grant had got so much into the habit of handling large sums that he gave away £10,000 to one person, £15,000 to another, and in fact distributed sums of this magnitude with as much ease as other people would have given half crowns' {*Economist* 26 Mar 1870}. A large amount, some £76,500, was used to push the shares of the land company on the very weak new issue market of March, 1866, mainly in the form of special commissions on share sales to London and provincial brokers. In order to maintain a premium on the land company's shares, so as either to attract further subscriptions or to create the right conditions in order to unload its own holding, the finance company itself bought shares before their allotment. The finance company's own commission consisted not only of cash but also of debentures of the land company. The readiness of the Crédit Foncier & Mobilier to accept paper for its promotional commissions and to buy shares of its progeny, for whatever reason, led it in 1867 to have 'locked up' £325,666 in the Imperial Land Co of Marseilles, £282,740 in the General Irrigation Co, and £243,615 in the City of Milan Improvements Co.

The Milan promotion led to Grant having the title of baron conferred on him by King Victor Emmanuel in 1868. The methods used to promote the City of Milan Improvements Co, which built the Galleria Vittorio Emmanuele, were very similar to those employed for the Marseilles land company.

The Crédit Foncier & Mobilier survived the 1866 crisis, but for the rest of the decade the energies of its board were absorbed in realising the company's frozen assets. These consisted of the paper of companies that had been floated in the 1860s boom, about £643,650 in 1870, and advances, such as those to Peto (qv) for the construction of the London, Chatham & Dover Railway and the Varna Railway, which still amounted to £1,504,598 in 1869. Grant's activities during the boom had been the subject of severe questioning by the finance company's shareholders at its annual general meeting of April 1866, held a month before the crisis. The impact of the crisis upon the company's balance sheet forced its voluntary dissolution on 15 August 1866, although it was reconstituted as the Crédit Foncier of England and surprisingly Grant became governor of the reformed institution, holding that position until July 1868 when he resigned due to 'impaired health'. The meeting which received Grant's resignation set up an investigative committee which found 'that the enormous profits shown in the books of the company as having been earned ... were no profits at all' {*Bankers Magazine* (1869) 65}. Grant settled the claims of the finance company against him by mortgaging his personal estate which allowed him to pay 'a very pleasant comfortable sum' but he 'utterly denied and repudiated the accusation of taking any money that he was not legally and strictly entitled to' {*ibid*, 377}. In addition the Crédit Foncier of England received £65,000 from six directors and pursued others through the Court of Chancery. The liquidation of the Crédit Foncier & Mobilier, Grant's creature, was finally closed in 1872.

Grant, as managing director of the Crédit Foncier & Mobilier, had become a major public figure, although the true nature of the company was known to some in the City at least three years before its unfortunate shareholders. Henry Hucks Gibbs (qv) of Antony Gibbs & Sons declined a loan for the Mexican Railway 'because although money is money, yet that company no huele bien, and we were not willing that they should publish a prospectus with our names to it, fathered by them' {Guildhall Library, Gibbs papers, Gibbs private letter book, 24 Nov 1866}.

On the basis of his public, rather than his private reputation, Grant became MP for Kidderminister in the 1865 election. He lost the seat in the 1868 election but was re-elected in February 1874 when he sat as a Liberal-Conservative being 'in favour of the largest measure of civil principles' {Dod (1874)}. Grant may have contributed £20,000 to the Carlton Election Fund and there are allegations that his 1874 campaign involved dealings in carpets, the purchase of the Music Hall at Kidderminister and its presentation to the Corporation, the payment of the working expenses of the sewerage and the water works, and the completion of the tower of the Catholic church. On a second petition, involving charges of corrupt bribery, Grant was unseated on 24 July 1874.

Grant had estimated publicly in 1867 that he was worth £500,000. He maintained a fortune until the mid-1870s by acting as a private banker, at first alone, and then from February 1872 in conjunction with his brother Maurice. Trading as Grant Brothers & Co at 24 Lombard Street, Albert and Maurice were responsible for the promotion of 19 new issues during the boom of the early 1870s consisting of four foreign mining companies, four foreign bond issues, three foreign railways, one public utility, two domestic industrial companies, and five issues on behalf of domestic railway companies.

Besides being a major financier, Grant was also a well known benefactor. In 1874 he bought Leicester Fields, a city rubbish dump, for £30,000, had it laid out as public gardens around a statue of Shakespeare, and presented it as Leicester Square to the London Metropolitan Board of Works. Similarly he acquired at Christies a portrait of Sir Walter Scott by Landseer for 800 guineas which he then presented to the National Portrait Gallery, his gift being prompted by the Government's inability to provide funds for the purchase.

The seal upon his position as a major public figure was self-applied, through his purchase in 1873 of a considerable area of slum land adjacent to Kensington Palace. He had this area cleared and then built Kensington House to the designs of Sir James Knowles; this was a palatial mansion set in landscaped gardens complete with an ornamental lake. This magnificence was paralleled by his personal collection of pictures.

One other area of his activities in the early 1870s was the purchase of the *Echo* newspaper from Cassells for £20,000 in 1874. There are indications that he may have considered publishing a halfpenny morning edition; he certainly was responsible for the introduction of advertising in the columns of morning papers. Subsequently the *Echo* was sold to Passmore Edwards.

Grant's promotional techniques in the early 1870s were little different from those he had applied during the 1860s boom and by June 1877-89 actions were pending with regard to his affairs. These legal cases began in 1872 with an action connected with Grant's promotion of the Emma Silver Mining Co. In *Rubery v Grant and Sampson*, it emerged that Grant was closely connected with Sampson, who was responsible for the daily Money

Market article in the *Times*, and so thereby may have been able to influence the commentary in that column regarding his own promotions and those of competing affairs. The most famous action was *Twycross v Grant* which is still a leading case in English company law. It centred upon disclosure in a company's prospectus, particularly section 38 of the Companies Act of 1867, a hurriedly drafted clause which had been a response to the *Overend, Gurney* case.

The action arose from the promotion of the Lisbon Steam Tramways Co, the prospectus of which had not disclosed a subsidiary contract between Grant and the Duke de Saldanha, directors and promoters of the company, and Clark & Co, who were to build the tramway, and which involved payments to the promoters of £90,000. In addition there had been share rigging by Grant, to ensure a premium before allotment, in which the contractors acted as ultimate underwriters. At the beginning of the action the judge refused to allow a withdrawal of pleas or a postponement, while the plaintiffs refused the damages claimed — some £1000 offered by Grant — and further the defendants' consent to a verdict was refused. This placed Grant in an invidious position which was compounded by all his counsel, led by Thesiger, QC, retiring. Consequently Grant was forced to conduct his own defence, during which he addressed the jury 'with remarkable ability' {Finlayson (1877) 42}. Grant's defence, which revealed so much about certain aspects of company promotion during the 1870s boom, 'was the talk of the town and congratulations poured in on him' {O'Hagan (1929) I, 37}. The promoter had his speech printed for private circulation; it was even rumoured that Grant was considering joining the Bar. However Grant lost the case before Lord Coleridge. Similarly the case in Banco went for the plaintiff, and although the judges in the Court of Appeal were equally divided, the appeal was abortive and judgement of the lower court was affirmed.

This case, and others, began to eat into Grant's fortune and he was forced to sell his pictures at Christies in April 1877 for £106,202, with many of them, such as Landseer's *Otter Hunt* having been auctioned off at almost 'knocked down' prices. Although bankruptcy began to stare him in the face, Albert Grant continued to try to act as a financier. Perhaps in an attempt to rebuild his wealth, he established in May 1878 the General Banking Co, 'one of the boldest things announced in the City for several years' {*Statist* 11 May 1878}, but his name was now too notorious for the company to have any chance of success. Of the company's 20,000 shares only 4,744 were taken up, including 1,000 founders shares held by Albert Grant. The General Banking Co lasted less than a year, going into liquidation in February 1879 and Albert Grant failed a week later. His bankruptcy almost coincided with the completion of his Kensington House, with the result that the residence was used only once for a function — the Bachelors' Ball of 22 July 1880. In 1883 it was demolished, the site was seized by Grant's creditors, while its grand staircase was incorporated into Madame Tussaud's exhibition.

Grant tried to continue as a banker in London, with offices at 5 Lothbury until 1888. His brother Maurice set up a separate establishment at 4 Moorgate and continued there until the 1890s. Albert was amongst those principally involved in the promotion of the ill-fated Lisbon-Berlyn Gold Mining Co in the Pilgrims' Rest district of the Transvaal in the mid-

1880s; this company was the first to introduce hydraulic mining on a large scale in South Africa. However in 1885 he appeared in the London Bankruptcy Court with accounts showing liabilities of £217,000 and assets of £74,000. Grant appeared again in the Bankruptcy Court days before his death on 30 August 1899. His life is thought to be the basis for Augustus Melmotte in Trollope's *The Way We Live Now* (1875).

P L COTTRELL

Writings:

Twycross v Grant and Others ... July 1876 (Waterlow & Sons, 1876).

Sources:

Unpublished

Guildhall Library, Gibbs Papers.

PRO, Company files BT 31: 398/1508 Mercantile Discount 898/1003c Crédit Foncier 904/1028c Crédit Mobilier 1011/1617c Crédit Foncier and Mobilier of England 1057/1871c General Irrigation and Water Supply Company of France 1214/2778c Imperial Land Company of Marseilles 1039/1765 City of Milan Improvements 1284/3218 Credit Foncier of England 1362/3712 The Consolidated Land Company of France 2425/12229 General Banking

Philip L Cottrell, 'Investment Banking in England, 1856-1882: Case Study of the International Financial Society' (Hull PhD, 1974).

Antonio L Vieira, 'The Role of Britain and France in the Finance of Portuguese Railways 1850-90. A Comparative Study in Speculation, Corruption and Inefficiency' (Leicester PhD, 1983).

Published

Bankers' Magazine 2 (1872), 5 (1874), 3 (1876), 4 (1879).

Banking Almanac and Directory.

Joyce Bellamy, 'A Hull Shipbuilding Firm, the History of C W Earle and Earle's Shipbuilding and Engineering Co Ltd' *Business History* 6 (1963).

DNB.

Dod's Parliamentary Companion.

The Economist, 11 Jan, 25 Oct 1873, 20 June 1874, 23 Jan 1875, 17 Feb, 9 June 1877, 18 May, 18 June, 13 July, 7 Sept 1878, 1 Feb 1879.

Paul H Emden, *Money Powers of Europe in the Nineteenth and Twentieth Centuries* (Sampson Low & Co, 1937).

William F Finlayson, *Liabilities of Promoters of Companies, Report of the Case of Twycross v Grant* (1877).

Albert Grant, *Twycross v Grant and Others, Speech of Albert Grant Esq* (pp, 1876).

Louis Hyman, *The Jews of Ireland from Earliest Times to the Year 1910* (The Jewish Historical Society of England and Israel Universities Press, 1972).

William Turrentine Jackson, 'The Infamous Emma Mine: a British Interest in the Little Cottonwood District, Utah Territory' *Utah Historical Review* 23 (1955).

Kidderminster Shuttle 7, 28 Feb, 7 Mar, 4 Apr, 11, 24 July 1874.

Wilfred T C King, *History of London Discount Market* (G Routledge & Sons, 1936).

Henry Osborne O'Hagan, *Leaves from my Life* (2 vols, John Lane, Bodley Head, 1929).

William P W Philmore and E A Fry, *An Index to Changes of Name, 1760 to 1901* (Philmore & Co, 1905).

PP, RC on the London Stock Exchange (1878) C2157 and C2157-I.

A Selected List of Companies, Foreign Loans and Miscellaneous Projects (Grobecker Son & Co, 1872).

Statist 11 May, 13 June 1878, 8 May 1879.

Times 13, 14, 15 Jan, 24 May 1875, 31 Aug 1899.

Alpheus F Williams, *Some Dreams Come True* (Cape Town: H B Timmins, 1948).

Stephanos Xenos, *Depradations; or Overend, Gurney & Co, and the Greek and Oriental Steam Navigation Company* (1869).

WWMP.

GRANTLEY, 1st Lord of Grantley
see **FURNESS, Christopher**

GRAY, Sir William

(1823-1898)

Shipbuilder and shipowner

William Gray was born in Earsdon parish near Blyth, Northumberland, being baptised on 3 March 1823, the younger son of Matthew Gray, a prosperous draper of Blyth, and his wife Jane. After attending Dr John Bruce's Academy in Newcastle upon Tyne, he joined his father's business but, at an early age set up his own drapery firm in West Hartlepool in 1844. West Hartlepool at this time was rapidly developing, and had an extensive programme of new harbour works in prospect. The young Gray, like his father, did not confine his activities to drapery, but also invested in wooden sailing ships, as did so many traders and others in the ports of North-East England.

Gray's business took him frequently to London where he met Dorothy Hall of Lewisham, whom he married in 1849. His father-in-law, Captain John Hall RN, was an experienced and lifelong seafarer, and no doubt this influence reinforced Gray's shipping interests. As a committee member of the Hartlepool & Durham Shipping Co, he came to know intimately John Dunshon Denton, a prominent and successful local shipbuilder who had already built some vessels for Gray's account.

In 1863, William Gray joined Denton in an informal partnership in the latter's shipbuilding business, each partner furnishing an equal share of the capital required, but sharing the profits in the proportion 55 per cent to Denton and 45 per cent to Gray. This arrangement was later altered in view of Gray's more active managerial involvement in the shipbuilding firm and Denton's ill-health. From 1863, the enterprise was known as Denton, Gray & Co, but there was a brief period during which Denton and Gray associated themselves with the shipbuilding and marine engineering firms of Richardson, Duck & Co, and T Richardson & Sons, the new company assuming joint-stock, limited liability structure, under the name of Richardson, Denton, Duck & Co Ltd. The financial crisis of 1866 terminated this venture which also precipitated the demise of the West Hartlepool shipbuilding firm of Pile, Spence & Co, whose premises Denton and Gray were subsequently to occupy.

Between 1866 and 1873, the firm traded as Denton, Gray & Co, but with Denton's failing health and subsequent death in 1872, the enterprise became known as William Gray & Co, and became a limited liability company in 1889. By the 1880s the firm had come to enjoy a considerable reputation as one of Britain's leading shipbuilders, and by 1884 was employing 2,000 men and paying wages weekly of £3,000. In that year Gray opened his Central Marine Engineering Works and thereafter not only built and outfitted sailing vessels and steamers, but also began the production of marine engines and boilers on an impressive scale.

In 1878, 1882, 1888 and in the year of Gray's death, 1898, the firm achieved the remarkable feat of constructing more tonnage than any other shipbuilding yard in the world. Gray's well-built tramp cargo ships were of innovative design and unsurpassed economy. His firm built one of the world's first bulk-carrying petroleum tankers, and provided Marcus Samuel (qv), the founder of Shell Petroleum, with the nucleus of his tanker fleet. Gray built innumerable well-decked tramp steamers and pioneered the installation of quadruple expansion marine engines in cargo vessels. Gray not only built ships on a very large scale, but was himself a shipowner of considerable importance. By 1887 he managed at least 12 steamers and had a substantial financial interest in about 70 more.

William Gray played a major part in both local and national affairs. The historian of West Hartlepool, Robert Wood, describes him as having 'made' West Hartlepool. He was a member of the West Hartlepool Harbour Commissioners, served on the town council, and had the unique distinction of being mayor of both Hartlepool and West Hartlepool. He stood unsuccessfully for parliament in 1891 in the Liberal-Unionist interest, but was narrowly defeated by his fellow-townsman, shipowner and shipbuilder, Christopher Furness (qv). His services to shipping were recognised in 1891 when he was made president of the Chamber of Shipping of the United Kingdom. He was a director of the North-Eastern Railway Co, and director of a number of marine insurance clubs in the North-East, including the Well-Deck Steamship Insurance Association. He was also a member of the Committee of Lloyd's Register. He was a JP and was knighted in 1890 and became High Sheriff for the County of Durham in 1892. He sat on the load-line Committee and gave evidence to the Royal Commission on the loss of life at sea in 1887. He died on 12 September 1898 leaving £1,534,704 gross and was survived by his youngest but only surviving son who later became Sir William Gray First Bt.

ROBIN CRAIG

Writings:

PP, RC Loss of Life at Sea (1887) C 5227.

Sources:

Unpublished

Northumberland RO, Earsdon parish registers.

PrC.

Published

Peter Barton, 'A Decade of Iron Shipbuilding' *Sea Breezes* 39 (1965).

Robin Craig, 'William Gray & Co: A West Hartlepool Shipbuilding Enterprise, 1864-1913' in P L Cottrell and D H Aldcroft (eds), *Shipping, Trade and Commerce: Essays in Memory of Ralph Davis* (Leicester: Leicester University Press, 1981).

Robert Wood, *West Hartlepool: The Rise and Development of a Victorian New Town* (West Hartlepool: West Hartlepool Corporation, 1967).

WWW.

GREATHEAD, James Henry

(1844-1896)

Consulting engineer

James Henry Greathead was born at Grahamstown, Cape Colony, on 6 August 1844, the son of a member of the Cape legislature. After attending college at Grahamstown, he came to England in 1859 to complete his education. About five years later he entered the office of Peter W Barlow, a prominent railway and civil engineer, brother of Henry Barlow (qv), a move which brought him into contact with the expanding world of Victorian engineering.

Greathead's first outside work was as assistant engineer at the extension of the Midland Railway to London in 1867, under William H Barlow and Benjamin Baker. A year later he went to work with the Tower Subway under the River Thames and there introduced the method of shield tunnelling with which his name has since been associated. Both Marc Brunel and P W Barlow had already experimented with tunnelling techniques which involved the use of shields or cast iron segments to hold back the material being excavated. Indeed, P W Barlow had patented the idea of shield tunnelling. Neither, however, had successfully put his ideas into practice: Brunel's disastrous experiences with flooding during the construction of the Thames Tunnel meant that the project, which was begun in 1825, had taken about seventeen years to complete and contractors became unwilling to undertake further projects beneath the river. In 1868, however, Greathead, as contractor under Barlow's chairmanship, tendered to build the tunnel for £9,400; work began the following year, with Greathead's circular shield, propelled by six powerful jacks, driving its way beneath the river. Completed within twelve months, the 1,350 foot long tunnel was convincing evidence that the shield system was technically and financially feasible.

Greathead set up as a consulting engineer in 1870 and continued to devote much of his time to tunnelling. The shield was adopted in several American projects — in New York in 1870 hydraulic presses were used to drive it forward. During 1873-77 Greathead returned to railway work, being resident engineer under F S Gilbert on the Metropolitan District's extension from Earl's Court to west of Hammersmith. He also drew up a scheme for an outer circle line following the Regent's Canal, and was associated with Richard Price Williams in a scheme to run another line to Brighton. In 1876 Greathead devised a complex arrangement, involving air-locks and hydraulic machinery for boring through water-bearing strata at Woolwich, though it was never put into effect.

From the early 1870s, Greathead's activities increasingly centred upon questions relating to passenger transport and the relief of traffic congestion in large cities. In 1884 the City of London & Southwark Subway Act was passed, with Greathead lending his considerable skills as parliamentary witness to the bill's advocates. Construction on the City & South London Railway — which eventually became the world's first electric underground line — was begun in 1886, with compressed air and the Greathead shield employed for the first time through water-bearing strata. For the first time too separate single-line tunnels were excavated so reducing the material to be removed and improving ventilation. Greathead also perfected a system of grouting, which used compressed air to force cement into the gaps between the cast iron tube and the excavated tunnel. The subway, running from King William Street to Stockwell, was opened by the Prince of Wales on 4 November 1890. The engineering success of the scheme, which established the superiority of electric traction produced many imitations. After the report of a joint-parliamentary committee on electric railways in 1892, before which Greathead was one of the principal witnesses, six different deep tunnel railways were authorised. In each case, Greathead, and eminent engineers such as Sir John Fowler and Sir Benjamin Baker (qqv), were chosen as consulting engineers.

Greathead did not confine his activities to deep tunnel lines. He was associated with Sir Douglas Fox and Francis Fox in the construction of the overhead electric railway at Liverpool — another pioneer undertaking in the field of electric traction, which was opened in 1893. He was greatly interested in hydraulic machinery and devised a new form of injector hydrant for the extinction of fires. Sir Henry Bessemer and Lord Armstrong (qqv) displayed an interest in these, and the latter undertook construction at Elswick.

Greathead was often involved in arbitration work, his most important case probably being the hearings between the Manchester Ship Canal Co and the London & North Western and Great Western railways, in which he appeared on behalf of the Canal Co, and ensured that the final award to the railways was very much below the amount claimed. Greathead acquired a considerable reputation as a parliamentary witness, where his engineering expertise, his clear exposition, and his ability to avoid petty disputes, served him to good effect. He was a member of the Institution of Mechanical Engineers from 1879, and of the Institution of Civil Engineers from 1881, serving on the council of the latter in 1894. Nevertheless, due to his retiring disposition, he seldom took part in the proceedings, although he did contribute notable papers, one of which, on the Liverpool overhead railway, was awarded the Telford medal by the Institution of Civil Engineers.

He retained his contacts with South Africa, and for years was consulting engineer for the Durban Tramway Co. In 1885 he married a Miss Coryndon, daughter of Mr Coryndon of Kimberley. A sufferer from acute dyspepsia, he died suddenly at his residence, Ravenscraig, Streatham, on 21 October 1896, in the midst of his work, leaving his colleagues to complete his designs for London's underground railway system. He left a widow and three children. His estate was valued at £18,874 gross.

GEOFFREY TWEEDALE

Writings:

'On Injector Hydrants for Fire Extinction' *Proceedings of the Institution of Mechanical Engineers* 1879.

(with Francis Fox) 'Liverpool Overhead Railway' *Minutes of the Proceedings of the Institution of Civil Engineers* 117 (1893-94).

'The City and South London Railway; with Some Remarks upon Subaqueous Tunnelling by Shield and Compressed-Air' *ibid* 123 (1895-96).

The proceedings of the parliamentary committees to whom Greathead presented evidence have not been published apparently.

Sources:

Unpublished

House of Lords RO, Commons Committee on City of London and Southwark Subway Bill.

PrC.

Published

Theodore C Barker and Michael Robbins, *A History of London Transport* (2 vols, George Allen & Unwin, 1963-74) I.

Engineer 82 (1896).

Engineering 62 (1896).

Alan A Jackson and Desmond F Croome, *Rails Through the Clay. A History of London's Tube Railways* (Allen & Unwin, 1962).

C E Lee, 'The Tower Subway' *Transactions of the Newcomen Society* 43 (1970-71).

John Marshall, *A Biographical Dictionary of Railway Engineers* (Newton Abbot: David & Charles, 1978).

GREENE, Edward

(1815-1891)

Brewer

Edward Greene was born in Bury St Edmunds, Suffolk, in 1815, the third son of Benjamin Greene (1780-1860), brewer and later West Indian merchant, and his wife Catherine née Smith. Benjamin had come to Bury

Edward Greene ca 1880 (courtesy of Dr R G Wilson).

around 1800 from Oundle, after completing his apprenticeship with Whitbreads, one of the great London brewers. The Greenes had been drapers and staunch Dissenters for generations in the South Midlands. Although his small Suffolk brewery was entirely unexceptional, Benjamin Greene was a controversial figure in Bury. Starting out a pillar of the Independent Chapel and marrying, as his second wife, the daughter of a famous Dissenting minister Rev Thomas Smith (pastor of the Howard Chapel in Bedford), he educated his five sons at Bury's prestigious Anglican grammar school, acquired and briefly ran an outspoken Tory newspaper (the *Bury and Suffolk Herald*), and took a notorious stance against the abolition of slavery after he became an estate proprietor in St Christopher in the mid-1820s. Buck & Greene's Westgate brewery remained small. In 1831 Benjamin reckoned it had an output of 3,000 barrels and a further 2,000 of table beer.

Edward Greene completely transformed his father's brewery between 1840 and 1870. He began work there in 1828 and in 1836, when his father moved to London to form a firm of sugar merchants, he became its sole owner on his coming of age. Unlike its bigger regional rivals in Norwich, Ipswich, Yarmouth and Colchester the brewery seems never to have possessed the protection of more than a handful of tied houses. Therefore Edward Greene's success was achieved entirely in the free trade before 1865. He sold his beers by a system of travellers and agents throughout East Anglia. Doubtlessly he was greatly aided by the railways after 1845 and rapidly rising beer consumption, even in agricultural areas, between 1830 and 1880. In some ways his brewery's expansion, without the aid of tied property, was not unlike that achieved by Guinness (qv) and the Burton brewers. An obituary of Edward Greene in the *London Star* put the secret of this success in a nutshell, 'He was one of the first country brewers to discover that beer need not be vile, black, turgid stuff, but brewed a bright amber-coloured liquid of Burton type, which he sold at a shilling per gallon, and made a fortune'. {quoted in the *Bury and Norwich Post* 21 Apr 1891} As a consequence of the popularity of his beers, output at Westgate increased to over 40,000 barrels a year by the 1870s. By this decade, according to the *Licensed Victuallers Gazette*, Greene's ales had become 'the accepted and most popular "tap" from Watton and Wymondham in the north to Colchester and Bishops Stortford in the south, and from Ely and St Ives in the west to Framlingham and Woodbridge in the east'. {quoted in the *Bury and Norwich Post* 17 Apr 1875}

As was usual in brewing which, with coal, was the major industry that underwent least technological transformation in the nineteenth century, Greene's increase in output was not matched by any significant modernisation of his plant. Of course it was extended several times: in 1845, 1856-58, 1865-66 and 1880. Except for a further steam engine in 1866, however, the additions were chiefly in malting and fermenting capacity. Indeed Edward Greene prided himself on his old-fashioned methods. With the traditional small labour force in breweries (he employed 18 men and three boys in 1851 and only 90 altogether by the early 1880s) modernisation mattered little so long as scrupulous cleanliness was observed and beers maintained a good reputation.

In 1887 Edward Greene merged his brewery with that of his neighbour,

Edward Greene's Westgate Brewery ca 1870 (courtesy of Dr R G Wilson) copyright Greene King & Sons plc.

Fred King. The latter's St Edmunds Brewery, literally adjacent to Greene's, was rapidly built up after 1869 from a century-old malting and wine and spirit business. By 1887 it had an output of over 20,000 barrels, just less than half that of its competitor. The reasons for the merger were two-fold. Greene and King both began purchases of tied public houses after 1870 which led them into serious rivalry. Between 1870 and 1887 Greenes' bought 91, Kings 52. These were early acquisitions pre-dating the more general scramble for tied houses in the late 1880s and 1890s. Secondly both Edward Greene and Fred King wanted to make adequate settlements for their families. The transformation of their firms into a private limited liabiltiy company allowed them to do this. The new company was a relatively early brewery to seek this status in the first real surge of brewing firms going public following Guinness's spectacularly successful conversion in 1886. Greene King's capitalisation of £550,000 was reckoned on a generous valuation. Ownership was almost entirely confined to eight individuals in the Greene and King families. Edward Greene became the first chairman of the new company, dying four years later.

Edward Greene's interests were predictable enough for a prosperous country brewer. He was an authority on horses, giving evidence in 1873 to a House of Lords committee on the supply of horses and was Master of the

Suffolk Hunt, 1871-75. After thirty years of total dedication to his brewery he became MP for Bury St Edmunds in 1865, representing the town in the Conservative interest until 1885, then the Stowmarket Division of Suffolk, 1886-91. He was also active as a JP and DL of Suffolk. At the outset of his parliamentary career he spoke quite often in the Commons, and remained for the next quarter of a century an extremely popular speaker throughout Suffolk. His speeches, delivered in a harsh, loud Suffolk accent, possessed an evangelical directness. Their themes were invariably agriculture, housing and religion. Disraeli reckoned him to be 'the fiercest Protestant in the House' {Zetland (1929) II, 62}. He opposed the introduction of ritualism and confession into the Anglican church and in one Commons speech asserted that the inmates of convents were in a worse situation than those in lunatic asylums. On housing he spoke from more experience. He was a member of the select committee on Artisans' and Labourers' Dwellings in 1866 and was himself a highly paternalistic employer. Certainly he practiced what he preached. By the mid-1880s he had acquired around 50 cottages in Bury to house around half his workforce. He insisted that all his cottages should have three bedrooms. 'How can you expect morality amongst the poor if you put them in hovels only fit for pigs? The first who have partaken of my prosperity are my poorer neighbours'. {Speech made in 1865, quoted in *Bury and Norwich Post* 21 Apr 1891}

Agriculture was Edward Greene's other great pursuit after 1865. He first began his farming ventures in 1854 on renting 150 acres on the edge of Bury. In 1865, when he set the seal on his election to parliament, by leasing the Ixworth Abbey estate he farmed a further 400 acres in a progressive manner. Nine years later he bought Nether Hall, Pakenham with 850 acres. He was principal innovator in experiments with steam ploughing in Suffolk in the late 1860s and also a county representative to the National Chamber of Agriculture after 1867. In 1870 he founded the Ixworth Farmers' Club. For the next twenty years it was the liveliest farmers' club in East Anglia. He was also chairman of the Bury & Thetford Railway Co, 1865-76. The venture, to provide an alternative outlet to Bury's Ipswich rail connection, was not very successful for its construction was a protracted affair, caught in the pincers of the 1866 financial crisis and the onset of agricultural depression.

Edward Greene was the archetypal, successful country brewer. But he never lost the common touch with his patently straightforward approach to life. He could speak about key issues in rural Suffolk in a way which everyone from Lord Bristol to the poorest agricultural labourer comprehended.

His immediate family connections were conventional enough. Edward's first wife Emily Smythies (d 1848), whom he married in 1840 was the daughter of a Huntingdonshire parson and magistrate; the second, Caroline Dorothea née Bunce whom he married in 1870, was the widow of Rear Admiral Sir William Hoste, Bt. His only son Walter, given in 1900 the baronetcy his father had been promised shortly before his death, was chairman of Greene King, 1891-1920, and Conservative MP for Bury St Edmunds, 1900-6. Sir Walter, a fair specimen of third generation business was addicted to stag hunting, steam yachting and partridge shooting. Edward Greene's brother, Benjamin Buck Greene, was Governor of the

Bank of England and few brewers can claim more impeccable literary connections: Christopher Isherwood is a great-grandson and Graham Greene a great-nephew.

Edward Greene died on 5 April 1891, leaving £356,945 gross.

R G WILSON

Writings:

PP, HC 1873 (325) XIV, Horses.

Sources:

Unpublished

Greene King & Sons PLC, Westgate Brewery, Bury St Edmunds, archives.

Family papers of the late Dr Raymond Greene.

MCe.

PrC.

Published

Bateman.

The Brewers' Journal after 1869

Burke's Landed Gentry 1937, 1965.

Burke's Peerage.

The Bury and Norwich Post 17 Apr 1875, 21 Apr 1891.

Bury Free Post passim and 21 Apr 1891.

Marquis of Zetland (ed), *The Letters of Benjamin Disraeli to Lady Bradford and Lady Chesterfield* (2 vols, Ernest Benn, 1929).

Richard G Wilson, *Greene King: A Business and Family History* (Heinemann, 1983).

WWMP.

'The Chairman', taken from Sacre cartoon (courtesy of British Petroleum Company plc).

GREENWAY, Charles

Lord Greenway of Stanbridge Earls

(1857-1934)

Petroleum company chairman

Charles Greenway was born in Taunton on 13 June 1857, the son of John David Greenway, a draper, and Lucy Emily née Whyte. Little information survives of his childhood and education. Apparently he left home as a young man to try his fortune. After some retailing and secretarial experience with Seton Laing as a junior market clerk, he joined the newly-opened London branch of Shaw, Finlayson & Co at Mark Lane, in June 1876. There he made the acquaintance of C W Wallace (qv) who was in charge of the office and who, only a couple of years older than Greenway, was to have such a dominant influence on his subsequent career and with whom he had an instinctive sympathy and a strong business relationship. This position also provided the basis for his practical business sense which was further developed when he left for India as a writer.

In 1884 the firm of Shaw, Finlayson & Co fell apart and Wallace and Greenway had to separate. Greenway made his first visit to India, joining the staff of Ralli Brothers, general merchants in Bombay. In March 1893 he joined the firm of Shaw Wallace & Co, which had been formed in 1886 and renewed his professional relationship with Wallace. At first he managed their combined import department.

Greenway's commonsense, initiative and energy was exercised in a succession of different posts of increasing responsibility. In 1891 Shaw, Wallace & Co acquired the Burmah Oil Co marketing agency in India. The first full ship's cargo reached Calcutta in 1896 and as partner and the manager of the agency Greenway acquired his first acquaintance with the oil trade, with which his subsequent career was so closely concerned. His respect and support for the managing agency as a method of administering British business overseas, particularly in the Indian sub-continent, was later to prove both a source of managerial strength and failure when applied to the technical operations of the Anglo-Persian Oil Co (APOC) in Persia.

It was a critical period for Burmah as a fledgling oil company: reorganised and with a new refinery and pipeline at Surinam, it faced fierce competition from the Asiatic Petroleum Co, the Standard Oil Co and Russian oil interests, primarily for the kerosene markets of the East, particularly India. Greenway must take much of the credit for the successful marketing of the products of the Burmah Oil Co which rose from 2 per cent of the market share in 1898-99 to 48 per cent in 1905-6.

It was Greenway, too, who was deeply involved in the Agreement of 1 October 1905, which ended the trade war between Asiatic Petroleum and Burmah Oil regulating the competition between them. However the negotiations were arduous and the animosity which was occasioned by them left bitter memories with Greenway, when he was later involved in discussions with the Asiatic Petroleum Co and the Shell management in London as the managing director of APOC.

Greenway returned to London in 1908 as a senior partner in R G Shaw & Co and was then asked by Wallace to assist him in the formation of the APOC, which he joined in autumn 1908. Greenway's administrative abilities and Wallace's persuasive talents were largely responsible for the successful incorporation of the APOC on 14 April 1909. Greenway became a director. On 31 January 1910, he succeeded Wallace as managing director and was appointed chairman on 11 July 1914 following the death of the first chairman, Lord Strathcona, in January. He held the position until his retirement on 27 March 1927. Greenway became the dominant figure of the APOC during its first formative decades and this was recognised by his colleagues who spoke of his 'courage, tenacity and wisdom . . . [which] have played an immensely important part in bringing this great Company to the position which it holds today' {Sir John Cargill 1927}.

He was almost a one-man managerial team, expanding to two principal assistants, H E Nicholson and Duncan Garrow during the First World War. Greenway organised the establishment of a firm of managing agents, Lloyd, Scott & Co Ltd, later Strick Scott & Co Ltd, based in Muhammarah, to provide the managerial expertise to administer the APOC's operations and marketing activities in Persia. Although his Burmah Oil Co colleague, James Hamilton, had initial responsibility for technical and financial affairs, Greenway gradually took charge and the Glasgow office was closed in 1915. He steered his company through the desperate technical difficulties which dogged the early refining processes and the almost crippling financial problems which nearly made it bankrupt. Greenway's initiative provided the basis for a long-term supply contract with the Admiralty for fuel and the justification for the acquisition by the British Government of a major shareholding in the APOC in 1914.

It was Greenway's purpose to create an integrated oil company, not just a purveyor of products to the Admiralty or confined to production in Persia. He wanted it to have its own tanker fleet, forming a company for that purpose in 1915, and a marketing organisation, acquiring the British Petroleum Co in 1917 as the basis for such activities and extensive world-wide oil interests beyond Persia. He also gained a 50 per cent shareholding in the Turkish Petroleum Co in 1914. A research establishment was formed in 1917. In these activities pursued with determination, even obstinacy, he incurred a mixed response from civil servants and politicians and encountered personal animosity and competition from his rivals. By his detailed advocacy and patient persistence, his achievement was considerable: the survival and independent existence of the APOC. From 1912 to 1918 there was a ten-fold increase in oil production in Persia from 80,800 tons to 897,402 tons and in 1919 production topped one million tons.

In the post-war period progress was maintained with world-wide exploration activities, with oil bunkering stations on the principal maritime routes and with the establishment of a marketing presence in most of the countries of Europe. Greenway faced opposition, doubts from some of his Burmah Oil colleagues on the board and uncertainties from the Government about whether it wished to remain as a shareholder in the APOC. In spite of financial difficulties, the first attempts to rationalise managerial responsibilities on a large scale both in Persia and elsewhere and emerging concessionary problems with the Persian Government, the expansion of activities continued. Consequently Greenway could claim to his satisfaction in 1924 at the annual general meeting that the APOC had achieved 'a record of development which, I am confident, has not been equalled in the same short space of time by any other concern in the commercial history of the World.' Securing his successor as chairman was not without its drama, before Sir John Cadman (qv) was appointed, but there was no doubt that Greenway's legacy was extraordinary. From an insignificant minor the APOC had become an impressive major oil company. He had faltered only once, in 1916, when there was an attempt to oust him by disgruntled government officials, but backed by the government directors, he survived to dominate the APOC for another decade.

In his recreations he was mostly an out-door man, enjoying most of all golf, fishing and shooting but he also relished playing bridge. He was hospitable and friendly and his house parties at his country seat at Stanbridge Earls in Hampshire were enjoyable rather than formal. Notwithstanding his formidable image of 'Chairman Charlie', top-hatted and bespatted, he was in private a friendly personality and deeply affectionate towards children. In public his business was his life. He was not a committee-man in public service.

Greenway was created a baronet in 1919 for his services during the war and in 1927 on his retirement he was elevated to the peerage as Lord Greenway of Stanbridge Earls.

In 1884 he married Mabel née Tower, daughter of Augustine Edwin Tower, a solicitor, at the Congregational Church in Selhurst near Croydon, Surrey, when he described himself as 'gentleman'. The marriage, a happy one, produced one son and two daughters. He died after a brief illness on 17 December 1934, leaving £298,953 gross.

R W FERRIER

Sources:

Unpublished

BCe.

MCe.

PrC.

Published

Sir John Cargill, 'The Retirement of Sir Charles Greenway' *The Naft* 1927.

T A B Corley, *A History of the Burmah Oil Company, 1886-1924* (William Heinemann Ltd, 1983).

Biplab Dasgupta, *The Oil Industry in India: Some Economic Aspects* (Cass, 1971).

R W Ferrier, *The History of the British Petroleum Company* Vol I *The Developing Years 1901-32* (Cambridge: Cambridge University Press, 1982).

Sir William Fraser, 'The Late Lord Greenway' *The Naft* 1935.

Geoffrey Gareth Jones, *The State and the Emergence of the British Oil Industry* (Macmillan, 1981).

Marian Kent, *Oil and Empire: British Policy and Mesopotamian Oil 1900-1920* (Macmillan, 1976).

Times 18 Dec 1934.

Sir Harry Townend, *A History of Shaw Wallace & Co and Shaw Wallace & Co Ltd* (Calcutta, 1965).

WWW.

Arthur Greenwood (from C Addison, Politics from Within *vol II).*

GREENWOOD, Arthur

(1845-1910)

Machine tool and machinery manufacturer

Arthur Greenwood was born in Leeds on 2 October 1845, the seventh child of Thomas Greenwood (qv), co-founder of the Leeds engineering firm of Greenwood & Batley, and his wife Joanna née Clapham. He was educated at a dame school in Leeds and later studied in France, where he acquired a fluency in French and other languages which is said to have helped the firm develop its foreign connections. At fifteen he was articled to his father's firm. When twenty-one he became foreman in one of his father's shops, was appointed under-manager two years later, and in 1870 was admitted as a partner. He was a leading figure in the firm from the death of his father in 1873; in 1888, when the partnership was transformed into a limited company, he became a major shareholder and managing director, having as co-managing directors his brother, George, his cousin Henry, and J H Wurtzburg, who had been closely associated with the designing and engineering departments. John Batley had retired from the business some years earlier.

Greenwood, like his father, was a prolific inventor. In 1888, for example, he held patents for machinery for printing, silk dressing, grinding, gunpowder pressing, oil cake making and firearms manufacture. His

GREG, Henry Philips

(1865-1936)

Cotton manufacturer

Henry Philips Greg was born on 13 August 1865, the fourth child of Henry Russell Greg and his wife Emily née Gair. He attended Rugby School and Trinity College, Cambridge.

The Greg family had long been established in the cotton industry. Samuel Greg had established Quarry Bank Mill at Styal, near Wilmslow, Cheshire, in 1784. By the early 1830s his firm, by then consisting of five mills, had emerged as one of the foremost coarse spinning and weaving concerns in the country. It consumed annually more than 1 per cent of the country's total raw cotton consumption. It was, however, not until 1847 that the Albert Mill, Reddish, was founded by Robert Hyde Greg, Henry Philips Greg's grandfather. The four storeyed mill concentrated on spinning and doubling yarns which were sold predominantly in Continental and Near Eastern markets. In 1856 Henry Russell Greg became a partner, taking full control of the mill after his father's death in 1875. Unfortunately he lacked the business flair of his father and indeed of his son and failed to develop the mill's full potential. When Henry Philips Greg joined the firm in 1887 very few changes had been made since Robert Hyde Greg's death.

On 12 September 1887 Henry Philips Greg started work at the Albert Mill as an office boy. He gradually proceeded through all branches of clerical work, reportedly paying exceptional attention to detail, both in his office work and in the duties of the 400 employees of the mill.

Henry Russell Greg died in 1894 leaving £60,232 gross. His son now took control of the Albert Mill. It was not long before the expansion and specialisation, so necessary to competitive survival in the cotton industry at this time, began. Emphasis was shifted towards the production of fancy yarn for use in upholstery fabrics and old machinery was scrapped in favour of ring spindles. In 1907 a new two storey mill was added and by the winter of 1913-14 fancy yarns had become so important that a new building, specifically for fancy doubling was erected, further expansion taking place in 1919. That R Greg & Co Ltd of Reddish was able to become and remain competitive during the difficult inter-war period was largely the result of the energy of its chairman Henry Philips Greg who retained the controlling interest after it became a private limited company in 1918.

In typical Greg tradition Henry Philips Greg took a close interest in the lives of his employees. He provided a reading room and recreation facilities as well as organising saving schemes. As early as 1915 the firm appointed a welfare secretary.

Henry Philips Greg's energies extended far beyond the confines of his own business. Indeed his efforts did have some lasting effects on the cotton industry as a whole. He was, for instance, a pioneer of the automatic loom. In 1904, on behalf of Ashton Brothers Ltd, he visited the United States and was responsible for the importation of 500 such looms. This led to the formation of the British Northrop Loom Co at Blackburn, of which firm he was later chairman, Denis Hollins (qv) being its managing director. He also became chairman of Ashton Brothers Ltd in 1907 and a year later faced a thirteen-week strike by the Weavers' Union over the conditions under which the new automatic looms might be introduced.

The period 1887-1936 was one in which the English cotton industry was facing growing foreign competition. Henry Philips Greg recognised that if the industry was to compete in a changing environment money was needed for research and development. As a result he was a prime mover in the formation of the British Cotton Industry Research Association as well as the Research Laboratories of the Shirley Institute at Didsbury near Manchester.

In addition to being an energetic manufacturer he also owned substantial landed estates in both Styal and Reddish.

Greg married in 1898 Jane Emily Dibblee, daughter of Frederick Lewis Dibblee, a civil engineer; they had five children. He died on 3 June 1936, leaving £136,623 gross.

MARY B ROSE

Writings:

Miscellaneous contributions to the journal *Fancy Yarns*.

Sources:

Unpublished

Manchester Central Library, Greg papers, accounts of Albert Mill, Reddish, title deeds of the Reddish Estate.

BCe.

MCe.

PrC.

Published

Burkes Landed Gentry.

Alan Fowler, 'Trade Unions and Technical Change: the Automatic Loom Strike, 1908' *North-West Labour History Society Bulletin* 6 (1979-80).

Obituary of Henry Philips Greg (R Greg & Co Ltd).

A M Grenfell (courtesy of Lady Maldigrave).

GRENFELL, Arthur Morton

(1873-1958)

Financier

Arthur Morton Grenfell was born in Mayfair, London, on 21 October 1873, sixth of the nine sons of Pascoe du Pré Grenfell (1828-96), of 69 Eaton Place, London, and Wilton Park, Beaconsfield, Buckinghamshire, by his wife and cousin Sophia (1833-98), daughter of John Pascoe Grenfell, vice-admiral in the Brazilian Navy. His father was a partner in Morton, Rose & Co (City financiers specialising in American railroads), deputy chairman of North British & Mercantile Insurance, trustee of the American Investment Trust, director of Alliance Marine & General Assurance, and on the London committees of the Anglo-Austrian Bank, the Bank of Romania and the Imperial Ottoman Bank; he left £125,252. Arthur Grenfell was nephew of Field Marshal Lord Grenfell and five of his eight brothers died as British soldiers on service. 'The Grenfells were a symbol of that landed gentry who made England a nation of sportsmen, pioneers and warriors', according to one guinea-pig director, 'When that type fails to be bred, but not until then, will England begin to sink downhill' {Winchester (1935) 167}. Arthur Grenfell was educated at Eton (1887-92) where he was a master of the beagles and won the steeplechase (1892). He was trained and set up in the City by the American financier Pierpont Morgan, for whom his second cousin E C Grenfell (qv) was London manager from 1900.

In 1896 Arthur Grenfell acted as London director of Willoughby's Consolidated Co, which was interested in Rhodesian development, during the absence in Africa (and gaoling for his part in the Jameson Raid) of Sir John Willoughby (1859-1918) and his partner Colonel Sir Weston Jarvis (1855-1939). Later, in 1899, Grenfell was briefly a director of North Bonsor Gold Mining, run by Willoughby and Jarvis, which owned 70 claims in the Selukwe district of Matabeleland and had £225,000 issued capital. Grenfell was also on the board for a time of another Willoughby company, Red & White Rose Goldmining, registered in 1899 with 76 claims near Bulawayo. Its other directors were two esurient noblemen, a courtier called Sir Seymour Fortescue (1856-1942) and the Hon Charles White (1860-1930), Chief Commissioner of Rhodesian Police 1892-95.

Grenfell in 1899 became a director of a merchant banking house which had been in existence under one name or another for about fifty years, and which was thereafter known as Chaplin, Milne, Grenfell (CMG). Ernest Chaplin (1849-1930), its senior partner, had been a member of the Morton, Rose firm together with Arthur Grenfell's father; its other partners were his nephew Eric (later Lord Chaplin, 1877-1949), George Grinnell-Milne (1853-1931) and his son Douglas (1886-1963), and R W Skipworth. Grenfell remained active in financing worldwide mining development. Some

GRENFELL Arthur Morton

concerns which he directed, such as the Freemantle Smelting Works, Kalgoorlie Southern Development Co or Oosten Rand Gold, were rapidly wound up. Others were more substantial. He was a director of United Excelsior Mines, which was formed in 1898 holding 1,040 claims on Mashonaland, and whose board included Horkheimer, the nominee of the powerful Frankfurt combine, Metallgesellschaft, controlled by the controversial Merton family. Grenfell was chairman of the Messina (Transvaal) Co registered in 1905 with 1,200 copper claims in the northern Transvaal, together with 21,200 acres of farmland. Under the chairmanship of Sir Robert Price MP (1854-1926), and with Sir Frederick Frankland, Tenth Baronet (1868-1937) as a co-director, Grenfell was on the board of United Africa Explorations floated in 1901 to conduct financial and trust business in Africa, Spain and America. He was also a director of the Charter Trust & Agency formed in 1902 to conduct trust and agency business for the British South Africa Co (his father-in-law Lord Grey was chairman of both), and for a period he was a director of Town Properties of Bulaweyo, a subsidiary of Rhodesia Ltd.

One important piece of Rhodesian finance was undertaken in 1902 by Grenfell for family reasons. His father-in-law, Lord Grey, 'the man that I loved better than anybody else' {Rhodes House, Grenfell to Lord Elton, 20 Jan 1954}, was a director of the British South Africa Co and was a prospective Governor General of Canada. The scandals of 1900-2 in Australian mining finance, centring on Whitaker Wright (qv), made Grenfell increasingly worried that similar trouble involving BSA Co would dash his father-in-law's chances of the Canadian post. He was anxious at the potential abuses in a company which had a controlling interest in the Rhodesian Government (with the sole right of granting concessions) and also benefited in the flotation of companies exploiting the concessions. On Cecil Rhodes's last evening in England before his final voyage to Africa in January 1902, Grenfell agreed to raise £1 million loan for Rhodesia on condition that these two functions of the BSA Co were separated. In the event, after Rhodes's death in March 1902, when Grenfell was already committed to issuing the loan, the surviving BSA Co directors reneged on the conditions of structural reform that had been agreed. However no Rhodesian scandal besmirched Grey's name, and in 1904 he was appointed Canadian Governor General.

This appointment turned Grenfell's interest toward Canadian financial promotions. By 1907 he was a director of the Western Canada Land Co, and he later joined the board of the Southern Alberta Land Co. After 1908, when Grenfell formed the Canadian Agency Ltd, he took a less active part in the direction of CMG. The Canadian Agency was his own private company, an issuing and financial house specialising in Canadian securities, and to this he devoted his main energies.

In 1909 Grenfell was the main promoter of the Chilean Longitudinal Railway Construction Co which had a concession to build a railway running the length of Chile. Grenfell appointed as his representative in Santiago a man called James Jaffray Williams who, unknown to Grenfell, tried to raise money fraudulently on the concession. Williams was then unmasked as an ex-convict called Harry Silverberg, 'a Moriarty of crime' described by Inspector McCarthy of Scotland Yard as 'the cheeriest, most versatile scamp that I ever came into contact with' {*Daily Express* 31

Dec 1909}. In the ensuing débâcle Silverberg fled and Grenfell lost the longitudinal railway contract to John Norton Griffiths (qv).

Grenfell also formed the Mexican Agency (1909) on the same principles as his Canadian Agency, and served as its chairman after 1911. He became a director of the Santa Gertrudis Co which held 600 acres of gold and silver mines in Pachuca mining camp at Hidalgo state in Mexico. Another Mexican mining company he directed was Tetela Mining, registered in 1904 holding 200 acres of gold and silver mines near Tetela de Ocampo in Puebla state. A further longstanding directorship of Grenfell was of Camp Bird Ltd, which owned goldmines at Ouray in Colorado. In 1913 he became a director of the British Bank of Northern Commerce (chaired by Lord Grey and associated with the Wallenberg family in Sweden) and chairman of Emba Caspian Oil, which owned oil rights in the Gurieff district of the Urals. He also joined the Burmeister & Wain Diesel Oil Engine Co after its formation in 1912 as a subsidiary of Harland & Wolff.

As part of the business of the Canadian Agency, Grenfell undertook heavy commitments in various Canadian securities. Chief among these were the Grand Trunk Railway and the Lake Superior Corporation (LSC). This large and complex metallurgical and chemical company hit a financial crisis in 1910, and underwent gradual reconstruction as the Algoma Steel Corporation. Grenfell's aid was sought, later controlled by Sir James Dunn (qv). The reforms in which he participated necessitated controlling a considerable amount of LSC stock, which Grenfell duly acquired. In December 1912 he had a serious riding accident which kept him from business for months, during which time his affairs were handled by his soldier brother, Riversdale Nonus Grenfell (1880-1914), who had joined Arthur's business in 1910. The Canadian Agency 'had had a career of meteoric brilliance' which 'aroused much jealousy' and was 'riding high speculative tides, where the hand of a skilled helmsman was badly needed'. Riversdale 'had to deal on his own initiative with intricate matters which he probably never understood, for his business training had always been sketchy and inadequate' {Buchan (1920) 182-83}: the Agency's business became gravely over-extended. When Arthur returned to work in 1913, he seemed to friends to have lost some of his knack: his difficulties were increased by the failure of LSC to pay its first mortage bonds in July 1913, by the civil war in Mexico where he held other investments, and by the Balkan War which depressed the London Stock Exchange and led Canadian securities to plummet.

By the spring of 1914 Grenfell's commitments, chiefly in Grand Trunk and LSC stock, amounted to a nominal value of several millions sterling, which he could not cover. An unregulated public failure, at a time of intense political tension in both eastern Europe and Ireland (where civil war seemed imminent), would have been catastrophic to City confidence, causing a major collapse on the Stock Exchange. To prevent this several powerful London finance houses intervened privately to prevent too drastic a liquidation and on 12 May it was announced that Grenfell's open account had been settled satisfactorily. (His personal loss on depreciated securities was £326,839.) Although a grave crisis was thus narrowly averted, Grenfell's personal position was irredeemable. In May, CMG announced that Grenfell had resigned as director with effect from 17 February, and on 6 June CMG and the Canadian Agency suspended payments. His shareholding of £127,400 in the agency became valueless. Later in the month Grenfell relinquished his other directorships, and sent for sale at Christies 67 of his pictures, including works by Cuyp, Uccello, Reynolds, Hoppner, Morland, Gainsborough, Lawrence and one attributed to Titian. Although the collection had cost Grenfell £112,111, it fetched only £48,974 since the auction fell in the week of the Austrian ultimatum when the art market was depressed. His bankruptcy hearings opened in August 1914, just after the outbreak of war, and his personal debts were found to total £1,097,178. The collapse of the Canadian Agency was incurred not by speculation, but by the fatal coincidence of Grenfell's riding accident and political crises at a critical moment in his attempts to reconstruct LSC. The crisis caused considerable worry and bitterness in the City, and came close to causing a major dislocation. Without the rescue operation, the Canadian Agency's failure might have had fatal consequences on the City nerves in both the Irish crisis and the early convulsions of the First World War.

A captain in the Royal Buckinghamshire Imperial Yeomanry from 1908, during the First World War Grenfell served as a major attached to the 9th Lancers (1915-17), and as a lieutenant colonel with the RAF (1917-18). He was twice wounded, mentioned in despatches three times and won the DSO on the Somme in 1916. Reputedly he was also recommended for the Victoria Cross. Grenfell returned from the war 'lamed, half-deaf, bankrupt and on the brink of middle-age, with a single-minded resolve to retrieve' his fortune and pay his creditors {*Times* 2 Dec 1958}.

He became interested in the development of Eastern Europe. In 1920 he organised the formation of the Danube Navigation Co which took over the fleets, coalmines and warehouses of the existing Danube navigation businesses (valued at £10 million by British accountants). Owing to his bankruptcy in 1914, Grenfell was not a director of Danube Navigation (almost half of whose shares were held by British interests), but the board included Sir Frederick Lewis (qv) the shipowner, Grenfell's brother-in-law Lord Grey, Sir Eric Hambro and Sir Charles Barrie (Lord Abertay), the financier and shipowner. As an extension of his Danube Navigation Scheme, Grenfell in 1921 formed syndicates to negotiate government rolling stock loans for Austria, Czechoslovakia and Hungary, and to create an international system of railway freight despatch. He was able to attract businessmen of importance to both syndicates, and it is clear that despite his misfortunes of 1914, he commanded confidence in the City, even if it was judged expedient to keep his name from the investing public. He persuaded Weetman Pearson (qv) to take responsibility for the construction and administration of any railways that he was able to finance in Czechoslovakia, Austria or Hungary, and other members of his financial group included the bankers Hambro, Cox and Robert Fleming, together with the shipowner, the Second Lord Furness (qv). More ambitious, and more successful, was Grenfell's Continental freight scheme. He wanted to create a freight network equivalent to the European sleeping-car monopoly Cie Internationale des Wagons-Lit (CIWL), headed by Sir Davison Dalziel (qv), and to this end he formed the G P Syndicate together with Sir William Petersen (1856-1925), a shipowner. Other members of the Syndicate included the Cunard Line, Swan Hunter, Lord Burnham of the *Daily Telegraph*, Sir Henry Thornton (general manager of the Great Eastern Railway), Sir George McLaren Brown of the Canadian Pacific Railway, Sir Charles Sykes (qv) and Sir Robert Nivison (Lord Glendyne) the government stockbroker. Grenfell also associated with the Syndicate's bankers from Denmark, Germany, Czechoslovakia, Austria, Hungary and elsewhere. In the autumn of 1921, after prolonged and delicate negotiations by Grenfell, the Trans-European Co Ltd was registered in London to take over the interests of the GP Syndicate. From the outset Trans-European held 40 per cent of the controlling shares of Mitropa, the German sleeping car company which had been set up under semi-official auspices before the war to challenge the Franco-Belgian CIWL. Grenfell wanted to develop Mitropa's competition with CIWL, and to that end made a concerted effort to oust CIWL from Austria when its monopoly came up for renewal in 1923. His aims for Trans-European were strenuously opposed by the French from the Baltic to the Balkans, and entailed diplomatic complications.

Grenfell had other interests in Eastern Europe, from which no great business eventuated, although in the 1920s he had success with a chrome mine investment in Serbia and later with a goldmine in Tanganyika. He obtained his discharge from bankruptcy in 1925, and became a director (1929) and then chairman (1932) of Trans-European. Also around 1932 he joined the boards of Grenfell Brothers and of Allatini Mines. Later he enjoyed some success in Kensington property development as a director from 1937 of Chesham Property Co (of which he was chairman at his death). But Hitler's war destroyed all his work in central European transport and mining together with his hopes of repaying his creditors or recovering his fortune. He seemed to accept this defeat with customary cheerfulness and stoicism.

Most men would have been broken by his misfortunes in 1914, but Grenfell with courage, persistence and boldness constructed for himself a second and honourable career. He was a man of great personal charm, with a strong power of persuasion, and a robust good humour: these advantages he used to overcome the suspicion and hostility of those businessmen who held the Canadian Agency disaster against him. Throughout he was indefatigible, ingenious and immune to discouragement. In appearance he was lithe, lean and alert, with the face of a Spanish grandee; and outside of business, his enthusiasm, courage and laughter made him widely-loved.

Grenfell married first, in 1901, Lady Victoria Sybil Mary Grey (1878-1907), god-daughter of Queen Victoria, eldest daughter of Albert, Fourth Earl Grey, and had two sons and a daughter. She died of typhoid contracted on a business visit to Mexico. He married secondly, in 1909, Hilda Margaret (1886-1972), second daughter of General Sir Neville Lyttelton, and had four daughters. His second wife was sister-in-law of Lionel Hichens (qv). Grenfell died on 24 November 1958 at Betteshanger, near Northbourne, in Kent, leaving £10,625.

R P T DAVENPORT-HINES

GRENFELL Arthur Morton

Writings:

letter on European recovery and stabilising Austrian and Czechoslovakian finances *Times* 4 Apr 1922.

letter on Empire pool of war debts *ibid* 8 Oct 1931.

letter on bodyline bowling *ibid* 27 Jan 1933.

letter on Abyssinian crisis and upholding the principles of 1914 *ibid* 20 Sept 1935.

letter on firefighting *ibid* 3 June 1941.

letter on aural aids *ibid* 17 June 1946.

Sources:

Unpublished

PRO, Kew, Foreign Office papers.

Rhodes House, Oxford, correspondence of A M Grenfell with Lord Elton, Mss Afr S 69 1/52-64.

BCe.

MCe.

PrC.

Information from Mrs Hermione Hichens and George Behrend.

Published

George H S Behrend, *History of Trains de Luxe* (Glossop: Transport Publishing, 1982).

John Buchan (Lord Tweedsmuir), *Francis and Riversdale Grenfell* (Thomas Nelson, 1920).

Burke's Peerage.

Daily Express 30, 31 Dec 1909.

Arthur C Fox-Davies, *Armorial Families* (2 vols, Hurst & Blackett, 1929-30).

Dolores Greenberg, *Financiers and Railroads 1869-1889: A Study of Morton Bliss* (Newark, Delaware: University of Delaware Press, 1980).

David S Macmillan (ed), *Canadian Business History* (Toronto: McClelland & Stewart, 1972).

Justinian Mallett, 'Railway Development in Canada' *United Empire* new ser 3 (1912).

R Tom Naylor, *The History of Canadian Business 1867-1914* (2 vols, Toronto: James Lorimer, 1975).

Stock Exchange Year-Book.

F Williams Taylor, 'Canadian Loans in London' *United Empire* new ser 3 (1912).

Times May, June 1914, 17 Jan 1925, 25 Nov, 2 Dec 1958.

Susan Tweedsmuir, *John Buchan by his Wife and Friends* (Hodder & Stoughton, 1947).

Marquess of Winchester, *Statesmen, Financiers and Felons* (Abbeville and Monte Carlo: F Paillart, 1935).

GRENFELL, Edward Charles

1st Lord St Just

(1870-1941)

Merchant banker

Edward Charles Grenfell was born in Pimlico, London on 29 May 1870, the son of Henry Riversdale Grenfell, MP and director of the Bank of England, and his wife, Alethea née Adeane. He was educated at Harrow School and at Trinity College, Cambridge, where he won the Greaves Essay Prize in 1891 and took a second class in history in 1892.

Grenfell joined the firm Brown, Shipley & Co, the London branch of an Anglo-American merchant bank, Brown Bros. Brown, Shipley specialised in acceptance credits for American customers of Brown Bros in New York, and Grenfell may have found that the work involved more administration than initiative, for in 1894 he moved to Smith Ellison's Bank at Lincoln, eventually becoming manager of the Grimsby branch.

Grenfell's family and social connections, however, encouraged his departure from Lincolnshire. Walter Hayes Burns and J P Morgan, partners in the Anglo-American firm of J S Morgan & Co, invited him in 1900 to become manager of their London house. He became a partner in 1904, and when, in 1909, because of the provisions of J S Morgan's will, the name of the firm had to be changed, the London house was renamed Morgan, Grenfell & Co. Grenfell remained the senior partner until his death.

During the First World War the firm acquired exceptional political importance. The New York house, J P Morgan & Co, became the Purchasing Agent in the United States for the War Office and the Admiralty, and the Financial Agent for the Treasury. Morgan Grenfell acted as liaison between the British Government and the New York organisation and Grenfell himself was largely responsible for relations with the Cabinet and the Treasury.

After the end of the war, Grenfell continued his interest in international financial affairs, ensuring that his house participated fully in the business developed by the New York house in Latin America, the Far East and Europe. He also helped to negotiate the currency stabilisation loans for Italy and Belgium, and in general fostered the firm's work as the British agent for foreign Governments wishing to borrow on the British market.

A by-election in May 1922 enabled Grenfell to continue a family tradition: both his father and grandfather had been MPs, and he served as MP (Conservative) for the City from 1922 until 1935, when he became Baron St Just. He concentrated on financial and international questions. He spoke against the Anglo-Soviet Treaty in August 1924 and against the French war debt agreement in July 1926, betraying some suspicion of both countries. His interventions during debates on Finance Bills were always on the side of caution; after 1927 he spoke infrequently.

Grenfell was a director of the Bank of England from 1905 to 1940, a position which could be nerve-wracking during the First World War: the Governor, Lord Cunliffe (qv), was of a dictatorial frame of mind and fought the Treasury over external financial policy. He was also a member of the board of the Sun Assurance Group, a director of Shaw, Saville & Co and a director of the White Star Line.

He was a Lieutenant of the City of London, and governor of Harrow School. His clubs were Brooks's, White's and the Beefsteak. E C Grenfell died on 26 November 1941. He was survived by his wife, Florence (the elder daughter of George Henderson, a merchant importer), whom he had married in 1913, and a son, Peter George. He left an estate of £880,332 gross.

KATHLEEN BURK

Sources:

Unpublished

Morgan Grenfell & Co Ltd, London, Archives

BCe.

MCe.

PrC.

Published

Kathleen Burk (ed), *War and the State: The Transformation of British Government 1914-1919* (George Allen & Unwin, 1982).

DNB.

PD, passim.

Richard S Sayers, *The Bank of England 1891-1944* (3 vols, Cambridge: Cambridge University Press, 1976).

Times 28 Nov 1941.

WWMP.

WWW.

Sir Nigel Gresley (courtesy of the National Railway Museum).

GRESLEY, Sir Herbert Nigel

(1876-1941)

Locomotive designer and builder

Herbert Nigel Gresley was born in Edinburgh on 19 June 1876, the son of Rev Nigel Gresley, an Anglican clergyman. He was educated at Marlborough College and, as a schoolboy railway enthusiast, obtained special leave from his housemaster to watch the work of converting the broad gauge to standard gauge on the nearby Great Western line.

On leaving school he was apprenticed at Crewe Works on the London & North Western Railway for a time, but later moved to the Lancashire & Yorkshire Railway as a pupil of Sir John Aspinall (qv) at Horwich Works. At the early age of twenty-seven he was appointed by Aspinall manager of the carriage and wagon works at Newton Heath. In 1905, whilst still under thirty, he was the successful applicant for the post of carriage and wagon superintendent of the Great Northern Railway, and on the retirement of H A Ivatt in October 1911, Gresley became locomotive superintendent at Doncaster.

On the grouping which created the London & North Eastern Railway in 1923, Gresley became chief mechanical engineer in preference to two other very distinguished engineers who might have been considered, Sir Vincent Raven (qv) of the North Eastern and J G Robinson of the Great Central. After Gresley's death, Robinson claimed that he had been offered the post but declined it and recommended the board to appoint Gresley. It is uncertain whether Robinson's memory of events was accurate at this advanced age.

Gresley was one of the last great steam locomotive designers and as such he is chiefly remembered; but his early work on carriage design was important and he remained deeply interested in this aspect of railway engineering all his life. He introduced the characteristic bow-end body shape, the principle of articulation whereby two carriage ends rest on a single bogie, the use (in British main-line stock) of the automatic buck-eye coupler and the wide, Pullman type of corridor connection or 'vestibule'.

GRESLEY Sir Herbert Nigel

LNER class A4 4-6-2 No 4468 'Mallard', one of the express passenger 'Pacifics' (courtesy of the National Railway Museum).

It is however, his locomotives which caught the public eye. Originally developed from Ivatt designs, for some time freight and mixed-traffic locomotives were his main products at Doncaster; but in 1922 the first two examples of a long series of successful express passenger 4-6-2 'Pacifics' appeared and immediately attracted attention. Large boilers and fireboxes to provide ample steam-raising capacity were associated with the use of three cylinders, the centre cylinder's valve events being derived from the outside valve gear by means of a conjugating 'two-to-one lever'. This device, to which Gresley adhered throughout the rest of his life with some obstinacy, was economical and effective with first-class maintenance, but gave trouble under conditions, such as those in the Second World War, of overwork and under-maintenance.

The Pacifics — steadily improved in details from the A1 series to the final streamlined A4 series (one of which, *Mallard*, achieved the world speed record for a steam locomotive of 126 mph) — were Gresley's most famous designs. He produced a very large number of other classes of locomotive, some highly successful, some — such as the P2 2-8-2 'Cock o' the North' and the 4-4-0 'Hunt' and 'Shire' class, rather less so. He did not embark upon standardisation such as Sir William Stanier evolved for the LMS, but tended to build relatively small batches of engines for particular duties. He was interested in design advances and tried out poppet valves and feed water heaters. He willingly accepted the merits of some other engineers' designs; he greatly admired, in particular, J G Robinson's 'Director' class for the Great Central, of which he ordered a number to be built for the LNER in preference to a design of his own.

Gresley's interest in diesel traction, especially the German 'Fliegende Hamburger' led him to design a British challenge with steam traction in the striking series of high-speed trains — the *Silver Jubilee*, the *West Riding Limited* and the *Coronation* of the later 1930s.

Although lively and downright by temperament, he was not an engineering prima donna such as F W Webb or Dugald Drummond (qv). After a brief initial clash, he had a cordial relationship with his chief

Writings:

letter on London beer prices *Times* 8 Oct 1909.

letter of State purchase of drink trade *ibid* 7 Apr 1917.

letter on Emigration Bill *ibid* 22 July 1918.

letter of Licensing Bill *ibid* 30 Apr 1921.

letter on Conservative party attitude to the Coalition *ibid* 3 Feb 1922.

letters on German reparations *ibid* 7, 13 Sept 1922.

letter on Conservative die-hards *ibid* 3 Jan 1924.

letter on Royal Household *ibid* 1 July 1925.

Report of the Committee of Enquiry into Government Printing Establishments (HMSO, 1927).

letters on naval armaments *Times* 9 Jan, 12 Apr 1930.

letter on Conservative policy *ibid* 18 Oct 1930.

letter of Finance Bill *ibid* 9 July 1931.

Sources:

Unpublished

Bodleian Library, Oxford, papers of J S Sandars.

BLPES, papers of Tariff Commission.

Churchill College, Cambridge, papers of Lord Croft.

Cambridge University Library, papers of Lord Baldwin of Bewdley.

House of Lords RO, papers of Lord Davidson, Bonar Law and Lloyd George.

Scottish RO, Edinburgh, papers of Sir Arthur Steel-Maitland.

Sheffield University Library, papers of W A S Hewins.

West Sussex County RO, Chichester, papers of Leo Maxse.

BCe.

MCe.

PrC.

Elliot research notes.

Published

Martin Gilbert (ed), *Winston S Churchill* 5, companion part 2 (Heinemann, 1980).

William A S Hewins, *Apologia of an Imperialist* (2 vols, Constable, 1929).

Times 4 June 1947.

WWW.

GRIFFIN, John Ross

(1863-1921)

Scientific instrument manufacturer

John Ross Griffin was born in Islington, London, on 22 June 1863, the son of William Griffin (1839-83) and his wife Emily née Soden. William Griffin and his brother Charles (1838-1900) had taken over the business of making scientific instruments founded in Glasgow by their father John Joseph Griffin (1802-77); the business, started as part of a publishing firm, was moved to London in 1848 and was known as John J Griffin & Sons after the founder's death.

Little is known of John Ross Griffin's education or training. When the firm was registered as a limited liability company in September 1889 he became the first company secretary and manager, although only twenty-six years of age. In the same year the business was transferred from Garrick Street to newly-erected premises at 20-26 Sardinia Street, Lincoln's Inn Fields.

Lean years followed the incorporation and the company had a struggle to survive a loss of £1,338 which it had accumulated by June 1894. The following year, however, marked a change in fortune when a profit of £122 11s 3d was recorded. In the same year a telephone was fitted on a trial basis and this undoubtedly helped. At the time of incorporation the firm had diversified its trade by setting up a photographic department which soon after acquired the Photographic Paper Works at East Molesey. In 1903, John Ross secured exclusive agency for the photographic papers of the celebrated Eastman Kodak Co of New York and this coup helped provide the business with impetus in the early years of the new century.

Set against this background John Ross Griffin was elevated to managing director in 1898 and, ten years later, to chairman, a position he retained until 1920. In 1906 he supervised, once more, the company's move to new premises, now at the corner of Kemble Street and Kean Street, a move due to the London County Council's plan to construct the Holborn Kingsway. From his new base John Ross forged new business links in the period before the First World War. Trade in equipment for science teaching and industrial laboratories was expanded by acquiring exclusive sales agencies, manufacturing licences and patent rights, often with American and German companies. But the war inevitably affected the volume of business and it is, perhaps, to John Ross's credit that the business survived at all.

During his lifetime John Ross Griffin married twice; first to Pearl Alexandra Barbara née Clark in 1892 and then to Charlotte Frances née Jervis in 1914. Lyndsay, a son of the second marriage, was killed at El Alamein. John Ross died in North Finchley on 9 February 1921, leaving £9,563 gross.

The business continued under Harold Desmond and Hilda, children of

Sardinia Street premises of John J Griffin & Sons Ltd c 1895 managed by John Ross Griffin.

the first marriage, and their step-mother, who inherited the family shares in the business. Neither of the living heirs, who eventually led active lives in New Zealand, seemed intent on following in their father's footsteps. Controlling interests, therefore, were passed to Thomas McKinnon Wood MP, a close relative of the Griffin family and firm shareholder. His eldest son, Major A L Sandison Wood, became director after John Ross's death and was responsible for a merger with the Scottish firm of Baird & Tatlock in 1926: in 1928 the style Griffin & Tatlock was adopted.

BRIAN GEE

Sources:

Unpublished

BCe.

MCe.

PrC.

H C Mayer, 'The History of Griffin & George Ltd' (Alperton-Wembley, 1980).

Private correspondence with James R Griffin, managing director of Charles Griffin & Co Ltd (Technical Publishers) in 1982.

Published

Griffin & Tatlock Ltd, *Souvenir Catalogue. British Instrument Industries Exhibition, Olympia, London 4-14 July, 1951. A Century and a Quarter* (The Company, 1951).

Sir John Norton-Griffiths, pencil and water-colour by James Kerr-Lawson (courtesy of the National Portrait Gallery).

GRIFFITHS, Sir John Norton

(1871-1930)

Engineering contractor

John Norton Griffiths, who took the surname of Norton-Griffiths in 1917, was born at Williton, Somerset, on 13 July 1871, the only surviving son of John Griffiths (1825-1891), by Juliet (1831-1926), daughter of Richard Avery. His father was a builder, based at Hammersmith, who left £153. He is sometimes said to have been educated at St Paul's School, Kensington, but in fact only attended its preparatory school, Colet Court, from April 1883 to July 1884, and subsequently was a pupil at Latymer School, Edmonton. At the age of fifteen he was articled to an architectural firm. Revolting against his father's bullying and narrow Nonconformity, and falsely giving his age as eighteen, he broke his articles and enlisted as a trooper in the Home Guards. He rebelled there too, and was bought out by Sir Henry Kimber, who sent him to South Africa with his son. Drought and tsetse fly defeated Griffiths and young Kimber as sheep farmers, and in 1891 he moved to the Transvaal where he beachcombed, sold buttons, bar-tended and did small-scale prospecting. He next got a job drilling shafts for Crown Reef Mines, but found conflict irresistible. In 1896 he went to Mashonaland as a captain in the British South Africa Police, and fought as a scout in the Matabele War of 1896-97 waged by Rhodes against King Lobengula (being mentioned in despatches thrice). Afterwards he collected mining claims in the Rhodesias, and floated the Rhodesian Mining & Development Co but suspended business on the outbreak of the Boer War. He commanded a company of Brabant's Horse in 1899-1901 and was a captain and adjutant of Lord Roberts's bodyguard in 1900-2. He fought at Paardeberg and Modder River, revelling in the campaign with its need of scouts and sharpshooters.

His Rhodesian concessions were meanwhile lost by default, and he anyway lacked mining qualifications, experience or cash. However in 1901 a company promoter called Henry Stoneham sent him to survey alluvial mines in French East Africa, and later paid him £5,000 per annum to manage goldfields on the Ivory Coast. Another syndicate sent him to report on a mining scheme in the Nile Valley, and around 1903 he became a mining consultant in London.

In 1905 Griffiths began his career as a contractor, building the Benguella railway in Portuguese Africa for a syndicate including Sir Robert Williams and Cecil Budd (qv). The plan was for the railway to run 1,000 miles from the Atlantic coast of Angola to the great mining areas of the Belgian Congo and then to connect with the Rhodesian copper-belt and the projected Cape to Cairo line first proposed by Rhodes and subsequently sought by Williams. Griffiths first employed Malay and Hindu coolies shipped from Natal, but finding them prone to illness and drink, he obtained Senegalese workers. At one time he had almost 11,000 coolies labouring on the project managed by Greeks and other Europeans (excepting Portuguese, whom he refused to employ). Griffiths chose Lobito as the railway terminus, and had completed the most difficult section of the railway by 1908 when a slump in copper shares obliged Williams's syndicate to stop work. He was at this time as 'powerful as a prize fighter, impetuous and passionate ... preserving cloaked, except in moments of rare emergency, a nature ruthless and in its crude force, entirely elemental' {Middlemas (1963) 258}.

In September 1908, after the suspension of the Benguella project, he formed the contracting firm of Griffiths & Co, with Lord Howard de Walden as chairman. The latter held £36,000 out of £100,000 worth of ordinary shares, while debentures amounted to £310,000. A large number of these were taken by Arthur Bellingham, who owned a distillery at Dalston; others were held by friends of Howard de Walden, such as Lords Clinton, Fitzwilliam, Harrowby, Leconfield and Newton. The company's first contract was in Chile, where the Government were constructing a longitudinal railway from Santiago to Puerto Montt, and wanted foreign capital to erect a northern extension from Santiago to Copiapo. The business was almost secured in 1909 by a syndicate led by Arthur Grenfell (qv), but their proposals were discredited when their Santiago representative was unmasked as an international swindler and 'Moriarty of crime' described by a Scotland Yard inspector as 'The cheeriest, most versatile scamp that I ever came into contact with' {Daily Express 31 Dec 1909}. In the confusion that followed Griffiths used the influence of Albert Pam (qv), of Venezuela salt monopoly fame, to win a contract for nearly 500 miles of railway. The Howard de Walden syndicate financed construction and delivered the line in sections in return for Chilean government bonds of 7 per cent; they were also entitled to operate the railway until Chile's debt was fully repaid after seventy years, although in the event its management was assumed by the Chileans around 1924. Between 1908 and 1914 Griffiths spent half of each year in Chile superintending the work, with costs escalating to £13 million. The roughness of the life is shown by the fact that the peons who built the railway averaged two murders a week.

At the same time Griffiths also built a sewer from Battersea to Deptford, and (with some trouble) an aqueduct 105 miles long through the Caucasian mountains to supply the Russian oil industry in Baku. He also unsuccessfully chased contracts for a trans-Sicilian railway and for the Syracuse-Ragusa-Vizzini railway. In 1913 he obtained a contract worth £1 million from Manchester City Corporation for a sewerage system.

In 1909 he was approached by Dudley Docker (qv), who had supplied the rolling-stock for the Benguella railway, to become Conservative parliamentary candidate at Wednesbury. The sitting Liberal MP was Sir Clarendon Hyde, partner of Griffiths' competitor Weetman Pearson (qv), whom Griffiths' intimate business friend Sir Laming Worthington-Evans was almost simultaneously adopted to fight in the Colchester constituency. Griffiths and Evans not only felt bitter business rivalry towards the Pearson firm, but as Imperial Protectionists detested the free trade principles of its partners. Evans coined the nickname 'Empire Jack' for Griffiths, and 'Empire Jack, with his business policy and John Bull style' was duly elected in 1910 {Midland Advertiser 22 Jan 1910}. With his Imperial League, Griffiths launched in 1911 a grandiose scheme to resettle the slum-dwellers of Wednesbury in Canada, and in parliament he campaigned for a Ministry of Commerce, imperial development and national defence. The Secretary of the Committee of Imperial Defence described Griffiths in 1917 as 'a clever man in a technical sense, but stupid, unpractical and visionary in his ideas' who led a small, obscure group of 'insufferable bores' in 'woolly' discussions about Imperial Federation {Roskill (1970) 423}.

In 1911 Griffiths formed a Canadian subsidiary, which later began to build the harbour at St John's in New Brunswick, the freshwater port on the Fraser River in British Columbia, public buildings in Calgary and the first skyscraper in Vancouver. Lord Howard de Walden's syndicate was however alarmed by aspects of the Chilean and Russian contracts, and refused to provide further finance for a large and complex railway contract which Griffiths signed with the New South Wales Government in 1913. After a public rupture, Howard de Walden resigned in October 1914 as chairman of the Griffiths Co, which 'was wound up in March 1915, everybody connected with it, except Norton-Griffiths, having lost heavily' {PRO FO 371/10092, Department of Overseas Trade memorandum of 1 Feb 1924}. Following this crisis Griffiths's only outstanding project, at St John's, was transferred to another firm; and although he adhered to the Australian scheme, little progress was made. Indeed his representatives in New South Wales made so many enemies that the Government there cancelled the contract in 1916, giving Griffiths compensation of £120,000, of which £80,000 was later recovered by the Howard syndicate.

In December 1913 he formed Norton Griffiths & Co in Canada, and in December 1914 J Norton Griffiths Ltd in London, and these companies remained the vehicles for his operations for the rest of his life.

In August 1914 Griffiths raised an irregular regiment, the Second King Edward's Horse, and hurled himself into war work. In the spring of 1915, under the aegis of the Royal Engineers, he organised eight tunnelling companies, which under appalling risks and terrible conditions, dug tunnels to the German lines under which they planted deadly mines. Their tunnelling methods had been evolved by Griffiths's workmen on the Manchester sewer contract. His men were wild and undisciplined, and he was abominated among fellow officers for his peremptory and flamboyant behaviour: he drove about Flanders in a two-ton Rolls Royce with a crate of champagne. He was briefly seconded to the Ministry of Munitions in 1916, and in November was sent on a lone mission to Romania to destroy their oilfields and corn-stores before the Germans could seize them. Despite Romanian objections, he raised a small team and within six days blew up 200 square miles of oilfields, which he left looking 'like the pits of hell in a medieval picture' {Middlemas (1963) 282}. He was estimated to have done £50 million worth of damage, excluding the hundreds of thousands of tons of grain which he also burnt or flooded. Later, in 1917-18, he built a slipway at Middlesbrough and a dry dock at Dublin for the Second Lord Furness (qv), Catterick aerodrome, Hickling Broad seaplane station, Knotty Ash Hospital Camp for the US Army, and extended Howden-on-Tyne shipyards. He received the DSO and was made a temporary lieutenant colonel in 1916. He was created KCB in 1917, when he was also awarded the Légion d'Honneur, the Order of St Vladimir of Russia and the Grand Star of Romania.

In 1918 he founded the Comrades of the Great War, intending to form a national network of clubs for ex-servicemen to prevent social unrest during demobilisation. It was subsequently annexed by Conservative politicians for party purposes, and merged with the British Legion in 1920.

Griffiths announced in 1914 that he would not stand again for Wednesbury, but was anti-coalition Unionist MP for Wandsworth 1918-24. In the campaign of 1918 the British Commonwealth Union subsidised his expenses, and he was fined by a magistrate for assaulting a heckler. After pressuring Austen Chamberlain, he received a baronetcy in 1922. He unsuccessfully implored Stanley Baldwin for a peerage in 1929, explaining that since Pearsons had ceased civil contracting work, 'my firm are the most active P[ublic] W[orks] Contractors ... always fighting Yanks, Italians, Germans etc and a Peerage would *materially* influence foreign business for the benefit of British Trade ... I am the only British firm — or all but — trying to keep the flag flying in S America'. He added slyly 'Cowdray helped his party (funds), but his party helped him to do so ... I can play the game and of course I should do much more if I am helped in this manner' {CUL, Baldwin papers vol 164}.

His first post-war contract was for Leixoes harbour to service Douro and Oporto in Portugal. In August 1921 he signed an agreement with the Angolan Government to reconstruct the harbour and facilities at Loanda. The estimated cost was £1 million, on which Griffiths was to receive 10 per cent. Everything went wrong. As with the New South Wales contract of 1913-16, Griffiths made disastrous selections of chief engineers in situ. The first was flagrantly anti-Portuguese; his successor 'had a peculiar temperament' and quarrelled with everyone. Plant and materials worth £56,000 were brought from Europe, but progress seemed far slower than with George Pauling's corresponding contract at Lobito; and the Portuguese came to suspect 'that operations were being deliberately held up and difficulties intentionally created so as to provoke a breach of contract . . . [by] the Government and so to give the firm an opportunity of claiming damages' {PRO FO 371/11091, despatch 14 of Alexander Byres Hutcheon, Consul General at Loanda, 17 Mar 1925}. Griffiths spent £164,000 to December 1924, including £62,000 on wages and salaries and £15,000 on commissions. In April 1925 he suspended work as the Angolans owed him nearly £30,000 and several years of litigation commenced. One of his British employees later told the Anti-Slavery and Aborigines Protection Society that on this contract natives were 'impressed as required, in batches, usually of 100, without regard to age or fitness for work' and that 80 per cent of their wages was siphoned off to the Finance Department in Loanda and never reached the workers {PRO FO 371/11136, Anti-Slavery Society to Foreign Office 10 Aug 1926}. His reputation in such matters was bad: on his Uasin Gishu railway contract in Kenya of 1920-23 the death rate among his forced labourers was 83 per thousand.

Throughout the 1920s he was notoriously broke. 'Nothing with which Sir John Norton-Griffiths had been connected appears to have prospered', wrote the Department of Overseas Trade in 1924, 'He ... [lacks] ... sufficient means behind him to justify any serious undertaking and ... no accepting house in the City would consider receiving his acceptance even for so little as £1,000' {PRO FO 371/10092, DOT memo 1 Feb 1924}. Thus in 1920 he signed a vast contract for dams, harbours, breakwaters and other installations in Brazil worth perhaps £17 million, and by 1923 was vainly beseeching help under the Trade Facilities Act to continue work. As at Loanda work was suspended and a lawsuit continued until after his death.

A director of Arsenal Football Club, Griffiths in the 1920s enlarged Clapham Common station, built a sewer from Highbury to Shadwell and an underground railway from Charing Cross to Kennington. The latter contract was worth £1 million, but he lost money on it. He became increasingly desperate for work. In 1926-29 he built two railways in Colombia, but significantly turned to New York and not London for finance, while the Foreign Office returned frosty replies to Colombian enquiries about his financial status. In 1928 he became enmeshed with an insane Eton schoolmaster who claimed to command Chinese railway and road contracts worth £15 million. In the same year he joined two men responsible for the Sheffield tool steel swindles of 1924 in a 'ridiculous' scheme to built Lithuanian railways which British diplomats averred would not assist 'British interests at all except that ... our old friend 'Empire Jack' will make a few thousand pounds to buy a new Rolls Royce' {PRO FO 371/13275, Joseph Addison to Sir Michael Palairet 10 Aug 1928}. Distrusted by the Colonial and Foreign Offices, he was in such straits that for a Bolivian railway contract of 1928 he could only make 'a half-hearted offer on a commission basis without complying with the stipulation of the Government that any tenderer ... make a deposit at the bank' {PRO FO 371/12741, despatch 23 of Robert C Michell, La Paz, 16 March 1928}.

Around 1911-12 Griffiths had visited Egypt with Worthington-Evans and offered Lord Kitchener to finance harnessing the power of the Aswan dam. Twelve years later he sought Ramsay MacDonald's 'personal — not official — blessing for such a scheme, doubtless hoping to entice a Labour Government subsidy on the pretext of the employment he would bring to Britain {PRO FO 371/10031, Norton-Griffiths to MacDonald 24 June 1924}. Subsequently a similar scheme was taken up by his friend Docker, representing the Belgian trust Sofina, and as part of the resultant interest in Aswan, Griffiths in 1929 won a contract to heighten the dam. His tender price of £1.96 million was £472,000 less than the next lowest tender, and it was immediately clear that he had mis-calculated his costs. He borrowed £265,000 from Solly and Jack Joel of de Beers Diamond Corporation, but the Wall Street crash and troubles with his multitude of sub-contractors aggravated the impossibility of his schedules and the unreality of his plans. Faced with bankruptcy, he stopped work on 21 September 1930, and on 29 September he paddled out to sea at Alexandria and shot himself in the temple. After some delay his estate was valued at £5,183.

Vehement, wild, rebellious and self-destructive, his hyper-excitement was almost demented. He was a poor judge of character, and as a public contractor he can be regarded as either a bad businessman or a dishonest one. His nemesis he brought entirely on himself. He married in 1901 Gwladys (1873-1974), daughter of Thomas Wood, of Bloomsbury, an engineer in the firm of Browning, Wood & Fox, they had two sons and two daughters. His grandson Jeremy Thorpe was Leader of the Liberal Party, 1967-76.

R P T DAVENPORT-HINES

Writings:

letter on Imperial Federation and Irish home rule *Times* 29 Oct 1910.

letter on proposed Imperial Council *ibid* 15 Mar 1911.

letter on standardised ships and building foreign ships in Britain *ibid* 17 June 1916.

letter on army manpower *ibid* 30 Oct 1916.

letter on formation of soldiers' association *ibid* 24 July 1917.

letter on dictating peace terms *ibid* 28 Aug 1918.

letter on general election candidatures *ibid* 21 Nov 1918.

letter on delay in army demobilisation *ibid* 7 Jan 1919.

letters on German war indemnities *ibid* 27 Mar 1919 and *Times* Trade Supplement 29 Mar 1919.

letter on construction costs of locomotives *ibid* 3 Sept 1921.

letter on ex-servicemen's claims *Times* 1 Oct 1921.

letter on developing Crown Colonies *ibid* 1 Oct 1921.

letter on Conservative Party attitude to National Party *ibid* 9 Mar 1922.

letter on Rutenberg concession in Palestine *ibid* 2 Aug 1922.

letter on coal industry *ibid* 3 May 1926.

Sources:

Unpublished

Cambridge University Library, papers of Earl Baldwin of Bewdley, vol 164.

PRO FO 371 and Colonial Office papers.

West Sussex County RO papers of Leo Maxse, letter of Brigadier Henry F E Lewin to Maxse, 7 Oct 1917, MP 474/238-9.

PrC.

Information from Rev Hugh Mead.

Published

DNB.

Simon E Katzenellenbogen, *Railways and the Copper Mines of Katanga* (Oxford: Clarendon Press, 1973).

R K Middlemas, *The Master Builders* (Hutchinson, 1963).

Midland Advertiser 1909-14.

Stephen W Roskill, *Hankey, Man of Secrets* (Collins, 1970).

WWW.

Sir William Griffiths (courtesy of J O Hitchcock).

GRIFFITHS, Sir William Thomas

(1895-1952)

Metallurgist and non-ferrous metal manufacturing company chairman

William Thomas Griffiths was born in Cardiff on 19 April 1895, the son of Rev Caradoc Griffiths, a Baptist minister, and his wife Elizabeth née Lewis. His early education was in Cardiff. He graduated in chemistry at University College, Cardiff in the early part of the First World War and joined the Royal Engineers, seeing service in the Gas Corps.

After the war he returned to Cardiff University and took an MSc degree in metallurgy. In 1922 he went to the Research Department, Woolwich Arsenal, then well known for its metallurgical expertise. At Woolwich he had the advantage of working with several distinguished metallurgists and published the results of some of the researches undertaken there.

These and activities in the Institute of Metals brought him to the attention of the Mond Nickel Co Ltd, formed by Ludwig Mond (qv) in 1901. Griffiths was recruited in 1926 to start a research and development department. The market for nickel had collapsed after the First World War since most of the nickel then produced had been absorbed in armaments and Mond nickel companies were looking for new applications to keep up with the International Nickel Co of Canada Ltd, their major competitor.

In his role of manager of the new department, Griffiths quickly assembled a research and development staff and established a laboratory in Birmingham. Research programmes were directed towards existing and new markets for nickel. One of his first objectives was to understand the role of nickel as an alloying element in steels — 80 per cent of the world's nickel production then went into alloy steels. It was also about this time that stainless steels were in the early stages of development. Griffiths quickly realised that research in this field could benefit the nickel industry, nickel being an essential element in the more advanced stainless steels. In these fields the laboratory in Birmingham made important contributions to fundamental knowledge. The laboratory also worked on the production of fabricated forms from nickel powder, on improved corrosion-resistant nickel-copper alloys, high-temperature alloys, alloyed cast irons, nickel plating, magnetic alloys and most fields where nickel was or could be used.

Griffiths's strength was his ability to attract outstanding men and the staff at the laboratory had such distinguished men as Dr L B Pfeil FRS the manager, Dr N P Allen FRS, Dr Richard (now Lord) Beeching and many others who became notable figures in the metallurgical world. Griffiths also realised that research was useless without development and his contribution to growth of the market for nickel (it grew from a world production of 38,000 tons in 1926 to some 160,000 tons in 1949) was his conviction that the results of research had to be communicated. Apart from field development work, he started a series of high-level publications, distributed to industry, including *The Nickel Bulletin*, an abstract journal, which was published monthly for nearly fifty years and only ceased when computerised information services made it obsolete. A pioneer in these fields, Griffiths's work was copied by other metal producers, including those of copper, tin, zinc, lead, vanadium and cobalt. A new laboratory in Birmingham was built for him in 1935 and led the field in Europe for many years.

On the outbreak of the Second World War, Griffiths immediately offered the services of the talented research staff to appropriate government departments. The laboratory's outstanding contribution was the creation of alloys which would withstand the high temperatures and stresses involved in the moving and fixed parts of the Whittle gas turbine jet engine. This work was so successful that the Whittle engine at last became feasible. For a paper describing this work Griffiths was awarded the 1947 Simms gold medal of the Royal Aeronautical Society, given annually for the best paper read to the Society on any science allied to aeronautics. The Nimonic series of alloys developed from these researches are now known world-wide. Other wartime researches included sintered nickel gaseous diffusion membranes (The Tube Alloys Project) and particularly steels for armoured fighting vehicles and other armaments.

The Mond Nickel Co Ltd and the International Nickel Co of Canada Ltd had merged in 1929 and in 1945 Griffiths was appointed chairman of Mond Nickel Co Ltd under the parentage of the International Nickel Co of Canada Ltd of which he was appointed director and vice-president. He was already familiar with North America having visited the USA twice during the war to brief colleagues there on the Birmingham work on high-temperature alloys and separately to advise the Combined Raw Materials Board on measures to conserve the use of nickel, then in short supply.

Griffiths was a dedicated man and demanded the same dedication from his staff, at times to the point of apparent harshness. He was intolerant of sub-standard performance which at times led to differences with his colleagues and staff, whom, however, he would defend at all times; typically he was quick to support those in trouble. After retiring in 1950 he subsequently undertook various consultancies in the metallurgical world.

During his career, apart from his pioneer work in the nickel industry, he believed in cooperative research and was a firm supporter of the British Non-Ferrous Metals Research Association, the British Cast Iron Research Association and the British Iron and Steel Research Association. He was president of the Institute of Metals in 1944-46 and a founder member of the Institution of Metallurgists formed in 1945 to improve the status of the profession of metallurgy, which he worked hard to achieve. He was a fellow of the Royal Institute of Chemistry and the Institute of Physics. Griffiths was knighted in 1946 for his services to the war effort having already received a DSc from University College, Cardiff.

In private life he enjoyed golf and photography. He married in 1922 Grace Jenkins, daughter of Henry Jenkins of Cardiff, a baker and confectioner. Grace was a great source of strength to him throughout his career. They had two daughters. Sir William Griffiths died on 30 July 1952 at the relatively young age of fifty-seven, leaving an estate valued at £53,009 gross.

JOHN O HITCHCOCK

Writings:

'The Change of Points in Some Nickel-Chromium Steels' *Journal of the Iron and Steel Institute* 1923.

(with J L Haughton) 'Some Uses of the Thread Recorder in the Measurement of Physical Properties' *Journal of Scientific Instruments* 1924.

'Note on Nitrogen as a Possible Factor in Temper Brittleness' *Journal of the Iron and Steel Institute* 1925.

'The Hardening of Steel: A Review and some Comments' *Metallurgist* 1926.

'Nickel Developments during the Past Twenty-One Years' *Metal Industry* 17 Jan 1930.

'Case-hardening and the Use of Nickel Steels' *Aciers Spéciaux Metaux et Alliages* Apr 1930.

'American and Continental Practice in Nickel Deposition' *Metal Industry* 6, 20 Nov 4, 18 Dec 1931.

(with D G Jones and L B Pfeil) 'Nickel-Copper Alloys of High Elastic Limit' *Journal of the Institute of Metals* 1932.

(with D G Jones and L B Pfeil) 'Precipitation-Hardening Nickel-Copper Alloys Containing Aluminium' *ibid* 1933.

'The Production of Specially Hard Cast Irons by Alloying and Heat Treatment' *Foundry Trade Journal* 1934.

'The Relationship between Embrittlement Caused by Prolonged Heating at 450-500 Degrees Centigrade and Temper Brittleness' *The Iron and Steel Institute Alloy Steels Research Committee* report 27 May 1937.

(with L B Pfeil and N P Allen) 'The Intermediate Transformation in Alloy Steels' *The Iron and Steel Institute Special Report* 24 May 1939.

'Determination of Transformation Characteristics of Alloy Steels' *ibid* 24 May 1939.

'The Problem of High-Temperature Alloys for Gas Turbines' *Journal of The Royal Aeronautical Society* Jan 1948.

'The Nickel Industry: Twenty Years on' Paper HI 5 to 4th Mining & Metallurgical Conference, July 1949, reprint.

Sources:

Unpublished

BCe.

MCe.

PrC.

Published

Times 1 Aug 1952.

WWW.

GROVE, Walter Patrick

(1914-)

Nuclear industry manager

Walter Patrick Grove was born in Thames Ditton, Surrey on 17 May 1914, the son of Thomas Grove, an accountant's clerk, and his wife Edna Mary née Sawer. He was educated at Brighton, Hove and Sussex Grammar School. His first job and practical experience with radioactivity began in 1931, when he worked as an assistant in the laboratory of The Radium Institute, London, under W L S Alton. Later Grove worked as a junior chemist under A J Ewins first at May & Baker Ltd, the pharmaceutical manufacturers, and then in the chemistry of precious metals and the production of radium appliances at Johnson Matthey & Co. During these years he studied chemistry as an evening student at Birkbeck College, London, and acquiring his BSc in 1937 took up an assistant lectureship in the Chemistry Department of University College, London; he subsequently gained a PhD in the magnetic properties of salts of the platinum metal group.

At the outbreak of war, Grove joined the Royal Naval Scientific Service Torpedo Establishment at Greenock. Thorium Ltd, a company which was formed in the First World War to manufacture thoria, and was owned jointly by ICI and Howard & Sons of Ilford, decided to set up a unit to extract radium from ores confiscated by the Ministry of Economic Warfare and to make luminous paint with it. Because of his practical experience with radium, Grove was released from Greenock by the Admiralty and joined Thorium Ltd in February 1940. Thorium bought a country house at Amersham, considered an ideal location since it was not far from the headquarters at Wembley, yet far enough from London to escape bombing. Later, of course, the site was particularly useful for its easy access to Heathrow Airport. However, the accommodation was primitive in the extreme and Grove started work from scratch with just three assistants. He set up a small laboratory in outbuildings to refine radium for use in self-luminous paints. Although facilities were very crude, they managed to produce a ton of luminising compound worth over £1 million during the war years.

In 1944 Grove spent four months at the wartime Anglo-Canadian atomic energy project in Canada, advising on the planning of a highly radioactive or 'hot' laboratory for the new site at Chalk River. He returned convinced that a national centre for natural and artificial radioisotopes should be set up in Britain, and he believed this could be done at Amersham. Grove was supported by Sir James Chadwick and Sir Henry Hall (both Nobel prizewinners) and by the firms Thorium Ltd and Johnson Matthey, and as a result the Radiochemical Centre was set up at Amersham in 1946, under the auspices of the Ministry of Supply, managed by Thorium as agents and directed by Dr Grove. Early in 1950 Thorium Ltd gave up the agency and the Centre became an outstation of the Atomic Energy Research Establishment at Harwell. Work on isotopes was divided at this stage between two groups. The Isotope Division, which already existed at Harwell, was to carry out the primary research and production of isotopes and pass on information to Amersham. The Radiochemical Centre was responsible for the separation, processing and distribution of all but the very short-lived isotopes and was also responsible for natural radioelements.

When the UK Atomic Energy Authority was set up in 1954, responsibility for the Isotope Division and The Radiochemical Centre passed from the Ministry of Supply to the UKAEA's Research Group. In April 1959, as a result of internal reorganisation in the UKAEA, The Radiochemical Centre took over all sales and most of the production from Harwell's Isotope Division, and became the single organisation for the production and marketing of isotopes in the UK. The Centre was still responsible to the Research Group and Grove remained the director. In 1964 the Centre was given its own board of management, although still under the UKAEA's umbrella. In April 1971 The Radiochemical Centre Ltd was formed as a separate company, still with Grove at the helm as managing director. He retired in 1979 and in February 1982, the Centre was privatised as Amersham International PLC.

Between the 1950s and the 1970s Dr Grove ran the Centre on commercial lines, and was in touch with every aspect of day-to-day management. The Harwell Isotopes Division's excellent public relations work in the early 1950s under Dr. Henry Seligman had laid a solid foundation by initiating the medical, scientific and industrial world into the use of isotopes and The Radiochemical Centre grew from strength to strength. Its major advantage was that it was able to stress the peaceful, beneficial and humanitarian uses of isotopes at a time when atomic energy was linked in the public mind with bombs and warfare. Isotopes are indeed now indispensable in the medical field, in the treatment of cancer, as tracers for diagnostic purposes and in the treatment of thyroid disorders: they have other valuable uses for example, in agriculture, biochemistry, chemistry, metallurgy.

The Centre's progress in terms of sales and prosperity is a testament to Grove's successful management. In the financial year 1954-55, total sales made by the Isotope Division at Harwell and Amersham were £450,000; and by 1965, sales from the Radiochemical Centre alone had reached £1.9 million of which 53 per cent went overseas. By 1972 group sales totalled £6 million with a pre-tax profit of £816,000, increasing to £37.8 million sales in 1979 with a profit before tax of £6 million. The number of staff employed by the Centre increased from 447 in 1965 to 1,337 in 1979.

Exports by 1979 had increased to 84 percent of total sales. Several joint companies were formed to promote business abroad; the Amersham-Searle Corporation was formed in 1968 to supply isotopes to West, Central and South America. In January 1977 The Radiochemical Centre bought up Searle's shares and the company became the Amersham Corporation (US). In November 1977 a joint venture was established with Buchler & Co, who had distributed Amersham's products in West Germany since 1961; the company was 60 percent owned by Amersham and 40 percent by Buchler. The Radiochemical Centre (Australia) Pty Ltd was also set up in 1977. As well as being managing director of The Radiochemical Centre, Grove was chairman of the American and Australian companies and director of the German one.

The Radiochemical Centre owes its success largely to the firm and steady guidance of Dr Grove, who, with the help of a highly able staff, provided an efficient and high-quality service. The Centre has won four Queen's Awards to Industry, including two for technological innovation in the production of Carbon-14 and its compounds, in 1970. Dr Grove was awarded the Sylvanus Thompson medal of the British Institute of Radiology in 1962 and the CBE in 1969. He retired in May 1979. He is a JP and a member of the governing bodies of Birkbeck College, London (of which he was elected a fellow in 1977) and of several local schools. He married in 1963 Joyce Mary Hide, daughter of Rev Stanley Hide.

STEPHANIE ZARACH

Writings:

'How Scientists Label Atoms' *Listener* 4 Aug 1949.

'Procurement of Labelled Compounds' *British Medical Bulletin* 8 (1952).

(with Sir John Cockcroft and Dr H Seligman) 'Atomic Energy in Industry and Agriculture' *Planning Ahead No 2*, 28 Mar 1952.

'By-Products of Atomic Energy' *Financial Times Annual Review of Industry* 1954.

'A Formidable Task of the Atomic Age' *Listener* 10, 15 Apr 1954.

(with B N Clack) 'The Measurement of Radon in Breath as a Control for Radium Workers' *British Journal of Radiology Supplement* 7 (1957).

'Products of the New Alchemy', The Sylvanus Thompson Memorial Lecture, delivered at the British Institute of Radiology 17 May 1962. Published in *British Journal of Radiology* 35 (1962).

'Recent Progress in Radioactive Chemical Manufacture' *Chemistry and Industry* 16 Jan 1965.

Sources:

Unpublished

United Kingdom Atomic Energy Authority. Annual Reports and Accounts (HMSO annually since 1954).

The Radiochemical Centre Ltd. Annual Reports and Accounts (since 1971).

BCe.

Published

Atom 104 (June 1965), 273 (July 1979).

E B Chain, 'Use of Radioisotopes in General Biochemistry' *Chemistry and Industry* 31 July 1965.

David Fishlock, 'Returns from Radioactivity' *Financial Times* 10 Nov 1976.

R F Glasscock, 'Some Examples of the Use of Radioisotopes in Agriculture' *Chemistry and Industry* 31 July 1965.

Margaret Gowing, *Independence and Deterrence. Britain and Atomic Energy 1945-1952* (2 vols, Macmillan, 1974) 2 *Policy Execution*.

'Isotope World. Leader in His Field. Dr W P Grove' *Nuclear Energy* Oct 1960.

Times 10 Dec 1980.

GUÉRET, Louis Jean Baptiste

(1844-1908)

Patent fuel manufacturer and coal exporter

Louis Jean Baptiste Guéret was born in Baccarat, Lorraine, France in 1844. Nothing is known about his early life. He came to Cardiff in 1868 to represent Messrs Tinel & Co, patent fuel manufacturers of Le Havre, at a time when the manufacture of patent fuel in Britain was beginning to receive serious attention. South Wales, because of the quality of its coal, rapidly became its major location. Tinel & Co had been receiving its supply of small coals from Cardiff, but in 1866 it set up the Anchor Patent Fuel Works there in order to process small coal and coal dust. Guéret took charge of these works and also of the company's shipping interests. Whilst continuing to operate as Tinel's agent, Guéret began to branch out on his own account, both as a coal and patent fuel exporter and as a pitwood importer. With the growth of the coal trade in general and the port of Cardiff in particular, Guéret gradually expanded into ship-brokering and ship owning. During the 1870s Guéret was joined in his business interests first by T J Callaghan in 1874 and then by his brother Henri in 1877, the brothers trading as L & H Guéret.

In 1879, Tinel & Co sold the Anchor Works to the Guéret brothers who remained the Cardiff coal agents of the Le Havre firm. The Anchor Works remained under the personal ownership of Louis until 1895 when a limited liability company, L Guéret Ltd, was formed to run Louis' interests (his brother having died by this time). With a nominal capital of £200,000 the firm remained essentially a private concern with Louis as chairman and T J Callaghan as deputy-chairman and manager. Due to ill-health, in 1908 Guéret disposed of the bulk of his ordinary shareholding in L Guéret Ltd and certain associated companies to T J Callaghan and David A Thomas (qv) — some of his interests thus becoming merged with those of the Cambrian Coal combine. By 1913 L Guéret Ltd was not only one of the largest exporters of Welsh coal and patent fuel, but also a major pitwood importer, part-owner of two collieries producing 1.5 million tons per annum and nine patent fuel works with an approximate capacity of 1 million tons per annum. Guéret's success in coal exporting and patent fuel manufacture would appear to have been partly due to a recognition of the potential in South Wales in the last decades of the nineteenth century. His forays into colliery ownership, however, were generally less successful than his other major activities possibly due to an inadequate knowledge of the various problems of coal mining.

Guéret, a Roman Catholic, was an energetic businessman with a reputation for being upright and fair. He was a principal founder of the Barry Railway Co, but took little part in public life. Having settled in Britain he became naturalised and married a Cardiff lady, who died some twelve years before him. Their only child, a daughter, married W Southwell Jones who continued to hold a position within the firm after Guéret's death.

Louis Guéret died on 7 November 1908 at the home of his son-in-law, near Weston-super-Mare. He left £420,272 gross.

COLIN BABER *and* TREVOR BOYNS

Sources:

Unpublished

PrC.

Published

Cardiff Times 14 Nov 1908.

South Wales Coal Annual 1913.

South Wales Weekly News 14 Nov 1908.

Western Mail 9 Nov 1908.

GUINNESS, Edward Cecil

1st Earl of Iveagh

(1847-1927)

Brewer

Edward Cecil Guinness (taken from P Lynch and J Vaizey, Guinness's Brewery in the Irish Economy *Cambridge University Press, 1960).*

Edward Cecil Guinness was born at St Anne's Clontarf, County Dublin on 10 November 1847, the youngest of three sons of Sir Benjamin Lee Guinness (1798-1868) then proprietor of the St James's Gate Brewery in Dublin, and his wife Elizabeth Guinness (d 1865), third daughter of Edward Guinness of Dublin. Edward Cecil was privately tutored at home, attending no school, before studying at Trinity College, Dublin where he took an ordinary BA with special merit in October 1869.

On the death of his father in 1868, Edward Cecil had hurriedly joined the management of the family brewery, receiving a general introduction to all aspects of the business, technical and financial. At first the brewery was jointly run by Edward Cecil and his elder brother Arthur (created Lord Ardilaun in 1880), with the help of an established, highly-competent and professional management which had served their father, but gradually Arthur moved out of business and into politics, particularly in Dublin and London. From the 1870s onwards Edward Cecil increasingly ran the brewery by himself, with Arthur as a sleeping partner, and eventually Arthur was bought out in the early 1880s.

In 1868 the average annual output of the brewery was in the region of 350,000 bulk barrels, produced from a single brewhouse and primarily sold in Ireland although with a small and growing trade in England. The main product was stout in a variety of forms. Annual profits were running at about £120,000 on average, and much of this was being ploughed back into the business to build up capacity. At this time the UK beer market was undergoing a particularly significant upheaval; after almost a century in which porter had been the dominant product of the large producers, ale,

The O'Neill Harp on which the design of the Guinness trade mark has been based (taken from P Lynch and J Vaizey, Guinness's Brewery in the Irish Economy. Cambridge University Press, 1960).

particularly from the new giants of the trade, the Burton brewers (Bass and Allsopp), was sweeping all before it. The consumption of porter appeared to be in terminal decline, and increasingly London brewers were switching their own production, and capacity, away from porter towards ale. To what extent this was the opportunity that Guinness required and to what extent they simply wiped out the opposition is not clear. At all events over the next twenty years the UK market for dark beer, porter and stout, was usurped almost entirely by Guinness alone. By 1875 Guinness's annual output had reached 725,000 bulk barrels, and by 1886 some 1.2 million bulk barrels, thus making the brewery the largest single producer not just in the British Isles but in the world.

This had been achieved primarily through explosive growth in England. Partly this was a result of narrowing its product range: from 1870 onwards only three different varieties were produced, each for a specific market — porter for Ireland, Extra Stout for Britain, and Foreign Extra Stout for the rest of the world. Targeted varieties were followed by a more targeted approach to marketing, wholesaling and retailing the brand. After decades of reliance on selling at arm's length through independent wholesalers and bottlers in the UK, Guinness now exerted a more direct influence and were prepared to set up their own agencies if necessary. The thought of such direct competition and the growing success of the brand rapidly encouraged mainland-based brewers to seek the agency for Guinness in self-protection. So increasingly Guinness's own success fuelled its system and motivated its agents. By the 1880s Guinness was firmly established as a brand, great advantage having been derived from the 1875 Trade Mark Registration Act in protecting the familiar buff coloured label with its harp motif. From that point on the brand became increasingly reliable, identifiable and unique. That uniqueness was probably a prime factor in its success, and was certainly an aspect of the brand which the company fought hard to protect.

The rapid expansion in output was achieved through a concomitant expansion in the capacity of the brewery itself. The first brewhouse was doubled in capacity in 1870, and the subsequent decade saw a new brewhouse in 1876, and the doubling of the old site by the purchase of new land between St James's Street and the River Liffey which allowed considerable extension to the existing facilities. By 1886 the site covered some 42 acres, supported by a fleet of barges running beer from the brewery to Dublin port. Between Edward Cecil's arrival and 1886 over £1 million was spent on capital projects, financed entirely from retained profits. By the mid-1880s the brewery had a 6 per cent share of the total UK beer market (probably, but not certainly, the largest of any company) and was generating profits of around £450,000 a year.

Effectively all this had been achieved under the proprietorship of Edward Cecil who was certainly the driving force and motivator behind the company from 1868 to 1886. His lieutenants were important, and Edward Cecil consistently chose extremely able men to work for him. The key man was J T Purser, inherited from his father's proprietorship in 1868, who continued as general manager of the brewery until 1886; Purser was probably responsible for the daily administration of the whole business until incorporation in 1886. Geoghegan, head brewer, was, however, another and was in part directly responsible, with Edward

Cecil's encouragement, for the technical and scientific development of the company. This culminated in the Guinness Research Laboratory set up in the 1890s and the steady evolution of Guinness's into the industry's most technically and scientifically enlightened brewery by the early twentieth century — with research including detailed work on raw materials as well as fermenting science. While these professional managers undoubtedly played a vital part in the growth of Guinness's, the primary credit still must be given to the proprietor who oversaw the whole enterprise.

Edward Cecil had briefly considered a sale of the business to the public in 1880 which would have allowed the family to realise some of their massive investment and would also have freed Arthur from the partnership agreement without the complex negotiations which were finally necessary. A meeting with Lord Rothschild (qv) was held in 1880, but the response from the banker was, at best, lukewarm and so the idea was dropped. In 1885 the idea was raised again, this time with Lord Revelstoke of Barings and progress was made. Revelstoke seems to have had a lower opinion of the value of the business than the family; Barings wanted to sell for less than a total capitalisation of £5 million, but Edward Cecil stood out for a price tag of £6 million, which was finally, though reluctantly, accepted. The sale went ahead in 1886, and was 20 times oversubscribed, the shares of Arthur Guinness & Son & Co Ltd rising to a 60 per cent premium on their first day of trading. In fact, a majority of the shares never went on public sale at all, as the merchant banks and family between them took a controlling interest from the start. Edward Cecil started with a significant minority holding but gradually bought his way back to a controlling stake again over the remainder of the 1880s. At first Edward Cecil was both managing director and chairman of the company, but it had always been his intention to step down from direct management as soon as possible and his period as managing director until 1889 was really little more than a guarantee to the investors that the family would continue to run the company despite the increasing reliance on professional managers in day-to-day operations. He was succeeded as managing director by Claude Guinness, although on the sudden death of Claude he did return to the position for a short time in the 1890s until a permanent successor could be found. He remained chairman and was very active until the First World War. Thereafter he was more of a figurehead (albeit one with the firmest views which were not lightly dismissed) until his death. The first publicly-declared profits after flotation were £543,000 in 1887, but growth continued rapidly thereafter, and profits reached £1,125,202 in 1913 and £2,175,816 in 1919. Equally volume produced rose steadily, mostly as a result of a burgeoning export trade and even greater penetration of the British market to 3 million bulk barrels a year around the time of Edward Cecil's death.

Although he remained closely in touch, and in distinct control of the company after 1900, the history of the company from around that time probably owed considerably less to his own abilities and initiative than to those of his carefully chosen professional managers who effectively ran the company for him. The major achievement of his business career might reasonably be said to have been completed by then, his chief monument being the conversion of Guinness from a provincial brewer of some influence to the largest and most influential brewer in the British Isles by

1900. This was marked when the newly-formed Brewers' Society in 1904 offered the chairmanship to him; although he refused, he did accept a life position as honorary vice-president. He did not believe in involving either himself or his company in trade politics; nevertheless Guinness's was a founder member of the Brewers' Society. A measure of Edward Cecil's success was that under his control Guinness's market share in the UK rose from around 3 per cent to well over 12 per cent on his death, which represented a dominant position in Ireland and virtual domination of the dark beer market in England and Wales.

Edward Cecil was never as active politically as other members of the family, such as his brother Lord Ardilaun, but he took a close and abiding interest in local social affairs. He was elected High Sheriff of Dublin City in 1876, and of County Dublin in 1885. This period also coincided with the first of his gifts to the two cities where he lived. In 1889 he donated £250,000 to social improvements in London and Dublin, and later a further £250,000 to the Bull Alley Clearance Scheme in Dublin. In 1907 the Iveagh Markets in Dublin were opened, named after him in recognition of his generous sponsorship of the scheme. These were just the largest and most publicised of his many similar donations to both cities. In recognition of his public work he received a steady flow of public honours; in 1885 he was created baronet, in 1891 (conveniently after his official retirement from direct involvement in business) he was created Baron Iveagh of Iveagh in County Down. In 1905 he was made Viscount Elvedon (named after the country house, Elvedon Hall in Suffolk which he had just bought) and finally in 1919 he received an earldom, taking the title the First Earl of Iveagh. He interested himself in academic and in scientific matters. He donated £250,000 to the Lister Institute of Tropical Medicine. He was elected Chancellor of Trinity College, Dublin in 1908. He received a special address of thanks from the City of Dublin in 1909. Other honours included the Knighthood of St Patrick (1896), the GCVO (1910) and FRS in 1906. In 1925 he rescued Ken Wood House for the nation, filling it with a large part of the remarkable private collection of pictures he had built up since the late 1880s on the proceeds of the business. On his death in 1927 the whole house and its collection were granted intact to the Nation in a bequest.

In retrospect his contribution to the brewing industry was immense in two ways. He demonstrated that even in the late nineteenth century there remained many opportunities to build up a brewery to national size. In that respect Guinness's was and is his prime monument. The rate of growth of the company finally outstripped that of Bass and Allsop, and was the wonder of the period. His social pre-eminence did much to build up the public image of the Guinness family which in turn contributed to the standing of the brewery itself, but that was not something in which he was actively concerned. While he rose rapidly to the greatest prominence as a businessman and a philanthropist in the period after the flotation of Guinness's in 1886, there can be little doubt that his major achievements lay in the period leading up to that. In 1886 he demonstrated that the public would clamour to buy shares in breweries and that the stock market was a potential route to urgently-needed capital funding for the industry. Ironically, Guinness's needed that funding far less than most of its competitors. However Guinness in 1886 set off a spate of such flotations and ultimately that alone, with its injection of vast capital resources into the trade, and the resultant rush for property, changed the face of the British brewing industry. Guinness's offer for sale in 1886 thus started the race for capital and property which, alongside the fall in demand for beer ultimately contributed to a major concentration of the industry in the early twentieth century.

Edward Cecil in 1873 married Adelaide Maud Guinness, a distant cousin, and the daughter of Richard Samuel Guinness of Deepwell House, County Dublin. They had three sons, one of whom, Rupert succeeded both to the title and to the chairmanship of the company in 1927. Lady Iveagh died in 1916. Edward Cecil himself died in London on 7 October 1927 leaving £13.486 million gross.

TOM CORRAN

Sources:
Unpublished

Guinness Co, St James's Gate Brewery, Dublin, archives.

Guinness family archives.

University of Dublin, Student Records Office, Information.

PrC.

Published

Tom H Corran, *The Brewing Industry in Britain 1830-1969* (forthcoming).

DNB.

Patrick Lynch and John Vaizey, *Guinness's Brewery in the Irish Economy, 1789-1876* (Cambridge: Cambridge University Press, 1960).

Statist.

WWW.

GUTHRIE, Edwin

(1841-1904)

Accountant

Edwin Guthrie was born in Bermondsey, London, on 22 June 1841, one of the four children of David Guthrie, an engineer, and Ann née Barker. His father probably worked for Guthrie Fisher Hill & Co, millwrights and engineers, in Bermondsey Street. While he was still a child his family moved to Liverpool. Nothing is known of Guthrie's education but by the age of nineteen he was working as a bookkeeper to a general merchant. Guthrie seems to have started his own business as a dealer in American wooden ware in 1864, later becoming a contractor in Birkenhead with his brother and in 1866 publishing a pamphlet advocating a Mersey ferry to connect the town to Liverpool.

During the early 1870s Guthrie left Liverpool for Manchester and in 1875 went into partnership as a public accountant with John Thomas and Charles Henry Wade as Thomas, Wade & Guthrie. All three men were founder members of the Institute of Chartered Accountants in England and Wales when it received its Royal Charter in 1880 and Guthrie was a member of the ICAEW council throughout his life.

The practice of accountancy in the 1880s was principally concerned with insolvency and in 1883 Guthrie visited New York in connection with a receivership. Unable to find any accounting firms who could assist him with his work he decided to seize the opportunity and create his own. Through his lawyers he was introduced to John Wylie Barrow, an English actuary, one of the Commissioners of Accounts for New York, and already engaged in auditing the American branch statements of several English insurance companies. Guthrie and Wade supplied the necessary working capital to found Barrow, Wade & Guthrie, the first British accounting firm in the United States.

Thomas, Wade & Guthrie opened a London office in 1886 but in Britain it remained primarily a Manchester-based practice. The major audit clients included the Fine Cotton Spinners & Doublers Association, together with a number of smaller companies in the cotton business, the Manchester Ship Canal, Manchester Liners, and for a time, the Corporation of Manchester. In New York the American firm became the auditors of the New York, Ontario & Western Railway Co, the first American railway to employ professional auditors, but in 1885 Barrow died and his assistant Morton attempted to wrest the business away from the English partners. Guthrie returned to New York in 1886 taking with him J T Anyon, who was put in charge of the practice after a legal action had been brought against Morton to regain control of the business. In the same year Guthrie proposed to all the American accountants who could be located that they form an American equivalent of the English Institute. The resulting body, the American Association of Public Accountants, was the first professional association of accountants in America and a predecessor of the American Institute of Certified Public Accountants.

Thomas retired from the firm in 1893 and Wade resigned, for reasons which are unclear, in 1895, leaving Guthrie with three partners, practising as E Guthrie & Co. The firm continued after Guthrie's death and in 1955 it became the Manchester office of Peat Marwick Mitchell & Co. Wade retained his share of the American firm until 1908 but Guthrie seems to have disposed of his interest in 1901. The firm of Barrow Wade & Guthrie survived them both and in 1950, by which time it had 17 offices and an annual fee income of $4.5 million, it merged with the American partnership of Peat Marwick Mitchell & Co.

Guthrie was a prominent figure in Liberal politics in Manchester and

GUTHRIE Edwin

was for many years chairman of South Manchester Liberal Association and chairman of the subcommittee on finance and organisation of the Manchester Liberal Union. A free-trader, supporter of decimal coinage and the amalgamation of Salford and Manchester, he was also the author of an ingenious scheme to solve the problems of Irish Home Rule, Imperial Federation and the powers of the House of Lords in one fell swoop. Guthrie was well-known as chairman of the finance committee of the Lancashire County Council from the Council's formation in 1889 until his death. He was closely identified with the formation of the Association of County Councils and in 1892 was the author of their recommendations on municipal accounts which were based on the use of professional accountants as auditors. He became a JP of Lancaster and of the City of Manchester. He was also a director of the Manchester Labourers' Dwelling Co, which provided tenements for people in Jersey Street, Ancoats, and was an honorary treasurer of the Mission to Seamen.

Guthrie was an active member of the Manchester Statistical Society, a council member from 1880 to his death and president in 1888-90. As well as the papers he delivered to that Society, he wrote some important papers on accounting, including a pioneering article on depreciation and an original article on accounting uniformity which had an unusual emphasis on principle and historical example, the latter quality, apparent in some of his other articles, not always being to the taste of some of his audience.

Guthrie married Augusta Strong, the daughter of a master mariner, in 1869. They had no children. He died at their home, Broughton Old Hall, Salford on 21 August 1904, leaving £14,199 gross.

M F BYWATER

Writings:

Bad Trade Considered in Relation to the Recent Condition of the Cotton Industry in England (Manchester: A Ireland, 1878).

'The Effect upon Trade of the Operation Called Cornering in Relation to Commodities' *Transactions of the Manchester Statistical Society* 1881-82.

'The Want of Uniformity in the Modes of Stating Accounts' *The Accountant* 8 (28 Oct 1882).

The Cotton Trade: Its Conditions and Prospects (Manchester: A Ireland, 1883).

'Depreciation and Sinking Funds' *The Accountant* 9 (21 Apr 1883).

The Political Problem: The Irish Question, Imperial Federation, the House of Lords-Proposed Solution (Manchester: J Heywood, 1886).

'Corporation Accounts' *The Accountant* 12 (30 Oct 1886).

Home Rule and Federation (Manchester: J Heywood, 1887).

Home Rule, Federation and the Crown (Manchester: J Heywood, 1889).

The Next Home Rule Bill. What Is It to Be? (Manchester: J Collins, 1891).

Guthrie's other papers on accounting are listed in: Institute of Chartered Accountants in England and Wales, *Library Catalogue (ICAEW, 1913)*. Guthrie's papers delivered to the Manchester Statistical Society are listed in T S Ashton *Economic and Social Investigations in Manchester 1833-1933* (P S King, 1934).

Sources:

Unpublished

BCe.

PrC.

Published

The Accountant 3 Sept 1904.

James T Anyon, *Recollections of the Early Days of American Accountancy, 1883-93* (New York: pp, 1925).

Peter F Clarke, *Lancashire and the New Liberalism* (Cambridge: Cambridge University Press, 1971).

James Kitchen and Robert H Parker, *Accounting Thought and Education: Six English Pioneers* (Institute of Chartered Accountants in England and Wales, 1980).

Manchester City News 27 Aug 1904.

Manchester Evening News 22 Aug 1904.

Manchester Guardian 22 Aug 1094.

T A Wise, *Peat Marwick Mitchell & Co, 85 Years* (New York: the firm, 1982).

GUTHRIE, Sir Giles

(1916-1979)

Airline executive

Giles Guthrie was born in Westminster, London, on 21 March 1916, the son of Connop Thirlwall Robert Guthrie, a lieutenant in the Grenadier Guards (who later had a distinguished military career, becoming a KBE in 1918 and a baronet in 1936), and his wife Mary Islay née McEacharn. Guthrie was educated at Eton and Magdalen College, Cambridge. At Cambridge he took up flying and in early 1936 entered a Vega Gull in the

Giles Guthrie (courtesy of British European Airways via British Airways).

King's Cup Air Race with Charles Gardner of the Redhill Flying Club, a wealthy young man, as pilot. Their 164 mph was the highest speed up till then for the race. Guthrie partnered C W A Scott, winner in 1934 of the famous Mildenhall-to-Melbourne Race, in the Portsmouth-Johannesburg Race of September 1936. They were the only team to complete the race, taking fifty-three hours, and received the £10,000 prize for what proved to be the last long-distance air race, before the Second World War stopped the sport.

Upon finishing Cambridge, Giles Guthrie went first to Eastleigh where he obtained his commercial pilot's licence and then to work for British Airways (1936) Ltd, a new company controlled by Sir Clive Pearson and the Whitehall Securities Group in competition with Imperial Airways. He was a traffic officer with the airline for only about a year before war broke out and he joined the Fleet Air Arm as a pilot. He was awarded the DSC in 1941 while serving on HMS *Ark Royal* as a fighter pilot and advanced to the rank of lieutenant-commander in 1943.

His father died in 1945 and Guthrie succeeded to the title and responsibility for the family's financial affairs, though still in the Fleet Air Arm working as a test pilot, for which he received the OBE. The following year he was released from the navy and returned to business full-time. He soon rose to be managing director of the merchant bankers, Brown Shipley & Co, deputy-chairman of North Central Finance Ltd, a director of Prudential Assurance Co Ltd, and of Radio Rentals Ltd, as well as of other companies.

More importantly, he was in 1959 appointed to the board of the nationalised British European Airways (BEA). Through the cross-linkage of that organisation with its rival British Overseas Airways Corporation (BOAC) and through his aviation and financial connections he became familiar with the workings of BOAC itself. It also happened that the Minister for Aviation (1962-64) Julian Amery, a fellow Etonian, was entangled in the whole discussion of cost analysis, efficiency ratings, and return upon investment in nationalised industries — a periodic debate which then occupied parliament's attention and demonstrated that the Treasury had little understanding of transport economics. Sir Matthew Slattery, the BOAC chairman, and Sir Basil Smallpeice (qv), the managing director of BOAC had asked for permission to write off the losses BOAC had made through introducing British aircraft (estimated at £80 million) and made proposals for changes in the airline's capital structure, but Amery delayed taking action until he received the secret Corbett Report. There then followed a political manoeuvre at the end of 1963 as a result of which both Slattery and Smallpeice resigned. Amery appointed Guthrie to the dual position of chairman and chief executive with their combined salaries and gave him all that Slattery and Smallpeice had asked for. But Guthrie cleverly got more than this, for he drafted a letter from the Minister to himself which Amery signed, known as the 'Magna Carta', which clearly spelt out that BOAC was to be run as a commercial corporation and that it would only give the national interest a higher priority if the Minister sent it a written Direction to do so. Thus when on 1 January 1964 Sir Giles walked into Speedbird House at Heathrow, he was in a very strong political position. Besides this, he was in an improving economic situation caused by not only the general upturn in

The controversial Vickers VC-10, much at the heart of Sir Giles Guthrie's commercialisation of BOAC starting in 1964 (courtesy of British European Airways via British Airways).

the airline business, but also by the hard work of his predecessors and the fact that he had a free hand to select economically viable aircraft regardless of manufacturer. He proceeded to fight the Government and Vickers. to cancel and get rid of the VC-10 and Super VC-10 order which had plagued BOAC since the 1950s and worked instead to create a fleet of aircraft with the lowest operating costs and highest profitability (Boeing in this case). Guthrie was also chairman of BOAC-Cunard Ltd, owned jointly with Cunards the shipping company, in order to exploit Atlantic transportation services; but this was dissolved in 1966 when Cunard, hit by a seamen's strike, could not raise its share of the capital needed to maintain a competitive aircraft fleet for the future.

Guthrie's five years to the end of December 1969 saw large profits, sufficient for BOAC to have paid off the £180 million debt that Sir Giles had persuaded the Government to restructure, essentially to wipe off. When he left, BOAC was a healthy, efficient airline, with a high morale and a good profit, in an environment of airline success in most parts of the world arising from the productivity of jets and opportunities of reduced fares against a rate of inflation that was not unreasonable. But change was on the horizon when the Edwards committee reported six months after Guthrie's departure at the end of 1968. Their report led to the partial dismemberment of BOAC in favour of British Caledonian's African ambitions. A few months earlier Guthrie had successfully negotiated the takeover of British United but had been frustrated in the end by the Labour Government's rejection for political reasons.

Sir Giles was easy to know, charming though quiet and shrewd. Of medium height, he had the ability to project his famous smile, and certainly one of the things that he and Lady Guthrie brought to BOAC was a clearer sense of purpose after the turmoil of the early 1960s and a better appreciation of management training and the well being of staff at all levels. Stressing the importance of profit, he voiced the view that in the airline world 'one aircraft too many was disaster, one too few was ideal'. Guthrie lacked the retiring stuffiness of the stereotyped merchant banker, projecting instead the image of the successful naval officer quite at home in the airman's world, which of course he was.

After he left BOAC Sir Giles was asked to set up an airline self-insurance company which was first established in Switzerland and then in Bermuda 1969-71. It was a part-time occupation and although he travelled to these countries, he lived in Jersey. Air Transport Insurance Ltd, of which he was chairman, was put in mothballs in 1971 for possible future use and he retired to Jersey, where he lived quietly with his wife. His outside involvements included service as a JP of West Sussex, 1955-63, and as a governor of the London Hospital, 1965-68, and its vice-chairman in 1968. Sir Giles Guthrie was interested in sailing, dendrology, walking, and conservation, as well as in several Jersey corporations. He was a Conservative and an Anglican.

In 1939 he married Rhona, daughter of Frederic Stileman of India. Sir Giles and Lady Guthrie had three sons, one deceased. The eldest, Malcolm Connop (born 16 December 1942), succeeded his father when Sir Giles died of a malignant brain tumour on 31 December 1979.

ROBIN HIGHAM

Sources:

Unpublished

BOAC annual reports, 1963/64 to 1968/69.

BCe.

Giles Guthrie, 'The British Overseas Airways Corporation — Its Task and Problems' (Edwards Seminar paper 365, 22 Feb 1966).

Personal knowledge.

Published

Burke's Peerage and Baronetage 1980.

Geoffrey Dorman, *Fifty Years Fly-Past* (Forbes Robertson, 1951).

Basil Smallpeice, *Of Comets and Queens. An Autobiography* (Shrewsbury: Airlife Publishing Ltd, 1980).

Times 3 Jan 1980.

WWW.